Buy-to-Let Property Handbook

Buy-to-Let Property Tax Handbook

General Editor
Mark McLaughlin CTA (Fellow), ATT (Fellow), TEP
Mark McLaughlin Associates Limited

Authors
Satwaki Chanda
Barrister at Law

James Darmon BA, ACA
Tax Consultant, The TACS Partnership

Malcolm Finney
Tax Consultant

Robert Maas FCA, FTII, FIIT, TEP
Consultant, CBW Tax Ltd

Lee Sharpe CTA, ATT
Sharpe Tax Consulting Ltd

David Smith
Policy Director, Residential Landlords Association; Partner, Anthony Gold Solicitors

Liz Syms
Connect IFA Ltd (Trading as Connect Mortgages)

Martin Wilson MA, FCA
The Capital Allowances Partnership Ltd

Ken Wright BA, CA, CTA

Bloomsbury Professional

Bloomsbury Professional
An imprint of Bloomsbury Publishing Plc

Bloomsbury Professional Ltd
41–43 Boltro Road
Haywards Heath
RH16 1BJ
UK

Bloomsbury Publishing Plc
50 Bedford Square
London
WC1B 3DP
UK

www.bloomsbury.com
BLOOMSBURY and the Diana logo are trademarks of Bloomsbury Publishing Plc

First published 2017

Reprinted 2017

© Bloomsbury Professional Ltd 2017

Bloomsbury Professional Ltd has asserted its right under the Copyright, Designs and Patents Act 1988 to be identified as Author of this work.

All rights reserved. No part of this publication may be reproduced or transmitted in any form or by any means, electronic or mechanical, including photocopying, recording, or any information storage or retrieval system, without prior permission in writing from the publishers.

While every care has been taken to ensure the accuracy of this work, no responsibility for loss or damage occasioned to any person acting or refraining from action as a result of any statement in it can be accepted by the authors, editors or publishers.

All UK Government legislation and other public sector information used in the work is Crown Copyright ©. All House of Lords and House of Commons information used in the work is Parliamentary Copyright ©. This information is reused under the terms of the Open Government Licence v3.0 (http://www.nationalarchives.gov.uk/doc/open-government-licence/version/3) except where otherwise stated.

All Eur-lex material used in the work is © European Union, http://eur-lex.europa.eu/, 1998-2017.

British Library Cataloguing-in-Publication Data

A catalogue record for this book is available from the British Library.

ISBN:	PB	978 1 78451 054 1
	Epub:	978 1 78451 055 8
	Epdf	978 1 78561 056 5

Typeset by Phoenix Photosetting, Chatham, Kent
Printed and bound by CPI Group (UK) Ltd, Croydon, CR0 4YY

To find out more about our authors and books visit www.bloomsburyprofessional.com. Here you will find extracts, author information, details of forthcoming events and the option to sign up for our newsletters

Preface

Welcome to the first edition of *Buy-to-Let Property Tax Handbook*.

Landlords of residential properties in the UK have seemingly been the target of some unwelcome government attention from a tax perspective in recent times. The inference appears to be that such landlords are at least partly responsible for a shortage in the UK housing market. Certain tax changes have prompted some existing residential landlords to consider selling their buy-to-let (BTL) property portfolios, whilst discouraging potential landlords from commencing BTL property businesses in the first place.

Two headline grabbing tax changes have caused many landlords of residential property particular concern. The first change was the introduction of a restriction in the deduction of finance costs to the basic rate of income tax, which is being phased in from 6 April 2017. This measure could turn individual landlords who would otherwise be basic rate taxpayers into higher rate taxpayers, and result in increased tax liabilities for those landlords who are already paying tax at higher rates. The second change was the introduction of higher rates of stamp duty land tax (SDLT) (ie 3% above the normal SDLT rates) on certain purchases of residential property by individuals who already own a dwelling and are not replacing a main residence (and also to first and subsequent purchases by companies etc). There is a similar 3% additional dwelling supplement in Scotland for land and building transactions tax purposes.

As if those measures were not bad enough, the basic and standard rates of capital gains tax (CGT) on most gains made by individuals, trustees and personal representatives are 10% and 20% respectively (for 2016/17), but gains on the disposal of interests in residential properties (that do not qualify for private residence relief) are instead subject to upper CGT rates of 18% and 28%. Thus individual landlords wishing to dispose of their residential property businesses are faced with a possible sting in the tail.

A potentially lower rate of corporation tax compared with marginal personal tax rates might make running a residential property business through a company seem attractive, along with freedom from the finance cost restriction mentioned above, which does not apply to companies. However, even company landlords are not without potential tax issues in relation to residential property, including the annual tax on enveloped dwellings (ATED) and ATED-related CGT in certain circumstances. Whilst there is relief from ATED for property rental businesses in most cases, the relief must still be claimed.

Apart from the daunting tax implications, landlords are faced with various commercial and (non-tax) legal issues in operating a BTL property business,

Preface

such as financing the acquisition of property, complying with landlord obligations and observing the rights of tenants.

The *Buy-to-Let Property Tax Handbook* is designed to be a 'one-stop shop' for tax practitioners, accountants and others who need to advise their clients and be aware of tax and non-tax aspects of running a residential BTL property business. The authors of this book include well-known and respected experts in property tax, finance and law. They bring a wealth of practical experience, which they have endeavoured to share with readers of this publication. The term 'handbook' in the title reflects that its purpose is to provide practitioners with practical guidance to help them in their exposure to issues covered in this publication. For example, the tax content includes chapters on topical subjects such as the finance cost restriction and incorporating the property rental business; the non-tax content includes chapters on BTL mortgages and landlord obligations and other considerations.

On behalf of all the authors, I would like to thank everyone at Bloomsbury Professional who has been involved in the production of the *Buy-to-Let Property Tax Handbook*, in particular to Claire McDermott for all her support and patience during its publication.

Last but not least, many thanks to you, the reader, for picking up and reading this publication. I hope that you find it a useful source of reference. Constructive comments and suggestions for future editions of *the Buy-to-Let Property Tax Handbook* will be welcome.

Whilst every care has been taken to ensure that the contents of this work are complete and accurate, no responsibility for loss occasioned by any person acting or refraining from action as a result of any statement in it can be accepted by the authors, the editor or the publishers.

The law in this book is stated as at 1 December 2016.

Mark McLaughlin
General Editor
Manchester, January 2017

Contents

Preface v
Table of statutes xxi
Table of statutory instruments and other guidance xxxi
Table of cases xxxv

PART 1   TAX ISSUES

Prologue: Starting a buy-to-let property business? What you need to know   1

Chapter 1   Commencement of a property business
Signposts   13
Basis of taxation   14
   Who is taxable on rental income?   14
Different entities   15
   Direct ownership in sole or joint names   15
   Trusts   15
   Apportioning taxable income between joint owners   16
   Partnerships and Limited Liability Partnerships   16
   Companies   18
When does a property business start?   19
Expenses incurred before letting commences ('pre-trading'/pre-letting expenses)   21
   Capital allowances and commencement   21
   A letting business usually starts only once   22
Expenses before first let – capital or revenue?   23
   Case Study – Classic cases   25
   Pre-letting expenses and the landlord's former home   27
Basis periods   27
Tax administration   28
   Requirement to notify HMRC   28
   Record keeping   29
   Finance costs – borrowing against non-business/private assets   30
Leases   31
   Lease premia on grant of lease/assignment of a lease   31
   The term of the lease is not always the term of the lease…   32
   Grant of a (short) sub-lease out of a short lease   33
   Lessee/tenant tax relief   34
   No premium received but capital costs incurred   35
   Assignment of a lease   35
   Reverse premia   37
   Stamp duty land tax (land and building transaction tax in Scotland)   38

Contents

Chapter 2   Calculating property business profits and losses
Signposts   39
Introduction   40
　What is property income?   40
　It depends…   41
Priority of rental income over trading income rules   42
Assessed as a business   42
Key differences between property investment income and trading income   44
Differences in property investment businesses for income tax versus
　　corporation tax   46
Hotels and similar establishments – a peculiar distinction?   47
Badges of trade   47
'Wholly and exclusively'   49
　Flip-flops or stethoscope?   49
Capital versus revenue   50
Interest relief and associated finance costs   51
　Unincorporated businesses: positive capital account is critical   51
　Companies and loan relationships   53
Change in intention/use of a property   54
　Moving from trading to investment   55
　Moving from investment to trading – developing an investment
　　property for onward sale   55
Transactions in UK land   57
　Criteria (following FA 2016)   58
　Impact for UK property businesses   58
　Limitations of scope   59
　'Slice of the action' arrangements   60
Non-commercial lettings   61
Proposals for a new cash basis for unincorporated property letting
　　businesses   61

**Appendix A   What expenses can be claimed for a buy-to-let
　property business?   63**

Chapter 3   Finance costs relief restrictions
Signposts   69
Restricting tax relief for residential lettings   71
　Introduction   71
　Overview   71
　The costs affected – restriction of the costs of a dwelling-related loan   73
　Extent of restriction – what are the 'costs of a dwelling-related loan'?   74
　Building or converting a dwelling for letting out   75
Far-reaching implications   76
Tax reduction mechanism overview – the relievable amount   80
　The tax reduction – calculation detail   81
Trusts and estates   86

Contents

    Interest in possession trusts   87
    Discretionary trusts   90
    Estates   91
Other issues   93
    Furnished holiday lettings (and hotels)   93
    Are houses in multiple occupation (HMOs) a 'dwelling house'?   94
    Beneficial loans and property investment businesses   95
    Loans to invest in a partnership with a property business   95
Finance costs – steps landlords can take to mitigate the effects   96
    Incorporation   96
    Increasing rental income   99
    Introducing family members   100
    Timing of expenditure   101
    Paying off capital   102
    Accelerating finance costs   102
    Pension/gift aid contributions   102
    Rationalising the business   104
    Diversifying the business   104
    Property development   105

Chapter 4   Capital allowances
Signposts   107
Introduction   108
Qualifying expenditure   108
Plant   109
    Integral features   110
    Other plant   110
    Annual investment allowance   111
Limitation of allowances on 'dwellings'   112
    What is a dwelling-house?   113
    Properties comprising more than one dwelling   113
    Communal areas in a block of flats   114
Allowances for furnished holiday lettings   115
    Letting conditions   116
    Averaging election   116
    Period of grace election   116
    Failure to meet the letting conditions   117
    Caravans   117

Chapter 5   Furnished lettings
Signposts   119
Introduction   120
Residential property   120
Commercial property   121
Replacement domestic items relief (from April 2016)   121
    Standard residential lettings   121

Contents

Fixtures in a dwelling   123
Fixtures and furniture in commercial properties   124
Wear and tear allowance   124
    Concession   125
    Legislation (April 2011 to April 2016)   125
Withdrawal of wear and tear allowance and interaction with replacement domestic items relief   126
Renewals basis   127
    Concessionary versus statutory basis   128
Chronology   130

Chapter 6   Furnished holiday accommodation/lettings
Signposts   133
Introduction   133
Advantages of furnished holiday lettings status   134
    Relevant earnings for pension purposes   135
    Capital allowances   135
    Profit split between spouses   136
    Capital gains tax reliefs   137
Disadvantages to FHL status   141
    Restriction of losses   141
    VAT   142
Conditions of furnished holiday accommodation status   142
    Relevant period   145
FHL losses   145
Inheritance tax and business property relief   146
HMRC guidance on FHLs   147

Chapter 7   Loss relief
Signposts   149
Income tax   150
    Overview   150
    Additional claims   153
    Uncommercial lettings   154
    Multiple businesses   154
    Capital allowances   155
    Agricultural expenses   156
    Furnished holiday lettings   157
Corporation tax   157

Chapter 8   Jointly-owned properties
Signposts   159
Introduction   161
Categories of ownership   163
    Legal title/ownership   163
    Beneficial ownership   164

Purchase of land 165
   Three stage process of acquisition 165
   Split of beneficial interests 166
   Land Registry protection of interests in land 167
   Overreaching 167
   Mortgages 167
Beneficial ownership 168
   Conversion from beneficial joint tenants to beneficial tenants in common or vice versa 168
   Joint tenants to tenants in common: severance 168
   Severance in lifetime or by will 169
   Tenants in common to joint tenants 169
Sole legal ownership: spouses and tax 169
   Sole legal ownership 169
   Inheritance tax and capital gains tax 171
   Income tax 172
Conversion from sole to joint legal title 173
Joint legal ownership: spouses and tax 173
   Income tax 173
   Income tax versus capital gains tax and inheritance tax 177
Manipulation of legal/beneficial interests: non-tax issues 179
Expenses 179
Sole and joint legal ownership: non-spouse and tax 181
Parent/child co-ownership 182
Grandparent/child co-ownership 183
Succession 183
Non-UK domiciled individual 185

Chapter 9 Non-resident landlords
Signposts 187
Introduction 188
Income tax 188
The non-resident landlord scheme 190
Capital gains tax 192
Non-resident capital gains tax 193
Relationship with ATED-related capital gains tax 199
How should a non-UK resident individual structure UK property investments? 203
Other taxes 204

Chapter 10 Corporate landlords
Signposts 206
Introduction 207
Why use a company? 207
   Commercial considerations 207
   Tax considerations 208

Contents

Offshore or onshore? 212
Profits of a property business 212
   Interest relief 213
Property losses 216
   Treatment of property losses and a comparison with trading losses 216
   A comparison of property losses between corporate and individual landlords 217
Annual tax on enveloped dwellings and related tax charges 218
   Background to the regime 218
   ATED – the annual charge 219
   Claiming relief for the ATED charge 221
   ATED and the 15% SDLT rate 224
   ATED-related capital gains – UK resident landlords 225
   ATED-related capital gains – non-UK resident landlords 226
Exit issues – disposal of the property portfolio 227
   Selling part of the portfolio 229
   ATED issues on exiting the business 231

Chapter 11   Capital gains tax

Signposts 233
Introduction 234
Rates of CGT 235
Time of disposal 235
Options 236
Capital gains and losses 236
   Computation 236
Allowable expenditure 238
   Gains accruing before 6 April 1965 238
   Losses accruing before 6 April 1965 238
   Time apportionment 239
   March 1982 rebasing 239
Part disposals 239
Small disposal proceeds 240
Allowable costs 241
   Use of losses 242
Losses: order of set off 242
Trading losses etc as capital losses 243
Partnerships 244
CGT reliefs etc 244
   Relief on gifts on which IHT is due 244
Incorporation relief 245
Compensation and insurance monies 245
Inter-spouse transfers 246
Private residence relief 246

Contents

Furnished holiday lettings   251
Other issues   252
   Leases   252
Exchange of joint interests   254
EIS deferral relief   254
Compulsory purchase of land   254
Compliance issues   254

Chapter 12   Inheritance tax
Signposts   256
Introduction   258
   The IHT charge   258
Ownership   259
   Introduction   259
   Sole owner   260
   Joint owners   260
   Trustees   261
   Companies   262
Investment or business?   263
   Introduction   263
   Partnerships   263
   Business property relief   264
Valuation   268
   General   268
   Discounts   269
   Liabilities   271
   Related property   273
Lifetime transfers   275
   Introduction   275
   Potentially exempt transfers   276
   Chargeable lifetime transfers   276
Gifts with reservation   277
   General   277
   Gifts of interests in land   279
IHT on death   281
   Introduction   281
   Liabilities   282
   'Fall in value' relief   284
   Post-death loss relief   285
Other points   288
   Instalments   288
   Pre-owned assets   289

Chapter 13   Incorporation of a buy-to-let residential property business
Signposts   291

Contents

Introduction   293
Is there a business?   295
   Background   295
   Case law   296
   The Ramsay case   298
Transactions in UK land   300
Capital gains tax   301
   Introduction   301
   Incorporation relief   303
   Relief conditions   303
   Non-statutory business clearance   311
Furnished holiday lettings   312
   Background   312
   Entrepreneurs' relief   312
   Section 165 relief   314
   Rollover relief   317
Stamp taxes   318
   General   318
   The market value rule   320
   Deemed non-residential property treatment   321
   Multiple dwellings relief   322
   Partnerships   325
Interest relief   331
Other issues   334
   VAT   334
   Capital allowances   334
   Payment of tax   338
   National Insurance contributions   338
   Employment related securities   340

Chapter 14   Stamp duty land tax and land and buildings transaction tax

Signposts   341
Introduction   344
   Rest of the UK   344
   Scotland   344
   SDLT   345
   LBTT   346
Chargeable consideration   347
   SDLT and LBTT charged on money or money's worth given for the property   347
   Debt as consideration   348
   Transfers to a connected company – market value rule   348
   Exchange of properties   349
   Partition of a property   349
   Partnerships   349

Contents

 Apportionment of chargeable consideration   350
 Contingent and uncertain consideration   350
SDLT payable on the acquisition of a buy-to-let property   351
Additional 3% rate of SDLT applies to the acquisition of buy-to-let
  properties   355
 SDLT Rates (excluding 3% surcharge)   356
 Enveloped residential properties – 15% slab rate of SDLT may apply   356
 Linked transactions   357
 Higher rates of SDLT (including 3% surcharge)   357
 Individuals – Interests in dwellings treated as owned by an
  individual for the purposes of the SDLT higher rates   362
 Joint purchasers   363
 Spouse or civil partner   363
 Dwellings held by trusts   363
 Dwellings held by a partnership   363
 Dwellings situated outside of England, Wales and Northern Ireland   364
 Dwellings acquired by inheritance   364
 Individual acquiring more than one dwelling as part of a single
  transaction   365
 Buy-to-let property acquired by a company   366
 Buy-to-let property acquired by a partnership   366
LBTT rates   369
 LBTT additional dwellings supplement (3%) applies to the
  acquisition of buy-to-let properties   369
 Leases   373
 SDLT rates on a grant of a new lease   373
 Grant of a new lease exempt from LBTT   375
 Acquisition of an existing lease   375
 Acquisition of bare land to build a buy-to-let property   376
 Reliefs   377
 Multiple dwellings relief   377
 Partnerships   380
Anti-avoidance provisions   383
Annual tax on enveloped dwellings   384
Transferring a buy-to-let property out of a company   384
Stamp duty and stamp duty reserve tax   385

Chapter 15   Other issues
Signposts   387
VAT   388
Construction industry scheme   389
Rents connected with a trade or profession   390
 Tied premises   390
 Other income from land not taxed under the rental business rules   391
Sale and leaseback of land   392

Contents

Transactions in UK land   392
   Taxation of chargeable gains   392
Beginning and end of a rental business   394
   The beginning of a rental business   394
Cessation of a rental business   394
Post-cessation receipts and expenses   395
   Post-cessation receipts   395
   Post-cessation expenses   395
   Post-cessation expenses but no post-cessation receipts   396

PART 2:   LEGAL ISSUES

Chapter 16   Buy-to-let mortgages
Signposts   397
Introduction   398
Different property types   398
   Residential property   398
   Buy-to-let property   399
   Commercial property   399
Comparison between a residential mortgage and a buy-to-let mortgage   399
   Residential mortgage   399
   Buy-to-let mortgages   400
Buy-to-let affordability calculations   401
Changes to buy-to-let affordability   402
Other borrowing criteria for a buy-to-let mortgage   403
   Applicant types   403
   Repaying a buy-to-let mortgage   404
   Age and term requirements for a buy-to-let mortgage   405
   Loan sizes   406
   Portfolio limits   407
   Income requirements   408
   Credit worthiness   408
   Property types   408
   Alternative ('bridge') finance   410
Costs associated with a buy-to-let mortgage   410
   Survey fee   410
   Mortgage lender fees   411
   Stamp duty land tax and land and buildings transaction tax   411
   Legal fees   411
   Mortgage broker fees   412
Other buy-to-let considerations   412
   Interest rates   412
   Early repayment charges   413
   Protecting the buy-to-let portfolio   413
Increasing the buy-to-let portfolio   414
   Further advances   414

Contents

    Re-mortgages   414
    Second charge or equity loans   415
    Bridging finance   415
Taxation and mortgage implications   416
    What types of company are acceptable?   416
    How is the mortgage underwritten?   417
    How do the mortgage products compare?   417
    Operating through a company   418
    Capital raising   420
    Commercial and semi-commercial properties   421
    Getting the lender right   421
The mortgage process via a broker   421
    Working with a specialist mortgage broker   421
    The accountant's role in the mortgage process   423
Alternatives to incorporation   423
    Summary   424

Chapter 17   Dealing with tenants and agents
Signposts   425
Considerations in buying a tenanted property   426
    Rent   426
    Costs   426
Introduction to tenancies   427
Fundamental aspects of being a residential tenant   427
Different tenancy types and what they mean   428
    England   428
    Wales   430
    Scotland   430
    Northern Ireland   430
Using an agent   431
    (a) Experience   431
    (b) Cost   431
    (c) Training   432
    (d) Accreditation   432
Redress, fees, and client money protection   432
    Scotland   433
    Wales   433
    Northern Ireland   433
Agency types   434
    (a) Let only   434
    (b) Rent collection   434
    (c) Full management   434
Inventory   435
    Consents   435
Advertising the property   436
Energy performance certificates   436

Contents

Key elements of the agency agreement   437
   (a) Fees   437
   (b) Services   437
   (c) Exclusivity   438
   (d) Consumer rights   438
Selecting a tenant   438
   Referencing   438
   Discrimination   438
Terms of the letting   439
   Rent   440
   Term   440
   Other tenancy terms   441
Deposits   441
Guarantors   442
Short letting   442
Rent to rent   443
Buying with a tenant in place   443

Chapter 18 Landlord obligations

Signposts   445
Introduction   445
Basic information requirements   446
   Scotland   446
   Wales   446
   Northern Ireland   447
Immigration and the right to rent   447
   Types of right   448
   Checking   448
   Re-checks   449
Licensing and registration   449
   England   450
   HMOs under the Housing Act 2004   450
   Registration and licensing in Scotland   452
   Registration and licensing in Wales   452
   Registration in Northern Ireland   452
Other landlord obligations   453
   Gas safety   453
   Electrical safety   454
   Scotland   455
   Fire safety   455
   Smoke and alarms   456
   Scotland   456
   Carbon monoxide   457
   Scotland   457
   Furniture   457
   Property standards   458

    Disrepair   458
    Housing health and safety rating system   459
    Wales   460
    Scotland   460
    Northern Ireland   461
Seeking possession   462
    Notices   463
    Tenant rights   463

Appendix B: Essential checklist for new landlords and new properties   465

Index   471

Table of statutes

[All references are to paragraph numbers]

Capital Allowances Act 2001	4.1; 5.7, 5.8, 5.18	Caravans Act (Northern Ireland) 1963	4.16
s 11	4.2	Caravan Sites and Control of Development Act 1960	4.16
13	1.21	Companies Act 2006	1.30; 10.2
13B	6.4	Pt 23 (ss 829–853)	10.2
15	1.20; 4.2; 6.4; 7.5; 13.66	Corporation Tax Act 2009	2.7
16	13.66	s 2(2A)	10.13
17	6.4; 13.66	5	10.4
17A	13.66	(2)	10.14
17B	6.4; 13.66	10	1.30
33A	4.4	37, 39	10.7; 15.14
35	1.20; 2.15; 4.1, 4.2, 4.7; 5.1, 5.15, 5.24; 6.4; 7.5, 7.12; 10.8; 13.66, 13.69	42	15.11
		45	10.7
		46, 47	2.7
		52	1.30
		53	2.15; 5.8; 10.4
		54	1.27; 2.7, 2.14; 10.4; App A
(2)	5.7, 5.32	61	1.19; 2.7; 15.18
38B	13.67	62	1.45
46(2)	13.67	63(3)	10.7
51A	4.6	68	5.25, 5.32, 5.34
55(2), (3)	13.68	96	1.49
(4)	13.67	157	2.24
56	4.5	201	2.5
61	13.68	Pt 4 (ss 202–291)	2.6
(2)	13.71	s 205	1.17, 1.22; 2.8
Table item 1, 7	13.68	206	1.17; 2.8
65(1)	13.67	210	1.1, 1.19; 2.6; 5.25, 5.32; 10.5; 13.60; 15.18
67	4.2		
88	13.69		
89	13.69	211	13.60
(4)	13.69	(1)	10.6
104D	4.4	217	1.40
187A, 187B	13.69	225	15.15
198	13.69	231	1.45
206, 208A	13.68	(2)	1.45
Pt 2 Ch 17 (ss 213–233)	13.68	243	1.41
s 213–215, 217, 218	13.68	248A, 248B	5.15, 5.21
266	13.69, 13.70	248C	5.15, 5.18, 5.21
(4)	13.69	250A	5.7
267	13.69	(7)	6.4
532	1.50	264	6.1
575	13.68		

Table of statutes

Corporation Tax Act 2009 – *contd*	
s 264(2), (2A)	13.43
265	6.16
266	6.22
267	4.12; 11.38
268	4.13; 6.18
268A	4.14; 6.19
280	15.22
Pt 5 (ss 292–476)	1.38; 2.20; 6.12; 10.6; 13.60; App A
s 292	1.38; 6.12
302(1)	10.6
307	10.6
348	2.21
456–463	10.6
Pt 6 (ss 477–569)	2.20; App A

Corporation Tax Act 2010	
s 37	10.7
39	10.7
45	10.7
62	7.17; 10.7, 10.8
(4)	1.24
63	7.17; 10.7, 10.8; 15.24
65	6.1, 6.4, 6.23; 10.7
66	7.18; 10.7, 10.8
67A	6.1, 6.23; 10.7
99	10.7
(1)(a)	10.7
(e)	7.17; 10.7, 10.8
Pt 8ZB (ss 356O–356OT)	2.26
s 356OC(3)	2.32
356OE(3)	2.32
356OL	2.32
704	7.18
719	7.18
Pt 18 (ss 815–833)	2.26
s 1000(1)	13.17
1064	2.9
1020	13.18
1122	10.11; 13.48, 13.55; 14.13, 14.28
(3)	10.11; 13.48
(4)	13.48
(7)	13.55

Equality Act 2010	17.18

Finance Act 1986	
s 79(4)	13.47
86	14.65
99(3)	14.65
102	12.34, 12.35, 12.40
(1)	12.35
(a), (b)	12.35
(3)	12.36, 12.40
(4)	12.34, 12.40
(5), (5A)–(5C)	12.37, 12.41
102A	12.34, 12.39, 12.40
(2), (3)	12.39
(4)(a), (b)	12.39
(5)	12.39
102B	12.34, 12.40
(3)(a), (b)	12.40
(4)	12.40, 12.59
102C	12.34, 12.41
(2)	12.41
(6)	12.40
103	12.44
(4)	12.44
104(1)(c)	12.45
Sch 20	12.34
para 6(1)(a)	12.38

Finance Act 1994	
s 189(2)	3.52

Finance Act 1998	
Sch 18	
para 2	1.34
21–23	1.35

Finance Act 1999	
Sch 13	
para 2	14.64
3	10.2; 14.64

Finance Act 2003	
Pt 4 (ss 42–124)	14.4
s 42	13.45; 14.2
47	14.14
51	14.18
53	13.48, 13.54, 13.58; 14.13, 14.56, 14.57
(2)	13.48
55	13.49; 14.21, 14.25, 14.51
(1A)	10.12
(2)	14.42
(b)	14.20
(3), (4)	14.20, 14.42
55A	14.26

Table of statutes

Finance Act 2003 – *contd*
- s 65 .... 14.13
- 75A 14.57, 14.58, 14.59, 14.60, 14.62
- 75B, 75C 13.58; 14.58
- 76 .... 14.2
- 81(1A) 10.12
- 90 .... 14.18
- 108 .... 13.46, 13.49; 14.20
- 116(1) 14.19
  - (7) 13.49, 13.50; 14.20, 14.26
- 117 .... 14.14
  - (5), (6) 14.42
- 122 .... 14.4
- Sch 4 .... 13.48; 14.11
  - para 4 .... 14.17
  - 5 .... 14.14
  - 6 .... 14.14, 14.15
  - 8 .... 14.12
    - (1A) 14.12
- Sch 4A 13.51; 14.26, 14.30
  - para 1(2) 10.12
  - 3(1) 10.12
  - 5 .... 13.50; 14.52
    - (1) 10.12
      - (a) 14.27
    - (2) 10.12
  - 5A 13.50; 14.52
    - (1) 10.12
    - (c), (e)–(h) 10.12
  - 5B–5F 13.50; 14.52
  - 5G 13.50; 14.28
    - (1)–(3) 10.12
- Sch 4ZA 10.12; 14.22
  - para 2(1) 14.23
    - (3) 14.32
  - 3 .... 14.30, 14.40
    - (1) 14.30
    - (4) 14.40
    - (6), (7) 14.38
  - 4 .... 14.39, 14.40
  - 5 .... 14.30, 14.38, 14.40
    - (5) 14.38
  - 6 .... 14.30
  - 8 .... 14.38
  - 9(1)–(3) 14.33
  - 11(1) 14.34
    - (2) 14.31
    - (3) 14.31

Finance Act 2003 – *contd*
- Sch 4ZA – *contd*
  - para 11(3)(a) 14.34
  - 13 .... 14.40
  - 14(1), (2) 14.35
    - (3) 14.35, 14.42, 14.55
  - 15(1), (2) 14.37
  - 16(1) 14.36
    - (2)(a) 14.36
  - 17(3)–(5) 14.23
- Sch 5
  - para 3 .... 14.44
- Sch 6B 13.50; 14.20, 14.52, 14.53
  - para 2(4) 14.20
    - (aa) 13.50
  - 5(6)(a) 13.50
- Sch 7 .... 10.16
  - para 2(1) 10.16
  - 3, 9 .... 10.16
- Sch 15 .... 12.10; 13.53, 13.55; 14.55
  - para 2(1)(a) 14.35
    - (b) 14.40
  - 18 .... 12.10; 13.53, 13.57
    - (2) 13.55, 13.56
  - 21 .... 13.57
    - (2), (3) 13.57
  - 22 .... 13.57
    - (1) 13.57
  - 34(2) 13.57
  - 39(2) 13.55
- Sch 16
  - para 1(1) 14.34, 14.40
  - 3 .... 14.31
- Sch 17A
  - para 7 .... 14.45
  - 11 .... 14.48
- Sch 20 .... 13.55

Finance Act 2004
- s 84 .... 12.58
- 57–77 .... 15.6
- 188(3)(a) 3.52
- 189 .... 2.8, 2.9
  - (2) 6.3
- 190(4) 3.52
- 228ZA 3.11, 3.52
- Sch 11 .... 15.6
- Sch 12 .... 15.6

Table of statutes

Finance Act 2004 – *contd*	
Sch 15	12.58
para 3	12.58, 12.59
4	12.58
(2)	12.59
5–9	12.58
10	12.60
11	12.60
(1)	12.60
(5)	12.60
(c)	12.59
21	12.60
Finance Act 2006	12.56
Finance Act 2008	
Sch 41	
para 1	1.33, 1.34
7(2)	1.33
(3)	1.34
Finance Act 2008	
Sch 41	
Finance Act 2009	
s 101–103	10.10
Sch 55	
para 1	10.10
Finance Act 2011	6.1; 13.7
Finance Act 2012	13.69
Finance Act 2013	10.9; 13.29; 14.61
Pt 3 (ss 94–174)	10.10; 13.51
s 99(4)	10.10
100, 101	10.10
106	10.10
132	10.11
133(1)(b)	10.11
134	10.11, 10.17
135	10.11
(2), (4), (5), (8)	10.11
136	10.11
(1)	10.11
(b), (e)–(h)	10.11
(7)	10.11
138	10.11
159A	10.11
(2), (3), (6), (7), (10)	10.11
172(1)	10.11
188	8.59
206–215	14.58
Sch 33	14.61
Sch 34	14.61
Sch 35	14.61
Sch 45	11.35

Finance Act 2014	
s 110	10.10
Finance Act 2015	
s 6	10.4
70	10.10
Sch 8	
para 3, 4	10.13
Finance Act 2016	1.31; 2.26, 2.28, 2.29; 3.1, 3.11, 3.12, 3.22; 5.7; 6.8; 7.1; 11.2; 13.1, 13.15, 13.49; App A; 15.17
s 1(2)	10.3
4	3.11
5	3.44
6	10.3
26	7.4
74	5.19
(3)	5.21
83	3.11
117(5), (6)	14.42
Finance Bill 2017	1.24; 2.38; 6.13; 7.19; 12.2
Finance (No 2) Act 2015	3.1, 3.11, 3.12, 3.15, 3.22, 3.52; 7.1, 7.4; 13.1
s 1	10.3
7	10.3, 10.4
24	10.6
Housing Act 1988	17.7
Housing Act 2004	4.9
s 254, 257	18.4
Housing (Scotland) Act 1988	17.7
Immigration Act 2016	18.3
Income and Corporation Taxes Act 1988	
s 74(d)	5.25
Income Tax Act 2007	
s 10	3.51; 6.3
(5A)	3.11
11	10.4
12B	3.11
18(3), (4)	3.16
19	3.16
Pt 2 Ch 3 (ss 22–32)	3.20
s 23	3.11, 3.16, 3.20; 13.62

Table of statutes

Income Tax Act 2007 – *contd*	
s 24	3.16
24A	7.6; 13.62
25(2)	3.20, 3.21
26	7.4
35	3.11
55B(2)(b)	3.11
55C(1)(c)	3.11
58	3.51
64	11.21, 11.22, 11.24
Pt 4 Ch 3 (ss 102–116A)	1.14
Pt 4 Ch 4 (ss 117–127C)	7.3
s 118	3.16, 3.35; 7.3, 7.10; 10.8
(3)	1.24
119	7.3, 7.10; 10.8
120	6.4; 7.5, 7.13, 7.14; 10.8
121, 122	7.5, 7.13, 7.14
123	7.5, 7.13, 7.14
(2)	10.8
124	7.5, 7.13, 7.14
(1)	7.6, 7.13
125	15.24
127	6.1, 6.23
(3), (3A)	6.4
127A	6.23
127ZA	6.1
128	11.21, 11.22, 11.24
181, 189	13.18
192(1)(d)	13.18
257DA	13.18
257HF	13.18
303(1)(d)	13.19
Pt 8 Ch 1 (ss 383–412)	13.61
s 383–387	13.61
392	13.61, 13.63
(2)	13.63
393	13.61
(3)	13.61
(4)	13.61, 13.62
393A(2), (3)	13.64
394	13.62
399	1.15
399A	3.42; 7.4
399B	3.42; 7.4
406, 407	13.62
Pt 9A (ss 517A–517U)	2.26; 13.15; 15.17
s 517B(7)	15.16

Income Tax Act 2007 – *contd*	
s 517C(3)	2.32
517E(3)	2.32
517L	2.32
517M	2.32
681A–681AN	15.15
Pt 13 Ch 3 (ss 752–772)	2.26; 15.17
s 756	15.16
809AZA	8.48
(1)(b)	8.48
836	3.46; 6.5; 8.30, 8.36, 8.38, 8.46, 8.47, 8.50, 8.51
(1)	8.30
(3)	6.5; 8.32, 8.33
837	3.46; 8.32, 8.33, 8.34, 8.36, 8.37, 8.38, 8.46, 8.47, 8.51
(1)	8.33
(5)	8.34
1011	8.31; 14.33
Income Tax (Earnings and Pensions) Act 2003	
Pt 3 Ch 5 (ss 97–113)	2.9
s 100A, 100B	2.9
Pt 3 Ch 7 (ss 173–191)	3.41
s 178	3.41
421J	13.77
421K(3)(a)	13.77
681B–681H	3.11, 3.45, 3.52
Income Tax (Trading and Other Income) Act 2005	
s 4	2.5
Pt 2 Ch 2 (ss 5–23)	13.76
s 19	15.11
25, 26	2.7
33	2.15; 5.8
34	1.27; 2.7, 2.9, 2.14, 2.17; App A
(2)	1.37; 3.6
57	1.19; 2.7; 15.18
58	2.17; 3.5
59	2.17
60	1.45
68	5.25, 5.32
101	1.49
172B	2.24; 3.9
Pt 2 Ch 15 (ss 196–220)	5.21

Table of statutes

Income Tax (Trading and Other Income) Act 2005 – *contd*
s 214–220	5.21
Pt 3 (ss 260–364)	2.6; 3.11
s 264	1.17, 1.22; 2.8
265	1.17; 2.8
Pt 3 Ch 3 (ss 268–275)	3.1
s 270	1.28
271	1.2
272	1.1, 1.19; 2.6; 3.1; 5.25, 5.32; 15.18
272A	3.1, 3.12, 3.25, 3.29, 3.30; 7.4; 10.6; 13.1
(1)–(4)	3.3
(5)	3.4
272B	3.54; 7.4; 13.1
(2)	3.6, 3.37
(3)	3.8
(4)	3.37, 3.54
(5), (6)	3.5
(7)	3.6
274A	3.12, 3.25, 3.30, 3.36; 10.6; 13.1
(2)	3.19, 3.31
(5), (7)	3.31
274AA	3.20, 3.25, 3.30, 3.36
(2)	3.35
(b)(i)	3.17
(4)	3.12, 3.19; 7.4
(6)	3.16
247B	13.1
274C	3.28; 13.1
275	1.28
276, 277	1.40
291	1.45
(2)	1.45
303	1.41
308A	5.15, 5.19, 5.32
308B	5.15, 5.18, 5.19, 5.32
308C	5.15, 5.19, 5.32
311A	5.7
(7)	6.4
322	6.1
323	4.12; 6.16; 11.38
324	6.21
325	4.12
326	4.13; 6.18
326A	4.14; 6.19
349	15.22

Income Tax (Trading and Other Income) Act 2005 – *contd*
Pt 5 Ch 5 (ss 619–648)	3.47
s 619	1.7
624	8.27, 8.36
626	8.27
Pt 5 Ch 6 (ss 649–682A)	3.32, 3.35, 3.54
s 649	3.34
656(4)	3.34
Pt 9 (ss 846–863L)	1.10
s 846	1.10
852	1.29
Inheritance Tax Act 1984	12.1
s 1	12.1
2	12.2
(1)	12.33
3(1)	12.1
(2)	12.17
3A	12.32
(1A), (5)	12.9
4(1)	12.2, 12.42
(2)	8.6
5(1)	12.3, 12.42
(2)	12.42
(3)	12.17, 12.23
(5)	12.17, 12.23, 12.43
6	12.4
(1)	12.2
7	12.2
(2)	12.1
(4)	12.32
18	8.59; 12.9, 12.37
(2)	12.31
19	12.31
22	12.37
43	12.8
(4)	12.8
Pt III Ch II (ss 49–57A)	12.8
s 49(1)	12.3, 12.8
52(1)	12.2
Pt III Ch III (ss 58–85)	12.8
s 94	12.9, 12.33
95–97	12.33
Pt V Ch I (ss 103–114)	6.24
s 103	12.12
104	12.12
(1)(a)	12.4
105	12.12; 13.11
(1)(a)	12.13

Table of statutes

Inheritance Tax Act 1984 – *contd*	
s 105(3)	6.24; 12.13, 12.16
106–114	12.12
131	12.46
(1)	12.48
(2ZA)	12.46
(2A), (3)	12.47
132–136	12.46
137	12.46, 12.49
(4)	12.49
138	12.46, 12.49
139, 140	12.46
142	8.57
160	12.17, 12.21
161	8.56; 12.25, 12.48
(1)	12.28, 12.29
(2)	12.25
(3)	12.26, 12.28, 12.29
(4)	12.28
162(1)–(5)	12.23
162A–162C	12.24, 12.43
163	12.21
175A	12.24, 12.43
(2), (4)	12.24
176	12.30
(3)	12.30
190	12.50
(1)	12.50
(4)	12.51
191	12.50
(1)	12.52, 12.54
(b)	12.52
(1A)	12.52
(2), (3)	12.51
192	12.50, 12.53
(1), (2)	12.53
193–196	12.50
197	12.50, 12.51
197A	12.50
(3)	12.53
198	12.50
202	12.33
227	12.56
(1C)	12.56
(3), (4)	12.57
234	12.57
267ZA, 267ZB	12.31
272	12.3
Land and Buildings Transaction Tax (Amendment) (Scotland) Act 2016	13.46, 13.50; 14.42
s 2(1)(d)	14.20
Land and Buildings Transaction Tax (Scotland) Act 2013	14.5
s 13	14.14
14(1)(c)	14.7
18–20	14.18
22	13.48; 14.13, 14.56, 14.57
23	13.48
24	14.41
26	13.49; 14.51
29, 40	14.6
41	14.18
57	13.49; 14.41
58	13.48
59	13.49
(8)	14.20
60	14.14
Sch 2	13.48; 14.11
para 4	14.17
5	14.14
6	14.15
8	14.12
(2)	14.12
Sch 2A	14.42
para 2	14.42
3	14.42
(1)–(3), (5)	14.42, 14.55
9	13.49; 14.20, 14.42, 14.53
10	13.49; 14.42, 14.53
Sch 5	13.50; 14.20, 14.52, 14.53
para 10A	13.49; 14.42
12	13.50
Sch 12	14.13
Sch 17	13.53, 13.55; 14.55
para 20–22	13.54
Sch 20	14.8
Landlord and Tenant Act 1985	
s 11	18.11
Land Registration Act 2002	
s 33, 43	8.14
Land Tenure Reform (Scotland) Act 1974	
s 8, 9	14.1

Table of statutes

Law of Property Act 1925
  s 1 .... 8.6, 8.11, 8.18
  2 .... 8.17
  34, 35 .... 8.4
  36 .... 8.4, 8.6, 8.19
  88, 89 .... 8.17
  104, 105 .... 8.17
  184 .... 8.6
  196 .... 8.19
  205 .... 8.1
Limited Liability Partnerships Act 2000 .... 1.12; 12.11; 13.53; 14.55
  s 2(1)(a) 12.11
  10 .... 1.12
  (1) 1.12
Limited Partnerships Act 1907 .... 12.11; 13.53; 14.55

Partnership Act 1890 .... 1.11; 12.11, 12.21
  s 1 .... 12.11
  2(1) 1.11; 12.11
  (a) 12.11
Private Housing (Tenancies) (Scotland) Act 2016 .... 17.7; 18.13

Rent Act 1977 .... 17.7
Renting Homes (Wales) Act 2016 .... 17.7; 18.2, 18.12, 18.13
Revenue Scotland and Tax Powers Act 2014 .... 14.5
  s 62–72 .... 13.58; 14.60

Small Business, Enterprise and Employment Act 2015 .... 13.47
Social Security Contributions and Benefits Act 1992
  s 2(1)(b) 13.74
  11 .... 13.74
  15(1) 13.76

Taxation of Chargeable Gains Act 1992 .... 11.1; 13.21
  s 2(1) 10.4, 10.14; 11.1
  (1A) 10.4, 10.14
  (7A) 10.13
  (7B) 10.14
  2B 10.13

Taxation of Chargeable Gains Act 1992 – *contd*
  s 2B(3) 10.13
  2C 10.13
  (4), (5) 10.13
  2D–2F 10.13
  4 .... 3.11; 10.3
  (2), (3) 11.2
  (3A) 10.13
  (3B) 10.14
  (4), (5) 11.2
  4B 10.3; 11.20
  (3A) 13.2
  4BB 11.2
  8 .... 1.30; 11.1
  10 .... 11.1
  14B 10.4
  14C 9.10; 10.4
  14D 10.4, 10.14
  (4) 10.14
  14E 10.4, 10.14
  14F 10.4, 10.14
  (2), (11) 10.14
  14G 10.4, 10.14
  14H 10.14
  16 .... 6.13
  17 .... 6.10, 6.11; 11.6, 11.17; 13.16
  18 .... 6.10; 11.6, 11.17; 13.16
  21(2) 11.12
  22(1)(c) 1.49
  23(4) 11.28
  28(1), (2) 11.3
  35(2) 11.11
  (3)(a)–(d) 11.11
  (4) 11.11
  38 .... 1.26; 11.7; 13.40
  (1)(b) 1.52
  42 .... 1.40; 11.12
  52A 3.44; 10.3
  58 .... 6.10; 11.6, 11.29
  59 .... 1.10
  127–139 .... 10.16
  144 .... 11.4
  152 .... 6.9; 13.18, 13.43
  (8) 13.43
  153, 154 .... 13.18
  155 .... 6.9; 13.18
    Head A 13.44

Table of statutes

Taxation of Chargeable Gains
Act 1992 – contd
s 156	13.18
157	13.18, 13.44
161	2.25
(2)	2.24
(3)	2.25
162	3.54; 11.27; 13.5, 13.7, 13.13, 13.14, 13.18, 13.19, 13.21, 13.22, 13.23, 13.24, 13.25, 13.26, 13.27, 13.29, 13.30, 13.31, 13.32, 13.39, 13.42, 13.47, 13.71, 13.77
(1)	13.20, 13.24
(3)	13.19
(4)	13.19, 13.27
162A	13.19
165	6.11; 13.7, 13.18, 13.36, 13.37, 13.40, 13.41, 13.42, 13.71
(1)(a)	13.38
(b)	13.39
(4)	13.38
(6), (7)	13.40
165A(14)	6.8
169H	6.7
169I	13.33
(2)	13.34
169K	13.33
169L, 169LA	13.34
169P	13.33
169S(1)	13.18, 13.34
171, 179	10.16
222	2.32; 11.30; 13.18
(1)(b)	11.31
(3)	11.31
(5)	11.36
223	2.32
(1)	11.32
(2)	11.33
(3)	11.34
(4)	13.18
224	2.32
(3)	11.37; 13.18
(4)	11.37
225, 226	2.32
241	6.7, 6.8, 6.9, 6.11, 6.12, 6.13; 13.7, 13.32

Taxation of Chargeable Gains
Act 1992 – contd
s 241(3A)	13.32, 13.34, 13.35
241A	6.7, 6.8, 6.9, 6.11, 6.12, 6.13; 13.7, 13.32
(5)	13.32, 13.34, 13.35
245	11.14
248A–248E	11.41
253	6.12
260	11.26; 12.39
261B	11.22, 11.23, 11.24
(2)–(4)	11.22
(7)(a)	11.22
(8)	11.24
286	11.6
(6)	13.16
Sch B1	
para 1, 2	9.10
4	9.11
8	9.11
Sch C1	10.14
Sch 3	
para 6	11.8
Sch 4ZZA	10.13
para 2	10.13
3	10.13
(3)	10.13
4	10.13
(3), (5)	10.13
5	10.13
6(2)–(4)	10.13
6A	10.14
Sch 4ZZB	10.14
para 2	9.14
13	9.18; 10.14
14	9.18; 10.14
15	10.14
23	10.14
Sch 5B	11.42
para 1(2)(b)	13.18
19(1)	13.18
Sch 5BB	13.18
Sch 7	
para 5, 6	13.41
Sch 7AC	6.13
Sch 8	1.47
para 1	1.42
2	11.39
5	1.41
(2)	1.42

Table of statutes

Taxes Management Act 1970	
s 7	1.31
(7)	1.32
12B	1.35
43(1)	13.39
59D(1)	13.73
Trustee Act 1925	
s 2, 14, 28	8.11
Trusts of Land and Appointment of Trustees Act 1996	8.4
Value Added Act 1994	
Sch 9	
Group 1	3.55; 13.65; 15.1

Table of statutory instruments and other guidance

[*All references are to paragraph numbers*]

STATUTORY INSTRUMENTS

Building Regulations 1991, SI 1991/2768	18.4, 18.8
Charge to Income tax by Reference to Enjoyment of Property Previously Owned Regulations 2005, SI 2005/724	12.60
reg 2	12.59
6	12.60
Childcare Payments (Eligibility) Regulations 2015, SI 2015/448	
reg 15	3.11
Childcare Payments (Eligibility) (Amendment) Regulations 2016, SI 2016/793	3.11
Education (Student Loans) (Repayment) Regulations 2009, SI 2009/470	
reg 29(4)	3.11
(a), (c)	3.11
Income Tax (Construction Industry Scheme) Regulations 2005, SI 2005/2045	15.6
Income Tax (Pay As You Earn) Regulations 2003, SI 2003/2682	
reg 69(1)	13.73
Inheritance Tax (Double Charges Relief) Regulations 1987, SI 1987/1130	12.34
reg 6	12.45
(3)(a), (b)	12.45
9	12.45
Land Buildings Transaction Tax (Tax Rates and Tax Bands) (Scotland) Order 2015, SSI 2015/126	10.2; 14.41
Private Tenancies (Northern Ireland) Order 2006, NISI 2006/1459	17.7
Value Added Tax Regulations 1995, SI 1995/2518 Pt XIV (regs 99–111)	15.2
Tax Credits (Definition and Calculation of Income) Regulations 2002, SI 2002/2006	
reg 11	3.11

HMRC GUIDANCE MATERIALS

Business Income Manual	
BIM 20315	2.26
BIM 33630	3.9
BIM 35430	2.16
BIM 35450	1.25
BIM 42701	App A
BIM 45510	App A
BIM 45665	2.19
BIM 45685	1.37
BIM 45700	2.18
BIM 45815	2.17
BIM 45820	2.17
BIM 46911	5.26, 5.33
BIM 46990	5.33
BIM 47820	App A
BIM 51625	3.9
BIM 60060	2.26
BIM 75010	App A
BIM 85025	11.24
Capital Allowances Manual	
CA11520	3.38, 3.39
CA 20020	7.12; 13.66
CA 23083	1.20
CA 29040	13.69
Corporate Finance Manual	
CFM 35110	2.22
CFM 35120	2.22

Table of statutory instruments and other guidance

Capital Gains Manual
- CG 15160 .... 1.46
- CG 15280 .... App A
- CG 27170 .... 13.8
- CG 61250 .... 13.44
- CG 64015 .... 13.35
- CG 64137 .... 13.40
- CG 64435 .... 11.32
- CG 65230 .... 2.12
- CG 65710 .... 13.24
- CG 65715 .... 13.14, 13.22
- CG 65720 .... 13.24
- CG 5715 .... 13.6

Employment Income Manual
- EIM 26135 .... 3.41

Employment Related Securities Manual
- ERSM 140040 .... 13.77

Enquiry Manual
- EM 4555 .... 1.32

Inheritance Tax Manual
- IHT 04073 .... 12.34
- IHTM 09734 .... 12.28
- IHTM 09737 .... 12.28
- IHTM 09739 .... 12.27
- IHTM 09754 .... 12.30
- IHTM 14318 .... 12.37
- IHTM 14336 .... 12.38
- IHTM 14626 .... 12.48
- IHTM 14663 .... 12.49
- IHTM 15044 .... 12.18
- IHTM 15091 .... 12.5
- IHTM 25271 .... 12.13, 12.15
- IHTM 25275 .... 12.15
- IHTM 25278 .... 6.24; 12.16
- IHTM 28029 .... 12.24
- IHTM 28030 .... 12.24
- IHTM 30363 .... 12.57
- IHTM 33000–330182 .... 12.55
- IHTM 33012 .... 12.52, 12.55, 12.55
- IHTM 33026 .... 12.51
- IHTM 33074 .... 12.50
- IHTM 33161 .... 12.53
- IHTM 33163 .... 12.53
- IHTM 4031 .... 12.3
- IHTM 44000–44116 .... 12.60

National Insurance Manual
- NIM 23800 .... 13.75

Property Income Manual
- PIM 1020 .... 5.11
- PIM 1030 .... 1.11; 3.46
- PIM 1040 .... 6.21
- PIM 2020 .... 1.25; 2.16
- PIM 2025 .... App A
- PIM 2030, 2040 .... App A
- PIM 2054 .... App A
- PIM 2205, 2210 .... App A
- PIM 2220 .... 2.37
- PIM 2330 .... 1.45
- PIM 2505 .... 1.17, 1.18; 15.21
- PIM 2500 .... 7.9
- PIM 25010 .... 15.21
- PIM 2510 .... 1.24; 7.9
- PIM 3205 .... 5.18
- PIM 4105 .... 6.16, 6.21
- PIM 4112 .... 6.17
- PIM 4120 .... 4.15; 6.4; 13.76
- PIM 4300 .... 2.5, 2.11; 3.10

Savings and Investment Manual
- SAIM 10230 .... 13.61
- SAIM 10250 .... 13.62

Stamp Duty Land Tax Manual
- SDLTM 04015 .... 14.49
- SDLTM 04020 .... 14.14
- SDLTM 29957 .... 3.40
- SDLTM 33310 .... 13.56
- SDLTM 34160 .... 13.54
- SDLTM 34170 .... 13.54

Trusts, Settlements and Estates Manual
- TSEM 4000 .... 3.47
- TSEM 4220 .... 1.6

EXTRA STATUTORY CONCESSIONS
- ESC B1 .... 5.28, 5.32
- ESC B47 .... 5.15, 5.17, 5.25, 5.26, 5.28, 5.30, 5.32
- ESC D32 .... 11.27; 13.24

REVENUE AND CUSTOMS BRIEFS
- 71/07 .... 12.28
- 05/13 .... 5.33

Table of statutory instruments and other guidance

STATEMENTS OF PRACTICE		VAT NOTICES	
D12	1.8; 13.8	709/3	6.15
SP/8/93	14.49		

Table of cases

[All references are to paragraph numbers or Appendix]

A

A-G v Cohen [1936] 2 KB 246, [1936] 1 All ER 583 .... 14.28
American Leaf Blending Sdn Bhd v Director-General of Inland Revenue [1979] AC 676, [1978] 3 WLR 985, [1978] 3 All ER 1185 .... 11.27; 13.9, 13.22
Arkwright (personal representative of Williams, dec'sd) v IRC [2004] EWHC 1720 (Ch), [2005] 1 WLR 1411, [2004] STC 1323 .... 12.28

B

Barclays Mercantile Business Finance Ltd v Mawson (Inspector of Taxes) [2004] UKHL 51, [2005] 1 AC 684, [2004] 3 WLR 1383 .... 13.29
Birmingham & District Cattle By-Products Co Ltd v IRC (1919) 12 TC 92 ..... 1.18
Burgess v Rawnsley [1985] Ch 429, [1975] 3 WLR 99, [1975] 3 All ER 142 ... 8.20
Burkinyoung's Exor v IRC [1995] STC (SCD) 29 .... 12.14; 13.11

C

C & E Comrs v Lord Fisher [1981] 2 All ER 147, [1981] STC 238 .... 12.14; 13.10, 13.21
Cairnsmill Caravan Park v R & C Comrs [2013] UKFTT 164 (TC) 2.16
Caledonian Rly Co v Banks (1880) 8 R 89, 1 TC 487 .... 5.26
Carlton v Goodman [2002] EWCA Civ 545, [2002] 2 FLR 259, [2002] Fam Law 595 .... 8.13
Carr-Glynn v Frearsons [1999] Ch 326, [1999] 2 WLR 1046, [1998] 4 All ER 225 .... 8.53
Charkham (dec'sd) v IRC [2000] RVR 7 .... 12.20
Chick v Comr of Stamp Duties of New South Wales [1958] AC 435, [1958] 3 WLR 93, [1958] 2 All ER 623 .... 12.38
Clarke (exors of Clarke, dec'sd) v HMRC [2005] STC (SCD) 823, [2005] WTLR 1465, [2005] STI 1758 .... 12.15
Conn v Robins Bros Ltd (1966) 43 TC 266 .... 2.16

D

Dunmore v McGowan (Inspector of Taxes) [1978] 1 WLR 617, [1978] 2 All ER 85, 52 TC 307 .... 8.30

F

Frost (Inspector of Taxes) v Feltham [1981] 1 WLR 452, [1981] STC 115, (1980) 55 TC 10 .... 11.32
Furniss (Inspector of Taxes) v Dawson [1984] AC 474, [1984] 2 WLR 226, [1984] STC 153 .... 13.29

G

G Pratt & Sons v R & C Comrs [2011] UKFTT 416 (TC) 2.16

Table of cases

Green v R & C Comrs [2015] UKFTT 334 (TC) 12.16
Griffiths (Inspector of Taxes) v Jackson [1983] STC 184, 56 TC 583, [1983] BTC 68 .... 2.11; 13.34

H

Halpin v R & C Comrs [2011] UKFTT 512 (TC) 8.30
Harris v Goddard [1983] 1 WLR 1203, [1983] 3 All ER 242, (1983) 46 P & CR 417... 8.19
Harthan v Mason [1980] STC 94, 53 TC 272, [1979] TR 369 .... 13.9
Hartland v R & C Comrs [2014] UKFTT 1099 (TC), [2015] STI 577 .... 2.12

I

IRC v Eversden [2003] EWCA Civ 668, [2003] STC 822, 75 TC 340 .... 12.37
IRC v George (exors of Stedman, dec'sd) [2003] EWCA Civ 1763, [2004] STC 147, 75 TC 735.. 12.15, 12.16
IRC v Gray (surviving exor of Lady Fox, dec'sd) [1994] STC 360, [1994] 2 EGLR 185, [1994] 38 EG 156 .... 12.21

J

Jarmin (Inspector of Taxes) v Rawlings [1994] STC 1005, 67 TC 130, [1994] STI 1373... 6.7

L

Law Shipping Co Ltd v IRC (1923-24) 17 Ll L Rep 184, 1924 SC 74, 12 TC 621.. 1.26

M

McKnight (Inspector of Taxes) v Sheppard [1999] 1 WLR 1333, [1999] 3 All ER 491, [1999] STC 669 .... 2.14
Mallalieu v Drummond (Inspector of Taxes) [1983] 2 AC 861, [1983] 3 WLR 409, [1983] 2 All ER 1095... 2.14
Marshall Hus & Partners Ltd v Bolton [1981] STC 18, 55 TC 539, [1980] TR 371... 1.30
Martin (exors of Moore, dec'sd) v IRC [1995] STC (SCD) 5 .... 12.14

O

Odeon Associated Theatres Ltd v Jones [1973] Ch 288, [1972] 2 WLR 331, (1971) 48 TC 257 .... 1.26; 5.26

P

Page (Inspector of Taxes) v Lowther [1983] STC 799, 57 TC 199, (1983) 127 SJ 786... 2.34
Price v R & C Comrs [2010] UKFTT 474 (TC), [2011] SFTD 52, [2011] WTLR 161 .... 8.56; 12.29
Project Blue Ltd (formerly Project Blue (Guernsey Ltd)) v R & C Comrs [2016] EWCA Civ 485, [2016] STC 2168, [2016] BTC 22 .... 14.58
Prudential Assurance Co Ltd v IRC [1993] 1 WLR 211, [1992] STC 863, [1992] EG 127 (CS)... 14.49

Table of cases

R

R & C Comrs v Pawson (dec'sd) [2013] UKUT 50 (TCC), [2013] STC 976, [2013] BTC 160 .... 6.24, 6.25; 12.16; 13.11

R & C Comrs v Salaried Persons Postal Loans Ltd [2006] EWHC 763 (Ch), [2006] STC 1315, [2006] BTC 423 .... 13.12

R (on the applicationof Wilkinson) v IRC [2005] UKHL 30, [2005] 1 WLR 1718, [2006] 1 All ER 529 .... 5.32

Ramsay v R & C Comrs [2013] UKUT 226 (TCC), [2013] STC 1764, [2013] BTC 1868 .... 12.10; 13.7, 13.13, 13.14, 13.21, 13.23, 13.31

Rashid v Garcia (Status Inspector [2003] STC (SCD) 36 [2003] STI 35 ...... 2.8; 13.12, 13.13

Riley v Read (1879) 1 TC 217 .... 4.8

Roelich v R & C Comrs [2014] UKFTT 579 (TC), [2014] STI 2891 .... 13.23

S

St Barbe Green v IRC [2005] EWHC 14 (Ch), [2005] 1 WLR 1722, [2005] STC 288 .... 12.43

Salisbury House Estates Ltd v Fry (Inspector of Taxes) [1930] AC 432, 15 TC 266 .... 13.34

Saunders v Vautier (1841) 41 ER 482, Cr & Ph 240 .... 8.42

Scorer (Inspector of Taxes) v Olin Energy Systems Ltd [1985] AC 645, [1985] 2 WLR 668, 58 TC 592 .... 1.36

Silk v Fletcher (Inspector of Taxes) [2000] STC (SCD) 565, [2000] STI 1655 . 2.19

Simmons (Liquidator of Lionel Simmons Properties Ltd) v IRC [1980] 1 WLR 1196, [1980] 2 All ER 798, [1980] STC 350 .... 2.3

Stack v Dowden [2007] UKHL 17, [2007] 2 AC 432, [2007] 2 WLR 831 .... 8.13

T

Taylor v Good (Inspector of Taxes) [1974] 1 WLR 556, [1974] 1 All ER 1137, [1974] STC 148 .... 2.3, 2.35

Terrace Hill (Berkeley) Ltd v R & C Comrs [2015] UKFTT 75 (TC), [2015] STI 1534 .... 2.12

Town Investments Ltd v Department of the Environment [1978] AC 359, [1977] 2 WLR 450, [1977] 1 All ER 813 .... 13.9

W

WT Ramsay Ltd v IRC [19982] AC 300, [1981] 2 WLR 449, [1981] STC 174 ... 13.29

Walker v Hall [1984] Fam Law 21, [1984] FLR 126, (1983) 80 LSG 2139 ...... 8.12

Wight & Moss v IRC (1982) 264 EG 935, [1984] RVR 163 .... 8.56

Williams v Hensman (1861) 1 John & H 546, 70 ER 862 .... 8.19

Wills v R & C Comrs [2010] UKFTT 174 (TC) 2.16

Woolnough, Re; Perkins v Bowden [2002] WTLR 595 .... 8.20

Y

Yarmouth v France (1887) 19 QBD 647 .... 4.3

Prologue

Starting a buy-to-let residential property business? What you need to know

Lee Sharpe CTA, ATT, Tax Consultant, Sharpe Tax Consulting Ltd.

SIGNPOSTS

- **Background** – The UK law relating to property has changed dramatically in the last few years. Many of the changes have potentially significant effects on buy-to-let residential property landlords. The following signposts are a summary of key developments for buy-to-let residential landlords. The tax measures are discussed further below. For non-tax issues, see **Chapters 16–18** (see **P.1–P.2**).

- **1 April 2013** – Annual tax on enveloped dwellings (ATED) introduced, to properties valued at more than £2 million (see **P.3**).

- **1/6 April 2013** – Purported abolition of renewals basis for loose furnishings in residential lettings (for income tax/corporation tax purposes respectively) (see **P.4**).

- **20 March 2014** – Purchases of dwellings by 'non-natural persons' attract 15% stamp duty land tax (SDLT), at lower threshold (see **P.5**).

- **6 April 2014** – Capital gains tax (CGT) principal private residence relief (or only or main residence relief) 'grace period' for final period of ownership reduced from three years to 18 months (see **P.6**).

- **4 December 2014** – SDLT on residential property reformed to apply on a progressive basis rather than a 'slab' basis (see **P.7**).

- **1 April 2015** – Land and buildings transaction tax (LBTT) applies in Scotland to replace SDLT. ATED applies to properties valued at more than £1 million (ie fall in *de minimis* threshold). Introduction of CGT on UK residential property owned by non-residents (see **P.8–P.9**).

- **1 October 2015** – Changed section 21 regime begins in England as a result of the *Deregulation Act 2014*. Smoke and Carbon Monoxide

- Regulations come into force in England, setting minimum standards for smoke alarm and carbon monoxide detectors.
- **23 November 2015** – New licensing and registration regime in Wales commences (not enforceable for one year).
- **1 January 2016** – New electrical testing regime begins in Scotland. New obligations in relation to smoke alarms and carbon monoxide alarms begin in Scotland.
- **1 February 2016** – Right to rent under the *Immigration Act 2014* comes into force throughout England.
- **16 March 2016** – Reform of SDLT for commercial (non-residential) properties (see **P.10**).
- **1/6 April 2016** – Reform of tax relief for furnishings in residential properties: abolition of wear and tear allowance for fully furnished properties; abolition of statutory renewals basis; 'new' relief for replacement of furniture, etc. (see **P.11**).
- **1 April 2016** – Extra 3% SDLT charge for 'additional' residential properties. ATED applies to properties valued at more than £500,000 (ie further fall in *de minimis* threshold) (see **P.12**).
- **6 April 2016** – Rate of CGT falls for 'non-residential property gains' (ie leaving residential property gains at an 8% disadvantage). Rent-a-room relief threshold extended from £4,250 to £7,500 (see **P.13–P.14**).
- **5 July 2016** – New regime for trading in and developing land; ostensibly to capture non-resident entities profiting from developing or dealing in UK land/property, but will in most cases catch as trading income development for onward sale at a profit (see **P.15**).
- **23 November 2016** – Rent smart Wales licensing and registration regime enforceable.
- **December 2016** – Right to rent checks given more teeth in England with the introduction of the *Immigration Act 2016*.
- **6 April 2017** – Progressive restriction of tax relief for finance costs (ie residential property businesses only) starts (ie year 1 of 4). New 'sharing economy' £1,000 allowance for letting incomes (see **P.15–P.16**).
- **April 2018** – Introduction of land transaction tax in Wales, and replacement of SDLT for Wales.
- **Through 2018** – Introduction of *Renting Homes (Wales) Act 2016* and replacement of current regime of residential tenancies in Wales. Introduction of *Housing (Private Tenancies) (Scotland) Act 2016*, replacing current regime of residential tenancies in Scotland.

Starting a buy-to-let residential property business? What you need to know

- **1 October 2018 onwards** – End of the transitional regime for *s 21* notices in England. All assured shorthold tenancies must now follow new *Deregulation Act* regime. CGT reporting and payment to be accelerated by 2019 (see **P.17**).

BACKGROUND
P.1

Focus

UK law relating to property has changed dramatically in the last few years. Many of the changes may affect only relatively few buy-to-let (BTL) residential landlords but some changes, such as the impending restriction of tax relief for mortgage interest and other finance costs for residential property landlords, seem likely to affect a substantial proportion of landlords, and certainly 'career' landlords with substantial portfolios, where 'gearing up' to expand the portfolio is very common.

This book aims to keep accountants and other advisers up-to-date as these changes develop. The book does *not* concentrate solely on tax, but also includes chapters on finance and landlord obligations, so that the reader can accrue a more rounded appreciation of the challenges currently facing investors in UK property.

Chronology – changes in the last few years
P.2

The pace and extent of change is such that landlords and their advisers might be forgiven for feeling a little harassed – most of the changes are intended to yield more money to the Exchequer (and by implication to cost landlords more money), or to increase landlords' duties and responsibilities. There are, however, one or two small comforts to be found.

The key developments in recent years are outlined below.

Annual tax on enveloped dwellings
P.3

ATED (*FA 2013, s 94*) is an annual tax charge on 'non-natural persons' that hold an interest in high-value UK residential property. 'Non-natural persons' include companies, partnerships that include companies, and collective investment schemes, since it was introduced to address concerns about SDLT

Starting a buy-to-let residential property business? What you need to know

avoidance using corporate structures; it is not affected by the company's tax residence.

> **Focus**
>
> ATED is particularly relevant to BTL landlords that own property through corporate structures, even where those companies are UK-resident.

The ATED charge was intended originally for high value properties held in a corporate wrapper, so a minimum value was set, at or below which ATED would not apply. However, that *de minimis* value threshold has quickly been reduced for the application of the charge, as follows:

- £2 million for ATED charges from 1 April 2013 (the initial value); then
- £1 million for ATED charges from 1 April 2015; then
- £500,000 for ATED charges from 1 April 2016.

The valuation applies to 'single dwelling interests' – in effect, the *de minimis* value test is not applied to a portfolio but to each single dwelling in which there is an interest. Hotels, guest houses, care homes and similar are not classed as 'dwellings' so do not fall within the scope of ATED.

Companies that own high-value property that would otherwise be caught but that is being used in a rental business may claim relief from ATED (by virtue of *FA 2013, s 133*). However, the relief must actively be claimed, since an ATED return is required if the value and ownership conditions are met. Similar reliefs are available for property developers and property traders. ATED returns are due generally within 30 days of the *commencement* of a chargeable period, which spans 1 April to 31 March – so by 30 April – or within 30 days of acquisition if the relevant property is acquired after 1 April in a year.

When ATED was originally introduced, a return/relief claim was required for each affected dwelling – and, since use might change in a year, more than one return might be required in a chargeable period. Fortunately for BTL landlords, it is now possible (since April 2015) to file a single relief claim encompassing all properties subject to a particular relief category. However, further acquisitions in a chargeable year may require further returns and claims.

Finally, companies within the scope of ATED may also be liable to a tax charge on ATED-related capital gains on property disposals since 6 April 2013 (*TCGA 1992, Sch 4ZZA*). Such gains generally accrue from 5 April 2013, to the extent that a property has been subject to an ATED charge. The ATED-related CGT charge is 28%. ATED-related CGT takes precedence over the more general non-resident CGT charge, for periods where there is a non-relieved ATED charge (*TCGA 1992, Sch 4ZZA, s 2C(4); Sch 4ZZB, para 12(5)*).

Further information on ATED can be found in **Chapter 10**. ATED-related CGT is also discussed in **Chapter 9**.

Tax relief for furnishings in residential lettings – removal of renewals 'concession'

P.4

Somewhen before 2013, HMRC reversed its earlier position that the cost of replacing furnishings in residential lettings would be covered by statute and said that, from April 2013, there would be no relief at all – unless the item was attached to the property such that it could be considered a replacement of part of the property itself and thereby a repair to a greater whole.

See **Chapter 5** for further information.

'Enveloped' dwellings: 15% stamp duty land tax threshold reduced

P.5

Since March 2012, purchases of high-value single use residential dwellings had attracted a premium SDLT rate of 15%, when bought by a 'non-natural person' – companies, partnerships including a company, and collective investment schemes. At the time, the rate was applied to residential properties costing more than £2 million.

There were (and remain) exceptions for rental businesses, property developers and property traders, farmhouses and others; also depending on the residential property itself.

The threshold was reduced for purchases completing on or after 20 March 2014, to apply to properties costing more than £500,000 (*FA 2014, s 111*). Property rental businesses will avoid this charge so long as profits are carried on (on) a commercial basis and with a view to a profit (*FA 2003, Sch 4A para 5*).

See **Chapter 14** for further commentary.

Private residence relief: final period of ownership rule restricted to 18 months

P.6

The regime for relieving the disposal of one's only or main residence from CGT (principal private residence or PPR relief) had long held a particularly useful exclusion for the last 36 months of ownership: they would qualify for the relief in almost any circumstances (except where, or to the extent that, the property was used exclusively in a trade or business).

This measure was intended to allow homeowners a decent amount of time to sell their previous main residence if they had moved into their new home but were struggling to sell, without having to sacrifice eligibility for their new home. (*TCGA 1992, s 223*).

Starting a buy-to-let residential property business? What you need to know

However, it was perceived to be overly generous and too easily manipulated to deliberately generate tax-free gains, which could be substantial over a three-year period in a volatile housing market. Landlords were free to benefit from these rules, provided they had occupied the property as their main residence at any time in their period of ownership.

While this part of the relief continues, its utility was curtailed by restricting the period to just 18 months, for disposals on or after 6 April 2014 (*FA 2014, s 58*).

Reform of residential property stamp duty land tax

P.7

SDLT was radically overhauled for residential property purchases that completed on or after 4 December 2014. The old 'slab' regime, whereby the relevant rate applied to the entire purchase price (resulting in large 'cliff-edge' hikes as the purchase price passed a new threshold) was replaced by a progressive regime that charges the rate applicable to the portion of consideration falling in the relevant band.

However, it was not all good news: the new regime also introduced higher tax rates and lower bands than beforehand. For example, a residential property costing up to £1 million would previously have been charged at only 4% whereas, from 4 December, anything costing more than £925,000 would be charged at 10%. The rates apply regardless of whether or not there is a property rental business.

See **Chapter 14** for further commentary on SDLT and LBTT.

Land and buildings transaction tax

P.8

The *Land and Buildings Transaction Tax (Scotland) Act 2013* was passed in July 2013, to replace in Scotland the SDLT regime that continues to apply in England, Wales (for now) and Northern Ireland. It broadly applies to property contracts settled on or after 1 April 2015, although there are transitional provisions for contracts that were entered into on or before 1 May 2012.

LBTT is very similar to the SDLT regime on which it is based – and it picked up the 'progressive' basis for charging residential properties that transformed SDLT as mentioned above. However, SDLT and LBTT are *not* the same, and notable distinctions between the regimes increase as new measures are introduced – such as the extra 3% that applies to additional residential properties (although largely similar across both regimes, there are several differences in the way it has been implemented in Scotland).

See **Chapter 14** for more detailed information on the SDLT and LBTT regimes.

Starting a buy-to-let residential property business? What you need to know

Non-resident capital gains tax on residential property interests

P.9

For many years, it was generally possible for non-resident persons to dispose of UK residential property without worrying about UK CGT (except where used in a trading activity), but this perceived unfairness was addressed in *Finance Act 2015*.

The non-resident CGT (NRCGT) rules apply for gains made on or after 6 April 2015 and, basically to:

- Individuals;
- Partners in a partnership;
- Trusts and estates;
- Companies.

There are exceptions for communally-occupied properties, such as hotels, care homes, etc. However, (and unlike ATED) there is no exception for property letting businesses, so non-resident landlords will generally be caught. A tax return and payment are generally required within 30 days of completion (a return is required even if there is no tax to pay).

The tax charge is supposed to apply only to gains accruing since 6 April 2015. For property already held at that date, the normal approach is to undertake a valuation as at 6 April 2015 and apply the charge to the uplift in value since then. Alternative calculation methods are available.

Since ATED can basically apply to companies wherever resident, and the NRCGT charge can apply to companies, there is a potential double-charge to CGT, which is resolved by giving primacy to ATED (which is chargeable at 28%, while standard corporation tax on capital gains is only 20%, and falling).

In the initial consultation document issued in March 2014 ('Implementing a Capital Gains Tax Charge on Non-Residents: Consultation'), it was proposed by the government that the general power to nominate which residence is one's main residence (*TCGA 1992, s 222(5)*) be abolished for all taxpayers, so that non-residents with only one residence in the UK tax net could not easily sidestep the new provisions by nominating their UK property for UK tax purposes.

The power to nominate which is one's only or main residence is extremely useful to 'ordinary' taxpayers with more than one property and, in many cases, to landlords. The government's proposal would have had some most unwelcome consequences for many more UK-resident taxpayers than the non-residents it was intended to target; ultimately an extra condition was imposed instead – that a nomination of a UK residence by a non-resident would be effective only if they and/or their non-resident spouse (where applicable) occupied the property (or other available properties in the UK) for at least 90 days in a tax year, tested at midnight (*TCGA 1992, ss 222B, 222C*).

For further information on NRCGT, see **Chapter 9**.

Reform of stamp duty land tax for non-residential transactions

P.10

Given that SDLT on residential properties can be so high (and we have not yet detailed the 3% surcharge on additional dwellings), there is some merit in considering commercial or 'mixed-use' properties, strictly 'non-residential' transactions, with their comparatively lower SDLT costs. However, perhaps the most useful aspect of the non-residential rates for residential property landlords is that even wholly residential property purchases will qualify for the lower non-residential rates, when acquiring six or more properties together (*FA 2003, s 116(7)*).

The reform of non-residential rates, like that of residential rates which preceded it, counts as something of a mixed blessing:

- The calculation moved from a 'slab' basis to a progressive, banded basis; but
- While purchases of properties at the cheaper end of the range may benefit from the abolition of the slab basis, the reform also introduced new, higher rates at the more expensive end of the range.

The change is intended overall to raise revenue for the Treasury.

Given that most BTL landlords are arguably likely to encounter the non-residential rates when dealing with six or more residential properties, it seems likely that they will in turn suffer, thanks to the higher rates that will almost certainly then apply (*FA 2016, s 116*, updating *FA 2003, s 55* and *Sch 5*).

See **Chapter 14** for further commentary on SDLT and LBTT.

Reform of tax relief for furniture in residential properties

P.11

Having 'abolished' the concessionary tax relief for the cost of replacing furnishings in residential lettings as outlined above, the government introduced further measures:

- Wear and tear allowance has been withdrawn. This very useful and straightforward relief allowed the landlord to claim a tax deduction of 10% of gross rental income (but after deducting those costs which were normally the tenant's burden, such as rates or council tax) to cover the cost of replacing furniture. Wear and tear allowance was available for individuals, partners and corporate landlords, and will be sorely missed. Relief will now be available only for the actual cost of replacing items of furniture, white goods, carpets, curtains, kitchenware and similar items.

- The statutory renewals basis – 'Replacement and alteration of trade tools' was also formally withdrawn, for both income tax and corporation tax purposes. However, a new measure, initially called 'replacement furniture relief' but now termed 'replacement domestic items relief' (introduced *FA 2016*) is essentially the renewals basis in all but name, but now available only to residential property landlords.

These measures have effect for expenditure incurred from 1 April 2016 for companies, and for 6 April 2016 for individuals, partners, trusts and other parties subject to Income Tax. (FA 2016 ss 68 and 69 removing *ITTOIA 2005, s 68* and *CTA 2009, s 68*; inserting new *ITTOIA 2005, s 311A* and *CTA 2009, s 250A*; *FA 2016, s 70 removing ITTOIA 2005, s 308A–C, CTA 2009 s 248A–C*).

See **Chapter 5** for further information.

SDLT: 3% extra charge for 'additional' dwellings
P.12

This measure was first announced in the 2015 autumn statement, and applied generally to purchases that completed from 1 April 2016. It is not aimed specifically at BTL investors, because it applies to anyone buying an additional dwelling; it does seem likely, however, that BTL investors will bear the brunt of the additional cost.

For individuals, the questions are two-fold:

(1) How many dwellings do you own at the end of the day of completion?

(2) If more than one, are you replacing your main residence?

If the answer to the second question is 'no', then the 3% charge will generally apply. Note that, if someone first buys an investment property and *then* their first main residence, then they will be caught on the second acquisition, even though it is their main residence. The rules also apply differently to corporate acquisitions: there is no 'additional' property and *any* acquisition will attract the 3% charge. There are useful transitional savings, and exclusions – most notably, that the test basically applies only at completion, so later development of bare or commercial land, into a dwelling, will not be caught (*FA 2016, s 117*, introducing new *FA 2003, Sch 4ZA*).

See **Chapter 14** for further commentary on SDLT and LBTT.

Starting a buy-to-let residential property business? What you need to know

Residential property capital gains tax

P.13

For disposals since 6 April 2016, the prevailing rates of CGT for individuals (ignoring ATED gains, as above) has fallen to 20%, and to just 10% to the extent that gains fall within whatever remains of the taxpayer's basic rate band. However, gains in respect of residential property (dwellings as per *TCGA 1992, Sch B1*) remain taxable at the 'old' rates of 28% and 18% respectively.

This effectively opens up an 8% CGT 'premium' on residential property gains, as compared to almost all other capital gains. Note that the legislation ensures that the capital gain is taxable at (what are now) the higher rates to the extent that the land/property has included a dwelling *at any time in the period of ownership*, since March 1982.

The stated intention of the new legislation (according to the accompanying Explanatory Note introducing it) is 'to provide an incentive for individuals to invest in companies over property', although commercial properties are not 'caught', nor are companies that own residential property (*FA 2016, s 72* and *Schs 11, 12*).

See **Chapter 11** for further commentary on CGT.

Rent-a-room threshold extension

P.14

The rent-a-room scheme allows a householder to let part of their main home (basically while still in occupation themselves), with various options:

- Receive up to the rent-a-room gross income limit without having to notify HMRC or to pay tax thereon;
- Where income is higher, deduct the rent-a-room gross income limit from that gross income received, and pay tax only on the net excess;
- Alternatively, it is possible simply to operate the normal regime for rental property businesses.

The taxpayer can choose differently each tax year. Clearly, if there is a deficit then the standard property business approach is likely to be preferred, in order to access and utilise those losses.

The scheme is of limited utility to property business professionals, but could, for example, benefit a bed-and-breakfast operation run from home.

The gross income limit was increased to £7,250 per year from 6 April 2016 by virtue of the *Income Tax (Limit for Rent a Room Relief) Order 2015*, which came into force on 13 August 2015, and amended *ITTOIA 2005, s 789*.

Restriction of tax relief for residential property business finance costs

P.15

This is perhaps the most controversial measure introduced in recent years. The basic approach is that, from 6 April 2017, residential property landlords will face a restriction in the amount of mortgage interest (and related finance costs) that they can claim as a deduction against their rental income. This will mean a loss in tax relief at whatever is the landlord's marginal tax rate. There will be compensation for the disallowance by way of a basic rate tax credit (ie reduction in tax liability)

While this will be sufficient to offset any increase in liability faced by investors whose marginal rate of income tax is only 20%, the disallowance will mean that some landlords who are currently only basic rate taxpayers will become higher rate taxpayers, so that the 20% tax reduction is no longer enough to balance the increased tax charge (and likewise some currently higher rate taxpayers will become exposed to additional rate tax, once their interest costs start to be added back).

Furthermore, the increase in tax-adjusted income may well affect other aspects of a landlord's tax position, such as student loans, the clawback of child benefit for high incomes, and even pension contributions

See **Chapter 3** for further information on the new regime for the restriction of tax relief for finance costs, which is being phased in over the next four years. The legislation itself was introduced in *F(No.2)A 2015* and was substantively overhauled in *FA 2016* following numerous criticisms by concerned parties *(F(No. 2)A 2015, s 24; FA 2016, s 26)*.

New regime for taxing profits from trading in and developing UK land

New legislation was introduced *very* late to *FA 2016 (ss 76–82)*, which set out to ensure (among other things) that offshore entities engaged in trading in or developing UK land were brought within the UK tax net – focusing on the fact that the land is in the UK, rather than on where the entity is situated.

The legislation was so late that it could not apply from 6 April 2016 but – broadly – from 5 July 2016 instead.

The wide scope of this legislation was afforded precious little scrutiny by reason of its late introduction and, despite assurances from HMRC that it would not affect BTL property investors when they came to sell their investment properties later on, investors should be very careful about the implications of developing an investment site or property for onward sale.

See **Chapter 2** for further commentary.

Starting a buy-to-let residential property business? What you need to know

£1,000 allowance against letting income (proposed)
P.16

The 2016 Budget announced two new allowances aimed principally at 'small incomes or micro-businesses'. One allowance is aimed at trading income, and the other at income from property – a good example of the latter being to share one's drive so that commuters might use it – for a fee – while the homeowner is away at work.

The general approach seems similar to the rent-a-room scheme: incomes from either category below £1,000 can be ignored and will be neither returnable nor taxable; where incomes exceed the relevant allowance, then £1,000 may be deducted from the gross income, leaving the balance to be taxed.

It seems likely, therefore, that there will be little appeal for normal property businesses, whose deductible costs are in turn likely to be well in excess of the £1,000 allowance, and who will generally be much better off sticking with the existing regime.

However, it *may* occasionally be of use to those who have just started to let out property towards the end of a tax year, and who might otherwise be caught out by a failure to notify chargeability under *TMA 1970, s 7*. (*Finance Bill 2017 Clause 19 and Sch 5*)

Capital gains reporting and payment to be brought forward
P.17

The Chancellor announced plans in the 2015 autumn statement to require taxable residential property sales to be returned within 30 days, alongside a payment on account of any tax due – basically emulating the regime that currently applies to non-residents who make gains on UK residential property.

Under the current rules, a gain made after 5 April 2017, in the 2017/18 tax year, will not be returnable or payable under self assessment until 31 January 2019 (at the latest); there is currently a minimum of roughly ten months to calculate the capital gain and allow for payment. While planned sales should allow sufficient time for a reasonable estimate of the CGT ultimately due, a 30-day window after an unplanned sale may prove inadequate. Consultation on the legislation was expected at the time of writing.

Chapter 1

Commencement of a property business

Lee Sharpe CTA, ATT, Tax Consultant, Sharpe Tax Consulting Ltd

SIGNPOSTS

- **How is a property business taxed?** – A property letting business is basically taxed according to trading principles, with some adjustments. It follows that the starting point for many property businesses will be a set of rental income accounts drawn up in accordance with UK generally accepted accounting principles (GAAP) (see **1.1**).

- **The business may be conducted in a variety of different entities** – eg, in sole or joint names, partnership or corporate entity (see **1.3–1.16**).

- **When does it start?** – There is some disagreement about when a property business actually commences. HMRC's stated position is that it commences when the first letting starts. However, if we follow trading principles, it can be argued that it actually commences before that point – once the landlord is in a position to let the property out, and is actively trying to do so (see **1.7–1.19**).

- **Pre-letting expenses** – Those expenses incurred before a property business begins are sometimes challenged on the basis that they should be considered capital, rather than revenue expenditure (see **1.20–1.22**).

- **Commencement** – There is (usually) only one property business, so the rules about commencement, pre-'trading' expenses, etc, apply only once. In other words, the expenses incurred in relation to a second or third property and beyond are subject to the rules for an ongoing business – although expenses may still be deemed capital improvements, etc, in relation to a particular property (see **1.23–1.25**).

- **Pre-letting: Capital or revenue?** – Expenses incurred at the outset of letting each new property can be substantial and are often subject to challenge by HM Inspector. However, it should not be assumed that substantial expenditure must be capital (see **1.26–1.27**).

1.1 *Commencement of a property business*

- **Basis periods** – These are almost universally on a tax year for unincorporated businesses, although where there is a formal partnership return, the rental basis period will follow that of the partnership. Companies are assessed to rental income according to their particular accounting period – usually twelve months (see **1.28–1.30**).

- **Administration/tax administration** – There are various administrative aspects to consider from a tax perspective, in terms of notifying HMRC and the requirement to keep records (see **1.31–1.35**).

- **Finance costs** – The arrangement of finance is critical to most property letting businesses but the source of the finance, and the security or collateral, are subordinate to the use or purpose of the finance (see **1.36–1.38**).

- **Lease Primia** – Lease premia (including reverse premia) are a complex area of property taxation; a relatively concise guide to the main aspects is included towards the end of the chapter (see **1.39–1.52**).

- **SDLT and LBTT** – New acquisitions will also be subject to Stamp Duty Land Tax (SDLT) – potentially at new, higher rates – or Land and Buildings Transaction Tax (LBTT) (see **1.53**).

BASIS OF TAXATION

1.1 For many years, the taxation of rental income has been 'harmonised' with that of trading entities. (This was not always the case, and the 'old' Schedule A rules comprised a quite separate regime for properties). The legislation now essentially dictates that trading taxation principles be applied to derive rental profits for tax purposes, with some exceptions. (*ITTOIA 2005, s 272* and *CTA 2009, s 210*)

Who is taxable on rental income?

1.2 The person liable for any tax charged is the person 'receiving or entitled to the profits' (*ITTOIA 2005, s 271*). The legislation allows HMRC to apply income tax (IT) to whoever 'owns' the profits, but also to tax (say) a letting agent who receives income on behalf of the landlord.

See **Chapter 2** for more on calculating property business profits and losses.

DIFFERENT ENTITIES

1.3

> **Focus**
>
> Most buy-to-let businesses are undertaken in sole or joint names. But some property businesses will be in partnership, while others will be in the format of a Limited Liability Partnership (LLP) or a company with limited liability.
>
> The following sections set out some of the issues to bear in mind when evaluating their suitability.

Direct ownership in sole or joint names

1.4 The individual owns the property or properties (or an interest therein). This is by far the commonest and most straightforward means of owning property. The individual is usually liable to income tax on their share of the net rental profits received, and capital gains tax (CGT) on the appropriate portion of any capital gains on the disposal of the investment properties.

Trusts

1.5 A person might also decide to put a property business into Trust. Trustees are then legally responsible for administering the Trust property on behalf of whoever the settlor designates as a beneficiary when they set up the Trust.

Trusts can be complex vehicles but, very broadly, they are taxed on a basis similar to that of individuals – ie, to income tax and CGT – albeit often at the highest rate that would apply to an individual. In some cases, however, and usually where the trustees have the power to accumulate income rather than having to pay it all out to beneficiaries, there is also an inheritance tax charge every ten years on the value of the assets in the Trust, and an 'exit charge' on value leaving the Trust in between those ten-year anniversaries.

1.6 *Commencement of a property business*

Apportioning taxable income between joint owners

1.6

> **Focus**
>
> Where properties are held jointly with other parties, the individual is generally taxed on the proportion of the income to which he or she is entitled. By default, this will be in proportion to the underlying ownership but this does not necessarily have to be the case, and a different split may have been agreed by the parties at the time (see PIM1020 and PIM1030).

1.7 While HMRC appears to accept that the agreed split in income need not necessarily follow underlying beneficial ownership, this would not necessarily prevent HMRC from arguing that the 'settlements legislation' (*ITTOIA 2005, s 619 et seq.*) applies, broadly so as to re-attribute the income according to underlying beneficial ownership. This would certainly be an issue to consider in terms of ownership between spouses and on behalf of minor children; otherwise it seems that HMRC accepts that there would be a requirement to demonstrate that the settlor may yet benefit from the diversion of funds – the following extract is from TSEM 4220, albeit specifically in relation to waiving entitlement to dividend income in favour of other shareholders:

> 'Where the person benefiting under the arrangement is not a spouse, civil partner or minor child the settlements legislation will not apply unless there are arrangements under which the money will be paid, or used to benefit the settlor (or spouse etc.).'

See also **Chapter 8**.

Partnerships and Limited Liability Partnerships

1.8 A general partnership may not be formally constituted, but may simply arise – 'Partnership is the relation which subsists between persons carrying on a business in common with a view of profit' (*PA 1890, s 1 (1)*).

There may be a formal agreement between the partners, or not. From a tax perspective, a partner is taxed on the agreed share in income, with similar provisions for CGT (that are explained in some detail in Statement of Practice D12). While the split of profits may again not necessarily need to reflect the underlying beneficial ownership in the assets, the split of capital gains almost certainly will.

1.9 Partners in a general partnership enjoy 'joint and several' liability in relation to the debts of the partnership – each partner is individually liable for up to the full amount of a partnership debt, and not just his or her notional 'share'.

1.10 From a tax perspective, while a partnership tax return is legally required to return details of its income and gains as a single entity, this is an administrative nicety, and income and gains are assessable at the level of each partner (*ITTOIA 2005, Pt 9, s 846 et seq.*; *TCGA 1992, s 59*).

Property Partnership or Joint Investment?

1.11

> **Focus**
>
> HMRC is quite adamant that most rental businesses carried on by more than one party will not be partnerships but merely jointly owned properties and, in the past, this has proved useful in as much as it relieved the joint owners of having to contend with the partnership tax filing regime, leaving them simply to account for their respective share of partnership income on their self assessment tax return.

In making HMRC's case, PIM1030 refers to the *Partnership Act 1890*:

> 'Joint tenancy, tenancy in common, joint property, common property, or part ownership does not *of itself* create a partnership as to anything so held or owned, whether the tenants or owners do or do not share any profits made by the use thereof' (*PA 1890, s 2 (1)* – emphasis added).

This would certainly make sense in the context of a jointly held bank account, share portfolio or even passively-held rental property, where the owners may, for example, appoint agents to look after the running of the property or properties. But many jointly-held property portfolios are very actively managed as a commercial business by some or all of their owners, and HMRC's position would seem quite tenuous in relation to such 'career' landlords, since, in the writer's opinion, the legislation clearly means here to exclude *only* jointly-held property that is *not* the subject of 'a business in common with a view of profit', as per **1.8** above.

Limited Liability Partnerships

1.12 Limited Liability Partnerships (LLPs) are actually corporate entities and, unlike simple general partnerships, cannot merely arise but must be constituted in accordance with the *Limited Liability Partnership Act 2000* (LLPA 2000). Nevertheless, its members are taxed almost exactly as if they were partners in a general partnership (*LLPA 2000, s 10*). Notable exceptions to that norm are when the LLP is either:

1. insolvent; or
2. not carrying on a business with a view to profit (*LLPA 2000, s 10(1)*).

1.13 *Commencement of a property business*

Many readers will be aware that there are numerous property business-based LLPs; it may ultimately prove difficult for HMRC happily to tax property LLPs as if they were general partnerships, while continuing to assert that the vast majority of joint property businesses are not general partnerships, given the remarkable consistency in the key criteria at (2) and **1.8** above.

1.13 The main benefit for members of LLP status is that, unlike the partners in a general partnership, they are not each jointly and severally liable for the LLP's debts but only to the extent of their capital invested. The implicit risk for potential creditors is why there are statutory reporting/filing obligations, similar to those for limited liability companies.

LLP losses and interest

1.14 One consequence of the reduced risk for LLP members is that their ability to set trading losses 'sideways' against other income is restricted to the amount of their accumulated respective contributions to their capital accounts, potentially including profits, not withdrawn to date. (*ITA 2007 Pt 4, Ch 3*).

This may be of little concern to property letting business owners, since property letting businesses are not trades and may generally only carry losses forwards in any event (see **Chapter 7**).

1.15 A further important issue for potential members of property investment LLPs is that interest paid individually by members to invest in investment LLPs is not allowable (*ITA 2007, s 399*). This differs to general partnerships, whose partners may normally deduct qualifying loan interest they have paid personally to invest in or fund a partnership (as distinct from borrowing at the partnership level) in their individual income tax calculations.

Where the borrowings are other than to acquire an interest in the partnership, then the funds have to be applied for the purposes of a trade or profession, so the distinction from a property business perspective lies in the relief potentially available for acquiring a share in a general partnership that carries on a property letting business.

Companies

1.16 Property businesses undertaken solely, in joint names, in a general partnership and even in a LLP (so long as undertaken with a view to profit) are all effectively 'transparent' entities for tax purposes, in that an appropriate proportion of either income or capital gains made at entity level is then taxed on the individual. Companies, however, are taxed as a distinct entity. The shareholders in the company (who are often also its directors in such small businesses as the buy-to-let landlord may envisage) *then* need to pay tax on any funds that they withdraw into their personal ownership, such as salary or bonus, as shareholder dividend, or potentially as capital on the disposal of their shares.

Simple examples of this so-called 'double tax charge' may be seen at **Examples 3.6** and **3.7** in **Chapter 3** – their key finding is that, mathematically speaking, companies are often *not* inherently superior to non-corporates for property businesses in terms of tax efficiency, unless there is some other factor such as the scheduled restriction of tax relief for finance costs, for unincorporated buy-to-let landlords.

WHEN DOES A PROPERTY BUSINESS START?

1.17 HMRC's Property Income manual states (at PIM2505):

'Normally a rental business will begin when the taxpayer first enters into a transaction that exploits their land or property in a way which gives rise to a receipt of some kind.

Where the rental business is letting property, the business can't begin until the first property is let. You need to distinguish between activities that are preparatory to letting and those business activities that are part of letting. Once a rental business has started, all activities will be [generally] treated as carried out in the course of one business…'

For HMRC to suggest that a property letting business commences only once the first property is first let is arguable.

The legislation at *ITTOIA 2005, s 264* states:

'A person's UK property business consists of –

(a) Every business which the person carries on for generating income from land in the United Kingdom, and

(b) Every transaction which the person enters into for that purpose otherwise than in the course of such a business.'

There are similar provisions for companies at *CTA 2009, s 205*, and for overseas property businesses (at *ITTOIA 2005, s 265* and *CTA 2009, s 206* respectively).

1.18 From the above, it is arguable that the commencement can be triggered earlier than when the first property is first let. If it be right to adopt trading principles, then commencement would normally be taken to be:

- When the person is in a position to let out property (ie, owns or holds property that is capable of being let out; and

- Does so, *or offers to do so.*

1.18 *Commencement of a property business*

This simple summary is derived from HMRC's own manuals, but this time from the Business Income manual at BIM80505.

Despite being a tax case involving a manufacturing process, *Birmingham & District Cattle By-Products Co. Ltd v IRC* (1919) 12 TC 92 is useful in than it held that trade commenced once all the key assets (including premises) were acquired and raw materials ordered. It did not require there first to be a sale.

> **Example 1.1 – When did the business commence?**
>
> Bill has for some time been mulling over whether or not to invest in property. He has undertaken copious amounts of research, spanning many months.
>
> In January 2016, he arranged for a mortgage facility to buy his first property. In March, he acquired a property with vacant possession, and he spent a few weeks re-decorating and generally getting the property in good order.
>
> He instructed a local estate agent to seek tenants at the beginning of April, and a suitable tenant was found within a few weeks, but did not want to move in until the beginning of June. Contracts were signed towards the end of May.

Based on these facts, and despite HMRC's stated position in PIM2505, the writer's opinion is that Bill's property business started for tax purposes at the beginning of April 2016, when he both had a property to let, and started to make it available for letting by seeking, or advertising for, prospective tenants. It did not start later on, when the first tenant signed the contract or when he moved in to occupy the property (clearly, HMRC may disagree with this position).

But nor did it start earlier: research into the viability of a business is not the business itself but is generally considered to comprise part of 'acts preparatory to' the commencement of a business; likewise, the seeking or raising of finance before one is in a position to deliver the service or product that makes the business.

In many cases, the actual date of commencement may not be of great concern, given that there is facility within the legislation for claiming 'pre-letting expenditure'. But if the run-up to actual commencement has been unusually long, then the precise date may be important.

EXPENSES INCURRED BEFORE LETTING COMMENCES ('PRE-TRADING'/PRE-LETTING EXPENSES)

1.19

> **Focus**
>
> The legislation provides that expenses incurred by the person who ultimately carries on the property business, up to seven years prior to the date on which the business commences, may be deducted from the rental income arising when the business does in fact commence.

The expenditure:

1. Must have been incurred no more than seven years before the date on which the business commenced; and

2. Cannot otherwise be allowable as a deduction, but *would* have been allowed as a deduction if incurred *after* the business had commenced.

Where expenditure satisfies these criteria, it will be treated as a deduction from the rental business on the first day of the rental business – the beginning of April in **Example 1.1** above (*ITTOIA 2005, s 57* by virtue *of ITTOIA 2005, s 272; CTA 2009, s 61* by virtue of *CTA 2009, s 210*; see also HMRC's Manuals at PIM2505 and BIM46355).

Capital allowances and commencement

1.20 Standard buy-to-let businesses involving residential property do not normally involve significant capital allowances claims because of an exclusion applying to property business plant or machinery for use in a dwelling house (*CAA 2001, s 35*). Nevertheless, an ordinary letting business is a qualifying activity for capital allowances (CA) purposes (*CAA 2001, s 15*). For CA in buy-to-let properties generally, see **Chapter 4**.

Where an otherwise eligible item is acquired before the rental business commences, the qualifying expenditure will likewise be treated as having been incurred on the first day of the new business (*CAA 2001, s 12*). In terms of eligibility for the annual investment allowance, this will not bring forward the date of expenditure from a date when such expenditure was non-qualifying, but it does not necessarily preclude a claim – see the examples at CA23083.

With ordinary buy-to-let businesses, claims are often limited to office and computer equipment, tools for maintenance and to motor vehicles, although any plant, etc, used for the business outside of the let dwelling(s) will potentially qualify (subject to any restriction for non-business use as may be appropriate).

1.21 Where the asset has *not* been bought specifically for the purposes of the rental business – say it was a laptop or similar that was owned and used

1.22 *Commencement of a property business*

personally beforehand – then it is usually the market value of the asset on the date of introduction to the business that will qualify as eligible expenditure for the purposes of capital allowances (*CAA 2001, s 13*)

A letting business usually starts only once

1.22

> **Focus**
>
> Since a UK property business consists of 'every business which the person carries on for generating income from land in the UK' (*ITTOIA 2005, s 264*; *CTA 2009, s 205*), then once the buy-to-let business starts, there are generally no further commencements – in other words, the aforementioned commencement rules do not apply every time that a new property is acquired for letting.

Similar rules apply for overseas letting: once that income stream starts, any further overseas property letting acquisitions merely add to the existing overseas property business. (There is also a separate business if there are one or more UK furnished holiday lettings and, lastly, EEA furnished holiday lettings).

1.23 Rental property held in a different capacity may, however, be a different rental business. A property investor may own his or her investment properties outright and some properties jointly with others (in HMRC's opinion, there are very few property partnerships – see **1.11**). Such activities will all fall into one property business, with appropriate proportions of any jointly-held property being aggregated alongside those held outright. But property held as Trustee, or in a 'genuine' partnership, would be considered a separate property business, with its own separate commencement.

1.24 It is also possible for a property business to cease, permanently, and then for a completely new property business to start some time later. Whether or not a property business has ceased altogether is a matter of fact, although HMRC will generally assume the old business continues where the gap between lettings is up to three years. At PIM2510, HMRC states:

> 'A general rule of thumb for rental businesses is that the old business stops where there is an interval of more than three years and different properties are let in the taxpayer's old and new activities. We offer this for guidance only. In practice, we will not normally suggest that the old business stopped where the gap is less than three years and the taxpayer was trying to continue. But the taxpayer would need to provide convincing evidence to show that the same business was carried on where the gap is three years or more.'

This will be relevant where the 'new' property activity is considered to be a new business in its own right, rather than merely a continuation after a pause or 'void period', because the losses of a property business may only be carried forward to set against future profits of *that* property business (*ITA 2007, s 118(3)*; while corporate UK property business losses are much more flexible – see **Chapter 7** – they too may be carried forward only so long as the same property business continues – *CTA 2010, s 62(4)* (but note that, at the time of writing, the Government had confirmed its intention to significantly overhaul corporate losses as originally set out in its Business Tax RoadMap for 2020 and beyond (legislation was included in the draft Finance Bill 2017 clauses published in December 2016), such that there may now be scope to carry forward property business losses once that business has ceased, as management expenses against future investment business income).

In the majority of cases, however, there will be a single continuing property business, and there will be only the one commencement. When new properties are added, costs incurred in getting them ready for letting will be the ongoing costs of a larger property business – subject to the general rules for whether or not expenditure is revenue or capital, or whether it has been incurred wholly and exclusively for the purposes of the property business. (See **Chapter 2**).

EXPENSES BEFORE FIRST LET – CAPITAL OR REVENUE?

1.25 Expenses incurred prior to the first let of a property are often challenged by HMRC on the basis that there must be some capital element to what is frequently a significant early cost.

Reading HMRC's Property Income and Business Income manuals, it is sometimes difficult to figure out why HMRC nevertheless picks up on pre-letting expenditure so frequently. For instance, while PIM2020 states:

> 'A landlord is most likely to incur capital expenditure before a property is let for the first time or between lettings. For example the landlord may decide to improve the property by creating ensuite facilities where there were none before. This is capital expenditure.'

It then goes on to state:

> 'Repairs to reinstate a worn or dilapidated asset are usually deductible as revenue expenditure. The mere fact that the taxpayer bought the asset not long before the repairs are made does not in itself make the repair a capital expense. But a change of ownership combined with one or more additional factors may mean the expenditure is capital. Examples of such factors are:
>
> - A property acquired that wasn't in a fit state for use in the business until the repairs had been carried out or that couldn't continue to be let without repairs being made shortly after acquisition.

1.25 *Commencement of a property business*

- The price paid for the property was substantially reduced because of its dilapidated state. A deduction isn't denied where the purchase price merely reflects the reduced value of the asset due to normal wear and tear (for example, between normal exterior painting cycles). This is so even if the taxpayer makes the repairs just after they acquire the asset.

- The taxpayer makes an agreement that commits them to reinstate the property to a good state of repair. For example, Fred is granted a 21-year lease of a property in a poor state of repair by his landlord that he, in turn, sublets. When Fred's landlord grants him the lease Fred agrees that he will refurbish the property. Fred's expenditure on making good will be capital expenditure and not allowable. But Fred's landlord may be chargeable on the value of the work under the premiums rules [see **1.39** below] and Fred may qualify for some relief. See below if payments for dilapidations are made to the landlord at the end of the lease.

It isn't necessary for all these factors to be present for the expenditure to be capital. The underlying principle is that the cost of buying a property in good condition is clearly capital expenditure. Hence the cost of buying a dilapidated property and putting it in good order is also capital expenditure.

Where the taxpayer is granted a lease of a property in good repair, the expenses they incur in keeping it in that state will normally be deductible. This generally includes a payment they make to their landlord at the end of their lease on account of repairs which were due but which they had not made. These over-due repairs are called "dilapidations".'

Also in HMRC's Business Income manual at BIM35450:

'Repairs remain repairs even if they have been deferred so long that an asset is in an extremely poor state of repair.

One potential exception to this is where an asset has been acquired in poor condition. In this situation the cost of the repairs may be capital expenditure as part of the cost of the asset. Whilst the cost of buying a basic version and upgrading to get the asset you want is clearly capital expenditure as part of the cost of acquiring the asset, the position is less clear with assets in poor repair.

If the work is simply routine maintenance work that recurs every few years, then it is allowable expenditure as a repair. For example, exterior painting of a building which has been deferred by the previous owner but which in the normal course of events falls to be expended shortly after the building is acquired, is allowable…

… if you would have treated the repairs as revenue if ownership had not changed, then the repairs are normally revenue when expended by the new

Commencement of a property business **1.26**

owner. The points that indicate that exceptionally the cost of the work is capital include:

- The asset was not in a fit state for use until the repairs had been carried out or could not continue to be used in the trade without being repaired shortly after acquisition.

- There is evidence in, for example, the contract for the sale of the asset or in negotiations leading up to the contract or in the surrounding circumstances that the purchase price was substantially less because of the dilapidated state of the asset. You should not attempt to deny relief where the purchase price merely reflects the reduced value of an asset due to normal wear and tear (for example between normal maintenance cycles).'

Focus

The guidance seems quite clearly to lend itself to the assumption that most repair costs incurred prior to first let should be allowed, and it will be only the more exceptional cases, where the property was sold at a substantial discount or otherwise clearly so dilapidated as to be unfit for use, that repair work might be considered capital expenditure.

Case Study – Classic cases

1.26 Algernon has decided to take his conventional pension savings on maturity and invest the funds into residential property. He acquires two detached homes, which were sold by their previous owner-occupiers. While the first property is going to be a standard buy-to-let, the second property is in an area particularly favoured by students, and is large enough to house up to five students as a House in Multiple Occupancy (HMO).

Property 1

The first property was previously occupied by an elderly couple, who had done little work on it for the last few years. The price has been discounted by a few thousand pounds in recognition of the updating required, but is essentially in line with the prevailing local market price for such a property.

A survey reveals damp in spots around the ground floor, that can be treated chemically without major work to the property. Algernon also decides that the bathroom and kitchen need to be replaced, with fixtures of a similar quality, and will re-decorate and re-carpet throughout.

Such work is typical when an investor takes on a new property: it makes commercial sense for the property to be renovated before installing a tenant.

1.26 *Commencement of a property business*

But the expenditure will frequently be relatively significant in aggregate, and could exceed one or even two years' rent.

To determine on basic principles whether the work is capital in nature, or revenue and thereby deductible against rental income, one need look no further than two of the best-known cases in tax law: *Law Shipping Co Ltd v CIR* (1923) 12 TC 621 and *Odeon Associated Theatres Ltd v Jones* (1971) 48 TC 257.

The former case concerned a second-hand ship, whose condition on purchase was so poor that it was considered unseaworthy, and basically required special permission to put out to sea, so that it might be repaired elsewhere. Its price was, notably, significantly discounted in recognition of the extent of the work urgently required in order to make if fit for purpose. The expenditure on that work was held essentially to be capital in nature.

The latter case involved a chain of cinemas that was acquired post-war, during which period repairs had been prohibited, such that they were in a poor state of when purchased. But the cinema facilities were nevertheless commercially fit for purpose immediately on acquisition – and were so used.

While Algernon has decided to incur the expenditure prior to first let, the property is clearly habitable, having been acquired from owner-occupiers, and is therefore lettable, even if not ideally so. It is not in a dilapidated state, nor is the asking price significantly lower than the market norm. A new bathroom and kitchen might enhance the value of the property for the time being, but will themselves need replacing again in a few years and, in effect, amount to no more than maintaining it to 'as-new' quality. Prima facie, all of this expenditure will be allowable as a revenue deduction on the first day on which the letting business commences.

Property 2

With regard to the second property, which Algernon wants to turn into an HMO, some structural work is required to the property to make the bedroom sizes more equal and, in line with local council regulations, Algernon has to:

- Install secondary 'fireproof' internal doors within individual bedrooms, with specified door-closing mechanisms;

- Upgraded electrical wiring, incorporating a hard-wired smoke detection and fire alarm system.

While it may be the case that the structural alterations could be reversed if Algernon wanted to sell the second property on as a family home at some point in the future, they represent a fixed and enduring change to the property and would therefore be considered capital expenditure.

The fire-rated doors are significantly more expensive than standard domestic internal doors, particularly with the door-closing mechanisms. They would not count as a 'repair', since they would represent a tangible improvement on the original doors. In a non-residential setting, the mechanisms might rank for capital allowances but not where they are used in a dwelling, as noted above – see **1.20**.

Commencement of a property business **1.28**

Given that the property was previously an 'ordinary' dwelling, the requirement to improve the electrical wiring in the property to a standard above that of a normal home will also constitute an enduring benefit – a capital improvement – that will not be eligible for tax relief against letting income; (although it might again have been eligible for CA in a property other than a dwelling); many advisers will be all too familiar with the difficulty of explaining to clients that, *just because an expense is necessary, or even required by law, does not guarantee that it will be allowable for tax purposes*. It follows that, while some of the work that Algernon undertakes to the second property will be allowable as repairs, he should not claim a deduction for the structural work, the fire doors or the electrical work. Of course, if the disallowed works are still present in the property when it is ultimately disposed of, Algernon may well be able to claim a deduction for CGT purposes, for his enhancement expenditure (*TCGA 1992, s 38*).

In summary, Algernon's pre-letting expenditure on the first property will be allowable as a deduction immediately that the property business commences, while the enhancement expenditure on the second property, as identified above, will not be deductible, as it will be considered an improvement.

A more general consideration of the capital/revenue divide is at **Chapter 2**.

Pre-letting expenses and the landlord's former home

1.27 Sometimes a landlord will let his or her former residence. Expenditure that has been incurred while the property is occupied as a private residence by the landlord, (or landlord-to-be), will usually be susceptible to challenge as to whether or not the expenditure has been incurred wholly and exclusively for the purposes of the business (*ITTOIA 2005, s 34; CTA 2009, s 54*), given that the landlord may benefit in a private capacity.

BASIS PERIODS

1.28

> **Focus**
>
> For individuals and Trusts, property business income is charged to income tax on 'the full amount of the profits arising in the tax year' (*ITTOIA 2005, s 270*). There are no basis periods for property income, as there are with trading activities subject to income tax, since property income is strictly investment income (but see **1.29** below).
>
> Property income accounts are almost always made up on a fiscal year basis. Where they are not, they should be apportioned so as to arrive at the profits or losses that correspond to the tax year (*ITTOIA 2005, s 275*).

1.29 *Commencement of a property business*

1.29 Property income arising to a partnership that carries on a trade or profession will, however, be taxed (alongside other untaxed investment income) according to the accounting period adopted by the partnership for trading purposes. Strictly, each partner is deemed to have his or her 'notional trade' that (aside from adjustments during individual commencements and cessations) aligns with the accounting date of the partnership, and untaxed income from the individual's notional business follows the same basis periods (*ITTOIA 2005, s 852 et seq.*).

1.30 Companies are charged to tax according to accounting periods. A company's flexibility in relation to choosing accounting periods is primarily subject to *CA 2006* but its accounting periods for tax purposes are usually the next earliest of:

- twelve months from the end of the last accounting period;
- ceasing to trade;
- the next accounting date;
- going into administration.

There are numerous other criteria but the above are the most common (*CTA 2009, s 10*).

It follows that where accounts are drawn up for a period in excess of twelve months then the period of account will be split into two accounting periods for tax purposes: usually the first being for twelve months and the second being the 'stub' remaining period.

Profits and losses are usually deemed to accrue evenly over the period of account, so are apportioned on a time basis between the two component periods (*CTA 2009, s 52*) but where a different basis of apportionment might give a more appropriate outcome, the Inspector may apply that basis instead (*Marshall Hus & Partners Ltd. v Bolton* Ch D 1980, 55 TC 539 – where a single set of accounts covered six years). This might be relevant where profits were highly seasonal, and simple time apportionment would not reflect how the profits actually accrued. Capital gains are taxed in the accounting period in which they arise, whichever that might be in a long period of account (*TCGA 1992, s 8*).

TAX ADMINISTRATION
Requirement to notify HMRC
1.31

> **Focus**
>
> If this is the taxpayer's first foray into property letting, it will constitute a new source of income, and it may well be his or her first source that requires to be notified to HMRC (*TMA 1970, s 7*). Where notification is required, it should be within six months of the end of the tax year – by 5 October following.

Commencement of a property business **1.35**

HMRC may try to avoid issuing a formal self assessment tax return where gross rental income is less than £10,000, and net income after allowable expenses is under £2,500, such that an informal assessment might be issued. (This is HMRC's current published policy, but it may well change once the rules for 'Simple Assessments' start to take effect, following *Finance Act 2016*).

1.32 Note that the legislation does not require notification if the taxpayer could not become liable to tax if he were to make a self-assessment (*TMA 1970 s 7(7)*). The Enquiry manual is disappointingly loose on this point at EM4551. Some comfort may be drawn from EM4555 ('No Liability Cases').

Late notification

1.33 If the taxpayer has not notified HMRC by 5 October as required, there is hope yet: the penalty for failure to notify is tax-geared, by reference to the total amount of tax due but unpaid by 31 January following. In other words, provided the taxpayer has settled the liability within the normal SA timeframe of 31 January following the tax year, the penalty will be reduced to nil (*FA 2008, Sch 41, paras 1, 7(2)*). There remains the possibility also of claiming a 'reasonable excuse', in the right circumstances.

1.34 For corporate landlords, it is rare that HMRC fails to request a corporation tax (CT) return but a company is nevertheless obliged to notify HMRC within twelve months of the commencement accounting period in the absence of a formal notice (*FA 1998, Sch 18, para 2*). Here, the penalty is geared by reference to any attributable underpayment still outstanding twelve months after the end of the accounting period – the deadline for notification itself (*FA 2008, Sch 41, paras 1, 7(3)*).

Record keeping

1.35 Individuals under the SA regime need to keep their business books and records until at least the 31 January, five years after the end of the tax year in question.

Partnerships have to keep their records for up to six years after the end of the relevant period of account.

These periods may be extended if an enquiry is opened into the tax return, or the tax return is filed late (*TMA 70, s 12B*).

Companies are obliged to keep all records for at least six years after the end of the accounting period in question (*FA 1998, Sch 18, paras 21–23*).

Perhaps unsurprisingly, HMRC is now perfectly amenable to digitisation of records, broadly so long as the information is accurately preserved and may be interrogated later (eg, commercial scanning of invoices and receipts).

The penalty for failure to keep records is up to £3,000 per year.

1.36 *Commencement of a property business*

Finance costs – borrowing against non-business/private assets

1.36

> **Focus**
>
> There is a popular misconception amongst some taxpayers that finance must be secured against business assets in order for the finance costs to be allowable. This is not the case. The purpose of the borrowings is of paramount importance – at the time the interest, etc is paid (*Scorer v Olin Energy Systems Ltd* [1985] 58 TC 592).

1.37 In IT cases, there is often a question of whether or not all of a loan has been applied for business purposes – for example, a landlord might extend his or her mortgage on the main home, partly to finance improvements to the property but also to fund the deposit on a new buy-to-let property. Where a proportion of the borrowings can be identified as being exclusively for business purposes, a reasonable apportionment is permitted (*ITTOIA 2005, s 34(2)*).

HMRC's Business Income manual also has the following (at BIM45685):

> 'The security for borrowed funds does not determine the use of those funds. It is very common in small businesses for loans to be secured on the proprietor's home, because that is the only substantial owned asset. This is not relevant to the consideration of the use of the funds borrowed. Similarly guarantees given by another person do not affect the use of the funds.'

Of course, the converse may also apply: a loan for a private purpose might be secured against the landlord's rental properties, in which case the private purpose determines that the finance costs not be deductible from rental income (but see also **Chapter 2**).

1.38 Corporate finance is governed by the loan relationships regime. Very broadly, any finance expense or loss will be allowable, provided it is for business purposes. In relation to a property business, such expenses will be allowed as 'non-trading loan relationship debits' basically as claimed in accounts as drawn up according to Generally Accepted Accounting Principles (GAAP). While this means that most expenses will be allowed, landlords will need to take care if there is private occupation, in case it may be arguable that the loan is at least partly for an unallowable purpose, and/or there may be a taxable 'benefit in kind'; likewise where debts are between connected parties (as defined specifically for the purposes of loan relationships) (*CTA 2009 Pt V, s 292 et seq.*; See **Chapter 2**).

LEASES

Lease premia on grant of lease/assignment of a lease

1.39

> **Focus**
>
> While the following sections cover the taxation of lease premia in some detail, they represent relatively straightforward scenarios and should be considered a basic guide to potentially quite complex issues.
>
> Although leases are of course very common in transactions involving flats and apartments, lease premia are more often encountered with commercial properties.

A lease may be summarised as a device by which the lessor gives the lessee the use and possession of the land/building, in exchange for payment or payments.

1.40 The grant of a lease may be distinguished from an assignment in that the grant of a lease out of the freehold, or of a sub-lease out of a lease, means that the grantor has retained some form of interest in the property, while the assignment of a lease is an outright disposal of one's interest in the lease.

The *receipt* of a one-off lump sum for the *grant* of a lease is generally taxable either as rental income, or as capital gains, or both. (The longer the lease, the less income and the more capital). But this 'lease premium' does not necessarily have to be paid to the grantor (it may, for instance, go to another party with a superior interest in the property), and can include any consideration paid in connection with the grant of a lease, other than rent itself.

Where the term of the grant of a lease exceeds 50 years, the lease premium on its grant is taxable as a capital gain, subject to the part-disposal rules because the grantor has retained an interest in the property. (The 'reversionary interest' has a value attributable to the freehold retained, and there is a right to receive rents from the lessee). (*TCGA 1992, s 42*).

Where the term of the grant of a lease is 50 years or less, then at least some of the receipt is taxable as income, and the shorter the lease, the greater the proportion taxed as income, rather than as a capital gain.

The amount of the premium to be treated as rental income in a short lease is:

$$\frac{\text{Premium} \times (50 \text{ years} - (\text{the number of } complete \text{ years' effective duration of the lease-1}))}{50}$$

This means that, where the lease term is 50 years exactly, then 1/50th of the premium will be taxed to income; if the lease is for a single year, (or up to but not including exactly two years), then all of the lease premium will be taxed as income. (*ITTOIA 2005, s 276, 277 et seq.; CTA 2009, s 217 et seq.*)

In either example, the balance of the receipt not taxed as income will be subject to CGT, as above.

1.41 *Commencement of a property business*

The term of the lease is not always the term of the lease…

1.41 Note that the term of the lease *may* need to be adjusted for the purposes of the calculation – typically where there are conditions in the lease (such as a break clause) that make it unlikely that the lease will endure for the full term; but it may be appropriate in some cases to assume that the duration may be extended, for instance where the terms for extension are particularly favourable to the tenant (*ITTOIA 2005, s 303*; *CTA 2009, s 243*).

There are also anti-avoidance provisions to counter arrangements where, for instance, the tenant may have a short lease with a high premium, followed by a much longer lease on similar terms with no premium (so the lease premium may instead need to be calculated across both leases).

Example 1.2 – Grant of a 'Short' Lease

Declan owns the freehold to a property and agrees to lease it out. He receives a premium payment of £20,000. The lease term is 20 years.

Income Element

Using the formula above, the income element of the premium is

£20,000 × (50–19)/50 = £12,400

Declan will be taxable on property income of £12,400, and have proceeds subject to CGT of £7,600, being the balance of the £20,000

Capital Element

The capital element represents a part-disposal of the property, being the lease, while Declan still retains the freehold interest, subject to that lease.

Declan bought the property for £50,000; the value of the reversion is (say) £60,000

His *cost* for CGT purposes is determined according to a slightly modified formula for part-disposals:

$$\text{Cost} \times \frac{\text{capital element of proceeds as already determined}}{\text{(total premium + reversionary interest)}}$$

In this case, his cost against the capital element of the lease will be:

£50,000 × £7,600/(£20,000+£60,000) = £4,750

Declan's capital gain is therefore £7,600 – £4,750 = £2,850

The modification to the standard 'A/(A+B)' calculation is that the numerator of the fraction for cost is not the total consideration received but only the capital element. (*TCGA 1992, Sch 8 para 5*) This is frequently missed by those unfamiliar with lease premium calculations

Grant of a (short) sub-lease out of a short lease

1.42 The grant of a sub-lease requires a complex calculation to determine the income element of the further grant, whereby the effective overlap of the income element already identified in the original grant is discounted from the income element charged on the sub-lessor.

> **Example 1.3 – Grant of a short sub-lease out of a short lease**
>
> Suppose that Declan's property as per the earlier example was leased to Deirdre, who then sub-lets to a third party for a term of ten years and for a premium of £10,000, with similar annual rent:
>
> **Income Element**
>
> Deirdre's standard calculation is:
>
> £10,000 × (50–9)/50 = £8,200 being the income element for a lease term of ten years
>
> Declan's income element has already been calculated:
>
> £20,000 × (50–19)/50 = £12,400 being the income element for a lease term of 20 years
>
> The proportion of Declan's income element duplicated in Deirdre's calculation is
>
> 10 years / 20 years × £12,400 = £6,200
>
> Deirdre's income element is reduced by the corresponding proportion of Declan's premium that has already been assessed as income, so
>
> Deirdre's adjusted income element = £8,200 – £6,200 = £2,000
>
> In this scenario, Deirdre will have the relevant details to calculate Declan's position, since it was she who paid the premium and agreed terms as the lessee. The legislation helpfully allows the income element of a corporate lessor to 'count' against a sub-lessor's income element, and *vice versa*.
>
> **Capital Element**
>
> Further complex calculations are required, because the gain arises on a wasting asset – basically, an asset (land) with an expected life of less than 50 years in accordance with TCGA 1992 Sch 8 para 1.
>
> Assume that Deirdre leased the property in year five of her 20-year term – which cost her £20,000 (Declan's premium). This means that her sub-lease, which will last for ten years, will end in year 15 of her lease term – when it has five years left to run. The proportion of Deirdre's own cost that she may set against the gain on her sub-lease premium is *not* calculated assuming that values deteriorate in a straight line but according to the

1.43 *Commencement of a property business*

factors in the table at *TCGA 1992, Sch 8, Para 1* (as required by para 4 of that Schedule):

$$\frac{\text{Factor for remaining term when sub-lease granted} - \text{Factor for remaining term when sub-lease expires}}{\text{Factor for term of lease when acquired}}$$

= (61.617–26.722)/72.770 × £20,000 = £9,590

Deirdre's CGT calculation is therefore:

Proceeds (premium received)	£10,000
Less: Apportioned Costs	£9,590
Gain	£410
But deduct Deirdre's *adjusted* income element above:	£2,000
Capital Gain	NIL

(Deirdre's deduction for her adjusted income element cannot create or increase a capital loss – similar to the old rule for Indexation Allowance – *TCGA 1992, Sch 8, para 5(2)*).

Lessee/tenant tax relief

1.43 The lessee may claim an amount of relief, against IT or CT, which relates to the amount assessed to income on the grant of a short lease, where the lessee is carrying on either a property business or a trade.

1.44 However, while the grantor is assessed to IT in the tax year of receipt of the premium, the tenant's or lessee's claim is 'spread' over the 'receipt period' (generally the term of the lease) and is deductible only – for the period(s) – that it is occupied for the purposes of the property business, etc.

The deduction is reckoned on a daily basis. If only part of the premises is used for a qualifying purpose, then the deduction is restricted accordingly.

The deduction may also need to be restricted, where the tenant receives their own income element of a premium received on the grant of the sub-lease, but also benefits from the restriction to that income element, by virtue of overlap with the (or a) superior landlord's own income element from a premium on a higher lease, as for Deirdre in **Example 1.3**. It would effectively be a duplication of relief if the income element of Deirdre's lease premium had been restricted by reference to overlap with Declan's taxed income element, but she got relief for the full amount of thee income element of the head lease over the term as well.

Commencement of a property business 1.47

1.45 Usefully, if the lease is assigned to another party, then that party is also able to benefit from the deduction, effectively standing in the shoes of the original lessee – a 'successor in title' (PIM2330). This would be distinguished from a sub-lease on the basis that an assignment is an outright disposal of the former lessee's interest.

Note that, HMRC's Property Income Manual states (at PIM2330):

'...the relief that the payer of a chargeable premium can have in computing rental business profits. It applies when the premises are used for the purposes of a rental business, *other than as a source of rents* – for example as offices to run the business from.' (emphasis added).

This contrasts with the legislation, which says that a deduction is available, where *either:*

- the tenant occupies the property for the purpose of carrying on the property business; or

- sublets the premises (*ITTOIA 2005, s 291(2); CTA 2009, s 231(2)*).

See *ITTOIA 2005 ss 60 et seq.* and *291 et seq.*; *CTA 2009 ss 62 et seq.* and *231 et seq.*

No premium received but capital costs incurred

1.46 The costs of negotiating a lease are not always deductible for IT purposes (see **Chapter 2**) and may instead comprise a capital cost, which is why landlords sometimes try to get the prospective tenant to pay both parties' legal fees. HMRC's Capital Gains manual notes at CG70822 that those costs may be incurred even when no premium is received but a lease is granted:

'If no premium is paid on the grant of a lease, and provided that the grant of the lease was an arm's length transaction, no chargeable gain will accrue.

However, if the landlord has incurred any expenditure allowable under TCGA92 s 38 (1) (c), see CG15160+, in granting the lease, a capital loss equal to the amount of that expenditure will accrue.'

Assignment of a lease

1.47 As mentioned above, an assignment of a lease is an outright disposal, in contrast to a grant, where an interest is retained. A disposal of a 'long' lease – with a remaining term of more than 50 years – is covered by a standard CGT calculation, with the cost being the premium paid.

An assignment of a 'short' lease – ie, with a remaining term of 50 years or less (regardless of its original term) – is more complex. Since the asset is a wasting asset, (see above), the original cost of the lease, being the premium, is deemed to dissipate over its term (otherwise one could create a substantial loss

1.47 *Commencement of a property business*

on a disposal just before the expiry of the lease). Simply put, the proportion of the original cost that has already been extinguished is excluded from the cost deductible when a short lease is assigned.

The calculation of deductible acquisition cost is further complicated if the lessee has used the property in his property business (or trade) – which will commonly be the case for buy-to-let investors – and has enjoyed tax relief as a short lessee on a premium already paid (see lessee/tenant tax relief above).

> **Example 1.4 – Assignment of lease**
>
> Asterix, who has a property business, acquired a 31-year lease of a property for use in his business on 6 April 2011, paying a premium of £25,000. On 6 April 2017, he sold the lease for £35,000. He has been able to claim tax relief on the income element of the premium as follows*:
>
> £25,000 × 50−(31−1)/50 = £10,000; (landlord's income element of premium)
>
> £10,000 × 6 years/31 years = £1,935 (cumulative amount Asterix has been able to claim before sale)
>
> *This should, strictly, be calculated on a daily basis
>
> However, he cannot now claim that element as part of his allowable expenditure:
>
> | | |
> |---|---|
> | Cost (premium originally paid) | £25,000 |
> | Less: Income Tax relief already enjoyed | £1,935 |
> | Net Expenditure | £23,065 |
>
> Asterix then has to derive the proportion of the (remaining) capital cost that may be deducted against the proceeds on his sale, again using *TCGA 1992, Sch 8*:
>
> Amount of cost of the premium to be excluded from relief:
>
> $$\frac{\text{Factor for duration of the lease at outset} - \text{Factor for remaining term at point of disposal}}{\text{Factor for duration of the lease at outset}}$$
>
> In this case:
>
> $$\frac{\text{Factor for 31 years: 88.371} - \text{Factor for 25 years: 81.100}}{\text{Factor for 31 years: 88.371}}$$
>
> = 0.082
>
> Amount to be excluded = £23,065 × 0.082 = £1,897; this representing the cost of the lease that has unwound prior to the disposal.

Commencement of a property business **1.50**

Therefore the net cost allowable is

£25,000 − £1,935 − £1,897 = £21,168

The gain on the assignment is therefore:

£35,000 − £21,168 = £13,832

If there were any enhancement expenditure attributable to the lease, then this would likewise have to be subjected to a similar adjustment but by reference to when the expenditure enhanced the lease. Where assignments do not arise conveniently on the anniversary of the original lease, then the corresponding nearest factors should be averaged accordingly.

Reverse premia

1.48 Having considered the tax implications of lease premia paid by the tenant, there are also scenarios where the owner may offer an inducement to a prospective tenant in order to secure a lease, or to change the terms of an existing lease. While a lump sum may be the most obvious example, HMRC considers that other examples may apply, so long as the benefit is in money's worth, such as:

- Writing off a tenant's existing debt;
- Paying or contributing to a tenant's fitting out costs or similar (without re-charging same in an elevated rent).

1.49 However, the following should not be caught as an 'inducement':

- Grant of a rent-free period;
- Replacement by agreement of an existing lease with one with a less onerous rent, or less onerous conditions.

The tax treatment of such reverse premia depends on the circumstances.

If to an existing tenant, such as to secure more favourable rental terms for the lessor, then it is likely to be considered a part-disposal of the lessee's interest in the existing lease – a capital asset, and therefore subject to CGT (*TCGA 1992, s 22(1)(c)*).

If the payment is to secure a new tenant, then it cannot be a capital gain because the tenant-to-be has not disposed of anything. (See CG70835). But it will normally be taxed as income (*ITTOIA 2005, s 101*; *CTA 2009, s 96 et seq.*).

If a tenant pays a third party to enter into a new lease with the landlord, so that the first tenant can get out of his lease, then that is not an inducement by the landlord or a party connected with him, so will not be a reverse premium.

1.50 Statutory exceptions to the charge include:

- Where the inducement is to occupy the property as one's main residence;
- Where the landlord is contributing to the recipient's expenditure that would qualify for CA (if the recipient cannot claim for the expenditure

1.51 *Commencement of a property business*

contributed by the landlord by reason of *CAA 2001, s 532*, and noting that the landlord may be eligible for CA for his own contribution by virtue of ss 537/8).

1.51

> **Focus**
>
> Where a reverse premium chargeable as income is received in the course of a trade or profession, etc, then it is taxed as trading receipt; otherwise it is a property business receipt and will be taxed as part of an ongoing property business if the recipient has one. Taxation of the receipt will usually follow GAAP, which would be to spread the receipt across the term of the lease or to first rent review to market rate, whichever is the sooner. However, the reverse premium will be taxable in full in the first period of receipt where the parties are connected and the arrangements do not follow normal commercial terms.

1.52 The scope for relief for the person making the payment may be limited. The legislation is concerned only to ensure that such receipts are taxed, rather than ensuring symmetry for the transaction. Property dealers and developers will generally be able to claim the cost of a reverse premium payment as a trading deduction. But property investors, including landlords, will need to fall back on CGT principles: the payment enhances the asset because it is made to secure an income therefrom. However, in order to claim the expenditure when the property is disposed of, the property investor will have to show that the enhancement is still present at the point of disposal (*TCGA 1992, s 38 (1)(b)*).

For excellent further analysis of the taxation of reverse premia, see the latest edition of *Property Taxes*, by Robert Maas (Bloomsbury Professional).

Stamp duty land tax (land and building transaction tax in Scotland)

1.53 SDLT and its Scottish equivalent LBTT will usually be payable when acquiring new property, be it at commencement or otherwise. Transactions involving the purchase of several dwellings together may potentially be eligible for either:

- Multiple Dwellings Relief which applies SDLT to the average price of the property acquired;
- Lower 'commercial property' rates where six or more properties are acquired in one go.

Most buy-to-let acquisitions now will also suffer the 3% additional charge on dwellings that are not replacing the buyer's main residence.

For further information on SDLT/LBTT, please see **Chapter 14.**

Chapter 2

Calculating property business profits and losses

Lee Sharpe CTA, ATT, Tax Consultant, Sharpe Tax Consulting Ltd.

> SIGNPOSTS
>
> - **Scope** – While the nature of income from property can depend on use and intention, property rental business income is generally calculated according to trading principles, with some key exceptions (see **2.1–2.5**).
>
> - **Treatment of corporates/non-corporates** – The taxation of corporate property businesses is similar to that for non-corporates – again, with some important exceptions (see **2.6–2.9**).
>
> - **Hotels, etc** – Hotels and similar establishments are generally considered to be operating a trade for tax purposes. The extent of services provided over and above the provision of a room, coupled with the fact that the owner generally continues to 'occupy' the property, can be key factors (see **2.10–2.11**).
>
> - **Badges of trade** – Certain attributes (or 'badges') may be of assistance in determining whether the activity is in the nature of a trade or investment (see **2.12**).
>
> - **Common Issues** – the 'wholly and exclusively' requirement and 'capital v revenue' distinction apply much in the same way as they do for ordinary trading activities (see **2.13–2.16**).
>
> - **Financing and collateral** – There is some flexibility in finance costs and loan collateral, that not all landlords utilise as comprehensively as the legislation comfortably allows (see **2.17–2.22**).
>
> - **Change of intention/use** – Taking an investment property to re-develop for onward sale has potentially significant tax implications; likewise property initially held for development being re-categorised as a letting investment property. Landlords developing former investment properties for onward sale need in particular to beware the Transactions in Land regime, as updated by *FA 2016* (see **2.23–2.35**).

2.1 Calculating property business profits and losses

- **Non-commercial lettings** – It is necessary to distinguish between commercial and non-commercial lettings, due to the different tax treatment of the latter category (see **2.36–2.37**).

- **Cash basis** – There is an alternative cash basis of taxation for quite modest letting businesses, although a more comprehensive cash basis is currently being developed (see **2.38–2.39**).

- **What expenses can I claim?** – A quick-reference list of typical letting expenses may be found at **Appendix A.**

INTRODUCTION

2.1 The taxation of property businesses is a broad topic. As the book focuses on the buy-to-let regime, the chapter does not cover the more unusual treatments, such as for wayleaves, tied premises, shooting rights, caravan sites, hotels, rent-a-room, etc.

For information on the tax treatment of buy-to-let rental business losses, see **Chapter 7**.

What is property income?

2.2 The categorisation of income from property is mutable, depending on the circumstances.

Property is an appreciating asset: it may be held as a long-term investment, with a reasonable expectation that it will increase in value over the period of ownership. While so owned, it may be exploited for rent or similar returns, without being consumed. In that regard, it is similar to money in a deposit account, or shares in a quoted company (it may be distinguished from a trading business that hires out equipment or similar, on the basis that the latter business' customers have no substantive interest in those assets, which may be considered to deteriorate over time or with use; it could be argued that property may also deteriorate over sufficient time, but there is in turn a question of to what extent the value attaches all but irreducibly to the land, or to the property that adorns it).

Tax law categorises such returns as 'investment income' which is essentially passive in nature. Much fun can be had trying to lecture a room full of career landlords that HMRC's starting position is that rental income is a passive investment activity!

> **Focus**
>
> Property can, on the other hand, be bought with a fixed intention to sell on at a profit. This latter approach may involve developing the land or existing property with a view to increasing the value of the asset, to assist in generating profit. Or, it may not: 'large' property developers may, for example, buy plots of bare land and consider them stock held for resale at a profit, no more or less so than a grocer buys tins of beans.
>
> Just like a grocer, or a business that builds laptops for sale, all such property businesses would be considered trading activities on basic principles (including the so-called 'badges of trade' – see **2.12**).

It depends...

2.3 The fact that land and property may fall into either category, depending on the circumstances, has and will continue to provide some quite interesting problems as regards the appropriate categorisation and corresponding tax treatment for property owners and their tax advisers.

While it may be said that a person's intentions as regards a property at the point of acquisition are very important (see, for example, *Lionel Simmons Properties Ltd v CIR* [1980] STC 350), one's intentions may change over time – whether the property should be recategorised as a result can sometimes be a difficult matter to resolve (the case *Taylor v Good* [1974] 1 All ER 1137 tussled with this issue all the way to the Court of Appeal).

2.4 Having recognised that the taxation of property income is not always straightforward, the simple rule of thumb is:

- Rental income is taxable as investment 'income from a property business';

- The sale of an investment property is a capital transaction subject to capital gains tax (CGT) or corporation tax (CT) on capital gains (but see **2.25–2.33** below in relation to developing investment property for onward sale);

- Buying property with an intention to sell it on for a profit, and property development for the purposes of resale, are taxable as trading activities.

2.5 *Calculating property business profits and losses*

PRIORITY OF RENTAL INCOME OVER TRADING INCOME RULES

2.5

> **Focus**
>
> Readers may be surprised to find that the legislation gives priority to the rental income regime, over trading rules. In other words, where income, etc might reasonably be considered to fall in either rental income or trading income category, it will in fact be taxed according to the rules for property income, not trading income (*ITTOIA 2005, s 4*; *CTA 2009, s 201*).
>
> There are exceptions to this rule, such as for overseas property businesses, where the reverse may apply.

One consequence of these rules is that rental income derived from property held for development purposes – for example, where new build homes are temporarily let out while looking for a buyer, or for the market to recover – may still be taxable as property income, despite the overwhelmingly trading nature of the overall enterprise – see HMRC's Property Income manual at PIM4300 – but note also the distinction in that section for the letting of temporarily surplus office space used in a trade or profession, where the rental receipts may be aggregated with trading income.

ASSESSED AS A BUSINESS

2.6 The income tax (IT) rules for the taxation of property investment income are to be found at *ITTOIA 2005, Pt 3 (s 260 et seq.)*.

The corporation tax (CT) rules for the taxation of property investment income are to be found at *CTA 2009, Pt 4 (s 202 et seq.)*.

For both IT and CT purposes, the starting point is that rental profits (and losses) are to be calculated in the same way as for trading profits (*ITTOIA 2005, s 272*; *CTA 2009, s 210*).

It can therefore be said that:

- The profits of both property investment businesses and trading businesses are derived according to the same core principles; and
- The profits for both unincorporated property investment businesses and their corporate equivalents are, likewise, derived on a similar basis.

However, there are exceptions – the more noteworthy for buy-to-let landlords being set out later in this chapter.

2.7 The legislation for both IT and CT purposes sets out in some detail where property business taxation borrows from trading principles; the more important of these, from a buy-to-let perspective, are set out below:

Calculating property business profits and losses **2.7**

Detail	Income tax (ITTOIA 2005)	Corporation tax (CTA 2009)
Profits are calculated in accordance with generally accepted accounting practice, subject to any adjustment required or authorised by law. The alternative 'cash basis' of accounting, which looks only at cash in and cash out in a period, rather than when income or expenditure is due, has been permitted for property letting businesses for several years where applied consistently, where gross receipts do not exceed £15,000 and the result is reasonable/does not differ substantially from the normal 'earnings' basis – see HMRC's Property Income manual at PIM1101 for further information, but see also **2.38** below for prospective changes.	s 25	s 46
Losses are to be calculated in the same way as profits.	s 26	s 47
Expenses not incurred 'wholly and exclusively' for the purposes of the activity are not allowable for tax purposes – but this does not prevent a deduction for an identifiable part or proportion of an expense that *is* incurred wholly and exclusively for such purposes. (See **2.13**). Eg for *unincorporated* businesses, adjustments are generally required if (and to the extent that) there is any 'private use or enjoyment' of an expense, such as where a property is occupied for two weeks by the owner, on holiday – a 1/26th add-back would be appropriate for some expenses, such as council tax, while other expenses, such as pre-letting inspections costs, might be unaffected. More precise apportionments might be appropriate in some cases (see **Appendix A** for more on this point).	s 34	s 54

2.8 *Calculating property business profits and losses*

Detail	Income tax (ITTOIA 2005)	Corporation tax (CTA 2009)
Pre-trading expenses (or pre-letting expenses). Expenses incurred by the person (who ultimately carries on the business) *up to seven years prior* to the date on which the business commences may be claimed as a deduction on the day of commencement – provided the deduction would be allowable, under normal principles, while the business were actually carried on. See **Chapter 1** for more information.	s 57	s 61

KEY DIFFERENCES BETWEEN PROPERTY INVESTMENT INCOME AND TRADING INCOME

2.8 The differences between property investment income and trading income include the following:

- A person's UK property letting business consists of 'every business the person carries on for generating income from land in the UK'. The legislation does not distinguish between locations, types of occupant, or category of property – even residential and commercial lettings are part of one and the same business. While a landlord may keep each property separate in his or her own books of account, the profits and losses across all properties are pooled, resulting in a single net amount – positive or negative (*ITTOIA 2005, s 264*; *CTA 2009, s 205*). This is quite different to the position for trades, each of which is identified and streamed separately, with its own capital allowances (CAs) pool, etc.

- Along similar lines, there is a separate pool for overseas letting activity – 'rest of world' (*ITTOIA 2005, s 265*; *CTA 2009, s 206*).

- For the special treatments of furnished holiday accommodation and non-commercial lettings, please see **Chapter 6** and **2.36** respectively.

Calculating property business profits and losses **2.8**

- HMRC considers property letting undertaken in a different capacity to be part of a separate pool, however – for example, where as a Trustee, or as a partner in a partnership (see **Chapter 1**).

- Relief for finance costs in relation to residential lettings is being restricted from April 2017 for unincorporated businesses; trading activities are not caught by the restriction (see **Chapter 3** for more detail on this point and **2.17** below for more on finance costs generally).

- For IT purposes, trades have a 'basis period' while property investment businesses are *almost* invariably taxed on a fiscal year basis; companies adopt a chargeable accounting period whether trading or investing (see also **Chapter 1**).

- Unlike ordinary trading businesses (including hotels), CAs are not available in relation to the cost of plant and machinery made available in ordinary residential lettings (see **Chapter 4**).

- Relief for the replacement/renewal of capital items has been withdrawn with effect from April 2016 for trading entities but ordinary residential letting businesses may claim the new replacement domestic items relief for eligible items (see **Chapter 5**). In the past, furnished residential lettings (but not furnished holiday lettings) were able to claim 'wear and tear allowance'

- Losses are relieved quite differently: the scope for relieving trading losses is generally more generous from an IT perspective. There are also different rules for CT losses (see **Chapter 7**).

- National Insurance contributions – for unincorporated businesses, property income profits are not 'earnings' for the purposes of NICs. HMRC has occasionally tried to argue to the contrary in relation to Class 2 contributions although they argued the opposite in *Rashid v Garcia* [2003] SSCD 36 and the realignment of earnings (in NICA 2015) should put the matter beyond doubt in future.

- There are specific rules for the taxation of lease premia and reverse premia (see **Chapter 1**).

- Ordinary property income arising to individuals (including in a partnership) does not comprise 'relevant earnings' as per *FA 2004, s 189*, so as to support pension contributions in excess of £3,600 per annum (but see **Chapter 6** and also **2.9**).

- Farmers' averaging does not apply to rental income receipts but only to trading income.

2.9 *Calculating property business profits and losses*

DIFFERENCES IN PROPERTY INVESTMENT BUSINESSES FOR INCOME TAX VERSUS CORPORATION TAX

2.9 There are certain differences in the treatment of property investment businesses for income tax and corporation tax purposes, including the following:

- Unlike unincorporated businesses, companies claim relief for finance costs through the loan relationships regime (see **2.20,** and see **2.17** for further information on tax relief for finance costs more generally). This distinction applies also to bad and doubtful debts. As noted above, companies are largely saved from the new restriction of finance costs in relation to the letting of dwellings (see **Chapter 3**).

- Property rental business losses are relieved differently, between IT and CT (see **Chapter 7**).

- The private use of a property in an unincorporated business would ordinarily be dealt with by a restriction of relevant costs under the general 'wholly and exclusively' rule set out in *ITTOIA 2005, s 34* (where apportionment is of course possible, as mentioned at **2.7**). In the corporate alternative, since a buy-to-let company's owners are likely to be its directors and therefore employees, private use may instead be caught by the 'benefit in kind' rules such as for the provision of living accommodation (*ITEPA 2003, Pt 3, Ch 5*). If the shareholder is *not* a director/employee, or not otherwise brought within the benefit in kind rules, and the company is a 'close' company, then there are provisions (at *CTA 2010, s 1064*) to treat an amount equivalent to the benefit in kind as a distribution in favour of the participator. As an aside, private overseas holiday homes owned through a corporate wrapper (commonly required for foreign ownership of properties in the former Eastern Bloc) are safe from a benefit in kind tax charge by virtue of *ITEPA 2003, ss 100A–100B*.

- Property income arising to individuals (including in a partnership) does not constitute 'relevant earnings' (*FA 2004, s 189*), so as to support pension contributions in excess of £3,600 per annum. But a company director's (or other company employee's) salary and taxable benefits in kind *will* ordinarily qualify as relevant earnings for pension purposes, despite being derived from rental income to the company.

HOTELS AND SIMILAR ESTABLISHMENTS – A PECULIAR DISTINCTION?

2.10 It is generally understood that running an hotel will be considered a trading activity, even though it principally orients around the provision of somewhere to stay.

> **Focus**
>
> The extent of services provided over and above the provision of a room, coupled with the fact that the owner generally continues to 'occupy' the property, are key factors. Both would be largely absent in a normal buy-to-let letting business with furnished holiday accommodation (see **Chapter 6**) inhabiting a 'middle ground' between the two – strictly still a letting (investment) business but eligible to access some of the reliefs otherwise available only to trades.

2.11 It is perhaps arguable that some such FHL businesses will provide a higher level of service than some of the more basic hotels; in *Griffiths v Jackson* [1982] 56 TC 583, Vinelott J said:

> 'It is a peculiar feature of United Kingdom tax law that the activity of letting furnished flats or rooms, while it may be a business, and in this case a demanding and time-consuming business, is not a trade.'

The following is from HMRC's Property Income manual at PIM4300:

> **'Whole Activity a Trade**
>
> The whole letting activity will only constitute a trade where the owner remains in occupation of the property and provides services over and above those usually provided by a landlord. The provision of bed and breakfast, for example, is clearly trading. Essentially the distinction lies between the hotelier (who is carrying on a trade) and the provider of furnished accommodation (who is not). An important difference is that in a hotel etc. the occupier of the room does not acquire any legal interest in the property.'

BADGES OF TRADE

2.12 Advisers will undoubtedly be on nodding terms with the 'badges of trade' as aggregate indicators of the presence (or not) of a trading activity.

With regard to those clients whose peculiar circumstances are such that they may actually be trading, a brief property-oriented review of the badges of trade follows.

- **Profit motive** – A clear intention, when a property is acquired, to sell property at a profit is a strong indicator of trading. See also **2.25** below;

2.12 *Calculating property business profits and losses*

Terrace Hill (Berkeley) Ltd v HMRC [2015] UKFTT 75 (TC) is an interesting case that focuses on intention – interesting not least because HMRC found itself in the relatively unusual position of trying to argue that the taxpayer's activity was trading (so as to deny relief for large capital losses).

- **Existence of similar trading transactions or interests** – Where a person is already an established property developer/trader, then a tribunal would require strong evidence to rebut an assumption that property acquired and then sold at a profit was not in fact trading. This is a line commonly adopted by HMRC in cases where property developers or builders repeatedly buy property, improve it, occupy it as a residence and then sell on at a significant gain: if it is a trading activity then it does not fall within the scope of CGT and the taxpayer is unable to access principal private residence relief (only or main residence relief – see, for example, HMRC's Capital Gains manual at CG65230; *Hartland v Revenue & Customs* [2014] UKFTT 1099 (TC) illustrates the dividing line between such cases).

- **The way the sale was carried out** – Property that is being marketed for sale as part of a development, off-plan or otherwise while being developed, would be indicative of a trading activity.

- **Method of acquisition** – A property that has been inherited or received by way of gift is unlikely to be considered an asset acquired for trading purposes (although intentions may change – see **2.25**).

- **Source of finance** – The normal test would be to consider whether or not the taxpayer has had to borrow in order to finance the acquisition of the property. But few taxpayers have sufficient wealth to be able to buy property outright, so borrowing is of course a common feature of property acquisition, be it for private occupation, buy-to-let or development. The *term* of the finance, and similar factors, may offer some indication although finance is generally relatively portable/mutable so is highly unlikely to be determinative on its own.

- **Interval of time between purchase and sale** – Most property transactions are long-term by ordinary standards: it may take many months or even years to develop a single property, depending on the resources available to the taxpayer. Perhaps more telling would be the interval between the completion of any development or refurbishment works and the onward sale of a given property. Many property developers decided to take their new properties off the market in 2008/09, when the recession started, to let on a short-term basis until the market had recovered. This did not affect their fundamentally trading status – although they would still have been assessed to rental business profits in the interim – see **2.5** above).

- **Number of transactions** – Given the funds potentially involved, a single property may comprise a substantial trade or an investment business. It may nevertheless be appropriate to consider a particular project in light of similar transactions that may have taken place before or since (or both).

- **Changes to the asset** – Property or home improvement seems to take up a good proportion of daytime television and appears to be a national pastime; work on the asset in hand is unlikely to be a strong indicator except perhaps where the work done is so radical as to imply a commercial aspect to the endeavour (although that will not necessarily preclude the property's being intended as a long-term source of investment income).

- **Nature of the asset** – Given that property may for the most part lend itself equally well to investment or trading, (and in many cases to private occupation) this 'badge' is unlikely to offer much to inform opinion on whether a business is trading or not.

'WHOLLY AND EXCLUSIVELY'

2.13 Here again, advisers will be familiar with the idea that an expense must be incurred 'wholly and exclusively' for the purposes of the property business in order to be tax deductible.

However, where an expense is incurred for more than one purpose, this requirement does not prevent a deduction for any identifiable part or proportion of the expense that is incurred wholly and exclusively for the purposes of the property business (investment or trading); in common with trades generally, an apportionment to recognise (say) private use leaving the remainder tax-deductible is both commonplace and acceptable.

Flip-flops or stethoscope?

2.14 There are very many tax cases which consider the concept of 'wholly and exclusively'. While *Mallalieu v Drummond* [1983] 2 AC 861 found against the taxpayer, arguably one of the most memorably perspicacious comments on this may be found therein, courtesy of Lord Brightman:

> 'The object of the taxpayer in making the expenditure must be distinguished from the effect of the expenditure. An expenditure may be made exclusively to serve the purposes of the business, but it may have a private advantage. The existence of that private advantage does not necessarily preclude the exclusivity of the business purposes. For example, a medical consultant has a friend in the South of France who is also his patient. He flies to the South of France for a week, staying in the home of his friend and attending professionally on him. He seeks to recover the cost of his air fare. The question of fact will be whether the journey was undertaken solely to serve the purposes of the medical practice. This will be judged in the light of the taxpayer's object in making the journey. The question will be answered by

2.15 *Calculating property business profits and losses*

considering whether the stay in the South of France was a reason, however subordinate, for undertaking the journey, or was not a reason but only the effect. If a week's stay on the Riviera was not an object of the consultant, if the consultant's only object was to attend on his patient, his stay on the Riviera was an unavoidable effect of the expenditure on the journey and the expenditure lies outside the prohibition.'

The point has a dash of seasoning added in *McKnight (Inspector of Taxes) v Sheppard* [1999] 1 WLR 1333. But to summarise, albeit a little tongue-in-cheek: what did the good doctor pack in his suitcase first – what was foremost in his mind: stethoscope, or flip-flops and Speedos? If the latter items comprised an afterthought, then their inclusion does not prevent (or even restrict) tax relief for the travelling expense (*ITTOIA 2005, s 34*; *CTA 2009, s 54*).

CAPITAL VERSUS REVENUE

2.15 Fundamentally, an expense is allowable to the extent that it results in income and therefore profit. Capital outlay is basically denied (*ITTOIA 2005, s 33*; *CTA 2009, s 53*), because it is not referable to the earnings of a particular period of assessment.

Capital expenditure is typically said to provide an 'enduring benefit'. Of course certain categories such as plant and machinery qualify for tax relief despite the general prohibition on capital expenditure – although the availability of such reliefs in normal buy-to-let dwellings themselves is significantly curtailed by reason of *CAA 2001, s 35*.

> **Focus**
>
> Typically in the context of property, the question will be whether or not the expense improves an asset so as to provide an enduring benefit to the business; also whether or not the expenditure would substantively affect the market value of the asset (albeit the latter may only prove indicative).

2.16 Advisers will be familiar with the 'capital v revenue divide' but from a property business perspective:

- For dwellings, it is generally accepted that the 'entirety of the asset' is the dwelling. Where a discrete asset is replaced in its entirety, then it is a capital expense. For ordinary trading businesses, this might be a car, a laptop, or a free-standing piece of equipment. Likewise in commercial buildings, it might be a kitchen cupboard, a washbasin or an air-conditioning unit. But replacing a washbasin in a standard residential property would normally be treated as a repair to the fabric of the building as a whole – unless the replacement item is of a meaningfully higher quality than the item it replaced (when that older item was originally installed), in which case it is the overall residential property that is being improved, much like a new, better graphics card might improve a laptop.

- Where an improvement is incidental to 'making good' then it is not necessarily capital – where an expense is incurred to maintain the property, and the use of modern and intrinsically superior materials or techniques means that there is an improvement, this will not necessarily preclude a revenue deduction. *Conn v Robins Bros Ltd* [1966] 43 TC 266 provides well-established case law, and *Wills v Revenue and Customs* [2010] UKFTT 174 (TC) serves to remind HMRC that the concept still holds good.

It is also useful that in *G Pratt & Sons v HMRC Commrs* [2011] UKFTT 416 (TC), additional kerbing to a replacement drive was accepted as updating to modern standards; in *Cairnsmill Caravan Park v Revenue and Customs* [2013] UKFTT 164 (TC) it was also found that the entirety of the asset in that case was the whole of the caravan park, (in excess of 51 acres), rather than a relatively small area of just three acres or so, whose grass surface had been replaced by hard-standing – which HMRC unsuccessfully contended comprised an improvement (perhaps because HMRC failed to raise the rather obvious question of *why* different materials had been selected). HMRC's own guidance can prove quite useful – see PIM2020, its Business Income manual at BIM35430 onwards, and BIM46900 onwards.

INTEREST RELIEF AND ASSOCIATED FINANCE COSTS

2.17 The following section considers the fundamental principles of claiming finance costs as an allowable expense. See **Chapter 3** for commentary on the new tax regime specifically for let dwellings, etc.

While the end result may be similar, the route to tax relief for finance costs differs markedly, depending on whether the business is subject to IT or CT.

The starting point for IT purposes is the general 'wholly and exclusively' rule at *ITTOIA 2005, s 34*. There are specific provisions for the claiming of incidental costs of obtaining loan finance at *ITTOIA 2005, ss 58, 59*, which include fees, commissions and the providing of security (although some expenses are specifically excluded – see BIM45815 and BIM45820 for HMRC's position).

Unincorporated businesses: positive capital account is critical

2.18 The source of the borrowing and the security for the loan are not normally relevant to whether or not tax relief is available (see also **Chapter 1**).

2.18 *Calculating property business profits and losses*

> **Focus**
>
> Usefully, the business may borrow, and the proprietor may then extract funds and the interest on the borrowings will remain allowable so long as the proprietor's capital account remains in credit. While this is the case, the borrowings are deemed to be funding the business even though the cash may have been withdrawn and used for private purposes.

The following extracts are from HMRC's Business Income manual (at BIM45700):

'This chapter applies for Income Tax purposes to the computation of trade profits and property income. References in the text to a "business" should therefore be taken to include both trades and property businesses…

A proprietor of a business may withdraw the profits of the business and the capital they have introduced to the business, even though substitute funding then has to be provided by interest bearing loans. The interest payable on the loans is an allowable deduction. This is on the basis that the purpose of the additional borrowing is to provide working capital for the business. There will, though, be an interest restriction if the proprietor's capital account becomes overdrawn…

Example 2

Mr A owns a flat in central London, which he bought ten years ago for £125,000. He has a mortgage of £80,000 on the property. He has been offered a job in Holland and is moving there to live and work. He intends to come back to the UK at some time. He decides to keep his flat and rent it out while he is away. His London flat now has a market value of £375,000.

The opening balance sheet of his rental business shows:

Mortgage:	£80,000	Property at Market Value:	£375,000
Capital Account	£295,000		
Totals:	£375,000		£375,000

He renegotiates his mortgage on the flat to convert it to a buy-to-let mortgage and borrows a further £125,000. He withdraws the £125,000, which he then uses to buy a flat in Rotterdam.

The balance sheet at the end of Year 1 shows:

Mortgage:	£205,000	Property at Market Value:	£375,000
Capital Account			
B/f	£295,000		
Withdrawn	(£125,000)		
	£170,000		
Totals:	£375,000		£375,000

Although he has withdrawn capital from the business, the interest on the mortgage loan is allowable in full because it is funding the transfer of the property to the business at its open market value at the time the business started. The capital account is not overdrawn.'

2.19 The guidance goes into further detail about the business capital account and borrows from *Silk v Fletcher (No 2)* SpC262 [2000] – noting that the capital account may be written up for depreciation and losses (amongst other things). See BIM45665 and subsequent sections.

Companies and loan relationships

2.20 The loan relationship regime (*CTA 2009, Pts 5–6*) governs the tax treatment of loan finance costs in relation to companies, etc, subject to CT. It does not apply solely to loans that have come about simply by the lending of money because adjustments in relation to money debts are also caught – in particular impairment losses in respect of unpaid business payments, such as bad debts.

2.21 The loan relationship regime is complex in the detail but some basic points in summary are as follows:

- Very broadly, the debits or credits on loan relationships follow the accounting treatment, so long as the financial statements are prepared in accordance with appropriate accounting standards. It follows that the traditional capital v revenue distinction is effectively ignored: the impairment of the capital element of a corporate loan balance may be tax-deductible.

2.22 *Calculating property business profits and losses*

- The most common exception to this approach is where the loan relationship is between connected parties, (as defined for loan relationships at *CTA 2009, s 348*).

- There is no real difference in treatment between interest itself and ancillary expenditure such as loan arrangement fees, commission or similar: essentially, a cost of finance (or loan relationship debit) for accounting purposes is a cost of finance for tax purposes as well, so long as accounted for appropriately (and the loan serves a business purpose).

- Loan relationships may be broken down into two categories: trading and non-trading. Trading loan relationships are basically treated as trading income or expenditure. A property letting business is not trading, and its loan relationships will fall in the other, non-trading loan relationship category. This means that:

    – Bank interest received will be a non-trading loan relationship credit.

    – Loan interest paid, related finance costs and bad debts (or corresponding provisions/impairment reviews) will be non-trading loan relationship debits.

    – Non-trading loan relationship debits and credits are extracted from the property business accounts for tax purposes, and aggregated. An overall credit is chargeable to CT; an overall debit is deductible against total profits of the same period, or it may be group-relieved, or set against non-trading loan relationship credits of earlier periods. Alternatively, it may be carried forwards, and set against non-trading profits – this includes capital gains. There is some flexibility as to how debits may be relieved – they do not *necessarily* have to be set against the first available non-trading profits.

2.22 The rules for connected party transactions effectively require (amongst a great many other things) that no relief is given for a loan relationship debit between such connected parties. For example, a group member that writes off a loan to another group member will not usually secure any tax relief for the write-off. (Although the debtor company will not have to recognise a credit for tax purposes if the loan is formally released, either). More detail on loan relationships can be found in HMRC's Corporate Finance manual.

The definition of 'connection' between parties in the context of loan relationships is perhaps narrower than might be expected – see for instance CFM35110 and CFM35120.

CHANGE IN INTENTION/USE OF A PROPERTY

2.23 Given that one's intentions regarding a property may change over time, it is possible that a capital asset may become a trading asset, or vice versa. A couple of basic examples:

- A property developer has struggled for several years to sell his new-build homes. Having let them for a few years, and having finally sold sufficient to cover his original finance costs, he decides to keep the remainder indefinitely as an investment portfolio – effectively as his 'pension'. When he decides to stop marketing them for sale and to retain them as an investment, the assets have moved from assets held for sale, to fixed assets of his business, ie, from trading assets to investment assets.
- A buy-to-let landlord owns a rental property with a substantial plot of land currently used as garden/grounds. She decides to level the property and develop the entire plot into six detached homes, for immediate sale (it may be the essential to the financing of the development). Although it could perhaps be argued that this is the mere enhancement of a capital asset, the intention to sell once complete is likely to result in its being categorised as a trading venture. (See **2.26**)

There are significant tax consequences in relation to such transactions or decisions. Practically speaking, it may be difficult to identify when a taxpayer's intentions change. Ideally, he or she will have taken advice comfortably before doing so.

Moving from trading to investment

2.24

> **Focus**
>
> Appropriating an asset from trading stock for any purpose, including to a fixed asset investment, will trigger a deemed sale for current market value (*ITTOIA 2005, s 172B; CTA 2009, s 157*).
>
> There is no election to hold over the deemed profit until the newly-capital asset is disposed of. The base cost for onward disposal of the asset will be the amount brought into the accounts of the trade for tax purposes, and therefore the market value on transfer (*TCGA 1992, s 161(2)*).

In the above example at **2.23**, the property developer has struggled to sell the properties so it may be that the market value is not so high that the transfer and deemed profit (if any) renders the transaction problematic from a tax perspective, and there may even be trading losses to utilise.

Moving from investment to trading – developing an investment property for onward sale

2.25 Appropriating a property from fixed assets to trading stock would also trigger a deemed disposal (this time for capital gains purposes) at current market value (*TCGA 1992, s 161*). CGT or (or CT on capital gains) may therefore be due on such an event.

2.25 *Calculating property business profits and losses*

> **Focus**
>
> Unlike with appropriations *from* trading stock as at **2.24**, the legislation *does* offer an election effectively to postpone the gain on transfer into trading stock (*TCGA 1992, s 161(3)*). The election reduces the value of the property when taken to trading stock so that the gain is nil, likewise reducing the cost of the asset for trading purposes.
>
> Businesses should, however, weigh up the implications of effectively converting a capital gain into a trading profit – particularly when moving from CGT to IT.

Example 2.1 – Appropriation of property to trading stock – expensive election

Katherine is a property investor and developer. She decides to demolish one of her existing rental properties and build a block of apartments for onward sale. The original property cost £400,000 and is now worth £1,000,000. After further build costs of £500,000, she reckons she will be able to sell the apartments for a total of £2,000,000. The project is a trading venture (see also **2.26** below).

It has been used as a dwelling throughout her period of ownership, so the CGT on the appropriation of the property to 'trading stock' (in 2016/17) would be:

£1,000,000 – £400,000 = £600,000 @ 28% = £168,000. (Katherine has used her CGT annual exemption and is already an additional rate taxpayer, so her residential gain is taxed entirely at 28%).

If Katherine were instead to elect (under *TCGA 1992, s 161(3)*) to treat the property's gain as reducing the 'purchase price' of the asset as transferred to stock to just £400,000, thereby reducing her capital gain to nil, then her trading profit after development costs would be subject to income tax and National Insurance contributions as follows:

£2,000,000 – £500,000 (development) – £400,000 (reduced cost) = £1,100,000 @ 47% = £517,000.

Alternatively, if Katherine does not make the election, her overall tax cost would be:

£1,000,000 – £400,000 = £600,000 @ 28% = £168,000

£2,000,000 – (£1,000,000 + £500,000) = £500,000 @ 47% = £235,000

£403,000

Calculating property business profits and losses **2.27**

In effect, the election would treat an extra £600,000 as being subject to IT (and NICs) instead of CGT, costing her:

£600,000 @ (45+2–28)% = £114,000

Note, however, that the election is equally valid if the market value has fallen between original acquisition and appropriation to trading stock. This has the potential to turn what may be a relatively inflexible capital loss into an allowable reduction of trading profits, in turn reducing amounts subject to IT and NICs. An alternative intention to let the newly-built apartments as part of her investment portfolio would retain the development within Katherine's existing (capital) investment business, rather than it becoming a trading activity.

TRANSACTIONS IN UK LAND
2.26

> **Focus**
>
> *Finance Act 2016* substantively re-wrote the transactions in land regime for both IT and CT purposes. While the main aim was apparently to extend the scope of the regime to ensure that offshore entities involved in UK land transactions were brought within the charge to UK tax, the new legislation arguably goes significantly beyond that, to affect even UK-based businesses. The following paragraphs are intended only to assist with a broad appreciation of the regime, insofar as it may impinge on buy-to-let landlords.
>
> *The FA 2016* measures apply to disposals on or after 5 July 2016 (*ITA 2007, Pt 9A, s 517A et seq.* replacing *Pt 13, Ch 3; CTA 2010, Pt 8ZB, s 356OA et seq.* replacing *Pt 18*). HMRC published guidance on the provisions in December 2016, which will eventually be included in its Business Income manual (see http://preview.tinyurl.com/HMRC-land-Dec16).

As mentioned at **2.23**, it could be argued that a project to develop a hitherto investment property for onward sale was not a trading venture but merely the enhancement of a capital asset, and subject to the capital gains regime. HMRC has sometimes run the counter-argument that a 'supervening trade' has developed (see for example BIM20315, and BIM60060 specifically in relation to land) but the transactions in land regime, while ostensibly introduced as anti-avoidance legislation, effectively acts to bring land or property disposals (that are not already caught as trading) within the scope of IT or CT, as appropriate.

2.27 These supposedly anti-avoidance measures were originally designed to treat the exploitation/development of land for a profit as being subject to

2.28 *Calculating property business profits and losses*

IT or CT. In doing so, their scope extended far beyond mere 'avoidance'. Simplistically, the importance of the regime to taxpayers and to HMRC depends on the difference in tax cost between a capital gain and now trading income – currently quite significant, although that has not always been the case.

Since the regime is aimed at anti-avoidance, it is broad and complex. A brief summary of the main points follows.

Criteria (following FA 2016)

2.28 Any of the following conditions must apply to be caught by the regime as now in effect:

1. The main purpose, or one of the main purposes, of acquiring the land was to realise a profit or gain from disposing of the land.
2. The main purpose, or one of the main purposes, of acquiring any property deriving its value from the land was to realise a profit or gain from disposing of the land.
3. The land is held as trading stock.
4. In a case where the land has been developed, the main purpose, or one of the main purposes, of developing the land was to realise a profit or gain from disposing of the land when developed.

Impact for UK property businesses

2.29 Finance Act 2016 replaced the old legislation with new provisions. One of the changes is that the legislation now requires affected transactions to be taxed as trading profits, instead of just applying IT or CT on deemed income. The pre-FA 2016 version of the legislation set a higher threshold in order to be triggered: the intention, at the point of acquiring/developing the land, to make a gain on its disposal had to be *the sole or main object* rather than just *one* of the main purposes (as now) in order for the disposal to be caught by the provisions.

Taken literally, it would not be unreasonable to say that the first new condition at **2.28** might be satisfied by many career buy-to-let landlords, who may well factor in a projected increase in a property's market value when considering whether or not to buy it. Arguably, the gain on a property's eventual disposal may therefore amount to 'one of the main purposes' of acquiring it in the first place; it no longer has to be *the* main purpose to fall within the scope of the transactions in land regime.

2.30 HMRC has said that it has no intention of applying the new provisions to catch simple property sales by buy-to-let investors, except in two scenarios:

- 'If the investor decides to undertake development prior to sale the profit on the developed part, from the date the decision to develop for sale, will be trading income. But that would be trading income without the new legislation; or

- If the investor sells the land in a contract with a 'slice of the action' clause (allowing them to benefit from changes in the future development of the property [see **2.34**] the slice of the action profit will be taxed under the new legislation – but it was previously taxed under the transactions in land legislation.' (Source: NLA website)

Such reassurance is arguably better than nothing, but some readers will already be aware that HMRC guidance has changed quite fundamentally in the past (see, for example, the history of the renewals basis in **Chapter 5**). Perhaps more worrying is HMRC's assertion, effectively, that 'property development to make a gain would be trading income anyway' since, if this were correct, criterion 4 above would seem to be redundant (see **2.28**).

2.31

> **Focus**
>
> Assuming HMRC's reassurances can be taken at face value, then practically, it is only the last of those criteria that will be relevant to a BTL investor, and only when there is a decision to develop an investment property with an objective of making a gain on onward sale. This will not normally affect previous capital value growth or earlier improvements to a property undertaken while the property was happily part of the property business, and effectively an investment asset.

Limitations of scope

2.32   The transactions in land regime will (still) not apply where:

- The transaction would be a trading activity anyway (*ITA 2007, s 517C(3); ITA 2007, s 517E(3); CTA 2010, s 356OC(3); CTA 2010, s 356OE(3)*).

- Where the gain on disposal of the property is partly attributable to a period before there was an intention to develop for onward sale, then the gain so attributable is exempt from the regime (*ITA 2007, s 517L; CTA 2010, s 356OL*).

- Where the gain in question would otherwise be eligible for relief on the disposal of an only or main residence under *TCGA 1992, ss 222–226* (or would be except for the restriction in relation to properties acquired partly to make a gain), the gain will not be deemed income as a transaction in land (*ITA 2007, s 517M*).

2.33   The second exception in **2.32** is likely to be relevant to many buy-to-let investors who, after having held an appreciating property for (say) many years, 'do it up' to sell it on, with the result that the new transactions in land regime deems the development project to be taxable as if a trading activity.

2.34 *Calculating property business profits and losses*

The potentially substantial gain that has accrued up to the point where the intention to develop the property has formed can be excluded from the deemed trading charge. This then leads to the potentially quite difficult question of *when* such an intention has in fact formed, which will turn on the facts of the case.

'Slice of the action' arrangements

2.34 A property investor may hold a substantial property or plot but not have either the expertise or financial resources to undertake a development project. Alternatively, a property developer may simply approach the investor with a proposal. The developer may offer the investor an initial lump sum, and then a commitment to pay over part of the profits on the onward sale of the developed property or properties. This arrangement is called a 'slice of the action' and HMRC will argue that the investor is actually participating in the developer's trading profits, rather than receiving simple deferred consideration.

The case *Page v Lowther* [1983] 57 TC 199 established the principle that the initial lump sum will be capital but that future sums contingent on successful development, etc, fall within the scope of the transactions in land provisions.

2.35 Any uplift in value from the investor's acquisition to the 'first intention date' should remain capital.

Further protection from the transactions in land provisions will be afforded where the property is also the individual's only or main residence and therefore eligible for relief, as already noted.

In line with *Taylor v Good* [1974] 1 AII ER 1137, HMRC accepts that planning permission is not itself 'development', a process which should entail physical adaptation or preparation for a new use (see BIM60460). The act of seeking planning permission may, however, be indicative of the investor's intention in relation to the property.

> **Example 2.2 – 'Slice of the action' arrangement**
>
> Freddie, a property investor, is approached by Brian the builder with a proposal to turn one of Freddie's larger properties into an apartment block, which Brian intends to sell on. Freddie and Brian agree terms, at which point the property is worth £1,250,000 on the open market. Brian offers to pay Freddie £1,000,000 up front and then a 'slice of the action' on subsequent apartment sales, such that Freddie stands to make a further £1,000,000, contingent on the sale of all of the apartments.
>
> Freddie's initial lump sum receipt is, of course, capital – in line with the above rules. But not all of the future receipts are taxable as trading income, because Freddie's property was already worth £1,250,000 at the time there was a firm intention to develop and that should be excluded from the trading income assessment. Freddie should therefore get a further £250,000 as a capital sum, out of the proceeds of sale, leaving only £750,000 to be taxable as income.

Calculating property business profits and losses **2.39**

NON-COMMERCIAL LETTINGS

2.36 A buy-to-let investor may let out a property at less than a commercial rate, perhaps because the tenant is a friend or relative. HMRC's position is that any expenses incurred in relation to a deliberately non-commercial letting are unlikely to have been incurred 'wholly and exclusively' for the rental business.

> **Focus**
>
> Strictly, they should not be allowed at all. However, HMRC's policy is to allow the expenses to offset the income from that property only. Any net income is still taxable, but any surplus expenses cannot be carried forwards as property losses, on that or indeed any other letting.

2.37 Simply offering to let out a property at a discount for the first year is not a non-commercial letting since the underlying motive is to let out at a commercial rate. It is the presence of a philanthropic or non-business motive that will trigger the restriction as outlined (see PIM2220).

PROPOSALS FOR A NEW CASH BASIS FOR UNINCORPORATED PROPERTY LETTING BUSINESSES

2.38 In August 2016, the Government issued a consultation on proposals to introduce a more comprehensive cash basis of taxation of rental business profits, modelled on the cash basis for unincorporated trades. This would see the taxpayer concentrate on receipts and payments only, in order to derive taxable profits, rather than working with invoices, provisions and accruals, etc.

The consultation proposed to introduce legislation for Finance Bill 2017 although it appears to have been omitted from the draft Finance Bill clauses published in early December 2016.

2.39 Amongst other things, the consultation document proposed:

- No monetary limit on eligible businesses: unlike with trading entities, property businesses of any monetary size will be eligible so long as carried on only by individuals or partnerships comprised only of individuals.

- Instead of a simple limit of £500 for allowable interest costs, interest will be allowable but the mortgages would need to be 'tied to property assets used in the business, be wholly and exclusively for business purposes and not exceed the value of the property'. If that means that the mortgages would need to be secured on the let properties, that would represent a significant restriction compared to the flexibility of the current regime, which is not overly concerned with how (or on what) finance is secured. Likewise, if no apportionment would be permitted to discount any private

2.39 *Calculating property business profits and losses*

use – ie, an 'all or nothing' approach. There will still be a restriction to the rate of tax relief available, insofar as it relates to the financing of residential lettings (see **Chapter 3**).

- Policy in relation to capital allowances is not fully formed, but would seem to permit an immediate write-down of any unrelieved allowances on transition to the cash basis, and no value limit on eligible expenditure (as distinct from the standard annual investment allowance which currently has an annual limit of £200,000 of eligible expenditure). Commercial property lettings are not excluded from the proposed new regime and the extent of eligible expenditure in some commercial properties can be very substantial. Scope for loss relief under the cash basis will, however, be limited to carry forwards only.

- While the capital gains element of any lease premium would continue to be taxed as a capital gain, the income element would be taxable immediately (see **Chapter 1**).

- Taxing even returnable deposits on receipt, because recognising the income only when it actually belongs to the landlord is just too complicated.

Appendix A: What expenses can be claimed for a buy-to-let property business?

The following table sets out a reasonably comprehensive list of the types of expenditure a landlord might expect commonly to incur in a buy-to-let business. Please see also **Chapter 2**.

Accountancy fees	Note HMRC's Property Income manual states (at PIM2205):
	'Cost of taxation accounts and negotiations
	Fees incurred on preparing accounts for commercial reasons and on many other accountancy services will meet the 'wholly and exclusively' test. Hence the cost can be deducted in computing rental business profits.
	Strictly, any additional fees incurred for computing and agreeing the tax liability on rental business profits are not deductible. But, under a long-standing practice, normal recurring legal and accountancy fees incurred in preparing accounts or agreeing the rental business tax liability can be deducted.
	This practice does not extend to other personal fees; for example, fees incurred on preparing a tax return or working out CGT due.'
	Note that the Capital Gains manual at CG15280 says that accountancy fees in relation to the ascertainment of market value or to any apportionment for the purposes of the CGT computation may be allowed, but that 'otherwise, fees for the computation of liability are not allowable'.
Advertising for tenants	Generally allowable under the 'wholly and exclusively' rule for business expenditure (*ITTOIA 2005, s 34*; *CTA 2009, s 54*).
Agents' fees/letting fees	Generally allowable where incurred in relation to ongoing let property (eg, as a monthly, quarterly or an annual cost) – but see **Legal and professional costs** below

Appendix A: What expenses can be claimed for a buy-to-let property business?

Bad and doubtful debts	Income should normally be recognised when it is due, rather than when it is received (unless operating the cash basis). However, where steps have been taken to recover a tenant's debt but without success, or it is otherwise reasonable to believe that a debt will not be paid, it is possible to write off or to provide for bad/doubtful debts accordingly. HMRC will, however, resist a simple provision that has not been gauged against a specific, or specific categories of, debtor (see BIM42701; PIM2054).
	Corporation tax works according to the rules for loan relationships, (*CTA 2009, Pt 5*) but the regime will basically allow relief for non-trading loan relationships in relation to the impairment of a relevant non-lending relationship (*Pt 6*) unless the parties to the loan relationship are deemed to be connected.
	For more on loan relationships, see **Chapter 2**.
Cost of collecting rents/enforcing debts	*Income tax*: Allowable in line with agents' and professional fees generally.
	Corporation tax: Similarly allowable, in line with the rules for loan relationships, as per **Bad and doubtful debts** above.
Cost of services provided, eg: • Cleaning/waste disposal; • Concierge; • Gardening; • Heat and light, gas, electricity; • Water rates; • Service charge (eg, for apartments)	Where the landlord occupies the property for part of the year, it will be appropriate to consider restricting the deduction for business expenses in line with the extent of business use. This may not necessarily be a simple time apportionment: if the property is occupied privately out of summer season, for instance, it may be appropriate to recognise a relatively higher private use proportion of heat and light due to less extensive consumption in the commercial period. Some expenses, however, such as cleaning, gardening and waste disposal, may be undertaken only directly before or after a commercial letting, in which case apportionment may not be necessary. See also **Service charges** separately below.
Council tax, rates	Generally deductible, although costs are usually borne by the tenant(s). Commonly incurred during void periods and therefore allowable if, at the time the cost is incurred, the property is held out for letting. See PIM2030.

Appendix A: What expenses can be claimed for a buy-to-let property business?

Insurance	Premia on insurance policies covering: • the risk of damage to the fabric of the property; • the risk of damage to the contents; and • loss of rents will be allowable if paid for the purposes of the rental business. Allowable deductions will include premia in respect of properties that are held for letting but vacant for the time being, as well as properties that are let. Amounts received are usually set against the costs incurred to make good damage, etc., while proceeds of a claim for loss of rents are taxable as rental income. See PIM2040 and BIM45510.
Interest – mortgage/ loan interest	Generally allowable; see **Chapters 2** and **3**.
Lease premium paid	See **Chapter 1**.
Legal and professional costs	Generally allowable on the basis that they are incurred for the purposes of the letting business. According to HMRC (see PIM2205), acceptable deductions include: • Obtaining a valuation for insurance purposes; • Arbitration to determine the rent of a holding; • Evicting an unsatisfactory tenant in order to re-let the property. However, note also the following (from PIM2205): 'The expenses incurred in connection with the first letting or subletting of a property for more than one year are capital expenditure and therefore not allowable. The expenses include, for example, legal expenses (such as the cost of drawing up the lease), agent's and surveyor's fees and commission. Expenses for a let of a year or less can be deducted.' Of course, there are conflicting demands in relation to the duration of letting arrangements. 'Where a replacement lease follows closely on a previous one, and is in broadly similar terms, a change of tenant will not normally make the associated legal and professional costs disallowable. Any proportion of the legal or other costs that relate to the payment of a premium on the renewal of a lease will, of course, remain disallowable.'

Appendix A: What expenses can be claimed for a buy-to-let property business?

Maintenance, repairs and decoration	Where related to general upkeep of a property, allowed as a deduction for either income tax or corporation tax purposes. See **Chapter 2**.
Motor expenses	If incurred for business travel, should be deductible; where capital allowances are claimed, a suitable restriction for private use should be considered. See also **Travelling expenses** below.
Office expenses: • Printing, postage, stationery; • Telephone and internet; • Use of home as office.	Expenditure on eligible equipment, such as laptops, office equipment, tools, etc, for use outside of let dwellings may be claimable for capital allowances, with a suitable restriction for private use, if appropriate. Business calls and broadband should be allowable. A restriction for private use may be appropriate unless private use is insignificant. See also HMRC's Business Income manual at BIM47820 and BIM75010.
Renewals basis	Replaced by new 'Replacement of domestic items relief' in *FA 2016*; see **Chapter 5**.
Rent as a cost, ground rent	Generally allowable (see PIM2025); claim may need to be restricted where there is also private occupation.
Service charges	Service charges may contain both ongoing running costs (generally allowable) and funds for capital improvements. Apportionment may be appropriate to reflect any periods of private use. Capital improvements may not be allowable as a revenue deduction on basic principles, but note that the restriction on capital allowances applies to dwelling areas, and not normally to common areas. Eligible expenditure in common areas, such as security installations, lighting and lifts may be claimable for capital allowances purposes; see **Chapter 4**.
Subscriptions	Subscriptions to associations representing the interests of landlords (see PIM2205).

Appendix A: What expenses can be claimed for a buy-to-let property business?

Travelling expenses	The cost of travelling to inspect or maintain properties, or to meet tenants or advisers, will normally be allowable. See PIM2210 for more on HMRC's position.
Wages	Where paid to family members, should be commercially justifiable. Normal rules for operating a payroll apply, regardless of whether to family members, eg: • RTI – where applicable; • Workplace pensions.
Wear and tear allowance	Not available after 1/6 April 2016 for corporation/income tax purposes; see **Chapter 5**.

Chapter 3

Finance costs relief restrictions

Lee Sharpe CTA, ATT, Tax Consultant, Sharpe Tax Consulting Ltd.

> SIGNPOSTS
>
> - **Scope** – The new regime restricting tax relief for finance costs for residential lettings applies to all residential property businesses subject to income tax. It is being phased in, in four equal tranches, commencing 2017/18 through to 2020/21. The normal deduction for affected interest costs, etc, is disallowed, but a basic rate (20%) equivalent tax reduction is allowed instead. However, the full 20% relief will not always be available (although where it is restricted, any unused excess should be carried forward). The restriction applies not only to interest itself but to all related finance cost (see **3.1–3.10**).
>
> - **Implications** – The practical consequences of disallowing (what for many landlords comprises) a very substantial cost can be far-reaching (see **3.11**).
>
> - **Tax reduction mechanism** – The rules relating to the basic rate tax reduction are complex, although significantly improved following revision in Finance Act 2016. Landlords and their advisers will need to be particularly careful where losses, reliefs and personal allowances, etc, can potentially restrict the amount of rental income that is taxable, or the amount of the new tax reduction (see **3.12–3.21**).
>
> - **Trusts and Estates** – These are subject to income tax, and are therefore within the scope of the finance cost restriction regime (see **3.22–3.36**).
>
> - **Other issues** – Not all types of residential property letting business are affected: companies and furnished holiday lettings (FHLs) are specifically excluded (but note the restriction is not applicable only to UK properties; overseas non-FHL properties are within the scope of the new regime). Employee loans used to fund personal buy-to-let businesses may previously have escaped a benefit-in-kind income tax charge on the director/employee but are now caught, with implications not only for the director/employee but also for the employing business. Loans to finance an interest in a partnership that has a residential property business are also specifically included in the regime (see **3.37–3.42**).

Finance costs relief restrictions

- **Incorporation** – Incorporating the residential property rental business will remove ongoing exposure to the potentially very significant cost of disallowed interest, etc, but there is often a very substantial threshold in the form of capital gains tax and stamp duty land tax, which cannot always be avoided. Companies will be neither necessary nor appropriate for all property businesses (see **3.43–3.44**).
- **Increasing rental income** – This is an obvious response to rising costs, but is potentially even more tax-inefficient (see **3.45**).
- **Introducing family members** – Where other (generally adult) family members can participate in the profits so as to utilise personal allowances and/or basic rate bands, this could help to mitigate tax costs (see **3.46–3.47**).
- **Timing expenditure** – It may be counterintuitive, but it is potentially beneficial to defer allowable expenditure until a later tax year, where the rise in taxable income might otherwise be particularly punitive (see **3.48**).
- **Paying off capital** – If paying off loan capital will reduce finance costs going forwards, then it makes sense to compare the potential lost income if the funds were deployed elsewhere, against the rising tax cost of mortgage interest, etc (see **3.49**).
- **Accelerating finance costs** – Increasing the amount of finance costs paid before the disallowance is 100% installed should reduce the proportion of costs disallowed, and be more tax-efficient overall (see **3.50**).
- **Pension contributions/gift aid** – Exposure to higher rates can, as usual, be mitigated by those payments that effectively extend both the basic rate and higher rate bands (and the respective points at which child benefit and the personal allowance start to be 'clawed back'). Scope for pension contributions may, however, be limited, where the buy-to-let investor does not have a source of relevant earnings (see **3.51–3.52**).
- **Rationalising the business** – Shedding the more highly-geared properties in a portfolio may help to mitigate the effects of disallowed interest costs, although capital gains tax will have to be considered (see **3.53**).
- **Diversifying the business** – Activities such as property development, management and maintenance might, if undertaken separately and in sufficient volume, be considered trades in their own right, such that associated finance costs escape the restriction for dwelling-related loans. But beware that 'carving out' business activity prior to incorporation might leave the residual investment portfolio ineligible for incorporation relief under *TCGA 1992, s 162* (see **3.54**).

RESTRICTING TAX RELIEF FOR RESIDENTIAL LETTINGS

Introduction

3.1 This chapter will concentrate on the new restriction of tax relief for finance costs for residential lettings, for non-corporates (primarily). It should be emphasised that the legislation is very new, and has rightly been criticised for poor drafting. Some of the finer detail may well require clarification by the tribunal. For further more general information on the deductibility of interest in the context of property businesses, see **Chapter 2**. The latter part of this chapter considers strategies for dealing with the new regime.

The announcement in the summer 2015 Budget that landlords' mortgage interest would soon be phased out for tax purposes sent shockwaves through the buy-to-let industry, and the tax profession that advises it. The rationale for the new regime is specious at best, since it purports to make things fairer for would-be homeowners who do not get tax relief on their mortgages while blatantly overlooking the fact that practically all other businesses *do* get such tax reliefs (butchers, bakers, candlestick-makers), regardless of how much those other businesses might 'compete' with homeowners.

Many landlords will find little to dissuade them from the perception that this is a thinly-veiled tax grab, hoping to exploit negative perceptions of the letting industry. Since the new regime does not distinguish between UK and overseas property businesses, it seems that the UK Government is happy to put the interests of French, American and Guatemalan homeowners (etc) before those of buy-to-let investors who are taxable in the UK.

Outrage aside, the regime (introduced in *F(No.2)A 2015*, and amended in *FA 2016*), effectively punishes borrowing to finance the business, and will undoubtedly act as a barrier to entry for prospective landlords, leaving mortgage-free and corporate landlords unaffected. The new legislation giving effect to these changes is to be found in ITTOIA *2005, Pt 3 Ch 3*, starting with new s 272A (s 272, ironically, being the section that says the taxation of property businesses should follow trading principles).

Overview

3.2 The new legislation will progressively disallow landlords' finance costs, starting 6 April 2017; to the extent that those costs are disallowed, there will be a corresponding reduction in the landlord's income tax liability, at the basic rate of 20%.

3.2 Finance costs relief restrictions

> **Focus**
>
> It follows that landlords who remain taxable at only the basic rate will not suffer any net tax 'penalty'. Of course, if a landlord's mortgage interest is substantial – which it is, in very many cases –the disallowance will mean that they are unlikely to remain mere basic rate taxpayers for long, once the new regime commences.

The new rules will be phased in from April 2017, as follows:

- 2017/18   75% of finance costs allowable, and 25% gets only 20% tax reduction;
- 2018/19   50% of finance costs allowable, and 50% gets only 20% tax reduction;
- 2019/20   25% of finance costs allowable, and 75% gets only 20% tax reduction;
- 2020/21   No finance costs allowed against rental profits; 100% gets 20% tax reduction.

Example 3.1 – Effect of interest relief restriction

Jennifer is already a higher-rate taxpayer, with a modest amount of rental income as a secondary source. She has a single property that generates £6,000 a year net rental income after £4,000 mortgage interest.

If we assume in this simple comparison that 2016/17 rates and allowances apply across all years, Jennifer's net income is affected as follows:

Tax Year	2016/17	2017/18	2018/19	2019/20	2020/21
	£	£	£	£	£
Earnings (say)	60,000	60,000	60,000	60,000	60,000
Net Rent after Mortgage	6,000	6,000	6,000	6,000	6,000
Add-back rental finance	0	1,000	2,000	3,000	4,000
Total	66,000	67,000	68,000	69,000	70,000
Tax Liability					
Initial (after int. add-back)	15,600	16,000	16,400	16,800	17,200
Rental 20% Tax Credit	0	−200	−400	−600	−800
Net Tax	15,600	15,800	16,000	16,200	16,400
Tax increase on 2016/17	0	200	400	600	800

Finance costs relief restrictions **3.4**

Using 2016/17 rates and allowances as the baseline, Jennifer's tax liability will be £15,600. The tax bill on her property income will be:

£6,000 × 40% = £2,400

All other things being equal, 25% of her interest costs (£1,000) will be added back in 2017/18, when the new rules start to apply. While this will initially cost £400 in additional income tax, the basic rate tax credit will reduce her tax bill by £200, meaning her net tax cost will increase by £200 as a result.

By 2020/21, the tax bill on Jennifer's property income only will be:

(£6,000 + £4,000 interest added back = £10,000) × 40% = £4,000;

but less the tax reduction of £4,000 × 20% = £800;

leaving her with a net property tax cost of £3,200 – ie, an increase of £800 on her original property tax cost of £2,400 in 2016/17.

The costs affected – restriction of the costs of a dwelling-related loan

3.3 The legislation initially sets out that, where a deduction would be allowed for a 'dwelling-related loan' in calculating the profits of a property business for the 2017/18 tax year, then only 75% of what would otherwise be deductible, will be allowed for income tax purposes (*ITTOIA 2005, s 272A(1)*).

Likewise 2018/19 but at only 50% deductible (*ITTOIA 2005, s 272A(2)*).

And 2019/20 but at only 25% deductible (*ITTOIA 2005, s 272A(3)*).

For 2020/21 *and any subsequent tax year*, no deduction is allowed for a dwelling-related loan (*ITTOIA 2005, s 272A(4)*).

3.4 From this it is clear that only property businesses that are subject to income tax are potentially affected by the new disallowance (note there is nothing to limit the new regime only to UK property businesses). The legislation applies the disallowance at the level of the business, rather than by reference to who (or what) carries on the business.

It follows that the legislation applies to:

- Individuals;
- Partnerships;
- Trusts and Estates.

Most companies are subject to corporation tax (CT) on their rental income, so will be unaffected. Companies that are subject to income tax (IT) (such

3.5 *Finance costs relief restrictions*

as those operating within the non-resident landlord scheme) are specifically excluded from the new measures, except to the extent that those profits are derived in a fiduciary or representative capacity (*ITTOIA 2005, s 272A(5)*).

Extent of restriction – what are the 'costs of a dwelling-related loan'?

3.5

> **Focus**
>
> Costs are held to include:
>
> - Interest;
> - Amounts economically equivalent to interest;
> - Incidental costs of obtaining finance by means of the loan (as defined in *ITTOIA 2005, s 58*).
>
> (*ITTOIA 2005, s 272B(5), (6)*)

3.6 A dwelling-related loan is defined as 'so much of an amount borrowed for the purposes of the business as is referable (on a just and reasonable apportionment) to so much of the business as is carried on for the purpose of generating income from land consisting of a dwelling house' or part thereof, or an estate, interest or right over such land (*ITTOIA 2005, s 272B(2)*), including any land occupied or enjoyed with the dwelling-house as its garden or grounds (*ITTOIA 2005, s 272B(7)*).

The definition can therefore be interpreted to mean that the precise purpose of the borrowing may not always be the only factor: rather it may be necessary to consider at least to some extent the proportion of the overall business that is given over to generating income from a dwelling, etc, so as to determine the proportion of the loan that is 'dwelling-related' and therefore falls within the scope of the regime.

For example, if a loan is taken out to acquire a new laptop for the property business, and the business lets only dwellings, then it could be argued that the loan is 100% 'dwelling-related'. Such a loan would not be financing the acquisition of dwellings themselves, but it would be financing an overall business whose income derived 100% from the letting of dwellings.

However, it may perhaps in turn be argued that it would not be 'just and reasonable' to apportion/restrict the costs of a loan that had been taken out specifically to finance the acquisition of a commercial property for letting out, even if the overall business let out both dwellings and commercial properties.

The explanatory notes that accompanied the introduction of the clause (24) in the summer 2015 Finance Bill said simply that a dwelling-related loan is

Finance costs relief restrictions **3.9**

'an amount borrowed for the purposes of generating income from residential dwelling', and *'where an amount is borrowed only partly for the purpose of generating income from residential dwellings then an apportionment on a just and reasonable basis is provided for'*.

In other words, the explanatory note appears not to follow the precise logic of the legislation itself, which also considers how much of the overall business is carried on for the purpose of generating income from dwellings, etc, HMRC has been questioned on this point – the CIOT raised the issue in communications with HMRC in September 2015 – but as yet, there is very little in the public domain. Nevertheless, it does seem that HMRC's position is as follows:

- Where a loan is for a specific purpose, that purpose is the determining factor (which is arguable).
- Where the loan is to acquire a 'mixed use' property, then apportion based on the respective initial values of the dwelling and non-dwelling parts.
- For financing general repairs to a mixed-use building, perhaps use floor areas.
- Where borrowing for general working capital, an apportionment will be required, perhaps by reference to comparing overall business income from dwellings against that from all other income.

As this is new legislation, this is a point that may ultimately need to be settled by the tribunal. Presumably, a loan taken out partly for a qualifying purpose and partly for other purposes, will be apportioned as normal in accordance with *ITTOIA 2005, s 34(2)* – see **2.17**. See **3.37** for dwelling-related loans in relation to furnished holiday accommodation.

3.7 A 'dwelling-house' is not itself defined in the legislation. See **3.38**, for further consideration of this point.

Building or converting a dwelling for letting out

3.8 A dwelling-related loan includes amounts borrowed to finance the creation of a dwelling-house, either by construction or adaptation for letting out, etc (*ITTOIA 2005, s 272B (3)*). It is difficult to support the logic of this condition, given the chronic national shortage of housing stock. Where a property has been developed for onward sale, then it will not normally be considered part of a buy-to-let business but a property development trade instead, on general principles, and should escape the restriction.

3.9 If a property developer subject to IT were at some point to decide he or she wanted to let a developed dwelling-house, such that it might from then on be considered part of a property letting business, then it seems likely that HMRC would consider any corresponding finance to be a 'dwelling-related loan' from that point (there would of course be a deemed sale to oneself as a result of removing the asset from stock held for resale, in accordance

3.10 *Finance costs relief restrictions*

with *ITTOIA 2005, s 172B* – see also HMRC's Business Income manual at BIM33630 and BIM51625, and **Chapter 2**).

3.10 Where a property developer is holding stock for re-sale but temporarily letting it out while looking for a buyer, HMRC's position is set out in the Property Income manual at PIM4300:

> 'Here, the rental receipts will fall into their rental business, or will create one if they did not already have one. Then:
>
> - Any revenue expenses of the letting of the trading stock must be deducted, in the first place, from the letting receipts.
>
> - Any net profit will be part of the rental business result.
>
> - Any excess of letting expenditure of the trading stock over the rental business receipts is an expense of their property dealing or developing trade.'

Here again, consideration of whether or not a trading loan to finance property development might temporarily transmogrify into a 'dwelling related loan' and, if so, how it might then be prioritised in terms of deduction against the deemed rental activity and/or the overarching trade, appears not to have been considered in any detail, in the legislation.

FAR-REACHING IMPLICATIONS
3.11

Focus

As mentioned above, the mechanism for disallowing dwelling-related loan costs has broad ramifications for those who find themselves affected. Taxable income is artificially created where, in reality, there is none. Claims that otherwise viable businesses will fail as a result of this new regime seem to be well founded.

Advisers should bear in mind the possible consequences for:

- **Tax credits** – The Tax Credits (Definition & Calculation of Income) Regulations 2002, reg 11 determines that the assessment of property income for the purposes of tax credits is in accordance with taxable property income (*ITTOIA 2005, Pt 3*). Any increase in taxable property income will have the potential to reduce a claimant's entitlement, subject to income disregards, etc.

- **Student loan repayments** – The Education (Student Loans) (Repayment) Regulations 2009, reg 29(4) states that a borrower's income (on which the quantum of repayments is to be based) is determined in accordance

Finance costs relief restrictions **3.11**

with *ITA 2007, s 23,* Step 1 – the aggregate amounts initially chargeable to IT. There is a minimum income threshold set by reg 29(4)(a) – currently £17,495 for 'Plan 1 Loans' and £21,000 for the more recent 'Plant 2 Loans' – and there is a threshold of £2,000 for unearned income at reg 29(4)(c), such that, if total investment income is below this level, then it is ignored. The repayment rate is 9% where the limits are breached. It follows that where the disallowance of what would otherwise be deductible dwelling related loan costs increases an individual's taxable income, it may exceed the limits which trigger loans to be repayable, and/or increase the amount of the loan.

- **Capital gains tax at the lower rate(s)** – the calculation of CGT has itself been transformed by *FA 2016* at least partly by the creation of a more favourable rate for gains that are, essentially, not on residential property. Capital gains are taxed at a lower rate to the extent that there remains a basic rate band unutilised by either taxable income or gains subject to entrepreneurs' relief (or the new investor's relief). Increased taxable property income will reduce the accessibility of those lower CGT rates (*TCGA 1992, s 4 et seq.*, as extensively updated by *FA 2016, s 83*).

- **Higher rate threshold** and:

    o **Eligibility for the full £1,000 'savings allowance'** – the Government left it rather late to admit that the so-called 'allowance' is in effect a nil-rate band applicable to the first £1,000 of taxable savings income, leaving advisers precious little time to prepare for the new regime. The £1,000 band is not fixed, and reduces to just £500 if the individual has 'higher rate income' (as defined specifically for the new 'allowance', but broadly as one might expect). Increased taxable rental income will feed into the calculation of whether or not the individual has such higher rate income, and therefore whether or not tax-free savings income will be restricted (*ITA 2007, s 12B*, as introduced by *FA 2016, s 4*).

    o **Ability to transfer tax allowance – the new 'marriage allowance'** – neither the transferor nor the beneficiary of the election may be (very broadly) 'higher rate' taxpayers under the regime which permits one spouse/civil partner to elect to sacrifice 10% of his/her personal allowance so that the other may claim a corresponding tax reduction at the basic rate of 20%. (*ITA 2007, s 55C(1)(c)* and *55B(2)(b)* respectively; the legislation is complicated thanks to the effects of the new savings and dividend 'allowances').

- **Child benefit clawback** – Where the taxpayer's 'adjusted net income' exceeds £50,000, any child benefit received by the taxpayer, or his or her 'partner' where applicable, starts to be clawed back at a rate of 0.01% for every £1 such income above the threshold (so that all child benefit is 100% forfeit as soon as adjusted net income reaches £60,000). It is always the higher earner of the couple (if there be one) who is subject to

3.11 *Finance costs relief restrictions*

the clawback, regardless of who receives the child benefit (*ITEPA 2003, s 681B–H*).

- **Loss of personal allowance** – at the rate of £1 for every £2 of 'adjusted net income' exceeding £100,000 (*ITA 2007, s 35*); and

- **Childcare payments** – where either parent has 'adjusted net income' in excess of £100,000, the new regime which 'tops up' eligible childcare provision will not be available; this is reduced from the original proposal which was to set the limit to the additional rate threshold (Childcare Payments (Eligibility) Regulations 2015 (SI 2015/448), reg 15, as updated by SI 2016/793).

- **Additional rate threshold** (*ITTOIA 2007, s 10(5A)*) and:

    o **Eligibility for £500 'savings allowance'** – the new 'savings allowance' is reduced to nil where the taxpayer has 'higher-rate income' as defined for the purposes of the new 'allowance' (*ITA 2007, s12B*, as introduced by *FA 2016, s 4*).

    o **Restriction of pension annual allowance** – very simply, where the taxpayer's 'adjusted income' exceeds £150,000, then their pension annual allowance (currently £40,000) starts to be tapered at a rate of £1 annual allowance for every £2 adjusted income above the threshold. 'Adjusted income' includes rental income, and is not limited to 'relevant earnings' (*FA 2004, s 228ZA*, as inserted by *F(No.2)A 2015*).

Case study – buy-to-let property portfolio

Jakob has a portfolio of several standard buy-to-let properties that yield £37,500 after mortgage interest of £45,000. He and his spouse have three young children (so they will continue to be eligible for child benefit for the next several years) and he has a large (Plan 1) student loan, having studied veterinary science at university. His spouse, who is a junior partner in a firm of architects, is currently the higher earner, on £48,000 a year. Jakob has no other income or outgoings of any significance.

Using 2016/17 rates and allowances, assuming child benefit for three children will remain at £2,500 a year, and the repayment threshold for Plan 1 student loans also remains at £17,495, Jakob's financial position over the next few years unwinds as follows:

Tax Year	2016/17	2017/18	2018/19	2019/20	2020/21
	£	£	£	£	£
Income:					
Net rent after mortgage	37,500	37,500	37,500	37,500	37,500
Add-back rental finance	0	11,250	22,500	33,750	45,000

Finance costs relief restrictions **3.11**

Tax Year	2016/17	2017/18	2018/19	2019/20	2020/21
	£	£	£	£	£
Income for tax purposes	37,500	48,750	60,000	71,250	82,500
Less: personal allowance	(11,000)	(11,000)	(11,000)	(11,000)	(11,000)
Taxable	26,500	37,750	49,000	60,250	71,500
Tax liability:					
Initial	5,300	8,700	13,200	17,700	22,200
Student loan payable	1,800	2,813	3,825	4,838	5,850
Child benefit clawback	0	0	2,501	2,501	2,501
Rental finance 20% tax reduction	0	(2,250)	(4,500)	(6,750)	(9,000)
Net tax, child benefit, student loan	7,100	9,263	15,026	18,289	21,551
Tax increase on 2016/17		2,163	7,926	11,189	14,451
Net income	30,400	28,237	22,474	19,211	15,949

Jakob's real income has not risen at all, but his tax costs (including the clawback of child benefit and increased student loan repayments) have a little more than trebled between 2016/17 and 2020/21.

His net income has broadly halved: by 2020/21, it has fallen to just 42.5% of the pre-tax income of £37,500 that he started with.

In 2017/18, Jakob's tax-adjusted income breaches the higher rate threshold for the first time, by £5,750. His costs increase by £11,250 × 9% + £5,750 × (40%−20%) = £2,163, being: the increased student loan repayment, and the marginal tax cost of the disallowed mortgage interest that falls within the higher rate band, so is not covered by the 20% tax reduction. He is now the higher earner in the couple, for tax purposes, but his adjusted net income does not exceed £50,000 so their entitlement to child benefit is unaffected.

In 2018/19, Jakob's deemed taxable income has risen to £60,000, meaning that the family's child benefit is 100% repayable through his tax return. His deemed extra taxable income of £11,250 is fully taxable at a marginal rate of (9% + (40% − 20%)), representing the student loan repayment and the marginal tax cost of the next 25% disallowance of his mortgage interest:

3.12 *Finance costs relief restrictions*

> £11,250 × (9% + (40% − 20%)) + £2,501 = £5,763, which is the increase in tax cost from 2017/18 to 2018/19.
>
> The next two years each see a further hike in tax cost of £11,250 × 29% = £3,263, being the marginal tax cost of each extra tranche of disallowed residential mortgage interest.
>
> Jakob's student loan will ultimately be repaid; it is assumed for the purpose of the case study that it is not fully paid off before 2020/21.

TAX REDUCTION MECHANISM OVERVIEW – THE RELIEVABLE AMOUNT

3.12 The original legislation in *F(No.2)A 2015* governing how the corresponding tax reduction should work was criticised by numerous parties, so was re-written for *FA 2016*. The following review is of the legislation as updated by *FA 2016*. This section considers individuals including partners and joint investors; the next section considers trusts and estates.

A reduction in IT liability is allowed where the individual has a 'relievable amount' in respect of a given property business. 'Relievable amount' includes both current year amounts and brought forward amounts in respect of that business, and any of the following components will suffice, either on its own or in combination, to make the individual eligible for a tax reduction (*ITTOIA 2005, s 274A; ITTOIA 2005, s 274AA(4)*).

- A current year amount arises where the new legislation has acted to disallow an amount of £A on (what would otherwise have been allowable as) a dwelling-related loan under the new *ITTOIA 2005, s 272A*, and the taxpayer is taxable on an N% share of the property business profits (so as to cover partnership and joint investment scenarios) – ie, N% of A, or the share of the disallowed amount at the property business level.

- A brought forward amount arises where the relievable amount in the previous year (which can itself include brought forward amounts, as above) exceeds the amount on which relief is given in that previous year; the excess becomes the brought forward amount for the next year.

- A current year estate amount – see **3.30** below.

3.13 Note that this relievable amount is in respect of the individual's relationship with a single property business. Although there is usually only one property business, it is possible that an individual might have more than one, such as where he or she is a buy-to-let investor but also a partner in a partnership that also lets residential property, and/or in receipt of estate income that also includes buy-to-let income.

3.14 Critically, while a current year amount depends on there being an amount of dwelling-related loan cost disallowed in that current year, the overarching relievable amount does not: any excess relievable amount in one year can become a relievable amount in its own right, indefinitely until it is fully relieved, or the property business ceases (this is relevant because the legislation as originally drafted in 2015 could have been construed as requiring a current-year disallowance in order for any carry-forward of unused relief to be effective: any unutilised tax reduction could not then have outlived the borrowings).

The tax reduction – calculation detail
3.15

> **Focus**
>
> The calculation seeks to give a tax reduction, equivalent to the amount of dwelling related loan disallowed at the basic rate. However, the calculation is devised so that none of this tax reduction may be given against tax due on savings income, such as bank interest or dividend income.

Noting that such income will now predominantly be paid gross, the rationale appears to be to encourage buy-to-let investors to apply such 'surplus' invested capital to pay down dwelling-related loans (although much of that investment income might well also be covered by the new savings and dividend so-called 'allowances' in any event, such that there might otherwise be a risk of the tax reduction's being wasted).

The legislation has also to cater for conventional property losses, and to ensure that the tax reduction is not effectively wasted against permitted non-savings income that will ultimately be covered by other tax reliefs or allowances. Clearly, the draftsman has struggled with the complexity of defining the amount of the tax reduction in terms of reliefs, deductions and allowances. But it is taxpayers and their advisers who must contend with the result. It may perhaps be some consolation to the reader that it could have been worse – and in fact it was, when originally enacted under *F(No.2)A 2015*.

3.16 The amount of relief ultimately given – to which the basic rate of 20% is applied – may be summarised as follows:

Firstly, calculate the individual's 'adjusted total income' (ATI) for the year as defined specifically for the purposes of calculating this tax reduction. It is essentially the individual's taxable income after losses and allowances and then net of chargeable savings and dividend income, but a fuller definition (albeit not entirely complete) follows:

> Take the individual's 'net income' for the year, (as defined at *ITA 2007, s 23* at 'Step 2'), being total taxable income but after offsetting the losses, reliefs, etc, in *ITA 2007, s 24*, which includes (amongst other things):

3.17 *Finance costs relief restrictions*

- Brought forwards property losses;
- Property loss relief against total income;
- Trade loss relief brought forwards;
- Trade loss relief against other income;
- Early trade loss relief;
- Terminal trade loss relief;
- Share loss relief;
- Interest payments.

But remove from the net income any savings income within *ITA 2007, s 18(3), (4)*, including (amongst other things):

- Interest;
- Some categories of purchased life annuity income;
- Accrued income profits; and
- Life assurance gains.

And remove dividend income (as per *ITA 2007, s 19*).

Then deduct from the balance those allowances, etc, given at *ITA 2007, s 23* 'Step 3' – personal allowance, blind person's allowance.

This is the individual's ATI (*ITTOIA 2005, s 274AA(6)*)

Second, calculate 'L', which is basically the default amount on which relief is to be given. This will ordinarily be just the amount of the individual's disallowed loan interest and related finance costs for the property business in question, but more precisely, L is the *lower of*:

- The relievable amount – being the sum of the individual's share (N%) of the disallowed costs (A) of dwelling-rated loans of the property business in question in the current year, and any as-yet unrelieved amounts brought forwards; and

- The taxable profits of the property business after adjusting for 'ordinary' property losses brought forwards under *ITA 2007, s 118*, or the individual's share of those adjusted profits, if a lesser amount, on which the individual is liable to IT (this section ignores estate amounts for simplicity; for further detail, applicable where the individual's income includes property income affected by the new finance costs restriction and that is derived from estates, see also **3.30** *et seq.* below).

3.17 Note that the second bullet point ensures that any unutilised tax reduction is forfeit after that property business has ceased, because the taxable profits of that property business will of course then be nil in later years (barring, perhaps, any adjustment for post-cessation income). While HMRC

Finance costs relief restrictions **3.19**

has historically been fairly relaxed about whether or not a property business has ceased and a new property business commenced, (see for example **Chapter 1**), the fact that potentially large amounts of tax relief may be forfeit, if a property business has in fact ceased, may not go unnoticed in future (*ITTOIA 2005, s274AA(2)(b)(i)*).

3.18 Where the individual's ATI is less than L, the amount on which relief is ultimately given 'AA' is restricted to ATI.

Where there is more than one default amount on which relief will be given L, (such as where there is more than one property business), then they are aggregated to S', and for each L, the amount on which relief is ultimately given is restricted in proportion:

$(L_n/S) \times ATI$

Having finally established the overall amount on which relief should be given, the amount of relief itself is:

AA × BR, the basic rate of income tax

3.19 Where the relievable amount exceeds the amount on which relief is ultimately given for that property business in the tax year, then that excess becomes the brought forward amount for the following tax year in respect of that property business (*ITTOIA 2005, s 274AA(4)*).

> **Example 3.2 – Tax reduction calculation**
>
> In 2021/22, Edith has the following income, etc:
>
> - Private pension of £6,500;
> - Residential property business profits for the year of £10,000, after loan interest paid of £8,000;
> - Residential property business losses brought forward of £15,000 – let us say that Edith's rental property was damaged by a previous tenant, requiring significant repair costs before it could be let out again;
> - Interest income of £10,000.
>
> After disallowing her loan interest but then claiming relief for her property losses, Edith's taxable rental income will be £10,000 + £8,000 – £15,000 = £3,000.
>
> The default amount by which her dwelling related loan cost tax reduction will be gauged will be the lower of:
>
> - The relievable amount – the loan interest disallowed of £8,000; and
> - The property business profits after deducting property losses brought forward, being £3,000.

3.20 *Finance costs relief restrictions*

(*ITTOIA 2005, s 274A(2)*)

However, Edith's tax reduction cannot exceed her ATI, which effectively carves out interest and dividend income from what would otherwise be taxable after reliefs and allowances, and in this example is:

£6,500 + (£10,000 + £8,000 − £15,000) − personal allowance of (say) £11,500 = £NIL.

Since Edith's net taxable income is only interest income, the tax reduction cannot apply, and must be carried forward (*ITTOIA 2005, s 274AA(4)*).

This will, however, usefully mean that in many cases the reduction will not be utilised inefficiently against income that will have no or a low rate of tax applied to it: the balance of Edith's personal allowance, starting rate for savings and new savings allowance would result in very little tax liability in 2021/22, to be covered by a tax reduction worth up to £8,000 @ 20% = £1,600 (but see **Example 3.3** below).

3.20 Landlords and their advisers will nevertheless need to be alert to some of the finer detail of the mechanism for calculating a taxpayer's liability, as set out in *ITA 2007 Pt 2 Ch 3*, notably to:

'…deduct the reliefs and allowances in the way which will result in the greatest reduction in the taxpayer's liability to Income Tax' (*ITA 2007, s 25(2)*)

Example 3.3 – Allocation of reliefs and allowances

Armon is self-employed and has a residential property business. His tax position in 2021/22 is as follows:

- Self-employed losses of £5,000;
- Residential property business profits of £10,500 after mortgage interest of £6,000;
- Dividend income of £10,000.

Note – assume the personal allowance remains at £11,500.

The default approach to allocating reliefs and allowances – ie, against earnings, etc, in preference to savings, in preference to dividends – may be compared to an alternative, as follows:

Finance costs relief restrictions **3.20**

	Approach #1	**Approach #2**
Rental income	10,500	10,500
Add back: mortgage interest	6,000	6,000
Less: rental losses b/fwd	–	–
Rental income net of property losses	16,500	16,500
Less: self-employed losses	(5,000)	–
Net rental income	11,500	16,500
Dividends	10,000	10,000
Less: Losses	–	(5,000)
Net dividend income	10,000	5,000

ITA 2007, s 23, Steps 1 and 2

Adjusted total income (ignores interest/dividend income):

Rental income	11,500	16,500
Less: Personal allowance (assumed)	(11,500)	(11,500)
Adjusted total income	–	5,000

Default amount L on which tax reduction is based:

Lower of:

Relievable amount	6,000	6,000
or		
Rental income net of property losses	16,500	16,500
Default amount:	6,000	6,000
But not more than adjusted total income	–	5,000
Actual amount on which relief given:	–	5,000

(ITTOIA 2005, s 274AA)

Of course, the taxable amount is the same in either scenario. But by deliberately setting losses against dividend income instead of against rental income, the amount of the dwelling related loan tax credit is different, and affects Armon's overall tax position as follows:

	Approach #1	**Approach #2**
Tax liability:		
Rental income	11,500	16,500
Dividend income	10,000	5,000
	21,500	21,500

3.21 *Finance costs relief restrictions*

	Approach #1	Approach #2
Less: Personal allowances (assumed)	(11,500)	(11,500)
Taxable income	10,000	10,000
Being:		
Rental income	–	5,000
Dividend income	10,000	5,000
	10,000	10,000
Tax thereon:		
(£10,000 – £5,000 'allowance') @ 7.5%	375	
£5,000 @ 20%		1,000
(£5,000 – £5,000 'allowance') @ 7.5%		–
Tax reduction for dwelling-related loan		
(£NIL / £5,000) @ 20%	–	(1,000)
Net Income Tax payable	375	–

In the default Approach #1, Armon is worse off because tax is due now, but his tax reduction would have been carried forwards to be used in later years. In Approach #2, Armon's liability is reduced to nil, although he has sacrificed a tax reduction worth up to £1,000 (£5,000 @ 20%) in order to reduce his tax bill by £375. Whether or not HMRC is alive to this quite fine point remains to be seen.

3.21 Finally, note that the approach required to calculate ATI – which effectively requires the taxpayer to net personal allowances, etc, against non-interest, non-dividend income, does not determine how the personal allowance should be allocated when calculating the taxpayer's actual liability. This is again determined in accordance with *ITA 2007, s 25(2)* – ie, the way which results in the greatest reduction in tax liability.

TRUSTS AND ESTATES

3.22 That, based on correspondence at the time of the July 2015 Budget, HMRC appeared not to have realised that applying the regime to all property businesses subject to IT (bar companies and furnished holiday lettings) meant that trusts and estates were also caught did not, alas, mean they were ultimately excluded. The legislation as originally drafted allowed the corresponding tax reduction only for individuals, effectively ignoring discretionary-type trusts. This was eventually addressed in *F(No.2)A 2015* but was re-written again in *FA 2016*.

3.23 Where the beneficiary has an immediate interest in the trust property business income, then the guidance below in relation to interest in possession trusts should be followed; where the trustees have discretion (or the power to accumulate) in relation to trust property business income, then the guidance in relation to discretionary trusts is applicable.

Interest in possession trusts

3.24 **Note:** guidance on the mechanism for interest in possession (IIP) Trusts has not been forthcoming from HMRC at the time of writing; the following must therefore be considered in light of HMRC's interpretation of the legislation, as and when it is eventually published.

3.25

> **Focus**
>
> The disallowance of relief for dwelling-related finance costs is set at the level of the business itself, so the trust (or more precisely its trustees) will suffer the additional IT arising as costs are denied (*ITTOIA 2005, s 272A*).

In circumstances where an individual has a right directly in the rental income from a property business undertaken by a trust of which he or she is a beneficiary, then that life tenant may benefit from the tax reduction for individuals, as already set out above, and which would appear adequately to cater for situations where the beneficiary has an interest in only a fraction of the rental income (*ITTOIA 2005, ss 274A, 274AA*).

> **Example 3.4 – Interest in possession trust**
>
> The Duralon trust has a residential property business, the income in which Junior Duralon has a 100% interest. The business has a net income of £10,000, after £5,000 of mortgage interest (assume for convenience that there are no other costs of any significance).
>
> By 2020/21, when the new regime is fully installed, the Duralon trustees will have the following tax position in relation to the residential property business income:
>
> (£10,000 add-back £5,000 interest) = £15,000 taxable profits at 20% = £3,000.
>
> Simply put, in relation to trust income in which a beneficiary has an immediate interest, the income effectively belongs to the beneficiary immediately that it arises – an interest in possession. The trustees have no powers of accumulation or discretion, so the income is not subject to the rate(s) applicable to trusts; basic rate tax is applied instead, at whatever level of income arises.

3.26 *Finance costs relief restrictions*

Having had to pay £3,000 tax on net profits of £10,000, the trustees will have £7,000 left physically to pay over to Junior Duralon.

Junion Duralon is deemed also to have received £15,000 of tax-adjusted income, despite having physically received only £7,000 from the Trust.

Assuming Junior Duralon is a basic rate taxpayer, he will personally be liable as follows:

£15,000 × 20% = £3,000.

In other words, his liability will be covered by the payment already made by the trustees (if he were a 40% higher rate taxpayer, his liability of £6,000 would be only partly met as to 20% by the trustees).

However, Junior Duralon is *also* entitled to the tax reduction, because he has a 100% interest in a property business that has had its dwelling related loan costs disallowed.

He is therefore entitled to a tax reduction of:

£5,000 @ 20% = £1,000. Assuming he has paid sufficient tax on his other income, he will get the £1,000 as a tax refund.

The result is that Junior Duralon's net income will be:

£7,000 from the Trust and £1,000 from HMRC = £8,000.

This is in order, because if Junior Duralon were to own the rental property business outright, then his 2020/21 net position would be:

(£10,000 add-back £5,000 of residential mortgage interest = £15,000) × 20% = £3,000.

But tax reduction of £5,000 × 20% = £1,000 gives:

Net tax cost of £3,000 − 1,000 = £2,000.

Net personal income to Junior = £10,000 − £2,000 Tax = £8,000 (the same as *via* the trust, as above).

Problems with the IIP mechanism

3.26 This arrangement has practical implications for the trustees. Even though an IIP trust pays tax at only the basic rate, the trust may have to finance a tax cost in excess of the net income actually received, and will not be able to offset the tax rises as the new regime progresses, because it is the beneficiary or beneficiaries who can claim the tax reduction.

Finance costs relief restrictions **3.26**

> **Focus**
>
> This may mean that the trustees are obliged to resort to other income, or even to capital, to meet the trust's ongoing IT liabilities. If there are other beneficiaries to the trust, this might be considered quite inequitable, since the other beneficiaries will be funding what is effectively the trust's payment on account of IT due on the life tenant's rental income.

Example 3.5 – Insufficient trust income

Trenton trust holds, amongst other things, a residential property business that yields £2,000 a year after £18,000 of mortgage interest. Widow Trenton has a 100% interest in that part of the trust's assets, for life. Assuming other costs are negligible, by 2020/21, the trustees' IT liability will be as follows:

(£2,000 add-back £18,000 interest) = £20,000 × 20% = £4,000.

But the trustees hold only £2,000 net rental income in funds, so the remaining £2,000 tax will have to be taken from trust assets belonging to other beneficiaries. Widow Trenton will physically receive nothing from the trustees.

Assuming Widow Trenton is a basic rate taxpayer already, she will be deemed to have received £20,000 in net rental income, just like the trustees, with a tax credit of £4,000, being the tax already paid by the trustees. This should be sufficient to meet her personal liability on that income.

But she will also benefit from the dwelling-related loan tax reduction allocated to her directly, of:

£18,000 disallowed interest at 20% = £3,600.

This will be repaid to her (assuming she has already paid sufficient tax on other sums).

In a life tenancy/interest in possession trust scenario, the life tenant should generally end up in the same position as if he or she had received the income directly – because the income 'belongs' to her. The trustees have to pay tax on that income, but it is effectively a payment on account of the life tenant's eventual liability. If Widow Trenton had owned the residential property business personally, then as a basic rate taxpayer, she would have had to pay:

(£2,000 add-back £18,000 interest) = £20,000 × 20% = £4,000.

But less the tax reduction of £18,000 × 20% = £3,600.

Leaves £400 net tax liability.

3.27 *Finance costs relief restrictions*

This makes sense, given that her 'real' net income would be £2,000 if she owned the property business herself, and she is a basic rate taxpayer. If she owned the property business herself, her net-of-tax income would be:

£2,000 – £400 tax = £1,600.

But Widow Trenton received £3,600, courtesy of a tax refund. The additional £2,000 is the extra 'contribution' provided, quite unfairly, by the other beneficiaries of the Trenton Trust.

Numerous representations have been made to HMRC in this regard. It remains to be seen whether or not this problem will be addressed – but the legislation may need to be changed, first.

Discretionary trusts

3.27 Where the trustees have discretion as to the income to distribute (or the power to accumulate income), the trustees are taxable on that income as to the rate(s) applicable to trusts. The beneficiaries have no direct interest in the income to the trust and, notably, the income that they receive loses its original 'identity' – it is simply 'trust income', regardless of whether or not it arose by virtue of residential property income in the hands of the trustees.

3.28

> **Focus**
>
> This in turn means that the individual cannot avail himself of the normal tax reduction rules available, such as would apply in relation to IIP Trusts as outlined above; there will be no trust *property business* income on the beneficiary's personal tax return against which a tax reduction might be claimed.
>
> HMRC has therefore had to create a separate tax reduction mechanism for discretionary trusts.

Broadly, the effect is that trustees will generally be exposed to a marginal rate of 25% on any dwelling related loan costs, being the standard rate applicable to trusts of 45%, but with a tax reduction of no more than 20%, as adjusted for property losses, etc.

3.29 First, the trust, will pay IT on the net property income, as usual. Likewise, given that the restriction of dwelling-related finance costs is at the property business level, it will be the trustees who will bear the additional tax due if and when any mortgage interest, etc, is disallowed. (*ITTOIA 2005, s 272A*).

Finance costs relief restrictions **3.31**

Second, the legislation that gives effect to the tax reduction for discretionary trustees is quite similar to that for individuals but is a little less complex, given that there are no personal allowances, etc, or adjusted total incomes. The amount on which relief is ultimately given (at the basic rate of 20%) in respect of a particular property business is restricted by reference to the *lower* of:

- The relievable amount (the current year amount – the trustees' N% share of property business profits × the disallowed amount A, as outlined for individuals above – combined with any brought forward amounts); and
- The profits of the property business for tax purposes after any adjustment for conventional property losses brought forwards (or the trustees' share therein, if less), on which the trustees are liable to IT and that comprise accumulated or discretionary income for the trustees.

Where the relievable amount does not end up being fully relieved, then the excess relievable amount may be carried forwards to augment the following year's relievable amount, as a brought forward amount (*ITTOIA 2005, s 274C*).

Estates

3.30

> **Focus**
>
> The legislation has been updated to reflect the complexities of estate Income:
>
> - The income may roll up and be distributed to beneficiaries for several years' worth at once;
> - The income paid to beneficiaries may be composed of different sources, which may or may not include a proportion derived from residential lettings, which may in turn have dwelling related finance costs that have been disallowed.

It may perhaps have been more straightforward to give the personal representatives the benefit of the tax reduction, as is the case for discretionary trustees above, but while the legislation disallows the dwelling-related loan costs at the business level (ie, in the estate) as usual – (see **3.3** above) – it permits a tax reduction in the hands of the beneficiary on receipt of a relevant distribution by the personal representatives (*ITTOIA 2005, s 272A, 274A, 274AA*).

Tax reduction – Estate income and the relievable amount

3.31 The aspects peculiar to estates orient around the tax reduction mechanism for individuals.

3.32 *Finance costs relief restrictions*

As noted at **3.12** above, an individual's relievable amount can include a 'current year estate amount' which is relievable on its own, or in aggregate with other amounts, albeit in respect of that same property business (*ITTOIA 2005, s 274A(2)*).

A current year estate amount for a particular tax year basically arises in relation to the individual beneficiary's receipt of relevant income from a given estate in that tax year, which may be traced to a property business that has suffered the disallowance of a dwelling related loan, when calculating the property business profits for a given tax year – the 'profits year' (*ITTOIA 2005, s 274A(5), (7)*).

3.32 That profits year may be the current year, or it could be any year beforehand (but since the introduction of this regime, clearly, so as to result in a relevant disallowance of residential property business profits). It is the individual's eventual receipt of such income which triggers his or her entitlement to a tax reduction in the year of receipt (or, more precisely, the individual's being deemed liable in a particular tax year for estate income *treated* as arising to that individual in that tax year, by reason of *ITTOIA 2005, Pt 5 Ch 6* – 'Beneficiaries' Income from Estates in Administration').

So if, for instance, the personal representatives distribute those rental profits that arose in 2019/20 a year later in 2020/21, the 'profits year' will have been 2019/20 but the beneficiary or beneficiaries will not be able to claim a tax reduction until 2020/21.

3.33 In any particular tax year, a beneficiary may receive one or more distributions from the estate that relate to several years' income from the residential property business in that estate, so it follows that the beneficiary's income in that tax year may relate to several 'profit years' by reference to the estate's property business. For that individual beneficiary, there will be a 'current year estate amount' in respect of *each* of those 'profit years'.

3.34 The formula in the legislation is that for each of those profit years that is comprised in the 'basic amount' of the individual beneficiary's estate income for a particular tax year, the individual has a current year estate amount of:

E% of the personal representatives' N% interest in the property business × A (the amount disallowed in the profit year by reason of the new finance costs restriction), where:

E% is the beneficiary's corresponding proportion reflected in his or her basic amount of estate income; 'basic amount' and 'estate income' as per *ITTOIA 2005, ss 656(4)* and *649* respectively.

N% is the personal representatives' share in the property business.

Estates and the calculation of the tax reduction

3.35 As above, the calculation is by reference to each property business, as follows:

The default amount "L" by which the individual's tax liability will be reduced at the basic rate of 20% is the lower of:

- The relievable amount – the sum of the current year amount, any brought forward amount and any current year estate amounts (broadly, disallowed dwelling related loan costs); and

- The total of:
  - The taxable profits of the property business after adjusting for 'ordinary' property losses brought forwards under *ITA 2007, s 118*, or the individual's share of those adjusted profits, if a lesser amount, on which the individual is liable to IT otherwise than under *ITTOIA 2005, Pt 5, Ch 6* – estate income; *and*
  - So much (if any) of the relievable amount as consists of current-year estate amounts, as now detailed (*ITTOIA 2005, s 274AA(2)*).

3.36 However, the relievable amount is still subject to the rule that the relievable amount cannot exceed the individual's ATI (see **3.16** above) so it seems plausible that any excess relievable amount – even of current year estate income – may roll forward to become a brought forward amount for the following year's calculation, albeit in relation only to that particular property business.

It will be interesting to see if HMRC accepts that such brought forward amounts may be used if and when a beneficiary of an estate inherits a property business and carries it on in his or her own name (solely or in joint with others). The legislation could easily be read to allow that there may be both estate amounts and 'ordinary' relievable amounts in a given tax year, (such as with the definition of the tax reduction itself), so transition seems possible (*ITTOIA 2005, ss 274A, 274AA*).

OTHER ISSUES

Furnished holiday lettings (and hotels)

3.37 Borrowings referable (on a just and reasonable apportionment, where appropriate) to furnished holiday accommodation (see **Chapter 6**) are specifically *excluded* from the definition of a dwelling-related loan (*ITTOIA 2005, s 272B(4)*). An hotel or similar establishment would not normally be considered a 'dwelling-house', so relevant finance costs would seem not to be caught by the definition of a dwelling-related loan in the legislation (*ITTOIA 2005, s 272B(2)*). See also **3.38** below.

3.38 *Finance costs relief restrictions*

Are houses in multiple occupation (HMOs) a 'dwelling house'?

3.38

> **Focus**
>
> HMOs are a good example of the potential uncertainty surrounding what does or does not constitute a 'dwelling house'. The legislation does not define a 'dwelling house' for the purpose of the new regime. It should therefore be inferred to take its ordinary definition. In this regard, HMRC has referred to the Capital Allowances manual CA11520.

That guidance suggests that a dwelling house is 'a building, or a part of a building; its distinctive characteristic is its ability to afford to those who use it the facilities required for day-to-day private domestic existence'.

The guidance suggests that university halls of residence may not qualify, but then says 'on the other hand, cluster flats or houses in multiple occupation, that provide the facilities necessary for day-to-day private domestic existence (such as bedrooms with en-suite facilities and a shared or communal kitchen/diner and sitting room) are dwelling-houses'.

3.39 Advisers familiar with HMOs and capital allowances will be well aware of the guidance issued in October 2010 HM Revenue & Customs Brief 45/10, which the guidance at CA11520 clearly follows; the guidance at the time stated:

> 'HMRC have concluded that the better view is that each flat in multiple occupation comprises a dwelling-house, given that the individual study bedrooms alone would not afford the occupants "the facilities required for day-to-day private domestic existence". In other words, the communal kitchen and lounge are also part of the dwelling-house. The common parts of the building block (such as the common entrance lobby, stairs or lifts) would not, however, comprise a "dwelling-house".'

It might therefore be argued that the relevant loan costs for an entire building or similar should be apportioned between 'dwelling-related loan' amounts and 'non-dwelling related loan' amounts, although perhaps only where the 'costs of the common parts of the building block' that may be considered not to comprise pare of a dwelling-house, are sufficient to make the exercise worthwhile.

3.40 Note also that for the purposes of SDLT 'multiple dwellings relief', in HMRC's SDLT manual at SDLTM29957:

> '[In] the case of a block of flats available only to students, each of which consists of individual study bedrooms with communal kitchen and bathroom facilities, each flat within the block will be treated as used, or suitable for use, as a single dwelling.'

Finance costs relief restrictions **3.42**

Beneficial loans and property investment businesses

3.41 Most readers will be aware that the benefit-in-kind rules for taxable 'cheap' (employment-related) loans (at *ITEPA 2003, Pt 3, Ch 7*) include an exception from charge where the loan would qualify for tax relief:

> 'A loan is not a taxable cheap loan in relation to a particular tax year if, assuming interest is paid on the loan for that year (whether or not it is in fact paid), the whole of that interest-...
>
> ...
>
> (d) is deductible in computing the amount of the profits to be charged to tax in respect of a UK property business...' (*ITEPA 2003, s 178*).

The implication is that, now that a deduction will be denied where (or to the extent that) the loan is deemed to constitute a dwelling-related loan, such loans will not be excluded from a benefit-in-kind tax charge for taxable cheap loans. The Employment Income manual explains how HMRC will apply the benefit in kind regime where a loan is only partly deductible, at EIM26135. A corresponding amount of interest relief is potentially deductible from the property business, to the extent that the individual is taxable on a cheap loan for benefit in kind purposes. Presumably, this potential deduction will now be subject to the new regime for disallowance, insofar as it relates to a property business whose purpose includes the exploitation of dwellings, etc.

While the employee may have an IT charge, it is the responsibility of the employer to return such details to HMRC, and there will be Class 1A NICs to pay at 12.8% on the benefit as well.

Loans to invest in a partnership with a property business

3.42 The costs of personal loans to acquire an interest in a partnership which in turn operates a property business that is carried on for the purpose of generating income from a dwelling-house, etc, are specifically included in the new regime for restrictions, again on a 'just and reasonable' basis. (*ITA 2007, s 399A*).

The legislation basically mirrors that of the main regime, although the mechanism for the tax reduction is much more straightforward, as the reduction for personal loan interest ignores the effects of losses, allowances, etc, and there is no provision to carry any unutilised reduction forwards (since this part of the IT legislation is descended from the regime for personal charges against income).

The amount of the tax relief is simply the basic rate of 20% × the 'relievable amount' – effectively the amount that would otherwise have been available for relief but for the new restriction (*ITA 2007, s 399B*). See also **1.14–1.15**.

3.43 Finance costs relief restrictions

FINANCE COSTS – STEPS LANDLORDS CAN TAKE TO MITIGATE THE EFFECTS
3.43

> **Focus**
>
> Having identified the nature and extent of the problem buy-to-let landlords face with the new interest relief restriction, we shall now look at some measures they might take to mitigate their increased costs. Some may be effective during the introduction phase of the new regime; others offer more lasting benefits.

The suggested measures will not be appropriate for all portfolios, nor in all circumstances.

Incorporation

3.44 It would probably be fair to say that most buy-to-let landlords who are aware of the new interest restriction regime will be aware of incorporation as a possible solution. But it is not a panacea. It would be broadly accurate to point out that, from a tax perspective at least, most property investment businesses would *not* be more tax-efficient if run through a company, were it not for the new interest disallowance rules. Incorporation brings its own costs – notably the new, more expensive dividend regime that applies to IT on dividends paid on or after 6 April 2016 (*FA 2016, s 5*) – and its own regime and administration overheads.

The following section will evaluate the potential benefit of incorporation from an ongoing tax efficiency perspective. **Chapter 13** examines the hurdles and the process of incorporation as an exercise, in more detail. Of course, new property investment ventures may benefit from incorporation from the outset, without the hurdles faced by long-established portfolio owners.

> **Example 3.6 – Individual versus company**
>
> Rose is a 'modest' property investor who is already a 40% taxpayer thanks to other earned income sources, with net rent of £15,000 after mortgage interest of £4,000. Assuming she were to take all of the residual funds from the corporate alternative in the form of dividends (given that she has no tax-free personal allowance left), the outcome would be:

Finance costs relief restrictions **3.44**

Tax Year	2016/17 £	2017/18 £	2018/19 £	2019/20 £	2020/21 £
Earnings (say)	60,000	60,000	60,000	60,000	60,000
Net rent after mortgage	15,000	15,000	15,000	15,000	15,000
'Real' income	75,000	75,000	75,000	75,000	75,000
Add: rental finance	–	1,000	2,000	3,000	4,000
Total	75,000	76,000	77,000	78,000	79,000
Tax liability					
Initial (after int. add-back)	19,200	19,600	20,000	20,400	20,800
Rental 20% tax credit	–	(200)	(400)	(600)	(800)
Net tax	19,200	19,400	19,600	19,800	20,000
Net income – personal ownership	55,800	55,600	55,400	55,200	55,000
(ignoring NICs)					
Or					
Corporate ownership					
Net rent (no add-back of interest)	15,000	15,000	15,000	15,000	15,000
Corporation tax	3,000	3,000	3,000	3,000	3,000
Residue – paid out as dividends	12,000	12,000	12,000	12,000	12,000
Earnings (as above)	60,000	60,000	60,000	60,000	60,000
'Real' income	72,000	72,000	72,000	72,000	72,000
Personal tax (earnings)	13,200	13,200	13,200	13,200	13,200
Dividends – net of £5,000 'allowance'	2,275	2,275	2,275	2,275	2,275
Total personal tax	15,475	15,475	15,475	15,475	15,475
Net income – corporate ownership	56,525	56,525	56,525	56,525	56,525
Net saving through incorporation	725	925	1,125	1,325	1,525

This model assumes that 2016/17 rates and allowances apply throughout. Corporation tax rates are of course set to fall to 17% by 2020/21, which would in turn increase the residue left for dividends to be paid out to Rose, increasing the net saving through incorporation. However, there are also likely to be higher 'running costs' in the corporate route.

The saving through incorporation is relatively modest, given that the cost of the new regime is only small in this example; it is perhaps unlikely, looking solely at these numbers, that a buy-to-let investor would want to go through the exercise of incorporating this business, given the potential tax costs, fees and effort involved.

3.44 *Finance costs relief restrictions*

Example 3.7 – 'Career' property business

If we take the example of a typical 'career' landlord with more extensive property interests and with higher levels of debt gearing, the potential ongoing savings of the corporate route become more apparent.

Rupinder has three young children (for whom she claims child benefit) and a residential property portfolio generating £36,000 of net rental income, but after £36,000 of mortgage interest. Assuming that the facts, personal tax rates and allowances stay the same from 2016/17 onwards (but this time observing the downward trend in CT to 17% by 2020/21 as mentioned above) and that she takes a modest salary of £8,000 to utilise her personal allowance/primary earnings threshold, Rupinder's results would be:

Tax Year	2016/17	2017/18	2018/19	2019/20	2020/21
	£	£	£	£	£
Net rent after mortgage	36,000	36,000	36,000	36,000	36,000
Add: rental finance	–	9,000	18,000	27,000	36,000
Total	36,000	45,000	54,000	63,000	72,000
Tax liability					
Initial (after int. add-back)	5,000	7,200	10,800	14,400	18,000
Child benefit clawback			1,000	2,500	2,500
Rental 20% tax credit	–	(1,800)	(3,600)	(5,400)	(7,200)
Net tax	5,000	5,400	8,200	11,500	13,300
Net income – personal ownership	31,000	30,600	27,800	24,500	22,700
Or					
Corporate ownership					
Net Rent (no add-back of interest)	36,000	36,000	36,000	36,000	36,000
Deduct salary	(8,000)	(8,000)	(8,000)	(8,000)	(8,000)
	28,000	28,000	28,000	28,000	28,000
Corporation tax (20/19/17%)	5,600	5,320	5,320	5,320	4,760
Residue – paid out as dividends	22,400	22,680	22,680	22,680	23,240
Earnings (as above)	8,000	8,000	8,000	8,000	8,000
'Real' income	30,400	30,680	30,680	30,680	31,240
Personal tax	1,080	1,101	1,101	1,101	1,143
Net income – corporate ownership	29,320	29,579	29,579	29,579	30,097
Net (cost)/saving via incorporation	(1,680)	(1,021)	1,779	5,079	7,397

Finance costs relief restrictions **3.45**

While it is clear that there is potentially significant ongoing tax efficiency for Rupinder in incorporating her residential property business:

- The results for 2016/17 and 2017/18 show that, in the absence of a significant interest-related tax adjustment, there is little benefit in incorporating a property business – in fact, there is a cost in doing so.

- The inherent 'double tax charge' of paying CT, then IT on the residue in order to withdraw the funds for personal use, makes incorporation expensive (in the absence of the NIC saving normally associated with trading enterprises).

- Incorporation might not be cost-effective in the first few years of the introduction of the new regime – the saving in 2018/19 may not be worthwhile.

- But, ultimately, the ongoing additional costs of a business with significant dwelling related loan exposure are so substantial that incorporation offers some comparatively substantial savings.

- *Very broadly*, greater efficiencies will be achieved with higher incomes and higher interest costs. For example, a doubling of the above mortgage interest costs results in a saving by 2020/21 of more than double Rupinder's outcome.

- The model assumes that Rupinder needs to withdraw all of the company's funds to meet her lifestyle demands – which is reasonable, given that her net funds are not actually going to increase under incorporation; the worst of the double tax charge may be avoided if some of the funds can be kept within the company.

- While not the focus of the examples, companies remain eligible for indexation allowance on their capital gains, thereby avoiding 'inflationary gains' (*TCGA 1992, s 52A et seq.*).

Increasing rental income

3.45 An obvious alternative solution to help to offset rising costs, which the Government seems nevertheless to think is highly unlikely, is to increase the rent charged to tenants.

For someone who is subject to 40% tax on their disallowed interest, any income increase will have also to be subject to 40% tax. In the simple example of Jennifer (see **Example 3.1** above, her net income fell by £200 a year. This would need to be grossed up by £200 × (100/(100−40)) = £333 per annum. Her gross rental income was £10,000 annually, (£6,000 a year net profit after mortgage interest of £4,000), meaning that a rent rise of roughly 3% per annum

3.46 *Finance costs relief restrictions*

from 2016/17 should prove more than sufficient, effectively compounding over the four-year introduction period.

In Rupinder's case (see **Example 3.7** above), the increase in tax is not consistent, as the introduction of the high income child benefit clawback (*ITEPA 2003, s 681B–H*) part-way through the restriction phase significantly increases the effective tax cost.

Over the four years 2017/18 through to 2020/21, Rupinder's net income falls by £8,300 (£31,000 – £22,700). A simple grossing up exercise will not suffice because of the additional clawback of child benefit, which results in much higher marginal tax cost applying in the interval.

All other things remaining equal, Rupinder's 2020/21 gross rental income would have to increase to £86,000 (including the £36,000 mortgage interest) in order to derive a net income of £31,099 if she were to remain unincorporated – slightly more than her original net income of £31,000 in 2016/17. This represents an increase of:

(£86,000 – £72,000)/£72,000 = c19.5% over the 4 years.

This is *broadly* equivalent to an increase of around 4.5% per annum for the four years from 2016/17.

(Note: in each scenario this is an increase on the *gross* rental income, not on the net rental profit).

Introducing family members

3.46

> **Focus**
>
> This would arguably be sound general tax advice, rather than a solution specifically for the restriction of dwelling related loan costs. With regard to the interest restriction, the aim is to minimise exposure to rates in excess of the basic rate band of 20%, at or below which the new tax reduction should be sufficient to make the restriction cost-neutral.

There are tax and non-tax implications to transferring income-producing assets between family members (and bearing in mind that it does not *necessarily* have to be an interest in the property business that is transferred so as to equalise taxable incomes; the transfer of other income-producing assets might yield a similar result) although transfers between spouses and civil partners who are living together can usually benefit from the 'CGT-neutral' transfer rules at *TCGA 1992, s 58*. Having said that, one of the inconveniences of investment property held between spouses, etc, is that IT law presumes a 50:50 split of income unless the underlying interests are different and are so notified to HMRC (*ITA 2007, ss 836, 837*).

Finance costs relief restrictions **3.48**

With regard to non-spousal joint ownership, it is potentially useful that HMRC admits a flexibility of arrangement at Property Income manual PIM1030:

> 'Where there is no partnership, the share of any profit or loss arising from jointly owned property will normally be the same as the share owned in the property being let. But joint owners can agree a different division of profits and losses and so occasionally the share of the profits or losses will be different from the share in the property. The share for tax purposes must be the same as the share actually agreed.'

3.47 This must, however, be seen in the light of potentially countervailing arguments in relation to what may broadly be termed the 'settlements' (anti-avoidance) legislation at *ITTOIA 2005, Pt 5 Ch 5 (s 619 et seq.)* and as per HMRC's Trusts & Estates manual at TSEM4000 onwards. These provisions are designed to ensure that the 'settlor' cannot transfer income away from himself, but continue to benefit from it. Where that is the case, the income is essentially deemed to remain in the hands of the settlor.

This is a complex area, but it is important to note that the main thrust of HMRC's attention is in relation to gifts, etc, to the 'settlor's' spouse and minor children and, while HMRC is confident that the anti-avoidance provisions may apply more widely than that, essentially the settlor (or his spouse or minor children) still has to be able to benefit from the diversion of income. See also **Chapter 1**.

Timing of expenditure

3.48 As a general rule, advisers work on the basis that taking tax relief sooner rather than later is a main aim of tax planning. However, it is sometimes appropriate to consider deferring expenditure so as to ensure that the tax reduction is comparatively greater, when claimed. This is commonly encountered with loss relief planning, and restricting claims to capital allowances.

Taking the example of Rupinder above (see **Example 3.7**), if she were contemplating a project to replace the bedrooms and bathrooms in her property portfolio (and setting aside any concerns as to whether or not that was allowable expenditure) to the tune of £15,000, that expenditure would save her:

2016/17	£3,000 – no more than £15,000 @ 20% basic rate = £3,000 – the cost itself
2017/18	£3,400 – as Rupinder's income was partly into the higher rate band
2018/19	£6,200 – as Rupinder's income was originally £11,000 into the higher rate band, with a £1,000 clawback of child benefit (£15,000 @ 20% + £11,000 @ (40–20)% + £1,000)
2019/20	£8,500 – ie £15,000 @ 20% + £15,000 @ (40–20)% + £2,500 child benefit recovered
2020/21	£6,751 – as only 30% of the child benefit clawback is recovered

3.49 *Finance costs relief restrictions*

Rupinder may prefer to get her tax relief as soon as possible, in which case she will recover £3,000 in tax relief. If, however, she (and perhaps her tenants) can wait until 2019/20, the saving will almost treble.

Paying off capital

3.49 Clearly, on the basis that paying off capital should reduce finance costs going forward, the negative consequences of finance costs should be ameliorated if the underlying loan capital is reduced.

Accelerating finance costs

3.50 Reducing the term of some or all of the mortgages will have the effect of both paying capital off more quickly and increasing the proportion of the remaining finance costs that apply over the shortened repayment period – which may in turn increase the proportion that escapes the full 100% disallowance, in 2017/18 to 2019/20.

Pension/gift aid contributions

3.51 Either measure will serve to extend both the basic rate limit and the higher rate limit – currently (2016/17) £32,000 and £150,000 respectively (*ITA 2007, s 10*). So where, for example, the dwelling-related loan cost disallowance takes taxable income above the basic rate limit, a qualifying contribution will reduce the exposure to higher rate tax, in favour of basic rate tax, saving the marginal rate of (40–20)% = 20%. If taxable income is sufficient, a similar saving can additionally be made at the higher rate limit, albeit at only (45–40)% = 5% (the marginal savings may of course be different if there is dividend income 'on top of' the rental income being considered).

> **Focus**
>
> Since both also feature in the definition of 'adjusted net income' (*ITA 2007, s 58*) they will likewise help to defer the onset of the forfeiture of child benefit, (assuming the landlord/landlady is the higher earner in a couple) and the tax-free personal allowance, at £50,000 and £100,000 adjusted net income, respectively.

3.52 Advice from a suitably qualified and experienced professional adviser is always recommended when contemplating whether or not to make pension contributions. There is no tax relief on pension contributions made by a taxpayer over the age of 75 (*FA 2004, s 188(3)(a)*).

Landlords without 'relevant earnings' (*FA 1994, s 189(2)*) – broadly employment, trading or furnished holiday letting income (see **Chapter 6**) – will have to limit their pension contributions to £2,880 net cash, or £3,600 deemed grossed-up of basic rate tax (*FA 2004, s 190(4)*) and the annual allowance (as accumulated, where relevant) will also feature when considering larger pension contributions

Finance costs relief restrictions **3.52**

(see also the new limits on pension annual allowance where adjusted income – not just relevant earnings – exceeds £150,000 (*FA 2004, s 228ZA* as inserted by *F(No.2)A 2015*).

As regard either contribution, the merits of marginal tax relief against the funds committed will have to be considered. If the landlord is of (or approaching) pensionable age, then the committed funds may be retrieved relatively quickly. But drawing down pension funds may have wider implications so, again, appropriate advice is strongly recommended.

Just as with the timing of expenditure above, maximum benefit can be derived where crossing tax bands or thresholds.

Example 3.8 – Pension contributions

Looking again at Rupinder in **Example 3.7**, she has no relevant earnings, so her maximum tax-relievable pension contribution is £2,880 in cash, equivalent to £3,600 after grossing up for basic rate tax deemed to have been deducted already from her contribution.

Assuming she makes the maximum payment each year, the savings are as follows:

2016/17 £Nil – she has no higher rate tax exposure, so there is no marginal saving.

2017/18 £400 – she has exceeded the basic rate limit by (£34,000 income – £32,000 Limit) = £2,000, so her saving is £2,000 × (40–20)% = £400

2018/19 £1,620 – the contribution saves tax at the marginal rate £3,600 × (40–20)% = £720 but the full £3,600 also reduces Rupinder's 'adjusted net income' within the band in which child benefit is clawed back (between £50,000 and £60,000), so:

£3,600 × 0.01% of Rupinder's child benefit of £2,500 = £900

£720 + £900 = £1,620

2019/20 £870

£3,600 × (40–20)% = £720

As regards child benefit, the contribution reduces her 'adjusted net income' as before but it now falls to £59,400, or only £600 below the upper limit set by *ITEPA 2003, s 681B–H*.

£600 × .01% of Rupinder's child benefit of £2,500 = £150

£720 + £150 = £870

2020/21 £720, being the standard marginal rate saving of £3,600 × (40–20)%

3.53 Finance costs relief restrictions

Rationalising the business

3.53 It may be appropriate in some cases to consider selling a part of the property portfolio, and to use the proceeds to pay down problematic dwelling-related loans. Many landlords and landladies will, however, face significant CGT costs: this may in turn reduce the amount of finance they are able to pay off, and the net benefit of reducing the dwelling-related loan tax restriction may be offset by a fall in net income after the portfolio has been 'downsized'.

It may be that certain properties are being retained that are not cost-effective – where an individual property is running at an income loss. This could be because the property's capital value is appreciating well so that it is worthwhile as a long-term investment. Or it could be because the property has already appreciated well, is standing at a significant capital gain but is highly geared so it is not economic to sell, settle the CGT and the mortgage.

In general terms, it would seem to make sense to target properties with the most punitive mortgage interest costs, but that have the least CGT exposure. It may be that older, more CGT-exposed properties do in fact have relatively generous interest rates, depending on when they were (re)mortgaged; more recent acquisitions may have more expensive mortgages but less CGT exposure. But each portfolio will need to be considered according to both tax and broader financial aspects, and the landlord's particular circumstances.

Diversifying the business

3.54 Finance costs are problematic only to the extent that they are attributable to dwelling-related loans, and although that includes developing or converting dwellings for the purposes of letting them out, (see **3.8**), it does not relate to borrowing for the purposes of a trading activity that is distinct from a property business, or to the extent that the property business is not carried on for (broadly) the letting of dwellings (*ITTOIA 2005, s 272B*).

The difficulty in interpreting the legislation in order to determine how to apportion a relevant loan – or, indeed, whether apportionment is necessary, has been covered in some detail (see **3.6** and **2.17**) and it seems likely that this will become a contentious area, while a corporate envelope as an alternative is either unattainable or undesirable for other reasons.

Nevertheless, the following activities may be distinguished:

- Property development (of any kind) for resale, which is excluded from a property business as it is a trading activity; this may include the development of former investment property as a 'supervening trade' (see **3.56** below);

Finance costs relief restrictions **3.56**

- Likewise a hotelier trading activity;
- Furnished holiday lettings within *ITTOIA 2005, Pt 3 Ch 6* – specifically excluded from the scope of 'dwelling related loans' by virtue of *ITTOIA 2005, s 272B(4)* (see **Chapter 6**);
- Commercial property investment, even though it may comprise part of the same property business as would the residential/dwelling-related part;
- Property estate management;
- Property maintenance.

Property estate management and property maintenance activities can occur naturally in the course of a normal property investment business, to a greater or lesser extent depending on the nature of the portfolio. It is not uncommon, however, for larger portfolios to develop a discrete trading activity that may be undertaken in a separate entity such as a limited company, or a general or limited liability partnership. HMRC is aware of this, and one might expect to see evidence of commercial arrangements including:

- Services provided on similar terms to unconnected third parties;
- Contracts or similar commercially-based arrangements between connected businesses.

Furthermore, if a buy-to-let investor hopes to attain CGT incorporation relief under *TCGA 1992, s 162*, then they will have to demonstrate that a substantive business is being conducted, potentially over and above that which might be expected to be incurred by an ordinary landlord – see **Chapter 13**. It follows that, rather than corralling active business management etc, into a separate function or entity, those buy-to-let investors should first be concentrating on ensuring that their properties are demonstrably being actively managed as an eligible business.

3.55 While the letting of residential property generally falls comfortably within the scope of exempt supplies of land in *VATA 1994, Sch 9, Group 1*, separate activities of property estate management and/or property maintenance would not; this applies also to hotels and furnished holiday lettings, and to the trade of property development (the development of new dwellings is zero-rated and registration *may* be excused). The letting of commercial property may be exempt or it may be taxable for VAT purposes depending on whether the landlord in question has 'opted to tax the property' – see **Chapter 15** for more on relevant aspects of VAT.

Property development

3.56 It may be that the property business extends into property development activity. Substantive property development for resale – even of

3.56 *Finance costs relief restrictions*

part of the existing investment portfolio – is likely to be considered by HMRC to be a separate trading activity, or caught by the "Transactions in Land" anti-avoidance regime; see **Chapter 2** for further information on this, and also for the CGT and IT implications of taking investment assets to trading stock, or *vice versa*. There will again be VAT aspects to consider (as to VAT generally, see **Chapter 15**).

Chapter 4

Capital allowances

Martin Wilson MA FCA, The Capital Allowances Partnership Ltd

> SIGNPOSTS
> - **Scope** – capital allowances are a way of giving tax relief for expenditure incurred on plant, as defined for tax purposes, for a range of businesses, including property rental. They are a mandatory alternative to accounting depreciation. They generally give tax relief over a number of years, although in some instances relief is due entirely in the first year (see **4.1**).
> - **Qualifying expenditure** – to qualify for capital allowances, expenditure has to be capital in nature and must be incurred for a qualifying activity. Property rental is a qualifying activity (see **4.2**).
> - **Plant** – there is no single definition of what constitutes plant for tax purposes, it can include small assets and large, from door handles to the whole electrical system. Plant is apparatus, or something which performs a function other than simply providing shelter (see **4.3–4.5**).
> - **Annual investment allowance** – if qualifying expenditure is below certain thresholds (currently £200,000 per annum) relief is given entirely in the first year (see **4.6**).
> - **Limitation** – there is a general ban on allowances for certain residential properties, known as 'dwelling houses'. It is often obvious whether a property is a dwelling house, but sometimes it can be complicated. A block of flats is not a dwelling house, but the individual flats are (see **4.7–4.9**).
> - **Communal areas** – in larger properties, such as blocks of flats, there may be significant expenditure in communal areas such as hallways, stairwells and lifts. Although plant in individual flats does not qualify for allowances, the amounts spent on plant in communal areas may lead to surprisingly large claims for tax relief (see **4.10**).
> - **Furnished holiday lettings** – Allowances for furnished holiday letting properties are available provided certain conditions are met. These are aimed at ensuring that tax relief is only given for genuinely commercial holiday rental activities, rather than for holiday homes which are rarely, if ever, let to the general public (see **4.11–4.15**).

4.1 *Capital allowances*

INTRODUCTION

4.1

> **Focus**
>
> Capital allowances provide tax relief for expenditure on plant. They can provide an immediate benefit, or accrue over a number of years. They save tax at the landlord's marginal rate (up to 45% for an income tax payer). Non-taxpayers cannot benefit.

Unless otherwise stated, all statutory references in this chapter are to the Capital Allowances Act 2001.

Capital allowances are a way of giving tax relief for expenditure incurred by taxpayers, including landlords. So far as the tax system is concerned, buy-to-let landlords will incur two types of expenses, called (somewhat confusingly) 'revenue expenditure' and 'capital expenditure'.

Revenue expenditure consists of those costs, whether recurring or not, which don't involve the acquisition of an asset, and which achieve only a short-term benefit. Examples include cleaning and maintenance, staff wages, rates or council tax, loan interest and so on.

Capital expenditure, on the other hand, creates a longer term benefit. Generally in the context of buy-to-lets, this means that the expenditure is on a fixed asset, such as the building itself, fixtures, equipment and furniture. Fixtures, equipment and furniture are examples of what the tax system calls 'plant'.

Taxpayers can deduct revenue expenditure from their income to work out their profit. However, they cannot deduct capital expenditure, nor can they deduct depreciation (an annual write-off of the cost of assets).

Instead, they can claim 'capital allowances'. Broadly speaking, capital allowances allow the cost of certain capital assets to be written off over a period against taxable profits.

Landlords should take note, however, that capital allowances are not available for plant which is let for use in a 'dwelling house' (*s 35*). In recent years, some purported 'specialists' (in reality part of the general claims industry) have persuaded residential landlords to make capital allowances claims, only for them to be rejected immediately by HMRC (see **4.7–4.9**).

QUALIFYING EXPENDITURE

4.2 In the context of buy-to-lets, for expenditure to qualify for capital allowances, it has to be capital expenditure (see **4.1**) in respect of 'plant' (see **4.3**) (*s 11*).

Capital allowances **4.3**

The expenditure additionally has to be incurred for a qualifying activity (*s 15* – property rental is a qualifying activity), and the plant has to belong to the person spending the money (*s 11*). This is not normally an issue where assets are purchased outright, and special rules exist that deem hire purchase (HP) assets to belong to the buyer as soon as he begins to use them, even if the HP agreement doesn't transfer ownership until all payments have been made (*s 67*).

There is, however, a caveat. Whilst property rental generally is a qualifying activity attracting capital allowances, there is an exception for assets which are actually inside someone's home (not necessarily the owner's), or as the legislation puts it, their 'dwelling house' (*s 35*) (see **4.7–4.9**).

Allowances are given at different rates according to the nature of the asset. However, for most landlords, the annual investment allowance (see **4.6**) will mean that relief on all expenditure will potentially be given in the year the expenditure is incurred.

PLANT

4.3

> **Focus**
>
> Plant can take many forms, from the obvious and commonplace to the unusual and unexpected. It includes most fixtures and fittings in a property.

There is no single definition of plant, and there is no definitive list of items that qualify.

Remarkably, the starting point is an 1887 public liability case about a drayman's horse! In it, the judge said:

> 'There is no definition of plant [...] but, in its ordinary sense, it includes whatever apparatus is used by a businessman for carrying on his business, not his stock-in-trade which he buys or makes for sale; but all goods and chattels, fixed or moveable, live or dead, which he keeps for permanent employment in his business' (*Yarmouth v France (1887) 19 QBD 647*).

So basically, 'plant' means apparatus of some kind, and it can be fixed or movable. This can be obvious machines like vacuum cleaners or heaters, but the term can also include many other assets, including some surprising ones. Many fixtures and even building services, for instance, count as plant and attract tax relief. Basically, 'plant' performs a function of some kind, other than simply housing the business.

If an asset is merely part of a building (for example, walls, floors, ceilings and doors), it is not counted as plant.

4.4 *Capital allowances*

The rate at which relief is given often depends on whether the items claimed count as 'integral features' (see **4.4**) or 'other plant' (see **4.5**).

Integral features

4.4   'Integral features' is a term used by the tax legislation with a very specific meaning. It does *not* mean, as some people assume, *all* assets that are integral to a building.

So-called 'integral features' attract relief at 8% per annum (*s 104D*). The relevant assets (*s 33A*) are:

- electrical systems (including lighting systems);
- cold water systems (plumbing);
- space or water heating systems (heating and hot water);
- ventilation and air conditioning systems;
- lifts; and
- external solar shading.

The 8% rate also applies to solar panels (*s 104A*).

An electrical system for this purpose does *not* include systems intended for other purposes, which may include wiring and other electrical components (eg communication, telecommunication and surveillance systems, fire alarm systems or burglar alarm systems etc).

Other plant

4.5   Plant that is not an integral feature, on the list above (see **4.4**) qualifies for relief at 18% per annum (*s 56*).

Such plant includes a multitude of assets, from small ones such as door locks to large ones, like complete alarm systems. The key thing is that they are assets which perform a function of some kind. The following list will give an indication of assets which can be plant, although such a list can never be complete.

- Aerials.
- Automatic exit doors and gates.
- Bicycle holders or racks.
- Blinds and curtains.
- Burglar alarms.
- Cable TV provision and ducting.

- Cameras.
- Car park illumination and barrier equipment.
- Carpets and other loose floor coverings.
- Cleaning cradles (including tracks and anchorages).
- Closed circuit television (CCTV) equipment.
- Conduit for security alarm systems.
- Fans and heaters.
- Fire alarms.
- Fire protection systems and sprinklers.
- Fire safety equipment.
- Garden furniture.
- Intercom installations.
- Internal signs.
- Laundry equipment (in communal areas).
- Loose floor coverings and doormats.
- Loose furniture.
- Racking, cupboards and shelving (in communal or staff areas).
- Sanitary installations.
- Signage.
- Smoke detectors and heat detectors.
- Soft furnishings.
- Sprinkler systems.
- Telecommunications equipment.
- Wash basins and associated plumbing.

Annual investment allowance

4.6

Focus

For most buy-to-let landlords, any expenditure they incur will attract tax relief in the first year (assuming of course that they have a tax liability). This applies for annual expenditure up to £200,000.

4.7 *Capital allowances*

As discussed above, tax relief is generally given at 8% per annum for integral features (see **4.4**) and 18% for other plant (see **4.5**). That means that the landlord has to wait a number of years before obtaining tax relief for even the majority of his costs. However, provided expenditure does not exceed certain limits, it can all qualify for tax relief in year one, ie the year the money is spent.

This is because of an allowance called the 'annual investment allowance' (AIA) (*s 51A*).

The AIA gives an annual 100% capital allowance on up to £200,000 of investment in plant and machinery per annum (CAA 2001, *s 51A*). Different thresholds (between £50,000 and £500,000) have applied at different times since April 2008, when the AIA was first introduced.

The AIA accelerates the tax relief that would otherwise be available compared to conventional capital allowances. In effect, it acts like a type of *de minimis* provision. Any additional expenditure above the maximum limit is written off under the normal capital allowances rules, at either 8% or 18% per annum.

> **Example 4.1 – Annual investment allowance and integral features**
>
> Bob owns a number of rental properties, and in the tax year 2016/17 he incurs £175,000 on integral features (see **4.4**) and £60,000 on other plant (see **4.5**).
>
> In that year he can claim up to £200,000 annual investment allowance (AIA). He allocates that AIA against his integral features first (£175,000) then the remaining (£25,000) against other plant. The balance of the other plant (£35,000) qualifies at 18% per annum, so Bob's allowances in year one are £206,300 (£200,000 @ 100% plus £35,000 @ 18%).

LIMITATION OF ALLOWANCES ON 'DWELLINGS'
4.7

> **Focus**
>
> Buy-to-let landlords should be wary of assuming all plant qualifies for allowances. In particular, plant does not attract allowances if it is used in a 'dwelling house'.

Expenditure on plant does not qualify for allowances if the plant is to be used in what the tax legislation calls a 'dwelling-house' (see **4.8**). This rule has existed for decades, and is now in *s 35*.

This means that capital allowances will not be claimable on many residential properties. In some shared properties, allowances will only be available for plant in communal areas.

What is a dwelling-house?

4.8 A dwelling-house used to be defined by the HMRC Manual as a building, or part of a building, which is a person's home (not necessarily the home of the owner). This is extended to a second or holiday home. In the old case of *Riley v Read* (1879), the meaning of 'to dwell' was described as 'to live in a house; that is, to live there day and night; to sleep there during the night, and to occupy it for the purposes of life during the day'.

However, in relation to capital expenditure incurred on or after 22 October 2010, HMRC's preferred definition changed, such that in its view the distinctive characteristic of a dwelling-house became its 'ability to afford to those who use it all the facilities required for day-to-day private domestic existence'.

So a single house, owned by a landlord and rented to a tenant, would be a dwelling house, and no capital allowances could be claimed. In most cases there should be little difficulty in deciding whether or not particular premises comprise a dwelling house, but in difficult cases the question is essentially one of fact.

Properties comprising more than one dwelling

4.9 A block of flats is not a dwelling-house although the individual flats within the block will be.

Consequently, allowances may be available for plant in communal areas, and for lifts, air-conditioning equipment, fire alarms and so on. HMRC guidance suggests that where a complex asset, such as a fire alarm, serves a block of flats as a whole, there is no requirement to disallow expenditure on those parts of the system (eg smoke detectors) which are within individual flats.

> **Example 4.2 – Residential flats and nursing home (published by HMRC)**
>
> Bob is a landlord. He owns a block of residential flats and a nursing home. He buys:
>
> - new cookers for the flats;
> - a new fire alarm system for the block of flats; and
> - new beds for the nursing home.
>
> His expenditure on the cookers is not qualifying expenditure and so does not qualify for PMAs because it is expenditure on assets for use in dwelling houses. The prohibition does not apply to the fire alarm system for the block of flats or the beds for the nursing home because they are not for use in a dwelling house.

4.10 *Capital allowances*

Nursing homes and accommodation used for holiday letting are *not* dwelling houses.

Student accommodation is problematical. In contrast to old-style halls of residence or colleges (neither of which counts as a dwelling house), many student residences are now indistinguishable from ordinary blocks of flats.

> **Example 4.3 – Student accommodation**
>
> Three students share a flat within a larger building. The flat provides each of them with a lockable study-bedroom, but they share a sitting room, kitchen and bathroom.
>
> The treatment of such accommodation follows HMRC's view that the distinctive characteristic of a dwelling-house is its ability to afford to those who use it all the facilities required for day-to-day private domestic existence. In effect, this means that the entire student flat (including the sitting room, kitchen and bathroom) are treated as part of the 'dwelling house'. Consequently, no allowances are available (allowances might be available for communal areas shared with other flats in the same block).

The same principle applies to other residential properties such as houses in multiple occupation (so-called HMOs; defined by the *Housing Act 2004*, broadly, as properties occupied by more than one household and more than one person). The genuinely communal areas in a HMO (that is to say, those areas excluded from being regarded as a dwelling house) are likely to be minimal in the extreme, such as corridors and staircases. Consequently the potential allowances for an HMO are rarely worth the cost of a specialist exercise.

Communal areas in a block of flats

4.10 Plant will qualify is it is in a communal area (but not actually in someone's dwelling).

Qualifying assets might therefore include:

- heating in corridors;
- boilers;
- lighting in corridors, and relevant wiring;
- switchgear;
- air conditioning (excluding items situated within actual flats);
- telephone cabling;
- TV aerials and cabling;
- Communal laundry equipment;

- Communal gym equipment;
- Lifts;
- Plant on the roof or in a plant room;
- Carpets in corridors;
- Door entry systems;
- Fire alarms;
- Intruder alarms;
- CCTV.

ALLOWANCES FOR FURNISHED HOLIDAY LETTINGS
4.11

> **Focus**
>
> A favourable system of allowances is available for properties let as furnished holiday accommodation, either in the UK or in most of Europe. Such properties do, however, have to meet strict criteria concerning availability for letting and actual letting.

Compared to other types of residential property, the advantage of furnished holiday accommodation is that it is not deemed to be a 'dwelling house', and so any plant contained will qualify for capital allowances.

Furnished holiday accommodation is defined by reference to its use and not its nature. So one half of a semi-detached house might be a dwelling house, but the other half might be in use as holiday accommodation.

Clearly a house, cottage or villa is accommodation and the HMRC has confirmed that the term may also include a caravan: the term will also embrace other structures or things capable of occupation, including flats or apartments.

The holiday property may be in the UK, but it can also be elsewhere in the European Economic Area (EEA). The EEA includes all EU members, plus Norway, Iceland and Liechtenstein. European countries excluded are Switzerland, Albania and (apart from EU members Croatia and Slovenia) the countries which were formerly part of Yugoslavia.

It should be noted that in order to qualify for allowances the property must meet certain conditions. The following is an outline of the conditions.

A separate chapter of this book covers furnished holiday lettings in more detail (see **Chapter 6**).

4.12 *Capital allowances*

Letting conditions

4.12   Accommodation is not holiday accommodation unless:

(a) it is *available* for letting to the general public as holiday accommodation, on a commercial basis, for at least 210 (formerly 140) days in a year (the 210 days need not be consecutive);

(b) it is *actually* let to the general public as holiday accommodation for at least 105 (formerly 70) days in a year; and

(c) for a period of at least 155 days during the relevant period it is not normally in the same occupation for a continuous period exceeding 31 days (*ITTOIA 2005 ss 323, 325* in relation to income tax and *CTA 2009, s 267* in relation to corporation tax).

The 210-day and 105-day requirements increased from 140 and 70 with effect from 6 April 2012.

Averaging election

4.13   Where accommodation is actually let for less than 105 days in the year of assessment, or the period of 12 months, it may nevertheless still qualify on the making of an 'averaging' claim. A person who lets two or more sets of accommodation may elect, within two years after the end of the year of assessment or period, to average the number of days let for each accommodation. If the average number of days let amounts to at least 105, all of the accommodation included in the claim is deemed to have been let for at least 105 days.

Accommodation may not be included in more than one such claim for any year of assessment or period. It is important to note that the election does not have to include all holiday properties let by that person. The lettings may be specified in the election on a selective basis so the lettings likely to reduce the average days below 105 may be excluded (*ITTOIA 2005 s 326* in relation to income tax and *CTA 2009, s 268* in relation to corporation tax).

Period of grace election

4.14   A so-called 'period of grace election' is permitted by *ITTIOA 2005 s 326A* and *CTA 2009 s 268A*. The election is intended to help businesses that fail to meet the letting conditions for up to two years.

This election allows a non-qualifying furnished holiday lettings (FHL) year to be treated as a qualifying year if the FHL qualified in the previous year.

If the property still fails the letting test in the next year the election can be made for a further year (provided the election was made for the first non-qualifying year) and it is even possible to make the claim if the property only qualifies in the first year as a result of an averaging election. If the property fails to meet

Capital allowances **4.16**

the letting test in the fourth year (after two years being treated as qualifying) then it will no longer qualify as an FHL.

It is important to note that there must be a genuine intention to meet the letting conditions for all years covered by the claim and the property must meet all the relevant conditions.

Failure to meet the letting conditions

4.15 Where a FHL property fails to meet the letting conditions (and a period of grace election – see **4.13**) is no longer possible, some commentators have suggested that the FHL business may be treated as permanently ceasing and capital allowances will no longer be available. Potentially, a balancing charge, based on the market value of the assets, will crystallise, but no sale proceeds will be received with which to pay the tax.

However, this interpretation relies on the failure to meet the conditions being regarded as tantamount to a permanent cessation of the FHL business. If the FHL business is continuing, with the intention that a qualifying level of letting may be achieved in future years, it is arguable that there has been no permanent discontinuance.

It is interesting to note that HMRC's Property Income Manual (at PIM4120) appears to allow for such wider concession:

> 'Strictly, if a property qualifies in one year but does not do so in the next, the disposal value of plant and machinery should be brought into account. If income from a property temporarily ceases to qualify solely because not all the conditions are satisfied for that year, capital allowances may be continued. But if a property is let on a long-term basis, or sold, or otherwise seems unlikely to qualify in the foreseeable future, disposal value should be brought into account.'

Caravans

4.16 A caravan is plant if it does not occupy a fixed site and is regularly moved as part of normal trade usage, even if it is only moved from its summer site to winter quarters.

In addition, HMRC accepts that a caravan, which is provided mainly for holiday lettings on a holiday caravan site, is plant whether it is moved or not. Caravans occupying residential sites do not qualify for capital allowances. As far as a holiday caravan site is concerned, HMRC regard a caravan as being anything that is treated as a caravan for the purposes of:

(1) the *Caravan Sites and Control of Development Act 1960* (CSCDA); or

(2) the *Caravans Act (Northern Ireland) 1963*.

4.16 *Capital allowances*

Those Acts give caravan a wider meaning than its normal one. In them, the term 'caravan' includes double units delivered in two sections and then joined together, and wooden lodges provided these are moveable. But it does not cover structures that are not moveable, even if these are otherwise identical.

In the 1950s an agreement was made with the National Caravan Council which has never been superseded. It applies to trades that consist of hiring out caravans or the provision of caravan sites and covers what capital expenditure qualifies or does not qualify as expenditure on plant or machinery.

Under the agreement expenditure qualifies for plant or machinery allowances if it relates to:

- water supplies (that is mains or other apparatus used to convey water to or around sites – and hot water systems);

- electricity supplies (that is heavy cables, distributive wiring and general electrical apparatus, and diesel generating apparatus); and

- sanitary fittings, baths and wash basins.

Under the agreement no allowances are due for expenditure on:

- roads;

- proposed sites for individual caravans;

- buildings erected as sanitary blocks; or

- sewage and drainage pipes installed as public health requirements.

Chapter 5

Furnished lettings

Lee Sharpe CTA, ATT, Tax Consultant, Sharpe Tax Consulting Ltd.

SIGNPOSTS

- **Scope** – There are special rules for claiming tax relief in respect of furnishings in standard residential dwellings, because items used in dwellings do not normally rank for capital allowances, for the ordinary letting business (see **5.1**).

- **Residential property** – Historically, a taxpayer has had a choice of alternative routes to tax relief. There have been numerous changes to the regime over the last several years, ending with the abolition of wear and tear allowance, and a new replacement domestic items relief (see **5.2–5.5**).

- **Commercial property** – Such lettings have also been affected by the abolition of the statutory renewals basis, since lettings of commercial property are ineligible for the narrower replacement domestic items relief (see **5.6**).

- **Replacement domestic items relief** – This relief is effectively the old renewals basis by another name, but is now limited in scope to free-standing items in a 'normal' residential letting that are ineligible for capital allowances (see **5.7–5.9**).

- **Fixtures in a dwelling** – As a general rule, fixtures in a dwelling (that are ineligible for capital allowances) are deemed to be part of the larger whole that is the building itself, so replacing a fixture will be considered a deductible repair, in the absence of substantive improvement (see **5.10–5.11**).

- **Fixtures and furniture in commercial properties** – Items in commercial property lettings will usually be subject to the capital allowances regime (see **5.12**).

- **Wear and tear allowance** – For many years, fully furnished residential lettings that were ineligible for capital allowances on their furnishings were able to secure a wear and tear allowance instead, that was available regardless of whether or not there had been any

5.1 *Furnished lettings*

> expenditure on furniture, etc, in the property during the chargeable period in question (see **5.13–5.18**).
>
> - **Withdrawal of wear and tear and interaction with replacement domestic items relief** – Wear and tear was withdrawn from April 2016, while the alternative replacement domestic items relief is available only for expenditure incurred from April 2016. In some cases, there may be a period where business expenses will get no income tax relief in 2016/17 because they were incurred before the operative date (see **5.19–5.21**).
>
> - **Renewals basis** – HMRC initially said that the renewals basis for the cost of replacing fixtures and fittings would be widely available, but then changed its mind and decided the renewals basis would be available only for minor items in let property. HMRC then formally abolished the renewals basis, introducing the replacement domestic items relief, which is significantly narrower in scope (see **5.22–5.28**).
>
> - **Chronology** – A history of changes to the regime over the last several years has been set out at the end of this chapter (see **5.29–5.36**).

INTRODUCTION

5.1 This chapter covers the more general tax treatment of furnishings in let property, and not the specific regime that applies to furnished holiday lettings (see **Chapter 6**).

> **Focus**
>
> The fundamental problem for property businesses in claiming tax relief on furniture, free-standing white goods and similar items used in dwellings is that the normal route, being capital allowances on such items, is specifically excluded where used by a property business in a let dwelling-house (*CAA 2001, s 35*).

RESIDENTIAL PROPERTY

5.2 The tax treatment of furnishings in general residential property lettings has undergone several changes in the last few years.

5.3 Many readers will be familiar with the 'wear and tear allowance', but unfortunately this was abolished with effect from April 2016 (1 April 2016 for corporation tax and 6 April 2016 for income tax purposes).

Historically, a good proportion of property business lettings were not so extensively furnished as to be eligible for the wear and tear allowance, so owners instead claimed for the cost of replacing free-standing items of furniture on a like-for-like basis – the 'renewals basis' – and, while HMRC only recently said that it had abolished the renewals basis for property lettings, there is now a 'replacement domestic items relief' that is indistinguishable from the renewals basis for property businesses, that HMRC had only recently abolished.

5.4 However, the general statutory provision for the renewals basis (that applied to trades and to property businesses) *has* now been formally withdrawn, meaning that where businesses are unable to avail themselves of the new replacement domestic items relief (typically, furnished holiday lettings, hotels and commercial lettings since these categories can generally access capital allowances within the let property), there will be no conventional revenue deduction at all, although capital allowances may well be available as an alternative.

5.5 It can therefore be broadly summarised that, having set out originally to abolish the renewals basis for residential lettings, the Government has ultimately succeeded in ensuring that the renewals basis is now the only remaining mechanism for securing tax relief for the replacement of discrete assets in ordinary residential lettings – albeit in the guise of replacement domestic items relief.

COMMERCIAL PROPERTY

5.6 Even commercial property lettings have not come out of this saga unscathed: commercial lettings would generally claim capital allowances on the cost of replacing items of furniture, appliances and equipment (fixed or movable) but in the past, were able to claim the renewals basis as an alternative; this second option is no longer available, now that the statutory renewals basis has been withdrawn.

REPLACEMENT DOMESTIC ITEMS RELIEF (FROM APRIL 2016)

Standard residential lettings

5.7 *Finance Act 2016* followed up on an announcement in the summer 2015 Budget, to introduce replacement domestic items relief, (*ITTOIA 2005, s 311A*; *CTA 2009, s 250A*), for the cost of *replacing* those items of furniture, kitchen appliances, etc, provided for use by a tenant in a dwelling and thereby excluded from capital allowances by the standard rule at *CAA 2001, s 35(2)*:

- For income tax purposes, for expenditure incurred from 6 April 2016; and

5.8 Furnished lettings

- For corporation tax purposes, for expenditure incurred after 1 April 2016.

The new legislation provides that a 'domestic item' means an item for domestic use, such as:

- Furniture and furnishings;
- Household appliances; and
- Kitchenware.

> **Focus**
>
> However, it does not include anything that is a fixture – plant or machinery (as per *CAA 2001*) that is installed or fixed so as to become part of the dwelling in law (specifically including boilers and standard radiators) – but see **5.10** below.

5.8 Relief will be given only where conditions A to D are met. These are broadly as follows:

(a) *Condition A* – a property business is carried on in relation to land which consists of or includes a dwelling-house.

(b) *Condition B* – a domestic item has been provided for use in the dwelling-house, and business expenditure is incurred on replacing that item with a new item, which is solely for the use of the lessee/tenant, and the old item is no longer available for use in the dwelling-house.

(c) *Condition C* – the expenditure is not prohibited by the standard 'wholly and exclusively rule' but would otherwise be blocked as it is capital expenditure within the meaning of *ITTOIA 2005, s 33* or *CA 2009, s 53*.

(d) *Condition D* – the expenditure is ineligible for relief through *CAA 2001* (thus preventing furnished holiday lettings, commercial properties, etc from accessing the relief).

5.9 The relief emulates the (now former) renewals basis for property businesses, with which many readers will already be familiar, but to recap:

- There is no deduction for the cost of the original item.

- Where the replacement item is substantially the same as the 'old' item, the allowable deduction is the replacement expenditure; where the replacement item is not substantially the same, then the expenditure actually incurred that is eligible for relief cannot exceed that which would have been incurred on a substantially similar replacement item.

- Incidental capital expenditure on the replacement item (or on the disposal of the 'old' item) increases the qualifying deduction, while proceeds on the disposal of the 'old' item, or consideration in part-exchange for the replacement item, serve to reduce the relief available.

Furnished lettings **5.11**

- Relief is not available for expenditure incurred in any tax year (or accounting period, where appropriate), in which the relevant dwelling-house has qualified as a furnished holiday letting (see **Chapter 6**) or where rent-a-room relief has been claimed.

Example 5.1 – Washing machine upgrade

Bill replaces a washing machine in one of his buy-to-let (BTL) properties with a washer-dryer, which cost £500. The washing machine-only version would cost just £400, so Bill can claim only £400 replacement domestic items relief.

However, when he comes in turn to replace that washer-dryer with a new model washer-dryer a few years later, this time for £650, then the full amount will be allowable, since it will then be a like-for-like replacement.

Example 5.2 – Replacement of fridge

Ben buys a new fridge to replace an older version in one of his BTL properties. The old fridge came with the property when Ben bought it; the replacement cost is £400 but the vendor charges Ben an additional fee of £25 to take away the old fridge; his relief includes the cost of disposing of the old item so totalling £425.

FIXTURES IN A DWELLING

5.10

Focus

While the new replacement domestic items relief is not available to fixtures in a dwelling, this should not normally present a problem, because replacing a fixture in a dwelling will generally count as a repair, unless the replacement is an improvement over the 'old' fixture.

While the replacement of 'an asset' is fundamentally capital in nature, HMRC accepts that, so far as residential property is concerned, 'the asset' is the entire property. It follows that replacing an integrated appliance, kitchen cupboards or even the whole roof of a dwelling would be akin to replacing a component in a computer used for business so as to constitute an allowable repair – unless the component represents a substantive improvement (see **Chapter 2**).

5.11 This does not apply to commercial premises, where each fixture would usually be considered an asset in its own right, and its replacement would be a capital transaction, rather than on revenue account (see HMRC's Property Income manual at PIM1020: 'Repairs to Let Property').

5.12 Furnished lettings

FIXTURES AND FURNITURE IN COMMERCIAL PROPERTIES

5.12 The dwellings-based approach that replacing integrated appliances and other fixtures will comprise the replacement of a component part in the overall asset (the building) and therefore potentially rank as deductible repair costs does *not* apply to commercial properties.

Just as with general trading activities, each identifiable asset – an item of furniture, a kitchen appliance or IT installation – will be considered separately and in many cases the cost of replacing an asset, although capital, will qualify for capital allowances instead.

> **Example 5.3 – Commercial property: replacement air-conditioning**
>
> Ronald has a small commercial unit that he rents out as office space to a local business. The air-conditioning needs to be replaced. If it were a standard BTL long-term residential letting, the replacement of air-conditioning on a like-for-like basis would be a repair, as it would be the replacement of just part of an asset – the overall property.
>
> However, because the property is commercial, the replacement of the air-conditioning will be treated as a replacement of an identifiable asset, covered instead by capital allowances – although Ronald should be able to claim the annual investment allowance (assuming he has not already used it elsewhere) to deduct 100% of his capital cost in the tax year.

WEAR AND TEAR ALLOWANCE

5.13

> **Focus**
>
> Wear and tear allowance has been a commonplace deduction for many years, but has been withdrawn from April 2016. It is included here for reference, and because there will still be scope to claim wear and tear for previous years, if it has been omitted.

5.14 There is a minimum level of furnishing in order to be eligible to claim.

It may be summarised as a deduction of:

10% × (rent – (council tax + water rates + any other costs paid by the landlord but which would ordinarily be the tenant's burden)).

Concession

5.15 Wear and tear was 'semi-formal' under Extra-Statutory Concession B47, but was put on a statutory footing by SI 2011/1037 (The Enactment of Extra-Statutory Concessions Order 2011) Art 11, introducing new *ITTOIA 2005, ss 308A–308C*, and *CTA 2009, ss 248A–248C*, to apply from April 2011 onwards.

ESC B47 itself was introduced to standardise the many different rates and regimes that had applied before the standard '10% of rent-less-rates' and, in one form or another, harks back as far as to 1977. It is clear from the wording of the concession that it was intended to address situations where the taxpayer was unable to access capital allowances by reason of the items being used in a dwelling in a property business (*CAA 2001, s 35*). Wear and tear was not available, where capital allowances were – such as for furnished holiday lettings, hotels or commercial premises.

The allowance was a tax deduction from residential letting profits, being 10% of the rent, net of any of the occupier's council tax and water rates paid by the landlord and any other material expenses borne by the landlord but which would ordinarily have been paid by the tenant.

ESC B47 also stated that, where the 10% allowance was given, no further relief was to be given for the cost of *renewing* furniture or furnishings such as suites, televisions, beds, carpets, curtains, linen, crockery or cutlery. However, the 10% allowance did *not* cover fixtures integral to the building, such as baths, washbasins, and the like – expenditure on renewing such items could be claimed alongside wear and tear.

5.16 Booklet IR150 (no longer in print) confirmed that the cost of *repairing* those assets covered by wear and tear was allowable, independently of the 10% deduction. This was entirely reasonable, since wear and tear was meant to cover those costs which capital allowances could not, and repair costs are not generally a factor in capital allowances (except perhaps for special provisions in relation to significant expenditure on integral features).

It also confirmed that a property would only be considered 'furnished' and therefore eligible for wear and tear allowance if the property were capable of normal occupation without the tenant having to provide their own essential items of furniture.

Legislation (April 2011 to April 2016)

5.17 The legislation for both income tax and corporation tax purposes basically emulates ESC B47 (which is unsurprising, given that was its purpose). The requirement that a property be 'fully' furnished became a requirement that the dwelling-house contain sufficient furniture, furnishing and equipment for normal residential use.

5.18 *Furnished lettings*

Also, the legislation required a restriction to the claim in respect of *any* expenses claimed by the landlord but which would ordinarily be borne by the lessee, while the concession required adjustment to be made only where such expenses were *material*.

5.18

> **Focus**
>
> One remarkable deviation, however, was that repairs were no longer claimable separately (ie in addition) to the wear and tear allowance, but were deemed also covered by the allowance. This is confirmed in the Property Income manual at PIM3205:
>
> 'This [Wear and Tear] election means that instead of claiming relief for replacing utensils, **or repairing furniture**, the taxpayers deduct an allowance calculated as a percentage of rents received.'

The legislative basis for this is found in either *ITTOIA 2005, s 308B* or *CTA 2009, s 248C*, which each say that on the making of the relevant election, no deduction is then allowed otherwise than under the wear and tear allowance, for expenses incurred in connection with the provision of furniture. This would be understandable if 'the provision of furniture' were still defined by reference to *CAA 2001*, but unfortunately it is not.

Whether the draftsman understood the change or its implication is unclear, but it does seem unfortunate that the mere enactment of an extra-statutory concession, introduced by Statutory Instrument, significantly changed the scope of the relief.

WITHDRAWAL OF WEAR AND TEAR ALLOWANCE AND INTERACTION WITH REPLACEMENT DOMESTIC ITEMS RELIEF

5.19 *Finance Act 2016, s 74* repealed the statutory allowance in *ITTOIA 2005 ss 308A–308C* with effect from 2016/17 onwards.

Property businesses subject to income tax usually run their accounts to a fiscal year (see **Chapter 1**), so this will normally be straightforward to administer: claim wear and tear allowance (or not) for 2015/16, and claim the new replacement domestic items relief for any expenditure incurred from 6 April 2016 onwards.

5.20 However, unincorporated businesses do not *always* run their property accounts to a fiscal year: for example, property business income to a trading partnership will be accounted for according to whichever is the basis period for the trading accounts. In such cases, it seems there may be a 'void' period in accounts which are assessable in 2016/17, as illustrated by the following example.

Furnished lettings **5.22**

Example 5.4 – Trading partnership with furnished lettings

The FixIt Partnership, which is a trading property development firm of many years' standing, also lets out a small portfolio of furnished residential properties, (not furnished holiday lettings), on which it has traditionally claimed wear and tear allowance.

The Partnership runs its trading accounts to 30 April annually. The accounts to 30 April 2015, including the property business results, will form the basis period for the 2015/16 tax year. No wear and tear allowance is permitted in 2016/17, but expenditure will be eligible for the new replacement domestic items relief for income tax purposes only if incurred after 6 April 2016.

Therefore, all expenditure on replacing eligible items of furniture, free-standing white goods, etc, in the period 1 May 2015 to 5 April 2016 is ineligible for the new relief, leaving only expenditure incurred between 6 April 2016 and 30 April 2016 potentially eligible.

5.21 If an entity such as in **Example 5.4** is particularly badly affected by the transition as above, it is potentially open to them to extend their 2015/16 basis period to 5 April 2016, or another suitable date (*ITTOIA 2005, Pt 2 Ch 15*, and in particular *ss 214–220*). However, this will usually bring more profits into charge (although overlap relief may be claimed).

Alternatively, they might choose to consider whether or not the statutory renewals basis is available instead for relevant expenditure incurred prior to 6 April 2016. It should be emphasised that this approach would run counter to HMRC's stated position in relation to the application of the statutory renewals basis – see below.

Finance Act 2016, s 74(3) withdrew *CTA 2009, ss 248A–248C* for accounting periods beginning on or after 1 April 2016. This time, there was specific provision for periods that straddle the operative date: the portion up to 1 April 2016 and the portion afterwards are treated as separate accounting periods, and amounts are apportioned to the two periods on a time basis (or on a just and reasonable basis, if more appropriate).

RENEWALS BASIS

5.22 The statutory provisions were repealed from April 2016 (but see replacement domestic items relief at **5.7** above).

The renewals basis has proved problematic for both HMRC and practitioners in recent years. However, practitioners (and taxpayers) have largely suffered only because of the Government's apparent inability to grasp the relief properly – which is unfortunate, given that the relief was well over 150 years old when it was withdrawn.

5.23 *Furnished lettings*

> **Focus**
>
> Despite its repeal, it may remain relevant to taxpayers and their advisers in relation to years up to 2015/16; also, potentially, for those property businesses with non-fiscal basis periods that may not be able to access the new replacement domestic items relief for all of the basis period that applies for 2016/17 (see **5.20** above).

5.23 The relief was straightforward enough: while no tax deduction was permitted for the cost of the original asset, the cost of a replacement was basically allowed in full, although any improvement element over the original was ignored.

Furthermore, it was logical, in that it permitted a deduction for the cost of replacing an asset that had been consumed by the business, albeit it might have taken several years.

The new replacement domestic items relief above is the renewals basis by another name, although it is now limited in scope only to movable assets in a normal residential letting (such that capital allowances are not available in the dwelling).

> **Example 5.5 – Renewal of dishwasher**
>
> Some years ago, Fred had a BTL property with an integrated dishwasher. As it was a capital item, Fred was prohibited from claiming a deduction for the initial cost; but when he paid £450 to replace the dishwasher with a similar model before April 2016, he was able to claim the full cost of the replacement under the renewals basis.
>
> Note that, unlike the original renewals basis, replacement domestic items relief is restricted to 'free-standing' items and is unavailable for fixtures, integrated appliances, etc.

5.24 The renewals basis fell out of favour with businesses in recent years only because capital allowances gave a measure of relief for the initial acquisition, and relatively quickly where first-year allowances, etc were available. But the renewals basis remained popular with residential property landlords because capital allowances are not available for assets provided in normal residential lettings (*CAA 2001, s 35*)

Concessionary versus statutory basis

5.25 The Government has contended that the broad scope of the renewals basis as set out in ESC B47 for furnished residential lettings was concessionary, and that the statutory basis set out in *ITTOIA 2005, s 68* and *CTA 2009, s 68* applied only to the replacement cost of small tools or items of very low value.

This was, in the writer's opinion, patently incorrect, since the tax law rewrite was not meant to change the law, and *ICTA 1988, s 74(d)* made no mention of tools or small tools, but referred instead to the replacement of 'any implements, utensils, or articles employed for the purpose of such trade' (or property business by virtue of what is now *ITTOIA 2005, s 272; CTA 2009, s 210*). It is, moreover, a complete *volte face* from HMRC's stated position in December 2011, when it initially confirmed that the statutory provisions would cover any relevant expenditure in a residential letting.

5.26 There is case law to demonstrate that the renewals basis had in the past been available in respect of very substantial trading business expenditure, such as *Caledonian Railway Company v Banks* (1880) 1 TC 487, where the taxpayer claimed £250,000 in 1879 for the repairs and renewals to its rolling stock. More recently, in the well-known *Odeon Associated Theatres Ltd v Jones* CA 1971, 48 TC 257, a sum equivalent to around £300,000 in today's money was allowed for the renewal of carpeting in a single venue.

This is relevant to BTL investors because ESC B47 was formally withdrawn in April 2013, and HMRC's position is that, from that date until the introduction of the new replacement domestic items relief for expenditure from April 2016, *no deduction is allowed for the cost of replacing free-standing appliances or similar 'high-value' items* (see, for example, Sophie's kitchen example in HMRC's Business Income manual at BIM46911).

Indeed, in the Government's overview of legislation and tax rates which accompanied the 2016 Budget, it said:

'Some businesses have recently sought to obtain relief under the renewals allowance provisions for expenditure on very large and expensive items of equipment. The renewals allowance was never intended to apply to expenditure of that nature and the measure protects that position.'

5.27 It is difficult to credit the Government's position on the renewals basis, given its established history such as in the cases mentioned above. The Government's continued determination to abolish one of the oldest reliefs that was available to offset against trading profits should perhaps be seen in the context of a marked reduction in the annual rate of capital allowances available in the alternative, over and above the 100% annual investment allowance.

The annual investment allowance is currently set at a quite generous £200,000, so a business will normally be able to claim 100% of the capital cost immediately in the year of acquisition, for qualifying expenditure of up to £200,000 per year. However, when the then-Chancellor George Osborne announced in the 2015 Summer Budget that the annual investment allowance would *not* fall to just £25,000, as originally scheduled, but instead be set at £200,000 every year, the accompanying Red Book clarified that this 'permanent' commitment was in fact only to the end of the current parliament, and it remains to be seen how much support the Government gives to the annual investment allowance beyond that date.

5.28 *Furnished lettings*

5.28

> **Focus**
>
> There will be cases where businesses are unable to access wear and tear allowance between the withdrawal of the concessions in April 2013 and the instatement of the new replacement domestic items relief in April 2016 – usually where the property did not count as being 'fully furnished'.

In the absence of any other avenue for tax relief, taxpayers and their advisers will need to balance the potential benefit of claiming the renewals basis for the cost of replacing free-standing furniture and white goods etc after April 2013 and up to April 2016 (fitted items generally remaining eligible for relief as repairs to the residential property – see **5.10**) against potential challenge by HMRC on the basis that its clearly stated position was that such relief was by concession only, and was effectively cancelled when ESCs B47 and B1 were withdrawn.

CHRONOLOGY

5.29

> **Focus**
>
> It may be useful for practitioners to have a timeline of the changes in this area, over the last few years, insofar as they relate to residential lettings.

5.30   For many years, as set out in ESC B47, landlords had the choice of:

- Claiming the 10% wear and tear allowance for 'fully furnished' residential lettings or, whether fully furnished or not; or
- Claiming the renewals basis on the cost of replacing furniture and free-standing appliances on an item-by-item basis.

In addition, landlords could claim:

- The cost of *repairing* assets covered by either wear and tear or the renewals basis; and
- The cost of renewing fixtures.

5.31   With effect from April 2011, the wear and tear allowance was put on a statutory footing. While essentially similar to the concessionary basis, there were one or two changes (for instance, repair costs were no longer separately allowable, as set out at **5.17** and **5.18** above).

5.32   In December 2011, HMRC published a technical document which said that several Extra-Statutory Concessions would need to be withdrawn and/or put on a statutory footing (this was as a result of an adverse ruling in the

House of Lords, which effectively found that HMRC did not have discretion to apply 'concessions' – *R v HM Commissioners of Inland Revenue ex p Wilkinson* [2005] UKHL 30). This included ESCs B47 and B1.

However, the following reassurance was given in relation to the withdrawal of ESCs B47 and B1:

> 'If the taxpayer's qualifying activity is an ordinary property business or an overseas property business, CAA 2001 s 35 (2) denies Capital Allowances for qualifying expenditure incurred in providing plant or machinery for use in a dwelling-house. In such cases, relief will be available either under ITTOIA 2005 s 68, or CTA 2009 s 68 or, for [fully] furnished lettings, under the Wear and Tear Allowance at ITTOIA 2005 s 308A to 308C.'

ITTOIA 2005, s 68 is entitled 'Replacement and alteration of trade tools' and was specifically referred to in *ITTOIA 2005, s 272*, being the broad provision that says that property business taxation follows trading principles (likewise *CTA 2009, s 210*).

ESCs B47 and B1 were withdrawn from 6 April 2013.

5.33 On 8 April 2013, HMRC published Revenue and Customs Brief 05/13, which included draft updated guidance on repairs and, notably, a new draft section BIM46990 which appeared to contradict the assurances given in the December 2011 technical release, including the following extract:

> 'Before the introduction of plant and machinery capital allowances, the renewals allowance was extended to machinery and plant assets outside the narrow range to which the legislation on renewals applies. This was sometimes termed the non-statutory renewals basis and was an extra statutory concession.
>
> Under the then legislation, the cost of such assets was capital expenditure and any relief was only due under the capital allowances plant and machinery code.'

There was also a draft example in the new guidance at BIM46911 – Refitting a Kitchen:

> 'Shortly afterwards, the fridge freezer breaks down and has to be replaced.
>
> This is not part of the building but is an asset in its own right. Sophia has not repaired an asset; she had incurred capital expenditure on a new asset. As the fridge freezer is used in a dwelling house it is not qualifying expenditure for capital allowances purposes.'

5.34 This apparent change in stance prompted much discussion in the professional press, including notably Mike Truman's excellent 'Renewals on Rails' in the 23 October 2013 edition of *Taxation*, which succinctly demolished HMRC's new-found contention that the 'broad' renewals basis was concessionary, (and now abolished), and the statutory basis was for relatively trivial items only.

5.35 *Furnished lettings*

The CIOT and ICAEW's Tax Faculty wrote jointly to HMRC in February 2014 and HMRC confirmed its position in April of that year, including:

> 'S68 ITTOIA 2005 relates only to items of a capital nature that are of a relatively low value and have a short useful economic life that would need to be regularly ... replaced in the ordinary course of business due to normal wear and tear. This would be on items such as crockery and rugs for instance, i.e., low-cost soft furnishings that might be expected to be replaced fairly regularly. However, it would not apply to carpets, for instance, as they are a capital item of potentially higher value that you would not expect to replace regularly. However, landlords may be able to get some relief on carpets if the expenditure qualifies as a revenue expense.
>
> White goods such as washing machines and fridges are not covered by the statutory renewals allowance as they are capital items not part of the entirety (the property). However, where white goods are fitted (i.e., integrated hobs and ovens), we recognise these as part of the entirety (the property) and so these would be deductible as a repair when replaced.
>
> To confirm, therefore, anything free-standing such as a fridge-freezer will not become part of the entirety (the property) for residential lettings and therefore would not be deductible under S68 ITTOIA 2005.'

Resistance to HMRC's new position continued in the professional press and it was clear that landlords themselves were unaware that the scope of renewals was under threat – a survey in early 2015 by the Residential Landlords' Association indicated that more than 75% of landlords had been unaware of the development. Nevertheless, HMRC continued to assert that there would be no tax relief for the cost of replacing free-standing items of furniture, white goods or appliances of any substantive value, for expenditure from 6 April 2013.

5.35 The 2015 Summer Budget announced in July 2015 that wear and tear allowance, which had of course only recently been put into statute, would be abolished from April 2016, because landlords could 'reduce their tax liability even when they have not *improved* the property' – representing either a very poor choice of words or further evidence of a failure to grasp the basic purpose of the regime. The Budget also said that a 'new' relief would be available instead, which would allow landlords to deduct only the costs actually incurred.

The 2015 Autumn Statement confirmed the intended repeal of wear and tear allowance from April 2016, together with a new relief that effectively re-instated the renewals basis but only for residential lettings – the statutory renewals basis would no longer be available for residential lettings (but see next).

5.36 The 2016 Budget introduced the new replacement domestic items relief for ordinary BTL businesses, and announced the repeal of the statutory renewals basis for all businesses, both effective from April 2016.

Chapter 6

Furnished holiday accommodation/lettings

Lee Sharpe CTA, ATT, Tax Consultant, Sharpe Tax Consulting Ltd.

SIGNPOSTS

- **Scope and advantages** – Furnished holiday lettings (FHLs) enjoy tax-favoured status, which can broadly be summarised as 'quasi-trading'. Given that FHL status sets some quite demanding conditions, some of those obstacles may be circumvented simply by achieving trading status outright (see **6.1–6.13**).

- **Disadvantages** – There are various potential disadvantages to FHL status (see **6.14–6.15**).

- **FHL conditions** – The FHL rules are quite onerous, and most buy-to-let properties will be unsuitable for FHL categorisation. However, the basic conditions can be relaxed in some circumstances (see **6.16–6.22**).

- **Losses** – FHL losses are treated as trading losses, but despite the flexibility normally attaching to such losses, FHL 'trading' losses may only be carried forward to set against the future profits of that FHL business (see **6.23**).

- **Inheritance tax** – FHLs are not guaranteed to be eligible for favourable inheritance tax treatment as relevant business property for business property relief purposes, but nor are they specifically excluded (see **6.24–6.25**).

- **HMRC guidance** – Helpsheet HS253 deals specifically with FHLs, but detailed guidance in HMRC's Property Income manual is awaited at the time of writing (see **6.26**).

INTRODUCTION

6.1 For almost 30 years up to the regime's significant overhaul in *FA 2011*, furnished holiday letting (FHL) status was broadly coveted, particularly

6.2 Furnished holiday accommodation/lettings

because losses on qualifying FHL businesses were allowed against general income.

In 2009, it was officially recognised that restricting FHL status only to UK properties was discriminatory from an EU law perspective. The original proposal was to abolish the FHL regime altogether, rather than have to permit such generous loss reliefs to be extended to similar properties throughout the European Economic Area (EEA). In the end, the regime was retained, but with more demanding thresholds imposed – and without such generous loss reliefs.

There are now potentially two separate FHL businesses carried on in the same capacity:

- A UK FHL business for UK properties; and
- An EEA FHL business – in relation to qualifying properties situated in the EEA (but elsewhere than in the UK).

This approach applies to both corporates and non-corporates (*ITTOIA 2005, s 322*; *ITA 2007, ss 127, 127ZA*; *CTA 2009, s 264*; *CTA 2010, ss 65, 67A*).

ADVANTAGES OF FURNISHED HOLIDAY LETTINGS STATUS

6.2 The potential advantages of properties qualifying for FHL status can be broadly summarised as follows:

- Profits from an FHL are 'relevant earnings' for pension purposes, so individuals are not restricted by the usual limit for buy-to-let investors (specifically, those who have no other relevant earnings such as trading profits or employment income) of £2,880 net, or £3,600 gross.

- Capital allowances may be claimed more widely – not subject to the exclusion that normally prohibits a claim for plant, etc, used in ordinary residential lettings.

- Spouses (or civil partners) who operate the business jointly are not constrained by the usual rule for joint spousal investments that stipulate profits should be split either 50:50 or by reference to the underlying interest: profits may broadly be split as desired.

- Various capital gains tax reliefs are available, that are not generally available to 'ordinary' letting businesses:
    - Entrepreneurs' relief;
    - Rollover relief;
    - Gift relief (gifts of business assets);
    - Relief for loans to traders;
    - Substantial shareholding exemption (for companies).

- FHLs are specifically excluded from the new measures to restrict income tax relief for finance costs in relation to residential lettings (see **Chapter 3**, **3.37**).

Some of these potential advantages are discussed further below.

Relevant earnings for pension purposes

6.3 Private pension contributions generally 'extend' the basic and higher rate limits, thereby reducing the amount of income that is taxed at higher rates (*ITA 2007, s 10*). Eligible contributions can also defer the onset of the clawback of child benefit, and forfeiture of the personal allowance.

Pension contributions are generally permitted up to £3,600 gross (£2,880 net), but where the individual wants tax relief for larger contributions, the taxpayer needs to have 'relevant earnings' at least as great as the total pension contributions in the year, in order to secure the tax benefit.

> **Focus**
>
> FHL profits qualify as relevant earnings for these purposes, and can secure tax relief on potentially much higher personal pension contributions where those profits are 'earned' personally (*FA 2004, s 189(2)*).

Capital allowances

6.4 Capital allowances are usually excluded in relation to any expenditure on plant to be used in a dwelling let out by an 'ordinary' property business (*CAA 2001, s 35*).

However, this exclusion applies only to 'ordinary' property businesses, and FHL businesses may claim capital allowances on plant and machinery in let dwelling areas – approximating a trading hotel (although hotel rooms would not normally comprise a dwelling) (*CAA 2001, ss 15, 17, 17B*).

The following points, however, should be noted:

1. FHLs are (were) ineligible for wear and tear allowance on furnishings, and are likewise ineligible for the new 'replacement domestic items relief' – See **Chapter 5** (*ITTOIA 2005, s 311A(7); CTA 2009, s 250A(7)*).

2. Capital allowances may need to be recalculated if assets used in an FHL effectively become part of an 'ordinary property business', or when they move from being used in an 'ordinary property business' to an FHL business.

    Typically, this would happen with eligible assets being used in an FHL property that failed the eligibility criteria and then by default became part of an 'ordinary property business' (or potentially *vice versa*).

6.5 *Furnished holiday accommodation/lettings*

The eligible assets are effectively treated as new assets, whose cost or 'notional expenditure' for capital allowances purposes is the lower of the following (*CAA 2001, s 13B*):

- Market value on the date of cessation of use in the 'old' business; and
- Expenditure actually incurred on the asset.

This will undoubtedly be practically difficult to administer, in terms of tracing eligible assets in properties that 'struggle' to meet the eligibility criteria from one year to the next (although see 'averaging' and 'grace periods' below at **6.18** and **6.19** respectively). Of course, assets in a dwelling may be eligible in an FHL but ineligible once the property becomes part of the 'ordinary letting business'. However, note HMRC's Property Income manual at PIM4120 for HMRC's interpretation of this rule:

> 'Non-qualifying years
>
> Strictly, if a property qualifies in one year but does not do so in the next, the disposal value of plant and machinery should be brought into account. <u>If income from a property temporarily ceases to qualify solely because not all the tests are satisfied for that year, capital allowances may be continued.</u> But if a property is let on a long-term basis, or sold, or otherwise seems unlikely to qualify in the foreseeable future, disposal value should be brought into account' (emphasis added).

3. Despite there being potentially much greater scope for capital allowances claims, it seems that the 'sideways relief' against total personal income available to ordinary property businesses under *ITA 2007, s 120* – broadly to the extent that the losses may be attributed to capital allowances – is not available for FHL losses (*ITA 2007, s 127(3, 3A)*). Similar restrictions apply in relation to corporate FHL losses (*CTA 2010, s 65*).

See **Chapter 4** for commentary on capital allowances generally.

Profit split between spouses

6.5 By default, the income from property that is held jointly by spouses/civil partners is split 50:50 between them (*ITA 2007, s 836*). FHLs, however, are the exceptions (D and DA) to this rule, broadly meaning that profits may be split as desired (*ITA 2007, s 836(3)*). See also HMRC's Property Income manual at PIM1030.

For commentary on jointly-held property, see **Chapter 8**. See also **1.7**, where incomes are not split according to underlying beneficial ownership in some cases.

Capital gains tax reliefs

6.6 The following paragraphs offer a summary of the key points in relation to the reliefs. While they may serve as a useful starting point for evaluation of relevance and eligibility, the reliefs can be complex in the detail, and further research is strongly recommended (eg see the latest edition of Capital Gains Tax Reliefs for SMEs and Entrepreneurs (Bloomsbury Professional)).

For commentary on capital gains tax generally, see **Chapter 11**.

Entrepreneurs' relief

> **Focus**
>
> It is rare for property investors to be able to access this highly-prized relief, which effectively reduces CGT from (as much as) 28% to just 10%. Entrepreneurs' relief is generally reserved for trading activities, but has been extended to cover FHLs.

6.7 Entrepreneurs' relief applies a 10% tax rate to qualifying disposals by *individuals* (including individuals who are partners in a partnership) of:

- A business or a part of a business (generally a trading business);
- An interest in a business – interest in a partnership, or similar;
- A qualifying holding in a trading company, (usually at least 5%), in which the individual shareholder is an employee or officer.

There is a £10 million cumulative lifetime allowance for each individual in relation to the maximum gains for which they may claim entrepreneurs' relief.

Note that the disposal of mere assets does *not* generally qualify for entrepreneurs' relief: there must be a disposal either of qualifying shares or an interest in an eligible business, or a disposal at the business level (nevertheless, assets held personally that are disposed of alongside such qualifying disposals may rank as 'associated disposals'). This means that entrepreneurs' relief will not normally be available for disposals of one or two FHL properties out of a portfolio unless perhaps they might be argued to comprise a separately distinguishable and self-sustaining part of the business, as per *Jarmin v Rawlings Ch D 1994, 67 TC 130; [1994] STC 1005*; HMRC is known to have argued in the past that there is, however, only one FHL business.

There are minimum periods in relation to the period for which the trade, the interest and the office/employment (where appropriate) must have been held. The relevant legislation – essentially a re-animation of 'retirement relief' – is to be found at *TCGA 1992, s 169H* onwards. *TCGA 1992, s 241* specifically provides that FHLs qualify as trades for the purposes of entrepreneurs' relief (*TCGA 1992, s 241A* for EEA FHLs).

6.8 *Furnished holiday accommodation/lettings*

6.8 Investors' relief was introduced by *Finance Act 2016*, effectively as an addendum to entrepreneurs' relief. The aim of this new relief is to offer similar incentives to passive investors – those who do not actively participate in the business – but basically only where they subscribe for shares and hold them for a minimum of three years. While investors' relief essentially follows entrepreneurs' relief, it appears *FA 2016* did not amend *TCGA 1992, ss 241, 241A*, to which *TCGA 1992, s 165A(14)* looks in order fully to define a 'trade' and to open the definition so as to include FHLs for the various CGT reliefs listed above. This would seem to be at odds with the general theme of giving FHLs special CGT status.

Rollover relief (replacement of business assets)

6.9 This provides an opportunity for the trader to postpone a capital gain on a qualifying asset into the acquisition of a new qualifying asset (*TCGA 1992, s 152 et seq.*). For the purposes of this relief, FHLs qualify as trades (*TCGA 1992, ss 241, 241A*). The relief is available to individuals and to companies.

The gain effectively resurfaces on the disposal of the replacement asset – although it may in turn be 'rolled over' into a further replacement asset. Both the old and the new asset must have been (and immediately be) used only for the purposes of the trade, otherwise the relief may be restricted or excluded.

The trader has to reinvest all of the proceeds from the sale of the asset on which the gain has been made, in order to postpone all of the gain. There is no need to trace specific funds: provided an amount is invested equivalent to the proceeds of sale within the eligible timeframe, the postponement should be effective. Basically, the investment can be up to three years after the relevant sale/disposal, or even up to one year beforehand.

The list of eligible asset categories includes land and buildings, goodwill, fixed plant and machinery, ships, aircraft, hovercraft, satellites, space stations and other items similarly esoteric. A list is available at *TCGA 1992, s 155* but for simplicity it is assumed that the 'trader' will contemplate only replacement FHL land and buildings

> **Example 6.1 – Rollover relief on replacement of FHL property**
>
> Lucia has an FHL property that she bought in 2010/11 for £100,000 and sells in 2016/17 for £200,000, realising a gain of £100,000. It has been used as an FHL throughout her period of ownership.
>
> She buys a replacement FHL property in 2016/17 for £190,000. As she has not reinvested all of the proceeds, some of her gain will be chargeable immediately in 2016/17:
>
> Proceeds £200,000 – Reinvestment £190,000 = £10,000 chargeable gain (but subject to her CGT annual exemption, assuming it has not already been used elsewhere).

The remaining gain (£100,000 – £10,000 = £90,000) is deemed to have been reinvested into the second FHL property, which reduces that property's cost for CGT purposes as follows:

Actual cost £190,000 – rolled over gain £90,000 = £100,000.

If the replacement FHL property is sold for £220,000 in 2018/19, then while the 'real' gain is only £30,000, for CGT purposes Lucia will be deemed to make a capital gain of:

£220,000 – £100,000 = £120,000.

This is of course the 'real' gain of £30,000, together with the deferred original gain of £90,000 that was rolled into the second property.

Gift relief (gifts of business assets)

6.10 Many taxpayers wrongly assume that CGT can be avoided by simply giving an asset away. It is of course true that assets transferred between spouses or civil partners (broadly, while living together) generally escape a charge to CGT by virtue of *TCGA 1992, s 58*. That is not, however, because it is a gift but rather because of the special relationship between the parties involved. Strictly, the fact that it may be a gift is irrelevant, because the rules for such transfers ignore any consideration actually received, or not.

Special reliefs, etc, aside, the main CGT rules require a gift (or sale at undervalue) to be treated as a disposal at the market value of the asset, because it was not an arm's length transaction (*TCGA 1992, s 17*). Simply put, while a non-arm's-length transaction (and therefore a disposal deemed by statute to be at market value) is generally assumed for transfers between connected parties, (such as relatives, as defined), the 'market value rule' should also be applied whenever there is a gratuitous element to the transfer, even if the parties are not connected (see also *TCGA 1992, s 18*).

6.11 It is of course entirely possible for two unconnected parties simply to make a 'bad bargain' that does not reflect an asset's fair market value, for any number of commercially-driven reasons and the legislation effectively accepts this, where the parties are not connected: however, where they *are* connected, market value should be used and the actual consideration, if any, is effectively ignored.

Focus

Business asset gift relief allows an individual to postpone CGT that would otherwise accrue to him on the gift of a qualifying business asset (*TCGA 1992, s 165*). FHLs are qualifying business assets for the purposes of this relief (*TCGA 1992, ss 241, 241A*). The mechanism is quite similar to that for rollover relief above.

6.12 *Furnished holiday accommodation/lettings*

> **Example 6.2 – Gift of FHL property**
>
> Lucas has an FHL property worth £330,000, which he inherited at a deemed (probate) value of £200,000 many years ago. It has been used as an FHL throughout his period of ownership. If he were to sell it on the open market, he would expect to make a gain of:
>
> £330,000 – £200,000 = £130,000.
>
> He decides to give the property to his son, Finlay. Lucas is therefore potentially exposed to CGT on the transfer of the property because it is between connected parties, so will be deemed to have been sold for market value, regardless of actual proceeds. The same would apply if the transfer were to an unconnected party, and it could be shown that Lucas wanted to confer some gratuitous element (as distinct from, say, a commercially-driven discount, or ignorance of the asset's true value). However, the property qualifies for business asset gift relief because it is an FHL.
>
> If Lucas were to sell the FHL to his son, Finlay would pay £330,000 for the property and *his* base cost would be £330,000. *TCGA 1992, s 17* would also fix Finlay's base cost at £330,000 (both parties apply market value if s 17 is in point). But as a gift of an FHL, the transfer is eligible for gift relief, and on making the election Finlay's base cost is reduced by the gain held over:
>
> £330,000 – £130,000 = £200,000.
>
> In effect, Lucas' son Finlay ends up with the same base cost as Lucas did when Lucas inherited the property, and Lucas' postponed gain will resurface as and when Finlay disposes of the property. Note that it is possible to manipulate the gain not held over – perhaps to utilise Lucas' CGT annual exemption – by paying some actual consideration for the property.

Relief for loans to traders

6.12 When a person is unable to recover all of the money lent to an eligible business for a qualifying purpose, he or she may be able to claim a capital loss under the 'loans to traders' provisions (*TCGA 1992, s 253*). The legislation also allows a similar claim where a person is required to make a payment under the terms of a guarantee he has given on such a loan.

Relief may be restricted or even denied, however, where the investor is deemed to have brought about the circumstances by which the loan becomes irrecoverable.

The legislation used to apply to companies as well as to individuals, but the loan relationships regime takes precedence for loans made by companies (see

Furnished holiday accommodation/lettings **6.14**

CTA 2009, Pt 5, at *s 292 et seq.*). Companies will generally be able to get some measure of tax relief for debits (including impairments) against their business loans, in accordance with the loan relationship rules – although tax relief is not normally given for losses between connected parties.

A qualifying loan is one made to a UK resident person, (including a company), and used wholly for the purposes of a trade or profession, etc (an FHL qualifies as an eligible business by virtue of *TCGA 1992, ss 241, 241A*). Having recognised that the FHL regime had to be overhauled to include EEA properties, it seems entirely plausible to the author that it could be argued that a claim should be allowed if the loan were to a person, etc, resident in the EEA, rather than just in the UK – although, given the UK's current direction of travel in relation to the EU, such arguments may not carry so much weight in future.

As to company landlords, see **Chapter 10**, and **10.6** in particular.

Substantial shareholdings exemption

6.13 The substantial shareholdings exemption (SSE) allows a company to dispose of an interest in another company without being taxed on a capital gain – the fundamental rationale being that it will allow the disposing company to preserve its funds to re-invest in new trading or otherwise approved business activities.

The regime is complex and heavy on detail (although it is expected to be simplified in certain respects by changes in *Finance Bill 2017*) but, very simply, the investing company needs to have held at least a 10% stake in a 'trading' company for at least a year (*TCGA 1992, Sch 7AC*). An FHL business will qualify for these purposes as a trade, by virtue of *TCGA 1992, ss 241, 241A*.

This is an exemption, rather than a postponement of relief. One consequence of this is that the symmetry of *TCGA 1992, s 16* therefore applies: without specific provision to the contrary, provisions that except a gain from being taxable also make a capital loss unallowable.

DISADVANTAGES TO FHL STATUS

Having already noted above that FHLs are unable to access replacement domestic items relief (see **6.4**), further disadvantages include:

Restriction of losses

6.14 The scope of losses is limited, in that they:

- May be set only against future FHL profits of the same business for income tax purposes; (see **6.23** for more information, including for companies).

6.15 *Furnished holiday accommodation/lettings*

- Potentially restrict the utilisation of losses deriving from capital allowances (see **6.4**).

VAT

6.15 The provision of 'holiday accommodation' is generally taxable, from a VAT perspective. See VAT Notice 709/3: Hotels & Holiday Accommodation. Depending on the overall level of taxable supplies, VAT registration may be required.

CONDITIONS OF FURNISHED HOLIDAY ACCOMMODATION STATUS

6.16

> **Focus**
>
> In order to qualify for FHL status, the following conditions must be satisfied, in relation to each of the properties (or parts thereof) let as FHL accommodation, for the 'relevant period' (basically a year, but see **6.21** below) (*ITTOIA 2005, s 323*; *CTA 2009, s 265*).

The properties must be:

(a) **Furnished** – the legislation requires merely that the occupant be able to use the furniture, although HMRC says at PIM4105, 'we would expect sufficient furniture to be provided for normal occupation'; it seems unlikely, however, that an FHL would be inadequately furnished yet be commercially viable.

(b) **Commercial** – the accommodation must be let on a commercial basis, with a view to the realisation of profits.

6.17 Furthermore, accommodation will only qualify if **all** of the following three conditions are satisfied:

1. Availability condition

The accommodation must be available as an FHL for at least 210 days in the relevant period.

2. Letting condition

The accommodation must actually be let to the public for at least 105 days in the relevant period, ignoring lettings in the same occupation exceeding 31 days unless it is due to illness, accident or similarly unusual/unforeseen circumstances.

The 210-day and 105-day conditions represent a 50% increase on the pre-2012/13 values of 140 and 70 days respectively.

Furnished holiday accommodation/lettings **6.18**

3. Pattern of occupation condition

The accommodation must not be occupied for more than 155 days in the relevant period, for periods in excess of 31 days; however, the test is based on the lessor's intentions, rather than actual occupation accidentally or occasionally exceeding 31 days, and this would not necessarily preclude extensive personal occupation by the owner 'out of season' – see PIM4112.

To help with these conditions in the face of what can often be a fleeting domestic holiday season, there are two saving provisions:

(a) Averaging election

6.18 If there is more than one property (or part thereof) being let as an FHL, then it is possible to test the letting condition against the average occupation rate for all or part of the FHL portfolio. This 'averaging election' may therefore save one or more FHLs that would otherwise fail individually. UK and EEA portfolios are two separate portfolios and cannot be mixed for averaging purposes. See also the 'period of grace' election at **6.19** below.

The election must be made no later than the second 31 January following the tax year in question (the normal time limit for amending a tax return). It must specify both the already-qualifying holiday accommodation to be included and any or all of the under-occupied furnished accommodation, but the qualifying holiday accommodation cannot be re-used, so as to feature in more than one averaging election per tax year; the approach for companies is similar except accounting periods replace tax years and the time limit for corporate elections is two years following the end of the accounting period (*ITTOIA 2005, s 326; CTA 2009, s 268*).

> **Example 6.3 – Averaging election**
>
> Charlotte has three holiday cottages, which satisfy the relevant conditions in 2016/17 as to all but actual occupation, with no period being in excess of 31 days, as follows:
>
> | | |
> |---|---|
> | Cottage A | 130 days |
> | Cottage B | 100 days |
> | Cottage C | 115 days |

Clearly, Cottage B fails the standard 105-day test. But the portfolio average is 115 days – comfortably above the minimum threshold. An averaging election would mean that Cottage B would qualify as an FHL for 2016/17.

6.19 *Furnished holiday accommodation/lettings*

(b)   Period of grace election

6.19   Where a property has passed the letting condition, either by virtue of actual occupation for 105+ days or by virtue of an averaging election as above, then a 'period of grace' election may safeguard that accommodation's FHL status for up to the next two tax years, provided:

- the accommodation would satisfy all other relevant conditions than actual occupation; and
- there was a genuine intention to meet the letting condition during the grace period; and
- if the grace period extends to two tax years, a valid election has been made for the first tax year of the grace period.

The election deadline is again the second 31 January following the relevant tax year.

The approach for companies is similar except accounting periods replace tax years and the time limit for corporate elections is two years following the end of the accounting period (*ITTOIA 2005, s 326A*; *CTA 2009, s 268A*).

6.20   Note that, while an averaging election can make accommodation qualifying so that the next two years may then benefit from a period of grace election, a period of grace election does not make accommodation qualify for the purposes of an averaging election, because only actual qualifying days of occupation are counted in an averaging election.

> **Focus**
>
> Nevertheless, an averaging election does not have to include all non-qualifying accommodation: it is possible, for example, to exclude from an averaging election any accommodation that has been saved under a period of grace election. This allows the averaging election to concentrate on properties that might otherwise fail, due to weaker averages.

Example 6.4 – Period of grace election

Charles has four holiday cottages that would pass all FHL criteria save for the actual letting condition, with actual occupation as follows:

Cottage A	2016/17 140 days	2017/18 120 days
Cottage B	2016/17 110 days	2017/18 115 days
Cottage C	2016/17 100 days	2017/18 61 days
Cottage D	2016/17 90 days	2017/18 100 days
Average	2016/17 110 days	2017/18 99 days

Furnished holiday accommodation/lettings **6.23**

> Clearly, an averaging election may be made across the entire portfolio for 2016/17, securing FHL status for Cottages C and D that would otherwise fail. But this would not be sufficient for 2017/18 because of Cottage C's poor occupation record. However, if (after having averaged in 2016/17) Charles in 2017/18 makes a valid 'period of grace' election in respect of Cottage C, and separately an averaging election for Cottages A, B and D, he will secure FHL status for all four cottages – the average occupation for A, B and D being comfortably above 105 days.

Relevant period

6.21 When determining whether or not the above conditions or criteria have been met, the relevant period is usually the tax year for income tax purposes, although where the FHL is let by a partnership whose trade or similar has a different basis year, then the basis year should be followed.

Where the accommodation was not let as furnished accommodation in the previous tax year, then the relevant period is the 12 months beginning with the first day in the tax year on which it is let as furnished accommodation.

Where the accommodation was let out as furnished accommodation in the previous tax year but not in the following tax year, the relevant period is the 12 months ending in the tax year, in which it was let as furnished accommodation (*ITTOIA 2005, s 324*, see also PIM4105 and PIM1040).

6.22 Companies will generally work to the relevant accounting period (or, if not a 12 month period, the 12 months ending with the last day of the accounting period) but:

- Where the accommodation was not let in the previous accounting period, then the relevant period is the 12 months beginning with the first day in the accounting period on which it was let as furnished accommodation.

- Where the accommodation *was* let as furnished accommodation in the 12 months immediately before the accounting period but not in the 12 months immediately after the accounting period, then the relevant year is the 12 months ending with the last day in the accounting period on which it is let by the company as furnished accommodation (*CTA 2009, s 266*).

FHL LOSSES

6.23 FHL losses are much more restricted under the 'new', post-FA 2011 regime. The losses are treated as trading losses, but despite the flexibility normally attaching to such losses FHL 'trading' losses may only be carried forward to set against the future profits of that FHL (pooled) business – noting

6.24 *Furnished holiday accommodation/lettings*

that there is a separate UK FHL pool, distinct from any EEA FHL pool (if there are any EEA FHL properties).

Therefore, a UK FHL pool loss may not even be set against EEA FHL profits, and *vice versa*, but only against future UK FHL pool profits.

At the time of writing, this summary applies equally for CT as it does for IT purposes, putting them at a significant disadvantage to 'ordinary' property business losses, which are much more flexible (*ITA 2007, ss 127, 127A; CTA 2010, ss 65, 67A*). However, a new, more permissive regime for corporate losses has been drafted in FB 2017. It seems that the Government intends that, out of all property businesses, only ordinary (non-FHL) property businesses should be affected, but it remains to be seen whether the new legislation affording more flexibility for trading losses arising from April 2017 (ie, they may in some cases be carried forwards against total profits rather than only profits of the same trade) successfully excludes FHL losses, which operate through the same parts of the legislation.

As to loss relief generally, see **Chapter 7**.

> **Focus**
>
> Considering that it is quite common for significant expenditure to arise on first acquiring a property, it may well be advantageous for the property to be made *not* to qualify as an FHL but as part of an ordinary property business asset instead, to incur those initial expenses which may then be pooled with other 'ordinary' property business properties, and later on to be taken to the FHL business.

This short term but potentially valuable advantage would have to be weighed against the implications for capital allowances and moving between non-qualifying/qualifying status; also the possible effect on future capital gains reliefs because the property may not be a qualifying asset for the entire period of ownership (see **6.6** above).

INHERITANCE TAX AND BUSINESS PROPERTY RELIEF

6.24 Unlike with IT and CGT, there is no specific provision for furnished holiday accommodation in relation to inheritance tax (IHT).

FHL owners have in the past been able to secure business property relief (BPR) for their businesses under *IHTA 1984, Pt V, Ch 1 (s 103 et seq.)* which, when granted, will usually remove 100% of the value of the business from the estate.

BPR is generally available to trading businesses, and it might reasonably be assumed that FHLs should qualify, given their 'quasi-trading' status. Indeed, HMRC used to agree with this, and old guidance in HMRC's Inheritance Tax manual used to confirm that BPR would be given where the lettings were short-term and there was substantial involvement with the activities of the holiday-makers.

Unfortunately, HMRC had a change of heart several years ago, which could be said to have manifested itself in the *Pawson* cases (see **6.25**).

> **Focus**
>
> The main problem for FHLs in terms of BPR is that a business – even with trading characteristics – is excluded if it consists wholly or mainly of making or holding investments (*IHTA 1984, s 105(3)*).

HMRC has concluded that the level of business activity has to be substantial in order to offset the investment aspect of an FHL business. HMRC has updated its guidance at IHTM25278, to state:

'Recent advice from Solicitor's Office has caused us to reconsider our [previously permissive] approach and it may well be that some cases that might have previously qualified should not have done so. In particular we will be looking more closely at the level and type of services, rather than who provided them.

Until further notice any case involving a claim for business property relief on a holiday let should be referred to the Technical Team (Litigation) for consideration at an early stage.'

6.25 In *HMRC v Pawson (Deceased)* [2013] UKUT 050 (TCC), the Upper Tribunal found against the taxpayer's claim for BPR, overturning the FTT's finding for the taxpayer. The activities which relate to letting property are at risk of being excluded since they can be categorised as being undertaken by ordinary property rental businesses, which *do* consist wholly or mainly of making or holding investments. Those running FHL properties – and even more mainstream buy-to-let properties – might argue with the distinction.

There are of course numerous hotels that offer 'no frills' accommodation; the growth of casual letting such as 'AirBnB' or similar, taken together with FHLs that offer considerably more than just accommodation make an unhappy confluence that HMRC and the courts may struggle to untangle to everyone's satisfaction. Certainly those FHLs that offer substantial levels of customer service should not take *Pawson* as the last word on eligibility for BPR and IHT relief.

For commentary on IHT generally, see **Chapter 12**.

HMRC GUIDANCE ON FHLs

6.26 With regard to the 'new' rules for FHLs from 2011/12 onwards, HMRC's Property Income manual states the following at PIM4113:

6.26 *Furnished holiday accommodation/lettings*

'The guidance for 2011–12 and following is available in Helpsheet 253 Furnished Holiday Lettings. It covers the changes to the rules for 2011–12 and for 2012–13 and following and is designed to provide help to most owners of furnished holiday lettings properties. Further more detailed technical guidance will be added to this manual in due course.'

Bearing in mind we are now in 2016/17, it is fortunate that HS253 makes a decent fist of the IT and CGT aspects of FHLs: www.hmrc.gov.uk/helpsheets/hs253.pdf. One can only hope that the manual guidance proper, once installed, proves to have been worth the wait.

Chapter 7

Loss relief

James Darmon BA Cantab ACA, Consultant, The TACS Partnership

> SIGNPOSTS
>
> - **Scope** – A property rental business is broadly treated as a single business. Losses are generally carried forward (see **7.1–7.4**).
>
> - **Loss relief against general income** – 'Sideways' relief for rental losses is available only in very limited circumstances (see **7.5–7.7**).
>
> - **Uncommercial lettings** – Losses from such lettings cannot be set off against rent and other income (see **7.8**).
>
> - **Multiple businesses** – An individual can obtain property income in a number of different capacities. However, rental business losses can only be set off against profits from the same rental business (see **7.9–7.11**).
>
> - **Capital allowances** – Losses may be set off against other income to the extent that they relate to capital allowances, although these are not available for plant installed in dwellings (this term excludes common areas of blocks of flats). Capital allowances may be available on the purchase of equipment, which in some cases may give rise to a loss (see **7.12–7.13**).
>
> - **Agricultural expenses** – Where agricultural land forms part of the rental business and a loss is incurred on that rental business, the taxpayer may set 'the agricultural part of the loss' against general income (see **7.14**).
>
> - **Furnished holiday lettings** – UK and European Economic Area (EEA) businesses are counted as separate businesses, so it is not possible to set off (say) losses in a UK furnished holiday letting business against profits of the EEA business (see **7.15–7.16**).
>
> - **Company losses** – Losses from UK property letting by a company are subject to relief in a specified order. The rules are modified in relation to overseas property (see **7.17–7.18**).

7.1 *Loss relief*

INCOME TAX

Overview

7.1 There are various ways of holding property for letting. It can be held by an individual, by two or more individuals together (in which case it may be a partnership), a trust (in which case the taxable person is the trustees as a body), or a company (either incorporated in the UK or overseas). For tax purposes these are all treated as persons. In the case of a UK resident company, the profits are assessed to corporation tax. In all other cases, they are assessed to income tax.

Losses are generally computed in the same way as profits.

> **Focus**
>
> Where a person owns two or more rental properties which are commercially let, this is treated as a single business (so the profit or loss is the total business profit or loss).

As noted in **Chapter 3**, income tax relief for finance costs related to residential property businesses (eg mortgage interest payable) is being phased out from 6 April 2017, and replaced with a basic rate tax credit.

These changes are being introduced over a four-year period. Once the changes have been fully implemented, it is likely that the loss relief rules will be of limited future benefit, because the major current deductible expense in computing rental income profit (mortgage interest on loans to buy, and often improve, the property) will no longer be deductible (but see **7.3** below).

The new rules were introduced in *Finance (No 2) Act 2015*, and amended in *Finance Act 2016*, and are discussed further at **7.4** below.

These restrictions for finance costs do not apply to companies. This has prompted many individual landlords, or landlords involved in property partnerships, to consider incorporating their buy-to-let property rental businesses (see **Chapter 13**).

7.2 Rental business losses are computed in the same way as profits for tax purposes. Where the property is let (or available for letting) at arm's length, relief is available for any resulting losses.

7.3 The first method of claiming loss relief is by way of carry forward (under *ITA 2007, ss 118, 119*). Losses are set against the first available rental business profits (ie rental income, less allowable costs, including repairs and legal costs – see **Example 7.1** below), and must be set in full to the extent that there are available profits. They cannot be set off against income other than rental income (with the limited exceptions noted at **7.5** below).

Loss relief **7.4**

Example 7.1 – Loss relief: current system

Fred has the following property business profits and losses:

2011/12	Loss	£(5,000)
2012/13	Profit	£3,000
2013/14	Loss	£(1,000)
2014/15	Profit	£8,000

Fred cannot make any of the claims to set off losses against other income described below.

Fred's rental profits for these years are as follows:

2011/12	No taxable profit	Loss of £5,000 to carry forward
2012/13	£3,000 profit set off against Loss brought forward	Loss of £2,000 to carry forward
2013/14	No taxable profit	Loss of £3,000 to carry forward
2014/15	Taxable profit of £5,000	No loss available to carry forward.

The rules for setting off losses from property businesses are contained in *ITA 2007, Pt 4, Ch 4* (ie ss 117 and following).

7.4 It is not possible to elect to claim a smaller amount than the total loss available for set off (for example, to take advantage of personal allowances).

In **Example 7.2** below, Fred could not claim to set off a lower amount than £8,750 in the year to 5 April 2017. It should be noted here that, since the main constituent of property business expenses has frequently been interest payments, the changes to tax relief for interest (ie a basic rate tax credit, rather than deductible expenses) may mean that the issue of losses is likely to be less relevant in future years for many residential rental property businesses.

Finance (No 2) Act 2015, s 24 introduced a gradual withdrawal of interest relief by deduction, commencing from 6 April 2017. The original provisions were subsequently amended in *Finance Act 2016, s 26*. To the extent that relief is not available as a deduction from rental income, it will be given by way of a basic rate tax credit. The detailed rules are set out in *ITTOIA 2005, ss 272A–272B; ss 274A–274C;* and *ITA 2007, ss 399A–399B*. The rules work in a similar way for partnerships and trustees, but do not apply to companies.

This restriction in relief for finance costs may result in many property businesses, particularly those which are highly geared, seeking to use the benefit of incorporation (see **Chapter 13**).

7.4 Loss relief

Example 7.2 – Loss relief and interest relief

Fred is a 40% taxpayer. He lets property, and has the following income and expenditure:

Year to 5 April	Net rental income	Interest cost	Profit/(loss)
2017	£5,000	£15,000	£(10,000)
2018	£20,000	£15,000	£5,000
2019	£20,000	£15,000	£5,000

It appears (subject to HMRC confirmation) that loss relief will work as follows:

Losses

2016/17:	Rental income	£5,000	
	Less Interest relief	£15,000	
	Loss to carry forward	£(10,000)	£(10,000)
	Taxable income	nil	
2017/18:	Rental income	£20,000	
	Less Interest relief (75%)	£11,250	
	Loss relief	£8,750	£8,750
	Taxable income	nil	
	Tax credit (20% of £3,750)	£750	
2018/19	Rental income	£20,000	
	Less Interest relief (50%)	£7,500	
	Loss relief	£1,250	£1,250
	Taxable income	£11,250	
	Tax at 40%	£4,500	
	Tax credit (20% of £7,500)	£1,500	
	Tax payable	£3,000	
	Losses carried forward	Nil	

The unused tax credit in 2017/18 (£750 above) will be set off against other income, or carried forward (*ITA 2007, s 26 and ITTOIA 2005, s 274AA(4)*).

Loss relief **7.6**

As an aside, it should be noted that, in the year to 5 April 2021, and assuming the rental income remains at £20,000, and interest at £15,000, Fred pays tax at an effective rate of 100%, as follows:

'Real' rental profit (as above)	£5,000
Tax at 40% on rental income of £20,000	£8,000
Less Tax credit at 20% of £15,000	£3,000
Tax charge	£5,000

Additional claims

7.5 In certain circumstances, relief for rental losses does not need to be restricted to future rental profits. It may instead be available (under *ITA 2007, ss 120–124* against general income to the extent that:

- the loss is due to certain types of capital allowance on plant and machinery; or
- the loss relates to certain agricultural expenses.

Whilst a UK property business is a qualifying business for capital allowances purposes (*CAA 2001, s 15*), capital allowances are not generally available to set off against rental income for plant installed in dwellings (see *CA 2001, s 35*). However, they can be claimed against plant installed in communal areas, for example in a block of flats. It should be noted that, where a taxpayer claims loss relief against general income (known as 'sideways' loss relief), they must take the full amount of the loss available up to the amount of general income. The claim must be for the full amount of the loss, up to the available income, or none. It is not possible to opt to take a defined quantity.

> **Example 7.3 – Use of losses**
>
> John has total income (before rental losses) for 2016/17 of £20,000.
>
> He owns a block of flats in which he has installed a new boiler, at a cost of £15,000, which attracts 100% relief.
>
> He cannot restrict the loss relief claim to £9,000, and use his full personal allowance: the claim must be for the full £15,000.

7.6 Any loss relief must be by way of claim, made by 31 January some 22 months from the end of the year of assessment (for example, for the year ended 5 April 2016, the claim must be made by 31 January 2018; see *ITA 2007, s 124(1)*). Where property business losses can be set off against general income, they are available to set off against income of the same year. If this does not

7.7 *Loss relief*

use up all the losses, the remainder can be set off against general income of the following year.

7.7 From 2013/14 onwards, there is an overall cap on loss utilisation of the higher of £50,000 and 25% of total income (under *ITA 2007, s 24A*). This includes property losses.

Relief against general income used to be available to the extent that the loss arose on furnished holiday lettings. However, this relief was discontinued in 2010/11.

Uncommercial lettings

7.8 The foregoing loss relief claim rules only apply where the loss arises from the commercial letting of property. Where property has been let on uncommercial terms (eg to a relative), any losses arising are not available to set off against the remaining rental property business.

> **Example 7.4 – Loss on property let on uncommercial terms**
>
> Diane owns five properties. She lets four of them on commercial terms, and the other is let to her partner, Jeremy, on generous terms.
>
> If the property let to Jeremy generates a loss, this loss is not considered part of the property business loss, and is not available for set off.

Multiple businesses

7.9 Rental business losses can only be set off against profits from the same rental business. Therefore, if that business ceases, the losses are lost, even if the taxpayer subsequently starts a new rental business. HMRC guidance on whether a business has ceased, and a new one commenced, or whether the same business continues, is set out in HMRC's Property Income manual at PIM2500-2510.

In addition, a taxpayer cannot set off losses incurred in one capacity (for example on property held in his sole name) against profits in another capacity (for example, as a member of a property investment partnership).

> **Focus**
>
> In cases, therefore, where rental income stops then restarts and the taxpayer has losses brought forward, it may be necessary to justify any claim that the 'new' rental business is in fact a continuation of the 'old' one.

Where appropriate, invoices, correspondence with letting agents, etc, should be retained to demonstrate the continuation of the business.

> **Example 7.5 – Continuing business**
>
> Andy owned a property for letting, but it stood empty for some period, so he decided to sell it. He spent £10,000 on repairs.
>
> If Andy makes clear to the estate agent that he intends to invest the proceeds in new property, and instructs the agent to look for such property, he should be able to make a case that the business is continuing, even if he cannot find a suitable property immediately. He should retain evidence of the search.

7.10 As indicated at **7.9**, an individual can obtain property income in a number of different capacities. For example, the individual could:

- hold property in their own name;
- be a partner in a partnership, and have a partnership share in the income of property owned by that partnership; and
- be a trustee of a trust which receives rental income.

> **Focus**
>
> These would all be treated as different rental businesses, and losses from one business cannot be offset against profits from another.

Any losses in a rental business are automatically carried forward, and can be set off against future rental business profits (*ITA 2007, ss 118, 119*).

Rental business losses cannot, however, be set off against the taxpayer's other income, except in the limited circumstances set out in **7.5** above.

7.11 The set off of losses brought forward against rental profits is automatic, and no claim is required. The taxpayer simply deducts losses brought forward when calculating the rental business profit for the current year. If that rental business profit is insufficient, or further losses are incurred in the following year, these losses are aggregated and set off against profits in the future years. The carry forward can be indefinite.

If any of the loss can be used against general income of that same year, that element is, of course, not available for carry forward. The amount available for carry forward is therefore correspondingly reduced.

Capital allowances

7.12 As noted at **7.5** above, losses may be set off against other income to the extent that they relate to capital allowances. As mentioned, capital allowances are not available for plant installed in dwellings (*CAA 2001, s 35*)

7.13 *Loss relief*

(this term excludes common areas of blocks of flats, as explained in the Capital Allowances manual at CA20020), but it is possible that equipment purchased for the business might be subject to capital allowances, giving rise to a loss.

Capital allowances are discussed in more detail in **Chapter 3**. Because capital allowances cannot be claimed for most residential property rental costs, losses attributable to capital allowances are fairly unusual.

7.13   The available loss is the lowest of:

- the taxpayer's total income for the year, after deducting any rental business losses brought forward, to the extent that rental business income has been set off against them, and after deducting any sideways relief for the previous year's loss;
- the amount of rental business loss made in the year;
- the net capital allowances after any balancing charge.

Such a set-off is subject to a claim, which must be made by 31 January, just less than 22 months after the year end. For example, for the year ended 5 April 2016, the claim must be made by 31 January 2018 – see *ITA 2007, s 124(1)*). The detailed rules are in *ITA 2007, ss 120–124*.

> **Example 7.6 – Losses attributable to capital allowances**
>
> Kevin owns a block of flats let to students. His rental income, less costs, is £30,000 per annum. He invests £50,000 in a new and improved heating system installed in the common areas, and claims 100% annual investment allowances on the whole of this expenditure, resulting in a loss of £20,000 for tax purposes.
>
> This loss is available to set off against Kevin's other income.

Agricultural expenses

7.14   When agricultural land forms part of the rental business and a loss is incurred on that rental business, the taxpayer may set 'the agricultural part of the loss' against general income, in the same way as losses attributable to capital allowances, and under the same legislation (*ITA 2007, ss 120–124*).

The agricultural part of the expenditure for this purpose comprises such matters as maintenance, repairs, insurance and management of the agricultural land, but not interest payable on any loan to buy it.

Again, this loss can be set off against the general income of either the tax year in which the rental loss was made, or the following tax year. The amount of loss relief available is the lowest of the three figures, calculated in the same way as that for capital allowance purposes.

Furnished holiday lettings

7.15 Historically, up to the 2010/11 tax year, taxpayers letting furnished holiday accommodation could claim any loss element against general income or capital gains.

For 2011/12 onwards, it is possible to have either an EEA holiday letting business (ie a holiday letting business in a European Economic Area territory), or a UK holiday letting business, depending on where the let property is located. UK and EEA holiday lettings are treated as two separate businesses.

If either incurs a loss, it is possible to set that loss against future profits of the same business. For this purpose, the UK and EEA businesses are counted as separate businesses, so it is not possible to set off (say) losses in the UK furnished holiday letting business against profits of the EEA business.

7.16 'Holiday letting' for this purpose means property which is:

Available for commercial letting	210 days (140 days for 2011/12 and earlier years)
Actually let commercially	105 days (70 days in 2011/12 and earlier years)
	Note – a period of longer-term occupation is not a letting as holiday accommodation (see below)
Pattern of occupation	No more than 155 days of longer-term occupation. This means occupation for a continuous period of more than 30 days.

Furnished holiday lettings are discussed in detail in **Chapter 6**.

CORPORATION TAX

7.17 Relief for corporation tax losses on property investment are discussed in more detail in **Chapter 10** (see **10.7–10.8**). The position (for 2016/17) is broadly summarised as below.

A company's UK property losses are given relief in the following order (*CTA 2010, ss 62, 63, 99(1)(e)*):

- Firstly, losses are set against the company's total profits for the same accounting period;
- If there are insufficient profits to relieve the loss, it is carried forward to subsequent accounting periods, to be set against total profits;
- Excess losses are carried forward in this way until the property business ceases. If there is still an excess loss at this point, it can be carried forward and treated as a management expense;

7.18 *Loss relief*

- Losses can also be surrendered to other group companies under the group relief provisions.

7.18 For investment in overseas property, the rules are modified so that losses are automatically carried forward to subsequent accounting periods. There is no set off against total profits as is the case with a UK property business (*CTA 2010, s 66*).

It should be noted that it is not possible to buy a company with property losses with a view to setting those losses off against property profits (*CTA 2010, s 704*). The losses are disallowed where there is a change of ownership, as defined in *CTA 2010, s 719*.

7.19 For periods after 1 April 2017, the Government proposes to legislate in *Finance Bill 2017* to remove the requirement to stream corporate losses between different activities. This will allow (for example) property losses to be set off against trading income of other group companies.

Chapter 8

Jointly-owned properties

Malcolm Finney, Tax Consultant

SIGNPOSTS

- **Introduction** – The concept of co-ownership of land involves ownership by two or more persons concurrently, not successively. The term 'land' includes any buildings on the land. Co-ownership of land involves the land being held under a trust (see **8.1–8.4**).

- **Categories of ownership** – Legal and beneficial ownership of land are two very different types of ownership. Legal ownership refers to legal title and can be held by persons only as joint tenants. Beneficial ownership, however, is capable of being held by persons as joint tenants or tenants in common. The form in which land is held beneficially has important tax and non-tax consequences (see **8.5–8.9**).

- **Purchase of land** – The purchase of land is typically a three-stage process involving exchange of contracts, transfer of the land and registration of ownership with Land Registry. On registration, co-owners agree their respective beneficial interests. Typically, most buy-to-let properties are mortgaged, which may have both tax and stamp duty land tax implications (see **8.10–8.18**).

- **Beneficial ownership: conversion and severance** – Land held beneficially as joint tenants or tenants in common can be subsequently changed from one form to the other quite readily. Normally, the conversion is from joint tenants to tenants in common involving severance of the joint tenancy. Severance can only be effected during a person's lifetime (see **8.19–8.22**).

- **Sole legal ownership: spouses and tax** – The various tax and non-tax implications of co-ownership vary as between land held by spouses and land held by non-spouses. Typically, for spouses, inter-spouse transfers of beneficial interests do not involve significant tax consequences. Invariably, entitlement to rental income simply follows beneficial entitlements; where this is not the case consideration of the income tax settlement provisions is required (see **8.23–8.27**).

Jointly-owned properties

- **Conversion from sole to joint legal title** – Usually, such conversion produces no immediate tax effects if the beneficial interests of the co-owners remain unchanged. If not, then there may be important income tax consequences and where the buy-to-let is mortgaged possible stamp duty land tax liabilities may arise (see **8.28–8.29**).

- **Joint legal ownership: spouses and tax** – The various tax and non-tax implications of co-ownership vary as between land held by spouses and land held by non-spouses. Typically, for spouses, inter-spouse transfers of beneficial interests do not involve significant tax consequences. Invariably, entitlement to rental income simply follows beneficial entitlements; where this is not the case consideration of the income tax settlement provisions is required. One of the key differences where legal title is held in one spouse's name as compared to where it is held jointly is that in the latter case specific legislation (*ITA 2007, s 836*) specifies for income tax (but not inheritance tax or capital gains tax) purposes how any rental income is to be split between the spouses irrespective of their respective percentage beneficial ownership; this, however, is subject to the possibility of a declaration being filed with HMRC (*ITA 2007, s 837*) (see **8.30–8.41**).

- **Manipulation of legal/beneficial interests** – Whilst often manipulation by spouses of their respective beneficial interests is undertaken to mitigate income tax liabilities on rental income, this can adversely affect future capital gains tax charges on a disposal (eg gift or sale). It is often forgotten by spouses that co-ownership involves land held under a trust and as trustees they (ie the spouses) have certain responsibilities (one of which is to act in the best interests of the beneficiaries). Thus, for example, a sole spouse trustee must act in the best interest of both spouse beneficiaries where each spouse has a beneficial interest in land (irrespective of the percentage held), not just in their own best interest (see **8.42**).

- **Expenses** – In calculating the taxable profit arising on rental income from a buy-to-let expenses may be deducted assuming, inter alia, they have been incurred wholly and exclusively for the purposes of the property business. Typically, expenses should be split in the same ratio as the rental income is split which in turn should ideally reflect the underlying beneficial interests in the buy-to-let (see **8.43–8.46**).

- **Sole and joint legal ownership: non-spouse and tax** – The legislative provision (*ITA 2007, s 836*) applicable for income tax purposes where a buy-to-let is legally jointly owned is inapplicable to non-spouse co-ownership. Furthermore, transfers of beneficial interests between non-spouses are not (of course) inter-spouse transfers; in which case, possible inheritance tax and capital gains tax charges may arise immediately on such transfers (unlike with respect to spouse transfers). However, the options available to non-spouses with respect to structuring legal and beneficial co-ownership are the same as for spouses (see **8.47–8.49**).

- **Parent/child co-ownership** – The age of the child is critical in determining the income tax consequences on co-owned property. In the case of minors (ie children below age 18) any rental income attributed to their beneficial share of the property may be subject to income tax on their parent(s) under the settlement provisions (*ITTOIA 2005, s 629*) (see **8.50–8.51**).

- **Grandparent/child co-ownership** – The age of the child is not critical in determining the income tax consequences on co-owned property. Any rental income attributed to the grandchild's beneficial share of the property is subject to income tax on the part of the grandchild (see **8.52**).

- **Succession** – A buy-to-let property is likely to be a valuable asset for the co-owner. Unfortunately, many co-owners who hold their beneficial interest as joint beneficial tenants overlook the fact that on death the survivorship rule applies to their beneficial interest, not their will. Whilst a post-death severance may be feasible for IHT purposes, a number of conditions need to be satisfied (*IHTA 1984, s 142*) (see **8.53–8.57**).

- **Non-UK domiciled individuals** – Non-UK domiciled individuals are able to own interests in buy-to-lets in exactly the same manner as a UK domiciled individual. One key difference is in connection with inter-spouse transfers for inheritance tax purposes. An inter-spouse transfer from a UK domiciled spouse to a non-UK domiciled spouse is not exempt without limit; there is an exemption limit currently equal to the nil-rate band (ie £325,000). Where a buy-to-let property is thus owned by a UK and non-UK domiciled spouse, on the death of the former an inheritance tax charge may arise, which would not normally occur (ie as between two UK domiciled spouses) (see **8.58–8.60**).

INTRODUCTION

8.1 Almost without exception all types of property can be held jointly. Land (realty/real estate) is just one kind of property which may be so held. A common alternative to the term 'joint ownership' is 'co-ownership' (both terms will be used in this chapter interchangeably).

8.2 Jointly-owned properties

Joint ownership typically refers to the position where two or more persons (which includes individuals) hold an interest (legal and/or beneficial) in land in possession at the same time ie their interests are concurrent not successive. By 'in possession' is meant that the interest is not in remainder or in reversion; it does not refer to physical possession.

Reference to 'land' includes any buildings on the land (*LPA 1925, s 205* provides: 'Land includes …buildings…..').

This chapter assumes all land is situated in England or Wales.

8.2 English law recognises two forms of property ownership: 'legal' and 'beneficial', and it is not uncommon for the legal ownership of land to be divorced from its beneficial ownership (ie held by different persons) although in many cases the legal *and* beneficial ownership are held by the same person(s).

8.3 Beneficial ownership gives the right of enjoyment of the land (including occupation and the right to any income therefrom) and the person who has the beneficial ownership owns an equitable interest in the property. Legal ownership refers to ownership of the legal estate. Legal ownership, without beneficial ownership, of land grants no rights of enjoyment of the land to the legal owner who is required to deal with the property only as the beneficial owner dictates.

Legal ownership, in essence, refers to the nominal or paper title to property; beneficial ownership, on the other hand, refers to the substantive ownership of property.

As indicated above, the legal and beneficial interests in the land may vest in one person or possibly two or more persons.

8.4 Co-ownership may, in principle, subsist either in the form of the joint tenancy or the tenancy in common.

Where co-ownership subsists the land is held under a trust of land (*LPA, ss 34–36*, as amended by TOLATA 1996; formerly under a trust for sale). The trust is imposed by statute, and in effect separates the powers of management and disposition of the land from enjoyment of it. The legal owner(s) possess the rights of power and disposition over the land, and the beneficial owners possess the rights of enjoyment of it.

The legal owners and beneficial owners may, or may not, be the same persons:

Example 8.1 – Identical legal and beneficial owners

X conveys the legal estate in land to A, B and C.

A, B and C hold the land under a trust of land for themselves as beneficial joint tenants.

> **Example 8.2 – Different legal and beneficial owners**
>
> X conveys the legal estate in land to A, B and C.
>
> A, B and C hold the land under a trust of land for beneficial tenants in common X and Y.
>
> **Example 8.3 – Mixture of legal and beneficial owners**
>
> X conveys the legal estate in land to A, B and C.
>
> A, B and C hold the land under a trust of land for beneficial joint tenants A, X and Y.

CATEGORIES OF OWNERSHIP

8.5 A person may hold the legal title to land, or may have a beneficial interest in land, or both the legal title and beneficial ownership may be combined in the one person.

Legal title/ownership

8.6 Legal ownership of land can only take the form of a joint tenancy; 'a legal estate is not capable of subsisting or of being created in an undivided share' (*LPA 1925, ss 1, 36*).

A key feature of a joint tenancy is that each co-owner is not treated as owning a distinct share in the land, although in aggregate all the co-owners own the whole property (thus one joint tenant cannot have a greater interest than another joint tenant).

This has the potentially very important consequence that it is not possible for a joint tenant to leave their interest in the land by will and thus, on death, that interest simply ceases to exist (ie is extinguished) and accrues (ie vests) automatically to the remaining (ie surviving) joint tenant(s) by survivorship (or, *jus accrescendi*).

> **Example 8.4 – Joint tenancy and legal title**
>
> A, B and C hold the legal title to land as joint tenants. A dies.
>
> The legal title automatically then vests in the survivors B and C.
>
> B then dies. The legal title then vests in C alone, the sole survivor.
>
> On C's death the legal title passes under C's will or intestacy.

8.7 *Jointly-owned properties*

Where it is necessary to ascertain who died first out of, say, two joint tenants in the case of contemporaneous deaths (eg a plane crash), *LPA 1925, s 184* provides that the younger is deemed to have survived the older (contrast this with the position for inheritance tax purposes as provided in *IHTA 1984, s 4(2)*).

Beneficial ownership

8.7 Beneficial ownership, unlike legal ownership, of land may take the form of joint tenants or tenants in common.

8.8 Beneficial ownership held as joint tenants follows the same rules in the same manner as where legal ownership is held as a joint tenancy (see **8.6** above); in particular, the right of survivorship applies on death of a co-owner.

However, beneficial ownership held as tenants in common, unlike a beneficial joint tenancy, confers on a co-owner a distinct beneficial share of the land which is capable of being left by will (failing which the laws of intestacy apply); thus, the other co-owners do not automatically take the deceased co-owner's interest on death by survivorship as is the case with a joint tenancy. This has potentially very important implications for structuring ownership of land both for taxation and succession purposes.

> **Focus**
>
> Land owned beneficially by a married couple as tenants in common may mean that on the death of one of the spouses the deceased spouse's beneficial interest may be left by will to someone other than the surviving spouse (eg to the deceased's spouse's two children from a former marriage), which may not be what the surviving spouse had expected to happen.

8.9 The distinct beneficial share owned by a tenant in common is an undivided share in the land and, as a consequence, each co-owner is in fact entitled to possession (albeit not exclusive possession) of the whole of the land not just that share (reference to an undivided share simply means that the property is not physically divided).

Although beneficial joint tenants always each own the same percentage of the land (see **8.6**), tenants in common may each hold a different percentage.

> **Example 8.5 – Joint tenants v tenants in common percentages**
>
> A, B, C and D own a piece of land as beneficial joint tenants. Automatically, each owns 25%.
>
> A, B, C and D also own another piece of land as tenants in common 10%, 20%, 40% and 30% respectively.

> **Example 8.6 – Percentage beneficial ownership**
>
> V conveys one piece of land to W and X to hold as joint tenants and another piece of land to Y and Z to hold as tenants in common.
>
> W and X automatically each own 50%.
>
> Y and Z agree to own the land in the ratio of 60%:40% respectively (ie Y holds 60% and Z holds 40% of the beneficial interest).

PURCHASE OF LAND

Three stage process of acquisition

8.10 The acquisition of the legal title to land is effectively a three-stage process:

- the *first* stage is the conclusion of a legally binding contract between vendor and purchaser (commonly referred to as 'exchange');

- the *second* stage is the conveyance/transfer of the legal title to the property to the purchaser (commonly referred to as 'completion'); and

- the *third* stage is the registration of the legal title of the purchaser with the Land Registry (until registration the vendor remains the legal owner of the property).

Where more than one purchaser effects the purchase, the legal title is registered in their respective names as co-owners in the form of a joint tenancy (recall it is not possible for the legal title to be held as tenants in common (see **8.6**).

> **Focus**
>
> Note that for capital gains tax purposes, generally, the disposal of land occurs at the date of 'exchange' whereas for SDLT purposes the relevant date is, generally, the date of 'completion'.

8.11 The maximum number of legal owners of land is four (ie only four joint tenants can hold the legal title; *TA 1925, s 34*), and any such individual holding title must be of full age (ie age 18 or over; *LPA 1925, s 1*). Where there are more than four persons the legal title is vested in the first four named in the conveyance. The law does not dictate the minimum number of trustees required. A sole trustee, however, cannot give a valid receipt for proceeds of sale arising on a disposal under a trust of land (*TA 1925, s 14*).

8.12 Jointly-owned properties

In addition, a purchaser of land from a sole trustee means that any prior beneficial interest(s) under the trust are not overreached (see **8.16** below) and remain binding upon the purchaser unless the purchaser can prove that he (ie the purchaser) had no notice of them (ie of the beneficiaries' interests); no overreaching conveyance can be made by fewer than two trustees of land (*TA 1925, ss 2* and *28*).

> **Focus**
>
> In practice, at least two trustees are normally therefore necessary to hold legal title.

Split of beneficial interests

8.12 On the acquisition of land by two or more persons agreement should be reached as to how the respective beneficial interests in the property are to be held (ie joint tenants or tenants in common *and*, in the latter case, in what proportions) and documented accordingly (see **8.13** below).

However, surprisingly, in practice this is not always the case and the courts are littered with decisions where the courts have been asked to form views as to how, on acquisition, the purchasers intended to own their respective beneficial interests and, if as tenants in common, in what proportions (eg *Walker v Hall* [1984] FLR 126 at 129).

> **Focus**
>
> Ensure that at the time of acquisition purchasers agree and document their respective beneficial interests (see **8.13** below).

8.13 On the purchase of land by two or more persons, the current version of the Land Registry (LR) Form TR1 ('Transfer of whole of registered title(s)') in Box 11 ('Declaration of trust') specifically provides for the purchasers to state how the beneficial interests in the land are to be held (eg as joint tenants; as tenants in common 60:40%, 80:30%, or 50:50%, etc.).

However, Box 11 is not always completed (strictly speaking, this is not necessary although it is highly desirable; *Carlton v Goodman* [2002] EWCA Civ 545). Lack of completion of Box 11(surprisingly) does not preclude acceptable registration of the purchased legal interest in the land with LR but leaves the beneficial interests as amongst the purchasers unresolved (in the absence of any other external documentation (eg an explicit declaration of trust) detailing the requisite ownership percentages).

Form TR1 in its current form was introduced on 1 April 1998. However, the earlier version did not provide an opportunity to provide information on the form in respect of the underlying beneficial interests (as was noted in the leading case of *Stack v Dowden* [2007] UKHL 17).

Land Registry protection of interests in land

8.14 The sole legal and beneficial owner of land (X) may, for example, subsequently decide to execute a declaration of trust in favour of himself and another individual (Y) (ie X is effecting a transfer of the whole or a percentage of the beneficial interests). In order to protect Y's beneficial interest Y may apply to the Land Registry to place a restriction on the proprietorship register (*LRA 2002, s 43*).

Such a restriction then precludes the Land Registry from registering the legal title acquired by a third party purchaser of legal title from X until the terms of the restriction are observed (ie the sale by X who possesses the legal title is effectively prevented without Y being made aware of the sale). Although as a beneficiary of the trust, Y cannot protect his beneficial interest by way of notice (*LRA 2002, s 33*).

8.15 It may be that the legal title is held jointly by X and Y who are also the beneficial owners of the land. On the death of X his beneficial interest is left under his will to Z. The legal title (held jointly) passes automatically by survivorship to Y. To protect Z's beneficial interest, Z would need to place a restriction on the proprietorship register at Land Registry. Although as sole trustee Y cannot provide a third party purchaser with a valid receipt for the proceeds of sale (see **8.11** above) this could be overcome by Y simply appointing another trustee to the legal title (without Z's knowledge).

Overreaching

8.16 Overreaching allows land which is subject to trust to be sold to a purchaser who buys free of any underlying beneficial interests in the land; any monies paid by the purchaser must be to at least *two* trustees holding the land. Although the beneficial interests *in the land* where overreaching applies no longer subsist, the beneficiaries interests are then interests in the sale proceeds held by the trustees.

Mortgages

8.17 Where two or more persons wish to borrow money on the security of their interests in land the legal estate is mortgaged by jointly executing a mortgage deed. Under the deed the land is charged with the debt by way of a legal mortgage. The underlying beneficial interests in the land mortgaged are normally of no concern to the mortgagee (ie the lender). The mortgagee's interest is in the legal title to the land. Thus, any changes to the legal title itself will require the prior mortgagee's consent (whereas changes to the beneficial interests usually do not). This is probably due to the fact that should the

8.18 Jointly-owned properties

mortgagee exercise his power of sale he is able to overreach the mortgagor's estate thus conveying the land free from any beneficial interests therein (*LPA 1925, ss 2, 88, 89* and *104*).

Where the mortgagee exercises the power of sale the sale proceeds (less related costs) are used to discharge any outstanding mortgage debt amount; any balance left over is paid to the mortgagor(s) (ie the borrower(s); *LPA 1925, s 105*).

BENEFICIAL OWNERSHIP

Conversion from beneficial joint tenants to beneficial tenants in common or vice versa

8.18 Whether beneficial interests are initially held as joint tenants or tenants in common a subsequent change from one to the other is perfectly feasible. However, as legal ownership of land can only be held by way of a joint tenancy, no change to tenants in common is feasible (*LPA 1925, s 1*).

Joint tenants to tenants in common: severance

8.19 A conversion from joint tenants to tenants in common may be achieved by the simple act of 'severance'. The act of severance can be achieved by a number of means (*LPA 1925, s 36*; *Williams v Hensman* (1861) 1 J & H 546). Perhaps the two most common are the serving of a notice of severance in writing by one joint tenant to the other(s) or doing something or some act with respect to the joint tenant's interest that is deemed to effect a severance (eg assigning the interest).

Thus, if land is held beneficially by two or more joint tenants any one or more of the tenants can sever their joint tenancy by simply writing to the other joint tenants notifying them of the intention to sever. Severance by way of written notice does not require the consent of the other joint tenants (*LPA 1925, s 196*; *Harris v Goddard* [1983] 3 All ER 242).

> **Example 8.7 – Joint tenants to tenants in common (I)**
>
> Land is held beneficially by four joint tenants A, B, C and D.
>
> One of them, namely A, decides to sever his joint tenancy with B, C and D. Thereafter A holds his interest (ie 25%) as tenant in common whereas B, C and D continue to hold their interest as joint tenants.
>
> **Example 8.8 – Joint tenants to tenants in common (ii)**
>
> Land is held beneficially by four joint tenants A, B, C and D.

Jointly-owned properties **8.22**

Two of them, namely A and B, decide to sever their joint tenancy with C and D and each other. Thereafter A and B each hold their interest (ie 25%) as tenants in common whereas C and D continue to hold their interests as joint tenants.

Example 8.9 – Mixed ownership

A and B hold their beneficial interests as tenants in common whereas C, D and E hold their interests as joint tenants.

Accordingly, A and B are free to dispose of their interests by will. But C, D and E continue to be subject to the survivorship rule (see **8.6**) unless and/or until one or more of C, D and/or E also choose to sever their interests as joint tenants.

Severance in lifetime or by will

8.20 Whilst severance in lifetime is possible, severance by will is not. This is because the principle of survivorship operates immediately on death ie prior to the will taking effect; in essence, the interest ceases to exist on death and there is as a consequence no interest to leave by will (*Re Woolnough, Perkins v Borden* [2002] WTLR 595; and *Burgess v Rawnsley* [1985] Ch 429).

Tenants in common to joint tenants

8.21 Less frequently is the conversion from tenants in common to joint tenants.

This is a simple exercise effected by the persons holding the legal title executing a new declaration of trust confirming that the beneficial interests are to be held as joint tenants.

SOLE LEGAL OWNERSHIP: SPOUSES AND TAX

Sole legal ownership

8.22 Co-ownership of land and the associated tax (inheritance, income and capital gains taxes) consequences is a complex matter. Planning to mitigate a capital gains tax charge on a future sale of land may adversely affect any income tax charge arising in the meantime on any rental income arising, and vice versa.

8.23 *Jointly-owned properties*

Structuring to minimise tax effects may also adversely affect succession issues, and vice versa.

It is therefore a balancing act when structuring co-owned land.

Co-owned land is often held by spouses but land may also be co-owned by non-spouses (eg two brothers; brother and sister; parent and children; co-habitees; etc). The tax effects are different in each case.

8.23   Possible structuring may be as follows:

- spouse ownership:
  - sole legal title;
  - beneficial tenants in common or joint tenants.
- spouse ownership:
  - joint legal title;
  - beneficial tenants in common or joint tenants.
- non-spouse ownership:
  - sole legal title;
  - beneficial tenants in common or joint tenants.
- non-spouse ownership:
  - joint legal title;
  - beneficial tenants in common or joint tenants.

8.24   In exceptional situations, the persons in joint ownership of a property may be treated as carrying on a business in partnership (with the attendant tax consequences; eg the accounting period of the partnership is the base period, not the tax year or year of assessment). However, invariably mere joint ownership of property does not, per se, create a partnership.

8.25   The purchase of land by two spouses may, on acquisition, be held (ie legal title) in the name of one spouse only. It is then for the spouses to decide how their respective beneficial ownership interests are to be held, and in what proportions. The spouse with legal title then executes a declaration of trust confirming their understanding.

> **Example 8.10 – Declaration of beneficial interests: joint tenants**
>
> Mr and Mrs Smith purchase a buy-to-let and legal title is held by Mr Smith alone.
>
> Mr Smith then executes a declaration of trust confirming that he holds the legal title on trust for himself and Mrs Smith as joint tenants.

Jointly-owned properties **8.26**

> **Example 8.11 – Declaration of beneficial interests: tenants in common**
>
> Mr and Mrs Smith purchase a buy-to-let and legal title is held by Mr Smith alone.
>
> Mr Smith then executes a declaration of trust confirming that he holds the legal title on trust for himself and Mrs Smith as tenants in common in the ratio of 60:40% respectively.

Inheritance tax and capital gains tax

8.26 The respective beneficial interests of each spouse may or may not reflect the respective financial contributions to the purchase price of each spouse.

Thus, for example, Mr Smith may contribute 60% of the purchase price whilst Mrs Smith contributes the balancing 40%. Nevertheless, the Smiths may agree that their beneficial interests should be equal (ie 50:50%) whether held as joint tenants or tenants on common.

For both inheritance tax and capital gains tax purposes, it is the beneficial (not legal) interests in the buy-to-let that determines any inheritance tax and/or capital gains tax liabilities on a disposal (eg sale or gift). Where, as indicated above, Mr and Mrs Smith contribute to the purchase price unequally (ie 60% and 40%) but agree a 50/50% beneficial split Mr Smith has effectively gifted a proportion of his beneficial interest (ie 10%) to Mrs Smith. This gift qualifies as an inter-spouse transfer for both inheritance tax and capital gains tax purposes. It is thus generally an exempt transfer for inheritance tax (ie no inheritance tax charge arises on the gift) and for capital gains tax purposes the transfer/disposal is treated as a transfer at neither gain nor loss, with the transferee spouse acquiring the transferred beneficial interest at its original cost to the transferor spouse precipitating no actual capital gains tax charge.

> **Example 8.12 – Inter-spouse transfer of beneficial interest**
>
> Mr and Mrs Smith jointly acquired a buy-to-let for £400,000 with Mr Smith providing 60% of the purchase price (ie £240,000) and Mrs Smith 40% (ie £160,000).
>
> Legal title is registered in Mr Smith's name alone but he executes a declaration of trust under which he states that he holds the legal title on trust for himself and his wife in the percentages 50/50%. Mr Smith has thus transferred 10% of his beneficial interest to Mrs Smith.

8.27 *Jointly-owned properties*

> No inheritance tax charge arises on the gift.
>
> No actual capital gains tax charge arises on the gift. Mrs Smith is treated as acquiring Mr Smith's 10% interest at its original cost to Mr Smith, namely, £40,000 (ie 10% of £400,000).

Capital gains tax issues in relation to buy-to-let property are discussed in **Chapter 11**. For commentary on inheritance tax issues, see **Chapter 12**.

Income tax

8.27 For income tax purposes each spouse is subject to income tax on their proportionate entitlement to any rental income which in principle follows the underlying beneficial interest in the buy-to-let. Thus, continuing **Example 8.12** referred to above, Mr Smith is subject to income tax on 60% of the rental income and Mrs Smith on 40%.

However, Mr and Mrs Smith could have agreed that although the beneficial interests in the buy-to-let are to be owned 60:40% their respective entitlements to any rental income are to be (say) 20:80% (ie Mr Smith is entitled to 20% of any rental income whereas Mrs Smith is entitled to 80%). This split may be agreed between Mr and Mrs Smith in order to reduce their aggregate income tax liability on the rental income as Mr Smith is subject to income tax at the additional rate of income tax (currently 45%) whereas Mrs Smith has no other income and thus will be subject to income tax on the rental income at the basic rate (currently 20%).

Unfortunately, there is a problem.

Although Mr and Mrs Smith have agreed a rental split of 20:80% in favour of Mrs Smith, Mr Smith has a beneficial interest of 60% in the buy-to-let and is thus in principle entitled to 60% of any rental income generated. By agreeing to Mrs Smith becoming entitled to 80% of the rental income he is effectively transferring 40% of his own entitlement to any rental income to Mrs Smith. Mr Smith will, for income tax purposes, be treated as having made a settlement the consequence of which is that any rental income transferred to Mrs Smith will continue to be subject to income tax on Mr Smith ie no income tax saving has been achieved (*ITTOIA 2005, s 624*; the exception provided for under *ITTOIA 2005, s 626* does not apply as the transfer of the 40% is 'wholly or substantially a right to [rental] income').

If Mr Smith and Mrs Smith's intentions are that she is to be subject to income tax on 80% of the rental income generated then she must own an underlying beneficial interest of 80% (not 40%).

> **Focus**
>
> Whilst it is therefore possible for spouses to purchase a buy-to-let and have legal title held by just one spouse with that spouse executing an appropriate declaration of trust confirming respective beneficial entitlements, rental income entitlements must follow those of beneficial entitlements for income tax purposes.

CONVERSION FROM SOLE TO JOINT LEGAL TITLE

8.28 Where a buy-to-let property has been purchased with legal title held in the name of one spouse only there is nothing to prevent that sole legal title being subsequently converted into a joint legal title held in the name of both spouses. A new declaration of trust will then need to be executed by the new joint legal owners.

Such a simple change in legal title gives rise to no tax consequences (see **8.29** below) although if at the time of any such change the buy-to-let is mortgaged it will be necessary, prior to effecting any change, that the mortgagee's (ie the lender's) permission is obtained.

8.29 However, if whilst changing the legal title, the underlying beneficial ownership percentages are also changed, a possible SDLT charge may arise on the part of the spouse who acquires a greater beneficial interest (but only if the buy-to-let is at that time mortgaged *and* the spouse acquiring a greater beneficial interest agrees to indemnify the transferring spouse or agrees to assume some part of the mortgage liability).

In addition, inheritance tax, capital gains tax and income tax consequences may also arise (see **8.26** and **8.30**).

JOINT LEGAL OWNERSHIP: SPOUSES AND TAX

Income tax

8.30 Where a buy-to-let property is purchased and legal title is held, *ab initio*, in joint spouse names (or where one spouse possesses legal title but converts it into joint legal ownership; (see **8.28**)) and a declaration of trust is executed under which each spouse has a beneficial interest in the buy-to-let, legislative provision is made as to the income tax consequences in relation to any rental income arising from the property.

It is specifically provided that any rental income arising from the property is automatically split 50:50% between the spouses for income tax purposes

8.31 *Jointly-owned properties*

(*ITA 2007, s 836*; *Halpin v HMRC* [2011] UKFTT 512 (TC) and *Dunmore v McGowan* [1988] 52 TC 307).

> **Example 8.13 – Spouses' beneficial interests**
>
> Mr and Mrs Brown purchase a buy-to-let property and register legal title in joint names.
>
> They execute a declaration of trust under which Mr Brown owns 70% of the beneficial interest and Mrs Brown 30%.
>
> The property is rented out producing gross annual rental income of £18,000.

In **Example 8.13** above it might be expected that for income tax purposes Mr and Mrs Smith would be subject to income tax on £12,600 of rental income (less expenses) and £5,400 respectively. However, *ITA 2007, s 836* provides that their respective income tax charges will be based on £9,000 of rental income each.

More specifically *ITA 2007, s 836(1)* provides:

'836 Jointly held property

(1) This section applies if income arises from property held in the names of individuals-

  (a) who are married to, or are civil partners of, each other, and

  (b) who live together.

(2) The individuals are treated for income tax purposes as beneficially entitled to the income in equal shares.'

8.31   It is to be noted that the automatic 50:50% split of rental income between spouses first requires that legal title of the buy-to-let is held jointly; second, that the spouses are living together (spouses are treated as living together unless they are separated under an order of the court or are separated by deed of separation or are in fact separated in circumstances in which separation is likely to be permanent (*ITA 2007, s 1011*); and third, that it is irrelevant what actual split of rental income may have been agreed between the spouses under the declaration of trust (but see **8.32** below).

The 50:50% rule is thus, inter alia, not in point if legal title rests in the name of one spouse only (see **8.26**).

8.32   There are certain specific legislative exceptions to this automatic 50:50% rule. These include where a declaration has been made by the spouses under ITA 2007, s 837 (ie a declaration of unequal beneficial interests; (see **8.33**)) or if the relevant income arises from furnished holiday accommodation (*ITA 2007, s 836(3)*).

Jointly-owned properties **8.33**

In addition, HMRC state that the 50:50% rule does not apply where the property is held by both spouses together with one or more third parties (TSEM 9810):

'Sometimes a married couple or civil partners hold assets jointly with others. The 50:50 rule does not apply in such cases. It applies only to income arising from property held in the names of individuals who are married to, or who are civil partners of, each other, and who live together'.

> **Example 8.14 – Ownership by spouses and third party**
>
> Mr and Mrs Blue purchase a buy-to-let with their friend Mr Black. All three names appear on the legal title.
>
> The 50:50% income tax rule does not apply to Mr and Mrs Blue.

8.33 As indicated at **8.32** the automatic 50:50% split with respect to any rental income arising from jointly held property may be displaced (*ITA 2007, s 836(3)* Exception B).

This may be achieved by both spouses making a joint declaration if one spouse is beneficially entitled to the rental income to the exclusion of the other spouse (ie a 100:0% per cent split) *or* if the spouses are beneficially entitled to the rental income in unequal shares *and* their beneficial interests in the rental income correspond to their beneficial interests in the property from which the income arises (*ITA 2008, s 837(1)*).

> **Example 8.15 – Joint declaration of beneficial interests**
>
> Mr and Mrs Bloggins purchase a buy-to-let registering legal title in their joint names.
>
> Under a declaration of trust executed by them they agree a split in the beneficial interests of 67:33% (which must thus be held as tenants in common) in favour of Mr Bloggins. Accordingly, their respective entitlement to any rental income is also in the same ratio (ie 67:33%).
>
> In the absence of a joint declaration by the spouses under *ITA 2008, s 837* Mr and Mrs Bloggins will each be subject to income tax on 50% of the gross rental income.
>
> However, should a joint declaration be made under *ITA 2007, s 837*, their respective income tax liabilities will be based on their actual rental income entitlements ie Mr Bloggins 67% and Mrs Bloggins 33%.

8.34 *Jointly-owned properties*

8.34 HMRC provide for such a declaration under *ITA 2007, s 837* to be made on Form 17 'Declaration of beneficial interests in joint property and income' (available at: http://tinyurl.com/HMRC-Form17).

To be effective for income tax purposes notice of the declaration must be given to HMRC within a period of 60 days from the date of the declaration and must be in the prescribed form, namely, Form 17. The declaration has effect for income arising on or after the date of the declaration and continues until there is any change in the beneficial interests of the spouses in either the income or the property from which the income arises (*ITA 2008, s 837(5)*); in effect, the declaration on Form 17 is irrevocable pending any future change in the beneficial interests in either the property or the income. A declaration on Form 17 requires the husband and wife to also be living together (see **8.31**).

Focus

Failure to file a declaration under *ITA 2007, s 837* with HMRC within the 60 days period invalidates (for income tax purposes) the desired rental income split thus resurrecting the automatic 50:50% split.

8.35 It is to be noted that even if one of the spouses possesses no beneficial interest in a buy-to-let (where legal title is registered in joint names of the spouses) a declaration may still be filed requiring that any income tax liability arising on any rental income is assessed on one spouse as to 100% and on the other spouse as to 0%. Indeed, a declaration must be filed if an automatic 50:50% allocation of the rental income as between the spouses for income tax purposes is to be avoided.

8.36 Where, however, one spouse owns 100% of the legal and beneficial interest in the buy-to-let and subsequently transfers the legal title into joint names and a declaration of trust is then executed under which the beneficial interest in the property is split, say, 100:0% but in addition declares that the rental income split is, say, 0:100% (ie the transferring spouse retains 100% of the underlying beneficial interest in the property but none of the rental income) a joint declaration under *ITA 2007, s 837* cannot be made (as the underlying beneficial interests in the property (100:0%) are not the same as the beneficial interests in the rental income (0:100%)). In such a case, prima facie, each spouse continues to be subject to income tax on 50% of any rental income.

However, this is not so. Effectively the transferor spouse has made a transfer (gift) of solely rental income (as to 100% of it) and has thus created a settlement (*ITTOIA 2005, s 624*) the consequence of which is that the transferor spouse continues to be subject to income tax on 100% of the rental income arising from the property despite an entitlement of 0% (the 'let-out' (ie providing that no settlement arises) contained in *ITTOIA 2005, s 626* is not satisfied).

Jointly-owned properties **8.40**

8.37 It may be that even where a husband and wife jointly purchase a buy-to-let and register legal title in joint names, with each spouse entitled beneficially to a different percentage, a declaration under *ITA 2007, s 837* achieves no income tax saving. This would be the case where, for example, each spouse is a higher rate taxpayer which remains the position after any rental income allocation is taken into account. In such circumstances there is no need for a declaration under *ITA 2007, s 837* to be made as no income tax saving occurs and an automatic 50:50% allocation (under *ITA 2007, s 836*) precipitates no adverse income tax consequences.

8.38 In a similar vein, another example might be where the husband is a higher rate taxpayer and possesses the sole legal title of a buy-to-let property. His wife is a non-taxpayer. The husband may not wish to transfer any significant beneficial interest in the property to his wife but would like to reduce his income tax liability on the rental income (to which he is 100% entitled).

He could therefore transfer legal title in his name into the joint names of himself and his wife who then jointly execute a declaration of trust under which the respective beneficial interests are to be 99% in his favour and 1% in his wife's favour. No declaration is made under *ITA 2007, s 837*. As a consequence, the automatic 50:50% rule under *ITA 2008, s 836* applies and each spouse is treated as entitled to 50% of the rental income and subject to income tax thereon despite the husband's actual entitlement to 99% of the rental income. The husband has thus effectively reduced his income tax liability on 50% of the aggregate rental income (as 50% is deemed allocated to his wife) whilst still retaining beneficial ownership of the bulk (ie 99%) of the property and joint legal title.

Income tax versus capital gains tax and inheritance tax

8.39 Whilst manipulation by spouses of both the legal and beneficial interests in a buy-to-let property (see **8.43**) may have unforeseen non-tax consequences it is also possible that in an attempt to mitigate any income tax charges on rental income such manipulation may have adverse capital gains tax consequences.

8.40 Capital gains tax applies to any capital gain arising on a disposal of a beneficial interest in a buy-to-let whether the disposal is by way of gift or sale and whether it involves a disposal of the whole of the beneficial interest or proportion of it.

However, where the disposal is between spouses who are living together (see **8.31**) it is treated as taking place at no gain or loss to the transferor spouse in which case no chargeable gain arises; the transferee spouse is deemed to acquire the interest at its original cost to the transferor spouse.

8.41 *Jointly-owned properties*

Example 8.16 – Inter-spouse transfer of property

Mrs Green acquired a buy-to-let property for a cost of £150,000.

She is an additional rate taxpayer whereas her husband is a basic rate tax payer. To save income tax on the rental income they decide to transfer her interest to her husband.

The whole of her beneficial interest is transferred to Mr Green at a time when the market value of the property is £250,000.

For capital gains tax purposes Mr Green is treated as having acquired the property at a cost of £150,000 (not £250,000). Mrs Green is correspondingly treated as having disposed of her interest for £150,000 and hence no gain arises.

In **Example 8.16** above if the buy-to-let property is then sold at a later date any capital gain is that of Mr Green (and his capital gain is based on a cost of £150,000). If, however, at the time of sale Mr and Mrs Green's circumstances had changed (for example, Mrs Green was no longer liable to income tax but her husband had become an additional rate taxpayer) the initial transfer designed to save income tax has created a greater capital gains tax charge. In such circumstances, there is nothing to prevent Mr Green transferring his interest back to Mrs Green prior to any sale. Mrs Green would be treated as having acquired the interest from Mr Green at no gain or loss to Mr Green ie £150,000.

However, the capital gains tax consequences just discussed would be different if the transferor and transferee were not spouses (eg two brothers; brother/sister; parent/child etc).

In **Example 8.16**, if the sequence of transfers were between, say, two brothers a capital gains tax charge would arise not only on the initial transfer from one brother to the other but also on the subsequent transfer back to the original brother. Using the same figures, on the initial transfer a capital gain of £100,000 (ie £250,000 less £150,000) would arise and on the later transfer a further capital gain of £275,000 (ie £525,000 less £250,000) would arise (assuming at the date of the transfer back the property had become worth £525,000).

8.41 It may therefore be that manipulation of beneficial interests to mitigate income tax charges on rental income could exacerbate any capital gains tax consequences in particular for non-spouses on future disposals. In addition, whilst for inheritance tax purposes inter-spouse transfers are exempt from any inheritance tax charge, transfers between non-spouses (eg two brothers) are potentially exempt transfers (so-called 'PETs'), which may become chargeable should the brother effecting the gift die within seven years of making the gift. This might be particularly expensive, in inheritance tax terms, should each brother die within the seven-year period from the date of each gift (depending upon their particular circumstances at the date of each death).

MANIPULATION OF LEGAL/BENEFICIAL INTERESTS: NON-TAX ISSUES

8.42 It seems to be commonly understood that as spouses owning a buy-to-let property that their respective legal and beneficial interests can be manipulated as and when they wish with impunity. This is not quite correct, and care needs to be exercised when doing so.

In particular, it needs to be appreciated that where one spouse, for example, owns 100% of both the legal and beneficial interest in the buy-to-let but subsequently declares that the legal title is to be held on trust for both spouses the beneficial entitlement of the transferee spouse cannot then be subsequently unilaterally changed by the transferor spouse.

The transferor spouse on declaring that the legal title is held on trust for both spouses has become a trustee and must henceforth act in the beneficiaries'(ie transferor and transferee spouse) best interests. In the case where the transferor spouse holds the legal title on trust for the transferee spouse 100% beneficially the transferee spouse as then owner of 100% of the beneficial interest in the property can demand that the legal interest (ie legal title) be transferred from the transferor to the transferee spouse, effectively bringing the trust to an end (*Saunders v Vautier* (1841) 41 E.R. 482), which may not be what the transferor ever intended.

Such may be avoided if the transferor spouse simply 1% of the beneficial interest (transferring 99%); this then precludes the transferee spouse ending the trust and taking sole legal title.

EXPENSES

8.43 For expenses incurred to be deductible in calculating the taxable profit arising on rental income from a buy-to-let they must, inter alia, be incurred wholly and exclusively for the purposes of the property business. The expense incurred must be a legal liability of the person incurring the expense.

For example, assume a buy-to-let property is purchased by husband and wife with legal title registered in the husband's name only and a declaration of trust has been executed under which the beneficial interest is split 80:20% in the husband's favour. It is also agreed that any expenses in respect of the property are to be similarly split between husband and wife 80:20% respectively. If the expense of repairing the roof is, say, £10,000 the husband is able to deduct £8,000 as a legitimate expense and the wife, £2,000.

8.44 *Jointly-owned properties*

If, however, the husband discharged the full £10,000 he is able to deduct the total £10,000 amount in calculating his taxable profit if, as would normally be the case, the contract to repair the roof was between the roofing contractor and both spouses (ie each spouse is jointly and severally liable to the roofing contractor for the full amount of £10,000). Under the agreement between the spouses the husband would have the right to seek reimbursement from his wife as to £2,000; should she reimburse her husband she then becomes able to deduct her £2,000 expense and the husband re-credits the £2,000 against his £10,000 expense).

8.44 In the above example the split of expenses not unnaturally reflected the respective beneficial interests in the buy-to-let (ie 80:20%). However, this does not seem to be strictly necessary. Thus, for example, despite the beneficial interest split of 80:20% in the husband's favour the expenses split could be different, for example, 60:40%.

However, some care needs to be exercised in such a situation. It is very unlikely, for example, that HMRC would accept a loss which arose due to one spouse being entitled to, say, only 1% of any rental income but was required to incur, say, 80% of any expenses. Perhaps the guiding principle, as between spouses, is to adopt the same conditions as two third parties might agree to in a negotiation at arm's length.

8.45 Mortgage interest is also in principle a tax deductible expense (although note the restriction in relief for finance costs (eg loan interest) related to residential property: see **Chapter 3**). However, deduction with respect to interest incurred on a mortgage may become problematic where one person who owns a buy-to-let subsequently marries and effects a transfer of a beneficial interest in the buy-to-let to the new spouse.

For example, H has the legal title to a buy-to-let property and a 100% beneficial interest therein; the property is mortgaged (the mortgage in H's name only). H subsequently marries W and transfers, say, a 50% beneficial interest in the property to W by declaring a trust to this effect; the declaration also states that W has agreed with H to assume joint liability for the mortgage (although W does not become a party to the mortgage agreement which remains between H and the mortgagee). However, any payment by W in respect of the interest charge on the mortgage is not deductible in calculating W's taxable profit arising from the property as W is not a party to the mortgage agreement; there is no borrowing incurred by W in respect of which W has a legal obligation to pay interest. W, in essence, has simply provided consideration (ie an agreement to contribute to the mortgage payments) in exchange for a beneficial interest in the property.

H, on the other hand, is able to continue to deduct 100% of the interest payments made by him to the mortgagee against his share of the rental income arising from the property.

Jointly-owned properties **8.47**

8.46 With respect to expenses incurred on a buy-to-let where legal title is held jointly by both spouses and *ITA 2007, s 836* applies (ie income is deemed to be split 50:50% with the spouses making no declaration under *ITA 2007 s 837*) it appears reasonable to assume that expenses are also automatically split 50:50% irrespective of which spouse actually incurs the expense. Although *ITA 2007, s 836* refers to 'income', not 'profit', it would nevertheless appear inconsistent for the section to split income but not expenses 50:50%.

SOLE AND JOINT LEGAL OWNERSHIP: NON-SPOUSE AND TAX

8.47 The basic co-ownership rules (eg joint tenancy; tenants in common etc) apply irrespective of the category of the co-owners, be they spouses or otherwise. However, with respect to income tax arising on rental income on a co-owned buy-to-let property the rule contained in *ITA 2007, s 836* (see **8.30**) does not apply.

Thus, co-ownership of a buy-to-let by persons who are not married (or married but not living together) are not subject to the automatic 50:50% rental income split which applies to spouses living together (*ITA 2007, s 836*) where legal title is jointly held (in the absence of a declaration under *ITA 2007 s 837*).

Hence, for example, two sisters jointly purchasing and owning a buy-to-let are each subject to income tax on their share of any rental income as agreed between the two of them.

> **Example 8.17 – Joint ownership by sisters (I)**
>
> Mary and Sue, two sisters, purchase a buy-to-let property for £300,000, each contributing £150,000.
>
> The legal title is registered in joint (ie both) names and under a declaration of trust confirm that the legal title is held in trust for them beneficially as tenants in common 50:50% and each sister is entitled to 50% of any rental income.
>
> **Example 8.18 – Joint ownership by sisters (II)**
>
> Jane and Sarah, two sisters, also purchase a buy-to-let property for £300,000 each contributing £150,000.
>
> The legal title is registered in joint (ie both) names and under a declaration of trust confirm that the legal title is held in trust for them beneficially as tenants in common 60:40% in favour of Jane (and so Jane is entitled to 60% of any rental income, and Sarah 40%).

8.48 *Jointly-owned properties*

> **Example 8.19 – Joint ownership by sisters (III)**
>
> Kate and Tamara two sisters, also purchase a buy-to-let property for £300,000 each contributing £150,000.
>
> The legal title is registered in joint (ie both) names and under a declaration of trust confirm that the legal title is held as tenants in common 60:40% in favour of Kate but, regarding the rental income, agree that Kate is entitled to 55% of any rental income, and Tamara 45%.

8.48 In each of the **Examples 8.17**, **8.18** and **8.19**, the sisters are free to agree how much each contributes to the purchase price; whether legal title should be registered in one or both names; the respective beneficial interest percentages; and the rental income split.

With respect to **Example 8.18**, Sarah has effectively gifted 10% of her beneficial interest to Jane (as she was entitled to a beneficial interest of 50% due to her contributing 50% of the purchase price). As a gift, it constitutes a potentially exempt transfer for inheritance tax purposes (see **8.41**), but no capital gains tax charge arises as the gift is made at the time of purchase (ie there has been no change in the market value of the buy-to-let property).

With respect to **Example 8.19** the matter is a little more complex. Tamara has effectively gifted not only 10% of her beneficial interest to Kate (as she was entitled to a beneficial interest of 50% due to her contributing 50% of the purchase price) but also 5% of her rental income entitlement. The gift of the 10% beneficial interest constitutes a potentially exempt transfer for inheritance tax purposes but no capital gains tax charge arises as the gift is made at the time of purchase. However, in addition, Tamara has given away 5% of her rental income entitlement.

On the basis that the agreement between Kate and Tamara has been negotiated at arm's length and there is no identifiable tax avoidance motive it seems difficult to argue that any tax consequences arise from this rental income stream transfer (although *ITA 2007, s 809AZA* may be relevant, it seems to be arguable that *s 809AZA(1)(b)* is not satisfied).

8.49 However, where rental income entitlement does not reflect the underlying beneficial entitlement, HMRC may take a closer look than might otherwise be the case.

PARENT/CHILD CO-OWNERSHIP

8.50 Co-ownership by parent(s) and child(ren) (aged 18 or over) are increasingly common. A classic example where this may occur in practice is where a son (or daughter) wishes to buy a buy-to-let property but cannot obtain a mortgage, for one reason or another. One (or both) of the parents agrees to purchase the property jointly with the son (or daughter) in order that a mortgage can be obtained; however, the parent makes no other contribution to the purchase price (all of which comes from the child). But as the parent/child are joint mortgagors they each must appear on the legal title; hence, the legal title, is held jointly (as joint tenants; see **8.06**).

Under a declaration of trust parent/child agree that they hold the legal title on trust as to 100% beneficially for the child and 0% for the parent ie the child is entitled to 100% of the underlying beneficial interest and rental income (*ITA 2007, s 836* not in point). The parent is thus not exposed to any income tax charge on the rental income (or indeed to any capital gains tax charge on a future disposal of the property).

In the event that the parent does, in addition to appearing as a joint borrower with respect to the mortgage, also contribute to the purchase price of the property (but acquires no beneficial interest in the property) the parent will have made a gift for inheritance tax purposes (see **8.41**).

8.51 With respect to minor children (ie below aged 18) the position is different. A minor is not capable of holding legal title to a buy-to-let (although may hold a beneficial interest in a buy to let property). The legal title is therefore necessarily registered in one or both parents' names. However, as stated above, typically the parent(s) holding the legal title will under a declaration of trust agree that they hold the legal title on trust as to 100% beneficially for the child and 0% for the parent ie the child is entitled to 100% of the underlying beneficial interest and rental income (*ITA 2007, s 836* not in point).

In this scenario a settlement arises for income tax purposes (*ITTOIA 2005, s 629*), albeit not for either inheritance tax or capital gains tax purposes.

The effect is that any rental income is subject to income tax on the parent(s) effecting the settlement, not the minor child.

GRANDPARENT/CHILD CO-OWNERSHIP

8.52 The settlement provisions are, however, not in point where a buy-to-let property is purchased by a minor's grandparents for the minor's benefit.

SUCCESSION

8.53 A buy-to-let property, after a person's main residence, is likely to be their second most expensive asset, albeit typically mortgaged. Care needs to be exercised to ensure that on death the property passes not only in the most tax-efficient manner, but in line with the wishes of the owner in particular where the property is co-owned (*Carr-Glynn v Frearsons* [1999] Ch 326).

8.54 *Jointly-owned properties*

8.54 A will is the key to ensuring that on death a person's estate (ie their assets less liabilities) passes as intended to the appropriate beneficiary or beneficiaries.

However, what is often forgotten is that a buy-to-let which is held beneficially in the form of a joint tenancy is not capable of being left by will. Where the property is held beneficially as a joint tenancy on the death of one of the joint tenants their beneficial interest in the property automatically passes to the surviving joint tenant(s) by survivorship (ie not by will). This may have unintended consequences.

For example, a man who is divorced from his first wife (with whom he had children) remarries. The buy-to-let property was (when he was married) and continues to be (following his divorce) owned as beneficial joint tenants with his former wife. On his death his beneficial interest automatically passes to his former wife, which he may not have wanted. If he had in fact wanted his interest to pass to, say, his children from his first marriage and/or his new wife he should have during his lifetime severed (see **8.19**) the joint beneficial interest converting it to tenants in common; a beneficial interest held as a tenant in common is capable of being left by will.

Another example would be where a purchase is effected by two friends (who individually cannot afford a purchase) who each intend that their share on death is to pass to their parents. Beneficial ownership as joint tenants would preclude this from happening.

8.55 On the other hand, where a buy-to-let is held as beneficial joint tenants, on death there is no need for probate. This may not, however, be sufficient reason to hold the beneficial interest as joint tenants.

8.56 For inheritance tax purposes, a deceased's interest in a buy-to-let property, whether held in the form of a beneficial joint tenancy or tenants in common, forms part of the deceased's estate and thus potentially liable to inheritance tax.

The valuation of an interest in a buy-to-let property for inheritance tax purposes is exactly the same irrespective as to how the property is held (ie joint tenants or tenants in common). However, where a buy-to-let is co-owned, the valuation of the interest held by one of the joint owners is likely to be subject to some form of discount (eg 10% to 15%), due to the fact that any person acquiring that interest would not have sole occupation rights (*Wight and Moss v CIR Land's Tribunal* [1982] 264 E.G. 935).

It is understood that HMRC do not accept such a discount applies to joint ownership of a buy-to-let property by spouses as the related valuation rules apply (*IHTA 1984, s 161*; *Arkright v CIR* [2004] S.T.C. (SCD) 89; *Price v HMRC* [2010] UKFTT 474 (TC)).

For commentary on inheritance tax, including in relation to related property, see **Chapter 12**.

8.57 Interestingly, whilst severance is not possible by will (only in lifetime), for inheritance tax purposes only severance by will is effectively possible.

In this regard, for inheritance tax purposes a fictional world is created, under which a beneficial joint tenancy may be deemed to have been severed immediately before the deceased's death by the surviving joint tenant(s) enabling a redirection by the surviving joint tenant(s) of the deceased's interest in the property. Such redirection may be to any other person(s) whether such person(s) is, or is not, a beneficiary(ies) under the deceased's will.

This inheritance tax fiction involves the use of an 'instrument of variation' more commonly referred to as a 'deed of variation' (*IHTA 1984, s 142*), whose purpose is typically (but not always) to reduce any inheritance tax charge arising on the deceased's estate.

> **Example 8.20 – Inheritance tax: deed of variation**
>
> Mr Tomkins and his son (a non-minor), Roger, own as beneficial joint tenants a buy-to-let property. The purpose is to provide Roger with a source of income whilst he attends university.
>
> Mr Tomkins dies and his joint interest in the property automatically passes to his son. Mr Tomkins' interest falls into his estate for inheritance tax purposes, which had not been his intention.
>
> Roger executes a Deed of Variation with respect to the 50% he inherits under which Mr Tomkins' 50% is redirected by Roger to Mrs Tomkins. Under the rules applicable to a deed of variation the effect of this is that for inheritance tax purposes it is assumed that Mr Tomkins had in fact left his 50% interest directly to his wife, which constitutes an inter-spouse transfer and no inheritance tax charge arises thereon.

There are, however, various conditions (*IHTA 1984, s 142*) which need to be satisfied for a deed of variation to be effective and reliance on its execution may not always be possible.

NON-UK DOMICILED INDIVIDUAL

8.58 Particular care is required when considering the form of buy-to-let property ownership where one spouse is UK domiciled and the other is non-UK domiciled. The issue is primarily one of inheritance tax.

8.59 Inter-spouse transfers are exempt for inheritance tax purposes and thus no charge arises thereon. This exemption applies in three out of four possible spouse combinations; thus, transfers between two UK-domiciled spouses, two non-UK domiciled spouses and transfers from a non-UK domiciled to a UK-domiciled spouse are all exempt transfers (*IHTA 1984, s 18*).

8.60 *Jointly-owned properties*

However, transfers from a UK domiciled to a non-UK-domiciled spouse may precipitate an inheritance charge (although, post FA 2013, an election for UK domicile status can be made in certain situations).

In relation to transfers (from a UK to a non-UK domiciled spouse) effected on or after 6 April 2013, the inter-spouse exemption only extends to £325,000 of such transfers (*FA 2013, s 188*; increased from the £55,000 exemption figure applicable to such transfers made before 6 April 2013). Transfers in excess of this amount are treated as potentially exempt transfers and thus may be subject to inheritance tax should the transferor spouse die within seven years thereof (subject to any available nil rate band; currently £325,000).

This lack of complete exemption with respect to such transfers may inhibit inter-spouse transfers from the tax planning perspective.

8.60 It is important therefore that transfers from a UK to a non-UK domiciled spouse do not occur 'accidentally'; if property is held as beneficial joint tenants the death of the UK-domiciled spouse automatically causes a transfer to the surviving non-UK domiciled spouse.

Chapter 9

Non-resident landlords

Robert Maas FCA, FTII, FIIT, TEP, Consultant, CBW Tax Ltd

> SIGNPOSTS
> - **Rental income** – Rents from UK properties are liable to income tax if the property owner is an individual or a trust. They are also chargeable to income tax, not corporation tax, if it is a company. None of the UK's double taxation agreements exempt non-residents from UK tax on rental income (see **9.1–9.5**).
> - **The non-resident landlord scheme** – Tax on rental income is collected by deduction at source, unless the non-resident registers for HMRC's gross payment scheme and agrees to complete UK tax returns (see **9.6–9.8**).
> - **Capital gains tax** – Non-UK residents are not normally within the scope of capital gains tax. However, there is an exception for residential property (see **9.9**).
> - **Non-resident capital gains tax** – Non-residents are taxable on gains on residential properties arising after 5 April 2015. Some special tax rules apply to such gains, which are called NRCGT gains (see **9.10–9.16**).
> - **ATED-related capital gains tax** – Some residential properties are subject to a special tax (the annual tax on enveloped dwellings (ATED)). Where ATED applies, the gain on the property is subject to ATED-related capital gains tax which has some different calculation rules to NRCGT. A property can be both within the scope of NRCGT and ATED-related capital gains tax if it is within ATED for part only of the period after 5 April 2015. Special rules apply to calculate the NRCGT in such circumstances to avoid double taxation (see **9.17–9.18**).
> - **Structuring property investments** – A non-resident should normally invest in UK residential properties through a company. A non-UK company can be more attractive than a UK one (see **9.19–9.20**).
> - **Other taxes** – There are other taxes that a non-resident investor in UK property may become liable to. These are summarised at the end of this chapter, but dealt with elsewhere in this book (see **9.21**).

9.1 Non-resident landlords

INTRODUCTION

9.1 Whilst a non-UK resident is not normally subject to tax in the UK, the UK does charge such people to tax on income from UK land, and on capital gains from the realisation of UK residential property.

INCOME TAX

9.2 Rents are chargeable to income tax. This is at graduated rates going up to 45%. A trust pays a flat rate of 45% unless a beneficiary has an interest in possession in the trust (ie a right to the income as it arises), in which case the trust pays income tax at 20% (as being the person in receipt of income belonging to another) and the beneficiary pays the full income tax rates subject to a deduction for the 20% paid by the trust.

It should particularly be noted that although UK companies are chargeable to corporation tax, not income tax, a non-UK company is chargeable to income tax on its rental income unless that income arises in the course of a trade. Investing in rental properties does not constitute a trade.

9.3 The UK has entered into a large number of double tax treaties with other countries. None of these treaties bar the UK from taxing UK rental income. Where, as is normally the case, the rental income is subject to tax in both countries the UK has the first taxing right with the other country being required to give credit against its own tax liability on the income for the UK tax paid.

9.4

> **Focus**
>
> A non-UK company is taxed at a flat rate of 20%. Accordingly, most investments by non-residents in UK property are held through overseas companies so as to limit the tax charge to 20%. That is not always the appropriate thing to do though, as if the investor is entitled to a credit against his domestic tax liability on the rental income for the UK tax paid he could well prefer that credit to arise in his personal hands rather than in a company.

9.5 A UK resident individual is entitled to claim a personal allowance in calculating his taxable income. Most non-residents are not entitled to claim the personal allowance, which is currently £11,000 (and will increase to £11,500 for the year to 5 April 2018). A non-resident can claim this allowance if:

(a) he is a national of an EEA (European Economic Area) country, namely the EU (Austria, Belgium, Bulgaria, Croatia, Republic of Cyprus,

Czech Republic, Denmark, Estoria, Finland, France, Germany, Greece, Hungary, Ireland, Italy, Latvia, Lithuania, Luxembourg, Malta, Netherlands, Poland, Portugal, Romania, Slovakia, Slovenia, Spain and Sweden), Iceland, Liechtenstein and Norway;

(b) he is a resident of the Isle of Man or the Channel Islands;

(c) he was previously a UK resident and is living abroad for the health of himself or of a member of his family who lives with him;

(d) he is (or has been) employed in the service of the Crown, eg, is a UK government employee;

(e) he is employed in the service of any territory under Her Majesty's protection. It is not clear if there are any longer any such countries as the last British Protectorate (Brunei) that gained independence in 1984;

(f) he is employed in the service of a missionary society, or

(g) his late spouse or civil partner was employed in the service of the Crown.

Even where a non-resident is entitled to claim the personal allowance, it may not be advisable to do so. This is because a person who claims the personal allowance becomes subject to UK tax on all UK source income (including interest and dividends) whereas we normally tax non-residents only on UK rents and earnings.

The rates of income tax payable by an individual for 2016/17 are:

First	£32,000	20%
Next	£108,000	40%
Excess over	£150,000	45%

These rates apply to the aggregate of the individual's UK taxable income, not simply to his rental income. Where the non-resident is entitled to claim the personal allowance, this exempts the first £11,000 of taxable income from tax in addition.

The rate payable by a company is 20%.

The rate payable by a discretionary trust is 45% although in practice if there are no UK beneficiaries, only the 20% rate is charged. The rate payable by a trust where a beneficiary has an interest in possession (such as a life interest) is 20%, but the beneficiary is then taxable at full income tax rates (less a deduction for the 20% paid by the trust).

9.6 *Non-resident landlords*

THE NON-RESIDENT LANDLORD SCHEME
9.6

> **Focus**
>
> There is an obligation on a tenant who pays tax direct to an overseas landlord to deduct tax at 20% from each payment of rent (less any expenses that he pays out of the rent) that he makes to the landlord. If he pays the rent to a UK agent or other intermediary, the obligation to deduct tax and account for it to HMRC falls instead on the intermediary or, if there is more than one intermediary, on the one who pays over the rent to the landlord or to someone else outside the UK. A payment direct into a UK bank account of the landlord is a payment to the landlord for this purpose and triggers the obligation to deduct tax.

This creates a number of problems for the landlord. The first is that the biggest expense is normally loan interest and that is rarely paid by either the tenant or rental agent. It is paid direct by the landlord, or the lender requires the rent to be paid into a UK bank account in the name of the landlord to which it debits the loan interest. This means that in most cases the 20% deduction exceeds the tax actually due. This particularly applies where the landlord is an overseas company so is taxable on the net income at 20%. It effectively means that the landlord has to reclaim the excess tax deducted from HMRC.

Another problem is that the tax is deducted on a receipts and payments basis, which rarely coincides with the accruals basis that applies to the non-resident tax return.

A third problem is that what is and is not an allowable expense is not always clear-cut. This particularly applies to building work – and from 6 April 2015 to the replacement of fittings – where the dividing line between a deductible repair and non-deductible improvements is very unclear. If a person is liable to account to HMRC for tax on someone else's income, he is unlikely to want to risk under-deducting the tax due. Accordingly he is likely to resolve grey areas in favour of HMRC rather than the landlord.

Deduction at source is also not wholly satisfactory to HMRC as private tenants – and even some agents who act only occasionally for non-residents – are not always aware of the obligation to deduct tax. This is not normally a problem with buy-to-let where the agent who acts for the non-resident purchaser is likely to understand the rules, but it can be a problem where a UK resident goes abroad temporarily and lets his house while he is away. A tenant who pays rent of more than £100 a week is required to register with HMRC, but a person who is unaware of his obligation to deduct tax is unlikely to be aware of his obligation to register.

9.7

> **Focus**
>
> The non-resident landlords scheme was designed to overcome all of these problems. It is an optional scheme. A non-resident needs to ask to join and will not be allowed to do so unless he is up to date on his UK tax obligations. A person's tax affairs will be up to date for 2016/17 if he has filed his 2014/15 tax return and paid the tax due. Most non-residents do not have any UK tax obligations at the time they let out their first property. Accordingly, there is a presumption that they meet this qualifying condition when they start their letting business.

By joining the non-resident landlord's scheme, the landlord is opting into the self-assessment system. He is undertaking to file UK tax returns annually and pay tax in accordance with the self-assessment rules. However, if the landlord allows tax to be deducted at source, he normally has to file a UK tax return to reclaim tax over-deducted, so volunteering to file such returns is unlikely to create an additional burden.

There has been a change of terminology since the scheme was introduced. HMRC now call the system of deduction of tax at source the non-resident landlord scheme and the option to join the self-assessment system the application to have UK rental income without deduction of UK tax. Accordingly to avoid confusion, the scheme will be referred to below as the gross payment scheme.

9.8 HMRC have the power to remove a landlord from the gross payment scheme if he does not continue to keep his tax affairs up to date. However, in practice this is fairly rare. The self-assessment system itself encourages compliance because the automatic penalties for non-compliance are severe – they amount to £1,350 if a return is six months late and become very severe after 12 months. In the absence of a return, HMRC also have power to 'determine' the tax due and seek to collect it. There is no right of appeal against an HMRC determination; it can be displaced only by filing the outstanding return to establish the tax actually due. HMRC tend to over-estimate the tax due when making a determination in order to incentivise the recalcitrant landlord to establish the amount actually due.

> **Focus**
>
> There are no special rules for the calculation of tax due from non-resident landlords. The taxable amount is calculated in the manner set out in **Chapter 2**.

When opting into the gross payment scheme, the landlord has to provide HMRC with a list of the properties that he owns and the names of the tenant

9.9 *Non-resident landlords*

and any agent who is acting for the landlord. Where there is an agent, the agent himself also needs to be registered with HMRC as a person entitled to operate the scheme. This is because HMRC want agents to help police compliance with the scheme.

The gross payment scheme does not of itself absolve the tenant or agent from the need to deduct tax. The procedure is that HMRC will give written notification to the tenant or agent that he is not required to deduct tax from any payment he makes to the landlord subsequent to the date of the notice. Because of this the landlord has to notify HMRC every time he acquires an additional property or there is a change in the identity of the letting agent or tenant, so that HMRC can authorise the new payer not to deduct tax.

The application for gross payment has to be made using an online form. The landlord can either register with the UK government and file the form using the Government gateway or can complete the form online, print it out and post it to HMRC. It is not possible to complete a paper form.

CAPITAL GAINS TAX

9.9 The UK does not normally charge non-residents to capital gains tax (CGT). The exception is residential properties. There are two potential CGT charges.

The first is to ATED-related CGT. This applies only to properties within the scope of the Annual Tax on Enveloped Dwellings (ATED) and taxes gains arising after 5 April 2013. ATED applies only to properties owned by a company (or a partnership or LLP (limited liability partnership) of which a company is a member) and properties held for letting are normally outside the scope of ATED. The exception is where the company's tenant is a shareholder in the company or an associated person of a shareholder. ATED-related CGT is at a flat rate of 28%. Where the property is owned by a company, an indexation relief can be claimed. This is a statutory uplift to the base cost of the property. It applies only to properties held in companies. ATED is covered in detail in **Chapter 10**.

The second is non-resident CGT (NRCGT). This is payable on gains arising after 5 April 2015. The rate of NRCGT is 28%. However, if the property is held by an individual and his UK taxable income for the year of disposal is under £43,000, the difference between the £43,000 cap and the income figure is taxed at 18% only. A non-UK trust (including an interest in possession trust) and a non-UK company both pay NRCGT at a flat rate of 28%.

NON-RESIDENT CAPITAL GAINS TAX
9.10

> **Focus**
>
> The UK does not normally charge non-residents to CGT. However, one of the few exceptions is in relation to residential property. Non-resident CGT (NRCGT) applies to gains realised by a non-resident on such property after 5 April 2015.

NRCGT is technically chargeable on a disposal of an interest in UK land where either the land has consisted of, or included, a dwelling at any time since acquisition (or since 5 April 2015, if later), or the interest in UK land subsists under a contract for an off-plan purchase (*TCGA 1992, s 14C* and *Sch B1, para 1*). An interest in UK land is any estate, interest, right or power in or over land in the UK, or the benefit of an obligation, restriction or condition affecting the value of any such estate, etc (*Sch B1, para 2*). The main types of interest are a freehold, a lease or sub-lease. However, a mortgage over land, a licence to occupy land, and a tenancy at will are specifically excluded from the scope of NRCGT.

It should particularly be noted that if a non-resident contracts to buy a flat off-plan and before the flat is built he sells on his right to acquire the flat, that sale attracts NRCGT. An option over land is also an interest in land, although if it is exercised the grant of the option and its exercise are treated as a single transaction taking place at the time the option is exercised and the consideration for which is the aggregate of the consideration given for the grant of the option and the amount payable on its exercise.

9.11 For the purpose of NRCGT a building is a dwelling at any time if it is either used as a dwelling or suitable to be used as a dwelling, or is in the process of being constructed or adapted for such use. Land occupied (or intended to be occupied or enjoyed with a dwelling as its garden or grounds must be treated as part of the dwelling (*Sch B1, para 4*).

Institutional style accommodation used as residential accommodation for school pupils or for members of the armed forces, or a children's home, old people's home, nursing home, hospital or hospice, a prison or similar establishment or any other institution that is the sole or main residence of its residents is not used (or suitable for use) as a dwelling. Nor is a hotel or similar establishment. Student accommodation is not a dwelling if it is either occupied solely or principally by persons for the purpose of undertaking a full-time course of further or higher education at a specific college or university and the university itself is the person managing or having control of the building (such as a university hall of residence), or the accommodation is purpose-built (or converted) as student accommodation, includes at least 15 bedrooms and is occupied by students on at least 165 days in the tax year.

9.11 Non-resident landlords

A building which becomes temporarily unsuitable for use as a dwelling must be treated as continuing to be a dwelling unless it cannot be used because the building was damaged (accidentally or by an event beyond the owner's control) and as a result was unsuitable for use for at least 90 consecutive days. Where this applies, the gain on disposal is not taxable to the extent that it relates to that 90-day or longer period of unsuitability. However, the building is regarded as remaining suitable for use as a dwelling if the accident, etc occurred in the course of work to the dwelling that made it unsuitable for use for 30 days or more.

Example 9.1 – NRCGT: Is the building a 'dwelling'? (I)

John had a buy-to-let property. He had an argument with a tenant who then set fire to the property. It took a year for the building to be restored so that it could be re-let. The building is not a dwelling during that 12-month period.

Example 9.2 – NRCGT: Is the building a 'dwelling'? (II)

Jack had a buy-to-let property. After the tenant moved out, Jack decided to completely refurbish the property. The refurbishment work was expected to take six weeks. After five days the builder caused an accident with a blowtorch as a result of which the building was damaged by fire. It took a year for the building to be restored so that it could be re-let. The building will continue to be regarded as a dwelling throughout the 12-months period even though Jack was not responsible for the accident.

If during the period of ownership, the building has undergone complete or partial demolition, or any other works, and as a result had either ceased to exist or was unsuitable for use as a dwelling, it can be treated as having ceased to be a dwelling not only for the period the work was being carried out but also for any period throughout which, for reasons connected with the work, the building was not used as a dwelling.

Example 9.3 – NRCGT: Demolition and replacement

Jill owned two adjoining houses at the end of a terrace. She decided to demolish them both and replace them with a single detached house. The tenant of one of the properties moved out on 8 December 2015. Jill knew then the lease of the second expired on 30 June 2016 and decided to board up the first property to keep out squatters until the second became vacant. She duly carried out the redevelopment. The new house was completed on 1 November 2016.

The first property is regarded as not being suitable for use as a dwelling from 8 December 2015 to 1 November 2016, even though it was factually so suitable from December 2015 to June 2016, because the reason it was not used in that period was in connection with the creation of the new

Non-resident landlords **9.12**

> dwelling. This exclusion for work applies only if any necessary planning permission or other consent for the works was obtained and the works were carried out in accordance with the planning permission (*Sch B1, para 8*). If this is not complied with, the building is treated as suitable for use as a dwelling even during the period that the works are being carried out so that as a question of fact it is not a dwelling. If consent is not obtained initially but is granted retrospectively, the exemption applies.
>
> Where a building is demolished, it is treated as ceasing to exist (so that it will no longer be a dwelling) only when it has been demolished completely to ground level (although the retention of a single façade or a double façade on a corner can be ignored if this is retained as a condition or requirement of the planning permission or development consent).

9.12 The rate of tax is normally 20% on a disposal by a company or 28% on a disposal by an individual or a trust. A lower rate of 18% can apply to the first part of the gains of an individual or trust but this applies only to the extent that the individual's UK taxable income for the year of disposal is below the higher rate income tax threshold, which for 2016/17 is £32,000. As the UK taxable income will include the rents from the property, this lower rate is unlikely to apply to buy-to-let landlords. An individual is entitled to claim the normal CGT annual exemption, which is £11,100 for 2016/17. Most trusts attract an annual exemption of £5,550, but where a settlor has created more than one trust, this figure has to be split equally between them subject to a minimum allowance of £555 for each trust.

A company is entitled to claim an indexation allowance. This is a proportion of the cost on 6 April 2015 value based on tables published monthly by HMRC and varies with the length of the period of ownership.

Where a property is disposed of under a contract, the date of disposal is the date of the contract, not the time of completion of the sale.

Focus

In that case, the tax can be paid on the normal self-assessment due date, which is 31 January following the end of the tax year. A non-resident landlord who has opted for gross payment in respect of rents will be within self-assessment. Where two or more properties are sold on the same day, they must be included in a single return. If a property is held jointly, each of the joint owners must make his own return. A return has to be made even if no tax is due or a loss arises and even if the non-resident is within the self-assessment system or ATED, so will have to make a tax return or an ATED-related CGT return in due course.

9.13 *Non-resident landlords*

If the non-resident does not have full details of the costs or disposal expenses available in the 30-day period, he needs to make the return to the best of his knowledge (using estimated figures). He can submit an amended return once the correct figures are available but this must be done within 12 months of the disposal.

If the taxpayer does not make the return, the same penalties apply as under self-assessment and, as with the failure to file a self-assessment return, HMRC can make a determination of the tax that they believe to be due. The amount shown by the determination is legally due and collectable unless and until the taxpayer files the return to displace the assessment.

If the property owned by an individual is sold during the tax year in which he either ceases to be resident in the UK or comes to the UK to take up residence, the tax year can be split into a resident and a non-resident part if specified conditions are fulfilled. Such a person is liable to CGT if the disposal occurs in the non-resident part of the year.

9.13 Where a residential property was acquired before 5 April 2015, the part of the gain arising before that date is not taxable; there are two alternative methods of calculating the gain. The default method is to use a valuation of the property at 6 April 2015, treating the property as if it had been acquired at that date at the valuation figure. This does not need to be a professional valuation. HMRC can challenge the valuation and ask the District Valuer (DV) for his opinion of the value. They are more likely to challenge a non-professional valuation than a professional one. Valuation is a matter of informed opinion. If the DV's figure differs from the taxpayer, it is usual to contact the DV and try to agree a compromise figure with him. If this cannot be agreed (which is fairly rare) HMRC will probably adopt the DV's figure, but the taxpayer has a right to challenge this before an independent appeals tribunal.

It needs to be borne in mind that what needs to be valued is what was held at the valuation date. That is normally a tenanted property. The value of a tenanted property is normally different from the value of the property with vacant possession. The tenanted value is normally lower, but this depends on the terms of the lease. It can be higher if the rent under the lease exceeds the market rent at the valuation date, but that would be unusual in the buy-to-let context.

9.14 The taxpayer can alternatively elect to use either straight-line time apportionment or the retrospective basis of computation (*TCGA 1992, Sch 4ZZB, para 2*). The retrospective basis taxes the entire gain over the period of ownership including the pre 6 April 2015 part. It is hard to see why anyone should opt for such a basis. However, as losses are calculated in the same way as gains, it can be attractive to elect for this basis if a loss arises by reference to the original cost.

Straight-line time apportionment calculates the actual gain or loss since acquisition and then splits this loss into two parts by reference to the ratio

Non-resident landlords **9.14**

which the number of days from 6 April 2015 to the date of disposal bears to the entire period of ownership. In practice, HMRC are normally happy to use months and fractions of months instead of days.

Example 9.4 – NRCGT: Default calculation versus Time – apportionment

Ken, who is resident in Hong Kong, bought a buy-to-let property on 10 May 2010 for £400,000 plus legal and estate agents fees and stamp duty land tax of £12,420. He contracted to sell the property on 20 July 2016 for £950,000. The legal and estate agency fees on the sale were £20,640.

The property was worth £875,000 at 6 April 2015.

The default calculation is:

Sale proceeds		£950,000
Less selling expenses	£20,640	
Value at 6 April 2015	£875,000	£895,640
Taxable gain		£54,360

The gain using time apportionment would be:

Sale proceeds		£950,000
Less selling expenses	£20,640	
cost of the property	£400,000	£895,640
acquisition expenses	£12,420	£433,060
		£516,940

Taxable gain:

period of ownership 74 and 1/3 months
period since 6 April 2015 14½ months
£516,940 × 14.5/74.33   = £100,842

Ken should clearly not elect to use time apportionment.

If the property is not used as a dwelling throughout the entire period of ownership (since 6 April 2015), the gain has to be time-apportioned to arrive at the taxable amount.

Example 9.5 – Period of non-dwelling use

Suppose that Ken had obtained planning permission to demolish the house and replace it with a block of flats, and on 20 May 2015 had demolished

9.15 *Non-resident landlords*

the property and marketed the vacant site, but that all the figures in the above example are unchanged.

The period since 5 April 2015 to the date of disposal is	15½ months
The part of that period for which it was a dwelling is	1½ months
The taxable gain is therefore:	£54,360 × 1.5/15.5 = £5,260

There is an exemption from NRCGT where the property owner is a diversely-held company, a unit trust scheme or an open ended investment company. NRCGT is not aimed at large publicly held entities but at private investors. A diversely-held company is one which is not under the control of five or fewer people.

However, control is very widely defined. In determining whether a person controls a company, the rights and powers of associates of his are treated as belonging to him. Accordingly, a company can have a large number of shareholders and still not be diversely held if more than 50% is owned in aggregate by the members of the families of five or fewer individuals, or by trusts created by such persons, or by companies controlled by them. Accordingly, even a publicly listed company can fail the diversely-held test.

There is also an anti-avoidance provision aimed at 'divided companies', such as cell companies, which are structured so that the ownership of the company itself meets the diversely-held test but the assets in an individual cell are under the effective control of five or fewer people. Each cell must be treated as if it were a separate company to apply the diversely held test.

9.15

> **Focus**
>
> Special rules apply if the property was the owner's principal private residence at some time during the period of ownership. A gain on a principal residence is exempt from UK domestic CGT. The NRCGT legislation seeks to preserve this exemption where the property was the individual's principal private residence for part of the period of ownership and, normally, that part was not wholly prior to 5 April 2015.

It is even possible for a non-UK resident to establish that his UK property qualified as his principal private residence for part of the period of ownership, but this is likely to be very rare. The individual needs to show that the UK house was occupied for at least 90 days in a tax year but that neither he nor his spouse or civil partner was UK resident for that year. In practice, it is difficult to spend 90 days in the UK without becoming resident here.

As these special rules are unlikely to apply to buy-to-let property, they are not considered here.

9.16

> **Focus**
>
> A special rule applies to groups of non-resident companies. The members of the group can jointly make a 'pooling election'. Once a pool is in place, companies that later join the group can elect to join the group pool. Where a pooling election is made, NRCGT is not payable on transfers between companies in the group pool. However, when a property is sold, the cost and acquisition date of the property is that which applied to the initial group company. Where any of the group pool companies have losses, the loss can be utilised against NRCGT gains made by other group companies.
>
> The downside of pooling is that all of the companies in the group pool are jointly and severally liable for the tax and interest on NRCGT disposals made by any of the group companies of residential property held at 5 April 2015.

RELATIONSHIP WITH ATED-RELATED CAPITAL GAINS TAX

9.17 ATED is an annual tax payable in relation to properties that are owned by a company and occupied by the owner of the company or a connected person. ATED applies only where the value of the property at 1 April 2012 exceeded £500,000 or the property was bought after that date and cost more than £500,000. There will be a revaluation on 6 April 2017. Properties worth less than £500,000 on that date but over £500,000 now will therefore be brought within the scope of ATED from 6 April 2018.

ATED was introduced from 6 April 2013. For the year to 5 April 2014 it applied only to properties worth £2 million or more, but this limit was reduced to £1 million from 6 April 2014, and to £500,000 from 6 April 2015. It applies to both UK resident and non-UK resident companies.

ATED is dealt with in **Chapter 10**.

> **Focus**
>
> If a property that was within ATED at any time during the period of ownership by the company is sold, the company has to pay ATED-related CGT. The gain is calculated in a similar way as for NRCGT with the obvious difference that it applies to the part of the gain arising after 6 April 2013 instead of 6 April 2015.

9.18 *Non-resident landlords*

> ATED-related CGT is payable at a flat rate of 28%. Accordingly, where a property has been within ATED continuously since 6 April 2013, the ATED-related CGT will always be at least equal to the NRCGT and in most cases will be at a higher rate. In such circumstances, only the ATED-related CGT is payable.
>
> ATED-related CGT is considered in detail in **Chapter 10**.

9.18 In many cases, a disposal by a non-resident company will attract both ATED-related CGT and NRCGT. Special rules are accordingly needed to ensure that the part of a gain that is subject to ATED-related CGT is not also subjected to NRCGT.

The calculation depends on when the property was acquired. If this was before 6 April 2015 and was worth over £1 million at that date, the NRCGT gain or loss is the 'special fraction' of the 'notional post-April 2015 gain or loss'. For this purpose, the special fraction is:

$$\frac{\text{number of days after 5 April 2015 the property was not within ATED}}{\text{period from 6 April 2015 to the date of disposal (or rather the day before)}}$$

The notional post-April 2015 gain or loss is the gain or loss that would have occurred on the ATED-related disposal had the property been acquired at 5 April 2015 at its market value at that date (*TCGA 1992, Sch 4ZZB, para 13*).

Example 9.6 – ATED-related gain

Kenhold Ltd, a Jersey company owned a house in London, which was acquired on 5 April 1998 at a cost of £800,000. The house was bought for occupation by its owner, Ken, when he visited London. The house was sold for £2 million on 5 May 2016.

The house was valued at £1.2 million at 5 April 2012, £1.5 million at 5 April 2015, and £1.8 million at 5 April 2016.

ATED-related gain

Disposal proceeds	£2,000,000
Less value at 5 April 2015 (when it came into ATED)	£1,500,000
Taxable Gain	£500,000

NRCGT gain

Special fraction

$$\frac{\text{months not within ATED}}{\text{period from 6 April 2015}} = \frac{0}{13}$$

Notional post-April 2015 gain

Disposal proceeds		£2,000,000
Less value at 5 April 2015	£1,800,000	
Indexation .016	£28,800	£1,828,800
		£170,200

As the special fraction is 0, there is no NRCGT gain. That is reasonable because the whole of the post 5 April 2015 gain is an ATED-related gain.

Example 9.7 – ATED-related gain and NRCGT (I)

Assume the same facts as in **Example 9.6**, but that Ken had moved out of the property on 5 May 2015, and it had then been let to an unconnected person.

ATED-related gain

Disposal proceeds	£2,000,000
Less value at 5 April 2015	£1,500,000
	£500,000
Period for which property was in ATED	
1 out of 13 months	
Taxable gain	£500,000 × 1/13th £38,461

NRCGT

Special fraction:	months not within ATED	12
	Months from 6 April 2015	13
Notional post-April 2015 gain (as before)		£170,200
Chargeable gain £170,200 × 12/13ths		£157,107

The same calculation is used if the property either was acquired after 5 April 2015, or the taxpayer has elected for the whole of the gain or loss since acquisition to be treated as ATED-related (or has elected for the entire gain or loss to be treated as an NRCGT gain or loss), with the actual cost being used in place of the 5 April 2015 value (*TCGA 1992, Sch 4ZZB, para 14*).

9.18 *Non-resident landlords*

Example 9.8 – ATED-related gain and NRCGT (II)

Lenco Ltd, a Guernsey company, owned a house in London which was acquired on 5 April 1998 at a cost of £300,000. The house was bought for occupation by its owner, Len, when he visited London. The house was sold for £800,000 on 5 May 2016.

The house was valued at £550,000 at 5 April 2012, £600,000 at 5 April 2015 and £675,000 at 5 April 2016.

ATED-related gain

Disposal proceeds	£800,000
Less value at 5 April 2016	£675,000
Taxable gain	£125,000

NRCGT

Notional post-April 2016 gain

Disposal proceeds		£800,000
Less value at 5 April 2016	£675,000	
Indexation 0.003	202	£675,202
		£124,798
Special fraction		
$\dfrac{\text{months not within ATED}}{\text{months within ATED}}$	$\dfrac{0}{1}$ = 0	
Chargeable gain	£ nil	

Notional pre-April 2016 gain

Value at 5 April 2016		£675,000
Less value at 5 April 2015	£600,000	
Indexation 0.013	7,800	£607,800
		£67,200
Special fraction	$\dfrac{12}{12}$ = 1	
Taxable gain		£67,200

As the NRCGT chargeable gain is a fraction of the NRCGT gain that does not relate to the period for which an ATED-related gain arises, the calculation is no different where time-apportionment is used. Time apportionment cannot be used to calculate an ATED-related gain.

Example 9.9 – NRCGT: Time-apportionment

Suppose that Ken in **Example 9.7** elects to use time-apportionment.

NRCGT gain

Disposal proceeds		£2,000,000
Less cost	£800,000	
Indexation 0.612	£489,600	£1,289,600
		£710,400
Period from 6 April 2015		13 months
Period of ownership		97 months
Taxable portion of gain 13/97ths		£95,208
Special fraction (as before) 12/13ths		
Chargeable gain £95,208 × 12/13ths		£87,884

As this is less than the £157,107 taxable under the valuation method, Ken should use time-apportionment.

HOW SHOULD A NON-UK RESIDENT INDIVIDUAL STRUCTURE UK PROPERTY INVESTMENTS?

9.19

> **Focus**
>
> Except where ATED applies, in most cases it makes sense for a non-UK resident to use a non-UK company to invest in UK residential property.

A company pays tax on the income at 20%, whereas if the property is held personally the rate of tax on the income can go as high as 45% on the top slice. Furthermore, from 2017/18 onwards the tax relief for mortgage and other loan interest and financing costs will be reduced, gradually limiting the relief to

9.20 *Non-resident landlords*

20% from 2020/21 onwards. That will increase the effective tax rate payable by an individual, but will have no effect on the rate paid by a company.

A company pays NRCGT at 20% as compared with the 28% normally payable by an individual. Using a company loses the benefit of the CGT annual allowance and in some cases the 18% band, but the saving on the excess gain on or over £43,100 (the £11,100 annual allowance and £32,000 basic rate threshold) and the indexation relief that applies only to companies are likely to outweigh these benefits. No tax on £11,100 saves £2,220 if tax is at 20%. The break-even point (assuming the individual is already a 40% taxpayer) is £38,850, ie:

Individual	**Company**
First £11,100	nil
Next £27,750 @ 28%	£7,770
£38,850 @ 20%	£7,770

That is a very low gain on a property transaction.

These figures ignore indexation relief. If annual inflation is (say) 4%, that increases the cost of a property that is held for, say, seven years (the average period for which residences are held) by 28% and reduces the tax payable by 20% of that figure.

If all that a company does is invest in UK residential properties, it does not really matter whether a UK company or a non-UK company is used. However, if the company might make other investments, for example, may invest surplus funds in stock exchange securities, using a UK company would bring both the income and gains on such investments into the UK tax net, whereas a non-UK company avoids this.

9.20 It needs to be realised that for UK tax purposes a company is resident in the country in which its central management and control takes place. This is normally, but not always, the place where board meetings are held. If the non-resident frequently visits the UK, care may need to be taken to ensure that HMRC cannot contend that management and control takes place in the UK. However, this is not normally a problem where an overseas company has non-resident shareholders and directors. With a property investment company, there is often very little need for any management of the company in any event – all it need do is buy the property, appoint a UK estate agent to manage it, and eventually sell the property.

OTHER TAXES

9.21 It should not be overlooked that a number of other taxes payable by UK investors can also be payable by non-residents owning UK properties, namely:

- **Stamp duty land tax (SDLT)** is a transfer tax which is payable on the acquisition of land and properties. The rates are graduated but the top slice is normally taxable at 15% and the 15% rate also applies to property acquisitions by companies. SDLT (and land and buildings transaction tax in Scotland) is considered in **Chapter 14**.

- **Construction industry scheme (CIS)** is a withholding tax on fees payable to building industry sub-contractors. It does not normally apply to property investors (unless the investor develops the property himself) but can do if the annual cost of repairs exceeds £1 million. CIS is considered in **Chapter 15**.

- **Inheritance tax (IHT)**, despite the name, is an estate tax. It is payable on a person's estate at death and is also payable on some lifetime gifts, the main exception being gifts to individuals if the donor survives for seven years after making the gift. It is based on domicile, not residence. Unless he was born in the UK, a non-resident investor is unlikely to be domiciled here. However IHT is payable on UK residential properties held by non-UK domiciliaries and, from 6 April 2017, on shares in a non-UK company that derives its value from UK residential property. IHT is dealt with in **Chapter 12**.

- **Value added tax (VAT)** is a form of sales tax. It is unlikely to be payable by a non-UK resident property investor but most expenditure, such as on repairs and building work attracts VAT at 20%. This tax is normally irrecoverable and is therefore an extra cost of maintaining a buy-to-let property portfolio. The VAT forms part of the expense on which it is charged and as such is deductible in calculating the taxable net rental income. VAT is dealt with in **Chapter 15.**

Chapter 10

Corporate landlords

Satwaki Chanda, Barrister at Law

SIGNPOSTS

- **Introduction** – The main differences between corporate and individual landlords is that the latter are subject to lower tax rates, and do not face the same restrictions on tax relief for borrowing costs (see **10.1**).

- **Why use a company?** – There are both commercial considerations and tax considerations in deciding whether to operate through a company, such as the advantages of limited liability for corporate shareholders, and whether a company is more tax-efficient than investing directly (see **10.2–10.3**).

- **Offshore or onshore?** – It may also be relevant to consider whether or not it is better to invest through a non-UK resident company (see **10.4**).

- **Profits of a property business** – There are important distinctions between how interest relief works for companies and individual landlords (see **10.5–10.6**).

- **Property losses** – There are also differences in how companies obtain tax relief for property losses compared with individual landlords (see **10.7–10.8**).

- **Annual tax on enveloped dwellings, etc** – Companies will need to consider the annual tax on enveloped dwellings (ATED), stamp duty land tax (or land and buildings transaction tax in Scotland) and ATED-related CGT, where appropriate (see **10.9–10.14**).

- **Exit issues** – Company owners considering the disposal of a property portfolio should plan ahead, and not leave exit issues until the point of sale (see **10.15–10.17**).

INTRODUCTION
10.1

> **Focus**
>
> Most of the tax and commercial issues relating to the buy-to-let sector apply equally to corporate landlords as they do for individuals. This chapter focuses on those features that are particularly relevant to corporate landlords.

In tax terms, the most obvious difference is the fact that UK companies are taxed at the lower rate of 20%, on both rental profits and capital gains. By contrast, individual landlords are subject to higher rates of 40%–45% on income profits, and 18%–28% on capital gains for residential property disposals.

Furthermore, corporate landlords do not face the same restrictions as individuals on tax relief for their borrowing costs (see **Chapter 3**).

This latter factor has generated interest amongst residential landlords as to whether a company should be the preferred vehicle through which to operate the buy-to-let business.

WHY USE A COMPANY?

Commercial considerations

10.2 The most common reason for operating through a company is that it affords limited liability to its shareholders. The company has its own distinct legal personality, and is fully responsible for the debts of the business. By contrast, the shareholders' liability is limited to any amounts unpaid on their share capital.

The concept of limited liability can be diluted in practice, especially for owner managed businesses. In the context of a buy-to-let business, bank borrowings will normally be secured by mortgage – however, the directors may be required to provide additional guarantees to secure the company's debts.

There are various other consequences that follow from adopting a corporate structure, but which do not apply to individual landlords:

- Companies have various reporting requirements to follow, as well as being obliged to follow certain procedures under the *Companies Act 2006* and related legislation;

- In particular, the directors have special duties to act in the best interests of the company ahead of their own, and must not use their position to gain a personal advantage. For example, a director who spots an investment

10.3 *Corporate landlords*

opportunity in his capacity as director is obliged to disclose this to the company; he is not permitted to make the investment for his own benefit;

- The company's assets belong to the company – its cash reserves cannot be treated as the shareholders' personal funds to draw from as and when they need to. There are specific rules which require the company to have distributable reserves before any distribution is paid (*CA 2006, Pt 23*).

The advantage of using a company becomes apparent as more properties are added to the portfolio. For example:

- By creating subsidiaries, it is possible to segregate and order properties by location or type, thereby facilitating a subsequent sale (see **10.15–10.17**);
- It is easier to allocate fractional interests in the portfolio to family members, by issuing or transferring the appropriate number of shares, or even by creating different classes of share capital.

In both cases, there is a stamp tax saving, as stamp duty on shares attracts a 0.5% charge as opposed to the higher stamp duty land tax (SDLT) or land and buildings transaction tax (LBTT) rates that would apply on transferring the relevant property interest directly (*FA 1999, Sch 13, para 3, FA 2003, s 55, Land and Buildings Transaction Tax (Tax Rates and Tax Bands)(Scotland) Order,* SSI 2015/126)).

Tax considerations

10.3 There are two tax reasons which, on the surface, make a corporate vehicle particularly attractive to residential property investors:

- UK companies are subject to lower tax rates – the current corporation tax rate is 20%, and is set to reduce to 17% by 2020 (see below);
- The restrictions on tax relief for borrowings, etc. being phased in from 2017/18 do not apply to corporate landlords (see **10.6**).

The lower tax rate for UK companies compares favourably to the rates applicable for individual landlords. For example, higher and additional rate taxpayers are subject to rates of 40–45% on their rental profits and 28% on capital gains (*FA 2016, s 1(2), F(No.2)A 2015, s 1, TCGA 1992, ss 4, 4B*).

For companies, a single rate of 20% applies to both income and capital gains – this rate is set to gradually decrease to 17% by 2020 (*FA 2015, s 6, F(No.2) A 2015, s 7*). Furthermore, for companies, capital gains are inflation proofed, while individual landlords are not eligible for the indexation allowance (*TCGA 1992, s 52A*).

However, any comparison of tax rates needs to take into account the fact that for corporate landlords, there is an additional layer of tax payable by shareholders when rental profits are distributed:

Corporate landlords **10.3**

- If investors intend to receive and enjoy the entire profits of the business as a separate source of income, a corporate vehicle adds little value compared to holding the properties directly;

- However, where part of the profits are retained for further reinvestment in the business, a company offers clear tax advantages.

This is illustrated by the following examples.

Example 10.1 – 100% of profits distributed to shareholders

The following table shows the tax position of a higher-rate taxpayer who invests in buy-to-let property, comparing the position between a direct investment on the one hand, and holding the properties through a company on the other.

The calculations assume that the company has sufficient distributable reserves to distribute its profits, and that the individual shareholder has exhausted all his various allowances.

	Individual landlord	Corporate landlord CT rate 20% (Financial year 2016)	Corporate landlord CT rate 17% (Financial year 2020)
Profit	100	100	100
Taxation 40%/20%/17%	(40)	(20)	(17)
Profit available to owners	60	80	83
100% distribution		80	83
Tax at shareholder level (higher rate) 32.5%		(26)	(27)
Amount of cash available	60 Effective rate 40%	54 Effective rate 46%	56 Effective rate 44%

Note that the adoption of a corporate structure actually yields a higher overall tax rate than is the case if the properties are held directly. This is the case even when the corporate tax rate comes down to 17% in 2020.

For an additional rate taxpayer, investing through a company also increases the overall tax rate.

10.3 Corporate landlords

	Individual landlord	Corporate landlord CT rate 20%	Corporate landlord CT rate 17%
Profit	100	100	100
Taxation 45%/20%/17%	(45)	(20)	(17)
Profit available to owners	55	80	83
100% distribution		80	83
Tax at shareholder level (additional rate) 38.1%		(30)	(32)
Amount of cash available	55 Effective rate 45%	50 Effective rate 50%	51 Effective rate 49%

Example 10.2 – 50% of profits distributed to shareholders

In practice, most businesses, including mature ones, do not distribute their entire profits to their owners – a part of the profits is normally retained for further investment.

For example, in the context of a buy-to-let business, profits which are not immediately paid out can be used to fund renovation work to existing properties, or the acquisition of additional rental assets. Furthermore, a company with retained earnings is better able to secure future dividend payouts in the event that rental profits do not increase sufficiently to support the income demands of investors.

The following tables compare the tax position of an individual landlord to that of an individual who invests through a company. However, in this example, only 50% of the annual net profits are paid out to the business owners, with the remainder being retained to fund future investment.

This is the position for a higher rate taxpayer:

	Individual landlord	Corporate landlord	Corporate landlord
Profit	100	100	100
Taxation 40%/20%/17%	(40)	(20)	(17)
Profit available to owners	60	80	83
Profit retained in business	(30)	(40)	(41)
Profits 'distributed'	30	40	42

Corporate landlords **10.3**

	Individual landlord	Corporate landlord	Corporate landlord
Tax at shareholder level (higher rate) 32.5%		(13)	(14)
Amount available after tax			
Amount 'paid' to owners (after tax)	30	27	28
Amount retained in business	30	40	41
Total	60 Effective rate 40%	67 Effective rate 33%	69 Effective rate 31%

The effect of retaining half the profits in the company leads to a lower overall tax rate compared to the position for an individual landlord.

Note also that the company's shareholders are only taxed on the amount of dividends that they actually receive. By contrast, an individual landlord must still pay income tax on the entire profits of the business, even though only half of those profits actually end up in his pocket.

The following table shows the position for an additional rate taxpayer:

	Individual landlord	Corporate landlord	Corporate landlord
Profit	100	100	100
Taxation 45%/20%/17%	(45)	(20)	(17)
Profit available to owners	55	80	83
Profit retained in business	(28)	(40)	(41)
Profits 'distributed'	27	40	42
Tax at shareholder level (higher rate) 38.1%		(15)	(16)
Amount available after tax			
Amount 'paid' to owners (after tax)	27	25	26
Amount retained in business	28	40	41
	55 Effective rate 45%	65 Effective rate 35%	67 Effective rate 33%

As with a higher rate taxpayer, the retention of half the profits in the company leads to a lower overall tax rate than for an individual landlord.

10.4 *Corporate landlords*

OFFSHORE OR ONSHORE?

10.4

> **Focus**
>
> In the past, it has been common practice for property investors to use an offshore vehicle, usually situated in a low tax jurisdiction such as Guernsey or Jersey. For UK tax purposes, there were distinct advantages compared to using a UK company, but these advantages have decreased in recent years.

In particular:

- Offshore companies investing in UK property do not pay corporation tax, but are subject to income tax at basic rate on their rental profits (*ITA 2007, s 11, CTA 2009, s 5*). Previously, basic rate income tax rates of 20% compared favourably to the top corporation tax rates of 30%. However, corporate rates have gradually decreased in recent years. The rate for the financial year beginning 1 April 2016 is 20% – this will come down further to 19% for the following three years and eventually decrease to 17% by 2020 (*FA 2015, s 6, F(No 2)A 2015, s 7*);

- Until recently, non-UK resident property investors were not subject to tax on capital gains (*TCGA 1992, ss 2(1), (1A)*). However, from 6 April 2015, offshore corporate landlords investing in residential property are potentially subject to CGT where the company is a close company, being under the control of five or fewer participators (*TCGA 1992, ss 14B–14G*).

Accordingly, the tax advantages of investing through an offshore vehicle are not as clear cut as they once were. In particular, owner-managed or family controlled businesses are probably better off using a UK resident company.

For further commentary on non-resident landlords, see **Chapter 9.**

PROFITS OF A PROPERTY BUSINESS

10.5 The principles involved in calculating the profits of the business are exactly the same as that which apply to individual landlords (see **Chapter 2**). In particular, there are two key principles that apply to determine whether expenses incurred in the business are tax deducible:

- Expenses must be incurred wholly and exclusively for the purpose of the letting business (*CTA 2009, ss 210, 54*); and

- Expenses must be of a revenue or income nature, as opposed to capital (*CTA 2009, s 53*).

Corporate landlords **10.6**

However, there are two key areas where the tax treatment of corporate landlords differs from that of individuals:

- Firstly, corporate landlords are subject to a different set of rules when determining the amount of tax relief is available for its borrowing costs (see **10.6**);
- Secondly, corporate landlords have a greater flexibility in using property losses to shelter taxable profits (see **10.8**).

These two areas are discussed in greater detail below.

Interest relief

10.6 The restrictions on tax relief for finance costs only apply to individual buy-to-let landlords (*ITTOIA 2005, s 272A* inserted by *F(No2)A 2015, s 24*, with effect from 18 November 2015); see **Chapter 3**.

A corporate landlord can still freely deduct its finance costs from its rental profits, but this advantage needs to be balanced against the possibility of banks applying higher mortgage rates.

For companies, the tax treatment of interest costs is governed by the loan relationship rules set out in *CTA 2009, Pt 5*. These rules apply to all corporate transactions relating to the 'lending of money' (*CTA 2009, s 302(1)*).

> **Focus**
>
> The overriding principle is that profits and losses arising from a company's loan relationships are calculated in accordance with credit and debit entries as they are recognised in the profit and loss account under generally accepted accounting practice (*CTA 2009, s 307*). Accordingly, credits and debits are netted off against each other, and the surplus taxed or the deficit is relieved, as the case may be.

It is important to note that the tax legislation specifically excludes a company's loan relationships when computing the profits of a property business (*CTA 2009, s 211(1)*). However, this does not mean that tax relief is unavailable for finance costs.

Relief is given by first computing the property profits and then setting off the relevant interest expenses, in accordance with the following rules (*CTA 2009, ss 456–463*):

- The company can make a claim to set off its net finance costs – all or part – against any of its profits earned during the current year;

10.6 Corporate landlords

- The company can also carry back all or part of its finance costs to set against interest income from the previous 12 months;
- The company can also surrender all or part of such costs to other group companies, who may use the deficit to shelter their own tax liabilities;
- Any amounts left over are automatically carried forward to future years to be set against the company's non-trading profits.

Technically, the carry forward rule has precedence, but is displaced by making an appropriate election for alternative treatment.

The effect of calculating the rental profits first and then relieving the company's interest expenses can be illustrated by the following example.

Example 10.3 – How tax relief is given for corporate borrowings

The first table shows the profits of a company investing in residential property, for three consecutive years, and assumes that it is in fact permitted to include interest costs in calculating taxable profits.

	2017 £	2018 £	2019 £
Property profits before deducting interest expense	30,000	1,000	3,000
Interest expense	(5,000)	(10,000)	(3,000)
Property profits/(loss)	25,000	(9,000)	Nil
Interest income (bank and intercompany loan)	14,000	Nil	Nil
Taxable profits	39,000	Nil	Nil

In 2018, the property business has made a loss of £9,000, which can either be set against current year profits or carried forward. But there are no other profits for the year and no profits in the following year to set against. It is not possible to carry back the loss into the preceding year 2017 and relieve it against the £25,000 profit.

The second table shows the actual position as required by the legislation, whereby interest costs are not regarded as part of the profits of the property business, but deducted only after those profits have been determined.

	2017 £	2018 £	2019 £
Property profits	30,000	1,000	3,000
Interest income (bank and intercompany loan)	14,000	Nil	Nil

Corporate landlords **10.6**

	2017 £	2018 £	2019 £
Interest expense	(5,000)	(10,000)	(3,000)
Net interest income/expense	9,000	(10,000)	(3,000)
Interest relief (current year profits)		(9,000)	Nil
Interest relief (carry back against net interest income)	(9,000)		
Taxable profits	30,000	Nil	Nil

For the year 2018, the property business made a profit of £1,000 even though there is an overall loss of £9,000. This is because the interest expense cannot be deducted in calculating the profits of the business.

However, the expense can be deducted against the profits once those profits have been determined, leaving an excess of £9,000 available for relief. Because the £9,000 excess is a loan relationship deficit, and not a property loss, it can be carried back to set against the interest income arising in the previous year. Accordingly, the company is actually better off as a result of being unable to include its interest expense as part of its rental profits.

This example also shows that a company is better off than an individual landlord:

- The first table also shows the position for an individual landlord before the interest relief restrictions came into force. Individuals were able to deduct their entire interest expenses in calculating rental profits – as a consequence, any excess interest is included in the resulting property loss which cannot be carried back (see **10.8**);

- The position is no better for individuals as a result of the interest relief restrictions. By 2020, none of the interest will be included in the profit calculation, but tax relief will be available at basic rate as a reduction against total profits. However, as with property losses, there are no provisions for any 'excess interest' to be carried back (*ITTOIA 2005, s 274A*). See **Chapter 3**.

10.7 *Corporate landlords*

PROPERTY LOSSES

Treatment of property losses and a comparison with trading losses

10.7

> **Focus**
>
> The treatment of property losses compares unfavourably with trading losses, with no facility to carry back losses to previous years. However, corporate landlords have advantages over individuals.
>
> For commentary on loss relief for individual landlords, see **Chapter 7**.

A company's UK property losses are given relief in the following order:

- Firstly, losses are set against the company's total profits for the same accounting period;

- If there are insufficient profits to relieve the loss, it is carried forward to subsequent accounting periods, to be set against total profits;

- Excess losses are carried forward in this way until the property business ceases. If there is still an excess loss at this point, it can be carried forward and treated as a management expense;

- Losses can also be surrendered to other group companies under the group relief provisions.

See *CTA 2010 ss, 62, 63, 99(1)(e)*.

For investment in overseas property, the rules are modified so that losses are automatically carried forward to subsequent accounting periods. There is no set off against total profits as is the case with a UK property business (*CTA 2010, s 66*).

Note that there are two important differences between the treatment of property losses and trading losses (*CTA 2009, ss 37, 39, 45*):

- There is no facility to carry back a property loss to a previous accounting period;

- In particular, terminal losses cannot be carried back to the three previous accounting periods as is the case with trading losses. Terminal losses are therefore stranded unless the company has another business, in which case, the terminal loss is treated as a management expense, which can then be carried forward (*CTA 2009, s 63(3)*).

The following table illustrates the differences between trading losses and property losses:

	Trading losses	**Property losses**
Carry forward	Yes, but only against same trade (*CTA 2010, s 45*).	Overseas property business – automatic (*CTA 2010, s 66*). UK property business – only after current year set-off (*CTA 2010, s 62*).
Set off against total profits	Yes – current year and carry back for one year (*CTA 2010, s 37*).	UK property business. But not for overseas property business (*CTA 2010, s 62*).
Carry back	Yes – one year/three years (*CTA 2010, ss 37, 39*).	No.
Group relief	Yes (*CTA 2010, s 99(1)(a)*).	Yes (*CTA 2010, s 99(1)(e)*).
Terminal losses	Yes – can carry back losses for three years (*CTA 2010, s 39*).	No. Terminal loss is treated as a management expense to be carried forward in the event that the company has another business (*CTA 2010, s 63*).

Note also that there are special rules where the company's business consists of furnished holiday accommodation. Although this is treated as a trade, losses can only be carried forward to subsequent accounting periods – no set-off against total profits or carry back to previous years is permitted (*CTA 2010, ss 65, 67A*). However, group relief is still available (under *CTA 2010, s 99*).

A comparison of property losses between corporate and individual landlords

10.8 For individual landlords, losses are relieved as follows:

- The general rule is that losses are carried forward against future profits of the same business (*ITA 2007, ss 118, 119*). By contrast, the general rule for corporate landlords is that losses are first set off against total year profits earned during the current year;

- However, individual buy-to-let landlords are unable to set off losses against general income. This is because for individuals, a general set off for property losses is only available to the extent that the loss is attributable to capital allowances, which are generally unavailable to residential property investors (*CAA 2001, s 35, ITA 2007, ss 120, 123(2)*);

10.9 *Corporate landlords*

- As with corporate landlords, there is no carry back facility, including a carry back for terminal losses;
- There is no provision to carry forward and treat excess losses on termination of the business as a management expense.

The following table illustrates the differences between corporate and individual landlords:

	Corporate landlord	**Individual landlord**
Carry forward	Overseas property business – automatic (*CTA 2010, s 66*). UK property business – only after current year set-off (*CTA 2010, s 62*).	UK and overseas property business – carry forward against profits of same business only (*ITA 2007, s 118*).
Set off against total profits	UK property business. But not for overseas property business (*CTA 2010, s 62*).	Not normally available for buy-to-let due to unavailability of capital allowances (*CAA 2001, s 35, ITA 2007, ss 120, 123(2)*).
Carry back	No.	No.
Group relief	Yes (*CTA 2010, s 99(1)(e)*).	Not applicable.
Terminal losses	No. Terminal loss is treated as a management expense to be carried forward in the event that the company has another business (*CTA 2010, s 63*).	No. Terminal losses are stranded.

ANNUAL TAX ON ENVELOPED DWELLINGS AND RELATED TAX CHARGES

Background to the regime

10.9

> **Focus**
>
> The annual tax on enveloped dwellings (ATED) regime is designed to discourage home ownership by individuals who use an intermediary such as a company or other 'non-natural' person to acquire and own the property. Corporate landlords should not be affected by the regime, provided that they can claim the relevant reliefs.

ATED was introduced by *FA 2013*, and was designed to counter stamp duty land tax (SDLT) avoidance by high net worth individuals in relation to high value residential property.

A typical scheme would involve an offshore company making the initial acquisition at standard SDLT rates. The company could then be sold to subsequent buyers intending to use the property as their own residence. Onward sales would be free of all stamp taxes since non-UK shares are not subject to stamp duty and SDLT is only payable in respect of real assets – the latter charge does not extend to shares where the property has been enveloped within the relevant company. In addition, the disposal of the property itself would have been tax free, since offshore investors were, at the time, outside the capital gains net.

There are three strands to the ATED regime:

- ATED itself – which is an annual charge paid by reference to the value of the property;
- A higher (15%) SDLT rate for residential property acquired by a non-natural person in circumstances where ATED related conditions apply;
- An ATED-related capital gains tax which applies to the disposal of the property.

These rules apply to 'non-natural persons' and include collective investment schemes and partnerships (with company members), as well as companies. Furthermore, they apply equally to resident and non-residents alike. However, it is unlikely that a company operating a buy-to-let business will be subject to an ATED charge – ATED is aimed at those who seek to live in the property themselves, rather then rent it out to others.

In Scotland, the ATED-related stamp tax rates do not apply to property transfers as SDLT was replaced by the land and buildings transaction tax (LBTT) from 1 April 2015. However, the other ATED related charges – the annual charge and the ATED-related CGT – continue to apply to the whole of the UK.

For HMRC's technical guidance on ATED, see www.gov.uk/government/publications/annual-tax-on-enveloped-dwellings-technical-guidance.

ATED – the annual charge

10.10 ATED is chargeable on companies, collective investment schemes and partnerships with company members who hold UK residential dwellings valued above a specified threshold on specified valuation dates (*FA 2013, Pt 3*). The threshold was set initially at £2 million but has been progressively reduced to £500,000 by April 2016.

ATED is based initially on the market valuation of properties at 1 April 2012. Thereafter, properties are revalued every five years, with each valuation applying to the next five chargeable periods beginning one year later. Additional valuations are required on the occasion of significant acquisitions or disposals (*FA 2013, ss 102, 103*).

10.10 *Corporate landlords*

For the chargeable periods beginning 1 April 2013, 2014, 2015 and 2016 respectively, the annual chargeable amount payable for a 'single-dwelling interest' is as follows (*FA 2013, s 99(4)*):

Chargeable period (1 April to 31 March)	2013–14	2014–15	2015–16*	2016–17**
Taxable value of property interest on relevant day	£	£	£	£
More than £500,000 but not more than £1 million	n/a	n/a	n/a	3,500
More than £1 million but not more than £2 million	n/a	n/a	7,000	7,000
More than £2 million but not more than £5 million	15,000	15,400	23,350	23,350
More than £5 million but not more than £10 million	35,000	35,900	54,450	54,450
More than £10 million but not more than £20 million	70,000	71,850	109,050	109,050
More than £20 million	140,000	143,750	218,200	218,200

* *FA 2015, s 70*

** *FA 2014, s 110*

It is important to note that the threshold is applied to each property separately and not (in general) to the total number of properties held. In the context of a buy-to-let business, if each property is valued at less than £500,000, ATED does not apply, even through the value of the whole portfolio is above this amount.

From 1 April 2016, there is a requirement to submit a return and pay the tax within 30 days of the beginning of the first day within the relevant chargeable period in which the ATED regime applies (*FA 2013, ss 159(1), (2), 163*).

For example, for the chargeable period beginning 1 April 2016, the tax must be paid and the return submitted by 30 April 2016. However, if the owner of the property does not come within the regime until 1 October 2016, the filing and payment date is deferred to 30 October 2016.

See www.gov.uk/government/publications/stld-annual-tax-on-enveloped-dwellings-ated for the ATED return form and guidance.

The ATED charge accrues day by day and, if it transpires that the payer is not chargeable for the full year, a repayment claim can be made (*FA 2013, ss 100, 106*). Late payment interest is charged on ATED paid late to HMRC, and repayment interest arises on ATED repaid late by HMRC (*FA 2009, ss 101–103*).

The amounts of annual tax payable are indexed each year in line with increases in the consumer price index (*FA 2013, s 101*). However, there is no provision for indexing the taxable value bandings, so there is an expectation that more and more properties will fall within the scope of ATED as values rise.

Penalties for late submission of an ATED return start at £100. If the form is 90 days late a £10 daily penalty applies; a further £300 is charged when the form is 6 months late. The total penalties due for one late ATED return can soon accumulate to £1,300 per form. One ATED form has to be completed per property, unless an ATED relief declaration form is submitted for a whole portfolio subject to the same relief (see **10.11**) (*FA 2009, Sch 55 para 1*).

Claiming relief for the ATED charge

10.11 Most corporate landlords are highly unlikely to fall within the ATED charge, as there is a specific relief available for residential properties which are let out on a commercial basis with a view to a profit (*FA 2013, s 132*). The relief is also available in respect of void periods as long as steps are being taken to let the property out again or to sell, demolish or convert the property without undue delay, subject to the following conditions (*FA 2013, ss 133(1)(b), 134*):

- If the property is being demolished with a view to replacing it with another dwelling, there must be an intention that the use of the new property will also qualify for ATED relief. There is no requirement to lease the new property and claim the same relief that applied to the old. For example, the company may sell the building on completion and claim relief as a property developer (*FA 2013, s 138*);

- The same rule applies if the property is converted to another dwelling – there must be an intention for the new dwelling to be used in a way that also qualifies for ATED relief;

- However, no conditions attach to selling the property or demolishing it completely without replacing it, or converting the property to non-residential use, provided that this is done without undue delay.

It is a further condition for the relief to apply that the property is not occupied by a 'non-qualifying individual', whether for rent or otherwise. A non-qualifying individual is one who is linked to the company in accordance with the legislation (*FA 2013, ss 135, 136*). This is particularly relevant in the context of owner managed or family run businesses. A non-qualifying individual includes (*FA 2013, s 136(1)*):

- Any individual who is connected to the corporate landlord, such as a controlling shareholder (*s 136(1)(b)*);

- The controlling shareholder's spouse or civil partner, as well as their relatives, and any spouse or civil partner of those relatives (*s 136(1)(e), (g), (h)*);

- The controlling shareholder's relatives as well as their respective spouses or civil partners (*s 136(1)(f)*).

See *FA 2013, s 172(1); CTA 2010, s 1122*.

10.11 *Corporate landlords*

For these purposes, a relative is either a brother, sister, ancestor or lineal descendant *(FA 2013, s 136(7))*.

Special care needs to be taken in respect of void periods, including the situation where the business has come to an end and any of the properties are empty (see **10.17**).

For example, permitting a relative to have use of the property while looking for a new qualifying tenant, or preparing the property for sale, demolition or conversion can have particularly adverse consequences:

- No relief is available in respect of the period for which the property is occupied. However, for the current and subsequent three chargeable periods, ATED relief only becomes available again when the property is let out to a tenant that is not linked to the company under the rules for non-qualifying individuals. It is not possible to argue that any prior period to finding the new tenant qualifies for relief on the basis that steps were being taken to fill the vacancy. This is the case even where the relative has vacated the property, leaving it void for a period before the new tenant is found *(FA 2013, ss 135(2), (8))*;

- Any period which falls within the current or preceding chargeable ATED period no longer qualifies for relief on the basis that steps were being taken to let it out, sell, demolish or convert the building. Accordingly, any relief previously given for these periods is withdrawn. However, this does not affect any previous relief given on the basis that the property was occupied by an unconnected tenant *(FA 2013, ss 135(4), (5))*.

Example 10.4 – ATED relief withdrawn for property made available to relatives

Molly Blackett is the sole shareholder of Beckfoot Ltd, a company that owns various properties around the Lake District area, which it leases out to tenants. The company owns Beckfoot, which used to be Molly's childhood home but which, for the last few years, has been leased to Professor Callum. The property is worth £3 million, and therefore falls within the ATED regime. However, relief is available on the basis that the company rents out the property on a commercial basis.

Professor Callum vacates Beckfoot on 31 May 2016. The property is advertised as available to let, but no new tenants appear. On 1 July 2016, Molly's two daughters. Nancy and Peggy move in to Beckfoot to stay for the summer holidays, leaving to return to university on 30 September 2016. The property continues to remain empty until 1 May 2017, when a new tenant, Dr Dudgeon signs a lease and moves in.

Analysis

Molly Blackett is connected to Beckfoot Ltd on the basis that she is the sole shareholder and therefore controls the company *(FA 2013, s 172(1); CTA 2010, s 1122(3))*.

Nancy and Peggy are her relatives, being lineal descendants (*FA 2013, s 136(7)*). They are therefore both non-qualifying individuals, being the relatives of a person connected to the company (*FA 2013, s 136(1)(f)*). Accordingly, no relief is available during their occupation for the three month period 1 July 2016 to 30 September 2016.

Unfortunately, the impact of allowing Nancy and Peggy the use of the property is not limited to the length of their visit. Relief for periods both before and after their stay is now at risk.

Chargeable period	Time period	Occupier
1 April 2015 – 31 March 2016	1 April 2015 – 31 March 2016	Professor Callum (tenant).
1 April 2016 – 31 March 2017	1 April 2016 – 31 May 2016	Professor Callum (tenant).
	1 June 2016 – 30 June 2016	Property empty.
	1 July 2016 – 30 September 2016	Nancy and Peggy Blackett (rent free).
	1 October 2016 – 31 March 2017.	Property empty.
1 April 2017 – 31 March 2018	1 April 2017 – 30 April 2017	Property empty.
	1 May 2017 – 31 March 2018	Dr Dudgeon (tenant).

Looking forward

No relief is available in respect of the property until Dr Dudgeon the new tenant moves in on 1 May 2017. This is the case in spite of the fact that the property was being advertised to let in the preceding months when it was empty. Relief would have normally been available for the 1 October 2016 to 30 April 2017 period, as the property is being advertised for sale. However, this is disallowed due to Nancy and Peggy using the property as their holiday home during the summer.

Note that the period for which relief is disallowed is not restricted to the chargeable period in which the 'disqualifying event' occurred (1 April 2016 to 31 March 2017). It extends to any period during the following three chargeable periods until such time as a new tenant is found.

Looking back

Relief would also have been available for the empty month of June 2016, shortly after Professor Callum vacated Beckfoot and when the property was first advertised to let. However, relief for this period is also disallowed due to Nancy and Peggy's subsequent visit.

10.12 *Corporate landlords*

In order to claim the relief, it is necessary to file a relief declaration return (*FA 2013, s 159A* and http://tinyurl.com/ATED-relief-return) which must state both:

- The fact that it is a relief declaration return; and
- The type of relief which is being claimed.

The return may be made in respect of more than one property, and there is no requirement to specify the details of each property on the claim form (*FA 2013, s 159A(2), (3)*). The return will also cover any additional properties that are acquired in the same chargeable period to which the return relates – there is no requirement for a separate filing (*FA 2013, s 159A(6), (7)*).

Even though no tax is payable on a successful claim for relief, there is still a requirement to file the return by the relevant dates applicable to a standard ATED return. Failure to do so may result in penalties applying (*FA 2013, s 159A(10)*). Note also that it is necessary to submit a form each year for the relevant chargeable period beginning on the 1 April.

ATED and the 15% SDLT rate

10.12 The higher SDLT rate of 15% applies to residential property acquisitions where conditions similar to the ATED charge are satisfied. Accordingly, properties acquired for more than £500,000 are potentially within the charge unless one of the reliefs is available (*FA 2003, s 55A, Sch 4A, para 1(2)*). The ATED-related charge displaces the standard and higher rates for additional dwellings (*FA 2003, s 55(1A)*).

As with the ATED annual charge, corporate landlords are unlikely to be subject to the 15% ATED rate. Note, however, that for properties worth more than £1.5million, a 15% charge could still apply under the rates applying to additional dwellings from 1 April 2016 (*FA 2003, Sch 4ZA*); see **Chapter 14**. However, the latter charge is calculated on a tiered basis, while the ATED related SDLT charge applies to the entire price paid for the property (*FA 2003, Sch 4A para 3(1)*).

Relief for the ATED-related SDLT charge should be available provided that the relevant property was acquired with the purpose of letting it out on a commercial basis, and with no intention of permitting a 'non-qualifying individual' to occupy the property (*FA 2003, Sch 4A, paras 5(1), 5(2)*). The definition of 'non-qualifying individual' is similar to that which applies for the ATED annual charge, and includes (*FA 2003, Sch 4A, para 5A(1)*):

- Any individual who is connected to the corporate landlord, such as a controlling shareholder (*FA 2003, Sch 4A, para 5A(1)(c)*);
- The controlling shareholder's spouse or civil partner, as well as their relatives, and any spouse or civil partner of those relatives (*FA 2003, Sch 4A, para 5A(1)(e), (g), (h)*);

Corporate landlords **10.13**

- The controlling shareholder's relatives as well as their respective spouses or civil partners (*FA 2003, Sch 4A, para 5A(1)(f)*).

The relief may be withdrawn if any of the following occur within the following three years (*FA 2003, Sch 4A, para 5G(1)–(3)*):

- The property (if still owned by the landlord) is no longer held exclusively for the purpose of the letting business. However, relief will not be withdrawn if the property is now being held for (re)development and/or resale in the course of a property trade;
- The latter condition extends to any property interest carved out of the superior interest acquired by the landlord and subject to the original relief. For example, the landlord cannot circumvent the condition by carving out a leasehold from a freehold interest;
- A non-qualifying individual is permitted to occupy the property (including any interest derived from the property such as a leasehold or sublease).

Failure to follow these conditions gives rise to an obligation to submit a further land transaction return within 30 days and to pay the correct amount of tax (*FA 2003, s 81(1A)*).

Note, however, that once the three year period is over, there is no further restriction. For example, a relative of the company's controlling shareholder could be permitted to live in the property without the SDLT relief being clawed back. However, this can still give rise to a clawback of the ATED annual charge (see **10.11**).

For further commentary on ATED, see **14.61**.

ATED-related capital gains – UK resident landlords

10.13 The third strand to ATED is the ATED-related CGT charge that arises on a disposal of the property (*TCGA 1992, ss 2B–2F, Sch 4ZZA*).

Corporate landlords are unlikely to be subject to any significant charge, on the basis that they are covered by the same reliefs applicable to the annual ATED charge (*TCGA 1992, s 2C(4)*). However, the CGT charge can still apply to the extent that the ATED relief is disallowed, such as when a property is occupied by family members (see **10.11**).

As a UK resident company, gains arising from the property portfolio will normally be subject to corporation tax at the rate of 20% for the financial year beginning 1 April 2016. However, to the extent that such gains are ATED-related, they are specifically excluded from corporation tax and charged to CGT at the higher rate of 28% (*CTA 2009, s 2(2A); TCGA 1992, ss 2B(3), 4(3A)*). It is therefore particularly important to avoid any situation whereby any of the rental properties fall within the ATED regime.

10.14 *Corporate landlords*

The ATED-related CGT charge arises on disposals made on or after 6 April 2013 where the consideration exceeds a specified threshold (*TCGA 1992, ss 2C(5), 2D)*). The threshold has been progressively reduced, as follows:

Fiscal year	*ATED-related CGT threshold*
	£
6 April 2013 to 5 April 2014	2 million
6 April 2014 to 5 April 2015	2 million
6 April 2015 to 5 April 2016*	1 million
6 April 2016 to 5 April 2017**	500,000

* *FA 2015, Sch 8, para 3*

** *FA 2015, Sch 8, para 4*

The threshold is reduced proportionately where the company owns only part of the property or disposes of part of it, thus ensuring that the charge cannot be avoided through fragmentation.

There are complex rules whereby the acquisition cost of the ATED property can be rebased to market value at various dates when the property was held, being 6 April 2013, 6 April 2015 and 6 April 2016 (*TCGA 1992, Sch 4ZZA, paras 2–4*). Alternatively, an election can be made to disapply the rebasing rules (*TCGA 1992, Sch 4ZZA, para 5*)).

The effect of rebasing is to ensure that only the subsequent growth in value of the property is taxed – however, this only applies to the calculation of the ATED related CGT charge. Any part of the property's gain that is not affected by ATED is taxed under the corporation tax regime in the normal way, without the benefit of this rebasing.

Indexation is unavailable for the ATED-related gain, since this is not subject to corporation tax (*TCGA 1992, Sch 4ZZA, paras 3(3), 6(2)*). The non-ATED part of the gain benefits from inflation proofing in the usual way (*TCGA 1992, Sch 4ZZA, paras 4(3), 4(5), 6(3), 6(4)*).

It is important to note that ATED-related gains and losses are ring fenced (*TCGA 1992, ss 2(7A), 2B*). In the context of a buy-to-let business, there will be few opportunities for sheltering any ATED gain that does arise. Most of the company's activities are outside the regime, and so losses are more likely to be standard losses subject to corporation tax treatment. As a consequence, such losses cannot be set against any ATED gains.

ATED-related capital gains – non-UK resident landlords

10.14 The position for non-UK companies is more complex. Before ATED was introduced in 2013, non-resident companies were not taxable on gains arising on buy-to-let properties since:

- Corporation tax is not payable by non-resident corporate investors (*CTA 2009, s 5(2)*); and
- Standard capital gains tax (CGT) did not apply due to the residence condition not being satisfied (*TCGA 1992, ss 2(1), (1A)*).

However, there are now two possible CGT charges on gains arising on investment properties:

- ATED-related CGT, which applies equally to non-UK resident companies at a rate of 28%. n theory, this should not be an issue for property investors, but it is always possible to inadvertently fall within the ATED regime (see **10.11**);
- For closely held non-resident companies, non-resident capital gains tax (NRCGT) applies to property disposals from 6 April 2015 (*TCGA 1992, ss 14D–14H, Sch 4ZZB*). The NRCGT charge is taxed at 20% for companies (*TCGA 1992, s 4(3B)*). A closely held company is controlled by five or fewer persons, except where the company itself (or at least one of the controlling persons) is a qualifying institutional investor (*TCGA 1992, ss 14F(2), (11), Sch C1*).

Both the ATED and NRCGT provisions contain complex rules whereby gains can be rebased to various dates, and which ensure that the same amount is not taxed twice. The higher rate ATED-related charge always takes precedence (*TCGA 1992, Sch 4ZZA, para 6A, Sch 4ZZB, paras 13–15*).

Gains subject to NRCGT benefit from indexation, unlike ATED related gains (*TCGA 1992, Sch 4ZZB, para 23*). However, NRCGT gains and losses are also ring-fenced (*TCGA 1992, ss 2(7B), 14D(4)*).

EXIT ISSUES – DISPOSAL OF THE PROPERTY PORTFOLIO
10.15

> **Focus**
>
> Careful planning for exiting the business should be undertaken as early as possible, and not left until the point of sale.

There are various ways in which an exit can come about. The simplest way is to sell the entire portfolio to a single buyer. On the other hand, the exit may be a gradual process involving selling the properties one by one, and distributing the proceeds to shareholders instead of recycling profits into new rental assets.

The lower rate on property disposals has already been mentioned as one of the tax advantages for operating through a corporate vehicle (see **10.3**). However, a lower tax rate does not always translate into higher profits, as the following example shows.

10.15 *Corporate landlords*

Example 10.5 – Sale of property portfolio – comparison between corporate and individual landlord

An individual P operates a buy-to-let business through BTL Limited of which he is the sole shareholder. In December 2016, he decides to sell the company to a buyer Q.

Assumptions:

	£
P's base cost in the BTL Limited shares	2 million
Value of property	10 million
The property is standing at a gain of	2 million
Mortgage debt owed by BTL Limited	1 million

In fixing a purchase price for BTL Limited, the buyer Q would expect to take into account the gains inherent in the underlying rental assets as well as the debt owed by the company. Therefore, Q would be expected to pay the following price:

Value of BTL Limited

	£
Value of property	10 million
Discount for corporation tax on property gain of £2m @ 20%	(0.4 million)
Mortgage debt owed by BTL Limited	(1 million)
Price paid	8.6 million

The amount of the net sale proceeds of the BTL shares after tax is therefore:

	£	£
Sale proceeds	8.6 million	8.6 million
Base cost	(2 million)	
Gain	6.6 million	
CGT at 20% on share sale	1.32 million	(1.32 million)
Net sale proceeds		7.28 million

However, if P had run the business as an individual landlord, his net sale proceeds would have been higher. The buyer would pay £10 million for the properties with no discount for the debt and tax charges inherent in the property:

	£
Sale proceeds	10 million
Repayment of mortgage debt	(1 million)
CGT on property gains of £2 million @ 28%	(0.56 million)
Net sale proceeds	8.44 million

The property portfolio may also be sold directly by the company, which is then liquidated, with any net cash balances being distributed to shareholders.

Example 10.6 – Sale of property portfolio – asset sale followed by liquidation

The same facts as in **Example 10.5**, but this time, BTL Limited sells the properties directly and is liquidated, with net cash balances distributed to P.

The net cash in the company after paying its debts and liabilities is calculated as follows:

	£
Sale proceeds	10 million
Repayment of mortgage debt	(1 million)
Corporation tax on property gain of £2 million @ 20%	(0.4 million)
Net sale proceeds	8.6 million

The net amount that P receives is:

	£	£
Capital distribution	8.6 million	8.6 million
Base cost	(2 million)	
Gain	6.6 million	
CGT at 20% on capital distribution	1.32 million	(1.32 million)
Net sale proceeds		7.28 million

Note that this last calculation is exactly the same as in **Example 10.5**. Accordingly the position (for P) between a share sale and asset sale is tax neutral.

Selling part of the portfolio

10.16 The examples in **10.15** are based on the assumption that the entire portfolio is to be sold to a single buyer. However, in practice, the buyer may not be interested in all the assets on sale.

10.16 *Corporate landlords*

In these circumstances, the obvious route would be for the company to sell the properties directly and retain the unwanted assets, to be sold as and when another buyer is found. The disadvantage of a direct sale is the fact that the property transfers attract SDLT charges, which can be as high as 15%, taking into account the 3% surcharge for additional properties (see **Chapter 14**). Is it still possible to effect a share sale instead?

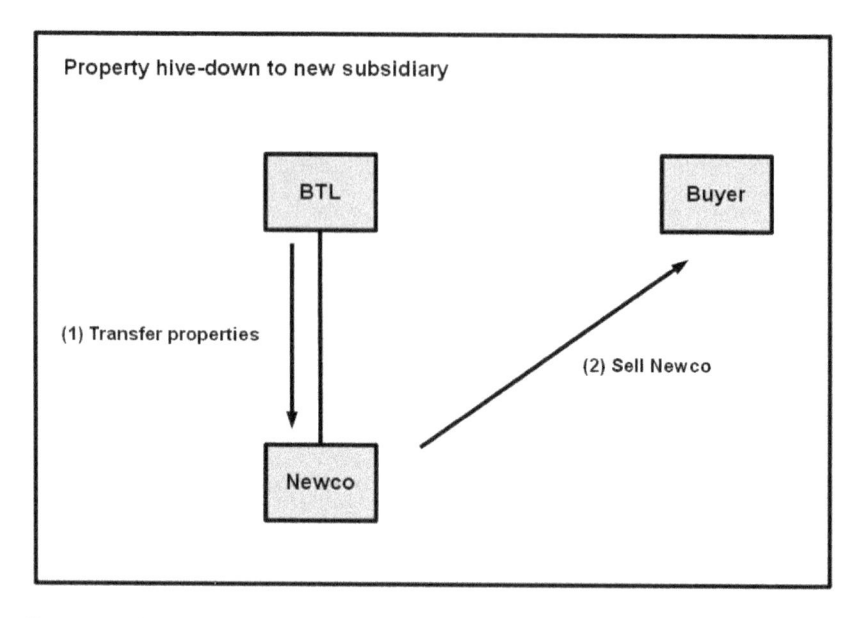

Property hive-down to new subsidiary

BTL → (1) Transfer properties → Newco → (2) Sell Newco → Buyer

For example, can the properties be transferred into a new subsidiary which is then sold on?

Unfortunately, this is not feasible due to the SDLT charge that applies when transferring the properties to the subsidiary. Intra-group relief is not available because at the time of the transfers, there are arrangements in place to sell the subsidiary to a third party (*FA 2003, Sch 7, para 2(1)*).

The solution lies in ensuring that any suitable tax planning takes place at an early stage of the business cycle, rather than at the point of sale. While it cannot be known at any point in time which properties a potential buyer will want to buy and which will remain on the reject list, certain steps can be taken at the point when it becomes clear how the portfolio is developing.

For example, the company may own a series of houses in a single street in addition to other assets elsewhere in the same town or city. Or the company could own properties in several different locations. In these circumstances, it may be worth considering splitting the portfolio by transferring each unit into a separate subsidiary.

Corporate landlords **10.17**

Property Reorganisation

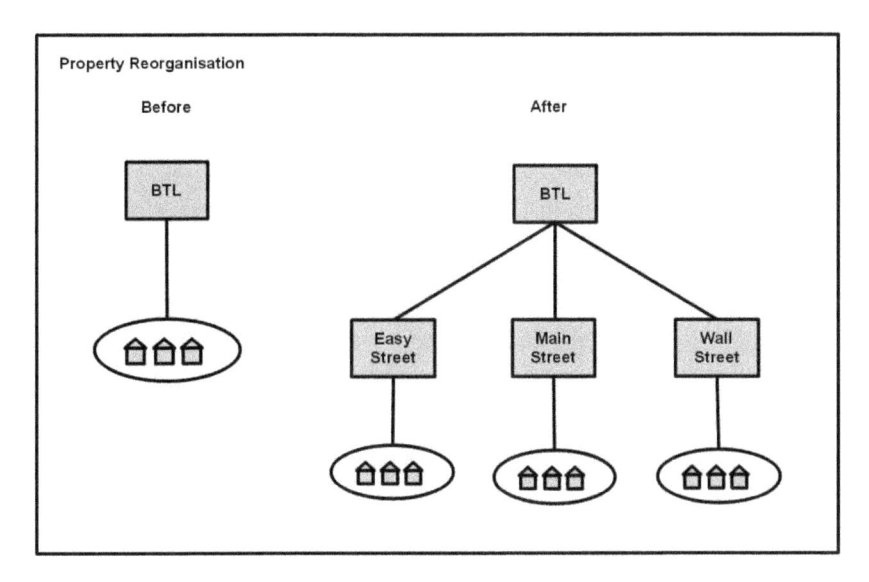

Before / *After*

[Diagram: Before – BTL company owns a portfolio of properties. After – BTL company owns three subsidiaries (Easy Street, Main Street, Wall Street), each holding properties.]

There are various tax reliefs available both in respect of taxable gains and SDLT charges that would otherwise arise on reorganising the portfolio (*TCGA 1992, ss 127–139, 171; FA 2003, Sch 7*). However, any restructuring must be undertaken early, as the reliefs can be clawed back if the relevant subsidiary is sold too quickly. For example:

- Where rental assets have been transferred to the subsidiary on a tax neutral basis, the latent gain is triggered if the subsidiary is sold within six years, and still holds the assets in question (*TCGA 1992, ss 171, 179*);

- Similarly, there is a clawback of SDLT reliefs in respect of the property transfers if the subsidiary is sold within three years while still holding the assets in question (*FA 2003, Sch 7, paras 3, 9*).

A detailed analysis of the restructuring provisions is outside the scope of this book, and the reader is referred to the latest edition of *Taxation of Company Reorganisations* (Bloomsbury Professional).

ATED issues on exiting the business

10.17 Under the ATED regime, a company owning high value residential property is subject to an annual charge, as well as an ATED-related CGT charge on disposal. Corporate landlords are unlikely to be affected, but need to be wary of inadvertently falling within the ATED regime (see **10.9–10.14**).

ATED issues are particularly relevant when planning an exit strategy. Careful planning is needed to ensure that the relief still applies to properties which are empty, or which become empty by the time that a buyer is found.

10.17 Corporate landlords

> **Focus**
>
> The relief should still apply if it is intended to sell the rental assets directly. This is on the basis that steps are being taken to sell the properties without undue delay (*FA 2013, s 134*, and **10.11**).
>
> However, if the focus is on selling the company itself, the relief could be withdrawn for empty properties that are left empty without taking steps to let them out again or put them up for sale.
>
> The solution would appear to be for the business owners to prepare for both an asset sale and a share sale at the same time.

Chapter 11

Capital gains tax

James Darmon, Tax Consultant, The TACS Partnership

> **SIGNPOSTS**
>
> - **General** – Capital gains tax (CGT) is charged on chargeable gains made by individuals, trustees and personal representatives. Companies generally pay corporation tax on chargeable gains, but are liable to CGT on 'ATED-related gains' and 'non-resident CGT' as appropriate. Residential property gains by individuals are subject to CGT rates of 18% and/or 28%; companies are liable to corporation tax at 20% (or in some cases CGT at 28%). The time of disposal of assets such as property is prescribed in the CGT legislation, which also includes special provisions in relation to options over assets (see **11.1–11.4**).
>
> - **Capital gains and losses** – Capital gains and losses arise on sales of chargeable assets, such as rental property. The gain or loss on each property is computed separately; all gains and losses in a tax year are then aggregated in determining an individual's CGT liability (if any). The capital cost of acquiring and enhancing the property can generally be taken into account, together with certain incidental costs of acquisition and disposal. There are specific provisions for part disposals, and also small disposal proceeds (see **11.5–11.18**).
>
> - **Capital losses** – Such losses are generally set off against future gains, to the extent that they cannot be set off against capital gains on the disposal of chargeable assets in the current year (see **11.19–11.20**).
>
> - **Trading losses etc and capital gains** – Aside from property rental activities, individual landlords will often have earned income, such as from self-employment or an employment. Losses may arise from those other activities, which may be the subject of a claim to offset against capital gains on (for example) rental property disposals, subject to certain computational rules (see **11.21–11.24**).
>
> - **Partnerships** – As a general rule, profits and losses accruing to partnerships are charged to the partners in their respective profit-sharing ratios. However, special rules can apply if a limited liability partnership ceases to carry on a business (see **11.25**).

11.1 *Capital gains tax*

- **CGT reliefs etc.** – Certain forms of relief from CGT may be relevant in the context of buy-to-let properties, including holdover relief for gifts on which inheritance tax is chargeable, and incorporation relief where a business is transferred to a company and certain requirements are met. A claim is also available in respect of compensation or insurance monies if (say) a property is destroyed. Inter-spouse transfers are generally subject to 'no gain, no loss' treatment for CGT purposes. Private residence relief (including 'lettings relief') may be available to individual landlords who have occupied the let property as an only or main residence at some time during their period of ownership (see **11.26–11.37**).

- **Furnished holiday lettings** – Favourable CGT treatment applies to furnished holiday lettings if certain qualifying criteria are met (see **11.38**).

- **Other issues** – Potentially relevant issues in respect of let properties include leases, exchanges of joint interests, EIS deferral relief, the compulsory purchase of land, and compliance issues (see **11.39–11.44**).

INTRODUCTION

11.1 The main legislation governing CGT is in the *Taxation of Chargeable Gains Act 1992* (*TCGA 1992*), and unless otherwise stated, all references to tax legislation in this chapter are to *TCGA 1992*.

CGT is charged on chargeable gains made by individuals and trustees. Companies are taxed on chargeable gains but their gains are subject to corporation tax not CGT (*s 8*).

Individuals who are resident in the UK are liable to CGT on disposals of all assets whether the assets are in the UK or elsewhere (*s 2(1)*).

Non-residents trading in the UK are liable to CGT on gains on business assets in the UK (*s 10*).

From 6 April 2015, non-residents are liable to CGT on disposals of UK residential property ('non-resident CGT', abbreviated to NRCGT). NRCGT is chargeable on the element of the gain which falls after that date. This is broadly done either by revaluing the property at 6 April 2015, or by time apportionment. 'Normal' capital losses cannot be used to set off against NRCGT gains: only NRCGT losses of the same year.

Where 'non-natural persons' (companies etc) own residential property valued at more than £500,000 at 6 April 2016 (reduced from £1 million at 6 April 2015), the Annual Tax on Enveloped Dwellings (ATED) needs to be considered.

Capital gains tax **11.3**

This Chapter mainly deals with CGT for individuals, although some of the considerations for individuals (eg the computation of gains) also generally apply to companies. For commentary on corporate landlords, see Chapter 10. In addition, the CGT position for non-resident landlords (including companies) in relation to UK residential property interests is discussed in Chapter 9.

A single chapter on such a wide ranging topic as CGT can only outline the basics. For further guidance on CGT generally, see *Capital Gains 2016/17*. For more detailed guidance on property tax issues (including CGT), readers are referred to the latest edition of *Property Taxes* (Bloomsbury Professional).

RATES OF CGT

11.2

> **Focus**
>
> From 6 April 2016, the CGT rates of 18% and 28% were reduced to 10% and 20% respectively. Finance Act *2016* amended *TCGA 1992, s. 4(2), (3), (4)* and *(5)* by substituting 10% and 20% for 18% and 28% where appropriate.
>
> However, this does not apply to 'upper rate gains'; essentially gains on disposals of residential property interests (*TCGA 1992, s 4BB*), which remain liable to CGT at either 18% or 28%. In other words, residential landlords remain generally subject to CGT at 18% or 28% on gains.

The normal CGT rate for trustees and personal representatives is 20% (*s 4(3)*) on gains other than 'upper rate gains. However, as noted above, gains on disposals of residential property interests remain taxable at 28%.

TIME OF DISPOSAL

11.3 All real estate must be bought and sold under the terms of a written agreement. Where a disposal is made under a contract, the time of disposal is usually the date of the contract, and not (if different) the time of completion (*s 28(1)*).

> **Focus**
>
> However, if the contract is 'conditional', the time of disposal is the date the condition (or, if more than one, the last condition) is satisfied (*s 28(2)*). For this purpose, a 'conditional' contract is one where completion of the contract is subject to a condition that the parties to the contract cannot control.

11.4 *Capital gains tax*

> **Example 11.1 – Conditional and unconditional contracts**
>
> Eric sells a property to Jack, subject to Jack obtaining satisfactory planning consent for the conversion of the property. The grant of planning consent is in the power of the local authority, so the date of disposal is the date planning consent is granted.
>
> By contrast, Billy sells a property to Frank, subject to Frank providing the cash to purchase it. This is within Frank's control (he is satisfying a term of the contract), so the contract is not conditional, and the date of disposal for CGT is the date of the contract.

OPTIONS

11.4 For this purpose, if an option is granted to buy the property, and the option is exercised, the option fee becomes part of the proceeds, and the date of disposal is the date of completion of the sale contract.

If the option is not exercised, its lapse becomes a disposal of an asset (the option), and the proceeds are subject to CGT (*ss 144ff*).

> **Example 11.2 – Option to buy property**
>
> Robert grants an option to Jimmy to buy his buy-to-let property for £250,000. Jimmy pays £50,000 for the option.
>
> If Jimmy exercises the option, Robert's proceeds are £300,000 (£250,000 + £50,000), and the date of disposal is the sale and purchase contract date.
>
> If Jimmy does not exercise the option, Robert's CGT proceeds are £50,000, and the date of disposal is the option date.

CAPITAL GAINS AND LOSSES

Computation

11.5 An individual or company which carries on a buy-to-let property business may from time to time sell properties. Such sales will give rise to capital gains or losses.

Capital gains tax **11.6**

For individuals, capital gains are calculated as follows:

	£	£
Sale Proceeds	x	
Less: Selling costs	x	
	x	A
Purchase price	x	
Purchase costs (including SDLT)	x	
Improvement costs	x	
Total costs	x	B
Capital Gain	x	**A–B**

The gain or loss on each individual asset is computed separately. All gains and losses in a tax year are then aggregated. Whether any tax is due on the aggregate gain depends on whether any relief is available against the gain. Gains may also be reduced or eliminated by the annual exemption or by losses.

11.6 The gain or loss on a disposal is calculated by taking the actual proceeds realised (or in some cases the deemed proceeds) and deducting from it the allowable expenditure. The following points should be noted in relation to disposals:

- In the straightforward case of a sale at full market value, the actual sales proceeds are used in the calculation. However, in the case of a gift of an asset, the sales proceeds are deemed to be the market value at the date of gift (*TCGA 1992, s 17*).

- Some disposals are treated as taking place at no loss or gain (eg most inter-spouse and civil partner transfers; see *s 58*).

- Disposals made for less than full market value consideration are also treated as being made for full open market value, again unless they are deemed to take place at no loss or gain (*s 17*).

- Transactions between connected persons are also deemed to take place at market value (*TCGA 1992, s 18*), unless the transfer is between spouses or civil partners.

An individual is connected with his spouse or civil partner and with any relative of himself or of his spouse or civil partner, and with the spouse or civil partner of any such relative (*TCGA 1992, s 286*).

'Relative' for this purpose means brother, sister, ancestor or lineal descendant.

If an individual is a partner in a partnership, he is connected with his business partners and each other's spouses, civil partners and relatives except in

11.7 *Capital gains tax*

connection with acquisitions and disposals of partnership assets made pursuant to bona fide commercial arrangements.

If an individual is a trustee, he is connected with the settlor of the trust, any person connected with the settlor, and any company connected with the settlement.

ALLOWABLE EXPENDITURE

11.7 The allowable expenditure which is deducted from the sales proceeds falls under four categories (*TCGA 1992, s 38*):

(1) The base cost or original acquisition cost of the asset.

(2) Improvement expenditure incurred for the purpose of enhancing the value of the asset and reflected in the state of the asset at the time of disposal.

(3) Expenditure incurred in establishing title to the asset.

(4) Incidental costs of acquisition or disposal.

In some cases, the base cost of an asset may not be the historical cost. For example, if the asset has been acquired as a gift or on a transfer between connected parties at less than market value, the market value used as sale proceeds for the transferor is the base cost to the transferee.

Gains accruing before 6 April 1965

11.8 Where a property was acquired before 6 April 1965 and disposed of after that date, part of the gain is treated as having accrued before the introduction of CGT. The overall gain is therefore reduced under the rules explained below, to eliminate that part of the gain that is treated as accruing before 6 April 1965. This is subject to 31 March 1982 rebasing.

The effect is that the gain or loss under the 6 April 1965 rules must then be compared with the gain or loss over the 31 March 1982 value (*Sch 3, para 6*).

Losses accruing before 6 April 1965

11.9 In the same way, capital losses are only allowable if they arise after 6 April 1965.

Time apportionment

11.10 The normal rule for eliminating any pre-6 April 1965 gain is to allocate the overall gain arising on the disposal between, and in proportion to, the period from the acquisition of the asset to 6 April 1965 and the period from that date up until its disposal.

March 1982 rebasing

11.11 Subject to the rules described below, gains and losses accruing on the disposal on or after 6 April 1988 of assets held on 31 March 1982 are computed as if those assets had been acquired at their market value on that date (*s 35(2)*). This is often referred to as 31 March 1982 rebasing.

There are several special provisions to accommodate conflicts between the old rules and the new:

- where there is a gain since 31 March 1982, but under the old rules there would have been a smaller gain, the rebasing rules will not apply (*s 35(3)(a)*);
- the rebasing rules will not apply where a loss would result but the old rules would produce a smaller loss (*s 35(3)(b)*);
- where the old rules (including those dealing with assets held on 6 April 1965) would produce a no gain/no loss position, the rebasing rules will not apply to give a different result (*s 35(3)(c), (d)*); and
- where the effect of the rebasing rules would be to substitute a gain for a loss, or vice versa, the relevant disposal will be deemed to give rise to neither gain nor loss (*s 35(4)*).

PART DISPOSALS

11.12 For capital gains purposes, a disposal includes a part disposal, which could be the disposal of a physical part of the asset or realising part of the value of an asset (*s 21(2)*).

In order to compute the gain on a part disposal, it is necessary to determine the allowable expenditure that can be deducted in the calculation (*TCGA 1992, s 42*).

Unless costs can be identified specifically to the part sold or the part retained, the costs attributed to the disposal are the following fraction of the total allowable costs:

$$A/(A+B)$$

Where:

A is the proceeds for the part disposal; and

B is the value of the part retained.

11.13 *Capital gains tax*

> **Example 11.3 – Part disposal of land**
>
> Mr C bought land to build a buy-to-let property in 2000, for £100,000. In 2016, he sells about half of the land for £80,000.
>
> The value of the land retained is £120,000.
>
> | | £ | £ |
> |---|---|---|
> | Sales proceeds | | 80,000 |
> | Cost of land | 100,000 | |
> | Attribute costs using A/(A+B) formula | | |
> | A | 80,000 | |
> | B | 120,000 | |
> | A/(A+B) | 0.4 | |
> | Attributable costs (0.4 × £100,000) | | (40,000) |
> | Gain | | 40,000 |
> | Cost of land retained (£100,000 less £40,000) | | 60,000 |

SMALL DISPOSAL PROCEEDS

11.13 The receipt of a capital sum derived from an asset is a disposal for CGT purposes, even though the person paying the capital sum does not acquire an asset.

There is provision for a taxpayer receiving a capital sum to elect that there is no disposal for capital gains tax purposes if the capital sum is less than 5% of the value of the asset. If the election is made, the capital sum is deducted from the allowable costs for future disposals (*s 122*).

> **Example 11.4 – Treatment of small capital sum**
>
> Mrs A has 50 acres of land, which cost £100,000 in 2005. In 2016, she sells one acre to Mr B for £2,500. The value of the remaining land is £150,000.
>
> Since the capital sum is less than 5% of the market value of the remaining holding, Mrs A can elect that there is no disposal and the allowable cost of the land for future disposals is reduced by £2,500 to £97,500.
>
> **Note** – This would only usually be advantageous to Mrs A if she has other gains to use her annual CGT exemption against.

11.14 There is a similar relief in *TCGA 1992, s 245* for capital sums where land is sold to a local authority under compulsory purchase powers, or where the authority could have exercised compulsory purchase powers. The conditions are that:

- the amount or value of the consideration for the transfer, or the market value if the transfer is not for full consideration in money or money's worth, is 'small as compared with' the value of the holding; and

- the transferor had not taken any steps by advertising or otherwise to dispose of any part of the holding or to make his willingness to dispose of it known to the acquiring authority or others.

HMRC normally accepts 5% of the full value as being 'small' for this purpose.

ALLOWABLE COSTS

11.15 Allowable costs are limited to:

- Costs of acquisition;
- Enhancement expenditure; and
- Costs of disposal.

The acquisition costs include the purchase price, together with stamp duty land tax (or land and buildings transaction tax in Scotland), legal costs of acquisition, survey costs and other costs of buying the property.

Enhancement expenditure includes any improvements or alterations to the property, provided they are reflected in the state or nature of the property on disposal. For example, an extant planning consent would be allowable, but a lapsed one would not.

Costs of disposal include advertising costs.

Any costs which have been claimed as revenue expenditure cannot be claimed as a capital deduction.

> **Example 11.5 – Allowable costs**
>
> Roger spends £20,000 on repairs and improvements to his property.
>
> He claims £12,000 as repair costs. The remaining £8,000 can be claimed as enhancement costs on disposal if the work is still reflected in the state of the property on disposal.

11.16 Where a company sells a property, it may deduct indexation allowance (ie the increase in the Retail Prices Index over the period of ownership, multiplied by each cost component).

11.17 *Capital gains tax*

For individuals, losses are calculated in the same way as gains. For companies, indexation allowance can never be used to create or increase a loss.

Use of losses

11.17 Capital losses arising on sales of buy-to-let properties may be offset against capital gains arising in the same or future years of assessment.

> **Focus**
>
> It should be noted that, where a loss arises on a sale to a connected person, or otherwise not at arm's length, HMRC has power to substitute market value for the actual sale consideration.
>
> Any losses arising on such sales may only be offset against capital gains or sales to the same person (*ss 17, 18*).

11.18 To the extent that capital losses are reported, these may also be set off against capital gains arising on disposals of other assets, such as shares and securities.

Where losses may be offset against more than one set of capital gains, the taxpayer may choose the order in which to set the losses off. This may be important, for example, if one of the gains qualifies for entrepreneurs' relief.

LOSSES: ORDER OF SET OFF

11.19 Where the taxpayer has chargeable gains in the year of assessment, he may deduct:

- any allowable losses accruing in that year of assessment. This must be done even if the net chargeable gain therefore falls below the annual exempt amount; then:

- any unused allowable losses brought forward from earlier years, but not so that the net chargeable gain is reduced below the annual exempt amount; then:

- excess losses carried back from the year of assessment in which the taxpayer dies, but again, not so as to reduce the chargeable gain below the annual exempt amount.

11.20 It should be noted that, where different gains are chargeable at different rates, *s 4B* provides that losses can generally be set off in a way that is most beneficial to the taxpayer.

Example 11.6 – Utilising capital losses

Robert has a gain of £50,000 on the sale of a buy-to-let property, and a gain of £30,000 on the sale of shares which qualified for entrepreneurs' relief. Robert has losses of £40,000 available to carry forward.

Robert can set the whole of the £40,000 against the gain on the sale of the buy-to-let property (which would otherwise be taxed at 28%).

He then sets the annual exemption against this gain to the extent possible, leaving only the gain on the sale of shares into a charge to tax, since these will be taxed at a rate of 10%.

TRADING LOSSES ETC AS CAPITAL LOSSES

11.21 In addition to operating a residential rental property business, the proprietor will often have earned income, such as from self-employment or an employment. Losses may arise from those other activities.

Where a claim for relief is made to set off trading losses (under *ITA 2007, s 64*) or employment losses under *ITA 2007, s 128*) against general income, the claimant may set any unused loss against capital gains for the same tax year.

If the trading or employment losses are claimed against the income of the year immediately preceding the year of the loss but there is insufficient income in that year to absorb the full amount of the claim, the excess loss may also be set against capital gains for that preceding year.

11.22 A claim to set unused losses against capital gains can be made:

- if relief is available under *ITA 2007, s 64* or *s 128* and a claim is made under that section to deduct the loss in calculating the claimant's net income for the year; or

- if relief is available as above, but the claimant has no taxable income for the year so that a claim for income tax relief would not be possible (*TCGA 1992, s 261B(2)*).

The claim under *s 261B* is to determine the 'relevant amount', ie the amount of the loss that has not been relieved against income for the year of loss and has not already been relieved for any other tax year under any other provision (*s 261B(3)*). Where that amount is 'finally determined', it is to be treated as an allowable loss for the tax year for which the claim under *s 64* or *s 128* was made (*s 261B(4)*). The relevant amount then ceases to be available for income tax relief (*s 261B(7)(a)*).

The relevant amount is finally determined when the amount of the loss can no longer be varied.

11.23 *Capital gains tax*

11.23 Having determined the relevant amount, the next stage is to compute the 'maximum amount' which is the upper limit on the amount of the unused losses which can be set against capital gains. This is the amount on which the claimant would otherwise be chargeable to capital gains tax ignoring:

- the annual exemption (thus a claim to relief under *s 261B* will mean that in some cases the annual exemption is wholly or partly wasted, as there is no provision permitting a partial claim to be made; it is an all-or-nothing claim); and

- any event occurring after the relevant amount has been finally determined, which results in the amount chargeable to capital gains tax being reduced, for example a rollover relief claim.

11.24 A claim for relief under *s 261B* must be made on the first anniversary of the 31 January following the end of the tax year in which the loss arose, in other words within 22 months of the end of that year (*s 261B(8)*). This is the same timescale as for claims under *s 64* and *s 128*. In practice a single claim under *ITA 2007 s 64* or *s 128* will be accepted, provided that it is made clear that it is also made under *TCGA 1992, s 261B* (see HMRC's Business Income manual at BIM85025).

PARTNERSHIPS

11.25 As a general rule, capital losses on sales of property by partnerships belong to the partners in their profit-sharing ratios. This includes limited liability partnerships. As a general rule, profits and losses accruing to any such partnership are charged to the partners in their respective profit-sharing ratios.

However, if an LLP ceases to carry on a business, losses are no longer distributed between the partners, but become losses of the LLP (essentially, the LLP loses its previous fiscally transparent treatment when it ceases business).

CGT RELIEFS ETC

Relief on gifts on which IHT is due

11.26 Holdover relief is available for gifts between individuals or trustees of a settlement on which inheritance tax is chargeable (*s 260*).

Gifts between individuals are usually 'potentially exempt transfers' and are not chargeable to inheritance tax in the terms of this relief. Therefore this relief mainly applies to transfers to and from trusts. The effect is that the transferee takes over the transferor's base cost.

Capital gains tax **11.28**

> **Focus**
>
> It should be noted that the relief still applies even if no inheritance tax is payable on the gift because the transfer is within the inheritance tax nil rate band.

INCORPORATION RELIEF

11.27 If a business is incorporated by transferring the business currently carried on by a sole trader or partnership to a company, there will normally be disposals for CGT purposes of the business assets. However, is possible to defer the gains arising using incorporation relief, if certain conditions are met (*s 162*).

In order for the relief to apply, the business, including all of the assets of the business (other than cash), must be transferred as a going concern in return for shares in the company it is transferred to. Sometimes the owners of a business may prefer to keep some business assets in their own name, such as business premises, but this will mean that the relief cannot apply.

If the conditions are met, the cost of the shares acquired is reduced by the postponed gain.

The relief is given automatically, and so there is no need to make a claim.

If the consideration is not only shares but, for example, includes a loan account, then the relief will be restricted and some of the gain will remain taxable.

HMRC do not treat the assumption of business liabilities by the transferee company as consideration for the transfer, however, this is not extended to include personal liabilities such as the tax liabilities of the unincorporated business (ESC D32).

Provided that a business is being carried on, within the meaning discussed in *American Leaf Blending CO Sdn Bhd v Director-General of Inland Revenue* [1978] 3 All ER 1185, HMRC accept that this relief applies to property investment businesses. However, the stamp duty land tax (or land and buildings transaction tax in Scotland) position requires careful consideration on such a transfer.

For more detailed commentary on the incorporation of a buy-to-let property rental business, see **Chapter 13**.

COMPENSATION AND INSURANCE MONIES

11.28 The loss or destruction of an asset is a disposal for CGT purposes. Where the owner of an asset receives compensation or insurance money

11.29 *Capital gains tax*

following the loss or destruction of an asset, and the proceeds are wholly, or wholly but for a small element, which is reasonably not so applied, applied in restoring the asset, those proceeds are not brought into account as disposal proceeds, if the recipient makes a claim (*s 23(4)*).

'Small' in this context means the greater of:

- £3,000; or
- 5% of the proceeds.

> **Example 11.7 – Compensation for damaged let property**
>
> Leonard bought a house for letting for £100,000. Following a fire some years later, he receives £200,000 compensation. He spends £198,000 restoring the house.
>
> On making a claim, he is not treated as making a disposal for CGT purposes.

INTER-SPOUSE TRANSFERS

11.29 Where a property is transferred from one spouse to the other, the transfer is treated as being for such consideration that no gain or loss arises (*s 58*).

A 'spouse' for these purposes means two people living together as husband and wife. It also includes the partners in a civil partnership.

PRIVATE RESIDENCE RELIEF

What is a dwelling-house?

11.30 A gain on the disposal of a property which is, or has at any time in the individual's period of ownership been, his only or main residence is exempt from capital gains tax (*s 222*).

There is no definition of what constitutes a 'dwelling-house' in the terms of the legislation so it can be a house, a flat or even a caravan or houseboat.

A 'dwelling-house' could be made up of more than one property. A detached garage or children's playroom would usually be part of the dwelling-house and it is possible that cottages occupied by domestic staff may also be part of a dwelling-house.

What are gardens or grounds?

11.31 The exemption is also extended to garden or grounds for 'occupation and enjoyment with that residence' (*s 222(1)(b)*).

The garden or grounds should normally be less than 0.5 hectares unless a larger area is required for enjoyment of the dwelling-house (*s 222(3)*).

'Garden or grounds' is not defined in statute. HMRC regard a garden based on a dictionary definition as:

> 'a piece of ground, usually partly grassed and adjoining a private house, used for growing flowers, fruit or vegetables, and as a place of recreation' (see HMRC's Capital Gains manual at CG64360).

Grounds are suggested to be:

> 'Enclosed land surrounding or attached to a dwelling house or other building serving chiefly for ornament or recreation.'

Based on the above, agricultural land used for a trade is not part of the garden or grounds but paddocks and orchards and overgrown land may be part of the garden or grounds.

What is a residence?

11.32 There is no definition in the legislation of 'residence'.

In simple terms, 'A residence is a place where somebody lives' as stated by Nourse J in *Frost v Feltham* Ch D 1980, 55 TC 10. A residence may be in the UK or abroad.

It appears that residence is a matter of quality rather than quantity and HMRC will not suggest any minimum period of occupancy which will mean that a property qualifies as a residence (CG64435).

However, in some limited circumstances from 6 April 2015 the taxpayer may have to meet a 'day count test' in order to qualify for the relief (see **11.35** below).

Focus

The exemption applies in full if the property has been the individual's main residence throughout the period of ownership although relief was always given for the final 36 months of ownership.

From 6 April 2014, the final period exemption reduced from 36 months to 18 months. Periods before 31 March 1982 are ignored (*s 223(1)*).

11.33 *Capital gains tax*

11.33 If the property has not always been the main residence, for example if the property was originally bought as a main residence, then let, then the relief is available for a fraction of the gain.

The fraction is calculated as the period of main residence (including the last 18 months of ownership even if not the main residence then) divided by the total period of ownership (*s 223(2)*).

> **Example 11.8 – Calculating the exempt fraction of a gain**
>
> Rachel buys a flat on 1 January 2004. She lives in the flat until 1 January 2012, then lets it. She sells the flat on 1 July 2016.
>
> The total ownership period is 12.5 years, of which the first 8 years were as her private residence, plus the last 18 months (1.5 years, making a total of 9.5 years).
>
> The exempt fraction of the gain is 9.5/12.5.

Permitted periods of absence

11.34 Certain periods of absence are 'permitted' and can be ignored in the calculations (*s 223(3)*):

- periods not exceeding in total three years;
- any period throughout which the taxpayer was employed outside the UK; and
- periods of up to four years in total when the taxpayer could not reside in the property because of the requirements of his employment.

In all cases it is important that the property is the main residence before and after the absence.

> **Example 11.9 – Absence whilst working abroad**
>
> Amy purchased a house in August 2000, from which date it was used as her only residence until February 2001, when she moved to Dubai to work for her employer. She returned to the UK in August 2005 when she again occupied the house as her only residence.
>
> In February 2006, she decided to put the house up for sale and moved back to live with her parents in their house. Unfortunately, her house was not sold until August 2015, when a gain of £90,000 was realised.

	Years	£
Gain		90,000
Total period of ownership		
August 2000 – August 2015	15.0	
Total period of residence		
August 2000 – February 2001	0.5	
Permitted absence		
February 2001 – August 2005	4.5	
August 2005 – February 2006	0.5	
February 2006 – August 2015		
Not residence but last 18 months deemed residence	1.5	
	7.0	
Relief – 7.0/15		(42,000)
Chargeable gain		48,000

11.35 From 6 April 2015, non-UK residents are subject to UK CGT on gains on disposals of UK residential property. If the property is the seller's main home, private residence relief may be available against the gain.

As a part of the introduction of these provisions, there are new rules *which apply to UK residents as well as non-residents*, which can restrict the availability of the relief where the property is located in a different territory to the one in which the taxpayer is resident.

A residence owned by a UK or non-UK resident will only be capable of qualifying for private residence relief if it is located in a territory in which the individual, their spouse or civil partner is resident or, where it is located in a different territory, the individual meets the 'day count test' in relation to the residence.

The 'day count test' will be met if the individual or their spouse/civil partner spent at least 90 days in the property in the tax year (although no one day can be counted twice by virtue of the individual and their spouse/civil partner both being there at the same time).

Where the individual or their spouse/civil partner has an interest in more than one dwelling in the territory in which the property is located, days spent in those other dwellings can be aggregated with days spent in the property in question to determine whether the 90-day threshold is met. However, it is only possible to nominate *one* property for private residence relief.

11.36 *Capital gains tax*

Where the individual owns the property for a part only of a tax year, the 90-day threshold in the day count test will be reduced pro rata.

If the 90-day rule is not met, the individual will be counted as away from the property for that tax year.

> **Focus**
>
> A non-resident individual who wishes to make sure they satisfy the day count test so that a property qualifies for PPR will have to be careful that they do not prejudice their residence status under the statutory residence test set out in *Finance Act 2013, Sch 45*; for example days spent in the UK is crucial in the 'sufficient ties test'.

More than one property

11.36 For the purpose of private residence relief, an individual and his spouse (or civil partner) can only have one main residence at any time (*s 222(5)*).

> **Focus**
>
> If a taxpayer owns several properties which are used as residences, then he may elect to specify which property is the main residence.
>
> The election must be made within two years of acquiring a second residence.
>
> If no election is made, a main residence will be determined based on the facts.

Let properties

11.37 Normally private residence relief will not apply to an investment property, such as a buy-to-let property.

It should be noted that there is a provision which disapplies private residence relief if a house was bought for the purpose of realising a gain (*s 224(3)*).

There is a specific 'lettings relief' which applies if a taxpayer has let the whole or part of his residence as residential accommodation for part of the period of ownership. Up to £40,000 of the gain which would otherwise be taxable can be exempt (*s 223(4)*).

Example 11.10 – Lettings relief in action

Charlotte sells her house making a gain of £60,000. 60% of the house has been used as her main residence and 40% has been let.

	£	£
Gain on sale of property		60,000
Private residence relief 60% of £60,000		(36,000)
Gain on let part		24,000
Letting relief		
Lowest of:		
(a) Statutory limit	40,000	
(b) Private residence relief	36,000	
(c) Gain on let part	24,000	(24,000)
Gain		0

Focus

Private residence relief was the subject of much press coverage in relation to the MPs' expenses scandal. With the reduction of the final period relief and the changes relating to properties abroad, the relief is now being restricted, possibly in response to this publicity.

FURNISHED HOLIDAY LETTINGS

11.38 It is possible (for 2011/12 onwards) to have either an EEA holiday letting business (a holiday letting business in a European Economic Area territory), or a UK holiday letting business, depending on where the let property is located. UK and EEA holiday lettings are treated as two separate businesses.

If either incurs a loss, it is possible to set that loss against future profits of the same business. For this purpose, the UK and EEA businesses are counted as separate businesses, so it is not possible to set off (say) losses in the UK furnished holiday letting business against profits of the EEA business.

'Holiday letting' for this purpose means property which satisfies certain letting and occupation conditions (*ITTOIA 2005, s 323*; *CTA 2009, s 267*):

11.39 *Capital gains tax*

Available for commercial letting	210 days (140 days for 2011/12 and earlier years)
Actually let commercially	105 days (70 days in 2011/12 and earlier years)
	A period of longer-term occupation is not a letting as holiday accommodation (see below)
Pattern of occupation	No more than 155 days of longer-term occupation. This means occupation for a continuous period of more than 30 days.

To the extent that furnished holiday lettings (FHLs) can be treated as a trade, hold over relief may be available for any transfer (for example, to a company) under the business assets rules. In addition, if the FHLs can be treated as a trade, other reliefs available to trading businesses (for example, entrepreneurs' relief, stamp duty land tax and CGT relief on reorganisations) can apply. These do not normally apply to landlords.

For detailed commentary on furnished holiday lettings, see **Chapter 5**.

OTHER ISSUES

Leases

11.39 The grant of a long lease out of a freehold interest or another long lease is treated as a normal capital disposal, however, the calculation recognises that the freeholder will get the property back at the end of the lease and so is taxed as a part disposal where A is the premium received and B is the residual value retained by the landlord plus the value of the right to receive the rent (*Sch 8(2)*).

> **Example 11.11 – Grant of a long lease**
>
> Mr B bought a freehold property in April 2000 for £200,000. In 2015, he decided to grant a 60-year lease of the property to Mr C for a premium of £120,000 and annual rent of £10,000 per annum.
>
> It was agreed that the value of the freehold reversion was £60,000 and the value of the right to receive the rent was £60,000.

Mr B's gain on the grant of the lease is calculated as:

	£
Proceeds	120,000
Allowable cost:	
fraction A/(A+B) is 120,000/(120,000+60,000+60,000)	
ie ½ of the original cost of £200,000	(100,000)
Gain	20,000

11.40 The calculation of the gain on a grant of a short lease out of a freehold or a long lease is modified as part of the premium for the grant is taxed as income and is therefore excluded from the calculation. This is easiest to show in an example.

Example 11.12 – Grant of a short lease

Mr C bought a freehold property for £45,000 some years ago.

In 2015, he granted a 46-year lease for a premium of £35,000 and a market rent.

The value of the freehold reversion was £50,000 (including the right to receive the rent).

The amount taxed as income is:	£
The premium	35,000
Less: the premium × (no. of years of the lease – 1)/50 ie £35,000 × (46–1)/50	(31,500)
	3,500
The calculation of the gain is:	
Premium received	35,000
Less: taxed as income	(3,500)
	31,500
Allowable cost	
(A – amount taxed as income)/(A+B) × cost ie (35,000–3,500)/(35,000+50,000) × 45,000	(16,677)
Gain	14,823

11.41 *Capital gains tax*

EXCHANGE OF JOINT INTERESTS

11.41 Where two or more people own land jointly, and wish to separate that land, this would strictly be two disposals, each at market value. However, where no cash passes, the gains can be held over in full, and the base costs or the divided land remain the same as the original base costs. The detailed rules are set out in *ss 248A–248E*.

Where an equalisation payment is made which exceeds the base cost, this will form the proceeds for a CGT computation.

EIS DEFERRAL RELIEF

11.42 Where a gain on any asset is reinvested in shares under the enterprise investment scheme (EIS) (*Sch 5B*) it can be possible to delay paying CGT on the amount of the gain equal to the amount you invested.

To receive this relief there is a period in which the taxpayer must invest in EIS shares – between one year before and three years after disposing of your original assets.

Income tax relief does not have to be claimed in respect of the EIS shares and, for deferral relief, an individual can be connected with the EIS company ie control of more than 30% of the company.

COMPULSORY PURCHASE OF LAND

11.43 Where a landowner disposes of land to a local authority, or other authority which has (or exercises) compulsory purchase powers, the owner took no steps to advertise the property for sale, and the owner uses the proceeds to buy new land (other than a dwelling on which any element of private residence relief is available), that part of the gain can be rolled over, and the tax deferred.

COMPLIANCE ISSUES

11.44 CGT is included on an individual or company's tax return. For individuals, the filing date is:

- 31 October following the end of the tax year if the return is submitted on paper.

    (**Note** – If HMRC do not issue a request for an individual to send in a tax return until after 31 July following the tax year in question, the submission date is extended to three months following the date that the request is received by the taxpayer.)

- 31 January following the end of the tax year if the return is submitted online.

(**Note** – If HMRC do not issue a request for an individual to send in a tax return until after 31 October following the tax year in question, the submission date is extended to three months following the date that the request is received by the taxpayer.)

The tax must normally be paid by 31 January following the end of the tax year.

Companies must file their corporation tax returns within 12 months of the end of the company's corporation tax accounting period. This is known as the 'statutory filing date'. Chargeable gains are included in a company's profits.

Payment of corporation tax is governed by separate rules depending on the size of the company, as follows:

- If the company's taxable profits are £1.5 million or less, tax must be paid within nine months after the end of the corporation tax accounting period (the 'normal due date'). For example, if a company's accounting period ends on 31 May, its corporation tax payment is due on or before 1 March the following year.

- If the company's taxable profits for an accounting period are at an annual rate of more than £1.5 million, corporation tax for that period is normally paid in instalments. If the company has a 12 month accounting period, these instalments are paid:

    - six months and 13 days after the first day of the accounting period;
    - three months after the first instalment;
    - three months after the second instalment (14 days after the last day of the accounting period);
    - three months and 14 days after the last day of the accounting period.

Companies with annual taxable profits of £20 million or more will, from 1 April 2017, have to pay under a revised quarterly payment system, paying corporation tax in quarterly instalments in the third, sixth, ninth and twelfth months of their accounting period.

Chapter 12

Inheritance tax

Mark McLaughlin CTA (Fellow), ATT (Fellow), TEP, Tax Consultant, Mark McLaughlin Associates Ltd

> **SIGNPOSTS**
>
> - **Scope** – Inheritance tax (IHT) can arise on chargeable lifetime transfers of assets such as buy-to-let property (eg gifts into most types of trust), and on the value of the estate on death, which may include such property. Individuals domiciled in the UK are liable to IHT on chargeable worldwide property. Non-UK domiciled individuals are also liable to IHT, but presently only on chargeable UK property (see **12.1–12.2**).
>
> - **Ownership** – The legal and beneficial owners of buy-to-let property will be the same in many instances. However, this will not automatically be the case. In many instances, buy-to-let property is held jointly, for example between spouses (or civil partners). Jointly-owned property (in England and Wales) can be held beneficially either as 'joint tenants' or as 'tenants in common', with different consequences of each type of ownership. A joint tenancy can be severed, with the owners holding the property as tenants in common. An alternative to the direct ownership of property by an individual is ownership by a company (see **12.3–12.9**).
>
> - **Investment or business**? – Particularly where individuals jointly own one or a small number of buy-to-let properties, those properties will normally be regarded as a passive investment. However, in some cases the letting activities may be organised in a business-like manner. A number of tax cases have considered whether such activities amount to a business, and if so whether the business is eligible for business property relief (BPR) for IHT purposes, or is excluded on the basis that the business consists wholly or mainly of making or holding investments. This exclusion from BPR has been held to apply to furnished holiday lettings (see **12.10–12.16**).
>
> - **Valuation** – As a general rule, an asset is valued for IHT purposes at the price it might reasonably be expected to fetch if sold in the open market at the time of transfer. However, the value of a lifetime gift is generally measured by reference to the reduction in value of the

transferor's estate as a result of the transfer (ie the 'loss to donor' principle). The practical approach to valuations of undivided shares of property may differ according to the particular circumstances. Factors to consider in valuing a joint owner's share can include the availability of discounts for co-ownership, and (in the case of joint ownership by spouses or civil partners) the 'related property' valuation provisions. Very often, the acquisition of buy-to-let property will be financed at least partly by a mortgage or other loan, and in such cases the extent of any deduction for liabilities in valuing a lifetime transfer or the death estate will need to be considered (see **12.17–12.30**).

- **Lifetime transfers** – A lifetime gift of property may be potentially exempt for IHT purposes (eg a gift from father to adult daughter), which becomes an exempt transfer if the donor survives for at least seven years. Conversely, the gift may be immediately chargeable (eg a gift into a discretionary trust) at the 'lifetime' IHT rate (20% for 2016/17) to the extent that it exceeds the transferor's nil rate band, after deducting any available reliefs and exemptions. Additional IHT at the 'death' rate (40% for 2016/17) generally applies to immediately chargeable lifetime transfers made within seven years from the death of the transferor (see **12.31–12.33**).

- **Gifts with reservation** – Anti-avoidance provisions can apply to lifetime gifts where an individual gifts an asset such as property but continues to have the use or enjoyment of it. Where those provisions apply, the gifted asset is treated as forming part of the donor's death estate. If the benefit is ended during his lifetime, the donor is treated as having made a potentially exempt transfer at that time, which becomes a chargeable transfer on death within the following seven years. There are certain exceptions and exclusions from an IHT charge under the gifts with reservation provisions in appropriate circumstances (see **12.34–12.41**).

- **IHT on death** – IHT is charged (subject to reliefs and exemptions, and the IHT threshold or 'nil rate band') on the deceased's estate as if, immediately before his death, he had made a transfer of value. The value transferred is deemed to equal the value of his estate immediately before death. There are specific rules for the deduction of liabilities from the estate. Certain reliefs may be claimed in appropriate circumstances, such as where the value of a lifetime gift has fallen between the time the gift was made and death ('fall in value' relief) and on the sale of an interest in land by 'the appropriate person' within a defined period following death for a genuinely lower value, subject to certain restrictions ('post-death loss' relief) (see **12.42–12.55**).

12.1 *Inheritance tax*

> • **Other points** – An IHT liability may be paid by ten equal yearly instalments (as opposed to under the general rules for the payment of IHT) on 'qualifying property' including land, where certain conditions apply. A 'pre-owned assets' income tax charge (which was introduced in response to certain IHT planning arrangements) can apply in some circumstances in respect of certain assets including property, subject to various exclusions and exemptions (see **12.56–12.60**).

INTRODUCTION

12.1 Property prices are such that the value of one or more interests in buy-to-let property owned directly or indirectly (eg through ownership of a company's shares) is likely to form a significant part of an individual's estate for inheritance tax (IHT) purposes in most cases. The IHT implications of property ownership are therefore an important consideration.

IHT is a tax on chargeable transfers (*IHTA 1984, s 1*; unless otherwise stated, all statutory references in this chapter are to *IHTA 1984*, unless otherwise stated). It applies to chargeable transfers of value made by an individual during lifetime (see **12.31**), and to the value of his estate on death (see **12.42**), subject to various exemptions, exclusions and reliefs.

A transfer of value is a disposition by a person resulting in the value of his estate immediately after the disposition being less than it would be but for the disposition. The amount by which his estate is reduced is the measure of the transfer of value (*s 3(1)*). This is sometimes referred to as the 'loss to donor' principle.

Chargeable lifetime transfers are charged at half of the rate on death (*s 7(2)*). The 'death rate' of IHT is 40% (for 2016/17) and, therefore, chargeable lifetime transfers above the nil rate band are charged at 20%.

The IHT charge

12.2 Individuals domiciled in the UK are liable to IHT on chargeable worldwide property. Non-UK domiciled individuals are also liable to IHT, but only on chargeable UK property (*s 6(1)*).

The government intends legislating to ensure that, from April 2017, IHT is payable on all UK residential property owned directly or indirectly by non-UK domiciliaries, with a view to blocking what HMRC describes as 'enveloping' (ie holding residential property indirectly through offshore structures). The relevant legislation (which will amend the definition of 'excluded property' for these purposes) is expected to be included in *Finance Bill 2017*.

IHT is broadly a cumulative tax charge on the value transferred by a chargeable transfer made by an individual during his lifetime within the preceding seven-year period (ie broadly the loss to the donor), and on the value of his estate on death. A 'chargeable transfer' is any transfer of value made by an individual, other than an exempt transfer (*s 2*). IHT is also charged on certain events relating to settlements (eg gifts to a discretionary trust).

The IHT charge on death (and in respect of certain settled property) is brought into charge by deeming a transfer of value to have been made immediately before death, equal to the value of the person's estate (and the value of the settled property, if appropriate) (*ss 4(1), 52(1)*).

Chargeable transfers within the seven-year period ending with the date of the latest chargeable transfer are cumulated, for the purposes of determining the IHT rate (*s 7*). Where chargeable lifetime transfers and the individual's death estate do not exceed the IHT threshold (or 'nil rate band', as it is more commonly known) there is no IHT liability.

OWNERSHIP

Introduction

12.3 IHT is quantified broadly by reference to a person's estate. An estate generally includes property to which the person is beneficially entitled (*s 5(1)*). 'Property' is defined as including rights and interests of any description (*s 272*), such as in respect of buy-to-let property.

HMRC guidance in its Inheritance Tax manual uses the term 'beneficially entitled' to mean that the estate only includes property to which a person is entitled, or in which they have an interest for their own benefit. In England, Wales and Northern Ireland this includes property which a person owns either legally or beneficially (nb different considerations apply in Scotland). A person is not beneficially entitled to property held purely in a fiduciary capacity (eg as a bare trustee) (IHTM4031).

> **Focus**
>
> Although the legal and beneficial owners of buy-to-let property will be the same in many cases, this will not automatically be the case. The absolute owner of a property may split the legal interest from the beneficial enjoyment. This can be done by (say) giving the legal ownership to trustees and the beneficial interest to a named beneficiary (or beneficiaries).

The meaning of beneficial entitlement is extended so that a person who is beneficially entitled to an interest in possession in settled property is treated as beneficially entitled to the property in which the interest subsists (s 49(1)). Thus the trustees of a qualifying interest in possession settlement may be the

12.4 *Inheritance tax*

legal owners of a property, but a beneficiary may be treated for IHT purposes as being beneficially entitled to the property.

Sole owner

12.4 An individual may acquire buy-to-let properties by more than one means. For example, the individual may have inherited one such property (eg from a deceased spouse or civil partner) and purchased a second property on the open market.

An inherited property will generally give rise to an immediate increase in the value of the recipient individual's estate for IHT purposes (unless, for example, the property is 'excluded property' because the property is situated abroad and the individual is not domiciled in the UK; (*s 6*)).

By contrast, the purchase of a buy-to-let property may, for example, result in the individual replacing one chargeable estate asset (ie cash) with a different asset (ie the property). In many cases, there will be little or no overall increase in the value of the individual's estate. However, the IHT position will probably change, as the value of the property can normally be expected to increase over time.

Where other assets are being sold to finance the purchase of a property, the individual should consider realising assets on which no IHT reliefs or exemptions are available, and retaining 'IHT efficient' assets, such as shares in a company on which 100% business property relief would be available to the shareholder (*s 104(1)(a)*).

To the extent that insufficient liquid assets are available, the individual may need to borrow funds to finance the purchase of a property. The deduction of liabilities (eg a mortgage or loan) in determining the value of the individual's estate is considered later in this chapter.

Joint owners

12.5 In many cases, buy-to-let property may be held jointly, for example between spouses (or civil partners).

Jointly owned property can be held beneficially either as 'joint tenants' or as 'tenants in common'. Ownership will be as joint tenants (in equal or identical interests) unless the owners declare otherwise. Separate categories of joint ownership apply under Scots law (see IHTM15091 and following), which is beyond the scope of this chapter.

The joint holding of property as joint tenants is the only form of co-ownership capable of existing in law (in contrast with beneficial ownership, ie in equity). By reason of the right of survivorship, the survivor takes the entire interest absolutely by operation of law.

Inheritance tax **12.8**

The interest of a joint owner passes upon death by survivorship to the remaining owner. Thus it is impossible (subject to severance, which cannot be by will but, as a matter of practice, can be achieved for IHT purposes by deed of variation) to make lifetime or death dispositions to third parties because this interest accrues automatically to the survivor.

As to partnership property, see **12.11** below.

12.6

Focus

A joint tenancy can be severed, with the owners holding the asset as tenants in common.

An important consequence of ownership as tenants in common is that the interest or share of any owner passes on death under their will or, if there is no will, under the rules of intestacy.

This type of holding is frequently found to be the most satisfactory from an IHT and practical perspective. In the case of joint ownership by a married couple, each spouse has a separate (eg half) share, which he or she can separately leave by will or dispose of during lifetime.

12.7 As to the joint ownership of buy-to-let properties in the context a partnership business (see **12.11**); see also **Chapter 8** (Jointly-owned properties).

Trustees

12.8 The words 'trust' and 'settlement' are often used interchangeably, implying that they share the same meaning. However, a settlement is widely defined for IHT purposes and can be created 'by instrument, by parol or by operation of law' (see *s 43*), whereas generally speaking, a trust is created and structured more formally, usually by a written document, either during an individual's lifetime (a trust 'deed' or 'instrument'), or perhaps to commence upon death (a 'will trust'). There are specific statutory provisions which apply to the definition of a settlement in Scotland (*s 43(4)*).

The typical characteristics of a trust may therefore be summarised as comprising: a donor (the 'settlor'); a transfer of property (the 'trust property'); to a person (the 'trustee'); on behalf of persons beneficially entitled (the 'beneficiaries'). As indicated (at **12.3**), the legal title to a property may be settled in the name of trustees, who hold it on trust for the beneficiaries who are the persons beneficially entitled to the property, subject to the terms of the trust.

The lifetime gift of a buy-to-let property to a relevant property trust (ie discretionary trusts and, since 22 March 2006, most types of interest in possession trusts) will normally be an immediately chargeable lifetime transfer. IHT at the lifetime rate (20% for 2016/17) may become due (subject to any

12.9 *Inheritance tax*

reliefs and exemptions) if the value of such gifts exceeds the donor's available nil rate band (£325,000 for 2016/17). Additional IHT becomes chargeable at the death rate (40% for 2016/17) in respect of an immediately chargeable lifetime transfer made within seven years from the settlor's death.

The IHT treatment of settled property is beyond the scope of this book. However, in very broad terms, the IHT legislation distinguishes between settlements with an interest in possession (*Pt 3, Ch 2*) and settlements without an interest in possession (*Pt 3, Ch 3*); the latter category are often referred to as 'relevant property' trusts.

An individual entitled to an interest in possession which came into existence before 22 March 2006 is generally deemed to own the settled property in which their interest subsists (*s 49(1)*). However, where a person becomes beneficially entitled to an interest in possession in settled property created on or after 22 March 2006, that property will only be treated as forming part of their estate for IHT purposes if the interest is an 'immediate post death interest', a 'disabled person's interest', or a 'transitional serial interest'. Otherwise, it will generally be relevant property.

Relevant property trusts are subject to their own IHT regime. For example, at each ten year anniversary from the date the trust was created, there is a 'principal' IHT charge (ie at a maximum of 6% on the value of the relevant property (ie assets after reliefs) in the trust). Furthermore, appointments out of the trust capital are liable to a 'proportionate' charge (commonly referred to as an 'exit charge').

For commentary on the IHT implications of trusts, see *Inheritance Tax 2016/17*, *Trusts and Estates 2016/17* and *Tax Advisers Guide to Trusts* (Bloomsbury Professional).

Companies

12.9 An alternative to the direct ownership of property is ownership by a company. An individual's estate in this context would comprise the company's shares, as opposed to the property itself.

The gift of a buy-to-let property from one individual to another is a potentially exempt transfer (PET) (ie which only becomes chargeable to IHT if the donor dies within seven years of making the gift; *s 3A(1A), (5)*). By contrast, a lifetime transfer of the property to a company cannot be a PET (ie it is an immediately chargeable lifetime transfer). IHT at the lifetime rate may become due (subject to any reliefs and exemptions) if the transfer of value exceeds the nil rate band.

However, a transfer of value is broadly measured for IHT purposes by reference to the loss in value of the donor's estate as the result of making it. Thus if (for example) the former property owner and the company shareholder are the same, there may be little or no diminution in value of the individual's estate.

On a 'gift' of property to a company in which the original owner and a spouse (or civil partner) are equal shareholders, the former owner will, on the face of it, lose half the value of the property, with a corresponding increase in the spouse's estate. However, in the case of husband and wife (both of whom are domiciled in the UK), transfers between spouses are generally exempt (*s 18*).

For commentary on the IHT implications of companies generally, including transfers by close companies (*s 94*), see *Inheritance Tax 2016/17*, and the latest edition of *Ray & McLaughlin's Practical IHT Planning* (Bloomsbury Professional).

INVESTMENT OR BUSINESS?

Introduction

12.10 Particularly where an individual jointly owns one or a small number of buy-to-let properties, those properties may be held largely as a passive investment.

However, in some cases (eg where a large portfolio of properties are let) the owner(s) may be involved in the letting of the properties to a significant degree, and/or the lettings activities may be organised in a business-like manner. The question then arises whether the lettings activity constitutes a business, as opposed to a mere investment.

Distinguishing a business from investment is generally advantageous from an IHT perspective if business property relief (BPR) is available in respect of the value of the business (or shares in a company undertaking the business). However, even if the property rental activity constitutes a business, that business will normally consist wholly or mainly of making or holding investments, which is not a qualifying activity for BPR purposes (see **12.12**).

It should be noted that establishing the existence of a property rental business may be important for non-IHT reasons, such as for capital gains tax purposes on an incorporation of the business (see *Ramsay v HMRC* [2013] UKUT 226 (TCC), or for stamp duty land tax purposes on the incorporation of a partnership's business (*FA 2003, Sch 15, para 18*).

Partnerships

12.11

> **Focus**
>
> The joint ownership of property (see **12.5**) will not of itself be sufficient to demonstrate the existence of a partnership business. Whether or not a partnership business exists will depend upon the facts.
>
> A general partnership (in England and Wales) does not have a separate legal identity. Partnership property is subject to the terms of the partnership, which may be set out in a partnership agreement, or otherwise imputed by virtue of *PA 1890*.

12.12 *Inheritance tax*

A partnership is defined (in *PA 1890, s 1*) as '…the relation which subsists between persons carrying on a business in common with a view to profit.' As indicated above, common ownership of property does not in itself constitute a partnership (*PA 1890, s 2(1)*). A partnership must arise from agreement between the parties, whereas co-ownership need not (eg siblings becoming joint owners as a result of inheriting a buy-to-let property from parents would not of itself constitute a partnership).

Although a partnership is not a separate legal entity (in England and Wales), its partners are agents for each other in respect of the business transactions, and each is bound by the acts of the others (by contrast, Scottish partnerships are separate legal persons).

Limited liability partnerships (LLPs) are legal entities registered in their own right (under *LLPA 2000*) and separate from their members. They have unlimited capacity and can do anything that an individual can do, such as enter into contracts and hold property. The incorporation of an LLP broadly requires (among other things) the carrying on of a lawful business with a view to profit (*LLPA s 2(1)(a)*). The existence of an LLP as a partnership is a matter of legal fact.

A further type of partnership, the limited partnership, can be created (see *LPA 1907*), under which the liability of one or more partners is limited to the amount of capital the partner has agreed to contribute. Such partnerships must have at least one general partner who is fully liable for the firm's debts. Limited partners cannot take part in the management of the partnership's business. A limited partner must be distinguished from a sleeping partner (ie an inactive partner).

Business property relief

12.12   BPR (*ss 103–114*) is an important and valuable relief from IHT. It reduces the value transferred by a transfer of value of certain types of business or business property by a specified percentage. The current rates of BPR are 100% and 50% respectively; the actual rate of relief applied to a transfer depends on the type of business property.

The relief applies to actual or deemed transfers. It is available for lifetime transfers, or to relevant business property included in an individual's estate on death. BPR also applies to settled property included in the death estate, and is available to trustees in respect of the periodic and exit charges that apply to discretionary trusts, and (following changes introduced in *FA 2006*) to most other types of trust.

BPR must be claimed, and a number of conditions must be satisfied before the relief is available. It applies if the value transferred by a transfer of value relates to 'relevant business property'. The most common categories of business property on which BPR is claimed are a business or an interest in a business, or unquoted shares in a company. In both cases, the rate of BPR is 100%.

12.13

> **Focus**
>
> As indicated (at **11.10**), business property is generally precluded from relief if the business consists wholly or mainly of dealing in securities, stocks or shares or land or buildings, or in making or holding investments (*s 105(3)*).

On the face of it, the letting of buy-to-let property constitutes the activity of 'holding investments'. Therefore even if the activity could properly be characterised as a business, it would be excluded from BPR. However, in some cases, the position might not appear so clear cut.

HMRC's approach to determining whether the letting of furnished accommodation (or a caravan site, a furnished holiday letting or letting commercial premises) is an eligible activity for BPR purposes is to apply two tests (see IHTM25271); firstly, whether the activities carried on constitute a business (for the purposes of *s 105(1)(a)*); and secondly, if they do, whether BPR is precluded because that business was wholly or mainly of holding investments (within *s 105(3)*).

12.14 On the first test of whether a business exists, in *Customs and Excise Commissioners v Lord Fisher* [1981] STC 238, heard in the High Court, Gibson J identified six criteria for determining whether an activity is a business:

(1) Whether the activity is a 'serious undertaking earnestly pursued';

(2) Whether the activity is an 'occupation or function actively pursued with a reasonable or recognisable continuity';

(3) Whether the activity has 'a certain measure of substance as measured by the quarterly or annual value of taxable supplies made';

(4) Whether the activity was 'conducted in a regular manner and on sound and recognised business principles';

(5) Whether the activity is 'predominantly concerned with the making of taxable supplies to consumers for a consideration'; and

(6) Whether the taxable supplies are 'of a kind which…are commonly made by those who seek to profit by them'.

Whilst *Lord Fisher* was a VAT case, HMRC considers that these indicators are equally applicable as a test for IHT purposes (IHTM25152).

A number of cases have considered what constitutes a 'business' for BPR purposes, including in the context of let property. For example, in *Martin and another (executors of Moore Deceased) v IRC* [1995] STC (SCD) 5, the business consisted of owning and letting industrial units on three-year leases at fixed rents. The activities included finding tenants, granting and renewing leases,

12.15 *Inheritance tax*

complying with the landlord's covenants under those leases and managing the premises. Notwithstanding that these activities went beyond straightforward investment activities, they were nevertheless held to be incidents of the business of making or holding investments. Thus, BPR was denied. It was the nature of the business that mattered, not the amount of effort that the owner put into it.

A similar decision to *Martin* was reached in *Burkinyoung's Executor v IRC* [1995] STC (SCD) 29. In that case, Mrs Burkinyoung let a number of properties and, on her death, her executors claimed BPR. In reaching his decision, the Special Commissioner noted that it was common ground (between the executors and the Inland Revenue) that Mrs Burkinyoung's owning and letting activity consisted of a business and, therefore, met the first test of relevant business property, although the claim failed on other grounds.

12.15 A number of cases (albeit in relation to caravan park businesses) may be helpful for the purposes of determining whether a business is substantially investment in nature due to rental receipts, or whether any trading (eg sales and service) components of the business is sufficient to enable it to qualify for BPR.

For example, In *IRC v George and another (executors of Stedman, dec'd)* [2004] STC 147, Lord Justice Carnwath accepted on the facts that a caravan site qualified, commenting that it was '… difficult to see why an active family business of this kind should be excluded from business property relief, merely because a necessary component of its profit-making activity is the use of land'.

HMRC's Inheritance Tax manual on BPR includes combined guidance on caravan sites and furnished lettings (IHTM25271 to IHTM25275), outlining its criteria for the exclusion from BPR for investment businesses to such businesses.

Similar difficulties can arise with the letting of dwellings generally. For example, in *Clark and Another (executors of Clark, dec'd)* v HMRC [2005] STC (SCD) 823, a company's business comprised rents from properties it owned (ie investment income), plus trading income from management charges in respect of a number of dwellings owned by family members. Viewed 'in the round', the company's business was held to consist mainly of investments. The company's maintenance of the rented properties was held not to constitute the separate provision of services, but was inherent in the property ownership.

12.16 In the context of furnished holiday lettings, HMRC generally examines BPR claims in respect of them to establish if the activity constitutes a 'business', and if so, whether it is wholly or mainly one of holding investments.

In *HMRC v Personal Representatives of N Pawson, Deceased* [2013] UKUT 050 (TCC), Mrs Pawson owned an interest in a large bungalow ('Fairhaven') on the Suffolk coast at the time of her death. Her executors claimed BPR in respect of the property. Their claim was on the basis that Fairhaven had been used for a holiday letting business, and that it was not disqualified (by *s 105(3)*) from being relevant business property on the basis of being a business consisting wholly or mainly of making or holding investments. The First-tier Tribunal allowed the executors' appeal ([2012] UKFTT 51 (TC)), finding that the exploitation of Fairhaven had constituted a business, which did not consist wholly or mainly of holding an investment. HMRC appealed.

The Upper Tribunal noted that some business activities carried on at Fairhaven naturally fell on the investment side of the line, but that certain additional services were provided to occupants as part of the holiday letting business. Those additional services comprised: a cleaner/caretaker to clean the property between each letting and carry out regular inspections of the property; space heating and hot water; a television and telephone at the property; being on call to deal with queries and emergencies; and minor matters such as the replenishment of cleaning materials as and when necessary, and the provision of an up-to-date welcome pack (laundry services were also provided, but only after Mrs Pawson's death).

The Upper Tribunal considered that the critical question was whether those additional services prevented the business from being mainly one of holding Fairhaven as an investment. The Upper Tribunal noted that the judgment in *IRC v George* (see **12.15**) made it clear that the provision of such services is 'unlikely to be material' in the case of a property letting business because they were not enough to prevent the business remaining 'mainly' one of property investment. The services provided were considered to be of a relatively standard nature. Looking at the business in the round, in the Upper Tribunal's view there was nothing to distinguish it from any other actively managed furnished holiday letting business, and there was certainly no basis for concluding that the services comprised in the total package were such that the business ceased to be one which was mainly of an investment nature. HMRC's appeal was allowed.

The decisions in *Pawson* (and *George*) were subsequently considered in *Green v Revenue and Customs* [2015] UKFTT 236 (TC), where it was held that lifetime transfers of interests in a furnished holiday lettings business to a settlement were not eligible for BPR, as the First-tier Tribunal decided that the business consisted mainly of making or holding investments.

Historically, HMRC's guidance in the Inheritance Tax manual indicated that BPR would normally be allowed if the lettings were short term (eg weekly or fortnightly) and there was substantial involvement with the holidaymakers both on and off the premises. This applied even if the lettings were for only part of the year. However, HMRC's guidance (IHTM25278) was amended in late 2008. HMRC's current approach suggests that the active involvement of the holiday lettings proprietor is of less importance than the degree of service and nature of services offered to guests. It would seem logical to draw the conclusion that the closer the comparison between the holiday accommodation and a hotel in terms of services provided, the better.

12.17 *Inheritance tax*

VALUATION

General

12.17 The general rule (but see below) is that assets are valued for IHT purposes at the price they might reasonably be expected to fetch if sold in the open market at the time of transfer (*s 160*). HMRC often scrutinise market valuations of property, especially where there might be development potential.

HMRC has produced a toolkit to assist tax agents and others when completing the account Form IHT400 (www.gov.uk/government/publications/hmrc-inheritance-tax-toolkit). The toolkit identifies particular areas of risk when completing an IHT400, and states: 'Valuations are the biggest single area of risk, accounting for a large part of our compliance checks'. HMRC considers valuation to be an area of 'high risk' in terms of the potential loss of IHT.

HMRC encourages taxpayers etc. to refer valuations to a qualified, independent valuer. However, this of itself may not be sufficient to satisfy HMRC that an asset has been valued satisfactorily. In its Inheritance Tax Toolkit, HMRC advises (subject to certain exceptions – see below) as follows:

> 'For assets with a material value you are strongly advised to instruct a qualified independent valuer, to make sure the valuation is made for the purposes of the relevant legislation, and for houses, land and buildings, it meets Royal Institution of Chartered Surveyors (RICS) or equivalent standards.'

In terms of engaging an independent professional valuer, HMRC strongly advises that this is done 'properly', and recommends the following:

- 'Explain the context and draw attention to the definition in section 160 Inheritance Tax Act (IHTA) 1984 (market value).

- Provide all the relevant details concerning the asset, in particular ensuring the valuer is aware of the need to take into account any points in the bullet points under 'Risk' above.

- Ensure that copies of relevant agreements, or full details where only an oral agreement exists, are provided so misunderstandings do not arise.'

Focus

However, the value of a lifetime gift is measured by the reduction in value of the transferor's estate as a result of the transfer (but not normally taking into account the value of any excluded property ceasing to form part of the estate (*s 3(2)*).

The loss to the estate for IHT purposes will not necessarily be the same as the value of the property transferred.

Liabilities are taken into account in valuing the estate at the date of transfer, if imposed by law or to the extent of being incurred for consideration in money or money's worth (*s 5(3), (5)*).

Valuations of property and property interests are normally undertaken by the Valuation Office Agency (VOA). When the extent of a co-owner's interest has been ascertained, the VOA's valuation approach in practice will be the same in each case (see the VOA's Inheritance Tax manual at section 18.1).

12.18 If joint tenants purchase land with the help of a mortgage, unless there is an agreement to the contrary, their beneficial interests will generally equate to their respective shares of the mortgage.

In addition, on the death of a joint owner of property, the survivor takes absolutely and by operation of law. Hence, it is impossible to make testamentary or lifetime dispositions to third parties (see **12.5**).

If the beneficial interests in land vary from the legal title, HMRC will require evidence of the parties' beneficial ownership (IHTM15044).

12.19 The practical approach to valuations of undivided shares may differ according to the particular circumstances. The two basic approaches commonly adopted by the VOA are: firstly, an 'entirety approach' (ie valuing the entirety and then deriving the value of a share by applying the appropriate arithmetical fraction (eg 1/2 in the case of a half share) and discounting the resulting figure to reflect the inherent disadvantages in owning a share compared with an entirety interest); and secondly, an 'income approach' (ie involving the capitalisation of income or notional income attributable to the share).

The VOA considers that neither approach will necessarily be correct in all circumstances, but that 'in most cases' the entirety approach will be preferable, although it is considered that in most cases the two methods should not produce a 'significantly different' result (see the VOA's Inheritance Tax manual, Practice Note 2, para 8).

Discounts

12.20 If the co-owner of a half share in a property (without rights of occupation as a main residence) is deriving some current benefit from the ownership of the share, guidance by the VOA indicates that this should normally be valued by taking the full value of the property and making an allowance of 10% from the share fraction (see the VOA's Inheritance Tax manual at para 18.6: http://tinyurl.com/VOA-IHT-section18).

However, in the case of property held by spouses or civil partners (whether as joint tenants or tenants in common, albeit that joint property passing by survivorship may be subject to the spouse exemption in any event), HMRC may seek to challenge any discount claimed, based on the 'related property' provisions (see **12.25**).

12.21 *Inheritance tax*

A co-owner may own only a minority interest in the property. The VOA accepts that in cases where the prospects of a Court granting an order for sale are thought to be less than 'highly likely', or the costs of such an action would be prohibitive, some greater discount than 10% may be appropriate; the actual level of discount may vary depending on factors such as the likely attitude of the other co-owners.

In *Charkham v IRC* [2000] RVR 7, an individual held minority interests in a number of investment properties. The Revenue considered that the value should be discounted overall by between 10%–15%. The taxpayer appealed. The Lands Tribunal held that there should be a single discount on each property, and that the appropriate discount should be 15% on some properties, and 20% or 22.5% on others.

However, the VOA envisages that only in very exceptional circumstances will the amount of such a discount exceed 20% (see the VOA's Inheritance Tax manual, Practice Note 2, paras 10.9–10.10).

A majority co-owner will normally be in a more powerful position than a minority one. However, the VOA accepts that ownership of a majority share still has its disadvantages, and that a discount of up to 10% should therefore be applied in normal circumstances (http://tinyurl.com/VOA-IHT-Majority).

12.21 For general partnerships (see **12.11**), the VOA's approach (based on the decision in *IRC v Gray (surviving executor of Lady Fox deceased)* [1994] STC 360) is to consider the valuation of an interest in the business carried on by the partnership by reference to the appropriate share of each asset. In arriving at the valuation the terms of the partnership agreement or (in the absence of any partnership agreement) the relevant provisions of PA 1890 should generally be taken into account.

A partnership agreement may include provisions regarding the freedom of individual partners to dispose of their interests. For example, there may be a provision that on the death or retirement of a partner any interest in partnership property is taken over by the other partners, for consideration which may not amount to market value (within *s 160*).

However, provisions in a contract (eg a partnership agreement) whereby the right to dispose has in some way been excluded or restricted are generally ignored in valuing the transfer to the extent that such exclusion or restriction is not for a consideration in money or money's worth (*s 163*).

This anti-avoidance provision is particularly designed to deter artificial arrangements in partnership agreements (eg as regards options below market value, or pre-emption provisions in articles of association of a company) that aim at artificially reducing the market value of the shares.

However, where a partnership comprises individuals who are not related to one another (other than in a business context) the VOA will generally presume the terms of a partnership deed to be for the mutual benefit of all the partners, with no intended gratuitous transfer of value from any one to another. By contrast, in the case of a family partnership, full account will be taken of the terms of the partnership agreement.

The valuation of a partnership interest should reflect the circumstances as they exist at the date of valuation. The VOA accepts that this will normally involve making some discount from the appropriate arithmetical share of the entirety value. However, the level of discount will not normally be regarded as great as in a case involving a similar sized undivided share held under a trust of land, as the purchaser of a partner's interest will normally be in a much stronger position to realise the full value of their proportionate share of the entirety than a tenant in common. The VOA therefore considers that the amount of any discount should not normally exceed 10% (see the VOA's Inheritance Tax manual, section 19.8).

12.22 The question of a discount may also arise when valuing shares in property companies. It should be noted the VOA considers that comparisons between valuations of undivided shares in property and the valuation of shares in property companies (ie where it is sometimes argued that large discounts from the entirety value are appropriate when valuing small shareholdings in unquoted companies) are misleading, and that no weight should be given to them (see the VOA's Inheritance Tax manual, Practice Note 2, para 12).

The valuation of shares in property companies (and property valuations generally) is outside the scope of this book. For detailed guidance on company share valuations, see the latest edition of *Practical Share Valuation* (Bloomsbury Professional).

Liabilities

12.23

> **Focus**
>
> Very often, the acquisition of buy-to-let property will be financed at least partly by a mortgage or other loan. Liabilities are normally taken into account in valuing a person's estate (ie on a lifetime transfer, or on death) if imposed by law, or to the extent of being incurred for consideration in money or money's worth (*s 5(3), (5)*).

The general rules for determining the amount or value of liabilities may be summarised as follows:

- A liability for which there is a right to reimbursement is taken into account only to the extent that reimbursement cannot reasonably be expected to be obtained (*s 162(1)*).
- If a liability will be discharged after the time at which it is to be taken into account, it must be valued when it is taken into account (ie at its discounted value (*s 162(2)*) – but see below regarding *s 162(3)*.

12.24 *Inheritance tax*

- In valuing the transferor's estate immediately after the transfer, his IHT liability is computed as follows (*s 162(3)*):

    (i) without making any allowance for the fact that the tax will not be due immediately; and

    (ii) as if any tax recovered otherwise than from the transferor were paid in discharge of a liability for which the transferor had a right to reimbursement.

- A liability which is an encumbrance on estate property must (as far as possible) be taken to reduce the value of that property (*s 162(4)*). However, this rule applies to the extent that the liability has not been taken into account against 'relievable property' under new s 162B (ie broadly business or agricultural property, or woodlands), if applicable (see below).

- A liability due to a person not resident in the UK which neither falls to be discharged in the UK nor is an encumbrance on UK property must (as far as possible) be taken to reduce the value of property outside the UK (*s 162(5)*). However, this rule is subject to the same further condition mentioned in the previous bullet point.

12.24 The deduction of liabilities is restricted by anti-avoidance provisions in relation to 'excluded property', 'non-residents' foreign currency bank accounts' and 'relievable property' (*ss 162A–162C*). For example, if a loan was incurred directly or indirectly to acquire (or maintain or enhance) an asset on which business property relief is due (eg unquoted shares in a trading company), the liability generally reduces the value of those shares, even if the loan was secured on a buy-to-let property.

A further potential restriction applies to liabilities on death. In determining the value of a person's death estate, a deduction for a liability is only allowed to the extent that it is repaid to the creditor out of the deceased's estate or from excluded property owned by the deceased immediately before death (and there are no other IHT provisions that prevent it from being taken into account) (*s 175A*).

However, there is a potential exception to this restriction (in *s 175A(2)*) where it is shown that there is a real commercial reason for not repaying the liability, securing a tax advantage is not a main purpose of leaving the liability outstanding, and it is not otherwise prevented from being taken into account. HMRC guidance (at IHTM28029) cites an example of a business being taken over by the deceased's beneficiaries, where the bank is prepared to allow any lending and overdraft facilities to continue.

If a liability is secured on an asset passing to the deceased's spouse (or civil partner) and the liability is not taken into account under *s 175A* in determining the value of the deceased's estate, it is also not taken into account in determining the extent to which the spouse's partner's estate is increased (*s 175A(4)*). In other words, the disallowed liability is ignored when considering the spouse exemption (see HMRC's example at IHTM28030).

Overall, the above measures are designed to block schemes and arrangements aimed at exploiting the IHT rules on liabilities to reduce the value of an estate. Such arrangements have previously involved obtaining a deduction for a liability and either not repaying the liability after death, or acquiring an asset which is not chargeable to IHT.

Related property

12.25 For valuation purposes, the value of 'related property' is generally taken into account when valuing a person's estate if this results in a higher valuation (*s 161*). This rule applies to lifetime and death transfers, and prevents the division of an asset into less valuable parts by means of exempt transfers to reduce overall IHT liabilities.

Property is broadly 'related' for these purposes if it is:

- in the spouse's or civil partner's estate; or

- is (or was during the preceding five years) the property of a charity (or a qualifying political party, housing association or national or public body, to which exempt transfers may be made) as the result of an exempt transfer (after 15 April 1976) by the individual, spouse or civil partner (*s 161(2)*).

The transferor's property and the related property are combined and valued as a single unit. The combined value of the estate property and related property is then apportioned to the estate property in the proportion that its value in isolation bears to the separate values when added together.

12.26 In the case of a jointly-owned property, the value of the combined unit is apportioned between the property in the individual's estate and the related property according to their separate values (*s 161(3)*).

> **Example 12.1 – Related property**
>
> Adam owns a block of apartments worth £1,200,000. His wife Brenda owns the surrounding grounds worth £300,000.
>
> The combined value is £2,000,000.
>
> The related property value of Adam's asset is:
>
> $$£1,200,000 \times \frac{£2,000,000}{(£1,200,000 + £300,000)} = £1,600,000$$

12.27 *Inheritance tax*

12.27 In the case of jointly-owned property, the question arises whether the value falls to be discounted to take into account the rights of the co-owner. HMRC's Inheritance Tax manual states (at IHTM09739):

'The related property rules apply because the interests of the spouses/civil partners are together worth more than the sum of their separate interests – the separate interests would normally be subject to a discount for joint ownership. The interests of the husband and wife, or civil partners, will normally be identical and will extend to the whole of the land and property so the value of the deceased/transferor's interest will be the appropriate proportion of the entirety value.'

However, it goes on to state: 'The rules do not apply where a deceased's interest in the jointly owned property passes to the other spouse or civil partner as the survivor in a joint tenancy, as spouse or civil partner exemption will apply.'

12.28 The value to be included in estate is the 'appropriate portion' of the value of the combined property (*s 161(1)*).

There are two methods of calculating the appropriate portion, ie what HMRC refers to (in IHTM09734) as the 'general rule' (s 161(3); see **11.26**) and the 'special rule' (*s 161(4)*; see below). HMRC's guidance points out that the general rule is used where the items of property being aggregated for valuation purposes are different (eg see **Example 12.1** above). The special rule is mainly used for calculating the value of shareholdings. However, HMRC may seek to use the special rule in other situations as well.

This point was considered (in the context of a family farm) in *Arkwright and another (Personal Representatives of Williams, deceased) v IRC* [2004] EWHC 1720 (Ch). In that case, Mr and Mrs W owned a freehold property as tenants in common. On Mr W's death, HMRC determined that IHT was due on 50% of the property's agreed open market value. The personal representatives appealed, contending that Mr W's interest should be valued at less than 50% of the vacant possession value, because his widow had the right to occupy the property and could not have it sold without her consent.

The Special Commissioner accepted this contention and allowed the appeal in principle, holding that the value of Mrs W's interest should be determined in accordance with *s 161(3)* (ie on the basis that both shares in the property were related, and that their values should therefore be aggregated, with the value of each property share being determined as if it did not form part of that aggregate). The Court of Appeal subsequently held that the Commissioner was entitled to conclude that the value of the deceased's interest in the property was not inevitably a mathematical one-half of the vacant possession value, rejecting HMRC's argument that *s 161(4)* applied to treat the land as 'units' and that the valuation ratio was one-half. However, the court considered that the value of Mr W's interest was a question for the Lands Tribunal to determine. The appeal was subsequently settled by agreement.

HMRC subsequently stated (in Revenue & Customs Brief 71/07) that, following legal advice, they would apply *s 161(4)* when valuing shares of land as related property in cases received after publication of that Brief (27 November 2007) and would consider litigation in 'appropriate cases'. This approach is confirmed in HMRC's guidance (at IHTM09737), which indicates that the 'special rule' will apply to undivided shares of property.

12.29 The 'general rule' was applied in *Price v Revenue and Customs Commissioners* [2010] UKFTT 474 (TC). In that case, the appellant (the executor and trustee of his late wife's estate) appealed against an IHT determination in respect of a property owned in equal half shares by husband and wife as tenants-in-common. The entire property was valued at £1.5 million, whereas the half shares of the property, valued independently, amounted to £637,500 each. The appellant argued (among other things) that 'the value of that and any related property' in *s 161(1)* meant the value of the two property interests valued independently of each other. HMRC argued that the above expression meant the totality of both interests treated as a single item of property.

The tribunal held that the related property provisions hypothesise a notional sale and that the property interests were to be valued on the basis that they are offered for sale together and at the same time. If this resulted in a greater price than if the interests had been offered individually, then (if the sale would not have required undue effort or expense) the greater price must be attributed to the two items by applying the formula in *s 161(3)*. The appeal was therefore dismissed.

12.30 A form of relief is available if related property is sold to an unconnected person within three years of death for less than the related property valuation. A claim is required. The effect of the relief is to recalculate the tax at death without reference to the related property (*s 176*).

The relief is subject to certain conditions, and applies to a 'qualifying sale' as defined (s *176(3)*; see IHTM09754).

The claim may be made by the deceased's personal representatives, or by persons in whom the property vested immediately after the death. It should be noted that 'related property relief' does not substitute the value of the property at the date of sale. The valuation date is immediately before the death.

LIFETIME TRANSFERS

Introduction

12.31 The beneficial owner of an interest in buy-to-let property may transfer all or part of that interest during their lifetime. The IHT implications of a transfer of value will broadly depend on factors such as the identity of the recipient, and the availability of reliefs or exemptions, such as the annual exemption of £3,000 (*s 19*).

12.32 *Inheritance tax*

In the case of transfers between spouses (or civil partners), there is a complete exemption for transfers (ie lifetime and on death) between UK-domiciled spouses. However, where the transferor spouse is UK domiciled but the transferee spouse is foreign domiciled, the exemption is restricted to a cumulative total of the prevailing nil rate band (£325,000 for 2016/17) (*s 18(2)*). There are provisions for an election to allow non-UK domiciled spouses to be treated as domiciled in the UK for IHT purposes so that the inter-spouse exemption is unlimited, but electing spouses are then generally subject to IHT on their worldwide estates (*ss 267ZA–267ZB*).

Anti-avoidance provisions can apply to lifetime gifts in certain circumstances involving the donor reserving a benefit in the gifted property (see **12.34**).

Potentially exempt transfers

12.32 Most types of gifts made during lifetime are potentially exempt transfers (PETs). A PET is broadly a lifetime transfer of value that satisfies the following conditions (*s 3A*):

- it is made by an individual on or after 18 March 1986;
- the transfer would otherwise be a chargeable transfer;
- for transfers of value before 22 March 2006, if it is either a gift to another individual or a gift into an accumulation and maintenance trust or a disabled person's trust;
- for transfers of value from 22 March 2006, if the transfer of value is made to another individual, a disabled person's trust or a 'bereaved minor's' trust on the ending of an 'immediate post-death interest' (ie lifetime gifts into the vast majority of trusts do not qualify as PETs from that date).

For example, the gift of a buy-to-let property from father to adult daughter is a PET that becomes an exempt transfer if father survives for at least seven years. Conversely, the gift becomes a chargeable transfer if made within seven years of death.

If the gift becomes chargeable, IHT is calculated at the death rates applicable at the time of death, subject to any taper relief (*see s 7(4)*). In addition, the transfer is cumulated with the death estate, and will also affect the individual's cumulative total of chargeable transfers.

Chargeable lifetime transfers

12.33 A chargeable lifetime transfer is a transfer of value made by an individual, which is not unconditionally or potentially exempt (*s 2(1)*). This includes transfers into relevant property trusts (eg the transfer of a property into a discretionary trust for family members). It also includes transfers by close companies, which can be charged on the shareholders in some cases (*ss 94–97, 202*).

A chargeable lifetime transfer is aggregated with other such transfers over a seven-year period, following which they fall out of the cumulative total. The rate of IHT is determined by reference to this total. Tax is charged at 20% (ie at half the 40% rate at death for 2016/17) on the transfer as the highest part of the cumulative total, to the extent that it exceeds the nil rate band (£325,000 for 2016/17), after deducting any available reliefs and exemptions.

Where the transferor bears the IHT liability, the tax represents a further loss in the value of his estate, and therefore the transfer must be grossed-up to arrive at the overall amount of the chargeable transfer.

Additional IHT becomes chargeable at the 'death rate' (40% for 2016/17) in respect of immediately chargeable lifetime transfers made within seven years from the death of the transferor. The gift is cumulated with immediately chargeable transfers and PETs in the preceding seven years. The resulting IHT (recalculated at the full death rate) is compared with the lifetime tax paid (if any), for the purposes of calculating any additional liability. However, if the recomputed figure is lower than the IHT paid at the time of transfer, no additional tax is payable, but the difference is not repaid.

GIFTS WITH RESERVATION

General

12.34 The gifts with reservation (GWR) anti-avoidance provisions (*FA 1986, ss 102–102C, Sch 20*) apply to lifetime gifts in certain circumstances. The rules are designed to prevent 'cake and eat it' situations, whereby an individual gifts an asset but continues to have the use or enjoyment of it.

Most lifetime gifts to individuals are PETs if not otherwise exempt, which only become chargeable if the transferor dies within seven years of the transfer. Without the GWR rules, if the transferor survived the transfer by seven years, the PET would become an exempt transfer, even though for all practical purposes the transferor may have continued to enjoy the gifted asset until their death.

The effect of the GWR rules is broadly to ensure that the property subject to a GWR is treated as forming part of the donor's death estate. If the benefit is ended during his lifetime, the donor is treated as having made a PET at that time (*FA 1986, s 102(4)*), which becomes a chargeable transfer on death within the following seven years.

However, because the PET is not actual but deemed (ie because there is no actual transfer of value when the GWR ceases) the annual exemption is not available to offset against it. The property transferred by the PET is valued on the basis of the loss to the transferor's estate (IHTM04073).

12.35 *Inheritance tax*

In the absence of provisions to the contrary, IHT could become chargeable on the initial lifetime transfer, and on the value of the relevant asset when the reservation ceased (eg upon death). However, the GWR rules are supplemented by regulations designed to prevent a double tax charge arising (*Inheritance Tax (Double Charges Relief) Regulations, SI 1987/1130*).

12.35 As indicated, the GWR provisions are anti-avoidance rules designed to stop taxpayers decreasing the value of their IHT estates by making gifts whilst leaving their overall circumstances effectively unchanged. The rules apply to gifts of property (on or after 18 March 1986) by an individual ('the donor') if:

- possession and enjoyment of the property is not assumed ('bona fide' as the legislation puts it) by the recipient of the gift ('the donee') at or before the beginning of the 'relevant period' (see below); or

- at any time in the relevant period the property is not enjoyed to the entire exclusion, or virtually to the entire exclusion, of the donor and of any benefit to him by contract or otherwise (*FA 1986, s 102(1)(a), (b)*).

The requirement that the donee must assume 'bona fide' possession and enjoyment of the gifted property to prevent a GWR means that the beneficial interest in the gifted property must be duly transferred, and the donee must have had actual enjoyment of that property (eg through physical occupation, or the receipt of income generated therefrom), instead of just the legal right of enjoyment.

The GWR rules can apply if the donor derives a benefit 'at any time' during the relevant period. The 'relevant period' is the period ending on the date of the individual's death and beginning seven years before that date, or (if later) on the date of the gift (*FA 1986, s 102(1)*).

For example, if the donor makes a gift of property eight years before his death (which satisfies condition (a) or (b) in *FA 1986, s 102*), the relevant period is seven years before his death. However, if the gift was made four years prior to death, the relevant period is four years.

12.36 As indicated at **12.34**, without the GWR rules, if an individual could make a PET of property and survive at least seven years, the property would fall outside his estate and he could continue to enjoy or benefit from the gifted asset with impunity for IHT purposes.

The GWR rules therefore provide that if property subject to a reservation would not otherwise form part of the donor's estate immediately before his death, it will be treated as such (*FA 1986, s 102(3)*). The gift is deemed for IHT purposes to be property to which the individual was beneficially entitled immediately before his death, and is therefore ineffective to reduce the value of his IHT estate. However, this GWR treatment does not apply to excluded property (IHTM04072).

12.37 The GWR rules do not apply to certain exempt transfers (*FA 1986, s 102(5)*), including transfers between spouses or civil partners (*s 18*; but see below) and gifts in consideration of marriage or civil partnership (*s 22*).

Before changes to the GWR rules were introduced (*FA 1986, ss 102(5A)–(5C)*), arrangements were possible to take advantage of the exception from the GWR provisions for exempt gifts between spouses (see IHTM14318). Certain arrangements (ie '*Eversden*' schemes) used the spouse exemption to avoid a GWR on the gift of an asset to a trust. Such schemes were blocked by the above GWR changes (with effect for disposals from 20 June 2003), and pre-existing schemes are potentially subject to an income tax charge under the 'pre-owned assets' regime (see **12.58**).

Whilst the GWR rules do not necessarily apply to a gift (eg to a discretionary trust) in which a benefit is reserved by the donor's spouse or civil partner (ie as a potential beneficiary), if enjoyment of the gift is effectively shared by the donor (eg if distributions from the discretionary trust are paid into a joint bank account of the donor and spouse/civil partner), the GWR provisions will need to be considered.

12.38 If the donor gives full consideration in money or money's worth there should generally be no reservation. There is a specific rule to this effect for land (and chattels). It provides that the retention of a benefit by the donor is disregarded if the donor is in actual occupation or actual enjoyment and pays full consideration in money or money's worth (*FA 1986, Sch 20, para 6(1)(a)*).

Note that this GWR exception applies specifically to land and chattels. Care should be taken with other assets. HMRC's Inheritance Tax manual (at IHTM14336) cites an example in which Alex, who is a partner, withdraws capital from his partnership capital account and gives it to Bella. Bella then lends the partnership an equivalent cash sum. HMRC consider that this is a GWR, and state that even though Alex may pay Bella a commercial rate of interest for the loan, this payment will not prevent the loan being a reservation (see also *Chick v Commissioner of Stamp Duties of New South Wales* [1958] AC 435).

Gifts of interests in land

12.39 It was possible (prior to 9 March 1999) to make arrangements for gifts of an interest in land whilst continuing to enjoy a benefit from it.

The GWR rules for gifts of interests in land (from 9 March 1999) provide that if the donor or spouse (or civil partner) enjoys a 'significant right or interest', or is 'party to a significant arrangement' in relation to the land during the 'relevant period', the gifted land interest is a GWR.

A right, interest or arrangement is 'significant' if it entitles or enables the donor to occupy all or part of the land, or to enjoy some right in relation to all or part of it, otherwise than for full consideration in money or money's worth (*FA 1986, s 102A(2), (3)*).

12.40 *Inheritance tax*

There are exceptions from the GWR rule if the right, interest or arrangement (as appropriate) is not 'significant', ie if:

- it does not and cannot prevent the enjoyment of the land to the entire exclusion, or virtually to the entire exclusion, of the donor (*FA 1986, s 102A(4)(a)*); or

- it does not entitle or enable the donor to occupy all or part of the land immediately after the disposal, but would do so but for the interest disposed of (*FA 1986, s 102A(4)(b)*);

- the right or interest was granted or acquired before the seven-year period ending with the date of gift (*FA 1986, s 102A(5)*).

Focus

The lifetime gift of a reversionary lease of (for example) a buy-to-let property owned by a parent for many years into trust for adult children (taking effect in, say, 20 years) has been advanced by some commentators as a potential application of this seven year exception, with the donor retaining entitlement to the rent until the end of that period.

Note that the gift will normally be an immediately chargeable transfer (ie at the lifetime rate, subject to the annual exemption and IHT nil rate band, if available) and the trust will be subject to IHT (eg ten-yearly charges) under the relevant property regime. Capital gains tax holdover relief (under *TCGA 1992, s 260*) is potentially available for lifetime gifts into trust which are not settlor-interested.

HMRC guidance on reversionary lease schemes established on or after 9 March 1999 (at IHTM44102) distinguishes between situations where the donor grants a reversionary lease within seven years after acquiring the freehold interest (in which case a GWR under *FA 1986 s 102A* may apply to the gift), and where the reversionary lease is granted more than seven years after acquiring the freehold interest (ie such that the exception from a GWR charge in the third bullet point above would be in point).

The pre-owned assets income tax provisions (see **12.58**) generally need to be considered in the context of reversionary lease arrangements. For example, if property subject to the reversionary lease is occupied by the disponer, there would be a potential pre-owned assets charge. However, assuming in the above example that the buy-to-let property is occupied by a third party tenant and not the parent, no such pre-owned assets charge arises.

12.40 The GWR rules were extended in FA 1999 to cover gifts of an undivided share of an interest in land (from 9 March 1999), such as where a sole freeholder gifts a half interest to another individual (*FA 1986, s 102B*). The share disposed of is a GWR (*FA 1986, s 102(3) and (4)*). It should be noted that *ss 102* and *102A* do not apply in cases to which *s 102B* applies (*s 102C(6)*).

There are exceptions from the GWR rule in *s 102B* if:

- the donor does not occupy the land (*FA 1986, s 102B(3)(a)*); or

- the donor occupies the land to the exclusion of the donee for full consideration in money or money's worth (eg a full market rent) (*FA 1986, s 102B(3)(b)*); or

- both donor and donee occupy the land, and the donor receives no (or negligible) benefit from the donee in connection with the gift (*FA 1986, s 102B(4)*).

The distinction between the gift of an interest in land (in *FA 1986, s 102A*) and the gift of a *share* of an interest in land (in *s 102B*) is an important one.

For example, a parent could give a residential investment property to his adult daughter, but retain the right to receive all the rent (nb the implications for taxes other than IHT are not considered in this example). The right to receive the rent would be 'significant' for GWR purposes (see **12.39**).

By contrast, if the parent gifts *a share* of the investment property but continues to receive all the rent, *FA 1986, s 102B(3)(a)* provides that no reservation of benefit arises where the donor does not occupy the land. However, the GWR (and pre-owned assets tax; see **12.58**) position following a subsequent sale of the property would need to be considered. The implications for other taxes should also be considered (eg there would be a disposal at market value by the parent of the gifted property share to the daughter for capital gains tax purposes in the above example).

12.41 Supplemental provisions (*FA 1986, s 102C*) linking the 'interests in land' rules with the general GWR rules provide that exempt gifts fall outside both sets of rules (*FA 1986, s 102C(2)*), including the exception for exempt transfers to spouses or civil partners (in *FA 1986, s 102(5)*). However, the spouse exemption is limited in its application for GWR purposes (*FA 1986, s 102(5A)–(5C)*) (see **12.37**).

For detailed commentary on the GWR provisions, see *Inheritance Tax 2016/17* and the latest edition of *Ray & McLaughlin's Practical IHT Planning* (Bloomsbury Professional).

IHT ON DEATH

Introduction

12.42 As indicated at **12.2**, IHT is charged on the deceased's estate as if, immediately before his death, he had made a transfer of value. The value transferred is deemed to equal the value of his estate immediately before death (*s 4(1)*).

12.43 *Inheritance tax*

The tax charged on the estate broadly depends on the aggregate chargeable lifetime transfers and PETs in the seven years preceding death. The estate generally consists of all the property to which the individual was beneficially entitled, less excluded property and liabilities.

The IHT liability will also depend on the identity of the legatees of the net estate, ie whether the recipient is a chargeable person (eg a son or daughter), or an exempt person (eg a UK-domiciled spouse, or a qualifying charity).

A person's estate consists of all the property to which he is beneficially entitled (but not excluded property or a foreign-owned work of art situated in the UK only for the purpose of public display, cleaning and/or restoration). The estate generally also includes property over which a person has a general power, together with certain settled property in which the person is beneficially entitled to an interest in possession (*s 5(1), (2)*).

Liabilities

12.43 A liability may be taken into account in valuing a person's estate (unless otherwise provided by tax law) if it is legally enforceable and is:

- imposed by law (eg income tax and capital gains tax up to the date of death, and IHT liabilities in respect of chargeable lifetime transfers discharged by the deceased's personal representatives); or

- incurred for a consideration in money or money's worth (*s 5(5)*).

Mortgages or secured loans can generally be deducted from the property they are charged against (but see below). If the mortgage is for more than the value of the property, the excess can generally be deducted from the deceased's other assets (see 'How to value the debts and liabilities of someone who has died' at www.gov.uk/valuing-estate-of-someone-who-died#2 under 'Debts and liabilities'). However, where a person with liabilities in excess of his assets is tenant for life of a fund his personal indebtedness cannot offset the value of the trust fund (*St Barbe Green v Inland Revenue Commissioners* [2005] EWHC 14 (Ch)).

Certain conditions and potential restrictions apply in respect of the deduction of liabilities such as mortgages, to the extent that the liability was used to acquire, maintain or enhance certain types of property (*ss 162A–162C*). In addition, the deduction of liabilities discharged after death is subject to certain requirements (*s 175A*) (see **12.24**).

A guarantee debt (ie a promise to pay the debts of a borrower if he is unable to repay those debts) to which the deceased agreed to act as guarantor may be deductible from the death estate if the loan remained outstanding at the time of death. However, before allowing a deduction, HMRC may seek to establish whether consideration was given for the debt.

As to liabilities generally, see **12.23–12.24**.

Inheritance tax **12.45**

12.44 An anti-avoidance rule in *FA 1986, s 103* ('Treatment of certain debts and encumbrances') restricts debts incurred or created by the deceased (on or after 18 March 1986) when determining the value of an estate immediately before death, to the extent that:

- the money borrowed originally derived from the deceased; or

- the money was borrowed from a person who had previously received property derived from the deceased.

> **Example 12.2 – 'Caught' by FA 1986, s 103**
>
> On 1 January 2009, Angela gifted a property (worth £550,000) to her brother Bob. On 6 April 2009, Bob took out a loan secured on the property, and lent the proceeds back to Angela.
>
> Angela died on 30 September 2016. The loan was still outstanding on her death.
>
> The lifetime gift of the property by Angela was a PET, which became an exempt transfer after seven years. However, no deduction is allowed for the loan in calculating the IHT liability on Angela's death relating to the money borrowed following the receipt by Bob of the property from Angela.

However, the above restriction does not apply if it can be demonstrated that:

- the original disposition by the deceased was not a transfer of value; and

- it was not part of associated operations (as set out in *FA 1986, s 103(4)*).

The disallowance of a debt may result in a double IHT charge. For example, suppose that on 1 April 2013, A gifted cash of £50,000 to B. On 30 September 2013, B lent £50,000 to A. On 1 January 2016, A died.

The cash gift from A to B is a PET, which becomes chargeable as the result of A's death within seven years. In addition, A's estate includes the £50,000 lent back to him, but a deduction for the debt is denied (under *FA 1986, s 103*), leading to a potential double IHT charge.

12.45 However, relief is given in such circumstances (*FA 1986, s 104(1)(c)*; *Inheritance Tax (Double Charges Relief) Regulations 1987, SI 1987/1130, reg 6*).

The effect is broadly that whichever of the two transfers results in the higher overall IHT liability remains chargeable, and the value transferred by the other is reduced (ie either the debt is disallowed and the gift is correspondingly reduced (*reg 6(3)(a)*), or the gift is taxed and the debt allowed (*reg 6(3)(b)*).

12.46 *Inheritance tax*

Examples illustrating the operation of these rules are included as a Schedule to *SI 1987/1130*, although they do not prevail over the regulations themselves (*reg 9*).

'Fall in value' relief

12.46   Tax (or additional tax) payable on transfers of any property (ie a failed PET or chargeable lifetime transfer) made within seven years before death may be relieved where the value of the gift has fallen between the time the gift was made and death.

If the market value of the transferred property at the time of the chargeable transfer (ie date of gift) exceeds its market value at 'the relevant date' (see below), the additional tax is to be calculated as if the value transferred were reduced by the amount of that excess. Thus, in effect, the lower value is substituted (*ss 131–140*).

'Relevant date' means:

- the date of death, where the transferee or his spouse still holds that property; or
- if that property is sold before the transferor's death, the date of a qualifying sale (namely an open market, arm's-length arrangement).

A claim for the relief must be made by a person liable to pay the tax (or additional tax) within four years of the date of the donor's death (*s 131(2ZA)*).

The relief does not affect the transferor's cumulative total (which remains at its original figure for the purpose of taxing any later lifetime transfers and the estate on death), or the tax originally charged at lifetime rates on an immediately chargeable lifetime transfer.

12.47   For the purposes of the relief in respect of transfers within seven years before death, it is important that the sale is a 'qualifying sale' (within *s 131(3)*). This broadly requires:

- the transaction was at arm's length for a price freely negotiable at the time of the sale;
- the vendor (or any person having an interest in the proceeds of the sale) is not the same as, or connected with, the purchaser (or any person having an interest in the purchase); and
- no provision is made, in or in connection with the agreement for the sale, that the vendor (or any person having an interest in the proceeds of sale) is to have any right to acquire some or all of the property sold or some interest in or created out of it.

In order to avoid giving too much relief, there is a special rule for calculating the relief where the property also qualifies for business or agricultural property relief (*s 131(2A)*). In this case, the market values of the transferred property on the two dates that are compared to establish the reduction in value must be taken as reduced by the percentage appropriate to any available business or agricultural property relief.

12.48 When valuing property transferred in order to ascertain whether relief may become available, no account should be taken of related property (under *s 161*; see **12.25**) or property passing under another title with which it was originally valued (IHTM14626).

In the case of a transfer that was immediately chargeable at lifetime rates, the relief does not give rise to a repayment or remission of the tax that has already become payable during the transferor's life.

The relief also does not apply where the property has before the death been given away by the transferee or his spouse.

> **Example 12.3 – 'Fall in value' relief**
>
> Peter gives an investment property to his daughter Maria in October 2013, which was then worth £250,000.
>
> Peter died in May 2015, when the value of the property had fallen to £200,000. This value can be substituted for relief purposes.
>
> However, if Maria had sold the property in March 2014 for £240,000, that would represent the substituted value instead (*s 131(1)*).

12.49 Specific rules apply to interests in land (*s 137*). An adjustment is made where a change takes place between the date of the chargeable transfer and the date of death or sale.

If the change (ie in the interest in the land, or the land itself) reduces the value of the transferred land, the relief is adjusted by increasing its market value at the date of death or sale by the difference between the market value of the interest in the land at the time of the transfer, and what that value would have been if the change had already taken place.

Conversely, if the change increases the value of the transferred land, the property is valued at the date of death or sale for relief purposes of the relief as if the change had not taken place (*s 137(4)*; see HMRC's example at IHTM14663).

An adjustment may also be necessary where the transferred property is a leasehold interest with not more than fifty years to run at the time of the chargeable transfer. In those circumstances, an adjustment is required to the market value of the property interest transferred at the date of death or sale (see *s 138*).

Post-death loss relief

12.50 IHT relief is available (see *ss 190–198*) broadly where an interest in land (including buildings) in a person's estate immediately before death

12.51 *Inheritance tax*

is sold by 'the appropriate person', ie the person liable for the IHT thereon (normally the personal representatives), within three years of the death at a genuinely lower value. That value is then to be the taxable value, subject to certain conditions.

Where an interest in land is sold within three years of death, a claim can be made by the personal representatives to substitute the sale value for the value on death (see **12.51**). If the appropriate person (acting in the same capacity) sells further interests in land within the fourth year of death, all the sales by that person are generally taken into account (under *s 197A*), unless the sale value would exceed the value on death (or in certain other circumstances; see IHTM33074).

An estate, interest or right by way of a mortgage or other security, is not an 'interest in land' for the purposes of loss on sale of land relief (*s 190(1)*).

12.51 A claim cannot be made if:

- the sale value differs from the value on death by less than the lower of £1,000 and 5% of the value on death (*s 191(2)*);
- the sale is by a personal representative or trustee to the following:
  - a person, who, at any time between death and sale, has been beneficially entitled to, or has an interest in possession in, property comprising the interest sold, or
  - the spouse, child or remoter descendant of such a person, or
  - a trustee of a settlement under which such a person has an interest in possession in property comprising the interest sold;
- the vendor (or any person in the three categories above) obtains a right in connection with the sale to acquire the interest sold or any other interest in the same land (*s 191(3)*).

Furthermore, HMRC guidance indicates that the relief is not available where the only sale is of an interest whose value on death is covered by agricultural or business relief (or both) at 100% (IHTM33026).

Expenses of sale (eg stamp duty land tax, estate agent fees, legal fees) cannot be deducted (*s 190(4)*).

Relief is available in respect of compulsory acquisitions (ie broadly where an interest in land is acquired from the appropriate person more than three years after the death by an authority possessing powers of compulsory acquisition) where certain requirements are met (see *s 197*).

12.52 A claim for the relief (on form IHT38) must be made by the appropriate person (*s 191(1)(b)*). The claim must be made within four years of the end of the three year period during which qualifying sales can be made (*s 191(1A)*).

Inheritance tax **12.54**

HMRC guidance helpfully points out that the appropriate person does not have to wait until all the property to be sold is sold before making a claim, but that making a claim too early may not work to the taxpayer's advantage if later sales are made for a higher price (IHTM33012). The claim cannot be withdrawn once it is made.

Form IHT38 ('Claim for relief – loss on sale of land') can be downloaded from HMRC's website: (www.gov.uk/government/publications/inheritance-tax-claim-for-relief-loss-on-sale-of-land-iht38).

> **Example 12.4 – Post-death loss relief**
>
> Joe died in August 2013. He lived in residential care, but rented out his former home, which was valued for IHT purposes on his death at £500,000.
>
> In April 2016, Joe's personal representatives sold the let property via an estate agent to an unconnected individual for £400,000.
>
> The personal representatives claimed relief (under *s 191(1)*). The value of the house at the date of death for IHT purposes was reduced by £100,000 to £400,000.

12.53 Where the appropriate person purchases an interest in land in the same capacity, the claim is reduced (see *s 192*). The aim of the relief for loss on sales of land is that it should apply only to the net loss. Thus if the purchase price (or aggregate purchase prices) is more than the sale price, no relief is due.

Purchases are taken into account only if they are made during the period beginning on the date of death and ending not later than four months after the last qualifying sale (*s 192(1)*) (ie a sale made within three years of the date of death; no account is taken of sales only in the fourth year: see *s 197A(3)*). The purchase price does not include expenses (IHTM33161).

The adjustment to the sale price is calculated by a formula (in *s 192(2)*), which broadly involves revisiting each interest in land to recalculate the relief. The adjustment for purchases is beyond the scope of this chapter, but HMRC's Inheritance Tax manual includes an example of the calculation (at IHTM33163).

12.54 If the land sold was held in joint ownership, care needs to be taken when making a loss relief claim if the value of the property was subject to a discount on death for IHT purposes (see **12.20**), as the discount does not apply post-sale.

12.55 *Inheritance tax*

> **Example 12.5 – Loss of relief claim and discount for joint ownership**
>
> Fred owned a half share of a rented property with his sister Glenda.
>
> On Fred's death, the property is valued at £300,000. Fred's half share is valued at £135,000 (after a 10% discount) for IHT purposes.
>
> The property is sold two years later for £290,000.
>
> The sale value of a half share of the property (for the purposes of *s 191(1)*) is £145,000.
>
> If a loss relief claim is submitted, additional IHT would be payable as a result of the sales value being £10,000 above the discounted value on death of £135,000.

12.55 As indicated at **12.52**, there are no provisions allowing for a claim to be withdrawn once it is made (see IHTM33013). Consideration should therefore be given to delaying the making of a claim if possible until the position becomes clear (ie until it becomes certain that there will be no further sales), subject to the statutory time limit for making the claim.

The post-death loss relief provisions are potentially complex, and an analysis of the rules is beyond the scope of this chapter. HMRC provides detailed guidance in its Inheritance Tax manual (at IHTM33000-IHTM33182).

OTHER POINTS

Instalments

12.56 As an exception to the general rules for the payment of IHT, a liability may be paid by ten equal yearly instalments on 'qualifying property' including land of any description (wherever situated), where certain conditions apply (*s 227*). The conditions are broadly:

- the transfer is made on death; or
- the tax is being paid by the person who benefits from the transfer; or
- the transfer comes within the 'relevant property' regime (which will be more common in the post-FA 2006 era) and either the tax is borne by the beneficiary or the property remains in the settlement.

The instalment option is also available on lifetime transfers (eg failed PETs) in certain circumstances (eg where the property was owned by the transferee from the date of the transfer to the death of the transferor (or, if earlier, of a transferee)) (see *s 227(1C)*).

12.57 An election is required for the instalment option, which is normally made when submitting the relevant IHT account to HMRC. If the instalment option applies in the case of a transfer on death, the first instalment is due six months after the end of the month in which the death occurred. In other cases, the first instalment is generally due at the time the tax would be due if it were not being paid by instalments.

Interest on the unpaid proportion of the IHT is added to each instalment (*s 227(3)*). However, there are various exceptions to this rule (see *s 234*); in such cases, instalments are 'interest-free' (ie interest is charged only from the date the instalment is payable).

In the case of land, instalments are interest-free only to the extent that the land is reflected in the value transferred by the transfer of a business or an interest in a business, or the value of the land is reduced by agricultural property relief (IHTM30363).

A person paying IHT by instalments may decide to pay the outstanding balance of the tax in one sum (with accrued interest) whenever they wish. Alternatively, the outstanding balance of the tax becomes payable in full immediately if (for example) the property is sold (*s 227(4)*).

For further commentary on the instalment election, see *Inheritance Tax 2016/17* (Bloomsbury Professional).

Pre-owned assets

12.58 The 'pre-owned assets' income tax charge (ie the 'charge to income tax on benefits received by former owner of property', or POAT) was introduced (by *FA 2004, s 84*, and *Sch 15*, and underpinned by subsequent Treasury Regulations) in response to certain IHT planning arrangements. The charge operates for 2005/06 and subsequent years, but applies with retroactive effect to 18 March 1986.

The typical circumstance will arise where an individual:

- owned an asset (eg a property);
- disposes of it as a gift or for less than full value (or provides funds for the purchase – but see reference to the seven-year period below); and
- continues to occupy or enjoy the asset in whole or part, but is not subject to IHT as a gift with reservation.

The tax, like IHT, is chargeable on worldwide assets where the individual is UK resident and UK domiciled or deemed domiciled for IHT purposes. The legislation sets out various formulae for calculating the charge (see *FA 2004, Sch 15, paras 3–5* (land), *paras 6–7* (chattels) and *paras 8–9* (intangible property)).

12.59 *Inheritance tax*

12.59 The POAT charge broadly applies if an individual occupies the 'relevant land' (whether solely or jointly), and either the 'disposal condition' or 'contribution condition' are satisfied (see *FA 2004, Sch 15, para 3*).

However, there are certain limited exemptions to the POAT charge (eg if the land was subject to acceptable 'sharing' arrangements for gifts with reservation of benefit purposes within *FA 1986, s 102B(4)*; see *FA 2004, Sch 15, para 11(5)(c)*).

The chargeable amount in respect of land for POAT purposes is the appropriate rental value, less any payments by the taxpayer to the legal owner of the land in pursuance of a legal obligation (eg a lease or licence) for its occupation (*Sch 15, para 4*). The 'appropriate rental value' is calculated using a formula (in *Sch 15, para 4(2)*).

For the purposes of valuing land (and chattels and intangible property) when calculating the deemed POAT benefit, the 'valuation date' is 6 April in the relevant tax year, or if later the first day of the 'taxable period' (*Charge to Income Tax by Reference to Enjoyment of Property Previously Owned Regulations 2005, SI 2005/724, reg 2*).

12.60 It should be noted that there are certain exclusions from the POAT charge (*Sch 15, paras 10, 11*). For example, the POAT charge does not apply if the relevant property (or property derived from it) is comprised in the individual's estate (*Sch 15, para 11(1)*).

Furthermore, there is no POAT charge if the GWR provisions (see **12.34–12.41**) apply (*FA 2004, Sch 15, para 11(5)*), or if an election is made (under *FA 2004, Sch 15, para 21*) to effectively 'opt out' of the income tax charge and into the GWR rules for IHT purposes.

A double IHT charge could arise if an election is made and the taxpayer dies within seven years of the original gift (ie both on the original transfer that must now be aggregated with the death estate, and on the property subject to the reservation). Double charge regulations (*Charge to Income Tax by Reference to Enjoyment of Property Previously Owned Regulations, SI 2005/724*) therefore prevent a double liability (ie on the original gift and the GWR); the higher amount of tax is charged (*SI 2005/724, reg 6*).

HMRC have published a section on pre-owned assets in their Inheritance Tax manual (IHTM44000–IHTM44116), albeit that the pre-owned assets regime relates to income tax, as opposed to IHT.

The POAT provisions are potentially complex, and an analysis of the rules is beyond the scope of this book. Further commentary on POAT can be found in *Inheritance Tax 2016/17* and the latest edition of *Ray & McLaughlin's Practical IHT Planning* (Bloomsbury Professional).

Chapter 13

Incorporation of a buy-to-let residential property business

Mark McLaughlin CTA (Fellow), ATT (Fellow), TEP, Tax Consultant,
Mark McLaughlin Associates Ltd

> **SIGNPOSTS**
>
> - **Scope** – The incorporation of buy-to-let residential property businesses has been in sharper focus since the restriction in the deduction of finance costs for individuals to the basic rate of income tax was introduced (in *F(No. 2)A 2015*) (and amended in *FA 2016*), and also in view of reductions in corporation tax rates. However, incorporation involves various potential tax (and non-tax) implications, which must be carefully considered in advance (see **13.1–13.4**).
>
> - **Is there a business?** – It will normally be important to consider whether the buy-to-let residential property activity constitutes a business, such as in determining whether capital gains tax incorporation relief (under *TCGA 1992, s 162*) is available. Unfortunately, there is no statutory definition of 'business' in the *Taxes Acts*, although some assistance may be derived from case law on the subject (see **13.5–13.14**).
>
> - **Transactions in UK land** – *Finance Act 2016* introduced legislation on transactions in UK land, which imposes an income tax charge in respect of dealing or developing land and property in the UK. The legislation resulted in concerns that individual buy-to-let property investors could potentially be subject to income tax as opposed to CGT on the disposal of such property, although it does not appear to be aimed at properties held purely for investment purposes to generate rental income (see **13.15**).
>
> - **Capital gains tax** – The transfer of chargeable assets (eg buy-to-let properties) from an unincorporated business to a company upon incorporation constitutes a disposal, which will normally be treated as made at market value for capital gains tax (CGT) purposes. However, CGT relief will be available in many cases, if certain requirements are met (see **13.16–13.18**).

Incorporation of a buy-to-let residential property business

- **Incorporation relief** – A specific form of CGT relief automatically applies on the incorporation of a business, if certain conditions are satisfied (*TCGA 1992, s 162*). However, the relief is subject to restriction in some circumstances, and therefore gains upon incorporation will not always be relieved in full (see **13.19–13.31**).

- **Furnished holiday lettings** – Favoured capital gains tax treatment is potentially available in respect of the commercial letting of furnished holiday accommodation (*TCGA 1992, ss 241, 241A*), by deeming the business to be a trade for various tax purposes. This treatment is not afforded to property rental businesses generally, but it is subject to a number of qualifying conditions (see **13.32–13.44**).

- **Stamp taxes** – Stamp duty land tax (SDLT) in relation to property situated in England, Wales and Northern Ireland, and land and buildings transaction tax (LBTT) in relation to property situated in Scotland, are generally charged on actual consideration in money or money's worth. However, there is an important exception to this general rule when property is transferred to a connected company. In that case, the chargeable consideration is the greater of the market value of the property and the actual consideration given. SDLT or LBTT may be subject to different calculation rules where multiple residential properties are acquired, depending on whether deemed non-residential property treatment applies (where six or more dwellings are acquired as part of a single transaction) or if 'multiple dwellings relief' is successfully claimed. Special rules apply to partnerships, the effect of which can sometimes be (if property is transferred from a partnership to a new company, and each of the partners is an individual 'connected' to that new company) that no SDLT or LBTT charge arises (see **13.45–13.58**).

- **Interest relief** – Financing the business will be an important consideration for most buy-to-let residential property business proprietors. In such cases, either the company itself must borrow, or the proprietor must do so. In the former case, the company would generally not be restricted on the quantum of tax relievable loan interest in the same way as unincorporated residential property business owners from 6 April 2017. In the latter case, if the director/shareholder was to incur any borrowings personally, the tax relief available is subject to various conditions and potential restrictions (see **13.59–13.64**).

- **Other issues** – Other potentially relevant issues include capital allowances, the timing of tax payments, and whether there are any reporting requirements under the employment related securities regime (see **13.65–13.76**).

INTRODUCTION

13.1 It may be instructive to consider the possible reasons why someone might want to incorporate a buy-to-let residential property business.

An unincorporated property letting business will derive gross rents against which may be set various expenses to arrive at a net property business profit. An individual in receipt of such a profit will be chargeable to income tax at his highest marginal rate as it arises. Getting the profits into a company has the obvious attraction of the ability to withdraw profits (possibly by way of dividend rather than salary) or to retain them, just as with a trading company.

A potentially lower rate of corporation tax compared with marginal personal tax rates might make incorporation seem attractive to some business owners, particularly in view of a standard corporation tax rate of 20% (for the financial year to 31 March 2017). Furthermore, the corporation tax rate was reduced to 19% for financial years beginning 1 April 2017, 1 April 2018 and 1 April 2019 in *Finance (No. 2) Act 2015*. The corporation tax rate for the financial year beginning 1 April 2020 was initially set at 18%, but was subsequently reduced to 17% in *Finance Act 2016*.

A company may therefore be seen as a useful vehicle in terms of sheltering retained profits at lower tax rates than the personal tax rates applicable to many sole traders and business partners. However, the future extraction of profits as dividends will be adversely affected in many cases by the reform of the dividend tax system in *Finance Act 2016*.

Furthermore, following the introduction (in *Finance (No. 2) Act 2015*, as amended in *Finance Act 2016*) of a restriction in the deduction of finance costs related to residential property to the basic rate of income tax, which is being phased in from 6 April 2017 (see *ITTOIA 2005, ss 272A–272B, ss 274A–274C;* see also *ITA 2007, ss 399A–399B* for property partnerships), individual landlords who are higher rate taxpayers may be attracted to incorporating the rental property business so that the company can claim unrestricted relief for such costs (albeit at corporation tax rates). The interest relief restrictions are discussed in **Chapter 3**.

13.2 The tax rates on profits from the disposal of property interests also merit comparison and careful consideration by the unincorporated business or putative company owner. For disposals in 2016/17, the basic and standard rates of CGT are 10% and 20% respectively (previously 18% and 28%) on most gains made by individuals, trustees and personal representatives. However, gains on the disposal of interests in residential properties that do not qualify for private residence relief (and also gains arising in respect of carried interest) are instead subject to upper CGT rates of 18% and 28%.

By contrast, capital gains on the disposal of investment properties by companies are generally subject to normal corporation tax rates. However, ATED-related gains are liable to CGT at the rate of 28% (*TCGA 1992, s 4B(3A)*).

13.3 *Incorporation of a buy-to-let residential property business*

Furthermore, business owners may perceive that there is a potential double tax charge by operating in corporate form. The company pays tax on its gain; the shareholder pays tax on extraction of the taxed profit.

For detailed commentary on capital gains tax issues, see **Chapter 11**.

13.3 As indicated, an unincorporated property letting business will derive gross rents against which may be set various expenses to arrive at a net profit. An individual receiving this will be chargeable to income tax at his highest marginal rate as it arises. Getting the profits into a company has the obvious attraction of them being subject to lower tax rates, and the ability to withdraw profits by way of dividend rather than salary, just as with any trading company.

The restriction in tax relief for loan interest incurred on personally-held buy-to-let residential property, with effect from 6 April 2017, to a basic rate tax deduction will also make a corporate property portfolio holding structure more attractive. However, it should be remembered that the corporation rate and basic rate of income tax (at least for 2016/17) are the same.

See **Chapter 10** (Company landlords) for commentary on the operation of a buy-to-let residential property business by a company.

13.4 This chapter considers potential tax implications upon incorporating a buy-to-let property business. It does not compare and contrast the tax position for the owner of an unincorporated property rental business and the same business operated through a limited company, as it is assumed for the purposes of this chapter that the decision to incorporate has already been made.

Corporate profit extraction issues (eg salary versus dividends) following incorporation are also not considered in this Chapter. Detailed guidance on such issues can be found in the latest edition of *Tax Planning for Family and Owner-Managed Companies* by Peter Rayney (Bloomsbury Professional). See also **Chapter 10** (Company landlords).

Accounting, legal and commercial implications of incorporation are also beyond the scope of this Chapter, but must not be overlooked. For example, professional fees are invariably a significant cost of the incorporation process. Where there is the transfer of several properties, conveyancing fees must be borne in mind, along with Land Registry charges. In addition, if the properties are subject to mortgages or other loans, financing issues will need to be addressed.

For detailed commentary on legal and commercial (eg financing) considerations of buy-to-let residential property businesses, including incorporation, see **Chapters 16–18**. Readers are also referred to the latest edition of *Incorporating and Disincorporating a Business* (Bloomsbury Professional).

Incorporation of a buy-to-let residential property business **13.7**

IS THERE A BUSINESS?

Background

13.5

> **Focus**
>
> Before looking at the tax implications of incorporating a buy-to-let residential property business, it is important to consider what constitutes 'a business' in tax terms.
>
> For CGT purposes, this will be relevant in determining whether incorporation relief (under *TCGA 1992, s 162*) is available where a non-trading activity is to be incorporated, and in particular when considering the incorporation of a property letting business.

13.6 What is a business? The term is not defined in the relevant *Taxes Acts* – and so, *prima facie*, should take its ordinary meaning. Dictionary definitions of 'business' include 'the activity of buying and selling goods and services', 'a person's regular occupation, profession, or trade' and 'commercial activity'. However, these definitions are not very instructive or useful in the context of this chapter.

However, it is clear from case law that 'business' is a wider term than 'trade', and that while a trade will always be a business, a business will not always be a trade.

For tax purposes, as mentioned there is no satisfactory definition of a 'business' in the *Taxes Acts*. In HMRC's Capital Gains manual (at CG65715), HMRC analyses some court decisions and concludes that although a business is somewhat wider than a trade, the passive holding of investments or an investment property would not amount to a business.

13.7 However, some assistance may be derived from *Ramsay v HMRC* [2013] UKUT 226 (TCC), particularly in the context of property rental businesses. The Upper Tribunal held on the facts in that case that Mrs Ramsay's activities in relation to a single building divided into ten flats were sufficient to amount to a business, for the purposes of incorporation relief under *TCGA 1992, s 162* (see **13.19**).

For CGT purposes, there is an exception to some of the potential uncertainties caused by property rental businesses, if the properties concerned meet the conditions to be treated as furnished holiday lettings. Various CGT reliefs are statutorily available to proprietors in respect of the commercial letting of furnished holiday accommodation in the UK, by treating the UK property business as a trade (*TCGA 1992, s 241*), including gift relief (under *TCGA 1992, s 165*; see **13.36**).

13.8 *Incorporation of a buy-to-let residential property business*

The furnished holiday lettings rules were extended in *Finance Act 2011*, resulting in the relevant CGT reliefs for furnished holiday lettings owners being available not only for furnished holiday accommodation in the UK, but also in respect of the commercial letting of furnished holiday accommodation in EEA states other than the UK (*s 241A*).

13.8 In general terms, a sole proprietor will personally own a collection of assets used for the purposes of the business. In the case of a partnership, these will normally be partnership property (in which case, in England and Wales at least, each partner will be deemed to own his proportionate share). See HMRC's *Statement of Practice D12* (reproduced at CG27170) as regards the CGT treatment of partnership assets.

Before the business is incorporated, and assets are transferred to the company, the CGT position of the business and its proprietors should be analysed carefully.

Case law

13.9 Lord Diplock described the term 'business' as 'an etymological chameleon; it suits its meaning to the context in which it is found' (in *Town Investments Ltd v Department of the Environment* [1977] 1 All ER 813).

In the Privy Council case of *American Leaf Blending Co v Director-General of Inland Revenue* [1978] STC 561, Lord Diplock said:

> '"Business" is a wider concept than "trade"…
>
> In the case of a private individual it may well be that the mere receipt of rents from property that he owns raises no presumption that he is carrying on a business. In contrast, in their Lordships' view, in the case of a company incorporated for the purpose of making profits for its shareholders any gainful use to which it puts any of its assets prima facie amounts to the carrying on of a business.
>
> The carrying on of "business", no doubt, usually calls for some activity on the part of whoever carries it on, though, depending on the nature of the business, the activity may be intermittent with long intervals of quiescence in between.'

In *Harthan v Mason* [1980] STC 94, the High Court judge (Fox J) agreed with the decision of the General Commissioners that activities carried on by the taxpayer in managing a row of terraced houses let to tenants did not amount to a 'business' for the purposes of a retirement relief claim for CGT (which excluded assets held as investments).

13.10 In the case of *Customs and Excise Commissioners v Lord Fisher* [1981] STC 238, heard in the High Court, Gibson J noted that, for VAT purposes, there was no definition of 'business', but went on to demonstrate six criteria for determining whether an activity is a business:

Incorporation of a buy-to-let residential property business **13.12**

(1) whether the activity is a 'serious undertaking earnestly pursued';

(2) whether the activity is an 'occupation or function actively pursued with a reasonable or recognisable continuity';

(3) whether the activity has 'a certain measure of substance as measured by the quarterly or annual value of taxable supplies made';

(4) whether the activity was 'conducted in a regular manner and on sound and recognised business principles';

(5) whether the activity is 'predominantly concerned with the making of taxable supplies to consumers for a consideration'; and

(6) whether the taxable supplies are 'of a kind which … are commonly made by those who seek to profit by them'.

13.11 For IHT purposes, in the context of business property relief (BPR) 'business' is defined as including 'a business carried on in the exercise of a profession or vocation, but does not include a business carried on otherwise than for gain. In addition, 'relevant business property' is defined as 'consisting of a business or interest in a business' (*IHTA 1984, s 105*).

In *Burkinyoung's Executor v IRC* [1995] STC (SCD) 29, Mrs Burkinyoung let a number of properties and, on her death, her executors claimed BPR. In reaching his decision, the Special Commissioner noted that it was common ground (between the executors and the Inland Revenue) that Mrs Burkinyoung's owning and letting activity consisted of a business and, therefore, met the first test of relevant business property. However, the claim failed on other grounds.

In *Revenue and Customs Commissioners v Lockyer (personal representatives of Pawson, dec'd)* [2013] UKUT 50 (TCC), the question of BPR entitlement for IHT was considered in relation to a property letting business.

In that case, the deceased had provided various services (including cleaning and gardening, advertising for lettings, etc) in relation to a bungalow which she owned and let as a holiday cottage. The First-tier Tribunal had found that this was a business (relying on the criteria referred to in *Lord Fisher*; see **13.10**), in particular that it was a serious undertaking earnestly pursued, there was reasonable continuity and the activities had a measure of substance.

However, the Upper Tribunal allowed HMRC's appeal on the basis that the tribunal had been wrong to find that the property was not held mainly as an investment.

13.12 In *Rashid v Garcia* [2003] STC (SCD) 36 (a National Insurance contributions case), the appellant sought to pay Class 2 contributions in respect of earnings from property letting. The Special Commissioner held that, whilst it was not free from doubt, the arrangements did not amount to a business. Rather, it was an investment which, by its nature, required some activity to maintain it.

13.13 *Incorporation of a buy-to-let residential property business*

In *HMRC v Salaried Persons Postal Loans Ltd* [2006] STC 1315 (a corporation tax case), a company passively receiving rents from a single property was held not to be carrying on a business at all.

The Ramsay case

13.13 The case of *Ramsay v Revenue and Customs Commissioners* [2013] UKUT 226 (TCC) is the first to be heard on a claim for incorporation relief (under *TCGA 1992, s 162*).

Mrs Ramsay owned a large house in Belfast, which was divided into ten flats and let to tenants. In 2004, she transferred the property into a newly incorporated company, in return for an issue of shares in the company, and claimed *s 162* relief from the capital gain which would have otherwise become chargeable.

The activities carried out by Mrs Ramsay included meeting the tenants, payment of electricity bills for the communal areas, changing insurance policy details, unblocking drains, oiling and re-attaching steel wires on garage doors, clearing debris from garages, returning post, ensuring compliance with fire regulations and installing fire extinguishers, etc. Refurbishment and redevelopment plans had also been made for the property when the incorporation took place.

TCGA 1992, s 162 requires that 'a person who is not a company transfers to a company a business as a going concern' in exchange for shares in the company. HMRC denied Mrs Ramsay's *s 162* claim on the basis that the property-letting activities did not constitute a business for these purposes.

The First-tier Tribunal dismissed the taxpayer's appeal. Judge Huddleston held that:

> '... the activities which have been cited by the Appellant are those which are normal and incidental to the owning of an investment property. They are not of a unique nature and applying the principles set out in *Rashid v Garcia* are those which arise by necessity when one owns a property, such as this, which is let out in flats.
>
> The reality was that the Moat House was a single investment property – albeit comprised of ten apartments – and the Tribunal finds that the scale of activities simply were commensurate with that size of property and the number of occupied apartments.'

13.14 However, the Upper Tribunal held that, as a matter of law, the First-tier Tribunal had erred in its approach and had addressed the wrong question. The question it should have asked was, 'whether the taxpayer's activities in relation to the property constituted a business,' and the tribunal concluded that, 'the degree of activity undertaken by the taxpayer ... was on the facts before the Upper Tribunal sufficient to amount to a business. The taxpayer's appeal would accordingly be allowed'.

The following key extracts from Judge Berner's decision are worth noting:

Incorporation of a buy-to-let residential property business **13.14**

- 'It is the degree of activity as a whole which is material to the question whether there is a business, and not the extent of that activity when compared to the number of properties or lettings. If an individual undertaking the letting of properties increases his portfolio, and as a result increases activities of a business nature in relation to his properties, those activities will not be prevented from being a business merely because the activity has only proportionally increased along with the enlargement of the portfolio, and so can be described as commensurate with the property holdings.'

- 'As I have described it earlier, in my judgment the word "business" in the context of *s 162*, TCGA should be afforded a broad meaning. Regard should be had to the factors referred to in Lord Fisher, which in my view (with the exception of the specific references to taxable supplies, which are relevant to VAT) are of general application to the question whether the circumstances describe a business. Thus, it falls to be considered whether Mrs Ramsay's activities were a "serious undertaking earnestly pursued" or a "serious occupation", whether the activity was an occupation or function actively pursued with reasonable or recognisable continuity, whether the activity had a certain amount of substance in terms of turnover, whether the activity was conducted in a regular manner and on sound and recognised business principles, and whether the activities were of a kind which, subject to differences of detail, are commonly made by those who seek to profit by them.'

- 'In my judgment, taking the activities of Mrs Ramsay as a whole, I am satisfied that these tests are satisfied. Certain of the individual activities by themselves have little impact on the issue, but overall, taking account both the day-to-day activities, and the work undertaken by Mrs Ramsay in respect of the early refurbishment and redevelopment proposals, I conclude that the activities fall within the tests described in Lord Fisher.'

- 'There remains, however, the question of degree. That is relevant to the equation because of the fact that in the context of property investment and letting the same activities are equally capable of describing a passive investment and a property investment or rental business. Although resolution of that issue will be assisted by consideration of the Lord Fisher factors, to those there must be added the degree of activity undertaken. There is nothing in the *TCGA* which can colour the extent of the activity which for the purpose of *s 162* may be regarded as sufficient to constitute a business, and so this must be approached in the context of a broad meaning of that term.'

- 'Applying these principles, in this case I am satisfied that the activity undertaken in respect of the Property, again taken overall, was sufficient in nature and extent to amount to a business for the purpose of *s 162, TCGA*. Although each of the activities could equally well

13.15 *Incorporation of a buy-to-let residential property business*

have been undertaken by someone who was a mere property investor, where the degree of activity outweighs what might normally be expected to be carried out by a mere passive investor, even a diligent and conscientious one, that will in my judgment amount to a business. I find that was the case here.'

HMRC comments on the *Ramsay* decision (at CG65715) as follows:

'That decision confirms that where the Courts have considered [the meaning of 'business'] elsewhere the particular context of the legislation involved often restricted the meaning compared with the less restricted use for incorporation relief. The First Tier Tribunal had misdirected itself by relying too much on such cases.' It also states: 'The *Ramsay* case endorsed the approach in *American Leaf Tobacco* set out above, confirming that for there to be a business for incorporation relief there has to be "activity" and that just a modest degree of activity would not suffice. It also shows us that it is the quantity not the quality of the activity that is important.'

TRANSACTIONS IN UK LAND

13.15 It has hitherto generally been assumed that the straightforward purchase and subsequent sale of buy-to-let residential property is a capital transaction, such that individual investors will be liable to CGT on gains made upon the disposal of such investments.

However, *Finance Act 2016* introduced legislation concerning 'transactions in UK land', which is broadly a specific income tax charge from dealing in or developing land and other immovable property in the UK (new *ITA 2007, Pt 9A*) which meet certain alternative conditions (A, B, C or D in the legislation). For example, Condition A is broadly that a main purpose of acquiring the land was to realise a profit or gain from disposing of the land.

If a profit or gain is 'caught' by these provisions, it is treated for income tax purposes as the profits of a trade carried on by the chargeable person, arising in the tax year in which the profits gain is realised. This applies to gains of a capital nature, in the same way as in relation to other gains.

Focus

The *Finance Bill 2016* legislation on transactions in UK land was published after the original Finance Bill clauses, and without consultation. Shortly after the *Finance Bill 2016* clauses on transactions in land were published, the Law Society of England and Wales published a representation regarding the draft legislation (http://tinyurl.com/Lawsociety-TIL).

It pointed out that the provisions as drafted could apply to many buy-to-let investors, and expressed the view that if this was not the government's intention, the draft legislation should be amended accordingly.

Incorporation of a buy-to-let residential property business **13.17**

Following the enactment of the legislation in *Finance Act 2016*, a letter from HMRC to the National Landlords Association offered the assurance that investors who buy properties to let out to generate rental income, and some years later sell the properties, will normally be subject to capital gains on their disposals rather than being charged to income on such disposals. However, HMRC added that in certain 'exceptional' cases (ie broadly involving development of property) the gains will be charged to income tax.

It therefore appears that the straightforward incorporation of a buy-to-let residential property business was not intended to result in a charge to income tax. However, HMRC guidance on the transactions in UK land legislation, which is expected to be published in its Business Income manual, was awaited at the time of writing.

CAPITAL GAINS TAX

Introduction

13.16 The transfer of chargeable assets in property from an unincorporated business to a company is a disposal for the purposes of CGT.

Furthermore, it is normally a disposal between connected persons. A company is connected with another person, if that person has control of it, or if that person and persons connected with him together have control of it (*TCGA 1992, s 286(6)*). It will be extremely rare that the proprietors of the former unincorporated business are different to the controlling shareholders of the company.

Where there are transactions between connected persons, the transaction is treated as a bargain not made at arm's length (*TCGA 1992, s 18*). This in turn brings *TCGA 1992, s 17* ('Disposals and acquisitions treated as made at market value') into play, such that the consideration for the business proprietor(s) disposal of the assets is treated as being at market value, and the company's corresponding acquisition value is also treated as being at market value.

Obtaining a contemporaneous professional valuation of the properties being transferred will generally be best practice. An application to HMRC for a post-transaction valuation check (on form CG34) could also be considered prior to submission of the proprietor's tax return for the year of disposal (see http://tinyurl.com/HMRC-CGT-CG34).

13.17 For CGT computation purposes, the chargeable assets of the business are therefore treated as passing at market value.

However, the actual consideration may be:

- shares in the company;
- loan stock in the form of a debenture or similar though (this tends to be rare, in the context of small private companies);

13.18 *Incorporation of a buy-to-let residential property business*

- cash (often left outstanding on a director's loan account); and
- nothing (if the business asses are gifted to the company).

On a sale of the properties to the company upon incorporation, as indicated at **13.15** the market value of the properties will normally prevail for CGT purposes. Care should be taken that the selling price does not exceed market value, to prevent any excess consideration being treated as an income distribution (*CTA 2010, ss 1000(1); 1020*).

13.18 If there were to be a large chargeable gain, with tax payable, this would amount to a significant disincentive to incorporation. Fortunately, CGT relief will be available in many cases.

The main form of CGT relief to alleviate this problem is *TCGA 1992, s 162* (Roll-over relief on transfer of business'), which is commonly referred to as 'incorporation relief' (see **13.19**).

Certain other forms of CGT relief may alternatively be available in the context of a qualifying furnished holiday lettings business. For example, a business of commercially letting furnished holiday accommodation is treated as a trade for the purposes of rollover relief for business assets (under *TCGA 1992, ss 152–157*) (see **13.43–13.44**), relief for gifts of business assets (under *TCGA 1992, s 165*) (see **13.36–13.42**) and entrepreneurs' relief (*TCGA 1992, s 169S(1)*) (see **13.33–13.35**).

A buy-to-let residential property may at some time during the business proprietor's period of ownership been their only or main residence. A measure of private residence relief (*TCGA 1992, s 222*) may be available on a disposal of the property to the company upon incorporation, including lettings relief (*s 223(4)*). However, various relief conditions and restrictions must be carefully considered. For example, relief is denied if the property was acquired wholly or partly for the purposes of realising a gain from its disposal (*TCGA 1992, s 224(3)*). For the purposes of this chapter, it is assumed that the rental properties have not been the business proprietor's only or main residence. For commentary on main residence relief, readers are referred to *Capital Gains Tax 2016/17* (Bloomsbury Professional).

Capital gains deferral relief for any gains resulting from the incorporation of a buy-to-let residential property business under the enterprise investment scheme (EIS) or seed enterprise investment scheme (SEIS) seems to be a non-starter. For EIS deferral relief purposes, the company must broadly be a qualifying company for EIS income tax relief purposes (*TCGA 1992, Sch 5B, paras 1(2)(b), 19(1)*). A 'qualifying company' must satisfy certain conditions, including a trading requirement (*ITA 2007, ss 181, 189*). As indicated elsewhere in this chapter, property rental activities do not come within the ordinary meaning of 'trade'. In any event, even if the letting of residential property amounted to trading, leasing (including the leasing of property) is an 'excluded activity' for EIS purposes (*ITA 2007, ss 192(1)(d), 303(1)(d)*).

Incorporation of a buy-to-let residential property business **13.21**

Similarly, one of the conditions for SEIS reinvestment relief (*TCGA 1992, Sch 5BB*) is that the investor is eligible for SEIS income tax relief. There is a trading requirement for SEIS income tax relief purposes, and also a 'new qualifying trade' requirement (*ITA 2007, ss 257DA, 257HF*). A 'qualifying trade' has the same meaning as for EIS income tax purposes, and therefore the leasing of residential property is also an excluded activity in the context of SEIS relief.

Incorporation relief

13.19

> **Focus**
>
> A specific CGT relief for incorporation purposes is contained in *TCGA 1992, s 162* ('Roll-over relief on transfer of business').
>
> The relief is mandatory and automatic if specified conditions are met, and therefore does not require a claim (although the person transferring the business can make an election under *TCGA 1992, s 162A* for incorporation relief *not* to apply). *Section 162(2)* simply states that the cost of the new assets (ie the company shares) shall be deducted from the chargeable gain. Correspondingly, *s 162(3)* gives the base cost of the new assets as reduced by the amount left out of the CGT computation on incorporation. There are provisions for apportionment where the consideration is not wholly in shares (*TCGA 1992, s 162(4)*).

Far too often, the incorporation of a business is purported to have taken place, but there is often no evidence that it actually has. Whilst a property transfer will be evidenced by a conveyance, do not forget that items such as office equipment attracting capital allowances as plant and machinery may need to be sold to the company at particular prices. All in all, some sort of document is often a sensible step to demonstrate what has taken place.

Relief conditions

13.20 The relief applies where three conditions (ie limbs of *TCGA 1992, s 162(1)*) are satisfied:

- a person who is not a company (ie sole trader, partner) transfers to a company a business as a going concern;
- together with the whole assets of the business, possibly excluding cash; and
- the business is so transferred wholly or partly in exchange for shares issued by the company to the person transferring the business.

13.21 With regard to the first condition above, it is important to ensure that what is transferred amounts to a 'business as a going concern'.

13.22 *Incorporation of a buy-to-let residential property business*

There is no definition of the term 'business' in *TCGA 1992*, for this or any other purpose of CGT. The question of what constitutes a business for these purposes has already been considered (see **13.5–13.14** above).

However, some assistance on its meaning may be derived from *Ramsay v HMRC* [2013] UKUT 226 (TCC) (see **13.13**). In that case, the Upper Tribunal allowed Mrs Ramsay's appeal against the decision of the First-tier Tribunal that she was not entitled to incorporation relief under *s 162*.

Mrs Ramsay had inherited a one-third share of a large single building, which was divided into ten flats (five of which were occupied at the relevant time). She subsequently made a gift to her husband of one-half of her own one-third share, and later purchased the remaining two-thirds share of the property from her brothers. Mr and Mrs Ramsay transferred the property to a company, in exchange for shares in it.

Taking the activities of Mrs Ramsay as a whole, the Upper Tribunal concluded that those activities fell within the business tests outlined in *Customs and Excise Commissioners v Lord Fisher* [1981] STC 238. The tribunal was also satisfied that the degree of activity undertaken in respect of the property overall was sufficient in nature and extent to amount to a business for the purpose of *s 162*.

13.22 HMRC guidance on the meaning of 'business' in the context of incorporation relief (at CG65715) refers to case law authorities including *American Leaf Blending Co v Director-General of Inland Revenue (Malaysia), PC* [1978] 3 All ER 1185, including the following extract from Lord Diplock's judgment: 'In the case of a private individual it may well be that the mere receipt of rents from property that he owns raises no presumption that he is carrying on a business.'

HMRC's guidance goes on to state:

'The Ramsay case endorsed the approach in American Leaf Tobacco… confirming that for there to be a business for incorporation relief there has to be "activity" and that just a modest degree of activity would not suffice. It also shows us that it is the quantity not the quality of the activity that is important.'

HMRC considers that there is a 'threshold' to be crossed for an undertaking to constitute a 'business', in terms of the quantity of the proprietor's activity in it. However, there will often be uncertainty as to whether this threshold test is met, as circumstances will vary.

This uncertainty will clearly be unsatisfactory for those taxpayers seeking to rely on incorporation relief under *TCGA 1992, s 162*. This has resulted in some taxpayers (or their advisers) seeking advance assurance from HMRC under the non-statutory business clearance service that their undertaking amounts to a business for these purposes (see **13.31**).

13.23 The second condition in *TCGA 1992, s 162* above not only requires the transfer of the business, but of the business as a going concern.

HMRC considers this requirement to indicate that something more than a collection of assets must be transferred (CG65710). Can a property rental

Incorporation of a buy-to-let residential property business **13.24**

business be a going concern? This issue was not raised in the *Ramsay* case, so presumably the answer is 'yes'.

In *Roelich v Revenue & Customs* [2014] UKFTT 579 (TC), the tribunal held that the business was transferred as a going concern, and was not merely the transfer of an income stream, as HMRC had contended (among other things). The taxpayer was perhaps fortunate on the facts of that case, in the sense that the incorporation of his business was conducted informally and there was very little documentary evidence of the transfer, whereas incorporation under *s 162* commonly involves some form of business transfer agreement.

13.24 Incorporation relief under *s 162* is very specific. All of the assets of the business (apart from cash which is, of course, not a chargeable asset) must be transferred to the company and this must be done wholly or partly in exchange for shares.

In fact, cash is not the only item which may be left out. HMRC's *Extra-Statutory Concession (ESC) D32* (reproduced below) indicates that relief under *s 162* is not precluded by the fact that some or all of the liabilities of the business are not taken over by the company.

Concession D32

'Where liabilities are taken over by a company on the transfer of a business to the company, the Inland Revenue are prepared for the purposes of the "roll-over" provision in Section 162 TCGA 1992, not to treat such liabilities as consideration. If therefore the other conditions of Section 162 are satisfied, no capital gain arises on the transfer. Relief under Section 162 is not precluded by the fact that some or all of the liabilities of the business are not taken over by the company.'

However, care is needed to ensure that liabilities remain within the terms of Concession D32. For example, if the company raises finance and uses the funds to pay the proprietors for the business to enable existing borrowings to be repaid, this will constitute (non-share) consideration for the business, resulting in any *s 162* relief being restricted.

Reference is made in *s 162(1)* to the transfer to a company of a business as a going concern, together with the whole assets of the business, or together with the whole of those assets other than cash. In this context, 'cash' includes sums in a bank current or deposit account (CG65710). In any event, consideration should be given to clearing out and closing unwanted bank accounts before the incorporation transaction proceeds.

If the consideration for the shares includes amounts left owing to the transferor as sums credited to a loan or current account with the company, HMRC's approach is to treat the amount of the loan or current account as consideration other than shares

13.25 *Incorporation of a buy-to-let residential property business*

(CG65720). The proportion of gains upon incorporation which is attributable to the loan or current account becomes chargeable in the tax year of disposal.

13.25 The third condition for s 162 purposes (see **13.20** above) is that the business is transferred wholly or partly in exchange for shares issued by the company to the person transferring the business.

Note that the shares must be issued to the transferor (of the business). This is not the time to do remuneration or inheritance tax planning. The shares should be issued to the business proprietor, and not also be issued to others (eg family members). Failure to satisfy this requirement would seem to preclude relief.

Example 13.1—Section 162 relief in action

Adam is a higher rate taxpayer who owns a portfolio of buy-to-let residential properties in the North of England. He commenced his property rental business in 2006. The balance sheet of the business at 5 April 2016 is summarised below:

		£	£
Fixed assets			
Properties	– at cost		750,000
	– revaluation uplift (see below)		390,000
			1,140,000
Office equipment			500
Current assets			
Debtors		600	
Cash		1,000	1,600
			1,142,100
Liabilities			
Creditors		500	
Bank loans (re properties)		550,000	(550,500)
Net assets			£591,600

The properties were professionally valued early in 2016. The balance sheet value is assumed to equate to market value for CGT purposes.

Adam incorporated his property rental business on 6 April 2016 (he retained the cash balance).

Incorporation of a buy-to-let residential property business **13.26**

The combined gains on the properties are as follows:

Market value	1,140,000
Less: Cost	(750,000)
	£390,000

Relief calculation – TCGA 1992, s 162

The base cost of Adam's shares in the property rental company (Adamsco Ltd) for CGT purposes is as follows:

Value of consideration shares (£591,600–£1,000)	590,600
Less: Section 162 relief (see above)	(390,000)
CGT base cost of shares	£200,600

13.26 It is important to note that the gain will not always be fully relieved. The business must be transferred as a going concern and must therefore reflect liabilities to be satisfied by the company.

> **Focus**
>
> An undertaking to satisfy these liabilities amounts to further consideration. *ESC D32* (see **13.24**) prevents the assumption of liabilities from being treated as consideration for the purposes of the *s 162* computation. However, this does not mean that the liabilities can be ignored in determining the market value of the assets transferred.
>
> Where the liabilities are relatively high (and are being transferred), the net asset value of the business (which equals the value of the shares issued) may be low. If the properties have large inherent capital gains it may be impossible to rollover all of the gain – the base cost of the shares cannot go below zero.

13.26 *Incorporation of a buy-to-let residential property business*

Example 13.2—Section 162 relief limitation

The facts are as in **Example 13.1**, except that the bank loans in respect of the properties amount to £820,000. The balance sheet is therefore summarised as follows:

		£	£
Fixed assets			
Properties	– at cost		750,000
	– revaluation uplift		390,000
			1,140,000
Office equipment			500
Current assets			
Debtors		600	
Cash		1,000	1,600
			1,142,100
Liabilities			
Creditors		500	
Bank loans		820,000	(820,500)
Net assets			£321,600

Relief calculation – TCGA 1992, s 162

Value of consideration shares (£321,600–£1,000)	320,600
Less: Section 162 relief*	(320,600)
CGT base cost of shares	£Nil

*The relief is limited to the value of the consideration shares.

CGT computation

Gains on properties	390,000
Less: Section 162 relief	(320,600)
	69,400
Less: Annual exemption (2016/17)	(11,100)
	£58,300
CGT at 28%	£16,324

Incorporation of a buy-to-let residential property business **13.27**

Thus a situation can arise where all the assets are transferred, only shares are issued and yet a chargeable gain still arises. It is therefore important to consider the level of potential gains arising, and to forecast the financial position of the company, in advance of the incorporation.

13.27 The consideration given is commonly entirely represented by an issue of shares. Occasionally, though, other consideration might be taken. Such consideration will often take the form of the creation of a director's loan account with a credit balance. In those circumstances, the gain which may be rolled over is limited to the following (*TCGA 1992, s 162(4)*):

A/B of the amount of the gain on the old assets where:

- A is the cost of the new assets (shares); and
- B is the value of the whole consideration received by the transferor in exchange for the business.

Example 13.3—Shares and other consideration

The facts are in Example **13.1** except that Adam transfers his residential property rental business to Adamsco Ltd in consideration of shares plus a director's loan account balance of £100,000.

	£
Net assets transferred	590,600
Gains on properties	390,000
Amount rolled over under s 162	
A/B × £390,000	
A = £490,600 (ie £590,600–£100,000)	
B = £590,600	
£490,600 × £390,000	(323,965)
£590,600	
Chargeable gain	66,035
Less: Annual exemption (2016/17)	(11,100)
	£54,935
CGT at 28%	£15,382
The base cost of Adam's shares in Adamsco Ltd is:	
Market value	490,600
Less: Amount rolled over under s 162	(323,965)
	£166,635

13.28 *Incorporation of a buy-to-let residential property business*

13.28 It may be possible to restrict the director's loan account credit balance to a level where the chargeable gain is covered by the individual's annual CGT exemption (assuming that the exemption has not been used elsewhere). However, the CGT saving should be measured against the loss of the director's loan account credit balance.

A loan account with the company at a relatively low CGT cost (eg in **Example 13.3** a loan account of £100,000 for a CGT cost of £15,382) might seem like an attractive proposition, with the loan being repaid by the company as funds allow. This may be seen as a cost-effective means of extracting funds from the company in some cases, compared with (for example) the rates of income tax applicable to a salary, or to dividends on the extraction of post-tax profits from the company following changes to the dividend tax regime from 6 April 2016.

The reduction in the base cost of the shares on a future disposal in those circumstances may be considered to be a price worth paying. However, the potential implications of a future increase in CGT rates should be borne in mind. Circumstances will vary, and there is no substitute for 'crunching the numbers' in each case.

13.29 The application of *s 162* is relatively inflexible, for two main reasons. First, it requires the transfer of all the business assets (with very limited exceptions) to the company. Secondly, most of the inherent value of the business is locked into the share capital of the company and cannot readily be extracted. Some commentators recommend that if there is a substantial capital account in the unincorporated business the proprietors should be advised to draw down on it before incorporation. Presumably, such a capital account exists in the first place in order to fund continuing business operations. If this is the case, then there is every likelihood that the funds withdrawn will be reintroduced into the company shortly afterwards by means of a credit to a director's loan account.

Perceived challenges to this process have often been said to stem from *Furniss (Inspector of Taxes) v Dawson* [1984] STC 153, in that the transactions are preordained and the intermediate one has no real purpose. The net effect is to recharacterise the transaction as if the business had been transferred for a consideration partly in the issue of shares and partly in cash. A counter-argument might be demonstrated by the incorporation agreement (assuming that there is one) showing the intention to transfer the entire assets of the business in return for shares. Could a similar challenge stem from the principle in *WT Ramsay Ltd v IRC* [1981] STC 174, notably that there is a circular series of transactions leaving the business in the same position as before it started? The significance of *Ramsay* was effectively relegated to a rule of statutory construction following *Barclays Mercantile Business Finance Ltd v Mawson* [2004] UKHL 51.

However, a general anti-abuse rule (GAAR) was subsequently introduced in *FA 2013*, and the Government can also introduce targeted anti-avoidance rules where it is considered necessary to do so. Nevertheless, it is difficult (for the author at least) to envisage business incorporations being affected by such measures.

13.30 A major asset retained from the business (commonly property) certainly prejudices the application of *s 162*. What about a minor one, though? It may be that the business proprietor would wish to retain personal ownership of an asset (eg a laptop, or a private car) outside the company. Although used in the business, such an asset may not have been on the balance sheet. However, it is not inconceivable that HMRC could use this as a reason to deny *s 162* relief. Positive steps ought to be taken to withdraw the asset from the business before incorporation, so that it has ceased to be an asset of the business before the time of transfer. Certainly, it ought not to be simply withheld.

Of course, it may be necessary to remove and retain part of the pre-incorporation capital account, for example to meet the tax liabilities of the unincorporated business. Provided that the final accounts of the unincorporated business have made full provision for outstanding tax liabilities, this should not be a problem.

Non-statutory business clearance

13.31

> **Focus**
>
> Despite the taxpayer's success in the *Ramsay* case (see **13.13**), a cautious approach is still to be advocated in relation to property portfolio incorporations. If one were to try such incorporation under *s 162*, and it was successfully challenged by HMRC on enquiry – being somehow distinguishable from the *Ramsay* case – then a very large unrelieved gain could ensue, with no cash having been generated to meet the liability.

It is therefore critical in cases where incorporation relief under *s 162* relief is being relied upon to ensure that what is being transferred to the company constitutes a *business*, and also that the business is a *going concern* (see **13.20–13.23**).

There is no statutory clearance on the availability of *s 162* relief. A non-statutory business clearance application to HMRC could be considered (see www.gov.uk/guidance/non-statutory-clearance-service-guidance) in advance of the incorporation taking place. HMRC provides a checklist of information ('Annex A') to be included in the clearance application.

An application under the non-statutory business clearance procedure has the advantage of potentially obtaining certainty on HMRC's position in terms of whether the conditions for *s 162* relief are satisfied. On the other hand, there is no statutory right of appeal against an adverse opinion by HMRC. There is

13.32 *Incorporation of a buy-to-let residential property business*

also anecdotal evidence that HMRC has been unwilling to provide its view in some cases, on the grounds that HMRC is unwilling to assist in tax planning exercises.

FURNISHED HOLIDAY LETTINGS

Background

13.32 As indicated at **13.18**, favoured CGT treatment is potentially available in respect of the commercial letting of furnished holiday accommodation (*TCGA 1992, ss 241, 241A*), which is not afforded to property rental businesses generally.

Such properties must meet certain conditions to be treated as furnished holiday lettings in order to be deemed a trade. Those conditions are discussed in **Chapter 6**, which also includes further commentary on the CGT reliefs discussed below.

Furnished holiday lettings in the UK are generally treated as forming a single trade, and similarly an overseas property business of furnished holiday lettings in one or more EEA states is generally treated as forming a single trade, for the purposes of the capital gains reliefs listed in *TCGA 1992, ss 241(3A), 241A(5)*.

Furthermore, incorporation relief under *TCGA 1992, s 162* (see **13.19**) is potentially available to furnished holiday lettings businesses, as it generally is to other types of property rental businesses.

As to the capital allowances position in relation to qualifying furnished holiday lettings businesses, see **13.62** and **4.11–4.14**.

Entrepreneurs' relief

13.33 Entrepreneurs' relief is a very valuable CGT relief for individuals. A CGT rate of 10% broadly applies to qualifying gains up to a lifetime limit of £10 million. It is therefore perhaps unsurprising that various conditions must be satisfied to be eligible to claim the relief when an individual makes a material disposal of business assets.

A 'material disposal of business assets' broadly includes the disposal of the whole or part of a business carried on by a sole trader or partnership. The business must be owned for at least one year ending with the date of disposal. The disposal of an asset used in the sole trade or partnership business upon cessation is also a material disposal if the one-year ownership requirement is met and the disposal takes place within three years after the business has ceased (*TCGA 1992, s 169I*).

Incorporation of a buy-to-let residential property business **13.34**

Entrepreneurs' relief is also available for qualifying disposals consisting of certain associated disposals. In the context of incorporation, an associated disposal broadly includes the disposal of an asset held by a partner personally and used in the partnership's business, where the disposal was associated with a 'relevant material disposal' by the partner of his partnership interest (within *TCGA 1992, s 169K*). Entrepreneurs' relief is subject to restriction or denial in respect of associated disposals in certain circumstances (see *TCGA 1992, s 169P*).

This chapter does not attempt to cover entrepreneurs' relief in any detail. For more detailed commentary on the relief generally, readers are referred to *Capital Gains Tax Reliefs for SMEs and Entrepreneurs 2016/17* (Bloomsbury Professional).

13.34 In terms of the incorporation of a buy-to-let residential property business, entrepreneurs' relief is generally a non-starter. As indicated, a qualifying business disposal includes a 'material disposal of business assets', which in turn includes a disposal of 'business assets' such as the disposal of the whole or part of the business, or assets used for the purposes of the business (*TCGA 1992, s 169I(2)*).

For entrepreneurs' relief purposes, 'a business' is defined as anything which is a trade, profession or vocation, and is conducted on a commercial basis and with a view to the realisation of profits (*TCGA 1992, s 169S(1)*). A buy-to-let residential property activity is capable of amounting to a business, but will not normally be treated as a trading activity.

HMRC relies on case law (*Salisbury House Estates Ltd v Fry* [1930] 15 TC 266 and *Griffiths v Jackson* [1982] 56 TC 583) as authority to support its view that income derived from rights of property in land is very unlikely to be trading income except in a hotel or guesthouse activity, where the whole income from guests is usually chargeable as trading income. The fact that the taxpayer spends a lot (or even all) of their working time in the letting business does not convert rental income into trading income in HMRC's view (see PIM1051).

However, an important exception to this general rule for entrepreneurs' relief purposes applies in the case of qualifying furnished holiday lettings (*TCGA 1992, ss 241(3A), 241A(5)*). This exception potentially provides the individual furnished holiday lettings business proprietor with the opportunity to sell the business to the company upon incorporation (in return for cash and/or a loan account balance with the company) and claim entrepreneurs' relief if the relevant conditions are satisfied. This may be a more tax-efficient means of extracting profits from the company than (for example) salary or dividends, although as always this will depend on the particular facts in each case.

The availability of entrepreneurs' relief on disposals of goodwill upon incorporation is restricted in respect of goodwill transfers to a close company, subject to certain limited exceptions (see *TCGA 1992, s 169LA*). The effect of the restriction is to exclude goodwill from the definition of 'relevant business

13.35 *Incorporation of a buy-to-let residential property business*

assets' comprised in a 'qualifying business disposal' for entrepreneurs' relief purposes (in *TCGA 1992, s 169L*), so that a gain on an affected disposal of goodwill to the close company (or a company that would be close if it were resident in the UK) is charged at normal CGT rates (subject to other reliefs being claimed). Consideration should therefore be given to whether there is any goodwill value in the business, including in the property itself.

13.35 Where the furnished holiday lettings business consists of a single property that is sold upon incorporation, clearly the business has ceased and there has been a disposal of the whole business.

However, as intimated at **6.7**, where the furnished holiday lettings business contains several let properties and there is a disposal of only some of those properties, a claim for entrepreneurs' relief may be challenged by HMRC, on the basis that there has been no disposal of part of the business (see HMRC's Capital Gains manual at CG64015 and following).

Section 165 relief

13.36 Relief under *TCGA 1992, s 165* ('Relief for gifts of business assets') broadly has the effect that a chargeable gain otherwise arising on the disposal of an asset is reduced by the held-over gain, and the amount of the company's capital gains base cost is also reduced by the held-over gain.

In the context of the incorporation of a buy-to-let residential property business, *TCGA 1992, s 165* relief is not generally available. This is because the relief permits the holdover of a capital gain where an asset is transferred at undervalue and the asset is used for the purposes of a trade, profession or vocation. As indicated at **13.34** above, a buy-to-let residential property activity will not normally be treated as a trading activity (or a profession or vocation).

13.37 However, as pointed out at **13.18** above, a qualifying furnished holiday lettings business is treated as a trade for the purposes of relief under *TCGA 1992, s 165* (see *TCGA 1992, ss 241(3A), 241A(5)*).

It is therefore possible for an individual to transfer a property used for furnished holiday letting at undervalue to a company and hold over a capital gain arising by making a claim under s 165. In other words, it is possible to incorporate a property-letting business which consists entirely of furnished holiday lettings without triggering a taxable capital gain.

13.38 The relief applies where the asset owner disposes of the asset by way of a bargain not at arm's length (*TCGA 1992, s 165(1)(a)*). The transfer of furnished holiday lettings from the rental property business proprietor to the company will normally be a connected party transaction.

Incorporation of a buy-to-let residential property business **13.40**

The effect of the relief is that a chargeable gain otherwise arising is reduced by the 'held over gain' and the amount of the company's CGT base cost is also reduced by the held over gain (*TCGA 1992, s 165(4)*).

13.39 Unlike incorporation relief under *TCGA 1992, s 162* (application of which is mandatory in the relevant circumstances), a specific claim is required for gift relief to apply (*TCGA 1992, s 165(1)(b)*). The claim must be made jointly by both the individual making the transfer and the company. HMRC require the claim to be made on the form contained in Helpsheet HS295 ('Relief for gifts and similar transactions') (http://tinyurl.com/HMRC-HS295). Claims for relief are possible without a computation of the gain on the gifted property, if both parties agree (see *Statement of Practice 8/92*).

No shorter time limit is specified, so the general time limit of four years from the end of the tax year in which the transfer takes place normally applies (*TMA 1970, s 43(1)*). In practice, claims will nearly always be made long before the end of this time limit (normally on the business owner's tax return for the year of incorporation), because otherwise CGT on the gain would become payable.

Note that *s 165* contains no requirement that the transfer shall be the whole of the business or even all of the assets used in the business. It must simply be 'an asset' used in a trade, profession or vocation. Thus there is a flexibility which is absent from the *s 162* process.

13.40 The amount of the gain which can be held over is as follows:

- in the case of a pure gift (ie no proceeds at all), the gain which would otherwise arise in deeming the proceeds to be market value (*TCGA 1992, s 165(6)*); or

- in the case of a transfer at undervalue, the amount by which the deemed gain exceeds the excess of the actual consideration over the costs deductible in the CGT computation (*TCGA 1992, s 165(7)*).

The costs deductible are those given by *TCGA 1992, s 38* ('Acquisition and disposal costs etc').

Care is needed in relation to the second bullet point above, if the furnished holiday lettings are being sold to the company at undervalue (eg cash or a director's loan account credit balance), as this could result in the relief under *s 165* being restricted.

13.40 *Incorporation of a buy-to-let residential property business*

Example 13.4 – Section 165 relief: Sale at undervalue

Brenda owns a qualifying furnished holiday letting. She decided to incorporate the business, and transferred the property to the company on 1 May 2016. Brenda acquired the property for £175,000 in 1992, out of the proceeds of an inheritance from her late father. The market value of the property upon incorporation was £380,000.

		£
(a)	Capital gain arising:	
	Consideration (market value)	380,000
	Less: Cost	(175,000)
		£205,000

(b) If Brenda gifts the property to the company the whole of the gain is held over. The base cost of the property for the company is:

	£
Market value	380,000
Less: Held over gain	(205,000)
Base cost for future disposal	£175,000

(c) If Brenda sells the property to the company for £150,000:

	£
Actual proceeds	150,000
Less: Allowable cost	(175,000)
Excess	£nil

The result is as in (b) above. This is probably not a realistic scenario as Brenda is missing the opportunity to take a further £25,000 tax free; the proceeds might as well be £175,000 – the result is similar.

(d) If Brenda sells the property to the company for £225,000:

	£
Actual proceeds	225,000
Less: Allowable cost	(175,000)
Excess	£50,000
Gross gain	205,000
Less: Excess	(50,000)
Gain held over	£155,000

Incorporation of a buy-to-let residential property business **13.43**

The excess is also the chargeable gain (subject to the annual exemption, if available). As indicated at **13.34**, entrepreneurs' relief is also potentially available for qualifying furnished holiday lettings disposals. *Section 165* relief and entrepreneurs' relief both require claims. HMRC's view is that *s 165* relief takes priority over entrepreneurs' relief (CG64137).

In the case of a disposal at undervalue, a claim to entrepreneurs' relief may therefore be possible in respect of the amount of any gain remaining chargeable.

The base cost of the property for the company is:

Market value	380,000
Less: Held over gain	(155,000)
Base cost for future disposal	£225,000

13.41 As indicated, relief under *TCGA 1992, s 165* is available broadly if the asset is used for the purposes of a trade (or deemed trade, in the case of furnished holiday lettings). The property has to have been in 'trade' use just before it is gifted. Previous periods of non-trade use will generally restrict the relief (*TCGA 1992, Sch 7, para 5*).

Similarly, if part of the property was used for the purposes of the trade and part of it was not, gift holdover relief is generally subject to a restriction on a 'just and reasonable' basis (*Sch 7, para 6*).

13.42 Incorporation of a furnished holiday lettings business potentially gives rise to a choice between incorporation relief, entrepreneurs' relief or gift relief. For the most part, there is no right or wrong answer, as all the circumstances of the business and proprietor must be taken into account before an appropriate decision can be made.

However, it is not possible to use both incorporation relief (under *s 162*) and gift relief (under *s 165*). We have seen that there may be circumstances in which *s 162* can leave a residual chargeable gain. This is not eligible for a claim under *s 165*, because there are actual market value proceeds (ie the shares).

For detailed commentary on *s 165* relief, readers are referred to *Capital Gains Tax Reliefs for SMEs and Entrepreneurs 2016/17* (Bloomsbury Professional).

Rollover relief

13.43 As indicated at **13.18**, CGT relief for the replacement of business assets ('roll-over relief') is one of the reliefs specifically made available to individual proprietors of qualifying furnished holiday lettings businesses, if

13.44 *Incorporation of a buy-to-let residential property business*

the relevant conditions are satisfied (*TCGA 1992, s 152*). The same applies to a company carrying on a business which comprises or includes the commercial letting of furnished holiday accommodation (*CTA 2009, s 264(2), (2A)*).

The 'trade' for rollover relief purposes includes all trades etc. carried on by the claimant either at the same time or successively as if they were a single trade (*s 152(8)*).

Upon the incorporation of the furnished holiday lettings business, the deemed trade will generally cease to be carried on by the individual(s), and will be carried on by the company instead. A claim for rollover relief would therefore not be available, as the persons carrying on the trade are different.

13.44 It is possible that ownership of one or more furnished holiday lettings may be retained by the individual, but still be used in the individual's personal company's 'trade'. The rollover relief provisions provide that a gain accruing to an individual on the disposal of qualifying assets may be rolled over into the cost of new qualifying assets in such circumstances if certain conditions are satisfied (see *TCGA 1992, s 157*).

However, in addition to the property being used by the company for the purposes of the trade carried on by it, HMRC guidance indicates that it must be 'occupied' by the personal company (CG61250). The rollover relief provisions require that land and buildings are occupied (as well as used) only for the purposes of the trade (*s 155, Head A*). HMRC's requirement for the company to 'occupy' the property in this context is therefore unclear. Furthermore, it is unclear on the face of it whether a tenant's occupation can be imputed to the company in these circumstances. Caution should therefore be exercised in the context of furnished holiday lettings.

STAMP TAXES

General

13.45 A major consideration in the decision whether to incorporate a buy-to-let residential property business will be the potential exposure to stamp duty land tax (SDLT) in relation to property situated in England, Wales and Northern Ireland, or land and buildings transaction tax (LBTT) in relation to property situated in Scotland.

SDLT applies to land transactions, ie broadly the acquisition or enhancement of interests in UK land and buildings (*FA 2003, s 42*). It has no application to land outside the UK. From 1 April 2015, SDLT ceased to apply to land in Scotland, where it was replaced by LBTT, which is administered by Revenue Scotland, the tax authority with responsibility for the taxes devolved to the Scottish Parliament, including LBTT.

The LBTT legislation borrows heavily from the SDLT regime and therefore in many situations the LBTT implications of a transaction may be the same, or

Incorporation of a buy-to-let residential property business **13.47**

similar, to the SDLT implications which would have arisen had the transaction been subject to SDLT. However, care must be taken as there are some fundamental differences between LBTT and SDLT. It is also possible that Revenue Scotland will take a different view of similar legislation compared to that taken by HMRC. Consequently, specific LBTT advice should normally be sought when dealing with a transaction over land in Scotland.

For a detailed consideration of SDLT and LBTT, including statutory compliance obligations such as in relation to tax returns and payments, see *Stamp Taxes 2016/17* (Bloomsbury Professional) and *Land and Buildings Transaction Tax 2016/17* (Bloomsbury Professional).

13.46 SDLT and LBTT are in point for land in the rest of the UK and Scotland, regardless of whether or not the transactions are effected inside or outside the UK.

The rates of SDLT and LBTT on consideration other than rent depend on the amount of the chargeable consideration, and whether the transaction is a residential property transaction or a non-residential property transaction. However, for the purposes of this chapter it is assumed that the incorporation only involves the acquisition of residential property.

If several transactions are linked (essentially part of one overall transaction involving the same vendor and purchaser or persons connected with them: *FA 2003, s 108; LBTT(S)A 2013, s 57*), the consideration must be aggregated to determine the rates of tax.

Higher rates of SDLT (introduced in *FA 2016*) apply to certain purchases of residential property by individuals who already own a dwelling (and are not replacing a main residence), and also to first and subsequent purchases by companies and other non-individuals. The higher rates are 3% above the normal SDLT rates. Similarly, in Scotland, an additional dwelling supplement (introduced by *LBTT(A)(S)A 2016*), which adds 3% to the standard LBTT rates, applies to certain purchases of additional residential (eg buy-to-let) properties by individuals and first and subsequent purchases by a non-individual, such as a company (see **13.49**).

For detailed commentary on the rates and mechanics of SDLT and LBTT, see **Chapter 14**.

13.47 Stamp duty is charged on 'instruments', broadly defined as documents, transferring title to stock or marketable securities (principally shares and securities).

Assets such as plant and machinery (but excluding 'fixtures', ie plant and machinery which in law has become part of the land and the transfer of which is potentially chargeable to SDLT or LBTT) may pass by delivery and therefore free of stamp duty.

Stamp duty now only applies to instruments transferring stock and marketable securities, the issue of bearer instruments and transfers of interests in

13.48 *Incorporation of a buy-to-let residential property business*

partnerships which hold stock and marketable securities. As regards bearer instruments, it should be noted that with effect from 26 May 2015 a UK incorporated company has been prohibited from issuing new bearer shares, and from 26 February 2016 all existing bearer shares issued by a UK incorporated company had to be converted into registered shares or cancelled (*Small Business, Enterprise and Employment Act 2015*).

Stamp duty reserve tax (SDRT) is effectively an alternative to stamp duty, which is charged when no document of transfer is presented for stamping.

In the context of incorporation, a stamp duty charge could arise in some cases where relief is sought under *TCGA 1992, s 162*. However, there is no stamp duty on the issue of shares as such; only in the event that the business assets transferred include shares or securities will there be a stamp duty liability (at 0.5%) on the amount or value of the consideration given for the acquisition of the shares or securities. It should be noted that there is an exemption (*FA 1986, s 79(4)*) for documents transferring certain categories of loan capital.

Stamp duty and SDRT are unlikely to be significant factors in the incorporation of buy-to-let residential property businesses, and are not discussed further in this chapter.

The market value rule

13.48

> **Focus**
>
> Both SDLT and LBTT are generally charged on actual consideration in money or money's worth, so a gift or distribution for no consideration should be free of SDLT or LBTT.
>
> The main exception is when a property is transferred to a connected company. In that case, the chargeable consideration is the greater of the market value of the property and the actual consideration given. This is the case whether the property is (for example) exchanged for shares, gifted or sold for cash at an undervalue.

The chargeable consideration for a land transaction is defined in *FA 2003, Sch 4*; *LBTT(S)A 2013, Sch 2*. In most instances, it will be the consideration given in money or money's worth for the transaction.

However, if land and buildings are transferred to the company upon incorporation, invariably the parties will be connected with each other. If so, the land and buildings are deemed to pass at a chargeable consideration not less than market value for SDLT purposes (*FA 2003, s 53*; *LBTT(S)A 2013, s 22*). There are certain exceptions to the deemed market value rule (see *FA 2003, s 54*; *LBTT(S)A 2013, s 23*), but these are unlikely to apply in the context of an incorporation of a buy-to-let residential property business, and are not considered further in this chapter.

The rule for connection is found in *CTA 2010, s 1122* for SDLT purposes (*FA 2003, s 53(2)*) and for LBTT purposes (*LBTT(S)A 2013, s 58*). This provides (at *s 1122(3)*):

'A company is connected with another person ("A") if—

(a) A has control of the company, or

(b) A together with persons connected with A have control of the company.'

Thus, for example, a controlling shareholder will be connected with the company. Whilst there may be some incorporation cases where the company has diverse shareholdings which will be outside the connection test in *CTA 2010, s 1122*, these are likely to be the exception rather than the rule.

Furthermore, two or more persons acting together to secure or exercise control of the company are connected with one another, and also any person acting on the directions of any of them to secure or exercise control of the company (*s 1122(4)*).

As a general rule, a partner in a partnership is connected with any partner in the partnership, the spouse or civil partner of a partner in the partnership, and a relative of a partner in the partnership. However, there is an exception from this general rule in relation to acquisitions or disposals of assets of the partnership pursuant to genuine commercial arrangements (*s 1122(7), (8)*). This exception will normally apply to the incorporation of a business.

Deemed non-residential property treatment

13.49 When several properties are acquired in a single transaction (or a series of linked transactions), it is normally necessary to aggregate the consideration to determine the SDLT or LBTT payable (*FA 2003, s 55; LBTT(S)A 2013, s 26*).

It should, however, be noted that where, as part of a single transaction (or a series of linked transactions), properties in the rest of the UK and Scotland are acquired, the acquisition of the rest of the UK properties is chargeable to SDLT, the acquisition of the Scottish properties is chargeable to LBTT, and the acquisition of the rest of the UK properties is not linked, for the purposes of either of the taxes, with the acquisition of the Scottish properties (and vice versa).

Transactions are 'linked' for these purposes if they form part of a single scheme, arrangement or series of transactions between the same seller and buyer (or persons connected with them) (*FA 2003, s 108; LBTT(S)A 2013, s 57*).

13.50 *Incorporation of a buy-to-let residential property business*

However, if six or more dwellings are being transferred as a single transaction upon incorporation, the dwellings are treated as being non-residential for the purposes of determining the SDLT or LBTT payable (*FA 2003, s 116(7); LBTT(S)A 2013, s 59*).

Under SDLT, the deemed non-residential property treatment applies automatically, subject to a claim for multiple dwellings relief (see **13.50**). In contrast, under LBTT, a claim must be made to exempt the transaction from the additional dwelling supplement (see **13.49**), if the 3% additional charge is not to apply (LBTT(S)A 2013, sch 2A, paras 9 and 10; see LBTT10040).

Consideration should also be given as to whether a claim for LBTT multiple dwellings relief (see **13.50**) would be beneficial since, where six or more dwellings are acquired as part of a single transaction, and a claim is made to exempt the transaction from the additional dwellings supplement, the normal rates of LBTT apply in calculating the tax payable when a claim for multiple dwellings relief is made (LBTT(S)A 2013, sch 5, para 10A). This is not the case for SDLT, as the higher rates of SDLT (3% above the normal SDLT rates) apply when calculating the tax payable on a claim for multiple dwellings relief.

This 'deeming' provision is potentially important in the context of incorporating a buy-to-let residential property business.

For example, to the extent that chargeable consideration exceeds £250,000, the maximum SDLT rate for non-residential property is 5%. By contrast, *FA 2016* introduced higher rates of SDLT for purchases of residential properties by individuals who already own another dwelling (and who are not replacing a main residence), and by any person who is not an individual (*FA 2003, Sch 4ZA, paras (4), (7)*), such as a company acquiring residential properties upon incorporation. Following those changes, if chargeable consideration exceeds £250,000, SDLT rates increase progressively from 8% to 15%. The 15% top rate matches the SDLT rate of 15% for properties valued at more than £500,000 which are subject to the 'higher rate transaction' regime; see **13.50** below.

Similarly, in Scotland to the extent that the purchase price exceeds £350,000, the maximum LBTT rate for non-residential property is 4.5%. By contrast, an additional dwelling supplement (introduced by *LBTT(A)(S)A 2016*) of 3% to the standard LBTT rates applies to certain purchases of additional residential (eg buy-to-let) properties in Scotland, which apply in circumstances including where the buyer is a non-individual such as a company. Where the 3% additional dwelling supplement applies, if chargeable consideration exceeds £250,000, the aggregate LBTT rates vary from 8% to 15%.

Multiple dwellings relief

13.50 For single or linked transactions involving the acquisition of an interest in more than one dwelling, the purchaser(s) may generally claim

Incorporation of a buy-to-let residential property business **13.50**

for the SDLT or LBTT payable to be determined on the basis of the average consideration per dwelling multiplied by the number of dwellings acquired (*FA 2003, Sch 6B; LBTT(S)A 2013, Sch 5*). The relief is called 'multiple dwellings relief' (MDR).

In relation to SDLT it is not possible for the rate to drop below 1% if MDR is claimed. Furthermore, the MDR calculation (following changes introduced in *FA 2016*) will need to take into account the higher rates of SDLT (ie 3% above the normal SDLT rates) for a transaction that is a 'higher rates transaction', which will apply to the acquisition of residential properties by a company in most cases (see *FA 2003, Sch 4ZA, Pt 2*).

However, properties with an individual value exceeding £500,000 are excluded from an MDR claim on the basis that the single SDLT rate of 15% would apply (*FA 2003, Sch 6B, para 2(4)(aa)*), subject to certain exceptions for properties used for businesses of letting, trading in or redeveloping properties and certain other categories of property; see *FA 2003, Sch 4A, paras 5–5F*); see **13.51** and **Chapter 14**. In relation to a buy-to-let residential property business it is likely that the exception from the single 15% SDLT rate for properties used for the purposes of a property letting business would apply, such that a claim for multiple dwellings relief could be made in respect of any properties with an individual value exceeding £500,000. However, the availability of the relief from the single 15% SDLT rate should be confirmed, and not just assumed. Furthermore, relief from the single 15% SDLT rate for lettings businesses is subject to withdrawal if certain requirements are not met for at least three years from the date of the transaction (see *FA 2003, Sch 4A, para 5G*).

In relation to LBTT, if MDR is claimed, the additional dwelling supplement of 3% must be taken into account, if appropriate. However, where six or more dwellings are acquired as part of a single transaction, and a claim is made to exempt the transaction from the additional dwellings supplement (LBTT(S)A 2013, sch 2A, paras 9 and 10), the normal rates of LBTT apply in calculating the tax payable where a claim for multiple dwellings relief has been made (LBTT(S)A 2013, sch 5, para 10A). Where a claim for MDR is made it is not possible for the tax charge in relation to the acquisition of the dwellings to be less than a 'prescribed minimum amount', ie 25% of the tax which would have been payable in respect of the dwellings had MDR not been claimed (including additional dwelling supplement if appropriate) (*LBTT(S)A Sch 5, para 12*).

The MDR provisions specifically disregard the deemed non-residential property treatment outlined in **13.49** for SDLT purposes (*FA 2003, Sch 6B, para 5(6)(a)*). A purchaser can therefore effectively choose between applying the non-residential rates or making a MDR claim, if the relevant conditions are satisfied.

13.50 *Incorporation of a buy-to-let residential property business*

Example 13.5 – Deemed non-residential treatment versus multiple dwellings relief

John owns a portfolio of ten houses and flats situated in the North West of England, which are let to tenants on short-term leases. John decides to transfer his buy-to-let residential property business to a new company, J Ltd. Six properties are valued at £100,000 each, the other four at £200,000 each.

Deemed residential property treatment

As this is a transfer to a connected company, SDLT is charged on market value (assuming the actual consideration is not higher). The residential property rates would not apply because a collection of six or more dwellings are being acquired in a single transaction (ie under a single contract between the same vendor and purchaser), which is treated as the acquisition of non-residential property *(FA 2003, s 116(7))*. The aggregate value is £1.4 million, so *prima facie* SDLT will be charged as follows:

	£
£150,000 × 0%	0
£100,000 × 2%	2,000
£1,150,000 × 5%	57,500
	59,500

The SDLT liability is therefore £59,500.

Multiple dwellings relief

If J Ltd makes a claim for MDR under *FA 2003, Sch 6B*, the SDLT payable is calculated as follows:

- The average chargeable consideration given per dwelling is £1.4 million divided by the number of dwellings acquired of 10, giving an amount of £140,000 per dwelling.

- The SDLT payable on the acquisition of a single residential property for £140,000 would be £4,500 (as the 3% higher rates of SDLT would apply – see below) which, multiplied by the number of dwellings acquired of ten, would give SDLT payable of £45,000.

- The SDLT payable cannot be reduced to less than 1% of the consideration payable for the dwellings. However as that only amounts to £14,000 (£1.4 million × 1%) this limit does not apply.

- As highlighted above, the transaction is a higher rate transaction, so an additional 3% is added to the normal SDLT rates for residential property in calculating the tax payable on the average consideration per property:

		£
£125,000 × 3%		3,750
£ 15,000 × 5%		750
		4,500
The SDLT liability is £4,500 × 10 houses		£45,000

A claim for MDR will therefore result in an SDLT saving for J Ltd of £14,500.

13.51 A punitive SDLT rate of 15% is charged on the transfer of a single dwelling with a value exceeding £500,000 to a company (*FA 2003, Sch 4A*). In addition, the company may be subject to the annual tax on enveloped dwellings (ATED) if the value of the property is more than £500,000 (from 1 April 2016) (see *FA 2013, Pt 3*).

However, relief from both may be available where the dwelling is held by a property trader, developer or a rental business or for certain other trading activities. If the conditions for relief are met, no charge should arise under these provisions on incorporation of such a business. Of course, SDLT charges will still apply, as outlined above.

In Scotland, there is no such punitive LBTT rate.

Partnerships

13.52 As indicated at **13.48**, the transfer of a property from a sole proprietor (or joint owners) to a new company with which the proprietor(s) is 'connected' will give rise to an SDLT or LBTT charge based on consideration of not less than market value.

However, transfers from a partnership to a new company, where each of the partners is an individual 'connected' with that new company, will generally be free of SDLT or LBTT.

> **Focus**
>
> It is important to first establish whether a partnership exists (as opposed to the properties merely being jointly owned).
>
> For commentary on the joint ownership of properties, see **Chapter 8**.

13.53 *Incorporation of a buy-to-let residential property business*

13.53 The UK tax system has always had difficulty working out how to deal with partnerships – in particular whether to treat them as separate entities distinct from their members, or as mere aggregations of separately taxed members – and both SDLT and LBTT continue that uncertainty. The SDLT rules are largely in *FA 2003, Sch 15*. The LBTT rules, which are virtually identical to the SDLT rules, are found in *LBTT(S)A 2013, Sch 17*.

Both regimes treat the three types of UK partnership (general partnership; limited partnership formed under the *Limited Partnerships Act 1907*; and limited liability partnerships formed under the *Limited Liability Partnerships Act 2000*) and overseas entities of a similar character in the same way. Normal arm's length purchases and disposals of property by a partnership are subject to SDLT or LBTT in exactly the same manner as purchases and disposals by other entities (ie normally by reference to the amount of the actual consideration given), although it is the partners rather than the partnership that are regarded as acquiring or disposing of the property.

13.54 There is an apparent conflict between the SDLT partnership provisions and *FA 2003, s 53*, which imposes a market value charge on transfer to a connected company. HMRC have confirmed that in this situation the partnership rules (*Finance Act 2003, Sch 15, para 18*) take precedence over the market value rule in *s 53* (see SDLTM34160).

In the Stamp Duty Land Tax manual, HMRC state (at SDLTM34170):

'Where the provisions of both *Finance Act 2003, s 53* and *para 18* apply to a transfer of a chargeable interest to a company, the provisions of *para 18* will take precedence to determine the chargeable consideration.'

The HMRC guidance at SDLTM34170 features an example, which indicates that the above SDLT provisions for partnerships will generally be more favourable than the market value rule in *s 53*, such as in circumstances involving the incorporation of a partnership.

For commentary on the application of the SDLT provisions in relation to partnerships, see *Stamp Taxes 2016/17* (Bloomsbury Professional).

At the time of writing, it is not known whether Revenue Scotland take a similar view regarding the interaction of *LBTT(S)A 2013, Sch 17, paras 20, 21* (transfer of land from a partnership) and the market value rule in *LBTT(S)A 2013, s 22*. It is suggested that until this point is clarified in Revenue Scotland's technical guidance, the views of Revenue Scotland should be sought in relation to any transaction where this is an issue.

13.55 When a partnership acquires or disposes of a property from/to a partner or someone connected with a partner, special rules in *Finance Act 2003, Sch 15* (or *LBTT(S)A 2013, Sch 17*) come into play to determine the amount of tax payable.

Incorporation of a buy-to-let residential property business **13.55**

When a property – possibly forming part of the assets of a business – is transferred from a partnership to a company (or vice versa), if the company is owned by one or more of the partners or persons connected with them, actual consideration is irrelevant. The consideration for SDLT purposes on a transfer of property out of a partnership to a company (and also for LBTT purposes) is calculated using a formula, which takes account of the market value of the property and the effective change in ultimate ownership, if any, by persons who are not individuals connected with the company. Provided that all of the partners are individuals who are connected (see *CTA 2010, s 1122*) with the company, this can mean that the chargeable consideration for a transfer is zero. For the purposes of the special rules for partnerships, the connection of individuals as partners (in *CTA 2010, s 1122(7)*) is ignored (*FA 2003, Sch 15, para 39(2)*).

However, it should be noted that there is no incorporation relief as such for partnerships. The SDLT or LBTT charge (which can be nil in appropriate circumstances) arises as a result of the application of the special rules for partnerships, and the method of calculating chargeable consideration where partnership properties are transferred to a company which is connected with the partners, who are individuals.

> **Example 13.6 – Incorporation from a partnership**
>
> Len and Margaret are married. They commenced their residential property rental partnership business in April 2008, sharing partnership profits equally. Their residential property rental portfolio (located in East Anglia) is worth £3.2 million. They decided to incorporate the business and transfer the property portfolio to a new company (LM Ltd) in September 2016.
>
> In the absence of special rules, Len and Margaret would need to calculate SDLT based on the aggregate market value of the property portfolio, subject to deemed non-residential property treatment (see **13.49**) or multiple dwellings relief (see **13.50**), as appropriate.
>
> Applying the special rules in *FA 2003, Sch 15*, the chargeable consideration is calculated as follows (*para 18(2)*):
>
> MV × (100 – SLP)%
>
> Where:
>
> MV is the market value of the interest transferred; and
>
> SLP is the sum of the lower proportions
>
> *Finding SLP*
>
> The 'sum of the lower proportions' (SLP) is calculated as follows (*Sch 20*):
>
> *Step One* – Identify the relevant owner(s).
>
> LM Ltd is the relevant owner, as immediately after the transaction it will be entitled to a proportion of the chargeable interest (ie the property portfolio) and immediately before the transaction it was connected with a partner(s).

13.55 *Incorporation of a buy-to-let residential property business*

Step Two – For each relevant owner, identify the corresponding partner(s).

The corresponding partners are Len and Margaret, as they were partners immediately before the transaction, and are individuals connected with the relevant owner (ie LM Ltd).

Step Three – For each relevant owner, find the proportion of the chargeable interest to which he is entitled immediately after the transaction. Apportion that proportion between any one or more of the relevant owner's corresponding partners.

LM Ltd is entitled to 100% of the chargeable interest after the transaction. This is apportioned between its 'corresponding partners', ie Len (50%) and Margaret (50%).

Step Four – Find the lower proportion for each corresponding partner in relation to the relevant owner(s). The 'lower proportion' is:

(a) The proportion of the 'chargeable interest' attributable to the partner. If the partner is a corresponding partner in relation to only one relevant owner the relevant proportion is any proportion of the chargeable interest apportioned to him at *Step Three* in respect of that owner, ie Len (50%) and Margaret (50%); or

(b) If lower, the 'partnership share' attributable to the partner (see **13.57**). In this case, the partnership shares are the same as the chargeable interests, ie Len (50%) and Margaret (50%).

Step Five – Add together the lower proportions of each corresponding partner in relation to the relevant owner, to arrive at SLP

SLP is 100% (ie Len (50%) and Margaret (50%) as per *Step Four*).

Applying the formula

Having established SLP, the formula in *FA 2003, Sch 15, para 18(2)* can be applied to calculate the chargeable consideration for the transaction. The total market value of the residential properties is £3.2 million. The incorporation will either be a single transaction or a number of linked transactions (see **13.49**), so the aggregate market value is used:

MV × (100 – SLP)%

£3,200,000 × (100 – SLP)%

£3,200,000 × (100 – 100)%

£3,200,000 × 0% = Nil

The incorporation of the residential property rental partnership business therefore gives rise to no SDLT liability for LM Ltd.

Incorporation of a buy-to-let residential property business **13.57**

13.56 It should be noted that the formula in *FA 2003, Sch 15, para 18(2)* uses the market value of the interest transferred. Neither actual consideration (if any) nor any related debt is taken into account for the above purposes (SDLTM33310).

In practice, the calculation of chargeable consideration can be complex, taking account of proportional partnership shares, other connections between the partners and whether the persons involved are individuals or companies. This chapter only deals with incorporations by partnerships of individuals, where all of the partnership properties are freehold interests (ownership of property in Scotland) which are transferred upon incorporation.

13.57 It is important to consider relevant historic changes in partnership shares and whether SDLT (or stamp duty) was paid on the acquisition of the property from a third party. Step four in determining SLP (see **13.55**) requires rules for the purpose of determining the partnership share attributable to each partner (*FA 2003, Sch 15, paras 21, 22*).

For most SDLT purposes, partnership share is defined as the proportion in which the partner is entitled to share in income profits (*Sch 15, para 34(2)*). A more complex analysis and calculation are required to determine the partnership share of any relevant partner, when this is required for the purposes of *Sch 15, para 18*. The complexity arises broadly from an attempt to negate early SDLT mitigation involving partnership structures.

In a straightforward case, if stamp duty or SDLT (based on market value or arm's-length consideration) has been paid on all properties acquired after 19 October 2003 and, where necessary, on transfers of partnership interests, the share of any partner should simply be the proportion in which he is entitled to share in income profits.

However, the calculation of the partnership share attributable to the partner involves working through various steps, as follows (*Sch 15, paras 21(2); 22*):

(1) Check whether the relevant chargeable interest which is the subject of the transfer:

    (a) Was transferred to the partnership before 20 October 2003, or

    (b) Was transferred to the partnership on or after that date, and either the instrument of transfer has been duly stamped or any SDLT payable on the transfer has been duly paid.

If *neither* (a) nor (b) applies, the partnership share of the partner is treated as zero (*Sch 15, para 21(3)*).

(2) Assuming the partnership share is not zero under (1) above, for the purposes of finding the partner's actual partnership share on the relevant date (see (3) below), establish the 'relevant date'. This is determined as follows (*Sch 15, para 22(1)*):

    (a) If (1)(a) above applies and the partner was a partner on 19 October 2003, that is the relevant date.

13.58 *Incorporation of a buy-to-let residential property business*

- (b) If (1)(a) applies and the partner became a partner after that date, the date (s)he became a partner is the relevant date.
- (c) If (1)(b) applies and the partner was a partner when the property was transferred to the partnership, the relevant date is the effective date of that transfer.
- (d) If (1)(b) applies and the partner became a partner after the property was transferred to the partnership, the relevant date is the date he became a partner.

(3) Find the partner's actual partnership share on the relevant date.

(4) Add to the share determined under (3) any increases in the partner's share in the period starting on the day after the relevant date and ending immediately before the date on which the transfer of property out of the partnership occurs, where:

- (a) If the increase resulted from a transfer which occurred on or before 22 July 2004, the instrument of transfer has been duly stamped with ad valorem stamp duty, and
- (b) If the increase resulted from a transfer which occurred after that date, any SDLT payable in respect of the transfer has been duly paid.

(5) Deduct from the result of (4) any decreases in the partner's partnership share during the period from the day after the relevant date to the day before the date on which the transfer of property out of the partnership occurs.

It can be seen that a great deal of historic information may be needed to determine what should be a simple matter of a partner's partnership share.

Detailed consideration of the various permutations is beyond the scope of this chapter. Specialist advice will generally be the best course of action.

13.58 It might seem attractive for a sole proprietor to seek an escape from the market value rule for SDLT purposes in *FA 2003, s 53* upon incorporation by (say) introducing one or more family members as partners in the business, prior to incorporating the rental property business in the hope of achieving SDLT savings through the operation of the special rules for partnerships outlined above.

However, it may be expected that HMRC will look carefully at any attempt to exploit these provisions to avoid a market value charge. There is no official 'safe' period between the sole proprietor introducing a partner in the business and the incorporation of the business.

Although the partnership rules contain no specific anti-avoidance rules which would impact such arrangements, it is possible that either the SDLT general anti-avoidance provision (*FA 2003, s 75A–75C*) or the GAAR could be applied.

LBTT is within the ambit of the Scottish GAAR, which can be found at *RSTPA 2014, ss 62–72*.

INTEREST RELIEF

13.59 An important issue for most proprietors of buy-to-let residential property businesses is financing the business. As indicated at **13.1**, the introduction of a restriction in the deduction of finance costs to the basic rate of income tax, which is being phased in from 6 April 2017, might result in individual landlords who are higher (or additional) rate taxpayers considering the incorporation of their rental property business. This would provide an opportunity for the company to claim unrestricted relief for such costs, albeit at corporation tax rates that are generally falling.

Large share capital is not a common feature of small private companies. There is generally no great advantage in financing the company this way. Thus an investment company is likely to have a relatively small share capital.

There are two ways of introducing more funds. Either the company itself must borrow, or the proprietor must do so.

13.60 The profits of a company's property letting business are calculated in accordance with the general principles of trading income, although the trading income provisions which specifically apply to the property business are limited to those set out in *CTA 2009, s 210*.

Relief for interest paid by a company generally falls within the 'loan relationship' rules of *Corporation Tax Act 2009* (*CTA 2009*), *Pt 5*.

However, the profits of a property business are generally calculated without regard to items giving rise to debits or credits within those loan relationship provisions (see *CTA 2009, s 211*). Consequently, rental profits are calculated first, prior to interest costs being considered. Such costs are generally tax deductible under the loan relationship provisions, but do not actually form part of the company's taxable profits as such.

Interest paid by the company on its own borrowings to purchase let property may therefore be deducted in computing its corporation tax liability.

It is likely that any bank funding a loan arrangement with the company would require personal guarantees from the directors/shareholders. However, the company would not be restricted on the quantum of tax relievable loan interest in the same way as unincorporated residential property businesses from 6 April 2017.

For commentary on interest relief for companies, see **10.6**. As to company landlords generally, see **Chapter 10**.

13.61 If the director/shareholder were to incur any borrowings personally, the tax relief available is more specific and limited. In particular, *ITA 2007,*

13.62 *Incorporation of a buy-to-let residential property business*

s 392 deals with interest incurred in relation to a close company (but note that if the property rental company is not 'close' – which is probably unlikely – no relief is available at all).

A relief claim is available for interest paid on a loan applied in the purchase of ordinary share capital in the company, if certain conditions are satisfied. Equally, a relief claim may be available where the money borrowed is lent on to the company and the company uses it wholly and exclusively for the purposes of its business (or that of a close 'associated company' qualifying under *ITA 2007, s 393*). Relief is also available for interest paid on a loan applied in paying off another loan if interest on that loan would have been eligible for relief if it had continued.

The interest relief provisions (*ITA 2007, Pt 8, Ch 1*) are detailed and potentially complex, but in broad terms relief is available (under *ITA 2007, ss 383* and *392*) provided that:

- The company is a close company (see **13.62**);

- The company is not a close investment-holding company when the interest is paid (see **13.63**);

- The 'capital recovery condition' is met (ie broadly the individual has not recovered capital from the company in the period from when the loan is used to when the interest is paid (other than recovered capital treated as a loan repayment; **13.62**));

- The individual either meets a 'material interest' condition when the interest is paid (**13.62**), or he owns ordinary shares in the company when the interest is paid, and works for the greater part of his time in the actual management or conduct of it (or of an associated company) between the loan being used and the interest being paid (*ITA 2007, s 393(3)–(4)*). Note that HMRC interpret the 'actual management or conduct' requirement strictly (see SAIM10230).

The interest must not relate to an overdrawn account or on a credit card or similar arrangement, and must not exceed a normal commercial rate (*ITA 2007, s 384*). Furthermore, the loan must be used for the specified purpose, within a reasonable time, and must not previously have been applied for another purpose (*ITA 2007, s 385*).

In the case of a 'mixed loan' (ie only part of the loan is for a qualifying purpose), only the 'qualifying part' of the loan is eligible for relief (*ITA 2007, s 386*). There are also provisions aimed at preventing tax relief being given twice, under the interest relief provisions and other tax rules (*ITA 2007, s 387*).

13.62 The determination of close company status is beyond the scope of this chapter. However, a close company for these purposes includes a company which is resident in the UK (or in another EEA state, if it would be close if it were UK resident) and is controlled by five or fewer participators (eg shareholders), or by any number of participators who are directors.

Incorporation of a buy-to-let residential property business **13.63**

The 'material interest' condition has two separate requirements. The first requirement is that the individual must have a material interest in the company. A 'material interest' is defined broadly by reference to beneficial ownership or control (ie direct or indirect) of more than 5% of the company's ordinary share capital, or to the possession of (or entitlement to acquire) rights to more than 5% of the assets available for distribution to participators on a winding up. Ownership by, or entitlement of, associates are taken into account in these 5% tests (see *s 394*).

The second material interest condition requirement applies if the company exists wholly or mainly to hold investments of the property. In these circumstances, either the individual must work for the greater part of his time in the actual management or conduct of the company (or of an associated company) between the loan being used and the interest being paid, or he must not use any property held by the company as a residence *(see s 393(4))*.

Interest relief is given against total income (under *ITA 2007, s 23*; see *s 383(4)*), but is subject to an overall limit of income tax reliefs in each tax year, being the greater of £50,000 or 25 per cent of the individual's adjusted total income *(ITA 2007, s 24A)*.

The relief is given as a deduction in computing net income of the tax year in which the interest is paid. Care is obviously necessary to ensure that sufficient taxable income is available so that tax relief can be obtained. If the interest exceeds the income from which it can be deducted, relief for the excess is generally lost.

The interest relief may be restricted where capital is recovered from the company *(ITA 2007, s 406)*. A nasty trap exists should the shares be gifted; capital is considered to be recovered not only if all or part of the share capital is sold or repaid, but also if it is given away *(s 407; see SAIM10250)*.

13.63 Interest relief is not available in respect of funds borrowed to acquire shares in a close company that is a close investment-holding company (CIHC), or to lend money to such a close company *(ITA 2007, s 392(2))*.

Furthermore, as indicated at **13.61**, interest on a loan within *s 392* is not eligible for relief if the company is a CIHC when the interest is paid.

A CIHC is essentially a close company which exists mainly to hold investments. A close company is automatically treated as a CIHC unless it falls within one of various stated exceptions to CIHC status (see **13.64**).

Historically, care was needed to ensure that a company wholly or mainly in receipt of property rental income was not a CIHC, as such companies were potentially subject to corporation tax at the main rate (although this would not be the case if, for example, all the properties were let to unconnected third parties).

However, a single corporation tax rate of 20% (for financial year 2016), and the abolition of the small profits rate for companies that do not have ring fence

13.64 *Incorporation of a buy-to-let residential property business*

profits (from 1 April 2015), means that there is longer a disadvantage to a company being a CIHC in terms of corporation tax rates.

13.64 The exceptions to CIHC status apply to close companies which exist wholly or mainly, throughout the accounting period under consideration, for one or more permitted purposes, such as carrying on a trade or trades on a commercial basis, or making investments in land (including buildings) which is, or is intended to be, let commercially (see *ITA 2007, s 393A(2)*).

The effect of the above exception for making investments in land etc. for commercial letting is that property investment companies are not CIHCs provided that they exist wholly or mainly to make 'commercial lettings'.

Property is let commercially unless it is let to a 'connected person', or to certain individuals such as the spouse, civil partner or relative of a connected person (see *ITA 2007, s 393A(3)*).

OTHER ISSUES

VAT

13.65 This book concerns residential property rental businesses. The grant of an interest in (or right over, or licence to occupy) residential properties is generally exempt for VAT purposes (*VATA 1994, Sch 9, Group 1*). Thus in **Example 13.6** above, VAT was not an issue (eg in the determination of market value).

However, VAT implications of incorporating a commercial rental property business are different. The VAT and other implications of commercial property and are outside the scope of this book.

Capital allowances

13.66 A separate chapter deals with capital allowances in relation to buy-to-let residential properties (see **Chapter 4**).

As indicated in that chapter, expenditure incurred in providing plant and machinery for use in a dwelling-house is not qualifying expenditure of a person carrying on an ordinary UK or overseas property business (*CAA 2001, s 35*).

Thus capital allowances claims for plant and machinery in such buy-to-let residential property businesses, and issues arising from their incorporation, are relatively limited compared with trading entities.

However, as indicated as **4.9–4.10**, property comprising more than one dwelling (eg a block of flats) is not a 'dwelling-house' (although the individual flats within the block will be). Consequently, plant can qualify is it is in a communal area (eg a lift or central heating system serving those communal areas; see CA20020).

Incorporation of a buy-to-let residential property business **13.68**

Furthermore, it should be noted that a furnished holiday lettings business (ie in the UK or EEA) is a qualifying activity for plant and machinery allowances purposes, subject to satisfying certain strict criteria (*CAA 2001, ss 15–17B*). See **4.11–4.14** and **13.32**.

Plant and machinery otherwise used for the purposes of the property letting business, such as office furniture and computers used in the business, are eligible for capital allowances.

13.67 Writing down allowances (WDA), annual investment allowances (AIA) and first-year allowances (FYA) are not available in the final chargeable period. Thus if the business incurs qualifying expenditure and incorporates very shortly afterwards, the opportunity to claim AIA and FYA may be lost. The timing of incorporation may therefore be a relevant consideration.

The final chargeable period is (for the main pool or a 'special rate' pool) the chargeable period in which the qualifying activity is permanently discontinued (*CAA 2001, s 65(1)*). WDA in the final chargeable period is prohibited by *CAA 2001, s 55(4)*, AIA is prohibited by *CAA 2001, s 38B*, General Exclusion 1, and FYA is prohibited by *CAA 2001, s 46(2), General Exclusion 1*.

13.68 In virtually every case, the new company will be connected with the proprietors of the unincorporated property business. In most cases, the company's shareholders and directors will be identical to the sole trader or business partners. Connection follows under *CAA 2001, s 575*.

The disposal value of plant and machinery is to be interpreted in accordance with the table in *CAA 2001, s 61* ('Disposal events and disposal values'). Incorporation will involve either a sale of the plant and machinery, or a transfer for nil proceeds.

If the plant and machinery is sold, the disposal value for capital allowances purposes will generally be the net proceeds of sale (*CAA 2001, s 61(2), Table item 1*). If there are no proceeds at all, so there is a pure gift, market value prevails (*s 61(2), Table Item 7*).

This bears careful consideration because there may be important planning advantages. The result is that there will be a balancing allowance or balancing charge. A balancing allowance occurs when the disposal value is less than the written-down value of the pool (*CAA 2001, s 55(2)*) and is given as a deduction in the income tax computation in a similar fashion to a WDA, AIA or FYA. A balancing charge occurs when the disposal value is more than the written-down value of the pool (*CAA 2001, s 55(3)*) and is treated as an addition to profit.

There are anti-avoidance provisions for capital allowances purposes (*CAA 2001, Pt 2, Ch 17*), which apply to 'relevant transactions' such as the sale of plant and machinery (*CAA 2001, s 213*), including transactions between connected persons (*s 214*). The effect is that no AIA or FYA is generally available for the buyer's expenditure (*s 217*), and the buyer's qualifying expenditure is potentially restricted (*s 218*).

13.69 *Incorporation of a buy-to-let residential property business*

In addition, the buyer's capital allowances are subject to adjustment (or other tax advantages such as in the timing of allowances may be cancelled out) where the transaction has an 'avoidance purpose' (as defined in *s 215*), or relates to a scheme or arrangement with such a purpose. However, particularly in the latter case it is difficult to envisage an ordinary incorporation having a main purpose of obtaining a tax advantage in respect of plant and machinery. Capital allowances are not normally a primary consideration, particularly in residential property rental businesses.

There is also a specific anti-avoidance rule to prevent the sale of a car allocated to a 'single asset pool' (ie within *CAA 2001, s 206*) at undervalue in order to generate a balancing allowance (*CAA 2001, s 208A*).

Finally, the taxpayer should consider whether there are significant assets which have hitherto been treated as 'main pool' plant and machinery, but which in the company's hands would be regarded as 'integral features' (see **4.4**), qualifying for a lower rate of allowances in the 'special rate pool'.

13.69 The parties do not necessarily have to suffer the balancing allowance or charge. Instead the transferor and transferee (the previous sole trader and the company) may make a joint election under *CAA 2001, s 266* that the plant and machinery are transferred at a price which gives rise to neither a balancing allowance nor a balancing charge.

There is nothing in *CAA 2001, s 267* to override the rules in *CAA 2001, ss 46, 38B* and *55* that prohibit a WDA, AIA or FYA in the final chargeable period. The trade of the former sole trader *is* discontinued at the point of incorporation. So, the plant and machinery is actually transferred at the tax written-down value at the *start* of the final period of account of the sole trade.

The above election generally fixes the value of plant and machinery at its tax written-down value, notwithstanding that the plant and machinery may be sold to the company, and for a different value (eg original cost). HMRC guidance confirms: 'When an election is made any sale or transfer price is ignored' (CA29040). An election may be made within two years from the date of incorporation (*CAA 2001, s 266(4)*).

If an election is made under *CAA 2001, s 266* and any of the assets are fixtures which are not subject to the general exception for plant and machinery allowances in a dwelling (*CAA 2001, s 35*; see **13.66**), a joint election is also required under *CAA 2001, s 198* ('Election to apportion sale price on sale of qualifying interest') in order that the company is able to claim capital allowances on the fixtures. This is due to the 'fixed value requirement' (see *CAA 2001, ss 187A–187B*), which was introduced (in *Finance Act 2012*) from April 2012.

An election under *CAA 2001, s 266* prevents a balancing adjustment in respect of the unincorporated business, whereas a *CAA 2001, s 198* election allows the company to claim capital allowances on any fixtures that are transferred. In many cases, an election under *s 266* will include both fixtures and other plant

Incorporation of a buy-to-let residential property business 13.70

and machinery; hence the amount specified in the *s 198* election should not exceed the amount in the *s 266* election.

A 'pooling' requirement also applies in relation to fixtures (from April 2014), whereby the availability of capital allowances to a purchaser of fixtures is generally conditional on the pooling of relevant expenditure prior to transfer.

For guidance on this potentially difficult area, readers are referred to the latest edition of *Capital Allowances: Transactions and Planning* by Martin Wilson and Steven Bone (Bloomsbury Professional).

An election for transfers between connected persons is also available in respect of 'short life assets' (SLAs), if made within two years following the chargeable period of disposal (*CAA 2001, s 89*). The transfer of SLAs between connected persons otherwise takes place at market value (unless there is a tax charge under *ITEPA 2003*) (*CAA 2001, s 88*). The effect of a connected person election is broadly to treat the disposal as taking place at the capital allowances pool value, so that the original SLA election continues with the purchaser. If no such connected person election is made, the purchaser is still treated as having made the original SLA election with its original terminal date (see *s 89(4)*), but a balancing allowance or charge will normally arise on the disposal.

13.70

> **Focus**
>
> The absence of any capital allowances at all in the final period of account means that care should be taken in selecting the date on which to incorporate.
>
> A tidy-minded adviser may favour incorporation at the traditional accounting date and make a *CAA 2001, s 266* election 'because it's easier'. This may result in the trader getting no capital allowances in the last period when, perhaps, there are substantial profits taxed at 40%, or possibly 45% (for 2016/17). The pay-off, of course, is that the company gets a higher writing down allowance in its first period of business but as companies generally pay corporation tax at 20% (for financial year 2016, commencing 1 April 2016), this may not necessarily be the most tax-efficient option.

Remember that capital allowances are given for a period of account (not a year of assessment). Where accounts have traditionally been drawn up to 5 April, incorporation on that date will mean the loss of AIA, FYA or WDA for a full accounting period. What about incorporating at 30 April instead? The final period of account in which no capital allowances can be given is therefore approximately one month – a far more acceptable proposition.

How short might the final period actually be? In theory, perhaps as little as a day (though this might be unduly provocative to HMRC); a month is probably realistic.

13.71 *Incorporation of a buy-to-let residential property business*

13.71 The above analysis (subject to the point about a sale and election in respect of plant and machinery at **13.69** above) applies to incorporation by the *TCGA 1992, s 162* route.

There is an alternative. This is to ignore the incorporation relief in that section and go for the alternative afforded by *TCGA 1992, s 165*. This relates to a gift of business assets, though payment of some proceeds is possible. The company could actually pay the proprietor for the plant and machinery. Where there are actual proceeds, they are taken as the disposal value under *CAA 2001, s 61(2)*, Table Item 1. Market value is not substituted even where the vendor and purchaser are connected.

The sale proceeds could be left outstanding on loan account with the company. The proprietor can then draw down on the loan account at a later date, without further tax charge.

Payment of tax

13.72 The timing of tax payments on rental profits will be different following incorporation.

The profits (or losses) of unincorporated buy-to-let residential property businesses will normally be measured on a tax year basis (ie 6 April to the following 5 April). For example, where a landlord draws up his property rental business accounts to 5 April each year, his tax liability for 2016/17 (ie based on the accounts for the year ended 5 April 2017) would be payable by two payments on account on 31 January 2017 and 31 July 2017, with a balancing payment on 31 January 2018.

The taxpayer will quite probably meet the 31 January 2018 bill out of incoming funds at the end of 2017, despite the fact that he began earning the relevant profits on 6 April 2016.

13.73 By contrast, following incorporation on (say) 1 April 2016, corporation tax on profits for the year ended 31 March 2017 would normally be due and payable by 1 January 2018, ie nine months and one day after the end of the accounting period (*TMA 1970, s 59D(1)*).

However, if the business owner draws a taxable salary from the company, income tax and NIC is normally payable only 17 days after the tax month of payment if paid electronically (or 14 days in any other case (*SI 2003/2682, reg 69(1)*).

An individual shareholder in receipt of dividends from the company will generally account for income tax under the self-assessment regime.

National Insurance contributions

13.74 Class 2 NICs are flat-rate contributions (£2.80 per week for 2016/17). Liability to Class 2 NICs arises broadly if 'an earner is in employment as a

Incorporation of a buy-to-let residential property business **13.76**

self-employed earner' in the relevant tax year and has relevant profits equal or exceeding the small profits threshold for that year. The small profits threshold is set at £5,965 for 2016/17 (*SSCBA 1992, s 11*).

A self-employed earner is defined as 'a person who is gainfully employed in Great Britain otherwise than in employed earners employment (whether or not he is also employed in such employment)' (*SSCBA 1992, s 2(1)(b)*). A person who is liable to income tax on the profits of a trade, profession, or vocation will generally be a self-employed earner for Class 2 NIC purposes.

13.75 HMRC considers that a person who is liable to income tax on the profits arising from the receipt of property rental income may be a self-employed earner for NICs purposes if the level of activities carried on amounts to running a business.

HMRC's published guidance in its National Insurance manual sets out circumstances in which property letting may be considered a 'business' (and the landlord a 'self-employed earner') for Class 2 NIC purposes (NIM23800). HMRC's guidance indicates that for a property owner to be a self-employed earner, their property management activities must extend beyond those generally associated with being a landlord. For example, HMRC considers that ownership of multiple properties, actively looking to acquire further properties to let, and the letting of property being the property owner's main occupation could be pointers towards there being a business for NICs purposes.

Furthermore, HMRC considers that if a property owner has an 'agent' (which can include family and friends, as well as a professional managing agent) who manages their property for them, the agent's activities should be attributed to the owner. However, HMRC's guidance adds that a property owner will only be a self-employed earner on this basis if the things that the agent does for them (ignoring any other clients they might have) are enough to count as a business or trade.

It is perhaps fortunate that this particular issue will not be relevant for much longer, in view of the Government's stated intention to abolish Class 2 NIC from April 2018.

13.76 Liability to Class 4 NICs generally arises on profits derived from trades, professions or vocations, which are chargeable under *ITTOIA 2005, Pt 2, Ch 2* ('Income taxed as trade profits'), and which are not carried on wholly outside the UK (*SSCBA 1992, s 15(1)*).

As indicated earlier in this chapter, property rental activities are capable of amounting to a business, but do not normally constitute a trade. Buy-to-let landlords are therefore generally outside the scope of Class 4 NICs.

In the case of furnished holiday lettings, although the income is treated for certain purposes as if it was from a trade, it remains assessable as rental income, so Class 4 NICs are not payable (PIM4120).

13.77 *Incorporation of a buy-to-let residential property business*

Employment related securities

13.77 There is a requirement (in *ITEPA 2003, ss 421J* and *421K(3)(a)*) to notify HMRC when shares in a company are issued to employees (including past or future employees). The relevant return (ie HMRC's 'other' template, previously form 42) must be made to HMRC by 6 July following the relevant tax year.

HMRC guidance states that no report is required where a company is incorporated and all founder shares are acquired at nominal value (NB the other requirements are that no form of security is required; the shares are not acquired by reason of, or in connection with, another employment; and the shares are acquired by a director or prospective director of the company (or someone who has a personal family relationship with the director) and the right or opportunity is made available in the normal course of the domestic, family or personal relationship of that person).

Furthermore, no report is required if further shares are allotted after a new company is incorporated, but before the commencement of business or transfer of assets to the company (broadly, where those shares are acquired by a founder shareholder or the person is a director or prospective director of the company, and the shares are acquired at nominal value and are not acquired by reason of, or in connection with, another employment).

However, if further shares are allotted after the company has commenced business, HMRC's view is that a return is required, albeit only in respect of those additional shares (see Example 3 at ERSM140040).

HMRC's requirement that the company's shares are acquired at nominal value effectively means that incorporations under *TCGA 1992, s 162* (ie under which the assets of the unincorporated business are transferred to the company wholly or partly in exchange for shares) will require a return to be made to HMRC.

An end of year return template, technical note and guidance notes can be accessed via the Gov.uk website (http://tinyurl.com/ERS-Template).

Chapter 14

Stamp duty land tax and land and buildings transaction tax

Ken Wright BA, CA, CTA

> **SIGNPOSTS**
>
> - **Scope** – This Chapter looks at the general rules for stamp duty land tax (SDLT) and land and buildings transaction tax (LBTT) and their application to the acquisition of buy-to-let property. It only considers the acquisition of residential buy-to-let properties and does not cover commercial buy-to-let properties. SDLT is a self-assessment tax with short reporting and payment deadlines. The tax is payable by the purchaser of the property. It applies to the acquisition of a buy-to-let property which is situated in England, Wales or Northern Ireland (referred to throughout this Chapter as the rest of the United Kingdom ('RUK')). SDLT is chargeable at progressive rates (like income tax) of up to 12% (where the purchase price exceeds £1.5 million). In most cases an additional 3% rate of SDLT will be applied to each of the tax rates bringing the top rate of SDLT to 15%. LBTT is also a self-assessment tax with equally tight reporting and payment deadlines, and is also payable by the buyer of the property. It is charged on a progressive basis at rates of up to 12% (where the purchase price exceeds £0.75 million) and in most cases the 'additional dwellings supplement' will apply which adds 3% to each of the tax rates, bringing the top rate of LBTT to 15%. The purchaser of a buy-to-let property will have filing and payment obligations for SDLT or LBTT purposes in most cases, subject to possible interest and penalties for non-compliance (see **14.1–14.9**).
>
> - **Chargeable consideration** – SDLT and LBTT are generally charged on the actual consideration in money or money's worth given for the acquisition of buy-to-let property (which can include the assumption of debt). The main exception is when a buy-to-let property is transferred to a connected company. In that case, the minimum deemed consideration is the market value of the property. There are specific provisions to determine the consideration on: an exchange of properties; partitions of a property; the apportionment of consideration when a property is acquired along with other assets;

Stamp duty land tax and land and buildings transaction tax

and contingent and uncertain consideration. There are also special rules in relation to partnerships (see **14.10–14.18**).

- **SDLT on the acquisition of buy-to-let property** – The acquisition of a buy-to-let property will normally be taxed as a residential property transaction. However, in certain limited circumstances it may instead be taxed as a non-residential property transaction (residential property rates of SDLT are higher than those for non-residential property). Where more than one dwelling is acquired the liability to SDLT may be reduced if a valid claim for multiple dwellings relief is made (see **14.19–14.21**).

- **SDLT rates and the 3% surcharge** – Higher rates of SDLT potentially apply to purchases by individuals of additional residential properties such as buy-to-let properties, subject to certain exceptions. The provisions also apply to first purchases of residential properties (including buy-to-let properties) by companies and other non-individual purchasers. A 15% 'slab' rate of SDLT applies where an interest in a single dwelling is acquired by a company, by a partnership whose partners include one or more companies, or on behalf of a collective investment scheme for a consideration of more than £500,000, subject to an exception if the dwelling is acquired exclusively for the purposes of a property rental business that is run on a commercial basis with a view to profit. The consideration for 'linked transactions' is aggregated to determine the applicable rate of tax (**14.22–14.40**).

- **LBTT rates and the 3% additional dwellings supplement** – A higher rate of LBTT potentially applies to purchases by individuals of additional residential properties, including buy-to-let properties. Like its SDLT equivalent, the 'additional dwelling supplement' also applies to first purchases of residential properties by companies and other non-individual purchasers. However, there are some important differences between the two regimes (see **14.41–14.43**).

- **SDLT on leases** – There are special rules for calculating the SDLT payable on the grant of a new lease. These special rules can be complex and are beyond the scope of this book. However, the basis for calculating the SDLT liability on the grant of a new lease and the SDLT consequences of acquiring an existing lease are considered in this Chapter. The grant of a new lease over residential property situated in Scotland, and the assignment of an existing lease over residential property situated in Scotland, is generally exempt from LBTT (see **14.44–14.48**).

- **Acquisition of bare land** – An investor may decide to purchase bare land and construct a buy-to-let property on that land. The acquisition of bare land will be taxed as the purchase of non-residential property so that the lower non-residential property SDLT rates will apply. However, care is needed to prevent the higher residential property SDLT rates applying instead (see **14.49**).

- **Exemptions and reliefs** – A buy-to-let property will generally be acquired from a third party and SDLT or LBTT will be chargeable based on the actual consideration given for the property. However, for example, a gift of a buy-to-let property from, say, one individual to another individual, in circumstances where no debt is assumed, is exempt from SDLT or LBTT. Multiple dwellings relief (see **14.51**), which can reduce the SDLT or LBTT payable, may be available where more than one dwelling is being acquired either as part of a single transaction or under two or more 'linked transactions' (see **14.28**). The rates of both SDLT and LBTT are generally lower on the acquisition of non-residential property compared to those charged on the acquisition of residential property. The acquisition of buy-to-let properties will generally be an acquisition of residential properties; however, where six or more dwellings are acquired as part of a single transaction, the lower non-residential tax rates may apply (see **14.20**). In addition, the non-residential rates of SDLT will apply if a mixed use property is acquired ie a property comprising both residential and non-residential property, or the property acquired is 'linked' (see **14.28**) to the acquisition of one or more other properties which include the acquisition of non-residential property (see **14.50–14.57**).

- **SDLT and LBTT anti-avoidance** – The acquisition of most buy-to-let properties should be structured in a straightforward manner, and the SDLT or LBTT liability should be clear. However, if the acquisition structure results in a reduced charge to SDLT or LBTT the potential application of the various anti-avoidance provisions, within both the SDLT and LBTT legislation, will have to be considered. The legislation governing both taxes includes a number of targeted anti-avoidance provisions and there is a general anti-avoidance provision within the SDLT legislation (*FA 2003*, s 75A). SDLT is also included within the scope of the UK general anti-abuse rule (*FA 2013, ss 206–215*) and is within the system for the disclosure of tax avoidance schemes (*FA 2004, Pt 7*). There is no specific general anti-avoidance provision within the LBTT legislation. However LBTT is subject to the Scottish general anti-avoidance rule (*RSTPA 2014, ss 62–72*). LBTT is not within the system for the disclosure of tax avoidance schemes (see **14.58–14.60**).

- **Annual Tax on Enveloped Dwellings (ATED)** – In principle, any buy-to-let property with a value of £500,000 or more, which is owned by a company, a partnership one of whose members is a company or a collective investment scheme could be chargeable to ATED.

14.1 *Stamp duty land tax and land and buildings transaction tax*

> It applies to properties located in both the RUK and Scotland. The 2016/17 annual charge varies from £3,500 for properties worth more than £500,000 but not more than £1 million through to £218,200 for properties worth more than £20 million. However, there is an exemption from ATED where the property is used for the purposes of a property rental business run on a commercial basis with a view to profit (see **14.61**).
>
> - **Transferring a buy-to-let property out of a company** – If the exemption from ATED for property rental businesses does not apply, a decision may be taken to transfer a property out of a company to prevent a future charge to ATED. Care is needed in such circumstances to avoid creating a liability to either SDLT or LBTT (see **14.62**).
>
> - **Stamp duty and stamp duty reserve tax (SDRT)** – Stamp duty broadly applies to instruments transferring 'stock and marketable securities', which would include an instrument transferring the shares of a company carrying on a property rental business. SDRT is effectively an alternative to stamp duty, charged when no document of transfer is presented for stamping (see **14.63–14.65**).

INTRODUCTION

14.1

Rest of the UK

Ownership of a buy-to-let property located in the rest of the UK (RUK) will normally be acquired either by: (a) the acquisition of the freehold interest in the land; or (b) the acquisition of an existing leasehold interest over the land. In principle a buy-to let property could also be 'acquired' by the grant of a new lease over the land, although this is likely to be less common. Each method of acquisition is likely to give rise to SDLT payment and filing obligations.

Scotland

In Scotland it is rare for a long lease to be granted over residential property (generally in Scotland it is now not possible to grant a lease over residential property for more than 20 years (*Land Tenure Reform (Scotland) Act 1974, ss 8–9*) and the buyer of a buy-to-let-property will normally acquire ownership of the land. The acquisition of the ownership of land in Scotland is likely to give rise to LBTT payment and filing obligations.

SDLT

14.2 SDLT applies to land transactions; ie, to the acquisition of interests in RUK land and buildings (*FA 2003, s 42*). For these purposes, the acquisition of an interest in land has a wide meaning and would include the three means of acquiring a buy-to-let property identified in **14.1**. SDLT has no application to land outside the RUK. From 1 April 2015, SDLT ceased to apply to land in Scotland, subject to certain transitional provisions (see **14.5**), where it has been replaced by LBTT, administered by Revenue Scotland.

SDLT is a self-assessment tax. The purchaser (the person acquiring the buy-to-let property) is responsible for notifying liability by completing a land transaction return and paying the tax (*FA 2003, s 76*). The normal deadline for notification and payment is 30 days from the 'effective date' (see **14.3**) of the transaction, with interest and penalties chargeable if the deadline is missed. It should, however, be noted that in the Chancellor's Autumn Statement on 25 November 2015 it was announced that the Government would consult on reducing the time limit for filing an SDLT return, and paying the tax, from 30 days to 14 days. The consultation document was issued on 10 August 2016 and it proposes that the change come into effect during 2017 to 2018. The exact date of implementation has yet to be confirmed but it is likely to be between 1 January 2018 and 1 March 2018.

14.3 The 'effective date', which triggers the SDLT payment and filing obligations, is usually the earliest of legal completion, taking possession of the property and payment of substantially the whole of the consideration (see HMRC's Stamp Duty Land Tax manual at SDLTM07950 – the latter is normally taken to be an amount equal to or greater than 90% of the total consideration due under the contract). In the case of a property subject to a lease, receiving or becoming entitled to any rent triggers the 'effective date'. Correct identification of the 'effective date' usually requires close liaison between the person dealing with SDLT, the lawyers dealing with the property law aspects of the acquisition of the buy-to-let property, and the parties to the transaction.

14.4 Numerous commonplace expressions are used in the SDLT legislation, but many of these are specifically defined and prove to be wider or narrower than their everyday meaning. There is a list of defined expressions at *FA 2003, s 122*. It may be important to consult the definition before concluding that a specific person or circumstance does not fall within the scope of a particular expression.

Most SDLT legislation is in *FA 2003, Pt 4*, but this has been substantially amended by many of the subsequent *Finance Acts*. It is therefore important to consult the latest version of the legislation. Further guidance on specific points is often available in HMRC's Stamp Duty Land Tax manual, available at www.hmrc.gov.uk/manuals/sdltmanual/index.htm: references to this are in the form SDLTM01234.

14.5 *Stamp duty land tax and land and buildings transaction tax*

LBTT

14.5 LBTT applies to transactions in relation to land situated in Scotland, with effect from 1 April 2015. The legislation can be found in the *Land and Buildings Transaction Tax (Scotland) Act 2013 (LBTT(S)A 2013)*, the *Revenue Scotland and Tax Powers Act 2014 (RSTPA 2014)* and various Scottish Statutory Instruments.

The tax is collected and managed by Revenue Scotland, a new tax authority with responsibility for the taxes devolved to the Scottish Parliament. There are transitional provisions (a copy can be downloaded from the Revenue Scotland website at www.revenue.scot) covering the move from SDLT to LBTT and, for example, some transactions over land in Scotland, with an effective date on or after 1 April 2015, are still chargeable to SDLT.

14.6 LBTT is similar to SDLT in many respects and some of the legislation borrows heavily from the corresponding SDLT law. LBTT, like SDLT, is a self-assessment tax. The buyer (the person acquiring the buy-to-let property) is responsible for notifying liability by completing a land transaction return and paying the tax *(LBTT(S)A 2013, ss 29, 40)*. Unlike SDLT, however, the tax must be paid at the same time as the land transaction return is filed. The normal deadline for notification and payment is 30 days from the 'effective date' (see **14.7**) of the transaction, with interest and penalties chargeable if the deadline is missed.

14.7 The 'effective date' is usually the earliest of settlement (completion) of the transaction, taking possession of the property and payment of substantially the whole of the consideration. However under LBTT, unlike SDLT, an 'effective date' will also be triggered, in relation to a contract to be completed by a 'conveyance', where there is an assignation, sub-sale or other transaction as a result of which a person other than the original buyer becomes entitled to call for a conveyance to that person *(LBTT(S)A 2013, s 14(1)(c))*. In the case of a property subject to a lease, receiving or becoming entitled to any rent triggers the 'effective date'.

14.8 Similar to SDLT, there are a number of commonplace expressions used in the legislation, but many of these are specifically defined and prove to be wider or narrower than their everyday meaning. There is a list of defined expressions at *LBTT(S)A 2013, Sch 20* . It may be important to consult the definition before concluding that a specific person or circumstance does not fall within the scope of a particular expression.

Further guidance on specific points may be found in the LBTT legislation guidance at www.revenue.scot.

For a detailed consideration of LBTT, please refer to *Land Buildings Transaction Tax 2016/17* published by Bloomsbury Professional as part of its Scottish tax series.

14.9 Some of the key differences between LBTT and SDLT are as follows:

Stamp duty land tax and land and buildings transaction tax **14.11**

- The tax rates and bands for the acquisition of residential property are different (see **14.29** and **14.43**). The SDLT liability on the acquisition of a buy-to-let property for consideration of up to £333,000 will be greater than the equivalent LBTT liability however, above £333,000, the charge under LBTT will be greater than that under SDLT. At the higher end of the buy-to-let property market the LBTT liability will be significantly higher than the SDLT liability. Under LBTT a rate of 15% applies to consideration over £750,000 whereas under SDLT the 15% rate does not apply until the consideration exceeds £1.5 million.

- LBTT must be paid at the same time as the land transaction return is filed which is not the case for SDLT.

- Multiple dwellings relief (see **14.51**) cannot reduce the LBTT payable to less than 25% of the tax that would have been payable on the acquisition of the dwellings had the relief not been available. Under SDLT a claim for multiple dwellings relief cannot reduce the tax to less than 1% of the total consideration given for dwellings.

- Under both SDLT and LBTT, on the acquisition of a buy-to-let-property, the rate of tax charged in each tax band is generally increased by 3%, however there are significant differences between the two additional rate regimes. The additional 3% rates are considered further at **14.22** and **14.42**).

CHARGEABLE CONSIDERATION

14.10

> **Focus**
>
> Both SDLT and LBTT are generally charged on the actual consideration in money or money's worth given for the acquisition of the buy-to-let property. The main exception is when a buy-to-let property is transferred to a connected company. In that case, the minimum deemed consideration is the market value of the property.

SDLT and LBTT charged on money or money's worth given for the property

14.11 The chargeable consideration for a land transaction is defined in *FA 2003, Sch 4*. The LBTT equivalent is *LBTT(S)A 2013, Sch 2*. In most instances, it will be the consideration given in money or money's worth for the buy-to-let property. There is no general rule substituting market value for actual consideration merely because the parties are connected.

Debt as consideration

14.12 Normally, any debt secured on a buy-to-let property will be settled prior to the acquisition of the property. However, if the property is transferred in satisfaction (or in return for the release) of a debt due to the purchaser or owed by the vendor, or in return for the purchaser assuming responsibility for a debt, the amount of the debt (including any interest due but unpaid) counts as consideration. Unusually, if the amount of the debt exceeds the market value of the property, the consideration is limited to that market value (*FA 2003, Sch 4, para 8*. The LBTT equivalent is *LBTT(S)A 2013, Sch 2, para 8*).

The position may be less clear where there is a debt secured on the buy-to-let property before the transfer, which remains in place after the transfer. In principle, it could be possible for the property to be transferred without the purchaser taking on responsibility for payment of the debt, in which case the debt should not be taken into account as consideration for the transfer.

However, with a view to the prevention of avoidance, it is provided that the amount of debt secured on the property *will* be taken into account as consideration if the rights or liabilities of any party to the transaction in relation to the debt are changed in connection with the transaction (*FA 2003, Sch 4, para 8(1A)*. The LBTT equivalent is *LBTT(S)A 2013, Sch 2, para 8(2)*).

Transfers to a connected company – market value rule

14.13 The acquisition of a buy-to-let property by a company from an unconnected party is taxed in the same way as an equivalent transaction not involving a company, although the additional 3% rate of SDLT or LBTT will generally apply (see **14.22** and **14.42**). However, if the purchaser of the buy-to-let property is a company which is connected with the vendor the consideration is taken to be the greater of the actual consideration and the market value of the property (*FA 2003, s 53;* the LBTT equivalent is *LBTT(S)A 2013, s 22*).

'Connected' is defined in accordance with *Corporation Tax Act 2010* (*CTA 2010*), *s 1122*. Thus the simple transfer of a buy-to-let property from an individual to a company 'connected' with that individual will lead to an SDLT or LBTT liability for the company based on the market value of the property (assuming that the actual consideration given is not greater than market value).

It should be noted that there is no general relief available where the transfer to a connected company occurs in the course of incorporation of a property rental business by a sole trader or unincorporated partnership. Other tax reliefs are available to ease the process of incorporation but, where the property rental business has substantial property assets, the SDLT or LBTT cost may act as a significant disincentive.

There is a very specific relief on a transfer from an unincorporated partnership to a limited liability partnership (*FA 2003, s 65*). The LBTT equivalent is *LBTT(S)*

A 2013, Sch 12.). Additionally, application of the special partnership rules may reduce the SDLT or LBTT on transfers between partners, partnerships and other connected persons, including companies in some cases (see **14.54** and **Example 14.9**).

Exchange of properties

14.14 Where interests in property are exchanged, this is treated as two land transactions. Assuming at least one of the interests transferred is a 'major interest' (see below), the consideration for each acquisition is the greater of (a) the value of the buy-to-let property acquired and (b) the value of the property given in consideration together with any other consideration given (*FA 2003, s 47, Sch 4 paras 5, 6*. The LBTT equivalent is *LBTT(S)A 2013, s 13, Sch 2 para 5*).

How to determine the chargeable consideration on an exchange for SDLT purposes is covered by HMRC at SDLTM04020. A 'major interest' for SDLT purposes covers interests generally referred to as freeholds, leaseholds and other tenancies (*FA 2003, s117*). For LBTT purposes a 'major interest' refers to the ownership of land or a leasehold interest (*LBTT(S)A 2013, s 60*).

Partition of a property

14.15 Where two or more persons hold a buy-to-let property jointly, whether as joint tenants or as tenants in common (broadly 'joint owners' or 'common owners' in Scotland), they are generally treated for SDLT and LBTT purposes as owning separate and distinct (but undefined) parts of the property. A property held in this way may be partitioned, so that each person takes a specific part. If this happens, the interest which each gives up is not treated as consideration for the part of which he or she becomes sole owner.

The only consideration for SDLT purposes will be any payment or other valuable consideration which one may give to another, perhaps to compensate for differing values of the parts taken by each (*FA 2003, Sch 4, para 6*. The LBTT equivalent is *LBTT(S)A 2013, Sch 2, para 6*).

Partnerships

14.16 The acquisition of a buy-to-let property by a partnership from an unconnected party is generally taxed in the same way as an equivalent transaction not involving a partnership (i.e. by reference to the actual consideration given in money or money's worth for the property). There are, however, special rules to determine the chargeable consideration when land is transferred to or from a partnership, respectively from or to a partner or someone connected with a partner (see **14.52** *et seq*).

14.17 *Stamp duty land tax and land and buildings transaction tax*

Apportionment of chargeable consideration

14.17 When a buy-to-let property is acquired along with other assets, the overall consideration must be apportioned amongst the assets in a just and reasonable manner (*FA 2003, Sch 4, para 4* – the LBTT equivalent is *LBTT(S) A, Sch 2, para 4*).

Neither HMRC nor Revenue Scotland will normally require professional valuations to be obtained for this purpose, but they will contest apportionments which appear to be skewed to obtain a tax advantage.

Contingent and uncertain consideration

14.18 In most cases, the consideration to be given for a buy-to-let property will be certain and not subject to any contingency. However, if the consideration to be given is contingent, uncertain or unascertainable there are special rules which need to be considered (*FA 2003, s 51*; the LBTT equivalent is *LBTT(S) A 2013, ss 18–20*).

If any amount of the consideration is contingent on some future event (for example, the obtaining of planning permission), it must initially be assumed to be payable and SDLT or LBTT paid accordingly. If the contingency fails to materialise, so that the consideration does not become payable, the purchaser may submit an amended return and claim repayment of the overpaid SDLT or LBTT.

If any amount of the consideration for the buy-to let property is uncertain or unascertainable at the 'effective date' (see **14.3** and **14.7**) of the transfer, a reasonable estimate must be made, and SDLT or LBTT paid accordingly. Then, once the consideration becomes ascertained, the amount of SDLT or LBTT payable must be revisited. If the original estimate was too low, an amended return must be made and the additional SDLT or LBTT paid within 30 days of the actual figure becoming ascertainable. If the original estimate was too high, the purchaser may make an amended return and claim repayment of the excess.

However, if any part of the consideration is contingent and/or uncertain *and* any part may fall to be paid more than six months after the 'effective date' (see **14.3** or **14.7**) of the transaction, the purchaser may apply to defer payment of SDLT or LBTT on the consideration which falls to be paid later (*FA 2003, s 90;* the LBTT equivalent is *LBTT(S)A 2013, s 41*).

Such an application must be made no later than the filing deadline for the SDLT or LBTT return; that is, 30 days after the 'effective date'. HMRC or Revenue Scotland as appropriate may be expected to refuse late applications.

SDLT PAYABLE ON THE ACQUISITION OF A BUY-TO-LET PROPERTY

> **Focus**
>
> The acquisition of a buy-to-let property will normally be taxed as a residential property transaction. However, in certain limited circumstances it may be taxed as a non-residential property transaction. The residential property rates of SDLT are higher than those for non-residential property (see **14.25** and **14.47**).

14.19 The SDLT payable on the acquisition of a buy-to-let property will depend upon the amount of the chargeable consideration given and whether the transaction is a residential property transaction or a non-residential property transaction. The acquisition of one or more buy-to-let properties will normally be a residential property transaction.

'Residential property' means property used or suitable for use as a dwelling (or in the process of being built or adapted for this purpose) and includes associated gardens, grounds, outbuildings and other rights which subsist for the benefit of the property – for example, access rights across adjacent property (*FA 2003, s 116(1)*). There is no definition of the term 'dwelling' in the legislation which must therefore take its ordinary meaning, that is a building which provides those who use it with the facilities required for everyday private domestic existence.

Non-residential property is any property which is not residential property (*FA 2003, s 116(1)*).

14.20 However, there are two situations in which the acquisition of a buy-to-let property may be taxed as a non-residential property transaction:

- The purchase of six or more dwellings as part of a single transaction is treated as the acquisition of non-residential property (*FA 2003, s 116(7)*), which limits the highest SDLT rate to 5%, subject to a claim for multiple dwellings relief (see **14.49**).

    The legislation does not define what is meant by 'a single transaction' but it is the author's view that it means one contract between the same vendor and purchaser (and not including parties connected with the vendor and purchaser) for the acquisition of the agreed number of properties. The term 'a single transaction' would not cover, for example, a situation where there are multiple independent contracts between the same vendor and purchaser, since in such a situation there would be a number of transactions, although they would be 'linked' (see **14.28**) for the purposes of *FA 2003, s 108*. The treatment of the purchase of six or more dwellings as the acquisition of non-residential property can be important given the higher rates of SDLT

14.20 *Stamp duty land tax and land and buildings transaction tax*

which generally apply to the acquisition of residential property, and the additional 3% rate which may apply to the purchase of a buy-to-let property (see **14.22**). Care will therefore need to be taken to ensure that where six or more dwellings are being acquired the deal is structured as a single transaction, and not a number of separate transactions, if non-residential property treatment is to be available. In such circumstances, however, it may also be beneficial to make a claim for multiple dwellings relief, although the higher rates of SDLT will normally apply when calculating the SDLT chargeable (see **14.49**).

- If the buy-to-let property is acquired along with non-residential property as part of the same transaction, or the acquisition of the buy-to-let property is 'linked' (see **14.28**) to one or more other transactions which include the acquisition of non-residential property *(FA 2003, s 55(2)(b) (3), (4))*.

Thus the tax rates for residential property will only be applicable if the transaction(s) under which the buy-to-let property is acquired consist(s) *entirely* of residential property.

Example 14.1 – Acquisition of six or more dwellings as part of a single transaction

Pamela enters into an agreement to acquire a block of eight flats situated in England and Wales, which are let to tenants on short-term leases. The purchase price of the property is £1,880,000. As six or more dwellings are being acquired as part of a single transaction, the transaction is treated as the acquisition of non-residential property *(FA 2003, s 116(7))*.

The SDLT chargeable on the transaction, if no claim for multiple dwellings relief (see **14.49**) is made, is calculated as follows:

Purchase Price (£)	Rate(%)	SDLT (£)
150,000	0	Nil
100,000	2	2,000
1,630,000	5	81,500
1,880,000		83,500

If Pamela makes a claim for multiple dwellings relief *(FA 2003, Sch 6B –* see **14.49**) the SDLT payable will be calculated as follows:

- The average chargeable consideration given per dwelling is £1.88 million divided by the number of dwellings acquired of eight, giving an amount of £235,000 per dwelling;

- The SDLT payable on the acquisition of a single residential property for £235,000 would be £9,250 (£125,000 at 3%, plus £110,000 at

5%) which, multiplied by the number of dwellings acquired of eight, would give SDLT payable of £74,000;

- The SDLT payable cannot be reduced to less than 1% of the consideration payable for the dwellings; however, as this is only £18,800 (£1.88 million × 1%), the SDLT chargeable is £74,000. By making the claim for multiple dwellings relief Pamela has reduced her SDLT liability from £83,500 to £74,000, a reduction of £9,500.

Had the block of flats been located in Scotland, if no claim for multiple dwellings relief (see 14.49) was made, but a claim was made under *LBTT(S)A 2013, Sch 2A, para 9* to exempt the transaction from the 3% additional dwellings supplement (see 14.42), the LBTT payable would have been calculated using non-residential property rates (*LBTT(S)A 2013, s 59(8)*) as follows:

Purchase Price (£)	Rate (%)	SDLT (£)
150,000	0	Nil
200,000	3	6,000
1,530,000	4.5	68,850
1,880,000		74,850

If Pamela makes a claim for multiple dwellings relief (LBTT(S)A 2013, *Sch 5* – see **14.49**) the LBTT payable should be calculated as follows:

- The average chargeable consideration given per dwelling is £1.88 million divided by the number of dwellings acquired of eight, giving an amount of £235,000 per dwelling.

- The LBTT payable on the acquisition of a single residential property for £235,000 would be £1,800 (£145,000 at 0% plus £90,000 at 2%) which, multiplied by the number of dwellings acquired of eight, would give LBTT payable of £14,400 (Note: The 3% additional dwelling supplement does not apply when calculating the LBTT chargeable on the average consideration per dwelling as account is to be taken of the claim made under *LBTT(S)A 2013, Sch 2A, para 9* to exempt the transaction from the additional dwellings supplement – see *Land and Buildings Transaction Tax (Amendment) (Scotland) Act 2016, s 2(1)(d)*).

- However, the LBTT payable cannot be reduced to less than 25% of the tax which would have been payable on the consideration given for the dwellings had no claim for multiple dwellings relief been made. As calculated above, the LBTT chargeable for the acquisition of the eight dwellings would have been £74,850 if no claim for multiple dwellings relief had been made, and therefore the LBTT liability cannot be less than £18,712 (£74,850 × 25%). Consequently, the LBTT chargeable is £18,712.

14.21 *Stamp duty land tax and land and buildings transaction tax*

By making the claim for multiple dwellings relief, Pamela has reduced her LBTT liability from £74,850 to £18,712, a reduction of £56,138.

Example 14.2 – Acquisition of mixed-use property

On 14 August 2016, George exchanges contracts for the purchase of a property situated in Wales which comprises a shop on the ground floor with two flats above. George already owns a property which he uses as his main residence and he intends to let out all three properties to third parties. The purchase price of the property is £350,000. The purchase of the property completes on 30 November 2016 without any prior event having taken place which would have 'substantially performed' (see **14.23**) the contract prior to that date.

The property acquired is mixed-use, ie it comprises both residential and non-residential property and, as a consequence, the non-residential property SDLT rates apply and the additional 3% rate (see **14.29** et seq) does not apply (*FA 2003, s 55(2)(b), (3), (4)*).

The SDLT chargeable on the purchase of the property is calculated as follows:

Purchase Price (£)	Rate (0%)	SDLT (£)
150,000	0	Nil
100,000	2	2,000
100,000	5	5,000
350,000		7,000

George must therefore file a land transaction return, and pay the SDLT due of £7,000 by 30 December 2016.

14.21 The SDLT payable in relation to a residential property transaction is calculated using a 'progressive system' (ie like personal income tax). This means that it is only that part of the chargeable consideration falling within each tax band that is taxed at the rate for that tax band.

The current SDLT rates and tax bands are shown at **14.25** (*FA 2003, s 55*).

Focus

With effect from 1 April 2016, a 3% surcharge is added to each of the SDLT rates, including the 0% rate, when an additional residential property is acquired including a buy-to-let property.

There are, however, certain circumstances in which the 3% surcharge will not apply (see **14.29 et seq**)

ADDITIONAL 3% RATE OF SDLT APPLIES TO THE ACQUISITION OF BUY-TO-LET PROPERTIES

14.22 At the autumn Statement on 25 November 2015, the Chancellor of the Exchequer announced that from 1 April 2016 higher rates of SDLT would apply to purchases of additional residential properties such as buy-to-let properties. In fact, the legislation is much wider than the original policy description and, for example, applies to first purchases of residential properties (including buy-to-let properties) by companies and certain trusts.

The legislation can be found in the new *FA 2003, Sch 4ZA* ('Stamp Duty Land Tax: Higher Rates for Additional Dwellings and Dwellings Purchased by Companies'), and it imposes an additional 3% SDLT charge on chargeable transactions falling within its provisions.

A transaction which falls within the legislation is referred to as a 'higher rates transaction' *(FA 2003, Sch 4ZA, para 2(1))*.

14.23 For the purposes of the higher rates legislation a dwelling is defined *(FA 2003, Sch 4ZA, para 17(2))* as a building or part of a building that is:

- used or suitable for use as a single dwelling; or
- in the process of being constructed or adapted for use as a single dwelling.

Land that is to be enjoyed with a dwelling such as a garden or grounds of the dwelling, including any building or structure on that land (for example a detached garage), and any land which subsists for the benefit of a dwelling, is treated as being part of the dwelling *(FA 2003, Sch 4ZA, para 17(3) and (4))*.

There is no definition of the term 'dwelling' in the legislation, which must therefore take its ordinary meaning, that is a building which provides those who use it with the facilities required for everyday private domestic existence. The term will cover holiday homes, including those which cannot be used all year round, and furnished lettings.

An 'off-plan purchase' will also count as the acquisition of a 'dwelling' if the following conditions are satisfied *(FA 2003, Sch 4ZA, para 17(5))*:

- a contract has been exchanged for the acquisition of a building which is to be constructed or adapted for use as a single dwelling;
- the contract is 'substantially performed' (broadly a contract to acquire a property will be 'substantially performed' if the purchaser takes possession of the property or pays 90% or more of the purchase consideration); and
- at the time of 'substantial performance' the construction or adaptation of the building has not yet started.

14.24 It will be a question of fact as to whether a single dwelling, or more than one dwelling, is being acquired. Generally, a self-contained building is likely to be a single dwelling if any-one living in that building can live independently of the residents of the rest of the building. This is likely to include having independent access to the building as well as cooking, toilet and washing facilities.

14.25 *Stamp duty land tax and land and buildings transaction tax*

This means that, for example, the acquisition of a main dwelling with an annex attached, or a so called 'granny flat' in the same grounds, is likely to be the acquisition of two dwellings.

SDLT Rates (excluding 3% surcharge)

14.25 If the additional 3% surcharge (see **14.29**) does not apply the rates of SDLT are as follows (*FA 2003, s 55*):

Consideration (£)	Current rates
Residential property – Progressive basis	
So much as does not exceed £125,000	nil
So much as exceeds £125,000 but does not exceed £250,000	2%
So much as exceeds £250,000 but does not exceed £925,000	5%
So much as exceeds £925,000 but does not exceed £1,500,000	10%
Above 1,500,000	12%

Enveloped residential properties – 15% slab rate of SDLT may apply

14.26 A 15% 'slab' rate of SDLT applies where an interest in a single dwelling is acquired by a company, by a partnership whose partners include one or more companies, or on behalf of a collective investment scheme for a consideration of more than £500,000 (*FA 2003, Sch 4A*).

It is not possible to take advantage of the relief for transfers of multiple dwellings to reduce the rate charged (see **14.49**). Anti-avoidance provisions do seek to prevent avoidance of the higher rate by fragmenting the purchase (*s 55A* and *Sch 4A*, inserted into *FA 2003* by *FA 2012, Sch 34*).

FA 2003, s 116(7) – reclassification of residential property as non-residential where six or more properties are transferred in a single transaction – has no application in determining whether the 15% rate applies to a transaction. This is because the 15% rate applies to the acquisition of an interest in a single dwelling for a chargeable consideration of more than £500,000, and it is irrelevant whether the acquisition of that single dwelling is part of a single transaction under which five or more other separate dwellings are acquired, such that *s 116(7)* would reclassify the transaction as an acquisition of non-residential property.

The stated purpose of this provision is to discourage the 'enveloping' of high value residential properties within corporate shells, a practice which allows future transfers free of SDLT. As such, it may be regarded as an anti-avoidance provision.

14.27 However, the 15% SDLT rate does not apply to the purchase of a dwelling for more than £500,000 by a company etc if the dwelling is acquired exclusively for the purposes of a property rental business that is run on a commercial basis with a view to profit *(FA 2003, Sch 4A, para 5(1)(a))*. See **14.65** for a list of indicators which HMRC consider may suggest that a property rental business is not being carried on on a commercial basis. It should be noted, however, that this exemption is not available if it is intended that the property be occupied by a 'non-qualifying individual', which would include the purchaser or an individual 'connected' with the purchaser.

This exemption from the single 15% rate of SDLT should apply to the purchase of a buy-to-let property by a company etc which intends to let the property out, on a commercial basis, to third parties. In any cases of doubt, specialist advice should be taken.

The relief from the 15% SDLT rate can be withdrawn if at any time in the period of three years from the 'effective date' (see **14.3**) of the acquisition of the buy-to-let property it ceases to be used exclusively for the purposes of the property rental business, or a 'non-qualifying individual' is permitted to occupy the dwelling *(FA 2003, Sch 4A, para 5G)*.

Linked transactions

14.28 If several transactions are 'linked' for the purposes of *FA 2003, s 108*, the consideration must be aggregated to determine the rates of tax applicable to the transaction. Transactions are 'linked' if they form part of a single scheme, arrangement or series of transactions between the same vendor and purchaser or, in either case, persons connected with them. Connected persons are as defined in *CTA 2010, s 1122*.

Whether transactions are linked is a question of fact, but transactions between the same vendor and purchaser which occur at similar times are likely to be presumed to be linked unless there is evidence to the contrary. In *Attorney General v Cohen* [1936] 2 KB 246, [1936] 1 All ER 583, several purchases of properties by the same purchaser from the same vendor at auction were held not to be part of a series of transactions, because each property was the subject of a separate bidding process.

In the case of linked acquisitions of residential properties, the amount of the SDLT liability may then be reduced if multiple dwellings relief is claimed (see **14.49**).

Higher rates of SDLT (including 3% surcharge)

14.29 The higher rates of SDLT (ie including the 3% surcharge) are as follows:

14.30 *Stamp duty land tax and land and buildings transaction tax*

Consideration (£)	Rate of SDLT on additional dwellings ('effective date' on or after 1 April 2016)
Not exceeding £125,000	3%
£125,001 to £250,000	5%
£250,001 to £925,000	8%
£925,001 to £1,500,000	13%
Exceeding £1,500,000	15%

As highlighted at **14.22,** with effect from 1 April 2016, the higher rates of SDLT detailed in the table above apply to the acquisition of additional residential properties including buy-to-let properties.

Generally, unless the purchaser is an individual who does not hold a 'major interest' in another dwelling, with a value of £40,000 or more, at the end of the day on which the buy-to-let property is acquired (see **14.31** to **14.37** for details of the person who is treated as holding a 'major interest' in a property), the higher rates are likely to apply to the purchase of a buy-to-let property. For these purposes a 'major interest' is a freehold or leasehold interest but excludes the acquisition of a lease originally granted for a term not exceeding seven years (*FA 2003, Sch4ZA, para 2(4)*). There are, however, certain circumstances in which the higher rates will not apply and these are considered below.

14.30 The SDLT higher rates will not apply to the acquisition of a buy-to-let property in the following circumstances:

- the consideration given for the buy-to-let property (dwelling) is less than £40,000;
- the purchaser is an individual who, at the end of the day on which the buy-to-let property is acquired, does not hold all or part of a 'major interest' (see **14.29**) in another dwelling which has a market value of £40,000 or more or, if he does hold a 'major interest' in such a dwelling, the interest held is subject to a lease which has more than 21 years to run at the date of the transaction. See **14.31** to **14.37** for the circumstances in which an individual is treated as owning a 'major interest' in another dwelling;
- the buy-to-let property being acquired is subject to a lease which has more than 21 years to run at the date of the transaction. This would be unusual as most buy-to-let properties are acquired unencumbered by any lease and are generally let for a much shorter period than 21 years;
- the buy-to-let property comprises mixed use property. For example, a shop with a flat above it or a farmhouse with agricultural land attached will both constitute mixed use property in which case the non-residential property SDLT rates should apply;
- six or more dwellings are being acquired as part of a single transaction in which case the non-residential property SDLT rates should apply (see **14.20**) subject to a claim being made for multiple dwellings relief (see **14.49**);

- the acquisition of a single dwelling by a company (or other non-natural person) for more than £500,000 if the single rate of SDLT of 15% applies to that transaction by virtue of *FA 2003, Sch 4A* and no relief applies (see **14.26** *et seq*);
- the acquisition of a caravan, houseboat or mobile home. This is on the basis that these items are generally moveable and not normally subject to SDLT;
- the buy-to let property is acquired under a contract entered into and 'substantially performed' (broadly a contract to acquire a property will be 'substantially performed' if the purchaser takes possession of substantially whole of the property or pays 90% or more of the purchase consideration) before 26 November 2015;
- the buy-to-let property is acquired pursuant to a contract entered into before 26 November 2015 and there has been: (a) no variation or assignment of rights under the contract on or after that date; (b) the transaction is not effected by the exercise on or after 26 November 2015 of any option, right of pre-emption or similar right; and (c) on or after 26 November 2015, there has been no assignment, sub-sale or other transaction relating to the whole or part of the land acquired under the contract as a result of which a person other than the original purchaser becomes entitled to call for a conveyance.

The higher rates of SDLT do not apply to the acquisition of a dwelling by an individual if that individual is replacing his or her only or main residence (*FA 2003, Sch 4ZA, paras 3 and 6*). However, that exemption is not considered in this chapter which covers the acquisition of buy-to-let property and not the acquisition of an individual's main residence. It is, however, possible that an individual may, either as part of a single transaction or a number of linked transactions (see **14.28**), acquire a dwelling which is replacing his or her main residence along with one or more buy-to-let properties. This scenario is considered below.

If, as part of a single transaction (ie a single contract between the same purchaser and vendor), an individual acquires two or more dwellings with at least two of the dwellings: (a) costing £40,000 or more; (b) not being subject to a lease with more than 21 years to run; and (c) not being 'subsidiary' (see **14.38**) to another of the purchased dwellings, then even though one of the dwellings may be replacing the individual's main residence, the higher rates of SDLT will apply to the entire transaction, including the acquisition of the dwelling which is the replacement main residence (*FA 2003, Sch 4ZA, para 5* – see **14.38**).

If instead, the transaction is structured so that the individual acquires the dwelling which is the replacement only or main residence under a separate transaction (ie under a separate agreement between the same purchaser and vendor), which would nevertheless be linked (see **14.28**) with the transaction under which the other dwelling or dwellings are acquired (which may be buy-to-let properties), then the higher rates of SDLT should not apply to the acquisition of the dwelling which is the replacement main residence, but will apply to the acquisition of the other dwelling or dwellings.

14.30 *Stamp duty land tax and land and buildings transaction tax*

Example 14.3 – Acquisition of two dwellings, under separate contracts, one of which is replacing an individual's main residence and the other is a buy-to-let property

On 11 March 2017, under separate contracts, Campbell agrees to acquire the freehold interest in two houses from a developer, one of which he intends to use as his main residence and the other he will let out to third parties. On 14 August 2017, Campbell sells his previous main residence and completes the contract for the purchase of his new main residence for a consideration of £450,000. On 24 November 2017 Campbell completes the purchase of the buy-to-let property for a consideration of £550,000.

Campbell must file a land transaction return, and pay the SDLT, on the acquisition of his new main residence by 13 September 2017. As Campbell is replacing his main residence, the normal SDLT rates apply and the liability is calculated as follows:

Purchase Price (£)	Rate (%)	SDLT (£)
125,000	0	Nil
125,000	2	2,500
200,000	5	10,000
450,000		12,500

Following completion of the acquisition of the buy-to-let property on 24 November 2017, Campbell must file a land transaction in relation to that transaction, by 24 December 2017, and pay SDLT at the higher rates as the following conditions are satisfied (*FA 2003, Sch 4ZA, para 3(1)*):

- The purchaser is an individual;

- The main subject matter of the transaction consists of a 'major interest' in a single dwelling (ie the freehold interest in the buy-to-let property);

- The chargeable consideration given for the buy-to-let property is £40,000 or more;

- The buy-to-let property is being acquired to let and therefore Campbell is not replacing his main residence;

- The land interest being acquired is not subject to a lease with an unexpired term of more than 21 years.

Campbell holds a 'major interest' (see **14.29**) in another dwelling at the end of the day which is the 'effective date' (see **14.3**) of the transaction under which the buy-to-let property is acquired and that interest has a market value of £40,000 or more and is not reversionary on a lease which has an unexpired term of more than 21 years.

Stamp duty land tax and land and buildings transaction tax 14.30

As the purchase of the main residence and the buy-to-let property are 'linked transactions' (see **14.28**), the SDLT liability on the buy-to-let property is calculated as follows:

Aggregate Purchase Price (£)	Rate (%)	SDLT (£)
125,000	3	3,750
125,000	5	6,250
675,000	8	54,000
75,000	13	9,750
1,000,000		73,750

The SDLT payable in relation to the buy-to-let property would therefore be £40,562 (£550,000/£1,000,000 × £73,750).

The revised calculation of the SDLT liability in relation to the new main residence, using the normal rates of SDLT, would be as follows:

Aggregate Purchase Price (£)	Rate (%)	SDLT (£)
125,000	0	Nil
125,000	2	2,500
675,000	5	33,750
75,000	10	7,500
1,000,000		43,750

The amended SDLT liability in relation to the acquisition of the new main residence would therefore be £19,687 (£450,000/£1,000,000 × £43,750). The total SDLT payable would therefore be £60,249 (£40,562 + £19,687).

However, if Campbell makes a claim for multiple dwellings relief it *is understood* that the SDLT liability should be calculated as set out below.

The average consideration per house would be £500,000 and the SDLT payable at the higher rates would be as follows:

Purchase Price (£)	Rate (%)	SDLT (£)
125,000	3	3,750
125,000	5	6,250
250,000	8	20,000
500,000		30,000

The total SDLT payable would therefore be £60,000 (£30,000 × 2 houses) and the amount payable on the buy-to-let property would be £33,000 (£550,000/£1,000,000 × £60,000).

14.31 *Stamp duty land tax and land and buildings transaction tax*

The SDLT payable at the normal rates based on an average consideration per house *of £500,000* would be as follows:

Purchase Price (£)	Rate (%)	SDLT (£)
125,000	0	Nil
125,000	2	2,500
250,000	5	12,500
500,000		15,000

The total SDLT payable would therefore be £30,000 (£15,000 × 2 houses) and the amount payable on the replacement main residence would be £13,500 (£450,000/£1,000,000 × £30,000).

The total SDLT payable if a multiple dwellings relief claim is made would therefore be £46,500 (£33,000 + 13,500), which compares to a liability of £60,249 if no claim for multiple dwellings relief is made. It is therefore beneficial for Campbell to make a multiple dwellings relief claim.

Campbell must also file an amended land transaction return by 24 December 2017, in relation to the purchase of his new main residence and pay the additional SDLT due of £1,000 (£13,500 – £12,500).

He must also file a land transaction return by 24 December 2017 in relation to the purchase of the buy-to-let property, and pay the SDLT due of £33,000.

The above is the author's understanding of how the calculation should be carried out in relation to linked transactions; however, until the matter is clarified by HMRC, it is suggested that confirmation of the calculation methodology be obtained from HMRC.

Individuals – Interests in dwellings treated as owned by an individual for the purposes of the SDLT higher rates

14.31 If an individual is the legal and beneficial owner of a 'major interest' (see **14.29**) in a dwelling they will own that interest for the purposes of the higher rates legislation. Equally, where an individual only has the beneficial ownership of a 'major interest' in a dwelling, with legal ownership held within a bare trust or by a nominee, the individual with the beneficial ownership is treated as owning the interest in the dwelling (*FA 2003, Sch 16, para 3* and *Sch 4ZA, para 11(2)* and *(3)*).

Joint purchasers

14.32 In circumstances where there are two or more individuals acquiring the dwelling as joint purchasers (either as 'joint tenants' or as 'tenants in common') the transaction will be charged at the higher rates if any of the purchasers holds a 'major interest' in another dwelling at the end of the day on which the buy-to-let property is acquired. It does not matter how small the interest of any purchaser is in the dwelling (*FA 2003, Sch 4ZA, para 2(3)*).

Spouse or civil partner

14.33 If the individual, who is purchasing the buy-to-let property, has a spouse or civil partner who they are living with on the 'effective date' (see **14.3**) of the transaction, and who is not a joint purchaser, the spouse or civil partner will be treated as though they were a joint purchaser in respect of the transaction.

Consequently, if the spouse or civil partner holds a 'major interest' in another dwelling worth £40,000 or more at the end of the day on which the buy-to-let property is acquired, the higher rates of SDLT will apply (*FA 2003, Sch 4ZA, para 9(1) and (2)*).

This treatment does not apply if the married couple are either legally separated (by court order or deed of separation) or they are in fact separated in circumstances in which the separation is likely to be permanent (*FA 2003, Sch 4ZA, para 9(3) and ITA 2007, s 1011*).

Dwellings held by trusts

14.34 Where a 'major interest' (see **14.29**) in a dwelling is held in a 'settlement' (ie a trust which is not a bare trust: *FA 2003, Sch 16, para 1(1)*), and under the terms of the trust the beneficiary is entitled to (a) occupy the dwelling for life, or (b) the income earned in respect of the dwelling, the beneficiary of the trust is treated as holding the interest in the dwelling for the purposes of the higher rates legislation (*FA 2003, Sch 4ZA, para 11(1) and (3)(a)*).

If the 'major interest' (see **14.29**) in the dwelling is held by the trustees of a trust and the beneficiaries are not entitled as described in the paragraph above, and it is not a bare trust (*FA 2003, Sch 16, para 1(1)*), then the trustees are treated as holding the dwelling for the purposes of the higher rates legislation.

Dwellings held by a partnership

14.35 The general rule is that in deciding, for the purposes of the higher rates legislation, whether an individual purchaser, who is a partner in a partnership, holds a 'major interest' in another dwelling, that individual will be treated as owning any 'major interest' held by or behalf of the partnership (*FA 2003, Sch 4ZA, para 14(3) and Sch 15, para 2(1)(a)*).

14.36 *Stamp duty land tax and land and buildings transaction tax*

However, a 'major interest' in a dwelling held by a partnership can be ignored for the purposes of the higher rates legislation if the individual purchaser is not acquiring the new 'major interest' for the purposes of the partnership, the partnership is carrying on a trade and the existing dwelling is being used for the purposes of the partnership's trade *(FA 2003, Sch 4ZA, para 14(1) and (2))*.

A property letting business carried on by a partnership is not a trade, and therefore, for the purposes of the higher rates legislation, an individual who is a partner in a partnership carrying on such a business, will be treated as holding all of the 'major interests' in dwellings held by the partnership.

Dwellings situated outside of England, Wales and Northern Ireland

14.36 In determining whether an individual purchaser holds a 'major interest' in another dwelling for the purposes of the higher rates legislation, an interest in a dwelling situated outside of England, Wales and Northern Ireland is to be taken into account *(FA 2003, Sch 4ZA, para16(1))*.

Other countries may have different land law concepts and it will be a question of fact whether an interest owned by an individual is equivalent to a 'major interest' (ie a freehold interest or a lease granted for a term of more than seven years – see **14.29**), whether any leasehold interest was originally granted for a term of more than seven years and whether the interest acquired is subject to a lease with more than 21 years to run *(FA 2003, Sch 4ZA, para 16(2)(a))*.

Dwellings acquired by inheritance

14.37 Where an individual becomes entitled to a 'major interest' (see **14.29**) in a dwelling in the three-year period before the 'effective date' (see **14.3**) of the acquisition of the buy-to-let property that interest can be ignored, in determining whether the acquisition of the buy-to-let property is subject to the SDLT higher rates (ie whether the purchaser held a 'major interest' (see **14.29**) at the end of the day on which the buy-to-let property was acquired), provided the following conditions are satisfied *(FA 2003, Sch 4ZA, para 15(1) and (2))*:

- the individual became the joint owner of the interest in the dwelling by inheritance; and
- the individual and any spouse or civil partner's combined interest in the dwelling has not exceeded 50% in the three-year period before the 'effective date' (see **14.3**) of the acquisition of the buy-to-let property.

However, if the interest in the dwelling was inherited more than three years before the acquisition of the buy-to-let property the individual will be treated as holding an interest in that inherited dwelling at the end of the day which is the 'effective date' (see **14.3**) of the acquisition of the buy-to-let property.

The date of inheritance is the date the individual becomes entitled to the 'major interest' (see **14.29**) which will normally be the date it is transferred to them.

In countries where property passes directly to heirs the date of inheritance will be the date of death.

Individual acquiring more than one dwelling as part of a single transaction

14.38 Where an individual acquires two or more dwellings under a *single transaction*, the SDLT higher rates legislation does not allow there to be a combination of higher rate and 'normal residential rate' transactions, and the transaction will either be a 'higher rates transaction' or it will not.

Thus, if two or more dwellings are purchased in the same transaction, and the consideration given for at least two of the dwellings is £40,000 or more, at least two of the dwellings are not subject to a lease with at least 21 years to run, and at least two of the purchased dwellings are not 'subsidiary' (see below) to another of the purchased dwellings, the transaction will be a 'higher rates transaction', and the higher rates will apply to all of the dwellings acquired under the transaction. This is irrespective of whether (a) the individual owns an interest in another dwelling at the end of the day on which the acquisition is made, or (b) one of the purchased dwellings replaces the individual's only or main residence (*FA 2003, Sch 4ZA, para 5* – see **14.30**).

The legislation does not define what is meant by 'a single transaction', but it is the author's view that it means one contract between the same vendor and purchaser (and not including parties connected with the vendor and purchaser) for the acquisition of the agreed number of properties. Thus if two or more dwellings are to be acquired from the same vendor, and those dwellings satisfy the conditions above, and one of the dwellings to be acquired is replacing, or may become a replacement for, the individual's only or main residence (see **14.30**), that dwelling which is to be the main residence should be acquired under a separate contract, which is legally independent from any of the other contracts, such that the higher rate should not apply to its acquisition, or that in due course, on a disposal of the previous main residence, a subsequent claim can be made that the higher rates do not apply (*FA 2003, Sch 4ZA, paras 3(6), 3(7) and 8*). See **Example 14.3**, in which two dwellings are acquired by an individual, under separate contracts, in circumstances where one of the dwellings is replacing the individual's main residence and the other is a buy-to-let property.

Where an individual is acquiring, as part of a single transaction, two dwellings one of which is a 'subsidiary' (within the meaning of *FA 2003, Sch 4ZA, para 5(5)*) to the other, the transaction will only be chargeable to the higher rates of SDLT if the individual holds a 'major interest' (see **14.29**) in another dwelling at the end of the day which is the 'effective date' (see **14.3**) of the acquisition of the main dwelling and the individual is not replacing his or her main residence. This is the so called 'granny flat' exemption. One dwelling is 'subsidiary' to another dwelling (ie the main dwelling) if it is within the grounds of, or within the same building as, the main dwelling, and the consideration apportioned on a just and reasonable basis to the 'subsidiary

14.39 *Stamp duty land tax and land and buildings transaction tax*

dwelling' is less than one third of the aggregate consideration given for both dwellings (*FA 2003, Sch 4ZA, para 5(5)*).

Buy-to-let property acquired by a company

14.39 The higher rates of SDLT will apply to any acquisition of a 'major interest' (see **14.29**) in a buy-to-let property (a dwelling) by a company if the purchase consideration is £40,000 or more, unless the property acquired is subject to a lease with more than 21 years to run (*FA 2003, Sch 4ZA, para 4*).

Buy-to-let property acquired by a partnership

14.40 A partner in a partnership is treated as a joint purchaser of any buy-to-let property acquired by or on behalf of the partnership (*FA 2003, Sch 15, para 2(b)*). This means that when a 'major interest' (see **14.29**) in a buy-to-let property costing £40,000 or more is acquired by or on behalf of a partnership, and the property is not subject to a lease with more than 21 years to run, the higher rates of SDLT will apply if any of the partners (who are individuals) holds a 'major interest' in a property at the 'effective date' (see **14.3**) of the acquisition of the buy-to-let property.

> **Example 14.4 – Calculation of SDLT chargeable on the acquisition of a buy-to-let property to which 3% higher rate applies**
>
> On 28 April 2016, John (who does not have a spouse or civil partner) exchanges contracts for the purchase of a buy-to-let residential property situated in England for a cash consideration of £550,000.
>
> John already owns a property which he uses as his main residence, and therefore the 3% additional rate charge (see **14.22 et seq**) applies to the transaction. Equally, as John acquires the property in his own right, and not through a company, a partnership with a corporate partner or a collective investment scheme, the single 15% rate of SDLT does not apply (see **14.26**).
>
> The purchase of the property completes on 30 June 2016, without any prior event having taken place which would have 'substantially performed' (see **14.23**) the contract prior to that date.
>
> The SDLT chargeable on the purchase of the property is calculated as follows:
>
> | Purchase Price (£) | Rate (%) | SDLT (£) |
> | --- | --- | --- |
> | 125,000 | 3 | 3,750 |
> | 125,000 | 5 | 6,250 |
> | 300,000 | 8 | 24,000 |
> | 550,000 | | 34,000 |
>
> John must therefore file a land transaction return, and pay the SDLT due of £34,000 by 30 July 2016.

Example 14.5 – Transactions to which the additional 3% SDLT rate does not apply

- Mark owns a buy-to-let property with his three brothers. The property is worth £156,000, with Mark's share being worth £39,000. Mark currently lives in a rented flat and does not own any other property. Mark decides to purchase a buy-to-let property in his own name, paying £200,000 for the property.

    The additional 3% rate will not apply to Mark's purchase of the property since, at the end of the day which is the 'effective date' (see **14.3**) of the purchase of the new buy-to-let property, Mark does not own all or part of a 'major interest' (see **14.29**) in another dwelling which has a value of £40,000 or more *(FA 2003, Sch 4ZA, para 3(4))*.

- Caroline owns a 25% share in a buy-to-let property. The property has a market value of £400,000 and Caroline decides to increase her share to 75% and pays £200,000 for the increased share. Caroline owns no other property.

    The additional 3% SDLT rate does not apply to the acquisition of the 50% share in the buy-to-let property, as at the end of the day which is the 'effective date' (see **14.3**) of the purchase of the increased share in the property Caroline does not own all or part of a 'major interest' (see **14.29**) in another dwelling which has a value of £40,000 or more *(FA 2003, Sch 4ZA, para 3(4))*.

- Elizabeth currently lives in rented accommodation and owns no property. She decides to acquire a buy-to-let property for £400,000.

    The additional 3% rate of SDLT will not apply to the acquisition of the property since, at the end of the day which is the 'effective date' (see **14.3**) of the purchase of the buy-to-let property, Elizabeth does not own all or part of a 'major interest' (see **14.29**) in another dwelling which has a value of £40,000 or more *(FA 2003, Sch 4ZA, para 3(4))*. This assumes that the lease which Elizabeth has over the rented property was not originally granted for a term exceeding seven years.

Example 14.6 – Transactions to which the additional 3% SDLT rate does apply

- Craig owns a property which is his main residence, and also owns a buy-to-let property with his brother Blair which has a value of £300,000. His brother's share in the buy-to-let property is worth £150,000 and Craig decides to buy his brother's share in the property for £150,000.

14.40 *Stamp duty land tax and land and buildings transaction tax*

The additional 3% SDLT rate will apply to the purchase of the share in the buy-to-let property (*FA 2003, Sch 4ZA, para 3*). This is because, at the end of the day which is the 'effective date' (see **14.3**) of the purchase of the buy-to-let property, Craig owns all or part of a 'major interest' (see **14.29**) in another dwelling which has a value of £40,000 or more ie his main residence.

- Tom and Linda are married and live together in a property which is worth £500,000 and is their only residence. The property is owned by Linda. Tom and Linda hold no other property. Tom decides to purchase a buy-to-let property in his own name for £250,000.

  The additional 3% SDLT rate applies to Tom's purchase of the buy-to-let property as, for the purposes higher rates legislation, Tom and Linda are treated as joint purchasers (see **14.33**) and Linda, at the end of the day which is the 'effective date' (see **14.3**) of the purchase of the buy-to-let property owns all or part of a 'major interest' (see **14.29**) in another dwelling which has a value of £40,000 or more (*FA 2003, Sch 4ZA, para 3*).

- Diana and Amanda decide to acquire a buy-to-let property for £350,000 and set up a limited company to make the acquisition. Diana and Amanda own no other property.

  The additional 3% rate of SDLT will apply to the acquisition, as the purchaser is not an individual, the transaction is for £40,000 or more and the buy-to-let property is not subject to a lease which has more than 21 years to run (*FA 2003, Sch 4ZA, para 4*).

- Alan, who owns the property which he currently uses as his main residence, decides to acquire two flats as part of a *single transaction* (ie both flats are acquired under a single agreement between the same purchaser and vendor). Alan intends to use one of the flats as his main residence whilst the other flat will be let out. He will sell his existing main residence at the same time as he acquires his new main residence. The flats will each be purchased for £195,000.

  The 3% additional rate of SDLT will apply to the acquisition of both flats, even though one of the flats is replacing Alan's existing main residence. This is because each of the flats costs £40,000 or more, neither of the flats is subject to a lease with more than 21 years to run, and neither of the flats is 'subsidiary' to the other flat (*FA 2003, Sch 4ZA, para 5* – see **14.38**). Had Alan acquired the replacement main residence under a transaction which was separate from the acquisition of the buy-to-let property then, even though both transactions would be 'linked' (see **14.28**) the higher rates of SDLT would not have applied to the acquisition of the replacement main residence.

- Cara and George are trustees of a discretionary trust, and the trust property does not include any residential property. They decide to acquire a buy-to-let residential property as an investment and the purchase price is £375,000.

  The additional 3% SDLT rate will apply to the purchase of the property. As the purchase is being made by the trustees of a 'settlement' (*FA 2003, Sch 16, para 1(1)*) the fact that the purchasers are individuals is ignored in determining whether the transaction is liable to the additional 3% SDLT rate (*FA 2003, Sch 4ZA, para 13*). Consequently, as the purchase price is £40,000 or more and the property is not subject to a lease with more than 21 years to run the additional 3% SDLT rate applies (*FA 2003, Sch 4ZA, para 4*).

LBTT RATES

14.41 The principal rates of LBTT are as follows (LBTT(S)A 2013, *s 24*; *The Land and Buildings Transaction Tax (Tax Rates and Tax Bands)(Scotland) Order 2015, SSI 2015/126*):

Consideration	Current rates
Residential property – Progressive basis	%
So much as does not exceed £145,000	nil
So much as exceeds £145,000 but does not exceed £250,000	2%
So much as exceeds £250,000 but does not exceed £325,000	5%
So much as exceeds £325,000 but does not exceed £750,000	10%
Above £750,000	12%

If several transactions are linked (essentially part of one overall transaction involving the same seller and buyer or persons connected with them: *LBTT(S) A 2013, s 57*), the consideration must be aggregated to determine the rates of tax.

LBTT additional dwellings supplement (3%) applies to the acquisition of buy-to-let properties

14.42 In response to the Chancellor's announcement that higher rates of SDLT would apply to the acquisition of additional residential properties including buy-to-let properties in the RUK, and ostensibly to avoid distortions

14.42 *Stamp duty land tax and land and buildings transaction tax*

in the property market between Scotland and the RUK, the Scottish Government announced that it would also introduce a higher rate of LBTT for purchases of additional residential properties, including buy-to-let properties.

Like its SDLT equivalent, the 'additional dwellings supplement' (ADS) is much wider than the policy description, and it applies to first purchases of residential properties by companies, individuals acquiring a dwelling as part of business of investing or dealing in land (either conducting the business as a sole trader or as a partner in a partnership) and certain trusts. The legislation can be found at the new *LBTT(S)A 2013, Sch 2A* ('Additional Amount: Transactions relating to second homes etc').

There are, however, some important differences between the two regimes including the following:

- Under SDLT, the higher rates do not apply to a non-residential property transaction. A transaction is a non-residential property transaction if the chargeable interest acquired under the transaction either consists of, or includes, a chargeable interest which is not residential property (ie is not a dwelling). If the transaction is one of a number of linked transactions (see **14.28**), it will be a non-residential property transaction if the chargeable interests acquired under any of the linked transactions consist of non-residential property *(FA 2003, s 55(2),(3) and (4))*. This means that a transaction which involves the acquisition of both residential and non-residential property, for example the acquisition of a shop with a flat above, will be a non-residential property transaction and the higher rates of SDLT will not apply to that transaction. Similarly if both residential and non-residential property are acquired as part of a number of 'linked transactions' (see **14.28**) each of the 'linked transactions' will be a non-residential property transaction and the higher rates of SDLT will not apply.

    In contrast under LBTT, the ADS would apply, with a just and reasonable apportionment of the consideration being made between the residential and non-residential elements of the transaction or transactions.

- Under LBTT, if six or more properties are being acquired as part of a single transaction there is a specific relief which can be claimed to exempt the transaction from the ADS *(LBTT(S)A 2013, Sch 2A, paras 9, 10)*, and if a claim for multiple dwellings relief (see **14.49**) is made, the normal LBTT rates for residential property apply and not the higher rates *(LBTT(S)A 2013, Sch 5, para 10A)*.

    This is not the case under SDLT, as the higher rates would apply when a claim for MDR is made in these circumstances.

- Under LBTT, the ADS applies to any purchase of a buy-to-let property by a partnership in which an individual is a partner, if the partnership is carrying on a business and its sole or main activity is investing or

Stamp duty land tax and land and buildings transaction tax **14.42**

dealing in property situated in Scotland. The ADS will apply irrespective of whether the individuals who are partners in the partnership own more than one dwelling at the end of the day which is the 'effective date' (see **14.7**) of the acquisition of the property by the partnership *(LBTT(S) A 2013, Sch 2A, para 3(1),(2) and (5))*.

Under SDLT, the higher rates will only potentially apply in these circumstances (other conditions must be satisfied – see **14.29** et seq) if one or more of the individuals who are partners in the partnership hold, or are treated as holding (see **14.31–14.37**), a 'major interest' in another dwelling, which has a value of £40,000 or more, at the end of the day which is the 'effective date' (see **14.3**) of the acquisition of the property by the partnership *(FA 2003, Sch 4ZA, para 14(3))*.

- The higher rates of SDLT do not apply to the acquisition of an interest in a dwelling if that interest is subject to a lease which has an unexpired term of more than 21 years as at the 'effective date' (see **14.3**) of the transaction under which the dwelling is acquired.

  There is no similar provision within the ADS legislation. However, it would be rare in Scotland for a lease, with a term of more than 21 years, to be granted over residential property.

- Under LBTT, when deciding whether the buyer owns more than one dwelling at the end of the day which is the 'effective date' (see **14.7**) of the transaction, any dwelling owned by a buyer's cohabitant is treated as owned by the buyer. For these purposes a person is a buyer's cohabitant if the two of them live together as though married to one another.

  This is not the case under SDLT, as the purchaser is not treated as owning any dwelling owned by their cohabitant.

- Under LBTT, the ADS will apply if the buyer is an individual acquiring a dwelling in the course of a property investment or dealing business carried on by that individual as a sole trader irrespective of whether that individual has ownership of another dwelling at the end of the day which is the 'effective date' (see **14.7**) of the transaction under which the dwelling was acquired *(LBTT(S)A 2013, Sch 2A, para 3(2))*. The property investment or dealing business carried on by the individual can comprise properties situated outside of Scotland as well as properties situated in Scotland *(LBTT(S)A 2013, Sch 2A, para 3(3))*. This means that if an individual acquires a buy-to-let property for the purposes of their property letting business, carried on as a sole trader, the ADS will apply to the acquisition of the first (assuming the 'effective date' (see **14.7**) of the transaction is on or after 1 April 2016) and any subsequent dwelling acquired for the purposes of that business.

  The Explanatory Notes to the *Land and Buildings Transaction Tax (Amendment) (Scotland) Act 2016* (which is the legislation that introduced the ADS) state, at paras 23 and 24:

14.42 *Stamp duty land tax and land and buildings transaction tax*

'When an individual buys a dwelling with the intention of renting it out, it will not necessarily be the case that this transaction is considered to be undertaken in the course of a business, the sole or main activity of which is buying or investing in property. If an individual works away from home, for example in the armed forces, and buys their first residential home to rent out, at least initially, then the purchase made by that individual will not be within paragraph 3 [i.e. the ADS will not apply], unless there are other characteristics of the transaction, for example business accounts drawn up, or a business plan, that bring it within it. The transaction will therefore be relevant to paragraph 2, and if the individual does not own an existing dwelling, the supplement will not be payable.

However, if an individual does not own an existing dwelling and buys a dwelling through a business they run and the sole or main activity of the business is dealing or investing in property, then the purchase will be relevant to paragraph 3 [i.e. the ADS will apply] and so the supplement will be payable. For example, the individual's business could already own a number of non-residential properties and when that business purchases its first dwelling, the supplement will be payable on the purchase price.'

Consequently, where the buyer is an individual, an important point under LBTT will be whether that individual acquires the dwelling for the purposes of a property investment or dealing business that they are carrying on and, if they do, the ADS will apply irrespective of whether that individual owns another dwelling at the relevant time.

This is not the case under SDLT and, if the individual does not own an existing dwelling at the end of the day which is the 'effective date' (see **14.3**) of the transaction, and buys a dwelling through a business they carry on as a sole trader whose sole or main activity is dealing or investing in property, the higher rates of SDLT would not apply to the acquisition of that dwelling.

- If the relevant conditions are satisfied (*LBTT(S)A 2013, Sch 2A, paras 2 and 3*), the ADS applies to a chargeable transaction where the missives for the transaction were concluded on or after 28 January 2016 if the 'effective date' (see **14.7**) of the acquisition of the dwelling is on or after 1 April 2016.

Under SDLT, if the relevant conditions are satisfied, the higher rates of SDLT will apply to the acquisition of a dwelling where the 'effective date' (see **14.3**) of the transaction is on or after 1 April 2016 (*FA 2016, s 117(5)*). However, the higher rates of SDLT do not apply where the contract for the acquisition of the dwelling was: (a) entered into and 'substantially performed' before 26 November 2015; or (b) entered into before 26 November 2015 and not excluded by virtue of certain events occurring on or after 26 November 2015 (*FA 2016, s 117(6)*).

14.43 Where the ADS applies, it adds 3% to each of the LBTT rates, including the 0% rate. The ADS, however, does not apply if the chargeable consideration for the transaction is less than £40,000.

The LBTT rates, if the ADS applies, are shown in the table below.

Purchase price	Additional rate
Up to £145,000	3%
£145,001–£250,000	5%
£250,001–£325,000	8%
£325,001–£750,000	13%
Above £750,000	15%

Example 14.7 – Calculation of LBTT chargeable on the acquisition of a buy-to-let property

The facts are as in **Example 14.4**, except that the property purchased by John is situated in Scotland. The purchase of the property completes on 30 June 2016, without any prior event having taken place which would have 'substantially performed' (see **14.7**) the contract prior to that date.

The LBTT chargeable on the purchase of the property is calculated as follows:

Purchase Price (£)	Rate (%)	SDLT (£)
145,000	3	4,350
105,000	5	5,250
75,000	8	6,000
225,000	13	29,250
550,000		44,850

John must therefore file a land transaction return, and pay the LBTT due of £44,850 by 30 July 2016. It can be seen (see **Example 4.4**) that the LBTT chargeable on the acquisition of a buy-to-let property for £550,000 is £10,850 (31.9%) higher than the SDLT chargeable on the acquisition of such a property.

Leases

SDLT rates on a grant of a new lease

14.44 If it is the buy-to-let landlord which is granting the lease to a tenant, it will be the tenant who is liable to pay any SDLT due and who has the obligation to file the land transaction return.

14.45 *Stamp duty land tax and land and buildings transaction tax*

When a new lease is granted, or deemed to be granted, SDLT is charged on any premium in the same manner described above in relation to the acquisition of a freehold interest or an interest in an existing lease.

In addition, there is an SDLT charge on any rent, at 1% of the net present value of the rent over the life of the lease. The method of calculating the net present value is set out at *FA 2003, Sch 5, para 3* as:

$$NPV = \sum_{i=1}^{n} \frac{r_i}{(1+T)^i}$$

where:

- NPV is the net present value;
- r is the rent payable in year i;
- i is the first, second, third, etc year of the term;
- n is the term of the lease;
- T is the temporal discount rate, which has been 3.5% per annum since SDLT was introduced.

14.45 If the lease is for more than five years, the rent for years six onwards is assumed to be the same as the highest rent for any consecutive 12-month period in the first five years (*FA 2003, Sch 17A, para 7*).

For a single standalone lease of residential property, the first £125,000 of NPV is not subject to SDLT. Consequently, if the NPV is £500,000, SDLT is charged on only £375,000 of it at a rate of 1%. If there are two or more leases and they are linked (see **14.28**), the £125,000 allowance is divided between them in proportion to the NPVs.

If it is possible for the rent to vary within the first five years of the term (eg because of a rent review, or some other variable), the lease is treated as being for unascertainable/contingent consideration (see *FA 2003, Sch 17A, para 7*). An initial return must be made on the basis of the known rent (including any contingent amounts, where a figure is available) at the outset, with a reasonable estimate being made where the rent is uncertain or unascertainable. At the end of the fifth year of the term of the lease or, if earlier, when the rent payable in the first five years ceases to be subject to a contingency, or uncertain or unascertained rent becomes ascertained, the SDLT must be recalculated. Any additional tax must be paid or if SDLT has been overpaid, the excess may be reclaimed.

If any part of the rent is contingent or uncertain, it is not possible to defer payment of SDLT on the contingent or uncertain element, even though it may fall to be paid more than six months later.

Stamp duty land tax and land and buildings transaction tax **14.48**

The Gov.uk website includes a calculator for determining the SDLT chargeable on lease transactions (www.hmrc.gov.uk/tools/sdlt/leases.htm).

Grant of a new lease exempt from LBTT

14.46 The grant of a lease over residential property situated in Scotland is exempt from LBTT, unless it is a lease which was originally granted for a period of more than 175 years and certain other conditions are satisfied.

Acquisition of an existing lease
14.47

> **Focus**
>
> It is important to check the history of any existing leasehold property to be acquired. In most cases, SDLT or LBTT will only be charged on the consideration given or the market value of the lease. However, if certain reliefs were claimed on the original grant of the lease, a subsequent acquisition may be treated as the grant of a new lease.
>
> The acquisition of an existing lease over residential property situated in Scotland should be exempt from LBTT unless the lease was granted for a term of more than 175 years and certain other conditions are satisfied.

14.48 The acquisition of an existing lease and the grant of a new lease will normally give rise to very different SDLT consequences:

- When an existing lease over a buy-to-let property situated in the RUK is acquired, SDLT is normally chargeable only on any actual consideration given by the purchaser for the lease. This is subject to the substitution of market value for consideration in the case of an acquisition by a connected company (see **14.13**). No further SDLT is normally chargeable in respect of rent payable under the lease, nor in respect of any premium previously paid on the original grant of the lease. However, if the SDLT on the original grant has not been finally determined when the lease is acquired (for example, because any rent payable is variable and the transfer occurs during the first five years of the lease), the transferee inherits the ongoing obligations to finally determine the SDLT liability and pay any further tax due.

- In contrast, when a new lease is granted SDLT is potentially chargeable on any premium paid and on any rent payable over the term of the lease (see **14.44**).

- In some circumstances, the acquisition of an existing lease is treated as the grant of a new lease, and SDLT is charged accordingly. This happens when one of a range of reliefs was claimed on the original grant of the

14.49 *Stamp duty land tax and land and buildings transaction tax*

lease, and the transfer is the first one since grant which does not qualify for one of the specified reliefs. The list of relevant reliefs is at *FA 2003, Sch 17A, para 11*. The list includes group relief, charities relief, and sale-and-leaseback relief.

Acquisition of bare land to build a buy-to-let property

14.49 Rather than acquiring an existing buy-to-let property, an investor may decide to purchase bare land and construct a property on that land. The acquisition of bare land will be taxed as the purchase of non-residential property so that the lower non-residential property SDLT rates will apply which are as follows:

Consideration (£)	**Non-residential property** ('effective date' on or after 17 March 2016)
Not exceeding £150,000	0%
£150,001 to £250,000	2%
Exceeding £250,000	5%

However, it will be important that what is acquired is bare land and that the construction of the buy-to-let property has not yet begun, otherwise the higher residential property SDLT rates will apply (see the definition of residential property at **14.19**).

If the construction of the property is carried out by a construction company or other party which is unrelated to the vendor of the land, SDLT will only be chargeable on the acquisition of the land and no SDLT will be chargeable on the cost of building the property.

However, where the property is to be constructed by the vendor of the land, or a person 'connected' with the vendor, the question which arises is whether what is being acquired is not bare land and separate construction services, but rather a completed property so that SDLT is chargeable on the cost of both the land and the construction services. In these circumstances it is necessary to consider the case of *Prudential Assurance Co Ltd v IRC* [1992] STC 863.

HMRC set out their view of the impact of this case at SDLTM04015. HMRC consider that the same principles apply as those set out in SP 8/93 in relation to the stamp duty liability in this kind of transaction. Provided the land purchase and the construction contracts are genuinely independent of each other, SDLT will be charged only on the price paid for the land. However, if there is, in reality, only one transaction – for example, if in truth the vendor will only sell the land if the purchaser agrees to engage the vendor (or a person connected to the vendor) to build the property, HMRC will seek SDLT based on the overall price for the land and the completed property.

Stamp duty land tax and land and buildings transaction tax **14.51**

Revenue Scotland accept that the same principles apply to LBTT, as they do for UK stamp duty and SDLT. In LBTT Technical Bulletin 1 (published on 14 October 2016), Revenue Scotland state:

> 'We will consider whether or not a contract for the sale of land and a contract for building services properly constitutes the sale of land with completed buildings such that the chargeable consideration for the transaction will be the aggregate consideration for the contracts. Generally, unless the purchase and development contracts are so inter-related that default of one will prevent completion of the other or would otherwise render one invalid, LBTT should be charged only on the consideration attributable to the land transferred (where necessary, apportioned on a just and reasonable basis).'

Consequently, provided the land purchase and building services contracts are genuinely independent of each other, LBTT should only be charged on the price paid for the land.

The LBTT rates on non-residential property are as follows:

Consideration (£)	Non-residential property
Up to £150,000	0%
£150,001–£350,000	3%
Above £350,000	4.5%

Reliefs

14.50

> **Focus**
>
> Few SDLT or LBTT reliefs are likely to be relevant to the acquisition of a buy-to-let property. However, if more than one dwelling is being acquired, a claim to multiple dwellings relief may reduce the amount of SDLT or LBTT payable.
>
> In addition, the special rules for partnerships may reduce any SDLT or LBTT charge below the expected amount when a buy-to-let-property is transferred by a partner, or a person 'connected' with a partner, to or from a partnership (see **14.52**).

Multiple dwellings relief

14.51 When several dwellings are acquired in a single transaction (or a series of linked transactions see **14.28**), it is normally necessary to aggregate the consideration for each of the transactions to determine the SDLT or LBTT

14.52 *Stamp duty land tax and land and buildings transaction tax*

which is payable (*FA 2003, s 55*; the LBTT equivalent is *LBTT(S)A 2013, s 26*).

It should, however, be noted that where, as part of a single transaction (or a series of linked transactions), properties in the RUK and Scotland are acquired, the acquisition of the RUK properties is chargeable to SDLT, the acquisition of the Scottish properties is chargeable to LBTT, and the acquisition of the RUK properties are not 'linked', for the purposes of either of the taxes, with the acquisition of the Scottish properties.

14.52 However, where more than one dwelling is acquired in this way, the purchaser(s) may claim for the SDLT or LBTT payable to be determined on the basis of the average consideration per dwelling multiplied (or in the case of LBTT the tax chargeable on each dwelling is summed) by the number of dwellings acquired (*FA 2003, Sch 6B*; the LBTT equivalent is *LBTT(S)A 2013, Sch 5*). The relief is called 'multiple dwellings relief' (MDR).

In relation to SDLT, it is not possible for the rate to drop below 1% if MDR is claimed. However, this limit is now largely superfluous, as the additional 3% rate of SDLT will apply to most MDR claims.

Under SDLT, any buy-to-let-properties with an individual value exceeding £500,000, which are acquired by, for example, a company, should not be excluded from a claim to MDR provided the exception from the 'slab' 15% rate for properties used for a letting business applies – see *FA 2003, Sch 4A, paras 5–5F* – see **14.26**).

14.53 In relation to LBTT, if MDR is claimed, it is not possible for the tax charge in relation to the acquisition of the dwellings to be less than 25% of the tax which would have been payable in respect of the dwellings had MDR not been claimed.

Under LBTT, unlike SDLT, where six or more dwellings are acquired as part of a single transaction, it is possible to make a claim to exempt the transaction from the 3% additional dwellings supplement (see **14.42** – *LBTT(S)A 2013,Sch 2A, paras 9, 10*).

If a claim is then made for MDR the tax payable on the average price of a dwelling is calculated using the normal rates of LBTT for residential property (see **14.41** and **Example 14.1**).

> **Example 14.8 – Multiple dwellings relief**
>
> Cameron enters into a single agreement to acquire a buy-to-let portfolio of five houses and flats situated in England and Wales, which are let to tenants on short-term leases. Three properties are valued at £250,000 each, the other two at £300,000 each.
>
> The SDLT chargeable on the transaction, if no claim for MDR is made, is calculated as follows:

Purchase Price (£)	Rate (%)	SDLT (£)
125,000	3	3,750
125,000	5	6,250
675,000	8	54,000
425,000	13	55,250
1,350,000		119,250

If Cameron makes a claim for multiple dwellings relief (*FA 2003, Sch 6B*), the SDLT payable will be calculated as follows:

- The average chargeable consideration given per dwelling is £1.35 million divided by the number of dwellings acquired of five, giving an amount of £270,000 per dwelling;

- The SDLT payable on the acquisition of a single residential property for £270,000 would be £11,600 (£125,000 at 3% plus £125,000 at 5% plus £20,000 at 8%) which, multiplied by the number of dwellings acquired of five, would give SDLT payable of £58,000;

- The SDLT payable cannot be reduced to less than 1% of the consideration payable for the dwellings however, as this is only £13,500 (£1.35 million × 1%), the SDLT chargeable is £58,000. By making the claim for multiple dwellings relief Cameron has reduced his SDLT liability from £119,250 to £58,000, a reduction of £61,250.

Had the houses and flats been located in Scotland, and if no claim for MDR was made, the LBTT payable would have been calculated as follows:

Purchase Price (£)	Rate (%)	LBTT (£)
145,000	3	4,350
105,000	5	5,250
75,000	8	6,000
425,000	13	55,250
600,000	15	90,000
1,350,000		160,850

If Cameron makes a claim for multiple dwellings relief (LBTT(S)A 2013, *Sch 5*) the LBTT payable should be calculated as follows:

- The average chargeable consideration given per dwelling is £1.35 million divided by the number of dwellings acquired of five, giving an amount of £270,000 per dwelling;

14.54 *Stamp duty land tax and land and buildings transaction tax*

- The LBTT payable on the acquisition of a single residential property for £270,000 would be £11,200 (£145,000 at 3% plus £105,000 at 5% plus £20,000 at 8%) which, multiplied by the number of dwellings acquired of five, would give LBTT payable of £56,000.

- However, the LBTT payable cannot be reduced to less than 25% of the tax which would have been payable on the consideration given for the dwellings had no claim for MDR been made. As calculated above, the LBTT chargeable for the acquisition of the five dwellings would have been £160,850 if no claim for multiple dwellings relief had been made, and therefore the LBTT liability cannot be less than £40,212 (£160,850 × 25%). Consequently, this limit does not apply and the LBTT chargeable is £56,000. By making the claim for multiple dwellings relief Cameron has reduced his LBTT liability from £160,850 to £56,000, a reduction of £104,850.

Partnerships

14.54

> **Focus**
>
> The SDLT and LBTT liability on the acquisition of one or more buy-to-let properties by a partnership from an unconnected party will be taxed in the same way as any other land transaction with an unconnected party, ie by reference to the consideration in 'money or money's worth' given for the property.
>
> However, the transfer of a buy-to-let-property, or the transfer of a number of buy-to-let properties, by a partner (or a person connected with a partner) to a partnership, or from a partnership to a partner or a person who has been a partner (or a person connected with a partner or a person who has been a partner), will result in SDLT or LBTT being charged on a proportion of the market value of the buy-to-let-property or properties. The actual consideration given for the transaction will be irrelevant.

14.55 The UK tax system has always had difficulty working out how to deal with partnerships – in particular, whether to treat them as separate entities distinct from their members or as mere aggregations of separately taxed members – and both SDLT and LBTT continue that uncertainty. The SDLT rules are largely in *FA 2003, Sch 15*. The LBTT rules, which are virtually identical to the SDLT rules, are found in *LBTT(S)A 2013, Sch 17*. Both regimes treat the three types of UK partnership (general partnership; limited partnership formed under the *Limited Partnerships Act 1907*; and limited liability partnerships formed under the *Limited Liability Partnerships Act 2000*), and overseas entities of a similar character, in the same way.

Normal arm's length purchases and disposals of a buy-to-let property by a partnership are subject to SDLT or LBTT in the same manner as purchases and disposals by individuals or other entities, ie normally by reference to the amount of the actual consideration given, although it is the partners, rather than the partnership, that are regarded as acquiring or disposing of the property. However, in deciding whether the additional 3% rate of SDLT applies to the purchase of a buy-to-let property by a partnership it is generally necessary for each individual who is a partner in the partnership to be tested to determine whether they hold, or are treated as holding (see **14.31–14.37**), a 'major interest' (see **14.29**) in another dwelling with a value of £40,000 or more, at the end of the day which is the 'effective date' (see **14.3**) of the transaction (*FA 2003, Sch 4ZA, para 14(3)*).

Under LBTT, the 3% 'additional dwellings supplement' applies to any purchase of a dwelling by a partnership, in which an individual is a partner, if the partnership is carrying on a business and its sole or main activity is investing or dealing in property. The property investment or dealing business carried on by the individual can comprise properties situated outside of Scotland as well as properties situated in Scotland. The additional dwellings supplement will apply irrespective of whether the individuals who are partners in the partnership own more than one dwelling at the end of the day which is the 'effective date' (see **14.7**) of the acquisition of the property by the partnership (*LBTT(S)A 2013, Sch 2A, para 3(1),(2) (3) and (5)*).

14.56 In contrast, when a partnership acquires or disposes of a property from or to a partner or someone connected with a partner, special rules come into play to determine the amount of SDLT or LBTT payable. When a property – possibly forming part of the assets of a property rental business – is transferred to a partnership from a partner or vice versa, actual consideration is irrelevant. The consideration for SDLT or LBTT purposes is calculated using a formula which takes account of the market value of the property and the effective change in ultimate ownership by individuals.

Where there is no change in ultimate ownership by partners who are individuals the chargeable consideration for a transfer can be zero.

The actual calculation can be complex, taking account of proportional partnership shares, other connections between the partners and whether the persons involved are individuals or companies. It may also be important to consider historic changes in partnership shares and whether SDLT or LBTT (or stamp duty) was paid on the acquisition of the property from a third party.

The following simple example deals with a situation where all of the partners are individuals who retain the same effective proportionate ownership of the buy-to-let business through shareholdings. Detailed consideration of the various permutations is beyond the scope of this book, and further advice will

14.57 *Stamp duty land tax and land and buildings transaction tax*

be necessary to determine whether the beneficial result illustrated is available in more complex situations.

Example 14.9 – Incorporation from a partnership

Jon and Ellie – two otherwise unconnected individuals – carry on a property rental business in partnership sharing profits and losses equally. They decide to transfer their business to a new company, D Ltd, in which each will be a 50% shareholder. This will involve transferring three properties, which are situated in England, with an aggregate market value of £600,000, to D Ltd.

In the absence of special rules, and assuming no claim to multiple dwellings relief is made, D Ltd would pay SDLT of £38,000 (£125,000 at 3% plus £125,000 at 5% plus £350,000 at 8%) on the transfer, in accordance with *FA 2003, s 53*.

However, the special partnership rules recognise that each of Jon and Ellie start with a direct 50% interest in the properties and end with an indirect interest of the same proportion. As a result, under the special rules the chargeable consideration is reduced to zero, and no SDLT is payable.

An equivalent result should arise for a transfer of a property from a company to a partnership of individual shareholders who are each 'connected' with the company, in the course of disincorporation.

A similar analysis should also apply for the purposes of LBTT, subject to the point discussed below in relation to the conflict between the LBTT partnership provisions and the market value rule in *LBTT(S)A 2013, s 22*.

14.57 There is an apparent conflict between the SDLT partnership provisions and *FA 2003, s 53*, which imposes a market value charge on a transfer to a connected company. HMRC have confirmed that in this situation the partnership rules take precedence (see SDLTM34160).

It may be expected that HMRC will look carefully at any attempt to exploit these provisions to avoid a market-value charge, for example by creating a partnership shortly before incorporating an essentially sole-trader property rental business. Although the partnership rules contain no specific anti-avoidance rules which would impact such arrangements, it is possible that either the SDLT general anti-avoidance provision (*FA 2003, s 75A*) or the GAAR could be applied (see **14.58 et seq**).

A similar conflict arises between the LBTT partnership provisions and *LBTT(S) A 2013, s 22*, which would impose a market value charge on a transfer of a buy-to let property to a connected company. To date, Revenue Scotland have not confirmed whether they accept that the partnership rules take precedence over the market value rule. Consequently, until such time as guidance is issued, it is suggested that confirmation be sought from Revenue Scotland that they agree that the partnership rules do in fact have precedence.

For commentary on the incorporation of a property rental business, see **Chapter 13**.

ANTI-AVOIDANCE PROVISIONS

14.58 SDLT is within the ambit of the general anti-abuse rule (*FA 2013, ss206–215*). In addition, there is an SDLT-specific general anti-avoidance provision and many reliefs or special treatments are hedged around with rules which are intended to prevent exploitation.

The SDLT-specific general anti-avoidance provision at *FA 2003, ss 75A–75C* does not contain any motive test. It simply provides that, if the SDLT payable on a transaction is less than the amount computed in accordance with those sections on a notional transfer, the higher liability is substituted. In general, SDLT on the notional transfer is computed by reference to the maximum amount paid by anyone or received by the vendor or others connected with the vendor, including substitution of market value where the transaction so requires. In principle this could apply to legitimate arrangements, but HMRC have stated that, in practice, they will only seek to apply the rules where there is an avoidance of SDLT motive.

However, in the case of *Project Blue Ltd (formerly Project Blue Guernsey Ltd) v Revenue and Customs Commissioners* [2016] EWCA Civ 485, it was confirmed that an SDLT avoidance motive is not required to fall within *FA 2003, s 75A* although the tax saving requirement, which would have to be satisfied for the section to apply, should mean that in practice SDLT would have been avoided.

This is an unsatisfactory situation as the Court of Appeal decision has made it clear that there is no need for an avoidance motive and the HMRC guidance remains in place stating that they will only apply the provision where there is an avoidance motive. Such a situation creates uncertainty for taxpayers, and potentially leaves the final decision, as to what constitutes avoidance, in the hands of HMRC.

14.59 *FA 2003, s 75A* is unlikely to impact on the straightforward acquisition of a buy-to-let property, unless it is one step in a larger series of transactions. For example, if a sole trader transfers a property rental business to a partnership shortly before incorporation in order to obtain the treatment outlined at **Example 14.8** there would be a risk of HMRC seeking to apply *s 75A* to disregard the formation of the partnership.

14.60 LBTT is within the ambit of the Scottish general ant-avoidance rule (the 'Scottish GAAR'), which can be found at *RSTPA 2014, ss 62–72*. Broadly, if an 'arrangement' is entered into with a main purpose (not necessarily *the* main purpose) of obtaining a reduction in a liability to LBTT (or a payment

14.61 *Stamp duty land tax and land and buildings transaction tax*

deferral or an acceleration of a repayment), and the 'arrangement' is 'artificial', then Revenue Scotland may seek to counteract the perceived tax advantage by applying the Scottish GAAR.

It is unlikely that the Scottish GAAR would be in point in relation to the straightforward acquisition of a buy-to-let property although, as discussed above in relation to SDLT, if a sole trader transfers a property rental business to a partnership shortly before incorporation in order to obtain the treatment outlined at **Example 14.8** there may be a risk of Revenue Scotland seeking to apply the Scottish GAAR.

There is no equivalent to *FA 2003, s 75A* within the LBTT legislation.

ANNUAL TAX ON ENVELOPED DWELLINGS

14.61 *Finance Act 2013, Pt 3* (*ss 94–174* and *Schs 33–35*) introduced a new tax known as annual tax on enveloped dwellings (ATED). Section and schedule references in this part are to *Finance Act 2013*, unless otherwise indicated.

> **Focus**
>
> ATED potentially applies to dwellings located in either RUK or Scotland, which have a market value in excess of £500,000 and which are held by a company, a partnership in which at least one of the partners is a company or a collective investment scheme.
>
> However, provided the company, partnership or collective investment scheme uses the dwelling for the purposes of a property rental business on a commercial basis with a view to profit it will be exempt from ATED.
>
> For further commentary on ATED, and also ATED-related CGT, see **10.9–10.14**.

TRANSFERRING A BUY-TO-LET PROPERTY OUT OF A COMPANY

14.62 If the exemption from ATED for properties used for a property rental business does not, for whatever reason, apply, a decision may be taken to transfer a property out of a company to prevent a future liability to ATED arising. Care is needed if this is to be done without creating a liability to either SDLT or LBTT. Provided the company is debt-free, the property can be transferred as a distribution in the winding-up of the company and no SDLT or LBTT charge will normally arise. However, if the company has debt – typically in the form of a mortgage secured on the property – care must be taken to avoid triggering a liability to either SDLT or LBTT.

Stamp duty land tax and land and buildings transaction tax **14.64**

In relation to SDLT, HMRC have confirmed that where the debt is owed to the shareholder, so that it simply disappears when the company is wound-up and the property transferred to that shareholder, this will not be regarded as the shareholder giving consideration, and no charge to SDLT will arise.

However, if there is a third-party debt due by the company and the shareholder provides funds for it to be paid off (whether by loan, gift or by subscription for further shares), HMRC will consider whether *FA 2003, s 75A* applies (SDLT general anti-avoidance provision – see **14.58** *et seq*). If they consider that the provision of the funds to pay off the third party debt is 'involved in connection with the disposal' of the property to the shareholder, they will seek to apply *s 75A* and charge SDLT as if the third party debt had been assumed by the shareholder. See SDLTM04042 for details of HMRC's views on this matter.

It is not known what approach Revenue Scotland will take (a) if the debt is due to the shareholder and the property is distributed to the shareholder subject to the debt, or (b) if the debt is due to a third party but the shareholder provides funds to the company to pay off the debt. In the Author's view, a shareholder taking steps to repay debt prior to the distribution of a property out of a company ought not to be an 'arrangement' to which Revenue Scotland would look to apply the general anti-avoidance rule (see **14.60**). Whilst there may be a 'tax avoidance arrangement', it would not seem to be 'artificial' and therefore it is considered that the general anti-avoidance rule should not apply. If that view is correct, and given that there is no equivalent of *FA 2003, s 75A* within the LBTT legislation, the analysis should be that no LBTT would be payable in these circumstances.

However, given that no specific guidance has been issued by Revenue Scotland on the mater, it is suggested that a formal opinion be sought from Revenue Scotland in circumstances where a property is to be extracted from a company and there is debt involved.

STAMP DUTY AND STAMP DUTY RESERVE TAX

14.63

> **Focus**
>
> In general stamp duty only applies to instruments transferring 'stock and marketable securities', which term would include an instrument transferring the shares of a company carrying on a property rental business.
>
> Stamp duty reserve tax (SDRT) is effectively an alternative to stamp duty, charged when no document of transfer is presented for stamping.

14.64 Stamp duty on transfers of shares is charged at 0.5% of the consideration given (*Finance Act 1999 (FA 1999), Sch 13, paras 2, 3*). If the

14.65 *Stamp duty land tax and land and buildings transaction tax*

shares in a UK incorporated company, carrying on a property rental business, are acquired then stamp duty at a rate of 0.5% of the consideration given for the shares will be payable. If the company carrying on the property rental business is not incorporated in the UK there should be no need, in practice, to pay the stamp duty on the acquisition of the shares. Neither SDLT nor LBTT should be payable if the shares of a company carrying on a property rental business are acquired. However, care should be taken to ensure that the acquisition of the shares does not trigger the withdrawal of an SDLT or LBTT relief previously claimed on any of the properties owned by the acquired company.

14.65 SDRT is a self-assessment tax on agreements to transfer chargeable securities (*FA 1986, s 86*). The term 'chargeable securities' broadly comprises shares, stocks or loan capital issued by UK incorporated companies (*FA 1986, s 99(3)*). It is charged mainly on stock market transactions which proceed electronically without production of a stock transfer form. If a property rental business is purchased by acquiring the shares of a UK incorporated company and the stamp duty charge is settled on a timely basis, the charge to SDRT, on the agreement to transfer the shares, is cancelled.

Chapter 15

Other issues

James Darmon BA, ACA, Tax Consultant, The TACS Partnership

SIGNPOSTS

- **VAT** – Rent is generally exempt, so VAT paid on property expenses is normally a cost to the business. Thus VAT planning for buy-to-let residential property businesses in essence involves minimising the amount of input tax payable. If fundamental changes to a property are being made, consideration should be given to whether reduced rates of VAT can be applied (see **15.1–15.5**).

- **Construction industry scheme** – In addition to building and construction companies etc., a business whose average annual expenditure on construction operations over a period of three years is £1 million or more counts as a 'contractor' for construction industry scheme (CIS) purposes. It is possible that larger property portfolios may require sufficient work for the business to be regarded as a 'deemed contractor', and therefore to be subject to CIS obligations (see **15.6–15.10**).

- **Rents connected with a trade or profession may be trading income** – Some employers may own premises (eg farm cottages) which are used, and required to be used, by employees for the better performance of their employment duties. Rents and expenses are generally taken into account based on trading principles. If the rents relate to a trade or profession, relief for any losses is more widely available than for other property rental activities (see **15.11–15.13**).

- **Beginning and end of a property rental business** – A property rental business normally starts when the first property is let. However, relief is potentially available for pre-lettings expenditure. A rental business generally ceases when the last let property is either disposed of, or starts to be used for some other purpose. If losses have arisen and a rental business ceases and recommences, it is a question of fact whether a new business has commenced or the old one has resumed (see **15.18–15.21**).

- **Post-cessation income and losses** – Receipts after the property rental business has ceased are taxable under special rules, provided

15.1 *Other issues*

> that they have not already been included in the computation of rental business profits. The business may also be able to claim relief for post-cessation expenses for which they have had no relief (see **15.22–15.24**).

VAT

15.1 The VAT system differentiates between taxable (including zero-rated) and exempt supplies. Input VAT (ie the VAT paid on goods and services supplied) attributable to taxable supplies can in general be recovered, but input VAT attributable to exempt supplies generally cannot. Therefore input VAT is a cost to an exempt business.

Rental Income from buy-to-let dwellings is generally exempt from VAT (*VATA 1994, Sch 9, Group 1*), so VAT is normally a cost to the business. A business which solely comprises letting residential property is not required to register for VAT.

15.2 Where a buy-to-let property is owned by a sole trader individual who is registered for VAT in respect of their other business activity, HMRC will argue that the exempt buy-to-let income should be included within the overall income of the business, meaning that the business is partially exempt, and input tax recovery should be restricted.

This restriction is subject to possible application of *de minimis* rules, whereby, if exempt input tax is below £7,500 per annum and 50% of total input tax, all input tax can be recovered (*SI 1995/2518, Pt XIV*).

See **Examples 1** and **2** below.

> **Example 15.1 – Full input VAT recovery**
>
> Joe is a plumber, registered for VAT, with a taxable turnover of £100,000. He has also bought two buy-to-let houses, from which he gets rent of £20,000 per annum. He incurs annual input tax related to the (fully taxable) plumbing business of £5,000. Input tax on overheads per annum is £1,200, and input tax on repair costs is £1,000.
>
> Joe's exempt input tax is:
>
> | | |
> |---|---:|
> | Directly attributable to exempt supplies: | £1,000 |
> | Overhead input tax apportioned: | |
> | $\dfrac{20,000 \times £1,200}{120,000}$ | £200 |
> | Total | £1,200 |

£1,200 is less than both £7,500 and 50% of total input tax (£7,200), so can be recovered.

Example 15.2 – No input VAT recovery

As in **Example 1**, but Joe spends £30,000 plus VAT of £6,000 on doing up one of the houses. The exempt input tax is now £7,200, which is more than 50% of total input tax (£13,200), so the VAT is not recoverable.

15.3 The examples above suggest that the most significant VAT cost to a property rental business may well be repairs and improvements to the building.

15.4 Essentially, VAT planning for buy-to-let residential property businesses involves minimising the amount of input tax payable. Whilst it may in some circumstances be possible to engage legitimately unregistered labour only subcontractors for certain jobs, this is not always practical.

15.5 One avenue to explore is where a building is purchased which is not, either wholly or partly, a dwelling at the time of purchase. The costs of converting non-dwelling areas to dwellings are generally subject to a lower rate (5%) of value added tax if the effect is to create additional dwellings. There are certain exceptions to this rule, and specialist advice should be sought where this situation arises.

Where a business makes a taxable (zero-rated) supply, any input VAT incurred may be recoverable. However, income tax, corporation tax and stamp duty land tax implications will need careful consideration.

Focus

In summary:

- For a buy-to-let property business, VAT will normally be a cost.
- Consider whether the *de minimis* rules can apply to benefit the business.
- Where fundamental changes to a property are being made, consider whether reduced rates of VAT can be applied.

CONSTRUCTION INDUSTRY SCHEME

15.6 Where a 'contractor' pays 'subcontractors' for 'construction operations', the operation of the construction industry scheme (CIS) must always be considered (*FA 2004, ss 57–77, Schs 11, 12; SI 2005/2045* as amended). The scheme requires contractors to deduct tax at 20% from payments, other than payments for materials, made to subcontractors.

15.7 *Other issues*

15.7 Building and construction companies and other firms are contractors for this purpose. Any business whose average annual expenditure on construction operations over a period of three years is £1 million or more also counts as a 'contractor' for this purpose.

15.8 The latter is commonly referred to by HMRC as a 'deemed contractor'.

15.9 HMRC does not regard property investment businesses as 'mainstream contractors' in the same way as property developers, because their business does not generally include large scale property development (and therefore construction) activities.

However, it is possible that large scale property investment activities may require sufficient work to be done on the estate and that the business spends an average of more than £1 million per annum over a three-year period. In such cases, a property investment business may be a deemed contractor.

For example, suppose a business has acquired properties which need substantial refurbishment before letting. It spends £200,000 doing up those buildings. This is unlikely, of itself, to cause the business to be regarded as a contractor.

If the property letting business then acquires a substantial dilapidated building, for example a hotel or office building, with a view to converting it to flats and letting it, this may cause it to be regarded as a mainstream contractor (not subject to the £1 million per annum *'de minimis'*) and as such will have to register.

15.10 If the business is obliged to register, it must inspect tax certificates for each subcontractor it engages. This is anyone it pays money to for construction operations.

> **Focus**
>
> Only buy-to-let residential property landlords with substantial portfolios will be potentially subject to the CIS rules. Where this may be an issue, landlords should ensure they keep expenditure records and check the limits.

RENTS CONNECTED WITH A TRADE OR PROFESSION

Tied premises

15.11 Where an employer owns tied premises (in other words premises which are used, and require to be used, by employees for the better performance of their jobs), the rent received counts as trading income (*ITTOIA 2005, s 19; CTA 2009, s 42*). This includes the taxable element of any premium received.

Other issues **15.14**

15.12 Equally, any expenditure incurred on the tied premises, which would be deductible under normal principles (for example, repairs) will be deducted in the computations as trading profits, and not included in the rental business.

15.13 The types of property might include farm cottages used by workers, mining cottages, and police houses.

> **Focus**
>
> Where the rents relate to a trade or profession, relief for any losses is more widely available under the trading losses rules.

Other income from land not taxed under the rental business rules

15.14 The categories of income from land which are not taxed under the rental business rules include the following:

- Income from the occupation of woodlands managed on a commercial basis;
- Income from cutting and selling timber from a woodland is not treated as income from land but is treated as trading income;
- Also:
    - income from mines and quarries;
    - income from iron works, gas works, salt springs or works;
    - canals, inland navigations, docks and drains;
    - fishing rights when operated on a commercial basis;
    - rights to hold markets, fairs, tolls, bridges and ferries;
    - railways and other similar businesses
    - hotels and guest houses;
    - caravan sites;
    - lodges or lodgers and tenants in your own home, if you do laundry and provide food, etc.

(ITTOIA 2005, ss11,12 and 261 for individuals; CTA 2009, ss 37, 39 for companies)

Where tenants change frequently, and extra services are provided for them, such as laundry, food etc, this may be sufficient to amount to a trade. This is essentially a matter of fact and degree, and should be examined on a case-by-case basis. The closer such a business is to a hotel business the more likely it is to be treated as a trade.

15.15 *Other issues*

> **Focus**
>
> Ensure that rental income is taxed on the correct basis.

SALE AND LEASEBACK OF LAND

15.15 For companies and individuals, where land is sold in return for a lease, tax relief can be restricted in certain circumstances. The form of the restriction depends on whether the lease granted is a short (less than 50 years) or long lease (*ITA 2007, ss 681A–681AN* for individuals; *CTA 2009, s 225* for companies).

The restrictions apply where land is sold to a property developer, and the vendor takes a lease of the property. In the absence of the restrictions, a taxpayer would be able to sell a parcel of land, subject to CGT, probably on much less than the full price received (because of the base cost), and get full income tax relief on the rental payments.

Where the lease is a long lease, the broad effect of the provisions is to restrict the rental deduction to a market rent.

Where the lease is a short lease, the broad effect is to treat a proportion of the premium received as subject to income tax.

These provisions are complex, and apply only in very limited circumstances to buy-to-let investors. The detailed rules are beyond the scope of this work, and any reader concerned by the issues raised here should seek appropriate specialist advice.

> **Focus**
>
> Ensure that sale and leaseback transactions are correctly taxed, and that income is correctly treated as income or capital.

TRANSACTIONS IN UK LAND

Taxation of chargeable gains

15.16 When land is sold, the profit is normally taxed under the chargeable gains rules. However, there are four circumstances under any of which the profit (or part of the profit) on the sale of land can be taxed as trading income. These are broadly as follows (*ITA 2007, s 756; s 517B(7)*):

(1) When land is acquired and the main purpose, or one of the main purposes, of acquiring it was realising a gain from disposing of all or any part of the land.

(2) When any property deriving its value from land is acquired and the main purpose, or one of the main purposes, of acquiring it was realising a gain on disposing of all or part of the land.

(3) When land is held as trading stock.

(4) If the land has been developed, one of the main purposes of the development was realising a gain from disposing of all or part of the land when developed.

15.17 When land is held as trading stock (in other words, purchased for resale) there is little doubt that any profit which arises is on trading account. It is more difficult, in many cases, to identify whether land which has been held for many years, or is otherwise treated as capital, should be regarded as subject to income rules in whole or in part.

For disposals prior to the introduction (in *Finance Act 2016*) of legislation on transactions in UK land, HMRC can apply the rules in *ITA 2007, Pt 13, Ch 3* ('Transactions in land') to 'override' capital treatment, and impose an income tax charge on any person holding or developing land, any person connected with such a person, or any person who is a party to, or concerned in, an arrangement or scheme which enables a gain to be realised by an indirect method or series of transactions. This rule does not apply to override gains otherwise subject to only or main residence relief (*TCGA 1992, s 222*).

The new anti-avoidance provisions on transactions in UK land (*ITA 2007, Pt 9A*) introduced in *Finance Act 2016* appear to widen the circumstances in which HMRC can seek to redesignate the profit as income (and therefore tax the profit at income tax, rather than CGT, rates).

Historically, HMRC have applied these rules under two main circumstances:

(1) The first is that an artificial series of transactions has reduced the amount chargeable to tax.

(2) The second scenario, which occurs more frequently in the author's experience in practice, is where land is sold to a developer and a 'slice of the action' scheme is entered into.

For further commentary on transactions in UK land, see **2.26–2.35** and **13.15**.

> **Example 15.3 – CGT or income tax?**
>
> Fred owns a parcel of land. He is approached by a builder who offers to buy the land for £5 million up front, or (if higher) £4 million plus a payment of £50,000 per house in excess of ten houses built on the land.

15.18 Other issues

The builder builds 50 houses on the land, so Fred receives a total payment of £6 million. £5 million of this is subject to CGT (the original fixed value) and the extra £1 million is subject to income tax as miscellaneous income.

> **Focus**
>
> The transactions in UK land rules can apply in many common situations, and can convert what the vendor thought were capital gains into (generally more highly taxed) income.

BEGINNING AND END OF A RENTAL BUSINESS

The beginning of a rental business

15.18 A rental business normally starts when the first property is let. Where a rental business incurs expenditure before the lettings can start, the legislation (*ITTOIA 2005, s 57,* as applied by *s 272; CTA 2009, s 61* as applied by *CTA 2009, s 210*) provides relief for the 'trading' expenditure.

Once a property has been let, all letting activities (other than those relating to properties let otherwise than at arm's length) are treated as a single letting business. As a result, once 'property 1' has been let, expenditure which is not capital, and is incurred wholly and exclusively for the purpose of the business, will be deductible even if it relates to 'property 2', which has been purchased with a view to being let.

For commentary on tax issues arising on the commencement of a property rental business, see **Chapter 1**.

CESSATION OF A RENTAL BUSINESS

15.19 Generally speaking, a rental business ceases when the last let property is either disposed of or starts to be used for some other purpose.

15.20 If there are any losses, and a rental business ceases and is later recommenced, it is a question of fact whether there is a new business or a resumption of the old one.

In cases where relatively few properties are involved, it is possible for there to be an interval between the end of an old let and the start of a new one. If the taxpayer can demonstrate that he was looking for tenants during this period, this interval should not necessarily cause the end of a rental business.

However, if the taxpayer states an intention to cease business, and then later recommences letting the property at a much later date, HMRC will probably

Other issues **15.23**

contend that the old business has ceased (and the losses have perished), and a new business has started.

15.21 Normally, HMRC is more likely to accept a continuing rental business if the interval is less than three years. Other factors include whether the same property was let before and after the dormant period. See HMRC guidance in its Property Income manual (at PIM2505 and PIM2510).

Focus

Landlords wishing to claim that a rental business is continuing (for example, to make use of losses) should ensure that evidence is retained to support the claim if the source of income ceases.

POST-CESSATION RECEIPTS AND EXPENSES

Post-cessation receipts

15.22 A receipt from a rental business after it has ceased is taxable under special rules provided it has not already been included in the computation of rental business profits. The business may also be able to claim relief for post-cessation expenses for which they have had no relief, as explained below.

The business may have post-cessation receipts where, for example, the rental business consisted of a single let property and, after it has been sold (so the rental business has ceased) they receive insurance proceeds under a policy which covers a tenant who defaults on the rents. The unpaid rent (or the insurance recovery) would have been taxable as business receipts while the rental business was continuing. Once the business has ceased, the receipt cannot form part of their rental business. Instead it is taxed separately (under *ITTOIA 2005, s 349; CTA 2009, s 280*).

Another common example of a taxable post-cessation receipt is the recovery of bad debts. These are taxable if the business previously claimed a deduction.

Post-cessation expenses

15.23 In arriving at the tax due on post-cessation receipts, the business can deduct any allowable business losses that were left unrelieved when the business ceased and any other expenses that would have been allowable had the business continued.

For example, if the business recovers a bad debt after cessation, it can deduct the costs incurred in collecting that debt. Another deductible expense would normally be the cost of heating empty premises to keep down condensation and so maintain the value of the property for later sale.

15.24 *Other issues*

Post-cessation expenses but no post-cessation receipts

15.24 Where the business has no post-cessation receipts they may still be able to claim relief against other income and gains of the same year for post-cessation bad debts and certain specific post-cessation expenses. A claim to relief must be made by 31 January following the end of the tax year in which the payment is made (*ITA 2007, s 125* for individuals). For corporation tax, if an investment company ceases to carry on a property business, any such costs are carried forward as expenses of management (*CTA 2010, s 63*).

Chapter 16

Buy-to-let mortgages

Liz Syms, MD of Connect IFA Ltd (Trading as Connect Mortgages), specialist mortgage advisor to property investors

> ## SIGNPOSTS
>
> - **General** – Properties in general potentially fall into different categories. This chapter explains from a mortgage or loan perspective what type of classification a property is given based on its use (see **16.1–16.4**).
>
> - **Residential and buy-to-let mortgages** – How do various types of mortgages compare? It is important for landlords to obtain the correct mortgage type based on the intended use of the property (see **16.5–16.6**).
>
> - **Buy-to-let affordability calculations** – In practice, lenders use a formula to calculate the loan size available from the investment returns. In September 2016, a supervisory statement was published by the Bank of England and Prudential Regulation Authority, which finalised the rules aimed at curtailing inappropriate lending and the potential for excessive credit losses (see **16.7–16.8**).
>
> - **Other borrowing criteria for a buy-to-let mortgage** – Different types of applicants potentially include first-time buyers, expats, consumers and companies. There are also different types of repayment schemes, age and term requirements, deposit sizes and loan limits, large portfolio holder limits, minimum income requirements, credit worthiness, lending implications for different property types and bridging finance to consider, as appropriate (see **16.9–16.32**).
>
> - **Costs associated with a buy-to-let mortgage** – A landlord will need to consider various costs in relation to the mortgage, such as survey fees, mortgage lender and broker fees, stamp duty land tax and legal fees. These costs need to be factored in when considering the profitability of the portfolio (see **16.33–16.37**).
>
> - **Other buy-to-let finance considerations** – This chapter explores how different interest rate types compare for example the difference between a fixed rate and a tracker rate. Investors should consider

16.1 *Buy-to-let mortgages*

> other mortgage features in relation to their strategy, such as penalties for coming out of a mortgage early, and should also look at a variety of protection plans for their portfolios (see **16. 38–16.40**).
>
> - **Increasing the buy-to-let portfolio** – To grow a portfolio, investors need access to additional funds. This Chapter explores the different ways to extract value from their existing property, and other tools investors can use to grow their portfolios (see **16.41–16.45**).
>
> - **Taxation and mortgage implications** – This chapter also looks at the types of companies accepted by lenders; how these are underwritten and how products compare between limited company and individual mortgages, including focus on security requirements; and information on mortgage requirements when considering incorporating an existing portfolio, including lender requirements around deposits (see **16.46–16.60**).
>
> - **The mortgage process via a broker** – The mortgage process from enquiry to completion can be difficult, and mortgage brokers and accountants often have an important role in the process. Certain documentation will be requested by typical lenders to support a mortgage application, including income verification documents that accountants can assist their clients in supplying (see **16.61–16.64**).
>
> - **Alternatives to incorporation** – Investors may decide to consider other strategies as an alternative to incorporation, such as rent reviews and higher yielding property types (see **16.65**).
>
> - **Summary** – Professional advice should be sought by a property investor from a suitably knowledgeable, qualified and experienced mortgage broker (see **16.66**).

INTRODUCTION

16.1 This chapter outlines the basics of mortgages, and considerations for individuals when evaluating their existing property portfolio or considering a property purchase. The chapter also focusses on the mortgages that investors use for the purchase of a buy-to-let property, and outlines some information around residential and commercial mortgages for comparative purposes.

DIFFERENT PROPERTY TYPES

Residential property

16.2 This is a property being used as an individual's principle primary residence.

Buy-to-let property

16.3 Also referred to as a 'residential investment property', buy-to-let (BTL) property may be owned by an individual or company, which is then subsequently let to 'tenants'. These tenants have an agreement to occupy the property as their home, via a contract such as an assured shorthold tenancy (AST) agreement.

An AST agreement is the legal contract between the landlord who is the owner of the property, and the tenant who occupies the property. This contract sets out the length of time the tenant may occupy the property for, the monthly rent they must pay and any other conditions the tenant and landlord must adhere to.

The term of the AST agreement will normally grant the tenant occupation for a minimum of six months, but could be agreed on a longer basis.

Commercial property

16.4 A commercial property is defined as property where the occupants are a business rather than an individual, such as shops, warehouses and offices. The property can be just a commercial premise or it may be of 'mixed use' or 'semi-commercial' by including a residential element on its legal title such as a residential dwelling above or adjacent to the commercial dwelling.

An individual or company may occupy the premises to run their own business, and this would be called a commercial trading property.

Alternatively, an individual or company may purchase the property to let to another business, and this would be called a commercial investment property. Similar to an AST agreement on a BTL property, a contract will be entered into between the owner and occupier of the property to set out the terms of occupation. The minimum term is usually three years, and will often be considerably longer.

COMPARISON BETWEEN A RESIDENTIAL MORTGAGE AND A BUY-TO-LET MORTGAGE

Residential mortgage

16.5 An individual looking to purchase a property to live in will need to arrange a residential mortgage. The loan approval amongst other things will be subject to the lender's affordability criteria.

In the past, some lenders have been guilty of adopting a relaxed attitude to assessing affordability. Some would offer loans that were based on an individual's own self-declaration of income, without requesting evidence of this income.

16.6 *Buy-to-let mortgages*

This and other lending practices were seen to contribute to the crash of the market. As a consequence, the industry regulators, the Financial Conduct Authority (FCA), conducted a review of the market and implemented tighter controls, particularly around affordability.

Each application to a lender for a residential mortgage now consists of an assessment of the applicant's income and outgoings to determine if the mortgage they require for a property they wish to live is affordable. The lender also requires full evidence of the declared income and declared outgoings to justify the decision and meet the regulator's requirements.

There are wide variants, however, between lender offerings in terms of how much they deem affordable and are prepared to lend. This is because each lender has created its own affordability model, and will assess affordability and risk based on their own interpretation and experience. An applicant looking to borrow a specific sum may be declined that sum by one lender but approved by another.

Whilst lenders do not share the algorithms around their own affordability model, many now have a 'calculator' on their website that an individual can use to get a guide of the mortgage amount that lender may consider.

Buy-to-let mortgages

16.6 BTL mortgages are used to buy a residential investment property. The BTL mortgage was specifically created for the residential investment market by residential lenders. BTL loans are similar to a residential mortgage; however, they are unique in that the lender gives specific permission within the loan agreement for the property to be let to a tenant.

The loan agreement may also specify conditions, such as the type of tenant. For example, not all lenders will allow lettings to tenants who are in receipt of housing benefits.

The loan agreement will specifically prohibit the borrower from occupying the property themselves. The reason for this is that the lender is not assessing the borrower's affordability to meet the monthly payments from their own income.

Instead, the loan approval is assessed based on the anticipated rent exceeding the expected monthly mortgage payment with an additional margin of typically 25–45% to cover running costs.

> **Focus**
>
> Because the lender is not assessing affordability, there is a risk that some borrowers may view a BTL mortgage as an easier way of obtaining a mortgage for a property they actually wish to live in. This risk is present because of the more stringent requirements implemented by the FCA around affordability for a residential loan, meaning some applicants are unable to borrow via residential mortgage.

BTL lenders are actively looking for risks of this nature, and may decline an application if they suspect the applicant does plan to occupy the property. They may be suspicious that this is the case in circumstances such as a proposed BTL purchase being of higher value than the applicant's current residence, or larger or closer to the applicant's workplace.

Lenders will also complete checks after the mortgage has completed, to determine who is occupying the property. Where it is found that the borrower has taken occupation, the lender is likely to demand that the loan is repaid and is also likely to share negative information about the borrower with other lenders, making it very difficult for that borrower to secure further loans.

BUY-TO-LET AFFORDABILITY CALCULATIONS

16.7 Lenders calculate if a BTL mortgage is affordable by the use of a formula that compares the potential rental income with the expected mortgage payment, and considers some running costs or mortgage payment increases.

The actual calculation method does vary between lenders, and is based on the lenders own affordability modelling and risk interpretation. One lender may require the rent payments to be 25% more than the actual proposed mortgage payment. Another lender may use a 'notional' or 'stressed' interest rate when calculating what a potential mortgage payment would be if rates were to rise, and then expect the rent to be at least 25% more than this projected higher mortgage payment.

This could make a significant difference to the size of mortgage that may be approved, as demonstrated in the following example.

Example 16.1—Affordability of a BTL loan

Property purchase price: £200,000

Loan required: 75% (eg £150,000)

Loan on an 'interest only basis' for 25 years

Lender one

Interest rate 4.09%

This lender calculates the affordability for the loan based on the actual monthly mortgage payment that the borrower will make.

Monthly mortgage payment:	£511.25 (£150,000 × 4.09%/12)
Rent needs to be at least 25% higher than this (say):	£639.06 (£511.25 × 125%)

16.8 Buy-to-let mortgages

Lender two

Interest rate 4.09%

Lender two takes a more cautious approach. Whilst the interest rate charged may be the same as lender one, they make an assumption that rates will increase to (say) 5.5%. They then calculate the mortgage payments that would be due on this rate and require that the market achievable rent is at least 125% of this figure

Monthly mortgage payment:	£511.25	(£150,000 × 4.09%/12)
Projected payments if increase to 5.5%	£687.50	(£150,000 × 5.5%/12)
Rent needs to be at least 25% higher than this:	£859.37	(£687.50 × 125%)

If the property could only achieve a market rent of (say) £750, clearly this would dictate which type of lender the borrower could approach, if they wished to achieve the full loan size of £150,000.

CHANGES TO BUY-TO-LET AFFORDABILITY

16.8 In March 2016, The Bank of England and the Prudential Regulation Authority (PRA) issued a consultation paper seeking views on its proposals around the standards that it felt lenders should adhere to when underwriting BTL mortgages. The aims of the proposals were to curtail inappropriate lending and the potential for excessive credit losses.

In September 2016, a supervisory statement was issued which finalised the rules. The rules require that the lenders should consider the impact of future rate rises and the additional costs that the tax relief changes could have on the borrower's future ability to meet mortgage payments.

The rules require lenders to apply special underwriting to portfolio landlords. Portfolio landlords they have determined are those that own four or more properties. The special underwriting should consider the makeup of the existing portfolio, such as the average loan to value (LTV), other assets and liabilities and how the new acquisition or refinance sits within the overall business plan.

One other key requirement is that BTL mortgages should be stressed tested at a rate of 5.5%, to allow for potential future rate rises. They then require the lender to further factor in the costs of running the portfolio, such as management and service fees, maintenance, future tax liabilities and voids. The reality, therefore, is that lenders may require the rent to be as high as 145% of an assumed mortgage payment at a rate of 5.5%

The rules do, however, allow for longer term fixed-rate mortgages of five or more years to be excluded from the minimum 5.5% stress testing, because of the security of payments against rate rises.

Thus, we have seen an increase of lenders offering five-year fixed-rate mortgages with rental calculations based on the actual rate taken. We have also seen lenders introduce products that allow personal income to make up any shortfall in rent. At this moment in time, therefore, the market has adapted to continue to offer mortgage products to serve investors who wish to buy a property for capital growth potential, rather than the strength of the rental income.

OTHER BORROWING CRITERIA FOR A BUY-TO-LET MORTGAGE

Applicant types

Owner occupiers

16.9 For BTL, in general, lenders prefer the applicant to be an existing home owner, and many of these lenders insist that there is also an existing residential mortgage in place.

It is common for a BTL landlord to hold a portfolio of property, yet be a tenant rather than the owner of the property they live in. There are some lenders who will cater for this type of borrower.

First-time buyer

16.10 Lenders in general are not keen to lend on a BTL basis to a first-time buyer. This is because of the perceived increased risk that the applicant may subsequently move in to the property.

Some lenders do offer a solution by assessing the applicant's individual affordability to meet the mortgage payments in addition to the rental assessment.

Other lenders (but not all) will allow a first time buyer to be a second applicant.

16.11 Identifying lenders who will consider first-time buyers as the main or second applicant may be useful for tax planning. It could be beneficial, for example, for a sibling of a property investor who is maybe a student or a low income earner to be added to the property to mitigate some tax.

Consumer buy-to-let borrower

16.12 This is a borrower looking to raise a BTL mortgage on a property they either currently live in or used to live in.

16.13 *Buy-to-let mortgages*

If this is the first BTL property they will own, and they are having to do this out of restricted choice (eg being unable to sell the property), this BTL mortgage will be treated as a 'consumer BTL.

Some, but not all lenders will consider consumer BTL applicants. If the lender accepts these types of applicants, it means the lender has some additional regulatory responsibility to ensure the loan is appropriate and lending is responsible.

The borrower would then qualify for some recourse via the Financial Ombudsman should problems arise in the future. A standard BTL mortgage in the main does not have such recourse with the Financial Ombudsman if they need to complain about the lender or mortgage adviser.

Expats and foreign nationals

16.13 An 'expat' is a UK citizen who no longer resides in the UK. There is a pool of lenders that do cater for an expat applicant looking to buy a BTL property in the UK. Sometimes, the criteria or products on offer from these lenders will be different to that on offer to UK residents.

Foreign nationals who wish to invest in a BTL property in the UK can also be catered for. However, lenders will decline applicants from sanctioned countries.

Companies

16.14 Many lenders (but not all) now have an offering for applicants who wish to purchase a property with their company or limited liability partnership as the purchase vehicle.

This has become increasingly popular due to taxation changes to mortgage interest relief, and so is explored in greater detail further on in this Chapter.

Repaying a buy-to-let mortgage

16.15 Whilst it is common for most BTL borrowers to take a BTL mortgage on an interest-only basis, all lenders do offer the choice of interest only or a capital and interest mortgage (often referred to as a repayment mortgage).

(a) A capital and interest mortgage is where the borrower pays a monthly payment that consists of both payments of capital sum owed and the cost of the interest for the loan. The amount of capital outstanding gradually diminishes over the mortgage term. A capital and interest mortgage is a guaranteed way to ensure that the mortgage is paid off in full at the end of the term, providing each required monthly payment is met in full, as it falls due.

Example 16.2—BTL mortgage illustration

£150,000 mortgage; interest rate 3.99%; mortgage term 25 years.

Total monthly payment £791.11

Mortgage point (subject to no interest rate changes)	Interest repaid	Capital repaid	Outstanding balance
Month one	£498.87	£292.25	£150,000
Month 60	£28,096.04	£19,370.67	£130,664.33
Month 180	£70,587.56	£71,844.05	£78,190.95
End of mortgage	£87,394.05	£150,035	Nil

(b) An interest only mortgage is where the monthly payment to the lender consists only of the interest on the loan amount, with no element of ongoing repayment of the outstanding capital.

Using the example above, the monthly payments for an interest only mortgage would be £498.75, subject to no changes in the interest rate.

The significant attraction of an interest only mortgage for BTL borrowers is that the monthly payments are considerably lower than a capital and interest mortgage. However, the whole mortgage debt will still be outstanding at the end of the mortgage term.

The total cost of the interest, however, over the 25 years would be £149,625, because nothing has been repaid off the capital during the 25 years.

Lenders are willing to offer this option to BTL borrowers as the property is not their main residence. The borrower could choose to sell the property at the end of the mortgage term to repay the loan. Lenders are far more cautious in offering an interest only option for a residential mortgage as the borrower may be forced to sell the property they actually live in to repay the mortgage at the end of the term, an issue they do not have for a BTL borrower.

Age and term requirements for a buy-to-let mortgage

Age

16.16 BTL is seen as a long-term investment. Investors are not always keen to sell their properties at retirement. Access to capital sums from pension schemes have fuelled the interest of older borrowers looking to invest in BTL property.

16.17 *Buy-to-let mortgages*

Due to demand therefore, more and more lenders have adjusted their criteria and look to accommodate older applicants. Whilst some lenders still have some catching up to do and offer mortgages that run to the maximum age of 65, others are willing to go to age 85 and beyond.

While it is legal for an 18-year-old to take a BTL loan, and some lenders will consider these applicants, BTL lenders typically prefer to lend where the applicants are over 21.

Term

16.17 A typical lender will offer a mortgage term between five and 25 years. Some lenders, however, do cater for terms as low as three years or as high as 35 years.

Most BTL mortgages are arranged on an interest only basis. This means that the monthly payments will remain the same, regardless of how long the mortgage is taken for. As the mortgage capital sum would, however, need to be repaid at the end of the term taken, selecting the longest possible term would provide the greatest flexibility over the longer term.

Loan sizes

Deposits

16.18

> **Focus**
>
> Currently, a borrower will need a minimum of 15% of the lower of the property's purchase price or property value as deposit in order to secure a BTL mortgage. This increases to 20%, if the borrower is not an existing landlord. A 15% deposit means a maximum loan size of 85% of the property purchase price or valuation and this is referred to as 85% loan to value (LTV).

LTV of 85% for a BTL mortgage is available from a limited panel of lenders. More lenders become available at 80%.

A higher deposit of say 25% (equating to a 75% LTV mortgage) will substantially increase the lender choice and the interest rates will become more competitive.

The most competitive mortgage interest rates, however, are available for loans at a 65% LTV or less.

16.19 Lenders will ask the applicant to provide documentary evidence to prove where their deposit is coming from. This is to mitigate any risks of money laundering or non-transparent transactions.

It is acceptable for the deposit to come from savings, refinance or sale of another property, and some lenders will also accept the deposit coming from gifts of money or equity from immediate family members.

Equity in an existing property

16.20 Many borrowers will look to start their property portfolio by raising some capital from the equity in their own home. This strategy can be used to either fund the purchase of one property outright or as the deposit for several purchases.

An 'offset' mortgage is a specific type of residential mortgage that is ideally suited to help property investors fund a deposit. In simple terms, an offset mortgage is secured on the residential home, but gives the option to draw down money in stages as and when required. This means the borrower will only pay interest on the specific monetary amounts as they are drawn down.

Loan size

16.21 Whilst the borrowing sum is dictated by the rent achievable on the property, lenders do also have minimum and maximum loan sizes, as well as minimum property values.

A property value of £50,000 would have a restricted lender choice, as would loan requirements that exceed £1,000,000.

Some lenders require a bigger deposit if the loan size is higher. They may, for example, lend up to 80% for loans sizes not exceeding £300,000, but limit the borrowing to 75% for loan sizes higher than this.

Some lenders favour higher loans more than others, so it is worth the investor shopping around if they are buying higher value properties.

Portfolio limits

16.22 If an investor is looking to build a portfolio, lenders will limit the number of loans that a borrower may have with them. This varies by lender, depending on the lender's own appetite to lend. The limit may be based on the number of loans, or a total monetary amount, or both. Once the lender's limit is exhausted, the borrower will need to find an alternative lender to continue to grow their portfolio.

It is important to note that some lenders also restrict the number of loans the applicant can have with other lenders. For example, they may refuse to lend if the applicant already owns ten or more BTL properties.

This type of lender is only targeting the smaller landlords, so professional landlords looking to grow substantial portfolios should look for lenders with no limit to the existing portfolio size.

16.23 *Buy-to-let mortgages*

Income requirements

16.23 Although the affordability for a BTL loan is based on the rental income covering the mortgage payments, many lenders do still require that the applicant is able to evidence an income. Whilst they may not complete an affordability assessment against this income, the level may be required to be of a minimum amount, such as £25,000.

It is also a requirement of some lenders that this income is derived from non-property related activities. This is to ensure that should the borrower struggle to rent a property, that they have other income sources with which to ensure they can meet the mortgage payments.

With the PRA proposals, it is likely that we will see more lenders considering applicants' overall financial profile as part of their underwriting.

When considering income, it is worth noting that lenders also have criteria in relation to how long the applicant has been employed or self-employed for. Applicants with self-employed status of one year or less will have a more limited pool of lenders to choose from.

Credit worthiness

16.24 The best mortgage rates will be available to applicants with good credit ratings. However, some lenders will now consider past credit blips, especially when these are historic.

The degree of the credit issues will dictate both the interest rate offered, and also the maximum LTV offered.

Property types

16.25 The location of a property, the type of property and how new or old the property is, can have an implication on the lenders and products that may be available.

Investors can increase their income by picking certain property types. Properties that are let to multiple tenants can increase the yield and profits that the property generates.

Properties in need of refurbishment can be a good investment to gain capital value, as can properties that can be added to or developed.

These types of properties require more specialist lenders and market knowledge.

Houses in multiple occupation

16.26 A property that is let to multiple individuals and unconnected tenants, such as student lets, may be classed as a house in multiple occupation (HMO).

Some HMOs require the landlord to hold a licence. The implications of this are that they would need to adhere to regulatory requirements, such as building and fire regulations.

It is mandatory for a landlord to have a licence on a property if there are three or more floors *and* five or more tenants *and* shared facilities. Where a mandatory licence is not required (eg a property with just two stories), the local authority can still require a licence by using additional or selective licencing powers.

If an investor plans to let to multiple tenants, he will need to check with the local authority for that property to establish the licence requirements.

16.27 It is important to understand the licence requirements prior to sourcing a mortgage, as this can dictate the lender's willingness to lend.

Where some lenders are happy to lend on all HMO types, some lenders will only consider HMO property that does not require a licence. Other factors of criteria are also taken into account, such as the number of tenants, if there are locks on the internal doors, if the tenants are all named on one tenancy agreement (AST) or several agreements, and also the experience of the landlord.

Many high street BTL lenders will consider a four-bedroom HMO to students all on one tenancy agreement, but a ten-bedroom HMO with locks on doors and needing a licence will mean a different and more specialist lender will be needed.

Properties in need of renovation

16.28 Many investors look to buy property that requires work which they hope will then create additional capital value. If the investor has cash available to them, the investor could simply purchase the property outright. Finance can then be arranged on the property when the renovations are complete or close to completion.

If the investor does not have cash available to purchase the property outright, he would need to consider some form of finance to assist.

Lettable condition

16.29 BTL mortgages are generally only available for properties that are in a 'lettable' condition. This means there will need to be a working kitchen, a bathroom, and the roof and windows etc. will need to be in a reasonable condition.

Even where the property is of a lower standard than the investor would like to live in for themselves, providing the lender's surveyor confirms it is 'lettable' and of a 'suitable security' they will be able to arrange a BTL mortgage on it.

16.30 The surveyor may still recommend that a retention is made until certain works, often damp proofing, is carried out. It is worth noting that the lender will only lend based on the property's value as it stands today, not the projected value after any work has been completed.

16.31 *Buy-to-let mortgages*

Light/cosmetic refurbishment

16.31 Some lenders offer a mortgage product where the valuer will give two valuation figures on the first visit to the property, one for its current condition, and one on the anticipated value once the schedule of works is completed. On this scheme, they will accept properties that are not in an immediately lettable condition, as long as the works can be completed in a short period of time (eg a maximum of three months).

When the work is complete, the investor can ask the lender to request that the surveyor revisits the property and checks the work that has been done. If the work has been done to the surveyor's satisfaction and the property value has increased as anticipated, the lender will release additional funds based on the increased value. This will be subject to the lender's rental calculation being met at the increased property value.

Alternative ('bridge') finance

16.32 If the property is deemed to be in a currently 'unlettable' condition a BTL mortgage will not normally be an option if it will take some time to bring the property up to a lettable condition.

This is because the affordability for the BTL loan is based on the rental income. If the rent cannot be received because of the work required, the mortgage will not be deemed affordable. Bridge lenders can offer short-term finance to enable the property to be purchased and then work can be carried out to bring the property up to lettable condition.

Short-term finance is typically offered between three and twelve months. The interest cost is higher than a BTL mortgage to reflect the shorter term the lender has to make a return and the additional risks involved.

A form of bridge finance is also used where a property is to be developed, for example the conversion of a three storey terrace into three flats.

The cost of the bridge finance has come down, but is still more expensive than a standard BTL mortgage, so work should be completed as quickly as possible.

Once the work is complete, the property can then be re-mortgaged to a standard BTL mortgage, although not every lender will allow an investor to do this until they have owned the property for a minimum of six months.

COSTS ASSOCIATED WITH A BUY-TO-LET MORTGAGE

Survey fee

16.33 It is a requirement of any BTL lender that the property is surveyed before they will approve the lending. The cost of the survey will vary depending on the property's value and the lender chosen, but is typically around £350 for a £100,000 property. This price is for a general valuation for mortgage purposes only, and although the borrower would normally get a copy of the report, there would be limited comeback in the event of future problems with the property, such as damp or structural issues.

A more comprehensive survey called a 'homebuyers report' could be considered, although this can cost up to twice the amount of a standard survey. This type of survey will provide the investor with greater detail about the property's general condition as well as the valuation for the lender.

Mortgage lender fees

16.34 Generally, all lenders have some sort of fee for providing a mortgage or loan. If the fee is described as an 'arrangement fee' it can often be added to the borrowing, but this will increase the loan and it will attract interest charges by becoming part of the overall loan amount.

If the fee is described as a 'booking fee' it is usually payable up front, when a full mortgage application is submitted to the lender. This fee is not normally refundable if the mortgage does not proceed for any reason.

Mortgage lender fees can range from several hundred pounds up to 3.5% of the amount being borrowed. Investors should add in the cost of these fees when comparing mortgage products.

Stamp duty land tax and land and buildings transaction tax

16.35 Stamp duty land tax (SDLT) is payable via the solicitor on the completion of a purchase. The SDLT cost is broadly calculated by multiplying the chargeable consideration against the percentage payable for each appropriate rate band (although a different basis of calculation will generally apply if an existing property portfolio is transferred to a company: see **Chapter 13**). From 1 April 2016, BTL and second home purchases are generally charged an additional 3%.

In Scotland, stamp duty land tax was replaced by land and buildings transaction tax (LBTT). An additional dwellings supplement of 3% applies to second home purchases in Scotland.

A useful tool to calculate SDLT can be found on the Gov.uk website (www.tax.service.gov.uk/calculate-stamp-duty-land-tax/#/intro).For detailed commentary on SDLT and LBTT, see **Chapter 14**.

Legal fees

16.36 Solicitor's legal fees will vary depending on the type of property transaction. For example, a solicitor may charge more for a commercial or bridging transaction than they would for a standard BTL transaction because of the different levels of complexity.

16.37 *Buy-to-let mortgages*

The solicitor's bill will always also include what is known as 'disbursements'. These disbursements include the Land Registry fees, telegraphic transfer fees and search fees. The amounts vary depending on the purchase price and location of the property, so investors should seek a quote for the costs in advance of instructing a solicitor.

For standard BTL mortgages, in many cases the lender will allow the solicitor that the client has picked for themselves to also act on the lenders behalf. There are some lenders however who restrict the solicitors they will allow to act for them and this could result in the investor paying for both theirs and the lender's solicitor fees.

Mortgage broker fees

16.37 A mortgage broker fee is normally charged for the expertise of researching and arranging a mortgage with the most appropriate and competitive lender. An independent mortgage broker can save the investor time and money by searching through the majority of the lenders in the market place and advising how each product differs with its rates and terms.

A good broker will also deal with all the paperwork and administration, plus liaise with all the associated professionals such as the solicitor, accountant and estate agent to help achieve a smooth completion.

OTHER BUY-TO-LET CONSIDERATIONS

Interest rates

16.38 All lenders have a standard variable rate (or reversion rate) which is priced at a margin above the Bank of England base rate, London interbank offered rate (LIBOR), or using their own method of calculation to give a variable rate.

As the Bank of England changes the base rate, lenders will increase or decrease their standard rate to maintain their profit margin. The current Bank of England rate is 0.25%. (August 2016). LIBOR is priced each quarter and is set by the banks themselves.

> **Focus**
>
> To attract business, lenders will often forgo some of their profit margin in the early years of the mortgage and offer an interest rate 'deal'.
>
> The two main types of mortgage rate 'deal' are explained below:

(a) Fixed: The lender will offer a fixed rate of interest that will not increase or decrease during the initial fixed-rate term, even if there are changes to their standard variable rate. If market interest rates rise, borrowers will benefit from cheaper than average payments; or if interest rates fall, they may end up paying over the odds. They will, however, have the security of knowing exactly what the monthly mortgage payments will be for a set period of time.

(b) Trackers (and discounts): Often slightly cheaper (but not always) than fixed rates. If the rate is lower than a fixed rate it will mean initial lower monthly payments. However, payments may go up during the initial rate term. Likewise, payments can also go down if interest rates are reduced. The terminology 'discount' means a discount is taken off the lender's standard variable rate. The terminology 'tracker' means that the interest rate is set at a margin above or below the current Bank of England base rate or LIBOR rate.

Early repayment charges

16.39 Many mortgage deals have an early repayment charge if the investor pays off some or all of their mortgage early. It is important to consider the impact of these charges against a purchase strategy.

For example, if a property is being purchased to renovate and sell on, it would be important to avoid any early repayment charges (ERCs), which can potentially run into thousands of pounds and severely impact on the profit margins.

Early repayment charges usually only apply for the period of time the investor takes an initial rate deal for. For example, there may be a penalty of 3% of the loan within two years on a two-year fixed rate.

Investors should also look out for mortgage product interest rates with an initial very attractive rate, but then have an early repayment charge that extends beyond the initial rate deal, committing the loan to a less competitive lender rate.

Protecting the buy-to-let portfolio

16.40 The only compulsory requirement in relation to insurance that is set by the mortgage lenders is that the property must be insured against fire, theft and subsidence. This plan, called buildings and contents insurance, can be taken with the lender or can be taken with any provider in the market.

The lender may charge an administration fee if their insurance plan is not used to cover the costs of 'checking' the plan is suitable to cover their security.

Borrowers should also consider a range of other insurances to protect their property. For an additional premium to the property insurance, borrowers can protect their rental income if a tenant doesn't pay.

Borrowers should also consider the impact to their portfolio in the event of death, serious illness or other incapacity. If ill-health causes financial difficulty in meeting personal commitments such as loans, credit cards or mortgage

16.41 *Buy-to-let mortgages*

payments this could affect the borrower's credit rating, and in turn affect their ability to raise further finance, or renegotiate finance on the portfolio.

Mortgages held in an individual's name cannot be transferred to another party and therefore would have to be repaid in the event of that individual's death. This could be through selling the property or through life cover.

INCREASING THE BUY-TO-LET PORTFOLIO

16.41 To build a substantial portfolio, investors will need access to additional funds on an ongoing basis to cover deposits and fees. This can be achieved using their existing portfolio in the following ways.

Further advances

16.42 If the property has increased in value, perhaps through refurbishment or a general inflationary increase over time, it is possible to go back to the existing lender and ask to borrow more money. This is called a 'further advance'.

A new survey will normally be required to check the current value of the property, and the loan will be restricted to the maximum LTV (loan to value) the lender offers. The rent will need to be sufficient to meet the lender's criteria for the higher amount of borrowing.

Most lenders will not allow further advances until the property has been owned by the investor for at least six months.

Re-mortgages

16.43 Where additional borrowing requirements cannot be met by the existing lender using a further advance, or perhaps if a competing lender offers a better interest rate, it may be possible to re-mortgage.

This means a new lender will grant a mortgage which will be used to repay the existing lender. If a higher loan sum is taken than needed to repay the existing lender, this is called 'capital raising'. The capital raised in this way could be used to fund additional property purchases.

As this is a new legal transaction, a new survey will be required and a solicitor will be needed to complete the legal work. The costs of the survey and legal work may make this option more expensive. However, some new lenders will offer to pay some or all of the costs to re-mortgage to them.

Many lenders will not normally allow a re-mortgage to them until the investor has owned the property for at least six months. There are some specialist lenders however who will consider re-mortgages at an earlier point.

Second charge or equity loans

16.44 These are loans that are secured on a BTL, residential or commercial property but sit behind the primary mortgage lender as a 'second charge' on the Land Registry.

The interest rates charged by these lenders are generally higher than a first charge mortgage. This is because in the event of a disposal of the property, the first-charge lender is always paid first from the proceeds. There may be insufficient funds to repay the second-charge lender once this is done, especially if the property has been repossessed.

These types of loans can be useful and attractive if the mortgage interest rate being charged by the first-charge lender is highly competitive, but this lender does not offer any further borrowing options.

It allows the investor to leave the first mortgage untouched, but still gain access to the equity in the property from capital raised for further property investment.

A standard second charge loan works in the same way as a mortgage in that monthly payments are made to cover the cost of the interest.

An equity loan, however, has no monthly payments. This is because instead of paying monthly interest, the lender benefits from a share of the growth in the value of the property from when the loan is taken until when the loan is repaid.

This is a useful way for investors to raise capital from their portfolio whilst still maintaining the property's cash flow. Because there is no rental calculation affordability test (as there are no monthly payments), it can increase the size of loan available when compared to other options.

Bridging finance

16.45 Bridging finance is a short-term loan raised on either a BTL, commercial or residential property. As a short-term solution, the loan term is usually for a maximum of 12 months. Bridging finance can usually be arranged much more quickly than BTL finance.

It can be used for a variety of reasons, but is often used when funds are required quickly. They are a suitable means of finance to acquire a property at auction, as a purchaser at auction often only has three or four weeks to complete on the property purchase.

Another common use for bridging finance is to fund the purchase if the property is not in a suitable condition for a normal BTL mortgage, such as a property requiring refurbishment or development.

In some cases, bridging can be used to arrange up to 100% of a property's purchase price, with a loan secured on the subject property and/or cross charged on one or more other properties in the existing portfolio.

16.46 *Buy-to-let mortgages*

TAXATION AND MORTGAGE IMPLICATIONS

16.46

> **Focus**
>
> Mortgage advisers should have a basic knowledge of the tax implications affecting a decision on how a mortgage is set up. However, they cannot give tax advice, so they should also look to recommend that the investors seek professional property tax advice from a qualified adviser, before proceeding with a mortgage.

Whether a mortgage is done in joint or single names or in the name of a company, the way the mortgage is set up in the first place is important, as changes cannot be done easily or without cost after the mortgage is in place.

The introduction of tax changes around mortgage interest relief etc for those investors who hold a property in their individual names (see **Chapter 3**) has resulted in mortgage advisers seeing increased enquiries for loans for companies.

In turn, more lenders have entered this market by introducing BTL loans for companies where they previously only offered the loans to individual applicants. Products and criteria available for company transactions have also become more competitive, increasing the availability of funding.

A survey earlier in the year by one of the lenders found that 40% of its landlords were now considering companies for their portfolios and future purchases.

What types of company are acceptable?

16.47 The company can be a new company, an existing company or a subsidiary.

Whilst some lenders will consider lending to an existing trading company, these are few and far between due to the complications of recovering the property if the trading business fails.

Most lenders prefer to lend to a special purpose vehicle (SPV) set up solely to own, buy, sell and let property.

At the start of the mortgage application, the company should be registered at Companies House and should also have an appropriate SIC code in place.

The SIC codes typically accepted by the lender are:

- 68100 – Buying and selling of own real estate;
- 68209 – Other letting and operating of own or leased real estate;
- 68320 – Management of real estate on a fee or contract basis;
- 68201 – Renting and operating of Housing Association real estate.

As with other criteria, this does vary from lender to lender, and should be checked in advance of a mortgage application.

If the location of the company is England or Wales, there will be a greater choice of lending options than if the company is located outside the UK. Whilst some lenders will consider offshore companies, this is a far more specialised area than a UK company and usually only available via more commercially minded lenders.

That said, an Indian national, living and working in Dubai and buying a property in the UK via an Irish company would still be able to source a lending option!

How is the mortgage underwritten?

16.48 Subject to the company meeting the lender's criteria in terms of its type and SIC codes, the remaining underwriting is identical to an individual BTL application as the underwriting is based on the applicants who will be the directors and shareholders.

The affordability is still calculated using the lender's rental calculation method, and the individual is still assessed in relation to their income and credit status.

The lenders will expect all directors of the company to be party to the mortgage, and will underwrite all directors in this way. Lenders may also expect all majority shareholders to be party to the mortgage. They deem this as typically any shareholder with 25% or more shared in the company. However, this can vary from lender to lender.

If one of the shareholders is another company, where the lender will consider this, they will insist on tracing back to the individual(s) who are the beneficial owners so that they can be underwritten in accordance with the lender's criteria.

> **Focus**
>
> It is worth noting that the individual directors and shareholders of the company will be required in almost all cases to offer a personal guarantee for the loan.
>
> In addition, the lender may also request a floating charge or a debenture against the company.

How do the mortgage products compare?

16.49 If, having spoken to their accountant, the investor decides that using a company is the most effective tax solution for new purchases going forward, the investor should then consider how the mortgage costs and features differ.

The below table outlines where there is no difference and where there are areas for consideration.

16.50 *Buy-to-let mortgages*

Mortgage feature	Individual loan versus a company loan
Interest rate	Range of rate types for both, but company rates typically slightly higher than individual rates
LTV (loan to value)	No difference, up to 85% for both company and individual applications
Age and term	No difference
Property types	No difference
Applicant income and credit status	No difference
Fees and costs	Lenders arrangement fees are typically a little higher and most lenders will not allow the applicants solicitor to act on the lenders behalf for a company loan resulting in higher legal fees.
Repayment method	No difference
Rental calculations	Some lenders calculations for companies are more favourable, due to the more favourable tax treatment.

The main consideration is costs in relation to mortgage fees and mortgage interest payments, which are in addition to any costs incurred for setting up and running a company.

The investor can ask the mortgage broker or lender to supply an illustration outlining the costs for both the most suitable lending option when taking out the mortgage in an individual name(s), and also the most suitable when taking out the mortgage in the name of a company.

That way, the additional mortgage costs can be compared and considered with the tax implications as part of a whole assessment.

If the demand for company mortgages increases, we are likely to see increased competition and a closer alignment between the interest costs and fees for company mortgages versus individual mortgages.

Operating through a company

16.50 If holding properties inside a company is decided as the correct solution for an investor, new purchases can be made fairly simply this way. However, moving an existing property or portfolio from the name of an individual to a company does come with potential additional costs and complications.

As the company is a separate legal entity to the individual name, the existing lender whom has lent money to the individual on that property, will not simply transfer the mortgage to the company.

The lender will treat the transaction as a sale of the property by the individual and a purchase of the property by the company.

Without any mitigation or planning, the incorporation of a property portfolio can create substantial costs in capital gains tax and SDLT (or LBTT in Scotland).

The tax issues of incorporating a residential rental property business are considered in **Chapter 13**.

If this route is chosen, investors should seek guidance on any strategies via advice from their tax specialist or their accountants that may help them mitigate such costs. However, care must be taken to ensure that any such strategies are transparent and acceptable to the lender.

16.51 One other example of complications relates to the deposit. The lender and solicitor will still require a transparent transaction that requires the company to have the required deposit as per the lender product chosen to make the purchase.

Clearly, if the company is a newly set up SPV, the funds are unlikely to be available in the company to demonstrate this. Lenders would normally look for a company's bank statement to demonstrate these funds.

Many lenders have given some consideration on how this potential complication can be overcome. The three main options that some lenders will consider approving are outlined below.

Director's loan

16.52 a director of the company that has been set up for the purchases could look to transfer money into the company as a director's loan.

This relies on the director(s) having sufficient capital of their own to be able to lend to the company. Again, for one or two small transactions this may be more viable than a larger number of transactions or larger value properties.

The director(s) would need to demonstrate the availability of the funds by showing a copy of their own personal bank statement.

16.53 It may be that they could have an option to take a director's loan by way of a loan to themselves first via another company if they are a director of another company that does hold sufficient funds.

As long as they can provide evidence via a paper trail of bank statements, the lenders will be satisfied with this.

Director's loan – 'Paper' transaction

16.54 Some of the more flexible lenders will allow the director's loan to be a 'paper' transaction.

16.55 *Buy-to-let mortgages*

This means they will take into consideration any retained profits held within the purchasing company or other companies connected to the director(s).

They will consider accepting this as evidence of deposit, subject to receiving confirmation from the applicant's accountants that the deposit will be managed through the accounts this way.

16.55 While the lender will instruct the solicitor managing the transaction of the acceptance of the source of deposit funds, the solicitor is also responsible for ensuring that they are happy with the transparency of the transaction.

Equity gift

16.56 One other option is to source a lender that will accept an equity gift as the deposit.

This means the current individual property owner 'gifts' equity to the company. As a gift of equity, this eliminates the need to demonstrate for either the individual or the company to have the capital for the deposit.

16.57 A lender will normally look to lend against the lower of the valuation of the property or the purchase price actually paid.

Instead, with an equity gift, they lend against the valuation. They will accept that the physical transfer of cash between the parties will be lower. The equity gift amount still needs to be at the sum required to at least cover the lender's minimum deposit required (eg 25%).

Example 16.3—Incorporation: equity gift

Value – £200,000

Equity gift (25%) – £50,000 (cash sums not required)

Mortgage loan – £150,000

Funds transferred to the individual by the company £150,000

The lender will, however, expect the Land Registry to reflect the total cost the company has had to pay to acquire the property, plus the value of the equity gift.

SDLT (or LBTT) implications will generally need to be considered in relation to funding issues (see **Chapter 14**).

Capital raising

16.58 Irrespective of the strategy adopted, the reality is that the sum actually paid by the company to the individual only needs to be enough to allow the individual to clear any existing mortgage held against the property in their own name.

They may, however, want to use the exercise to capital raise additional funds for further property investment. Most lenders are happy to lend additional sums for this purpose within their LTV limits and subject to satisfactory rental income to meet their affordability requirements.

Commercial and semi-commercial properties

16.59 It is worth noting that properties meeting the definition of a commercial property, that is being let to or occupied by a business rather than an individual on a residential basis, fall outside the tax relief restriction for finance costs as discussed in **Chapter 3**.

Therefore, these type of properties held in individual names may not need to consider incorporation, if the sole or main purpose of incorporation would otherwise be to continue to benefit from tax relief for interest payments.

Applicants for commercial loans are very similar to BTL loans. Commercial loans are offered by lenders who specialise in commercial lending, and include both high street banks with traditional commercial offerings and specialist 'challenger' banks who offer products with more flexibility and are similar to BTL lenders, for example, higher LTVs and interest only terms.

In addition to the standard BTL underwriting, applicants looking for a commercial loan will typically need to show experience in their field and a business plan.

Getting the lender right

16.60 It is important for an investor to consider the strategy in advance of making an application to a lender. The lenders' criteria vary greatly in respect of the deposit requirements.

If a lender is selected that does not allow, for example, gifted equity, and this is the only option for the transaction to be successful, the lender will decline the application. There is a risk that this does not get uncovered until the legal point of the transaction, by which time legal and mortgage costs, as well as time, will be lost.

It is expected that the lender criteria will continue to develop and change over the coming years, as more investors look to incorporate their portfolios as the finance costs restriction is gradually phased in.

THE MORTGAGE PROCESS VIA A BROKER

Working with a specialist mortgage broker

16.61 A mortgage broker that specialises in mortgages for property investment should be able to help the property investor navigate through the

16.62 *Buy-to-let mortgages*

lenders' criteria on all points, to reach the most suitable lender for the overall circumstances and requirements.

The mortgage process is outlined below.

- The mortgage broker completes a full fact-find on the investor.
- The fact-find includes basic details, an income and outgoings assessment and details of any existing properties and mortgages.
- The details of the proposed transaction are gathered.
- Research is completed by the broker, and a lender is sought that meets the applicant's requirements from the fact-finding.
- An independent broker will source options from the range of products and lenders available in the market.
- The broker makes a recommendation of the most suitable option found through the research.
- The broker applies to the lender for a decision in principle' on the applicant's behalf.
- The lender completes a credit check and considers the merits of the application information submitted, and if satisfied, confirms an agreed decision in principle.
- The broker collates with the applicant the supporting documents required by the lender. This typically includes identity and address proof, income evidence, deposit evidence and bank statements.
- The broker submits a full mortgage application to the lender with the supporting documents the lender requires, on behalf of the applicant.
- The lender instructs a surveyor to complete a valuation of the property.
- The surveyor prepares a property report and sends it to the lender.
- The lender's underwriter assesses all the documents and the survey report to make a lending decision.
- The lender issues a binding mortgage offer outlining the terms of the loan.

The above applies to all mortgage applications, regardless of whether they are purchase or re-mortgage transactions, and also regardless of whether they are residential, BTL or commercial transactions.

16.62 Once the mortgage offer has been issued, the applicant's solicitor will complete the legal work required, such as searches, Land Registry and drafting contracts. It is at this point, for purchases, the deposit requirements will need to be satisfied.

The mortgage broker will be less involved during the legal stage, but will liaise with the solicitor to assist if any lender issues arise.

Once the legal work is completed, the funds will be released by the lender and legal completion will take place.

The accountant's role in the mortgage process

16.63 The accountant can assist their client by researching suitably knowledgeable mortgage brokers to whom they can refer their clients.

This can often be a reciprocal arrangement as mortgage brokers, in light of the various tax complexities, are looking for accountants that are knowledgeable in property tax to refer their own clients to.

Accountants can also assist brokers greatly when gathering information about an applicant's income or company details.

16.64 Whilst applicants will have an understanding of their income, it is not uncommon (but perhaps understandable) for applicants to be unable to recall, for example, their exact net profit for the last three years. An application submitted to a lender without accurate information stands a much higher potential to be declined by that lender when the documentary evidence does not match the initial proposal.

Whilst applicants can produce employed income evidence easily such as payslips and P60 certificates, the documents required from self-employed applicants or company directors are often more complex.

A lender may request any combination of the below documents as income evidence for a self-employed applicant or a director:

- Form SA302;
- Tax summary and calculation documents;
- Tax return;
- Accounts;
- Management accounts and projections.

Where a mortgage broker can work directly with the accountant to gather the correct income details and documents, this can greatly increase the application's chances of success.

ALTERNATIVES TO INCORPORATION

16.65 The investor may conclude, after seeking advice, that whilst new purchases should be made via a company, it is not practical or financially viable to incorporate the existing portfolio.

16.66 *Buy-to-let mortgages*

Some options an investor could consider to cover the increased taxation costs include:

(1) Re-evaluate the mortgages on the existing portfolio. Can the properties be re-mortgaged to benefit from lower mortgage interest costs?

(2) Is there margin to increase rents? Demand is strong in a number of areas, and the rents on properties with long standing tenants may not have been increased regularly to the market level.

(3) Consider incorporating a clause in future tenancy agreements that outlines a regular review and increase of the rent.

(4) Where a property is held in joint names between husband and wife and one party has a lower tax rate than the other, consider transferring the ownership into the owner with the lower tax rate. This is called a 'transfer of equity' and it is usually accepted by the lender, although lender approval will need to be sought.

(5) Investors could consider converting or extending existing properties, so that they can be let on a multiple occupancy basis, potentially generating higher rental yields.

Summary

16.66 The information supplied in this chapter is based on the lender offerings in the market place at the time the publication was produced. The lender offerings do change on a regular basis and lender by lender, often in response to market conditions. The information is supplied for general guidance purposes only, and should not be taken as a recommendation of a particular course of action. Professional advice should be sought by a property investor from a suitably knowledgeable, qualified and experienced mortgage broker to determine the best course of action on a case by case basis.

Chapter 17

Dealing with tenants and agents

David Smith, Policy Director, Residential Landlords Association;
Partner, Anthony Gold Solicitors

SIGNPOSTS

- **Buying property to rent** – When buying a property to let, careful consideration should be taken in terms of achievable rent levels versus the costs involved (see **17.1–17.4**).

- **Core rights of tenants** – Tenants have several fundamental rights which must be respected. These rights vary, depending on whether the property is in England, Scotland, Northern Ireland or Wales. Most, but not all, residential tenants are protected by statute. It is important to identify them, as they will have more rights (see **17.5–7.7**).

- **Regulation of agents, etc.** – Many landlords will use an agent. Agents are increasingly restricted, and may have to be members of various schemes or be licensed (see **17.8–17.15**).

- **Selecting a tenant** – This is very important, and doing so with care could avoid a lot of problems later on (see **17.16–17.18**).

- **Terms of a tenancy** – Many tenancy terms are standard, but there are key elements which need to be considered (see **17.19–17.21**).

- **Deposits from tenants** – It is common for landlords to take a deposit from the tenant as a security for them complying with the terms of the tenancy (see **17.22**).

- **References and guarantors** – If a tenant cannot produce sufficient references, a guarantor, who is prepared to take that financial risk for the tenant's benefit, is often sought (see **17.23**).

- **Short-term lets** – If landlords want to let their property on a short-term basis, there are restrictions to be aware of (see **17.24**).

- **'Rent to rent' arrangements** – These should be undertaken with care (see **17.25**).

- **Buying with a tenant in place** – When considering buying with a tenant already in place, a review of the tenancy agreement and deposit should be carried out, as well as assessments regarding the tenant themselves and the current repair of the property (see **17.26–17.29**).

17.1 *Dealing with tenants and agents*

CONSIDERATIONS IN BUYING A TENANTED PROPERTY
17.1

> **Focus**
>
> When buying a property to let, the considerations are very different from buying a house to live in.
>
> In buying a home, the main issues are affordability and whether or not it is personally attractive as a place to live. In buying a rental property, the main issue is whether it is one that can be rented profitably.

Rent

17.2 Careful research should be done into rent levels in the area and those for the same property type. Estate agents are often very optimistic with rent levels when selling property, and these may not in fact be achievable.

If the property is in a new development, it may also be very hard to rent or achieve a much lower rent level while the rest of the development in being completed, as amenities will be missing and the area will be less attractive.

Costs

17.3 Most new landlords fail to properly appreciate the costs involved. The rent paid by the tenant is not the same as the figure that the landlord will have left at the end or have available to pay the mortgage. As well as mortgage payments, it is necessary to consider the costs of:

- Annual gas safety certificates and boiler servicing;
- Energy performance certificates;
- Repairs to the property;
- Electrical tests and safety certificates in areas where these are required;
- Landlord licences and compulsory training courses;
- Service charges for flats to maintain the common parts;
- Charges for consent to let from superior landlords, insurers, mortgage companies etc;
- Letting agent fees;
- Accountant fees; and
- Solicitors fees (where the worst happens).

17.4 On top of these costs, it is important to remember the risks of rent arrears and tenant damage, which can also further erode the profitability of the enterprise. These costs are not optional, and some landlords think that being genuinely able to say they cannot afford them provides some sort of justification for not having paid or done the necessary work. This is not accurate, and so they must be considered as fundamental costs alongside the mortgage payment each month.

For further information on these obligations, please see below and **Chapter 18**.

INTRODUCTION TO TENANCIES

17.5 Tenancies have existed for a long time in British history, almost as long as we have had ownership of land. They have evolved from feudal origins into modern, highly sophisticated, legal relationships.

As such, tenancies have a great deal of law which govern their operation, and contain many traps for the unwary landlord.

FUNDAMENTAL ASPECTS OF BEING A RESIDENTIAL TENANT

17.6

> **Focus**
>
> Tenants have several fundamental rights. Some of these exist because of long-held legal convention or custom, and some are provided specifically by various statutes.
>
> In general, residential tenants have a very high level of protection from unreasonable interference and harassment in the UK, much more than commercial tenants.

A tenancy is essentially a right for the tenant to use the property exclusively as if it were their own for a set period of time. This is particularly important, as it creates two of the key rights that tenants enjoy. That is the right to exclusive possession of the property, which means that the tenant has the right to exclude every other person from access, including the landlord. Linked to this right is the right of quiet enjoyment. This is not a right to silence but a right to enjoy the property quietly, that is without interruption or hindrance from the landlord or anyone else employed by him.

The key point here is that when a landlord lets a property to a residential tenant, they give up much of their control of the property for the duration of the tenancy, and they will only be able to take back that control in serious situations. From a practical point of view, this means the landlord will not be able to go to the property without permission, cannot stay there overnight for their convenience, cannot use it for storage, and cannot use it as a mail drop.

17.7 *Dealing with tenants and agents*

The other very important right that all residential tenants (as indeed do almost all residential occupiers) have is that they cannot be removed from their property without an order of the Court, whether the County Court in England, Wales, and Northern Ireland or the Sheriff's Court in Scotland. This means that there is no right for a landlord to demand that a residential tenant or other occupier leave a property, and it is harassment to do so.

DIFFERENT TENANCY TYPES AND WHAT THEY MEAN
17.7

> **Focus**
>
> There are several different types of tenancy and occupancy right available in the sector. It is important to establish what sort of tenancy a tenant is in possession of, in order to fully understand their rights.

It is also important to understand that different occupiers may all be tenants, but the statutory regime which applies to their tenancy will vary. It is possible that tenants can move between statutory regimes in some cases. They will still be tenants, but the statutory protections will apply in a different way.

It should be noted that it is not normally possible to avoid a specific statutory regime by stating that it will not apply, even if the landlord and tenant have agreed to this. The statutory regimes will apply in the majority of cases, unless the situation falls into one of the specific exceptions; it is not possible to manufacture these to avoid the regime.

The statutory regimes vary across the UK, as housing is devolved to the various regional parliamentary bodies. Accordingly, the situation is in a state of flux in both Wales and Scotland, as new regimes in these areas will come into force at some point prior to 2020.

England

Historically, tenancies in England and Wales were covered by the *Rent Act 1977*. This provided a very high level of protection to tenants indeed as they were tenants for life, were almost impossible to evict and benefited from strict state limits as to the level of their rent and the ability to increase it, which meant that tenants were charged a rent which was far below market levels. It is no longer possible to create these tenancies, and they are dying out as the tenants themselves leave the properties they are in or die; however, there remain a small number (estimated to be less than 100,000) in England and Wales. Where a landlord is dealing with a tenant protected by the *Rent Act 1977* they should be seeking specialist advice as these tenancies are very complex, and the tenant has a great deal of protection.

The vast majority of tenancies fall under the *Housing Act 1988*, which protects most residential tenancies in England and Wales at the current time. This applies to tenancies which were commenced on or after 15 January 1989. Any tenancy that started before that date will fall under the *Rent Act 1977* provisions. The *Housing Act 1988* creates two tenancy types. Assured tenancies were the norm initially, unless a specific notice (called a 'section 20 notice') was served by the landlord on the tenant, telling them that it was not to be an assured tenancy. If a section 20 notice was served on the tenant or the tenancy began after 28 February 1997, the tenancy is very likely to be an assured shorthold tenancy (AST). An assured tenancy is a tenancy for life but at a full market rent. The landlord can only end the tenancy for specific reasons, mainly relating to non-payment of rent and other misbehaviour by the tenant.

If the tenancy is an AST, and the overwhelming majority of residential tenancies in England and Wales are ASTs, the tenancy is one at a full market rent, and the landlord can end it much more easily.

As well as the right to end the tenancy for breaches, the landlord can also bring it to an end at the end of any fixed term agreed with the tenant, although the tenancy cannot normally be ended until the tenant has been in the property for at least six months. If the landlord does not formally bring the tenancy to an end, it will continue until such time as the landlord does formally end the tenancy.

Specific tenancies are excluded from the *Housing Act 1988*. There are a number of exclusions, but the most common are:

- Lettings to tenants who are not individuals or groups of individuals. This would include any situation where the tenant is a limited company;

- Lettings where the tenant is not living in the property as their main home. This would include holiday properties, *pied a terre* or other part-time accommodation;

- Lettings where the rent exceeds £100,000 per annum pro rata. This will usually only apply to the most valuable properties;

- Lettings of properties where the premises includes land which is rated as agricultural land and which makes up more than two acres.

Example 17.1 – Assured shorthold tenancy

Naveen lets a property on a tenancy for one year to Simon and Taran for £700 per month as their main home. They are both individuals and so the tenancy will be an AST.

If she had rented to Simon and Taran's company, Bitza Pizza Ltd, for them to occupy it would not have been an AST because the tenant would have been a company, which is not an individual or group of individuals, even though the final occupiers are unchanged.

17.7 Dealing with tenants and agents

Wales

At the time of writing, the tenancy types in Wales are the same as they are in England. However, the *Renting Homes (Wales) Act 2016* is expected to come into force in 2017/18. This will replace the entire assured tenancy and AST regime in Wales, and after that time no new assured tenancies or ASTs will be created. Any existing tenancies will be converted to the new regime.

The new regime is very similar in that tenancies will be at a market rent, and can only be terminated for breaches of the agreement by the tenant and at the end of any fixed tenancy term. The regime is still to be fully set up, and so information on it is limited at the time of writing. A specialist in Welsh housing law should be found to advise.

Scotland

Scottish tenancies are mostly governed by the *Housing (Scotland) Act 1988*. Most residential tenancies will fall into this regime. The *Housing (Scotland) Act 1988* creates two tenancy types. There are assured tenancies, which are essentially the same as assured tenancies in England; and Short Assured Tenancies (SATs), which are essentially the same as ASTs.

Most tenancies will be SATs, provided that a notice was served on the tenant in advance of the tenancy telling them that the tenancy would be a SAT. The same exclusions apply from the *Housing (Scotland) Act 1988* regime as in England, except that in Scotland there is no maximum rent limit. However, it is not common for a tenancy in Scotland to be for a sum of over £100,000 per annum. As with England, a tenancy will normally be for a minimum of six months, although it can be ended if the tenant breaches the agreement. At the end of a fixed-term tenancy, the tenancy will continue if the landlord has not taken steps to terminate it, and because of a special process in Scotland (called tacit relocation), if the tenancy is not terminated a fresh tenancy will be granted for the same term as the original tenancy or for 12 months, whichever is the shorter.

Scotland is introducing an entirely new tenancy regime through the *Private Housing (Tenancies) (Scotland) Act 2016*. This is likely to come into force at some stage in 2018/19. As with Wales, once the new regime comes into force no new assured tenancies or SATs can be created, and existing tenancies will be migrated into the new regime. The new regime will only allow tenancies to be ended in very limited circumstances, mainly where the tenant is in breach of the agreement, and so landlords will have to have a good reason to end the tenancy. The regime is still to be fully set up and so information on it is limited at the time of writing. A specialist in Scottish housing law should be found to advise.

Northern Ireland

The majority of tenancies in Northern Ireland are governed by the *Private Tenancies (Northern Ireland) Order 2006*. Under this regime, the tenancy

Dealing with tenants and agents **17.8**

continues for whatever time the landlord and tenant agree, and will continue after the end of any fixed term until the landlord takes steps to terminate it. The rent is set at a market level.

USING AN AGENT
17.8

> **Focus**
>
> Landlords are perfectly entitled to let and manage their properties themselves. However, many choose to use a letting agent.
>
> It is important to remember that letting agents are not licensed or regulated, and so agent selection can be of particular importance.

When choosing an agent a landlord should consider a number of different things:

(a) Experience

This is very important. An agent should have experience both in the industry and in the local area. They will need to understand which properties are good and which not so good in the local rental market and the reasons for this, and what can be done to maximise rental returns.

If the property is of a specific type or a specific type of letting is being targeted, it is important that an agent is experienced in this area. For example, lettings to students are very different from those to families, and an agent catering to students will have a very different skill set.

(b) Cost

Cheapest is not always best! Most agents will charge a commission calculated as a percentage of the rent received, which will usually be somewhere between 7% and 17% of the monthly rent, depending on exactly what services are on offer. This is changing, and more agents are offering fixed-price models. However, agents charging lower commission or a low fixed fee may have other hidden charges, and may charge extra for things that are built in to higher-priced services. Some agents may have a lower fee but add a fee for repairs or take a substantial commission on repairs and management from the contractor carrying out the work, so it is important to ask what commission is being taken, if any.

Some agents will offer valuable additional services, such as insurance against loss of rent if a tenant does not pay or against legal fees on eviction. These items may not seem important initially, but can be very valuable if there is a problem later on. Where commission is being charged, it will often be charged for the entire time a tenant is in the property, and this could mean the landlord will be paying the agent for an extended period, so it is important to understand precisely what the agent is charging for, and for how long that charge will be payable.

Agents will also be charging fees to tenants, and these are very variable. In some cases, it has been suggested that agents are effectively charging the landlord and tenant for the same thing. Therefore, landlords may also wish to consider what the agent is charging the tenant for, and how much those charges are.

(c) Training

Good agents will be making sure they keep up-to-date with changes in the law, and will be advising their landlords on matters which affect them.

The landlord is often relying on the agent for advice in complying with their responsibilities, so it is important that the agent is knowledgeable and up-to-date.

(d) Accreditation

While there is no formal licensing of agents, they are able to join professional bodies. These offer codes of conduct, protection for client money, and other benefits which are useful to landlords.

REDRESS, FEES, AND CLIENT MONEY PROTECTION

17.9 All letting agents in England are now required to offer access to free redress schemes run by government approved, independent bodies. This is enforced by penalties issued by local authorities.

Additionally, all agents in England must state on their website and in their offices which scheme they belong to. In the same place, agents must also have a list of their fees for landlords and tenants, so that everyone can see what is being charged.

> **Focus**
>
> Redress schemes are very powerful. They can order agents to pay compensation for losses they have caused, or for bad service.
>
> If a landlord believes they have had bad service, a redress scheme is a very good way of starting to deal with this. The agent must be written to first though and given a chance to respond to the complaint, before the redress scheme is approached.

The Government has also passed legislation which gives it the power to require all agents to offer client money protection. This means that if the agent become insolvent or they steal money, the protection scheme will protect landlords and tenants from money that the agent was holding being lost. The government is consulting on the exact form of these schemes, and they are expected to come into operation during 2017/18.

Scotland

Landlords are required to register with the government in Scotland. Agents are not required to register, but landlords must tell the government about the agents they use, and agents must be assessed by the government as being fit to fulfil that role.

To avoid this being repeated time and again, most reputable agents are registered with the government, and have a registration number the landlord can use.

Wales

In Wales, there are new requirements for agents to be licensed. It is an offence to use an agent who is not registered to manage a property.

All registered agents will have to have completed a training course, so they will have an assured minimum level of knowledge. They will also have to comply with a code of practice, to ensure a minimum standard of service and they can be prosecuted if they fail to do this.

Northern Ireland

In Northern Ireland, landlords need to be registered with the government (see below), but there is no requirement for agents to do so. There is no redress schemes or client money protection available, other than those offered by professional bodies to their members.

> **Example 17.2 – Agent registration**
>
> Dee runs a lettings agency, which has offices in Bristol and Newport. The office in Bristol must be registered with a redress scheme approved in England.
>
> The office in Newport must be registered with the Rent Smart Wales scheme as an agent, and must also be licensed with that scheme to manage property.

17.10 *Dealing with tenants and agents*

AGENCY TYPES

17.10   Most agents offer more than one service type. The fees are usually different for each service and some of them may be charged on fixed fees, while others may be charged on a commission basis by taking a percentage of the rent.

There are three main categories that most agency services tend to fall into, and the majority offer at least two of them. These are:

(a)   Let only

This is the most basic service, and is focused on finding a suitable tenant only. It is increasingly offered as a fixed fee service, but may also be charged as a commission. In some cases, the commission will continue to be payable if the tenant stays in the property after the initial fixed term agreed between the landlord and tenant.

This service will normally include:

- a valuation of the property;
- marketing of the property with internet portals and possible local newspapers and magazines – photography to support those adverts may be charged separately;
- negotiation over the terms of the tenancy with the tenant;
- the taking up of references for the tenant (see below);
- the preparation of a tenancy agreement;
- arrangement of an inventory of the property – the cost of the inventory may be charged separately;
- arranging necessary safety checks for the property pre-tenancy – again, the actual cost of the checks may be separate.
- collection of the initial rent and deposit;
- registration of the deposit with an appropriate scheme if required (see below).

This service will not include ongoing management of the tenancy, and this will be up to the landlord to deal with.

(b)   Rent collection

This service will normally include everything provided for a let only service, with the additional feature that the agent will manage the collection of rent and will chase the tenant where it is not paid.

(c)   Full management

This is usually the most expensive service, and is almost always charged on a commission basis. This will usually include everything in the let only and rent collection service, along with the management of repairs and other issues in the property. This service will usually also include visits to the property to make sure the tenant is looking after it, but landlords should check carefully whether this is part of the service and how many visits are being offered.

This service will not normally include management of the property when it is not tenanted (known as a 'void period'), and this will usually incur an extra charge.

INVENTORY

17.11

> **Focus**
>
> Damage to the property, or it being dirty at the end of the tenancy, are the biggest causes of complaint by landlords against their tenants. It is important to have an inventory to prove that the property has been returned in a worse state than it was when it was let.

It is usual practice to conduct a comprehensive inventory of the property and all of its contents to show its condition at the beginning and end of the tenancy.

An agent will usually arrange this with an independent inventory clerk or conduct it themselves. Some landlords do not bother with this, but without a full inventory at the start and end of the tenancy it is almost impossible to show that the condition of the property has deteriorated, and so deductions from a tenant's deposit are not likely to be possible.

Consents

> **Focus**
>
> Many landlords overlook the need to obtain consent to let. A range of people are interested in every property as they have investment in it, and they may well need to give permission. If there are co-owners they will not necessarily have to give consent to let, but they are entitled to share in the earnings from the property.

17.12 Mortgage companies will usually require consent from them for letting, and this may involve fees or a change in the mortgage type. Some lettings will be prohibited altogether.

Insurance companies will also expect to be told, and will normally charge an increased premium to reflect the higher risk in a let property. If the property is a flat or there is some form of superior landlord, that landlord will also usually need to be asked for permission to let. Again, this may well come with a fee.

17.13 *Dealing with tenants and agents*

ADVERTISING THE PROPERTY

17.13 Property adverts must be accurate and non-misleading. It is an offence to suggest that a property has a feature it does not in fact have, or to conceal something that a reasonable person would consider a detrimental feature.

For example, not mentioning that permission had been given to build a cement factory next door or timing property viewings to avoid the passing of a noisy goods train would be unacceptable.

More commonly, taking photographs from specific angles to conceal a feature or, even worse, changing them with a computer programme would also not be permitted. This would include the use of loose language such as saying a property benefited from 'good schools' when the local schools were average, or that it was good for commuters if the local train station did not have appropriate commuter services.

This type of false advertising is a criminal offence, and carries an unlimited fine. More importantly, it also allows a tenant to leave the property inside the first month of their occupancy and have all of their money returned in full, effectively living in the property rent free. A line needs to be walked between showing a property in a good light and a degree of advertising 'puff', and being downright misleading.

Before a property can be advertised it will also need to have an energy performance certificate.

> **Example 17.3 – False advertising of property**
>
> Sarah is advertising her property to let. She takes all the photographs to ensure that the high-tension electricity lines running immediately behind the house are not visible.
>
> In one photograph she uses a computer programme to hide part of the leg of the pylon by putting in a shrub that does not exist. This is likely to be an offence.

ENERGY PERFORMANCE CERTIFICATES

17.14

> **Focus**
>
> All properties marketed for rental in the UK require an energy performance certificate (EPC) to be produced for them. This is intended to make the issue of energy efficiency more of a focus, and create a market in more efficient properties.

The EPC uses a mathematical model, which gives an estimate of the cost to heat and light the property for a year, and this is then reduced to a letter from A to G. The EPC, as well as giving an estimate of current cost to light and heat the property, is also required to give some recommended works, if possible, and what the EPC rating would be if those works were carried out.

From 2018, landlords in England will not be able to rent properties that have an EPC rating below E, in other words F and G rated properties. There is an exception if there is no reasonable possibility of improving the rating. This will mean that energy efficiency improvements will have to be carried out in those premises before they can be rented.

More information can be found at:

- England and Wales: www.gov.uk/buy-sell-your-home/energy-performance-certificates.

- Scotland: www.gov.scot/Topics/Built-Environment/Building/Building-standards/enerperfor/epcguidance.

- Northern Ireland: www.nidirect.gov.uk/articles/energy-performance-certificates.

KEY ELEMENTS OF THE AGENCY AGREEMENT

> **Focus**
>
> When entering into an agreement with a lettings agent a landlord will want to consider their terms of business, which will set out all the key matters in the relationship.

17.15 Important points to consider in the agreement include:

(a) Fees

The level of commission fee payable is fairly obvious. However, it is more important to review the additional fees and charges payable and consider what the total agency fee is likely to be. In addition, consideration should be given to the ongoing fee basis, and whether a fee is payable if the tenant remains in the property for an extended period.

(b) Services

Careful consideration should be given to the services on offer and what is included or extra.

17.16 *Dealing with tenants and agents*

(c) Exclusivity

The majority of agency agreements will have a period of exclusivity, where the agent is the sole agent entitled to obtain a tenant. The length of this period and how it is brought to an end is very important to know, because if a tenant is found during a period of exclusivity the agent is entitled to claim a fee, irrespective of whether they found the tenant or not.

(d) Consumer rights

If a landlord is a consumer and the agency agreement was made outside the agent's office, the landlord has a right to cancel the agreement for 14 days, and they should have been provided with written information about that right.

The 14 day right to cancel does not begin until such time as the information is provided, so if the information is not provided the landlord can cancel at any time and pay nothing at all, even if the agent has found a tenant in the meantime!

SELECTING A TENANT

17.16 The majority of landlords will have more than one possible tenant to choose from. Sometimes the choice will be obvious, but sometimes it can be harder to decide.

Speaking to the prospective tenants can be useful. Many landlords overlook the value of simply talking to a tenant and forming a view of what they are like to deal with as a person.

Referencing

17.17 It is common for agents to obtain some sort of reference in respect of a tenant. Few landlords do this for themselves. It should be remembered that a reference is not any form of promise of the future good behaviour of a tenant, but is merely a statement that there is no negative information on their past behaviour.

References can be of several types. Some are nothing more than credit references. This will not say a lot about a tenant other than that they have not been the subject of previous court orders.

Some referencing involves the taking up of employer references and comments from previous landlords. These can give extra comfort, but there will tend to be a reluctance to say anything negative, and so it is sometimes necessary to read between the lines of comments made.

Discrimination

17.18 Landlords are allowed to be selective in respect of their tenants. However, they may not carry out unlawful discrimination in breach of the

Equality Act 2010, or in Northern Ireland a range of Orders and Acts dealing with different types of discrimination.

Discrimination can be direct, such as a refusal to let to people of colour, or indirect where a set of conditions are imposed which have the effect of discriminating against a group.

It is acceptable to discriminate against some specific criteria. Landlords can discriminate by refusing to let to people on state benefits, for example. However, it is unlawful to discriminate against people on the basis of:

- Race, including colour and nationality;
- Disability;
- Sex;
- Sexuality;
- Gender reassignment;
- Religious belief, including a lack of belief;
- Marriage or civil partnership.

When deciding not to let to a person, a landlord should be clear in their own minds as to why they are not suitable, and be certain that those objections are well-founded on a clear and reasonable set of criteria.

It should also be noted that disabled tenants are entitled to ask for reasonable adjustments to a property, which includes adjustments to non-structural items.

For example, they could seek changes to doorbells or wall colours, but could not ask for a stair lift. It is not permissible to refuse a disabled tenant on the basis that they might, or have, asked for alterations. Disabled tenants are also entitled to ask for permission to make other changes, and this should normally be given provided that they make good the damage.

If there is a reason why permission cannot be given, such as a superior landlord needing to give consent, the landlord must take reasonable steps to obtain that consent themselves.

TERMS OF THE LETTING

17.19

Focus

Many tenancy terms are standard, but there are key elements which need to be considered. The two most important will be the rent and the length of the tenancy.

17.20 *Dealing with tenants and agents*

Rent

The rent will normally be based on the market advice given by the agent. It is important to remember that the market for a let property, just like anything else, is what people are prepared to pay for it. Many landlords make the mistake of setting the rent at the level of their mortgage.

In some cases, the mortgage may be considerably more expensive than the local market rent and setting at that level will mean the property simply stands empty.

Likewise, making improvements to property that the market does not value will cause the same problem. Many landlords have found themselves unable to understand why they are not able to command a premium rent to reflect premium fittings such as inbuilt televisions or sound systems while ignoring the simple fact that the property is not in a desirable area.

Term

17.20   Tenancy terms cannot usually be practically less than six months. The market tends to offer six-month or twelve-month tenancies. However, some landlords and agents have looked more carefully at tenant desires, and offer 18 months to two-year tenancies which tends to more closely reflect tenant's wishes.

It is important to bear in mind that if a tenant enters into an agreement for a two-year tenancy with a landlord, neither landlord nor tenant will find that agreement easy to get out of unless they both agree to do so. Thus a landlord may find the property hard to sell, and the tenant may be trapped in a house that no longer fits their needs.

To reduce this risk, it is not uncommon to have a break clause in a tenancy, which permits one or other side to terminate the tenancy earlier than the fixed term. If a landlord wants to rely on such a clause, it will not be valid if it undermines the tenant's basic right to reside in the property, and it will also need to be reasonably balanced. So a break clause that allowed the landlord to terminate the tenancy at any time on two months' notice, but only allowed the tenancy to give six months' notice on a specific date, would be unlikely to be acceptable. These clauses are very important, because they are strictly interpreted by the courts, so if they are not written properly they can be useless.

Tenants also sometimes seek a clause that allows them to extend the tenancy further, commonly known as an option to renew. If a tenant has such a clause, he or she will be allowed to extend the tenancy whether the landlord agrees or not, provided there is no serious breach of the terms of the agreement at the time the extension takes place. Many landlords think that these clauses allow them to refuse the extension, but they usually do not, and landlords should think very carefully before agreeing to them.

Other tenancy terms

17.21 Tenancies contain a range of other terms that control the behaviour of tenants. It is important to bear in mind that a landlord cannot reasonably control every aspect of a tenant's behaviour and clauses which contain overly strict provisions, such as requiring tenants to remove their shoes for example, will not be enforceable.

While it is possible, in England at any rate, to let out a property without any formal written agreement and in other jurisdictions with very little agreed, it is generally best to be fairly detailed in a tenancy agreement to provide a clear understanding of what a landlord expects from the tenant.

While breaching the terms of a tenancy is not always grounds to remove a tenant from the property, without terms of agreement which the tenant can be shown to have breached, a landlord will not be able to claim any losses caused by the tenant from the deposit.

DEPOSITS

> **Focus**
>
> In order to cover possible losses and to give the tenant an investment in the property landlords will take a sum of money, refundable at the end of the tenancy, as a deposit.
>
> In all UK jurisdictions deposits are regulated and must be protected with an approved scheme.

17.22 It is common for landlords to take a sum of money from the tenant as a security for them complying with the terms of the tenancy. This is called a deposit. It is usually around four to six weeks of rent, but there is no reason why it cannot be more or less. In Scotland, there is a restriction on deposits in that they cannot exceed three months' rent, but no such restriction exists elsewhere in the UK. A deposit can only be cash and, it is not permissible to take goods as an alternative.

A tenancy deposit is required to be registered with an approved tenancy deposit protection scheme in all UK jurisdictions, and the tenant must be given information about the scheme protecting the deposit and how it can be recovered. All the schemes also offer free adjudication to help resolve disputes over deductions from deposits.

It is very important that the rules of these schemes are complied with, as there are substantial penalties for failing to do so. Even relatively small technical breaches of the scheme rules will lead to a tenant being able to recover their deposit in full and usually other money as well, so understanding the rules that apply and following them rigorously is very important.

17.23 *Dealing with tenants and agents*

More information can be found at:

- England and Wales: www.gov.uk/tenancy-deposit-protection/overview.
- Scotland: www.gov.scot/Topics/Built-Environment/Housing/privaterent/landlords/tenancy-deposit-schemes.
- Northern Ireland: www.housingadviceni.org/advice-private-tenants/deposit-protection.

GUARANTORS

17.23   Where a tenant cannot produce references, or if their references cast doubt on whether they can afford to rent the property, it is common to ask for someone else who can afford it to stand as a guarantor. This person agrees to ensure that the tenant obeys the terms of the tenancy agreement, and to compensate the landlord if any money is left owing from rent arrears or property damage.

Guarantors are often the parents of the tenants, but can also be anyone who is prepared to take that financial risk for the tenant's benefit. It is important that a guarantor is chosen and referenced carefully, as they are the last line of defence a landlord has against a failure by the tenant to make payment. It is also important that a clear agreement is entered into, to ensure that the guarantor understands and accepts their role and the liability that goes with it.

In some cases, tenants will try to deal with the guarantor themselves and the landlord or agent will not have much to do with them. This is very dangerous. There have been numerous cases where guarantors were told by the tenant that they were only signing a reference and not a guarantee, or where the guarantor's signature was forged by the tenant and the guarantor knew nothing about it. It is important, therefore, that guarantors are engaged with directly, and care is taken to ensure they really do agree with their role.

SHORT LETTING

17.24   An increasing number of landlords are looking to rent their properties on a short-term basis, often to tourists, using a range of websites which specialise in this.

Care should be taken with these arrangements. Inside London, short letting is restricted, and requires planning permission if it is to be undertaken for more than an aggregate of 90 nights in any one year.

It is also a common restriction in mortgages, and in the leases for flats that they will not be used for business purposes, and short letting is held by the courts to be a business use.

RENT TO RENT

17.25 There is a growing trend for people to approach landlords on an individual basis or by way of a structured business, and offer to rent their property for an extended period with a guarantee of payment. These tenants will then rent the same property out for more money, taking the difference as their fees and profit. This is usually done by way of letting out each room separately.

For some landlords, the certainty of a regular income each month, albeit slightly lower than they might otherwise obtain, can be attractive. However, care must be taken with the agreement entered into and the use being made of the property. Some rent to rent organisations may be breaking the law by not having a suitable property licence for the use they are putting the property to, or by not having the right planning permissions. It is also the case that this kind of sub-letting will breach mortgage terms or the lease of a flat.

While some rent to rent organisations are very good and highly skilled, others have a very limited understanding of the law and what they are doing.

BUYING WITH A TENANT IN PLACE

17.26

> **Focus**
>
> When a purchase is being contemplated with a tenant already in the property, there are a range of important issues to consider. These have less to do with the financial situation and more to do with the legal aspects of the tenant that is in place.

A copy of the tenancy agreement should be obtained at the earliest possible opportunity. This should be reviewed to ensure that it is not granting a tenant unexpected rights, or misses key elements which will protect the landlord or ensure recovery of possession.

Consideration should also be given to where the tenancy is in its lifetime, and whether the tenant has the ongoing protection of a fixed-term agreement.

Finally, thought should be given to any provision around raising the rent and when this can be done.

17.27 The tenancy deposit will need to be considered. All UK jurisdictions have systems for protecting tenant's deposits, and there are penalties for breaching these. If the deposit has not been protected properly in the past, the new owner may find themselves liable for this failure. In that case, an indemnity may be needed from the previous owner.

17.28 *Dealing with tenants and agents*

In all UK jurisdictions there are some elements of property licensing. A check will need to be made as to whether the property has previously been licensed, and a new licence will need to be sought for the new owner prior to the sale being completed. If the property has not been licensed previously, it might also need improvements made to satisfy current licensing standards, and this will need to be factored into the cost of purchase.

17.28 An assessment of the repair of the property should be made, to make sure that it is likely to meet the legal obligations of the landlord to the tenant in the specific jurisdiction. There may be substantial costs to face if this has not been done.

17.29 An assessment of the tenant should also be carried out. Ideally, the vendor should provide a schedule of the rental payments made by the tenant for at least the last year. Inconsistent, late, or missed payments should be a source of concern, and should trigger further enquiries.

Chapter 18

Landlord obligations

David Smith Policy Director, Residential Landlords Association;
Partner, Anthony Gold Solicitors

> SIGNPOSTS
>
> - **General** – Landlords have a range of important obligations to their tenants and to the state. They can be prosecuted or end up paying money to their tenant if they do not obey these (see **18.1**).
>
> - **Basic information for tenants** – Tenants are entitled to some basic information about their rights, their tenancy, and where their tenancy deposit is held (see **18.2**).
>
> - **Landlord licensing and registration** – Landlords have obligations to check that tenants have the right immigration status to rent a property, and may be required to hold a licence or be registered as a landlord (see **18.3–18.4**).
>
> - **Other landlord obligations** – There is a range of important safety and repairing duties that landlords must comply with (see **18.5–18.12**).
>
> - **Seeking possession** – Tenants can only be forced to leave a property by way of a court order (see **18.13**).
>
> - **Essential checklist for new landlords and new properties** – A list of some useful tips and mandatory requirements that landlords should consider when setting out in business, or letting (or re-letting) their properties, can be found at **Appendix B**.

INTRODUCTION

18.1 Landlords have an extensive range of obligations to their tenants and the state due simply to them being landlords. In general, these have increased over the last five to ten years, and are continuing to grow.

Some of these obligations are punishable by criminal fines, and some are implied into the contract between landlord and tenant, so the tenant can seek damages if they are not fulfilled. These obligations are some of the most important, and

18.2 Landlord obligations

most commonly breached, and having the organisation and systems in place to fulfil them efficiently is the hallmark of a really good landlord.

BASIC INFORMATION REQUIREMENTS
18.2

> **Focus**
>
> Tenants have several fundamental rights. Some of these exist because of long held legal convention or custom, and some are provided specifically by various statutes.
>
> In general, residential tenants have a very high level of protection from unreasonable interference and harassment in the UK, much more than commercial tenants.

In England, all tenants are entitled to details about their tenancy deposit, a copy of the relevant gas safety certificate and a copy of the property energy performance certificate. In addition, all tenants must be given a copy of the government published guide 'How to Rent: A Checklist for Renting in England'. This is available at: www.gov.uk/government/publications/how-to-rent.

If the information above is not provided, the landlord will not be able to serve a tenant with an eviction notice under section 21 (see below).

There is no absolute requirement for a written tenancy agreement in England, but it can be very difficult to evict tenants without one. In addition, tenants are entitled to request a written copy of the key terms of their tenancy.

Scotland

Scotland requires landlords to give tenants a detailed tenant information pack, which sets out their rights at the beginning of a tenancy. This guide is regularly revised and updated. The guide must also include basic details about the landlord and property, and must be signed by the landlord to confirm that it is accurate.

The guide can be found at www.gov.scot/Publications/2016/02/7185.

Wales

Wales currently has no specific prescribed information requirements at the time of writing. At some point in 2017/18, when the Welsh government brings the *Renting Homes (Wales) Act 2015* into force, a tenant will be required to be provided with a written tenancy agreement. This will need to contain information about their rights, and may also have to be accompanied by further documents, which the Welsh government may set out. At the time of writing, it is not clear precisely what will be required or when this will come into force.

More information can be found on the Welsh government's 'renting homes' web page at: http://gov.wales/topics/housing-and-regeneration/legislation/rentingbill/?lang=en.

Northern Ireland

In Northern Ireland, all tenants with tenancies of 12 months or more must be given a written tenancy agreement. All tenants must be given a rent book, regardless of how long their tenancy is, and regardless of how and when they pay their rent. This agreement and rent book have government specified information in them, which sets out many of the tenant's key rights. Failure to provide either of these documents is a criminal offence punishable by a fine.

More information can be found on the Northern Ireland government website here: www.nidirect.gov.uk/articles/private-rent-and-tenancies.

IMMIGRATION AND THE RIGHT TO RENT

18.3

> **Focus**
>
> Landlords are under an obligation to check that their tenants and other occupiers are legally entitled to be in the UK and to rent property. This requirement is initially for England only, but is spreading to all parts of the UK.

In England, landlords are under an obligation to make sure that people they rent to are not in the country unlawfully. At the time of writing, the same requirement does not apply in Scotland, Wales or Northern Ireland, but the government remains committed to applying the same processes in all UK jurisdictions, and so landlords in these areas should check to make sure that it has not been imposed on them.

The requirement is to ensure that no person residing in the property with the consent of the landlord is in the country unlawfully. Landlords can gain protection against such a person being found in their property by carrying out checks on people's status to confirm that they have a right to rent prior to a tenancy being granted and, in certain cases, at specified interval thereafter.

These provisions apply to all private sector tenancies and licences, and will also apply to lodgers living in the landlord's home with them. They only apply to people who are living in a property as their only or main home, so it will not apply to those with second homes or to lettings for holiday purposes. Additionally, the requirement only applies to adults, so there is no need to

18.3 *Landlord obligations*

carry out checks on persons under 18, although a landlord will need to satisfy themselves that the person is under 18 and may need to see evidence to that effect.

The Secretary of State may give a civil penalty notice to a landlord in a variable amount of up to £3,000 for any contravention. From December 2016, it additionally became an offence in England to knowingly rent to person who did not have a right to rent.

The primary obligation to do checks is on the landlord, but they are entitled to pass that obligation to an agent. It is important to bear in mind that the obligation can only be passed in writing, and so landlords must be very sure that they have agreed with an agent that the agent will do the checks.

Types of right

There are two types of right to rent, ie permanent and time-limited. Their names are largely self-explanatory.

The permanent right is established by someone who has a right to reside in the UK without restriction. This applies to UK, EEA (that is the EU plus Iceland, Liechtenstein, and Norway) and Swiss nationals, along with those who have acquired such nationality (by marriage, for example, or who have gained a permanent right to reside in an EEA country).

The time-limited right is for those whose right to reside in the UK is limited in time, and so it is primarily oriented toward those persons present in the UK on a visa. However, it also deals with asylum seekers who have a time-limited asylum claim. It is possible for someone with a time-limited right to obtain a permanent right (by marrying an EU citizen, for example).

Checking

Landlords must check for a right to rent by examining documents provided by the prospective occupiers. All the adults that the landlord reasonably expects to be occupying the property must be checked. The document check requires looking at original documents (not copies) and this must be done in the presence of the document holder or with them available on a video link.

There are specific lists of documents that must be used to establish the right. In general, there is only the need to see one document if it is one which clearly identifies a person and establishes their citizenship. Thus a UK passport is sufficient to establish a permanent right alone. If a person cannot produce such a document then, for permanent rights only, there is a secondary list of lesser documents, and any two documents from this list will suffice.

There is also a telephone and online service called the landlord's checking service, which is only for checking those persons who claim that they have an ongoing asylum claim or appeal with the Home Office, and are not yet in possession of documents.

A check must look for inconsistencies between documents and between the document and the individual, expiry dates, identity and obvious signs of tampering or forgery. Copies of documents must be made and retained for one year after the end of the tenancy. These must be made in colour and for biometric documents both sides of the document must be copied.

The checks must be done in the 28 days preceding the day before the tenancy is entered into.

Re-checks

If a permanent right is established, it is established once and for all, and will not need to be confirmed again.

However, if a time limited right is established, it must be checked again once the time limit on the document runs out or 12 months has passed, whichever is the later. Prior to the expiry of a time limited right, efforts must be made to re-establish the right, and if that cannot be done a report must be made to the Home Office before the current time-limited right ends.

There is no obligation to evict at the time of writing, but the *Immigration Act 2016* does require eviction within a reasonable period of time after detection of an illegal immigrant.

LICENSING AND REGISTRATION

18.4

> **Focus**
>
> All parts of the UK have some form of requirement for landlords to be licensed, but which landlords it applies to and how rigorous the licensing process is varies substantially.

The UK has a very confused picture when it comes to the licensing and registration of landlords and let properties.

Some jurisdictions have landlord registration systems, and some of these go further and become systems to licence landlords and ensure they meet certain standards in terms of training and behaviour. In addition, all areas carry out some form of property licensing in respect of certain houses which are in multiple occupancy, and there is also discretion in some areas for local authorities to licence other properties which are deemed to be high risk.

Frustratingly, a lot of licensing occurs at local government level, so there is not a great deal of consistency in each of the devolved government areas, and landlords will need to look closely at the requirements of the specific local authority where the property is to be found.

18.4 Landlord obligations

England

England does not have any form of blanket landlord registration or licensing, and only deals with individual properties at a local government level.

HMOs under the Housing Act 2004

A House of Multiple Occupation (HMO) is one occupied by a group of people who do not form one household. This is defined in *s 254* of the *Housing Act 2004*. There are a series of tests for whether a property is an HMO.

These tests can be complex but in general terms a property:

- which has three or more occupiers;
- where those occupiers form more than one household;
- where rent is being paid;
- in which one of the occupiers lives in the property as his or her principal home; and
- where at least two of the households share basic amenities (such as cooking or washing facilities),

will be considered an HMO. Many properties may be HMOs, but only a subset of these will require licensing. This test can be altered by the government, and consideration is being given to doing so at the time of writing.

There is an additional and entirely separate definition of an HMO under *s 257* of the Act. This states that a whole building is an HMO for the purposes of that section where:

- It is a building which was a single dwelling but has been converted into multiple dwellings;
- The conversion does not accord with the *Building Regulations 1991* and is still not in accordance with it;
- One third or more of the properties are let out on leases of less than 21 years.

The fact that a building is an HMO under *s 257* has no connection with whether the flats within it are HMOs under *s 254*. In other words, a building could be a *s 257* HMO and one or more of the flats within it could also be *s 254* HMOs, depending on their occupancy.

Households

The definition of a household is slightly counter-intuitive, and is focused around families and cohabiting couples. People will be regarded as forming a single household where they are a couple, or where they are related as parents, children, siblings, uncles, aunts, nephews, nieces, grandparents, grandchildren or cousins. Foster, half and step relationships all count as full relationships.

There is nothing to stop two individuals in a property from being two households, and the age of the occupiers is totally irrelevant. Therefore the household test has nothing to do with how the property is being used by the occupiers and everything to do with the familial relationships between them.

Storeys

When calculating the number of storeys in a property, it is necessary to include basements or attics which are converted or adapted for use as part of the living accommodation (as opposed to merely used for storage) or are being used in that manner, mezzanines which are more than mere access to another level, any separate floor which includes the main entrance to the property, or any business premises above or below the property irrespective of whether they are connected in any way.

The High Court has held that storeys used for residential purposes should not be counted, and that there is only a need to count other storeys which are business premises. It should be remembered though that where a business premises is present above or below it must be counted as a storey included within the HMO, irrespective of whether it is in separate ownership or even if it is several storeys removed from the residential premises.

HMO licensing

Not all HMOs require licensing but those that do must be licensed, otherwise the landlord or any other person collecting or receiving the rent for the property will be committing an offence.

Larger HMOs which have five or more occupiers (adults and children of any age all count as one occupier) and extend over three or more storeys must all be licensed. In addition local housing authorities can elect to licence other HMOs with fewer occupiers or extending over a smaller number of storeys.

This is an area which is subject to change, and landlords should check carefully what licensing is in operation in their local area. This is also an area which is retrospective, and where a licensing scheme is brought into force landlords who are already renting properties which fall into a licensing scheme will need to apply for a licence.

Selective licensing

Individual local authorities can also choose to licence all landlords in some or all of their area of responsibility. Not having a licence for a rented property is an offence.

18.4 *Landlord obligations*

Selective licensing schemes can come into force on relatively short notice, and landlords should check carefully what licensing is in operation in their local area. As with HMO licensing this is retrospective, and where a selective licensing scheme is brought into force landlords who are already renting properties which fall into the scheme will need to apply for a licence.

Registration and licensing in Scotland

In Scotland, all landlords must be registered with their local authority. Every property they own must be registered individually, but there is a discount for multiple property registrations. The local authority can refuse to grant a licence if it does not consider that the applicant is a fit and proper person to hold a licence, or if the owner or his agent is disqualified from holding a licence.

Although registration is with each local authority, there is a central registration management system operated through www.landlordregistrationscotland.gov.uk, which also provides more detail on the process.

HMOs also require separate licensing in Scotland. An HMO is any property:

- occupied by three or more persons from three or more families; and
- occupied by them as their only or main residence; and
- involving the sharing of cooking or washing facilities.

HMO licensing is handled by individual local authorities using their own arrangements, and they should be contacted directly to establish what their licence application arrangements are.

Registration and licensing in Wales

Wales operates the same HMO and selective licensing schemes as England. However, it also has its own separate landlord registration scheme, operated by Cardiff Council under the brand name 'rent smart Wales'. All landlords in Wales must register with the scheme and they must also be licensed if they wish to carry out any form of property management, including of their own properties. To obtain a licence there is a compulsory training requirement, as well as satisfying the scheme that the person is suitable to be a manager.

There is a range of criminal and financial penalties for failing to register or licence, or for using an unlicensed managing agent. Registration and licence applications as well as more information can be found at www.rentsmart.gov.wales.

Registration in Northern Ireland

In Northern Ireland, all landlords must be registered and must provide their registration number to tenants on all written communication. It is an offence not to be registered.

Landlord obligations **18.5**

More information on registration is available and applications can be made at: www.nidirect.gov.uk/articles/landlord-registration-scheme.

HMOs in Northern Ireland also need to be licensed separately. A house that:

- has three or more occupiers; and
- those occupiers form three or more families; and
- is the principal place of residence of at least one of the occupiers,

will be an HMO that must be licensed. Licensing applications can be made on the internet at www.nihe.gov.uk/hmo_application_form_3.pdf.

OTHER LANDLORD OBLIGATIONS

Gas safety

18.5

> **Focus**
>
> Deaths from gas appliances have been substantially reduced over the years by requiring all landlords to obtain certificates proving that the installation and appliances are safe.

Gas appliances have the capacity to kill, both by way of explosion or by poisoning from carbon monoxide. They can also cause long-term problems at lower levels with carbon monoxide poisoning which goes unrecognised. To help combat this, it is compulsory throughout the UK for landlords to have gas appliances checked and approved regularly by authorised inspectors.

All inspectors have to be authorised by the gas safe register, and they should be carrying a card to confirm that they are authorised. It is important that this is checked as there have been reports of fake inspectors, and landlords are liable for the inspection.

The requirement covers all gas installations and appliances, including those with bottled or tank-supplied gas as well as mains gas. All residential landlords must comply unless the gas installation is not within their control. This exception might apply where there is a communal gas boiler serving a number of flats which is dealt with by a superior landlord.

Checks must be carried out prior to the tenant moving in, and they must be given a copy of the inspection certificate when moving in. The check must be repeated every 12 months without fail, and the tenant supplied with a copy of the new inspection certificate within 28 days after the re-check. Where tenancies are for less than 28 days, such as holiday lettings, the certificate must be posted in the property in a prominent place. Landlords are required to keep their old certificates for at least two years, but they are allowed to do so

18.6 *Landlord obligations*

by scanning them rather than keeping paper copies, as long as the scan can be printed easily.

If a tenant will not allow access for a gas safety certificate to be carried out, the prosecuting authorities have made clear that they will be unlikely to pursue a prosecution where a landlord can show that they have made at least three clear efforts to make an appointment and access the property to carry out the safety checks.

A breach of this legislation is punishable by an unlimited fine and prison in the most serious cases. If a person is severely injured or killed, a landlord could reasonably expect to go to jail for a considerable period if the gas safety regulations had been breached.

In England it is now not possible to serve most residential tenants with a notice requiring the property back (a 'section 21 notice') unless a valid gas safety certificate has been given to them first (see below).

More information on the scheme, along with a list of approved inspectors, is available at www.gassaferegister.co.uk.

There are no obligations on landlords for the testing or certification of oil-fired appliances that are analogous to the gas safety requirements.

Electrical safety

18.6   In most of the UK there are no specific requirements that require a landlord to obtain certification of electrical safety. Scotland is different, and does require electrical testing (see below).

In England and Wales, a property which is an HMO does require a regular electrical inspection in respect of the fixed wiring, but not for appliances. These inspections must be carried out every five years and failure to do so is an offence punishable by an unlimited fine.

However, landlords should remember that they are under a general duty to ensure that the electrical installation is safe, and that any electrical appliances are safe. Even where testing is not required, a landlord who injured or killed his tenant due to an electrical fault would be liable to prosecution as well as a claim for damages from the tenant concerned. It should also be remembered that one of the most common causes of fire is faulty electrical installations and appliances. A landlord would be liable to the tenant for any losses or injuries caused by a fire caused by a faulty electrical installation or appliance.

In England only, the government has passed new legislation allowing regulations to be made requiring landlords to have the electrical installation and any electrical appliances tested. At the time of writing, the government is consulting over how this is to be implemented, what should be inspected, and how often that needs to occur. It is likely that these changes will be implemented in 2017/18.

Scotland

As indicated above, Scotland has a different electrical testing regime. In Scotland, landlords are required to give their tenants a certificate confirming that they have had the fixed electrical installation checked, called an electrical installation condition report (EICR), and this is required to be renewed every five years. Landlords must also carry out portable appliance testing (PAT). The tested appliances must have a sticker placed on them and a record must be kept of this. PAT must be repeated at an interval to be determined by the inspecting electrician.

All inspections must be done before a tenancy commences (if they have not been done before) and then repeated at the relevant intervals. The tenant must be provided with the EICR and PAT record before they move in and when they are renewed.

Failure to carry out these inspections and tests will mean the house does not meet the repairing standard (see below), and the landlord will be liable to pay the tenant compensation as well as be subject to orders requiring him to carry out the inspections and tests.

Fire safety

18.7

> **Focus**
>
> Fire safety is very difficult to ensure in residential property, especially as landlords cannot control every aspect of their tenant's behaviour.
>
> However, there is an increasing interest in making sure that the landlord has given thought to this area and done what they can to ensure that a tenant will receive warning of a fire and that its spread will be slowed down.

There is a general requirement on properties to be fire safe and to have adequate means of escape in case of fire. In relation to HMOs in England and Wales there is a specific requirement as regards fire safety.

However, what is fire safe is open to argument. The Local Authorities Coordinators of Regulatory Services (LACORS) have previously produced a guidance document for properties in England and Wales suggesting appropriate standards and this is used by most enforcement bodies, but LACORS has now ceased to exist and the document is increasingly hard to find. In general terms, a property which corresponds with current building regulations is likely to be fire safe.

Particular emphasis is given to ensuring:

- that there is a clear protected escape route from bedrooms to an external exit which is viable for at least 30 minutes;

18.8 *Landlord obligations*

- that doors are fireproof for at least 30 minutes and are fitted with automatic closing devices;
- stairways are protected so that they can be used safely during a fire; and
- that there is reliable mains-powered smoke and heat detectors which are interlinked and have a battery backup.

For larger HMOs it may be necessary to have a separate fire alarm system, emergency lighting, and escape signs but these cases are best dealt with by seeking specialist advice.

It is advisable for landlords to carry out a written fire risk assessment. This need not be complex, and there are kits and other advice to help landlords in doing this. They should consider providing written instructions to tenants as to how to operate any fire safety equipment provided and what they should do in the event of fire. It is also advisable to consider the provision of fire blankets in kitchens and possible small dry powder extinguishers to deal with immediate fires. If extinguishers are provided they must be serviced in line with the manufacturer's recommendations.

Smoke and alarms

18.8 Independently of the general fire safety requirements, some UK jurisdictions require a specific level of smoke or carbon monoxide alarm to be fitted. These are generally a minimum requirement and fall below what would ordinarily be considered to be fire safe.

All landlords in England are required to ensure that every storey of their property has at the least a battery-powered smoke alarm fitted if that storey has any room used partly or wholly as living accommodation. This means that a mezzanine which is only a turn in the stairs does not need anything fitted but one with a room does. Bathrooms and toilets are also counted as living accommodation. The alarm must be a smoke alarm and a heat detector is not an acceptable substitute.

This alarm must be checked to make sure it is in working order on the first day of the tenancy. Failure to fulfil this obligation allows the local authority to serve an enforcement notice requiring alarms to be fitted, and if this is not complied with they can issue an on-the-spot fine.

Scotland

In Scotland, the fire alarm requirement is the same as that set out in the *Building Regulations*. This requires that there be at least one interlinked alarm in each:

- room which is used by the occupants for general daytime living purposes;
- common circulation space, such as hallways and landings; and
- kitchen.

Failure to meet this standard will mean that the property is in breach of the repairing standard (see below) allowing the tenant to potentially seek damages and the landlord can be ordered to fit the necessary alarms.

Carbon monoxide

18.9 In England, landlords must ensure that there is a carbon monoxide alarm fitted in any room that is used partly or wholly as living accommodation which also contains any appliance which burns, or is capable of burning, solid fuel. This would include log and coal burning stoves and open fires, even if they are not normally in use, but does not include gas and oil boilers.

As with smoke detectors, failure to fulfil this obligation allows the local authority to serve an enforcement notice requiring alarms to be fitted, and if this is not complied with they can issue an on-the-spot fine.

> **Example 18.1 – Alarm requirements**
>
> Pav has a two-storey house which has a gas boiler in the kitchen and a log-burning stove in the sitting room, which she is letting to Taran.
>
> She will need to ensure that both the ground and first floor have at least one battery-powered smoke alarm fitted, and also that there is a carbon monoxide alarm fitted near the log-burner.

Scotland

In Scotland, the carbon monoxide obligations are more rigorous. In any property which contains any appliance (other than a cooking appliance) which requires combustion, a carbon monoxide detection system must be installed. This will include all forms of boiler or water heater unless they are powered by electricity. As a minimum this will require one alarm, which may be battery powered provided the battery is a fixed one which operates for the life of the detector.

These detectors must be in each place where a combustion appliance operates and in any high risk areas (such as bedrooms) where a flue passes through. There are a range of requirements regarding specific detector placement, and an expert should be consulted on this issue.

As with smoke alarms, failure to meet this standard will mean that the property is in breach of the repairing standard (see below) allowing the tenant to potentially seek damages, and the landlord can be ordered to fit the necessary alarms.

Furniture

18.10 All soft furniture and furnishings must comply with the appropriate fire regulations. These specify a set level of resistance to ignition and also

18.11 *Landlord obligations*

that the furniture will tend to stop burning on its own. Any modern furniture supplied within the UK should meet these standards, and should have labels attached to it to confirm this.

The same standards of safety and labelling to confirm this is required before the furniture is supplied to the tenant as part of the tenancy. Breaching these requirements is a criminal offence, and is punishable by a fine which can be unlimited as well as by prison.

These standards have been present in the UK for some time and so most landlords will find it difficult to obtain furniture that does not already meet the necessary standards, but some imported or very old furniture may not meet the standard.

Property standards
18.11

> **Focus**
>
> The standard to which a property must be repaired is something that varies widely between the different parts of the UK.
>
> In general, the devolved assemblies are moving to far stricter and more comprehensive repairing standards than in England.

In England, there are a number of obligations on landlords to ensure that properties are in repair and meet a minimum standard of quality and fitness.

Disrepair

It is a term implied into all residential tenancy agreements that a landlord will keep the rented property at a minimum level of repair. This level is not high, and is primarily focused on things that deteriorate during the tenancy. It does not generally require a landlord to improve a property beyond the standard it was at when the tenancy began.

The minimal repairing standard is imposed by the *Landlord and Tenant Act 1985, s 11* and requires a landlord to:

- keep in repair the structure and exterior of the dwelling-house (including drains, gutters and external pipes);

- keep in repair and proper working order the installations which supply water, gas and electricity and for sanitation (including basins, sinks, baths and sanitary conveniences, but not other fixtures, fittings and appliances for making use of the supply of water, gas or electricity); and

- keep in repair and proper working order the installations in the dwelling-house for space heating and heating water.

Landlord obligations **18.12**

It is important to note that these minimal obligations do not require a landlord to keep in repair white goods or other items that he or she has supplied to the tenant. However, many tenancy agreements will include clauses which do oblige a landlord to keep any additional items he has supplied in repair.

The repairing obligation does not arise until the landlord is notified of disrepair by the tenant, unless that disrepair is obvious to the landlord. The landlord is also entitled to a reasonable amount of time to deal with the disrepair, which will depend on the date it is reported and the nature of the problem. For example, a failure of a boiler on Christmas Eve is unlikely to be repaired before New Year, although it may be reasonable to expect a landlord to make a small patch repair to at least get hot water flowing.

A landlord is entitled to reasonable access on 24 hours written notice to inspect a property and carry out repairs. If this access is not given, the obligation to repair does not arise. So a tenant who reports a problem but then obstructs access to deal with it cannot claim that their property is in disrepair.

The repairing obligations in *s 11* are implied automatically, and will override any other statement in the tenancy agreement. The obligation to repair is a contractual one, and so a breach of it will give a tenant a right to make a financial claim against the landlord for breach of contract. In general this will be limited to the loss of value in the property caused by the disrepair for each day between the date the repair should have been carried out until the day that it was.

Example 18.2 – Leaking roof

Naveen is letting a two storey house out to Dee. There is a leak in the roof which is making the upstairs main bedroom unusable.

If Naveen does not get this repaired reasonably promptly after being told about it by Dee, she is breaching an implied contractual term with Dee, and Dee can claim damages for each day that this is not done.

The damages would usually be calculated based on the difference between the actual rent being charged and the lower rental value of the property without the unusable room.

Housing health and safety rating system

18.12 The housing health and safety rating system (HHSRS) is a different and higher standard. The HHSRS arguably represents one of the most significant and far-reaching repairing obligations in existence from the point of view of residential lettings. It creates strong powers for local authorities to inspect property, a range of criteria by which improvements can be sought, and couples this with substantial enforcement powers. It is aspirational in scope, and actually seeks to improve the quality of property in England and Wales.

18.12 *Landlord obligations*

The HHSRS is based on evidence derived from studies relating to housing health and analysis of accident statistics. It therefore purports to be scientific and evidence based. However, the quality of the evidence has been doubted, and the level of individual discretion given to environmental health officers (EHOs) in practice has meant that the claims for objectivity of the HHSRS have ended up being questioned.

The HHSRS uses a three-stage approach:

1. A residential property is inspected.

2. Individual 'hazards' are identified and a hazard score is generated for each hazard, based on the likelihood of an occurrence resulting from that hazard and the level of harm that could result from that occurrence. This assessment is based on an average property and notional occupiers, so the actual occupation is not relevant.

3. The most appropriate form of action for those hazards is selected, taking into account the impact on tenants, landlord cooperation, and the seriousness of the issues. The actions can range from notifications of risks, through orders requiring specific improvements, up to bans on the use of the property altogether.

Due to the powers to demand improvements or ban the use of property, the HHSRS give local authority EHOs tremendous powers to control the use of property.

Wales

At the time of writing, Wales has the same requirements around repairs and fitness standards as England and also uses the HHSRS.

When the *Renting Homes (Wales) Act 2016* comes into force in 2018, this will change. The HHSRS will continue unchanged, but there will be a new repairing standard in Wales known as the fitness for human habitation standard. This requires that a property must meet all the 29 hazard areas under the HHSRS at a minimal level, and if it is seriously deficient in any of those areas it will not meet the fitness standard.

At the time of writing, this standard is in an early stage of consultation, and so the exact manner of assessment is yet to be decided.

Scotland

In Scotland, landlords are required to meet a repairing standard both at the start of and throughout the tenancy. The repairing standard requires that:

- The property must be wind resistant, watertight and fit for human habitation;

- The structure and exterior of the property, including the drains, gutters and external pipes, should be in a reasonable state of repair and in proper working order;
- The installations in the property, including gas, electricity, sanitation, space heating and water heating, should be in a reasonable state of repair and in proper working order;
- The fixtures and fittings and appliances in the property should be in a reasonable state of repair and in proper working order;
- The furnishings should be able to be used safely for the purpose for which they were designed;
- There should be satisfactory provision made for the detecting of fire and for giving warnings.

Before the start of the tenancy landlords must provide tenants with information about the landlord's obligation to comply with the repairing standard as part of the Tenant Information Pack. If the landlord fails to comply with the repairing standard, the tenant or the local authority can apply to the Housing and Property Chamber of the First-tier Tribunal (previously the Private Rented Housing Panel or PRHP). If the Chamber is of the view that the landlord is failing to comply with the standard, it can order him to do so by requiring specified works to be done on the property. Not complying with this allows the Chamber to make a rent relief order which can be for up to 90% of the rent, as well as to impose fines.

Northern Ireland

Northern Ireland has a minimum fitness standard which requires that all properties must at least:

- be structurally stable;
- be free from serious disrepair;
- be free from dampness which could damage your health;
- have adequate provision for lighting, heating and ventilation;
- have an adequate piped supply of wholesome water;
- have enough space and facilities to prepare and cook food, including a sink;
- have a suitably located toilet for the exclusive use of the occupants;
- have either a bath or shower with hot and cold water; and
- have effective, working drains.

If a tenant believes this not to be the case, they can seek an inspection from a local authority. If the authority is not satisfied with the standard of the property,

18.13 *Landlord obligations*

they can issue a notice requiring repairs and failure to comply with this is an offence punishable by a fine. Older properties built before 1 January 1945 which have not been modernised must have a compulsory fitness inspection before they are rented. If they do not have this, they can only be rented under a restricted rent set by the state.

Unlike in England and Wales, repairing obligations in residential property in Northern Ireland do not automatically default to the landlord, as long as the property meets the minimal fitness standard at the start of the tenancy. Landlords and tenants are free to agree their own division of repairing obligations between themselves. Where there is no provision as to repairs in the tenancy agreement made between the landlord and tenant the law will impose a set of repairing obligations on the landlord, which are the same as those found in England so the landlord will be required to:

- keep in repair the structure and exterior of the dwelling-house (including drains, gutters and external pipes);
- keep in repair and proper working order the installations which supply water, gas and electricity and for sanitation (including basins, sinks, baths and sanitary conveniences, but not other fixtures, fittings and appliances for making use of the supply of water, gas or electricity); and
- keep in repair and proper working order the installations in the dwelling-house for space heating and heating water.

SEEKING POSSESSION

18.13

> **Focus**
>
> Most landlords and tenants have an amicable relationship, and the tenant leaves happily at the end of their tenancy.
>
> If this does not happen, the landlord may need to take action to remove the tenant from the property. This can only be lawfully done by the landlord asking the court to remove the tenant from the property for him.

In all UK jurisdictions, possession of a residential property can only be obtained through the courts. Any other route is likely to be an unlawful eviction unless the tenant has voluntarily given up possession. Seeking possession is time consuming and will take at least two to three months in most cases and will incur significant costs, in court fees if not in legal costs.

In general, an amicable settlement in which the tenant leaves voluntarily is to be preferred in most cases but this will often not be possible, not least because local authorities will frequently tell tenants that they will be seen as having made themselves intentionally homeless if they leave before a court order has

Landlord obligations **18.13**

been obtained and executed and that they will therefore render themselves ineligible for housing assistance. Specialist advice should be sought in all cases where a possession action is being considered.

As well as obtaining a court order for possession this will need to be executed and this can only be done through a properly authorised court officer. This process will also take some time, usually at least a month.

In all cases, landlords will need to consider their financial situation and make sure that they have made arrangements with mortgage lenders and others, as they will have no real prospect of accelerating the process due to their own financial difficulties.

Notices

Prior to seeking possession in the courts, it will be necessary to serve formal notices on the tenants. These notices will be different depending on the jurisdiction involved, but fall into two types.

The first group is available where the fixed term of a tenancy has come to an end and the landlord simply wishes to recover the property for their own purposes. These notices usually require a longer notice period and are increasingly restricted, as they do not require a landlord to have any reason to recover the property. They are often used as a weapon to ensure compliance with other legislation, and so a landlord who is not properly licensed or registered or who has not protected a tenancy deposit will have some difficulty in serving such a notice.

In England, this notice is known as a 'section 21 notice'. In Scotland, it is called a 'section 33 notice', but this notice will disappear at some stage in 2018 as changes made by the *Private Housing (Tenancies) (Scotland) Act 2016* come into effect. In Northern Ireland, the 'notice to quit' is used, while Wales currently uses the section 21 notice, but will have a new notice structure once the *Renting Homes (Wales) Act 2016* comes into force.

The second group of notices deal with situations where the landlord has a specific right to recover possession. The most usual use of such notices is where the tenant is in arrears of rent but there are other circumstances where such a notice would be appropriate. These notices usually have shorter time limits, but the criteria for them are relatively strict and the landlord will need to fit within them. In England and Wales, this is the 'section 8 notice', although this will disappear in Wales as the *Renting Homes (Wales) Act 2016* comes into effect. Northern Ireland has no formally named notice for this situation, while Scotland's notices are subject to change.

Tenant rights

While going through the possession process, it is important to remember that all of a landlord's other obligations, such as repairs to the property, continue

18.13 *Landlord obligations*

unchanged and that the tenant will, in most cases, remain a tenant up until the court makes an order for possession and it is executed by an authorised officer. Therefore landlords may still be under an obligation to carry out repairs at a property, even when the tenant is not paying the rent and refusing to do so will be an offence and will allow a potential claim to be made by the tenant for disrepair. Likewise, deliberately cutting off the electricity or threatening the tenant to make them leave will be a criminal offence.

In addition, the tenant can ask the court to order that they be allowed back into the property, and can seek damages from the landlord.

> **Example 18.3 – Non-payment of rent: tenant's ongoing rights**
>
> Dee is letting a property to Pav, and Pav has failed to pay the rent this month. Rather than go to court, Dee cuts off the electricity by removing all the fuses and then changes the locks when Pav goes out to work.
>
> Pav can go to court to seek an injunction that she be allowed back in to the property, and also seek damages from Dee, which will likely exceed the rent arrears. She will also be able to recover her legal costs in doing so.

Appendix B: Essential checklist for new landlords and new properties

With thanks to the Residential Landlords Association for their kind assistance in compiling this checklist.

The following list sets out some useful tips and mandatory requirements that a landlord should consider when setting out in business, or letting (or re-letting) his or her properties. Please also see **Chapter 1**.

1. AGENTS DUTIES TO PUBLICISE FEES/THEIR REDRESS SCHEMES

Under the *Consumer Rights Act 2015* it is now a legal requirement for all letting and managing agents in England and Wales to publicise details of their fees, and to say whether they have client money protection. They must also give the name of the redress scheme of which they are a member. Membership of a redress scheme is compulsory for agents.

The intention is that there should be full transparency, to deter double charging to both the landlord and the tenant, and enabling tenants and landlords to shop around.

For further information, see: http://tinyurl.com/RLA-Agent-Duties.

2. BANK ACCOUNT

Consider setting up a separate property bank account for your property business. Very simply put, HMRC has the right to review business records within the scope of its very extensive information and enquiry powers, and may ask for information or documents 'reasonably required' to check the taxpayer's tax position, while the taxpayer has some quite limited protections for personal information.

If a landlord wants to keep his or her private bank account private, by far the most practical approach is to ensure that business transactions are undertaken in an entirely separate bank account – but note that even then, privacy is by no means guaranteed.

Appendix B: Essential checklist for new landlords and new properties

3. CARBON MONOXIDE AND ALARMS IN NON-HOUSES IN MULTIPLE OCCUPATION

Landlords in England are required to provide smoke alarms on every floor of their property, and a carbon monoxide alarm in every room with a solid fuel source.

This applies to most tenancies, but further guidance on exceptions and best practice is available at www.rla.org.uk/landlord/guides/carbon-monoxide-requirements.shtml.

4. DEPOSITS

Where your market allows, consider taking six weeks as a minimum for a deposit. This is hopefully a sufficient amount for a month's rent arrears and any damages/cleaning that may occur at the end of the tenancy. Be aware that taking two months or more as a deposit triggers the tenant's right to sublet without your permission.

If you take a deposit from a tenant under an assured shorthold tenancy, the deposit must be protected under one of the three tenancy deposit schemes, and the prescribed information regarding the deposit must be given to the tenant and all who have contributed to it, within 30 days of receiving the deposit.

For a full explanation of tenancy deposits, see: www.rla.org.uk/landlord/tenancy_deposits.

5. ELECTRICAL APPLIANCES

Where a property is provided with electrical appliances, it is the landlord's responsibility to make sure that they are safe at the outset of letting.

6. ELECTRICAL INSPECTIONS

If your property is a house in multiple occupation (HMO) of any kind, you must have a five-yearly electrical safety check carried out by a competent electrician, even if you do not need a licence.

This will cover shared houses, flats in multiple occupation, bedsits, hostels and certain converted blocks of flats. These are blocks of flats which are not converted in compliance with 1991 (or later) building regulations and fewer than two thirds of the flats in the block are owner-occupied.

7. ENERGY PERFORMANCE CERTIFICATES (EPCS)

Before a tenant moves in, there must be an energy performance certificate (EPC) in place, for most types of property. A copy of the certificate must be

Appendix B: Essential checklist for new landlords and new properties

given to any tenant who moves in to the property. If not, you cannot serve a 'Section 21 notice' for a new tenancy in England after 1 October 2015. (*HA 1988, s 21*: notice seeking possession of the property, sometimes referred to as a 'Notice to Quit').

For further details regarding EPCs, see www.rla.org.uk/landlord/guides/epc.

8. FIRE ALARM SYSTEMS AND FIRE PRECAUTIONS IN HOUSES IN MULTIPLE OCCUPATION

Where fire alarm systems are provided in an HMO, the landlord is responsible for ensuring fire alarms are checked regularly. You must also make sure that the means of escape from the property (normally the halls, stairs and landings) are unobstructed. HMOs include shared houses, flats in multiple occupation, bedsits and certain types of converted flats.

For information about the *HMO Management Regulations*, which impose these requirements, see: www.rla.org.uk/landlord/guides/housing_act/firesafety.shtml.

9. FIRE SAFETY ORDER

Where a landlord controls flats, bedsits or hostels there must be a risk assessment in place to comply with the fire safety order. It should be in writing. A statutory risk assessment is not required for shared houses or single dwelling lets.

For further information on the fire safety order, see: www.rla.org.uk/landlord/guides/housing_act/firesafety.shtml.

10. GAS SAFETY

Where there are any gas appliances in the property provided by the landlord, the landlord must ensure that annual gas safety checks are carried out. These checks must be carried out by a gas fitter/engineer who is registered on the Gas Safety Register (which has replaced Corgi). A copy must be given to the tenant before the tenant moves in and the check must have been carried out within the 12 months before the new tenant takes up occupation. Checks must be done annually at no more than 12 month intervals and copies of all certificates for checks must be handed over to the tenant. If landlords fail to do this, they may lose their 'Section 21 rights' in England as of 1 October 2015.

For further details on gas certification, see: www.rla.org.uk/landlord/documents/gas_safety/gas_safety.shtml.

11. GUARANTOR

Ask the tenant(s) for a guarantor. By having a guarantor you can contact them for any rent arrears problems that may occur during the term of the tenancy.

Appendix B: Essential checklist for new landlords and new properties

A home owner and/or someone in stable employment is a good guarantor to fall back on if required. The guarantor(s) should be credit checked.

For further information, see: www.rla.org.uk/landlord/documents/preLet/doc_gl4_guarantor.shtml.

12. ILLEGAL EVICTION/HARASSMENT

Landlords must not harass their tenants. It is unlawful to evict a tenant without a Court Order. Landlords cannot throw a tenant out because he is in arrears with his rent or breaking the terms of his tenancy. They must go to court to get a possession order. Any possession order obtained must be enforced by the Court Bailiff.

For more information about harassment or illegal eviction, see: www.rla.org.uk/landlord/documents/useful/DYK_11_Unlawful.shtml

13. INSURANCE

Appropriate insurance should be in place for building, public liability and rent guard (rent insurance).

For more information, see: www.rla.org.uk/landlord/insurance.

14. INVENTORY

Complete an inventory (photographic) and make sure the tenant(s) sign to agree the condition of the property. If they do not sign the inventory, write to the tenant(s) and give them seven days to confirm back, otherwise it will be taken that the inventory is agreed by both parties.

For more information on inventories, see: www.rla.org.uk/landlord/landlord_inventory/landlord_inventory.shtml.

15. KEYS

Do not hand over any keys to the property until a tenancy agreement has been signed, and the first month/week rent in advance and security deposit have been received.

16. LEGIONELLA ASSESSMENT

Landlords are required to perform a risk assessment for Legionnaires' disease. If they don't do this, they could be issued with a fine. However, the extent of risk assessment required depends on the type of property and landlords should be wary of claims that all properties need extensive water sampling tests.

Appendix B: Essential checklist for new landlords and new properties

For more information on this, as well as information packs and risk assessment forms, see: www.rla.org.uk/landlord/guides/legionnaires_disease.shtml.

17. LICENSABLE HOUSES IN MULTIPLE OCCUPATION

If the property is an HMO (eg bedsits, shared house or a shared flat) then an HMO licence may well be needed from the local authority. Landlords should check with their local authority what licencing requirements, if any, they have.

If they do not, they may not be able to serve a 'Section 21 notice' after 1 October 2015.

18. NOTIFY HMRC OF A NEW SOURCE

If this is a new source of income for the taxpayer – his or her first rental property – it may need to be notified to HMRC in accordance with *TMA 1970, s 7*; see **Chapter 1**.

19. PAYMENTS OF RENT/ADMINISTRATION FEES

It is very important that advance payments of rent and non-returnable administration fees are not confused with deposits. Landlords should always make clear to tenants what the money is being taken for; otherwise it could be regarded as a deposit and be protected under one of the deposit protection schemes.

For more information regarding advance payments of rent and non-returnable administration fees, see: www.rla.org.uk/landlord/tenancy_deposits/tds-Alternatives.shtml.

20. PRESCRIBED INFORMATION TO TENANTS IN ENGLAND

As of 1 October 2015, upon starting a tenancy, landlords are now required to provide the most up to date copy of *How to Rent: The Checklist for Renting in England*.

If they do not, they will not be able to serve a valid 'Section 21 notice' in England.

21. REFERENCE CHECKS

Carry out reference checks on the tenant(s). This will highlight any previous CCJ's the tenant(s) may have, and confirm the details the prospective tenant has given you in their application.

For further information, see: www.rla.org.uk/landlord/creditcheck/index.shtml.

Appendix B: Essential checklist for new landlords and new properties

22. TENANCY APPLICATION FORMS

Ensure that you get an application completed by the tenant(s) with the last three years' residence details, with their birth date, National Insurance number and next of kin details. If you can get a copy of the birth certificate, driving licence or any other proof of identity, that would help you also in processing details about your tenant(s).

For further information, see: www.rla.org.uk/landlord/documents/preLet/tenancy-application-form.shtml

23. VAT REGISTRATION

For standard buy-to-let properties, it is neither desirable nor indeed possible to register for VAT, since the provision of let accommodation for use as an ordinary dwelling is an exempt supply.

Furnished holiday lettings and similar may however 'count' as taxable supplies for VAT purposes, and VAT registration is mandatory when taxable supplies exceed the VAT registration threshold in a period of 12 months or less (2016/17 £83,000).

The position for commercial properties is more complex, and registration may be desirable in some cases. It is possible to 'opt to tax' an interest in a commercial property, such that future supplies of renting out or onward sale are taxable and would count towards the registration threshold; the freehold sale of a new commercial property (or one that is less than three years old) is often taxable and might trigger a requirement to register.

Index

[All references are to paragraph numbers]

Additional dwellings supplement
  acquisition by companies, 14.39
  acquisition by partnerships, 14.40
  background, P.12
  civil partners, 14.33
  company acquisitions, 14.39
  excluded acquisitions, 14.30
  generally, 14.29–14.30
  inherited dwellings, 14.37
  interests in dwellings treated as owned by individual, 14.31
  introduction, 14.22–14.24
  joint purchasers, 14.32
  multiple dwellings as part of single transaction, 14.38
  partnership acquisitions, 14.40
  partnership-held dwellings, 14.35
  rest of the UK dwellings, 14.36
  spouses, 14.33
  trust-held dwellings, 14.34
Advertising
  properties for let, 17.13
Agency agreement
  properties for let, 17.15
Agents
  accreditation, 17.8
  agency agreement, 17.15
  client money, 17.9
  consent to let, 17.12
  cost, 17.8
  experience, 17.8
  fees, 17.9
  inventory, 17.11
  redress, 17.9
  mortgage company consent, 17.12
  training, 17.8
  types, 17.10
Agricultural expenses
  loss relief, 7.14
Annual investment allowance (AIA)
  capital allowances, 4.6

Annual tax on enveloped dwellings (ATED)
  corporate landlords
    background, 10.9
    capital gains, and, 10.13–10.14
    charge, 10.10
    claims for relief, 10.11
    disposal of property portfolio, and, 10.1
    SDLT, and, 10.12
  generally, 9.9
  introduction, P.3
  meaning, P.3
  relationship with NRCGT, 9.17–9.18
  stamp duty land tax, 14.61
Anti-avoidance provisions
  stamp duty land tax
    annual tax on enveloped dwellings, 14.61
    generally, 14.58–14.60
    stamp duty reserve tax, 14.63
    transfer buy-to-let property out of company, 14.62
Apportionment of consideration
  stamp duty land tax, 14.17
Arrears of rent
  considerations on purchase of property for rental, 17.4
Averaging election
  furnished holiday lettings, 6.18

Badges of trade
  calculation of property business profits and losses, 2.12
Bare land
  stamp duty land tax, 14.49
Beneficial loans
  finance costs, 3.41
Beneficial ownership
  declaration of trust, 8.21
  introduction, 8.7–8.9

Index

Beneficial ownership – *contd*
  joint ownership
    declaration of trust, 8.21
    generally, 8.18
    severance, 8.19–8.20
  meaning, 8.3
  overview, 8.2–8.3
  severance, 8.19–8.20
Boilers
  replacement domestic items relief, 5.7
Block of flats
  capital allowances
    communal areas, 4.10
    generally, 4.9
Borrowing against assets
  generally, 1.36–1.38
Bridging finance
  generally, 16.32
  increases to portfolio, 16.45
'Business'
  case law, 13.9–13.12
  generally, 13.5–13.8
  Ramsay case, 13.13–13.14
Business property relief
  furnished holiday lettings, 6.24–6.25
  generally, 12.12–12.16
  introduction, 12.10
Buying properties for rental
  advertising, 17.13
  agency agreement, 17.15
  buying with tenant in place, 17.26–17.29
  client money, 17.9
  consent to let, 17.12
  considerations on purchase
    arrears of rent, 17.4
    costs, 17.3
    introduction, 17.1
    rent, 17.2
    tenant damage, 17.4
  deposits, 17.22
  discrimination, 17.18
  duration of tenancy, 17.10
  energy performance certificates, 17.14
  guarantors, 17.23
  introduction, 17.5
  letting agents
    accreditation, 17.8
    agency agreement, 17.15
    client money, 17.9

Buying properties for rental – *contd*
  letting agents – *contd*
    consent to let, 17.12
    cost, 17.8
    experience, 17.8
    fees, 17.9
    inventory, 17.11
    redress, 17.9
    mortgage company consent, 17.12
    training, 17.8
    types, 17.10
  references, 17.17
  rent to rent, 17.25
  selection of tenant
    discrimination, 17.18
    introduction, 17.16
    referencing, 17.17
  short letting, 17.24
  tenant's rights, 17.6
  term of tenancy, 17.10
  terms of letting
    duration, 17.10
    generally, 17.19
    other, 17.21
  types, 17.7
Buy-to-let property business
  additional dwellings SDLT, P.12
  annual tax on enveloped dwellings
    generally, P.3
    meaning, P.3
  background, P.1
  basis of taxation, 1.1–1.2
  basis periods, 1.28–1.30
  beginning of
    basis of taxation, 1.1–1.2
    basis periods, 1.28–1.30
    choice of entity, 1.3–1.16
    date, 1.17–1.18
    introduction, 15.18
    pre-letting expenses, 1.25–1.27
    pre-trading expenses, 1.19–1.24
    tax administration, 1.31–1.53
  calculation of profits and losses
    assessment as a business, 2.6–2.7
    badges of trade, 2.12
    capital-revenue distinction, 2.15–2.16
    cash-basis proposals, 2.38–2.39
    change of use of property, 2.23–2.25

472

Index

Buy-to-let property business – *contd*
  calculation of profits and losses – *contd*
    differences between income rules, 2.8–2.9
    finance costs, 2.17–2.22
    hotels, and, 2.10–2.11
    interest relief, 2.17–2.22
    introduction, 2.1–2.4
    non-commercial lettings, 2.36–2.37
    priority of income rules, 2.5
    reform proposals, 2.38–2.39
    transactions in UK land, 2.26–2.35
    'wholly and exclusively', 2.13–2.14
  capital gains tax
    non resident's residential property interests, P.9
    'new' residential property gains, P.13
    principal private residence relief, P.6
    reporting and payment reforms, P.17
  cessation of
    generally, 15.19–15.21
    subsequent expenses, 15.23–15.24
    subsequent receipts, 15.22
  choice of entity
    companies, 1.16
    direct ownership, 1.4
    introduction, 1.3
    joint ownership, 1.4
    partnerships, 1.8–1.15
    sole ownership, 1.4
    trusts, 1.5
  chronology of recent changes, P.2
  commencement of
    basis of taxation, 1.1–1.2
    basis periods, 1.28–1.30
    choice of entity, 1.3–1.16
    date, 1.17–1.18
    introduction, 15.18
    pre-letting expenses, 1.25–1.27
    pre-trading expenses, 1.19–1.24
    tax administration, 1.31–1.53
  corporate ownership, 1.16
  considerations on purchase of property for rental
    arrears of rent, 17.4
    costs, 17.3
    introduction, 17.1
    rent, 17.2
    tenant damage, 17.4

Buy-to-let property business – *contd*
  date of commencement, 1.17–1.18
  developing UK land, P.15
  direct ownership, 1.4
  enveloped dwellings
    annual tax, P.3
    stamp duty land tax, P.5
  finance costs, P.15
  furnishings in residential lettings
    removal of 'concession', P.4
    statutory renewals basis, P.11
    wear and tear allowance, P.11
  incorporation of
    See also **Incorporation of letting business**
    'business', 13.5–13.14
    capital allowances, 13.66–13.71
    CGT, 13.16–13.31
    employment-related securities, 13.77
    furnished holiday lettings, 13.32–13.44
    interest relief, 13.59–13.64
    introduction, 13.1–13.4
    NICs, 13.74–13.76
    payment of tax, 13.72–13.73
    stamp taxes, 13.45–13.58
    transactions in UK land, 13.15
    VAT, 13.65
  joint ownership
    apportionment of taxable income, 1.6–1.7
    generally, 1.4
  lease
    assignment, 1.47
    capital costs incurred, 1.46
    grant of sub-lease out of short lease, 1.42
    lessee tax relief, 1.43–1.45
    premium, 1.39–1.42
    reverse premium, 1.48–1.52
    tenant tax relief, 1.43–1.45
    term of lease, 1.41
  letting income allowance, P.16
  limited liability partnerships
    generally, 1.12–1.13
    losses, 1.14–1.15
  non resident capital gains tax on residential property interests, P.9

473

Index

Buy-to-let property business – *contd*
partnerships
generally, 1.8–1.10
joint investment, 1.11
limited liability partnerships, 1.12–1.15
post-cessation expenses, 15.23–15.24
post-cessation receipts, 15.22
pre-letting expenses
generally, 1.25–1.26
landlord's former home, 1.27
pre-trading expenses
capital allowances, 1.20–1.21
capital expenses, 1.25
case study, 1.26
introduction, 1.19
landlord's former home, 1.27
no further commencement, 1.22–1.24
revenue expenses, 1.25
principal private residence relief, P.6
profits from trading in or developing UK land, P.15
renewals allowance
removal of 'concession', P.4
statutory basis, P.11
rent-a-room scheme, P.14
replacement domestic items relief, P.11
residential property business finance costs, P.15
Scottish land and buildings transaction tax, P.8
sole ownership, 1.4
stamp duty land tax
additional dwellings supplement, P.12
enveloped dwellings, P.5
generally, 1.53
non-residential property, P.10
residential property, P.7
tax administration
borrowing against assets, 1.36–1.38
finance costs, 1.36–1.38
late notification, 1.33–1.34
lease premium, 1.39–1.52
notification requirement, 1.31–1.32
record keeping, 1.35
stamp duty land tax, 1.53

Buy-to-let property business – *contd*
taxation
administration, 1.31–1.53
basis, 1.1
basis periods, 1.28–1.30
pre-letting expenses, 1.25–1.27
pre-trading expenses, 1.19–1.24
taxable persons, 1.2
trading in UK land, P.15
trusts, 1.5
wear and tear allowance, P.11

Calculation of property business profits and losses
acquisition methods, 2.12
assessment as a business, 2.6–2.7
badges of trade, 2.12
capital-revenue distinction, 2.15–2.16
cash-basis proposals, 2.38–2.39
change of intention/use of property, 2.23–2.25
change to asset, 2.12
corporation tax, 2.6–2.7
differences between income rules, 2.8–2.9
finance costs, 2.17–2.22
finance sources, 2.12
hotels, and, 2.10–2.11
income tax, 2.6–2.7
interest relief, 2.17–2.22
interval between purchase and sale, 2.12
introduction, 2.1–2.4
loan relationships, 2.20–2.22
nature of asset, 2.12
non-commercial lettings, 2.36–2.37
number of transactions, 2.12
priority of income rules, 2.5
profit motive, 2.12
'property income', 2.2–2.4
reform proposals, 2.38–2.39
rental income
assessment as a business, 2.6–2.7
differences from income rules, 2.8–2.9
priority of rules, 2.5
sale methods, 2.12
similar trading transactions or interests, 2.12

474

Calculation of property business profits and losses – *contd*
  'slice of the action' arrangements, 2.34–2.35
  source of finance, 2.12
  trading income
    assessment as a business, 2.6–2.7
    differences from income rules, 2.8–2.9
    priority of rules, 2.5
  transactions in UK land
    criteria, 2.28
    generally, 2.26–2.27
    impact, 2.29–2.31
    limitations of scope, 2.32–2.33
    'slice of the action' arrangements, 2.34–2.35
  'wholly and exclusively', 2.13–2.14

Capital allowances
  annual investment allowance, 4.6
  block of flats
    communal areas, 4.10
    generally, 4.9
  capital expenditure
    generally, 4.2
    introduction, 4.1
    plant, 4.3–4.5
  caravans, 4.15
  communal areas, 4.10
  furnished holiday accommodation
    caravans, 4.15
    failure to meet letting conditions, 4.14
    generally, 4.11
    letting conditions, 4.12
    overview, 6.4
    period of grace election, 4.13
  incorporation of buy-to-let business, 13.66–13.71
  introduction, 4.1
  limitation for 'dwellings'
    'dwelling-house', 4.8
    introduction, 4.7
    properties comprising more than one dwelling, 4.9
  meaning, 4.1
  nursing home, 4.9
  plant
    annual investment allowance, 4.6
    generally, 4.3

Capital allowances – *contd*
  plant – *contd*
    integral features, 4.4
    other plant, 4.5
  pre-trading expenses, 1.20–1.21
  qualifying expenditure, 4.2
  revenue expenditure, 4.1
  student accommodation, 4.9

Capital expenditure
  capital allowances
    generally, 4.2
    introduction, 4.1
    plant, 4.3–4.5

Capital gains tax
  allowable costs
    generally, 11.15–11.16
    use of losses, 11.17–11.18
  allowable expenditure
    gains accruing before 6 April 1965, 11.8
    introduction, 11.7
    losses accruing before 6 April 1965, 11.9
    rebasing (March 1982), 11.11
    time apportionment, 11.10
  annual tax on enveloped dwellings
    generally, 9.9
    relationship with NRCGT, 9.17–9.18
  capital gains and losses
    allowable expenditure, 11.7–11.11
    computation, 11.5–11.6
    trading losses, 11.21–11.23
  compensation, 11.28
  compliance issues, 11.44
  compulsory purchase of land, 11.43
  corporate landlords
    non-UK resident landlords, 10.14
    UK resident landlords, 10.13
  costs
    generally, 11.15–11.16
    use of losses, 11.17–11.18
  EIS deferral relief, 11.42
  entrepreneurs' relief, 13.33–13.35
  exchange of joint interests, 11.41
  furnished holiday lettings
    background, 13.32
    entrepreneurs' relief, 6.72, 13.33–13.35
    generally, 11.38

Index

Capital gains tax – *contd*
  furnished holiday lettings – *contd*
    gifts of business assets relief, 6.10–6.11, 13.36–13.42
    introduction, 6.6
    loans to traders, 6.12
    replacement of business assets, 6.9
    rollover relief, 6.9, 13.43–13.44
    substantial shareholdings exemption, 6.13
  gains
    accruing before 6 April 1965, 11.8
    allowable expenditure, 11.7–11.11
    computation, 11.5–11.6
  gifts of business assets relief, 13.36–13.42
  gifts on which IHT is due, 11.26
  incorporation of buy-to-let business
    entrepreneurs' relief, 13.33–13.35
    furnished holiday lettings, 13.32–13.44
    gifts of business assets relief, 13.36–13.42
    incorporation relief, 13.19–13.31
    introduction, 13.16–13.18
    overview, 13.2
    replacement of business assets relief, 13.43–13.44
    roll-over relief, 13.43–13.44
    roll-over relief on transfer of business, 13.19–13.30
    s 162 relief, 13.19–13.30
    s 165 relief, 13.36–13.42
  incorporation relief
    conditions of relief, 13.20–13.30
    generally, 13.19
    introduction, 11.27
    non-statutory business clearance, 13.31
  insurance monies, 11.28
  inter-spouse transfers, 11.29
  introduction, 11.1
  leases, 11.39–11.40
  losses
    accruing before 6 April 1965, 11.9
    allowable expenditure, 11.7–11.11
    computation, 11.5–11.6
    order of set-off, 11.19–11.20
    trading losses, 11.21–11.23
    use,. 11.17–11.18

Capital gains tax – *contd*
  non resident landlords
    ATED, 9.9
    introduction, 9.9
    NRCGT, 9.10–9.18
  non resident's residential property interests (NRCGT)
    generally, 9.10–9.16
    introduction, 9.9
    overview, P.9
    relationship with ATED, 9.17–9.18
  'new' residential property gains, P.13
  options to buy, 11.4
  order of loss set-off, 11.19–11.20
  part disposals, 11.12
  partnerships, 11.25
  private residence relief
    dwelling-house, 11.30
    garden or grounds, 11.31
    introduction, P.6
    let properties, 11.37
    more than one property, 11.36
    permitted periods of residence, 11.34–11.35
    residence, 11.32–11.33
  rates, 11.2
  rebasing (March 1982), 11.11
  relief
    compensation, 11.28
    gifts on which IHT is due, 11.26
    incorporation relief, 11.27
    insurance monies, 11.28
    inter-spouse transfers, 11.29
    private residence relief, 11.30–11.37
    replacement of business assets relief, 13.43–13.44
  reporting and payment reforms, P.17
  roll-over relief
    replacement of business assets, 13.43–13.44
    transfer of business, 13.19–13.30
  s 162 relief
    conditions of relief, 13.20–13.30
    generally, 13.19
    non-statutory business clearance, 13.31
  s 165 relief, 13.36–13.42
  set-off, 11.19–11.20
  small disposal proceeds, 11.13–11.14
  time apportionment, 11.10

Index

Capital gains tax – *contd*
  time of disposal, 11.3
  trading losses, 11.21–11.23
Caravans
  capital allowances, 4.15
Carbon monoxide
  landlord obligations, 18.10
Carry forward
  loss relief, 7.3
Cessation of rental business
  generally, 15.19–15.21
  subsequent expenses, 15.23–15.24
  subsequent receipts, 15.22
Change of use of property
  calculation of property business profits and losses, 2.23–2.25
Child benefit
  finance costs, and, 3.11
Childcare payments
  finance costs, and, 3.11
Choice of ownership entity
  companies, 1.16
  direct ownership, 1.4
  introduction, 1.3
  joint ownership
    apportionment of taxable income, 1.6–1.7
    generally, 1.4
  limited liability partnerships
    generally, 1.12–1.13
    losses, 1.14–1.15
  partnerships
    generally, 1.8–1.10
    joint investment, 1.11
    limited liability partnerships, 1.12–1.15
  sole ownership, 1.4
  trusts, 1.5
Client money
  properties for let, 17.9
Commercial property
  furnishings relief
    fixtures and furniture, 5.12
    generally, 5.6
Communal areas
  capital allowances, 4.10
Companies
  See also **Corporate landlords**; **Incorporation of business**
  choice of entity, and, 1.16

Companies – *contd*
  mortgages, and
    acceptable types, 16.47
    alternatives to incorporation, 16.65
    capital raising, 16.58
    choice of lender, 16.60
    commercial properties, and, 16.59
    deposits, 16.51–16.57
    director's loans, 16.52–16.55
    equity gift, 16.56–16.57
    introduction, 16.47
    operating through a company, 16.50–16.57
    product comparison, 16.49
    SIC codes, 16.47
    underwriting, 16.48
Compensation
  capital gains tax relief, 11.28
Compulsory purchase of land
  capital gains tax relief, 11.43
Consent to let
  properties for let, 17.12
Consideration
  stamp duty land tax
    apportionment, 14.17
    contingent sums, 14.18–14.21
    debt, 14.12
    exchange of properties, 14.14
    introduction, 14.10
    market value, 14.13
    money or money's worth given, 14.11
    partition of property, 14.15
    partnerships, 14.16
    transfers to connected company, 14.13
    uncertain sums, 14.18–14.21
Construction Industry Scheme (CIS)
  generally, 15.6–15.10
  non-resident landlords, 9.21
Contingent consideration
  stamp duty land tax, 14.18–14.21
Conversion of dwelling
  finance costs, and, 3.8–3.10
Corporate landlords
  See also **Companies**
  advantages, 10.2
  annual tax on enveloped dwellings
    background, 10.9
    capital gains, and, 10.13–10.14

477

Index

Corporate landlords – *contd*
  annual tax on enveloped dwellings – *contd*
    charge, 10.10
    claims for relief, 10.11
    disposal of property portfolio, and, 10.1
    SDLT, and, 10.12
  capital gains
    non-UK resident landlords, 10.14
    UK resident landlords, 10.13
  commercial considerations, 10.2
  disposal of property portfolio
    ATED, and, 10.17
    generally, 10.15
    sale of part of portfolio, 10.16
  distribution of profits, 10.3
  exit issues
    ATED, and, 10.17
    generally, 10.15
    sale of part of portfolio, 10.16
  interest relief, 10.6
  introduction, 10.1
  limited liability, 10.2
  losses
    comparison with individual landlords, 10.8
    generally, 10.7
  non-UK resident landlords, 10.14
  offshore companies, 10.4
  profits
    generally, 10.5
    interest relief, 10.6
  reporting requirements, 10.2
  stamp duty land tax, 10.12
  tax considerations, 10.3
  trading losses, 10.7–10.8
  use of company, 10.2–10.3
Corporation tax
  calculation of property business profits and losses, 2.6–2.7
  incorporation of buy-to-let business, 13.1
  loss relief, 7.17–7.19
Costs
  capital gains tax
    generally, 11.15–11.16
    use of losses,. 11.17–11.18
  mortgages
    legal fees, 16.36

Costs – *contd*
  mortgages – *contd*
    mortgage broker fees, 16.37
    mortgage lender fees, 16.34
    stamp duty land tax, 16.35
    survey fee, 16.33
  purchase of property for rental, 17.3
Death
  inheritance tax
    'fall in value' relief, 12.46–12.49
    introduction, 12.42
    liabilities, 12.43–12.44
    post-death loss relief, 12.50–12.55
    rate, 12.1
Debt
  stamp duty land tax, 14.12
Deposits
  properties for let, 17.22
Developing UK land
  generally, P.15
Discretionary trusts
  finance costs, and, 3.27–3.29
Discrimination
  properties for let, 17.18
Disposal of property portfolio
  ATED, and, 10.17
  generally, 10.15
  sale of part of portfolio, 10.16
Distribution of profits
  corporate landlords, 10.3
Duration of tenancy
  properties for let, 17.10
Dwelling-house
  capital allowances, 4.8
EIS deferral relief
  capital gains tax, 11.42
Electrical safety
  landlord obligations, 18.7
Employment-related securities
  incorporation of buy-to-let business, 13.77
Energy performance certificates (EPC)
  properties for let, 17.14
Entrepreneurs' relief
  furnished holiday lettings, 6.72
  incorporation of buy-to-let business, 13.33–13.35

478

Enveloped dwellings
annual tax
generally, P.3
meaning, P.3
stamp duty land tax
generally, 14.26–14.27
introduction, P.5
Estates
finance costs, and
calculation of tax reduction, 3.35–3.36
introduction, 3.30
relievable amount, 3.31–3.34
Exchange of joint interests
capital gains tax, 11.41
Exchange of properties
stamp duty land tax, 14.14
Existing leases
stamp duty land tax, 14.47–14.48

'Fall in value' relief
inheritance tax, 12.46–12.49
Finance costs
accelerating repayment, 3.50
affected costs, 3.3–3.4
beneficial loans, 3.41
building dwelling for letting out, 3.8–3.10
calculation of property business profits and losses, 2.17–2.22
child benefit, and, 3.11
childcare payments, and, 3.11
calculation of tax reduction
estates, 3.35–3.36
generally, 3.15–3.21
converting dwelling for letting out, 3.8–3.10
costs affected
dwelling for letting out, 3.8–3.10
dwelling-related loan, 3.5–3.7
generally, 3.3–3.4
discretionary trusts, 3.27–3.29
diversifying the business, 3.54–3.55
dwelling-related loan, 3.5–3.7
estates
calculation of tax reduction, 3.35–3.36
introduction, 3.30
relievable amount, 3.31–3.34
furnished holiday lettings, 3.37

Finance costs – *contd*
generally, 1.36–1.38
Gift Aid contributions, 3.51
hotels, 3.37
houses in multiple occupation, 3.38–3.40
incorporation of business, 3.44
increasing rental income, 3.45
interest in possession trusts, 3.24–3.26
introducing family members, 3.46–3.47
introduction, P.15
legislative basis, 3.1
loans to invest in partnership, 3.42
mitigation of effects of interest relief restriction
accelerating repayment, 3.50
diversifying the business, 3.54–3.55
Gift Aid contributions, 3.51
incorporation of business, 3.44
increasing rental income, 3.45
introducing family members, 3.46–3.47
introduction, 3.43
paying off capital, 3.49
pension contributions, 3.51–3.52
property development, 3.56
rationalising the business, 3.53
timing of expenditure, 3.48
overview, 3.2
paying off capital, 3.49
pension annual allowance, and, 3.11
pension contributions, 3.51–3.52
personal allowance, and, 3.11
property development, 3.56
rationalising the business, 3.53
relief restrictions
costs affected, 3.3–3.4
effect, 3.2
estates, 3.30–3.36
extent, 3.5
implications, 3.11
introduction, 3.1–3.10
mechanism, 3.12–3.21
mitigation of effects, 3.43–3.56
other issues, 3.37–3.42
trusts, 3.22–3.29
relievable amount
calculation detail, 3.15–3.21
estates, 3.31–3.34
generally, 3.12–3.14

Index

Finance costs – *contd*
  savings allowance, and, 3.11
  student loan repayments, and, 3.11
  tax credits, and, 3.11
  timing of expenditure, 3.48
  trusts
    discretionary trusts, 3.27–3.29
    IIP trusts, 3.24–3.26
    introduction, 3.22
Finance sources
  calculation of property business profits and losses, 2.12
Fire safety
  carbon monoxide alarms, 18.10
  furniture, 18.11
  generally, 18.8
  smoke alarms, 18.9
Fixtures
  furnishings relief
    commercial property, 5.12
    residential property, 5.10–5.11
Furnished holiday accommodation or lettings
  See also **Furnishings relief**
  advantages of status
    capital allowances, 6.4
    capital gains tax relief, 6.6–6.13
    introduction, 6.2
    relevant earnings for pension purposes, 6.3
  availability condition, 6.17
  averaging election, 6.18
  business property relief, 6.24–6.25
  capital allowances
    caravans, 4.15
    failure to meet letting conditions, 4.14
    generally, 4.11
    letting conditions, 4.12
    overview, 6.4
    period of grace election, 4.13
  capital gains tax relief
    entrepreneurs' relief, 6.7
    generally, 11.38
    gifts of business assets relief, 6.10–6.11
    incorporation of buy-to-let business, and, 13.32–13.44
    introduction, 6.6
    loans to traders, 6.12

Furnished holiday accommodation or lettings – *contd*
  capital gains tax relief – *contd*
    replacement of business assets, 6.9
    rollover relief, 6.9
    substantial shareholdings exemption, 6.13
  conditions
    availability, 6.17
    introduction, 6.16
    letting, 6.17
    pattern of occupation, 6.17
    relevant period, 6.21–6.22
    saving provisions, 6.18–6.20
  disadvantages of status
    introduction, 6.13
    restriction of losses, 6.14
    VAT, 6.15
  finance costs, and, 3.37
  HMRC guidance, 6.26
  incorporation of buy-to-let business, and
    background, 13.32
    entrepreneurs' relief, 13.33–13.35
    gifts of business assets relief, 13.36–13.42
    roll-over relief, 13.43–13.44
  inheritance tax, 6.24–6.25
  introduction, 6.1
  letting condition, 6.17
  loss relief, 7.15–7.16
  losses, 6.23
  pattern of occupation, 6.17
  period of grace election, 6.19–6.20
  profit split between spouses, 6.5
  relevant earnings for pension purposes, 6.3
  relevant period, 6.21–6.22
  restriction of losses, 6.14
  VAT, 6.15
Furnishings relief
  boilers and radiators, 5.7
  commercial property
    fixtures and furniture, 5.12
    generally, 5.6
  fixtures
    commercial property, 5.12
    residential property, 5.10–5.11

Furnishings relief – *contd*
  furniture
    commercial property, 5.12
    residential property, 5.7–5.9
  household appliances, 5.7
  introduction, 5.1
  reform chronology, 5.29–5.36
  renewals basis
    generally, 5.22–5.28
    overview, P.4, P.11
  repairs to fixtures, 5.10–5.11
  replacement domestic items relief
    generally, 5.7–5.9
    interaction with wear and tear allowance, 5.19–5.21
  residential property, 5.2–5.5
  wear and tear allowance
    concession, 5.15–5.16
    introduction, 5.13–5.14
    legislative basis, 5.17–5.18
    overview, P.11
    withdrawal, 5.19–5.21
Furniture
  landlord obligations, 18.11

Gas safety
  landlord obligations, 18.5
Gift Aid
  finance costs, and, 3.51
Gifts of business assets relief
  furnished holiday lettings, 6.10–6.11
  incorporation of buy-to-let business, 13.36–13.42
Gifts with reservation
  generally, 12.34–12.38
  interests in land, 12.39–12.41
Grant of new lease
  stamp duty land tax, 14.44–14.45
Guarantors
  properties for let, 17.23

'Higher rate transactions'
  acquisition by companies, 14.39
  acquisition by partnerships, 14.40
  background, P.12
  civil partners, 14.33
  company acquisitions, 14.39
  excluded acquisitions, 14.30
  generally, 14.29–14.30
  inherited dwellings, 14.37

'Higher rate transactions' – *contd*
  interests in dwellings treated as owned by individual, 14.31
  introduction, 14.22–14.24
  joint purchasers, 14.32
  multiple dwellings as part of single transaction, 14.38
  non-UK dwellings, 14.36
  partnership acquisitions, 14.40
  partnership-held dwellings, 14.35
  spouses, 14.33
  trust-held dwellings, 14.34
HMRC guidance
  furnished holiday lettings, 6.26
Hotels
  calculation of property business profits and losses, 2.10–2.11
  finance costs, and, 3.37
Household appliances
  replacement domestic items relief, 5.7
Houses in multiple occupation
  finance costs, and, 3.38–3.40
  landlord obligations, 18.4
  mortgages, 16.26–16.27

Income tax
  administration, 1.31–1.53
  basis, 1.1
  basis periods, 1.28–1.30
  calculation of profits and losses, and assessment as a business, 2.6–2.7
  badges of trade, 2.12
  capital-revenue distinction, 2.15–2.16
  cash-basis proposals, 2.38–2.39
  change of use of property, 2.23–2.25
  differences between income rules, 2.8–2.9
  finance costs, 2.17–2.22
  hotels, and, 2.10–2.11
  interest relief, 2.17–2.22
  introduction, 2.1–2.4
  non-commercial lettings, 2.36–2.37
  priority of income rules, 2.5
  reform proposals, 2.38–2.39
  transactions in UK land, 2.26–2.35
  wholly and exclusively', 2.13–2.14

Index

Income tax – *contd*
  capital allowances
    See also **Capital allowances**
    generally, 4.1–4.15
    loss relief, 7.12–7.13
  furnishings
    See also **Furnishings relief**
    generally, 5.1–5.36
  loss relief
    additional claims, 7.5–7.7
    agricultural expenses, 7.14
    capital allowances, 7.12–7.13
    furnished holiday lettings, 7.15–7.16
    multiple businesses, 7.9–7.11
    overview, 7.1–7.4
    uncommercial lettings, 7.8
  non-resident landlords, 9.2–9.5

Incorporation of letting business
  'business'
    case law, 13.9–13.12
    generally, 13.5–13.8
    Ramsay case, 13.13–13.14
  capital allowances, 13.66–13.71
  capital gains tax
    entrepreneurs' relief, 13.33–13.35
    furnished holiday lettings, 13.32–13.44
    generally, 11.27
    gifts of business assets relief, 13.36–13.42
    incorporation relief, 13.19–13.31
    introduction, 13.16–13.18
    overview, 13.2
    replacement of business assets relief, 13.43–13.44
    roll-over relief, 13.43–13.44
    roll-over relief on transfer of business, 13.19–13.30
    s 162 relief, 13.19–13.30
    s 165 relief, 13.36–13.42
  corporation tax, 13.1
  employment-related securities, 13.77
  entrepreneurs' relief, 13.33–13.35
  finance costs, and, 3.44
  furnished holiday lettings
    background, 13.32
    entrepreneurs' relief, 13.33–13.35
    gifts of business assets relief, 13.36–13.42
    roll-over relief, 13.43–13.44

Incorporation of letting business – *contd*
  gifts of business assets relief, 13.36–13.42
  incorporation relief
    conditions of relief, 13.20–13.30
    generally, 13.19
    introduction, 11.27
    non-statutory business clearance, 13.31
  interest relief
    generally, 13.59–13.64
    introduction, 13.1
  introduction, 13.1–13.4
  loan interest relief, 13.3
  mortgages, and
    acceptable types, 16.47
    alternatives to incorporation, 16.65
    capital raising, 16.58
    choice of lender, 16.60
    commercial properties, and, 16.59
    deposits, 16.51–16.57
    director's loans, 16.52–16.55
    equity gift, 16.56–16.57
    introduction, 16.47
    operating through a company, 16.50–16.57
    product comparison, 16.49
    SIC codes, 16.47
    underwriting, 16.48
  national insurance contributions, 13.74–13.76
  payment of tax, 13.72–13.73
  purpose, 13.1
  replacement of business assets relief, 13.43–13.44
  roll-over relief
    replacement of business assets, 13.43–13.44
    transfer of business, 13.19–13.30
  s 162 relief
    conditions of relief, 13.20–13.30
    generally, 13.19
    non-statutory business clearance, 13.31
  s 165 relief, 13.36–13.42
  stamp taxes
    deemed non-residential property treatment, 13.49
    generally, 13.45–13.47
    market value rule, 13.48

Index

Incorporation of letting business – *contd*
  stamp taxes – *contd*
    multiple dwellings relief, 13.50–13.51
    partnerships, 13.52–13.58
  tax implications
    capital allowances, 13.66–13.71
    capital gains tax, 13.16–13.44
    employment-related securities, 13.77
    interest relief, 13.59–13.64
    introduction, 13.1–13.4
    national insurance contributions, 13.74–13.76
    stamp taxes, 13.45–13.58
    value added tax, 13.65
  tax rates, 13.2
  transactions in UK land, 13.15
  value added tax, 13.65
Inheritance tax
  business property relief
    generally, 12.12–12.16
    introduction, 12.10
  charge to tax, 12.2
  chargeable lifetime transfers, 12.33
  death
    'fall in value' relief, 12.46–12.49
    introduction, 12.42
    liabilities, 12.43–12.44
    post-death loss relief, 12.50–12.55
    rate, 12.1
  discounts, 12.20–12.22
  'fall in value' relief, 12.46–12.49
  furnished holiday lettings, 6.24–6.25
  gifts with reservation
    generally, 12.34–12.38
    interests in land, 12.39–12.41
  instalments, 12.56–12.57
  introduction, 12.1
  investment properties, 12.10
  liabilities
    death 12.43–12.44
    valuation, 12.23–12.24
  lifetime transfers
    chargeable, 12.33
    gifts with reservation, 12.34–12.41
    introduction, 12.31
    potentially exempt transfers, 12.32
    rate, 12.1
  limited liability partnerships, 12.11

Inheritance tax – *contd*
  nil rate band, 12.2
  non-resident landlords, 9.21
  ownership, and
    companies, 12.9
    introduction, 12.3
    joint owners, 12.5–12.7
    sole owners, 12.4
    trustees, 12.8
  partnerships, 12.11
  post-death loss relief, 12.50–12.55
  potentially exempt transfers, 12.32
  pre-owned assets, 12.58–12.60
  rates, 12.1
  valuation
    discounts, 12.20–12.22
    generally, 12.17–12.19
    liabilities, 12.23–12.24
    related property, 12.25–12.30
Instalments
  inheritance tax, 12.56–12.57
Insurance monies
  capital gains tax, 11.28
Interest in possession trusts
  finance costs, and, 3.24–3.26
Interest relief
  calculation of property business profits and losses, 2.17–2.22
  incorporation of buy-to-let business
    generally, 13.59–13.64
    introduction, 13.1
Inter-spouse transfers
  capital gains tax, 11.29

Jointly-owned properties
  apportionment of taxable income, 1.6–1.7
  beneficial ownership
    declaration of trust, 8.21
    generally, 8.18
    severance, 8.19–8.20
  capital gains tax, and, 8.39–8.41
  choice of entity, and
    apportionment of taxable income, 1.6–1.7
    generally, 1.4
  declaration of trust, 8.21
  expenses, 8.43–8.46
  forms, 8.4
  grandparents and grandchildren, 8.52

483

Index

Jointly-owned properties – *contd*
  income tax, and, 8.30–8.38
  inheritance tax, and, 8.39–8.41
  introduction, 8.1
  legal ownership
    capital gains tax, and, 8.39–8.41
    income tax, and, 8.30–8.38
    inheritance tax, and, 8.39–8.41
    introduction, 8.28–8.29
    non-tax issues, 8.42
    tax issues, 8.30–8.41
  non-spouses, 8.47–8.49
  non-tax issues, 8.42
  non-UK domiciled individual, 8.58–8.60
  parents and children, 8.50–8.51
  severance
    generally, 8.19
    lifetime, in, 8.20
    will, by, 8.20
  succession, 8.53–8.57
  types, 8.4

Land and buildings transaction tax (LBTT)
  additional dwellings supplement, 14.42–14.43
  anti-avoidance provisions
    annual tax on enveloped dwellings, 14.61
    generally, 14.58–14.60
    stamp duty reserve tax, 14.63
    transfer buy-to-let property out of company, 14.62
  apportionment of consideration, 14.17
  chargeable consideration
    apportionment, 14.17
    contingent sums, 14.18–14.21
    debt, 14.12
    exchange of properties, 14.14
    introduction, 14.10
    market value, 14.13
    money or money's worth given, 14.11
    partition of property, 14.15
    partnerships, 14.16
    transfers to connected company, 14.13
    uncertain sums, 14.18–14.21
  contingent consideration, 14.18–14.21

Land and buildings transaction tax (LBTT) – *contd*
  debt consideration, 14.12
  exchange of properties, 14.14
  generally, 14.5–14.9
  grant of new lease, 14.46
  introduction, 14.1
  market value, 14.13
  money or money's worth given, 14.11
  overview, P.8
  partition of property, 14.15
  partnerships, 14.16
  rates, 14.41
  relief
    existing lease acquisitions, 14.47–14.48
    introduction, 14.50
    multiple dwellings, 14.51–14.53
    partnership acquisitions, 14.54–14.57
  transfers to connected company, 14.13
  uncertain consideration, 14.18–14.21

Land-related income
  generally, 15.14

Landlord obligations
  basic information requirements, 18.2
  carbon monoxide alarms, 18.10
  electrical safety, 18.7
  fire safety
    carbon monoxide alarms, 18.10
    furniture, 18.11
    generally, 18.8
    smoke alarms, 18.9
  furniture, 18.11
  gas safety, 18.5
  houses of multiple occupation, 18.4
  Housing Health and Safety Rating System, 18.13
  introduction, 18.1
  legal right of person to rent, 18.3
  licensing, 18.4
  possession, 18.14
  property standards
    disrepair, 18.12
    HHSRS, 18.13
  registration, 18.4
  repairs, 18.12
  smoke alarms, 18.9

Late notification
  tax administration, 1.33–1.34

Index

Leases
  assignment, 1.47
  capital costs incurred, 1.46
  capital gains tax, 11.39–11.40
  grant of sub-lease out of short lease, 1.42
  lessee tax relief, 1.43–1.45
  premium, 1.39–1.42
  reverse premium, 1.48–1.52
  tenant tax relief, 1.43–1.45
  term of lease, 1.41
Legal ownership
  capital gains tax, and, 8.26
  conversion from sole to joint title, 8.28–8.42
  expenses, 8.43–8.46
  generally, 8.22–8.27
  income tax, and, 8.27
  inheritance tax, and, 8.26
  introduction, 8.6
  joint ownership
    capital gains tax, and, 8.39–8.41
    income tax, and, 8.30–8.38
    inheritance tax, and, 8.39–8.41
    introduction, 8.28–8.29
    non-tax issues, 8.42
    tax issues, 8.30–8.41
  meaning, 8.3
  non-spouses, 8.47–8.49
  non-UK domiciled individual, 8.58–8.60
  overview, 8.2–8.3
  purchase of land
    generally, 8.10–8.11
    Land Registry protection of interests in land, 8.14–8.15
    maximum number of legal owners, 8.11
    mortgages, 8.17
    overreaching, 8.16
    split of beneficial interests, 8.12–8.13
    stages, 8.10
  structure, 8.23
  succession, 8.53–8.57
Lettable condition
  mortgages, 16.29–16.30
Letting agents
  accreditation, 17.8
  agency agreement, 17.15

Letting agents – *contd*
  client money, 17.9
  consent to let, 17.12
  cost, 17.8
  experience, 17.8
  fees, 17.9
  inventory, 17.11
  redress, 17.9
  mortgage company consent, 17.12
  training, 17.8
  types, 17.10
Letting income allowance
  generally, P.16
Licensing
  landlord obligations, 18.4
Lifetime transfers
  chargeable, 12.33
  gifts with reservation, 12.34–12.41
  introduction, 12.31
  potentially exempt transfers, 12.32
  rate, 12.1
Limited liability
  corporate landlords, 10.2
Limited liability partnerships
  generally, 1.12–1.13
  inheritance tax, 12.11
  losses, 1.14–1.15
Linked transactions
  stamp duty land tax, 14.28
Loan interest relief
  incorporation of buy-to-let business, 13.3
Loan relationships
  calculation of property business profits and losses, 2.20–2.22
Loans to traders
  furnished holiday lettings, 6.12
Loss relief
  See also **Losses**
  capital gains tax
    accruing before 6 April 1965, 11.9
    allowable expenditure, 11.7–11.11
    computation, 11.5–11.6
    order of set-off, 11.19–11.20
    trading losses, 11.21–11.23
    use,. 11.17–11.18
  corporation tax, 7.17–7.19
  income tax
    additional claims, 7.5–7.7
    agricultural expenses, 7.14

Index

Loss relief – *contd*
  income tax – *contd*
    capital allowances, 7.12–7.13
    furnished holiday lettings, 7.15–7.16
    multiple businesses, 7.9–7.11
    overview, 7.1–7.4
    uncommercial lettings, 7.8

Losses
  See also **Loss relief**
  calculation of
    assessment as a business, 2.6–2.7
    badges of trade, 2.12
    capital-revenue distinction, 2.15–2.16
    cash-basis proposals, 2.38–2.39
    change of use of property, 2.23–2.25
    differences between income rules, 2.8–2.9
    finance costs, 2.17–2.22
    hotels, and, 2.10–2.11
    interest relief, 2.17–2.22
    introduction, 2.1–2.4
    non-commercial lettings, 2.36–2.37
    priority of income rules, 2.5
    reform proposals, 2.38–2.39
    transactions in UK land, 2.26–2.35
    'wholly and exclusively', 2.13–2.14
  capital gains tax
    accruing before 6 April 1965, 11.9
    allowable expenditure, 11.7–11.11
    computation, 11.5–11.6
    order of set-off, 11.19–11.20
    trading losses, 11.21–11.23
    use,. 11.17–11.18
  corporate landlords
    comparison with individual landlords, 10.8
    generally, 10.7
  corporation tax, and, 7.17–7.19
  furnished holiday lettings, 6.23
  income tax, and
    additional claims, 7.5–7.7
    agricultural expenses, 7.14
    capital allowances, 7.12–7.13
    furnished holiday lettings, 7.15–7.16
    multiple businesses, 7.9–7.11
    overview, 7.1–7.4
    uncommercial lettings, 7.8

Market value
  stamp duty land tax
    generally, 14.13
    incorporation of buy-to-let business, 13.48

Mines and quarries
  generally, 15.14

Mortgages
  accountants, 16.63–16.64
  affordability calculations
    changes, 16.8
    generally, 16.7
  age requirements, 16.16
  alternative finance, 16.32
  applicants
    companies, 16.14
    consumer borrower, 16.12
    expatriates, 16.13
    first-time buyer, 16.10–16.11
    foreign nationals, 16.13
    owner occupiers, 16.9
  associated costs
    legal fees, 16.36
    mortgage broker fees, 16.37
    mortgage lender fees, 16.34
    stamp duty land tax, 16.35
    survey fee, 16.33
  borrowing criteria
    age, 16.16
    alternative finance, 16.32
    applicants, 16.9–16.14
    creditworthiness, 16.24
    deposit, 16.18–16.19
    equity in existing property, 16.20
    houses in multiple occupation, 16.26–16.27
    income requirements, 16.23
    lettable condition, 16.29–16.30
    loan size, 16.21
    portfolio limits, 16.22
    property type, 16.25–16.31
    refurbishment, 16.31
    renovation needs, 16.28
    repayment, 16.15
    term, 16.17
  bridging finance
    generally, 16.32
    increases to portfolio, 16.45
  broker fees, 16.37
  buy-to-let mortgages, 16.6

Mortgages – *contd*
  buy-to-let property, 16.3
  commercial property, 16.4, 16.59
  company applicants, 16.14
  comparison
    buy-to-let mortgages, 16.6
    residential mortgages, 16.5
  consumer borrower, 16.12
  costs
    legal fees, 16.36
    mortgage broker fees, 16.37
    mortgage lender fees, 16.34
    stamp duty land tax, 16.35
    survey fee, 16.33
  creditworthiness, 16.24
  deposit, 16.18–16.19
  early repayment charges, 16.39
  equity in existing property, 16.20
  equity loans, 16.44
  expatriates, 16.13
  fees
    legal, 16.36
    mortgage broker, 16.37
    mortgage lender, 16.34
    stamp duty land tax, 16.35
    survey, 16.33
  first-time buyer, 16.10–16.11
  foreign nationals, 16.13
  further advances, 16.42
  houses in multiple occupation, 16.26–16.27
  income requirements, 16.23
  increases to portfolio
    bridging finance, 16.45
    equity loans, 16.44
    further advances, 16.42
    introduction, 16.41
    re-mortgages, 16.43
    second charge, 16.44
  interest rate, 16.38
  introduction, 16.1
  legal fees, 16.36
  lender fees, 16.34
  lettable condition, 16.29–16.30
  limited companies, and
    acceptable types, 16.47
    alternatives to incorporation, 16.65
    capital raising, 16.58
    choice of lender, 16.60
    commercial properties, and, 16.59

Mortgages – *contd*
  limited companies, and – *contd*
    deposits, 16.51–16.57
    director's loans, 16.52–16.55
    equity gift, 16.56–16.57
    introduction, 16.47
    operating through a company, 16.50–16.57
    product comparison, 16.49
    SIC codes, 16.47
    underwriting, 16.48
  loan size, 16.21
  mortgage broker fees, 16.37
  mortgage lender fees, 16.34
  owner occupiers, 16.9
  portfolio limits, 16.22
  process via broker
    accountants, 16.63–16.64
    generally, 16.61–16.62
  property type
    generally, 16.25
    houses in multiple occupation, 16.26–16.27
    lettable condition, 16.29–16.30
    refurbishment, 16.31
    renovation, 16.28
  protection of portfolio, 16.40
  refurbishment, 16.31
  re-mortgages, 16.43
  renovation needs, 16.28
  repayment, 16.15
  residential mortgages, 16.5
  residential property, 16.2
  second charge, 16.44
  stamp duty land tax, 16.35
  survey fee, 16.33
  taxation, and, 16.46
  term requirements, 16.17
  types of property, 16.2–16.4
Multiple businesses
  loss relief, 7.9–7.11
Multiple dwellings relief
  stamp duty land tax
    generally, 14.51–14.53
    incorporation of buy-to-let business, 13.50–13.51

Index

National insurance contributions (NICs)
incorporation of buy-to-let business, 13.74–13.76
Nil rate band
inheritance tax, 12.2
Non-resident landlords
annual tax on enveloped dwellings
generally, 9.9
relationship with NRCGT, 9.17–9.18
capital gains tax
ATED, 9.9
introduction, 9.9
NRCGT, 9.10–9.18
capital gains tax on residential property interests (NRCGT)
generally, 9.10–9.16
introduction, 9.9
overview, P.9
relationship with ATED, 9.17–9.18
Construction Industry Scheme, 9.21
general scheme, 9.6–9.8
income tax, 9.2–9.5
inheritance tax, 9.21
introduction, 9.1
stamp duty land tax, 9.21
structuring UK property investments, 9.19–9.20
value added tax, 9.21
Nursing home
capital allowances, 4.9

'Off-plan purchase'
stamp duty land tax, 14.23
Offshore companies
corporate landlords, 10.4
Options to buy
capital gains tax, 11.4
Ownership of properties
beneficial ownership
conversion between joint tenancy and tenancy in common, 8.18–8.21
declaration of trust, 8.21
introduction, 8.7–8.9
meaning, 8.3
overview, 8.2–8.3
severance, 8.19–8.20

Ownership of properties – *contd*
categories of ownership
beneficial ownership, 8.7–8.9
introduction, 8.5
legal ownership, 8.6
choice of entity, and
companies, 1.16
direct ownership, 1.4
introduction, 1.3
joint ownership, 1.4
partnerships, 1.8–1.15
sole ownership, 1.4
trusts, 1.57
expenses, 8.43–8.46
grandparents and grandchildren, 8.52
introduction, 8.1–8.4
joint beneficial ownership
declaration of trust, 8.21
generally, 8.18
severance, 8.19–8.20
joint legal ownership
capital gains tax, and, 8.39–8.41
income tax, and, 8.30–8.38
inheritance tax, and, 8.39–8.41
introduction, 8.28–8.29
non-tax issues, 8.42
tax issues, 8.30–8.41
joint ownership
beneficial ownership, 8.18–8.21
expenses, 8.43–8.46
forms, 8.4
grandparents and grandchildren, 8.52
introduction, 8.1
legal ownership, 8.28–8.42
non-spouses, 8.47–8.49
non-UK domiciled individual, 8.58–8.60
parents and children, 8.50–8.51
succession, 8.53–8.57
types, 8.4
joint tenancy
conversion, 8.18–8.21
declaration of trust, 8.21
generally, 8.4
severance, 8.19–8.20
'land', 8.1
legal ownership
capital gains tax, and, 8.26

Index

Ownership of properties – *contd*
  legal ownership – *contd*
    conversion from sole to joint title, 8.28–8.42
    expenses, 8.43–8.46
    generally, 8.22–8.27
    income tax, and, 8.27
    inheritance tax, and, 8.26
    introduction, 8.6
    meaning, 8.3
    non-spouses, 8.47–8.49
    non-UK domiciled individual, 8.58–8.60
    overview, 8.2–8.3
    purchase of land, 8.10–8.17
    structure, 8.23
    succession, 8.53–8.57
  non-spouses, 8.47–8.49
  non-UK domiciled individual, 8.58–8.60
  parents and children, 8.50–8.51
  purchase of land
    generally, 8.10–8.11
    Land Registry protection of interests in land, 8.14–8.15
    maximum number of legal owners, 8.11
    mortgages, 8.17
    overreaching, 8.16
    split of beneficial interests, 8.12–8.13
    stages, 8.10
  severance of joint tenancy
    generally, 8.19
    lifetime, in, 8.20
    will, by, 8.20
  succession, 8.53–8.57
  tenancy in common
    conversion, 8.18–8.21
    declaration of trust, 8.21
    generally, 8.4
    severance, 8.19–8.20
  types, 8.2–8.3

Part disposals
  capital gains tax, 11.12
Partition of property
  stamp duty land tax, 14.15
Partnerships
  capital gains tax, 11.25

Partnerships – *contd*
  generally, 1.8–1.10
  joint investment, 1.11
  inheritance tax, 12.11
  limited liability partnerships
    generally, 1.12–1.13
    losses, 1.14–1.15
  stamp duty land tax (acquisitions)
    consideration, 14.16
    generally, 14.40
    relief, 14.54–14.57
  stamp duty land tax (held dwellings), 14.35
Payment of tax
  incorporation of buy-to-let business, 13.72–13.73
Pension annual allowance
  finance costs, and, 3.11
Pension contributions
  finance costs, and, 3.51–3.52
Period of grace election
  furnished holiday lettings, 6.19–6.20
Personal allowance
  finance costs, and, 3.11
Plant
  capital allowances
    annual investment allowance, 4.6
    generally, 4.3
    integral features, 4.4
    other plant, 4.5
Possession
  landlord obligations, 18.14
Potentially exempt transfers
  inheritance tax, 12.32
Pre-letting expenses
  generally, 1.25–1.26
  landlord's former home, 1.27
Pre-owned assets
  inheritance tax, 12.58–12.60
Pre-trading expenses
  capital allowances, 1.20–1.21
  capital expenses, 1.25
  case study, 1.26
  introduction, 1.19
  landlord's former home, 1.27
  no further commencement, 1.22–1.24
  revenue expenses, 1.25
Principal private residence (PPR) relief
  dwelling-house, 11.30

Index

Principal private residence (PPR) relief – *contd*
  final period of ownership rule restriction, P.6
  garden or grounds, 11.31
  let properties, 11.37
  more than one property, 11.36
  permitted periods of residence, 11.34–11.35
  residence, 11.32–11.33
Profit motive
  calculation of property business profits and losses, 2.12
Profit split
  furnished holiday lettings, 6.5
Profits
  calculation of
    assessment as a business, 2.6–2.7
    badges of trade, 2.12
    capital-revenue distinction, 2.15–2.16
    cash-basis proposals, 2.38–2.39
    change of use of property, 2.23–2.25
    differences between income rules, 2.8–2.9
    finance costs, 2.17–2.22
    hotels, and, 2.10–2.11
    interest relief, 2.17–2.22
    introduction, 2.1–2.4
    non-commercial lettings, 2.36–2.37
    priority of income rules, 2.5
    reform proposals, 2.38–2.39
    transactions in UK land, 2.26–2.35
    'wholly and exclusively', 2.13–2.14
  corporate landlords
    generally, 10.5
    interest relief, 10.6
  trading in or developing UK land, from, P.15
Property development
  finance costs, and, 3.56
'Property income'
  calculation of property business profits and losses, 2.2–2.4
Property standards
  disrepair, 18.12
  HHSRS, 18.13
Purchase of land
  generally, 8.10–8.11

Purchase of land – *contd*
  Land Registry protection of interests in land, 8.14–8.15
  maximum number of legal owners, 8.11
  mortgages, 8.17
  overreaching, 8.16
  split of beneficial interests, 8.12–8.13
  stages, 8.10

Quarries and mines
  generally, 15.14

Radiators
  replacement domestic items relief, 5.7
Rebasing
  capital gains tax, 11.11
Record keeping
  tax administration, 1.35
References
  properties for let, 17.17
Refurbishment
  mortgages, 16.31
Registration
  landlord obligations, 18.4
Relief
  capital gains tax
    compensation, 11.28
    gifts on which IHT is due, 11.26
    incorporation relief, 11.27
    insurance monies, 11.28
    inter-spouse transfers, 11.29
    private residence relief, 11.30–11.37
  furnishings relief
    commercial property, 5.6
    fixtures, 5.10–5.12
    furniture, 5.7–5.9
    introduction, 5.1
    reform chronology, 5.29–5.36
    renewals basis, 5.22–5.28
    replacement domestic items relief, 5.7–5.9
    residential property, 5.2–5.5
    wear and tear allowance, 5.13–5.18
    withdrawal, 5.19–5.21
  private residence relief
    dwelling-house, 11.30
    garden or grounds, 11.31
    introduction, P.6
    let properties, 11.37

Relief – *contd*
  private residence relief – *contd*
    more than one property, 11.36
    permitted periods of residence, 11.34–11.35
    residence, 11.32–11.33
  replacement domestic items relief
    generally, 5.7–5.9
    interaction with wear and tear allowance, 5.19–5.21
  stamp duty land tax
    existing lease acquisitions, 14.47–14.48
    introduction, 14.50
    multiple dwellings, 14.51–14.53
    partnership acquisitions, 14.54–14.57
Renewals allowance
  generally, 5.22–5.28
  overview, P.4, P.11
Renovation
  mortgages, 16.28
Rent
  considerations on purchase of property for rental, 17.2
Rent-a-room scheme
  threshold extension, P.14
Rent-to-rent
  properties for let, 17.25
Rental income
  calculation of property business profits and losses
    assessment as a business, 2.6–2.7
    differences from income rules, 2.8–2.9
    priority of rules, 2.5
Repairs
  furnishings relief, 5.10–5.11
  landlord obligations, 18.12
Repayment of capital
  finance costs, and, 3.49
Replacement domestic items relief
  generally, 5.7–5.9
  interaction with wear and tear allowance, 5.19–5.21
  overview, P.11
Replacement of business assets relief
  furnished holiday lettings, 6.9
  incorporation of buy-to-let business, 13.43–13.44

Residential property business finance costs
  restriction of tax relief, P.15
Revenue expenditure
  generally, 4.1
Right to rent
  landlord obligations, 18.3
Roll-over relief
  furnished holiday lettings, 6.9
  incorporation of buy-to-let business
    replacement of business assets, 13.43–13.44
  transfer of business, 13.19–13.30
Sale and leaseback of land
  generally, 15.15
Savings allowance
  finance costs, and, 3.11
Scottish land and buildings transaction tax (LBTT)
  additional dwellings supplement, 14.42–14.43
  anti-avoidance provisions
    annual tax on enveloped dwellings, 14.61
    generally, 14.58–14.60
    stamp duty reserve tax, 14.63
    transfer buy-to-let property out of company, 14.62
  apportionment of consideration, 14.17
  chargeable consideration
    apportionment, 14.17
    contingent sums, 14.18–14.21
    debt, 14.12
    exchange of properties, 14.14
    introduction, 14.10
    market value, 14.13
    money or money's worth given, 14.11
    partition of property, 14.15
    partnerships, 14.16
    transfers to connected company, 14.13
    uncertain sums, 14.18–14.21
  contingent consideration, 14.18–14.21
  debt consideration, 14.12
  exchange of properties, 14.14
  generally, 14.5–14.9
  grant of new lease, 14.46
  introduction, 14.1

Index

Scottish land and buildings transaction tax (LBTT) – *contd*
  market value, 14.13
  money or money's worth given, 14.11
  overview, P.8
  partition of property, 14.15
  partnerships, 14.16
  rates, 14.41
  relief
    existing lease acquisitions, 14.47–14.48
    introduction, 14.50
    multiple dwellings, 14.51–14.53
    partnership acquisitions, 14.54–14.57
  transfers to connected company, 14.13
  uncertain consideration, 14.18–14.21
Section 162 relief
  incorporation of buy-to-let business
    conditions of relief, 13.20–13.30
    generally, 13.19
    non-statutory business clearance, 13.31
Section 165 relief
  incorporation of buy-to-let business, 13.36–13.42
Set-off
  capital gains tax, 11.19–11.20
Severance of joint tenancy
  generally, 8.19
  lifetime, in, 8.20
  will, by, 8.20
Short letting
  properties for let, 17.24
'Sideways' relief
  loss relief, 7.5–7.7
'Slice of the action' arrangements
  calculation of property business profits and losses, 2.34–2.35
Smoke alarms
  landlord obligations, 18.9
Spouses
  stamp duty land tax, 14.33
Stamp duty land tax (SDLT)
  additional dwellings supplement
    acquisition by companies, 14.39
    acquisition by partnerships, 14.40
    background, P.12
    civil partners, 14.33
    company acquisitions, 14.39

Stamp duty land tax (SDLT) – *contd*
  additional dwellings supplement – *contd*
    excluded acquisitions, 14.30
    generally, 14.29–14.30
    inherited dwellings, 14.37
    interests in dwellings treated as owned by individual, 14.31
    introduction, 14.22–14.24
    joint purchasers, 14.32
    multiple dwellings as part of single transaction, 14.38
    partnership acquisitions, 14.40
    partnership-held dwellings, 14.35
    rest of the UK dwellings, 14.36
    spouses, 14.33
    trust-held dwellings, 14.34
  annual tax on enveloped dwellings, 14.61
  anti-avoidance provisions
    annual tax on enveloped dwellings, 14.61
    generally, 14.58–14.60
    stamp duty reserve tax, 14.63
    transfer buy-to-let property out of company, 14.62
  apportionment of consideration, 14.17
  bare land acquisitions, 14.49
  chargeable consideration
    apportionment, 14.17
    contingent sums, 14.18–14.21
    debt, 14.12
    exchange of properties, 14.14
    introduction, 14.10
    market value, 14.13
    money or money's worth given, 14.11
    partition of property, 14.15
    partnerships, 14.16
    transfers to connected company, 14.13
    uncertain sums, 14.18–14.21
  contingent consideration, 14.18–14.21
  corporate landlords, 10.12
  debt consideration, 14.12
  'effective date', 14.3
  enveloped dwellings
    generally, 14.26–14.27
    introduction, P.5
  exchange of properties, 14.14

Stamp duty land tax (SDLT) – *contd*
existing lease acquisition relief, 14.47–14.48
generally, 14.2–14.4
grant of new lease, 14.44–14.45
'higher rate transactions'
  acquisition by companies, 14.39
  acquisition by partnerships, 14.40
  background, P.12
  civil partners, 14.33
  company acquisitions, 14.39
  excluded acquisitions, 14.30
  generally, 14.29–14.30
  inherited dwellings, 14.37
  interests in dwellings treated as owned by individual, 14.31
  introduction, 14.22–14.24
  joint purchasers, 14.32
  multiple dwellings as part of single transaction, 14.38
  non-UK dwellings, 14.36
  partnership acquisitions, 14.40
  partnership-held dwellings, 14.35
  spouses, 14.33
  trust-held dwellings, 14.34
incorporation of buy-to-let business
  deemed non-residential property treatment, 13.49
  generally, 13.45–13.47
  market value rule, 13.48
  multiple dwellings relief, 13.50–13.51
  partnerships, 13.52–13.58
introduction, 14.1
linked transactions, 14.28
market value
  generally, 14.13
  incorporation of buy-to-let business, 13.48
money or money's worth given, 14.11
mortgages, and, 16.35
multiple dwellings relief
  generally, 14.51–14.53
  incorporation of buy-to-let business, 13.50–13.51
non-resident landlords, 9.21
non-residential property, P.10
'off-plan purchase', 14.23
overview, 1.53
partition of property, 14.15

Stamp duty land tax (SDLT) – *contd*
partnership acquisitions
  consideration, 14.16
  generally, 14.40
  relief, 14.54–14.57
partnership-held dwellings, 14.35
rates
  general, 14.25
  higher, 14.29–14.30
relief
  existing lease acquisitions, 14.47–14.48
  introduction, 14.50
  multiple dwellings, 14.51–14.53
  partnership acquisitions, 14.54–14.57
residential property, P.7
Scotland, 14.1
spouses, 14.33
stamp duty reserve tax, 14.63
tax administration, 1.53
transfer buy-to-let property out of company, 14.62
transfers to connected company, 14.13
trust-held dwellings, 14.34
UK, 14.1
uncertain consideration, 14.18–14.21
Stamp duty reserve tax (SDRT)
stamp duty land tax, 14.63
Student accommodation
capital allowances, 4.9
Student loan repayments
finance costs, and, 3.11
Substantial shareholdings exemption
furnished holiday lettings, 6.13
Succession
generally, 8.53–8.57

Tax administration
borrowing against assets, 1.36–1.38
finance costs, 1.36–1.38
late notification, 1.33–1.34
leases
  assignment, 1.47
  capital costs incurred, 1.46
  grant of sub-lease out of short lease, 1.42
  lessee tax relief, 1.43–1.45
  premium, 1.39–1.42
  reverse premium, 1.48–1.52

Index

Tax administration – *contd*
  leases – *contd*
    tenant tax relief, 1.43–1.45
    term of lease, 1.41
  notification requirement, 1.31–1.32
  record keeping, 1.35
  stamp duty land tax, 1.53
Tax credits
  finance costs, and, 3.11
Tenancies in common
  conversion, 8.18–8.21
  declaration of trust, 8.21
  generally, 8.4
  severance, 8.19–8.20
Tenant damage
  considerations on purchase of property for rental, 17.4
Tenant selection
  discrimination, 17.18
  introduction, 17.16
  referencing, 17.17
Tenanted properties
  advertising, 17.13
  agency agreement, 17.15
  buying with tenant in place, 17.26–17.29
  client money, 17.9
  consent to let, 17.12
  considerations on purchase
    arrears of rent, 17.4
    costs, 17.3
    introduction, 17.1
    rent, 17.2
    tenant damage, 17.4
  deposits, 17.22
  discrimination, 17.18
  duration of tenancy, 17.10
  energy performance certificates, 17.14
  guarantors, 17.23
  introduction, 17.5
  letting agents
    accreditation, 17.8
    agency agreement, 17.15
    client money, 17.9
    consent to let, 17.12
    cost, 17.8
    experience, 17.8
    fees, 17.9
    inventory, 17.11
    redress, 17.9

Tenanted properties – *contd*
  letting agents – *contd*
    mortgage company consent, 17.12
    training, 17.8
    types, 17.10
  references, 17.17
  rent to rent, 17.25
  selection of tenant
    discrimination, 17.18
    introduction, 17.16
    referencing, 17.17
  short letting, 17.24
  tenant's rights, 17.6
  term of tenancy, 17.10
  terms of letting
    duration, 17.10
    generally, 17.19
    other, 17.21
  types, 17.7
Terms of letting
  duration, 17.10
  generally, 17.19
  other, 17.21
Tied premises
  generally, 15.11–15.13
Timber
  generally, 15.14
Trading income
  calculation of property business profits and losses
    assessment as a business, 2.6–2.7
    differences from income rules, 2.8–2.9
    priority of rules, 2.5
Trading in UK land
  generally, P.15
Trading losses
  capital gains tax, 11.21–11.23
  corporate landlords, 10.7–10.8
Transactions in UK land
  chargeable gains, and, 15.16–15.17
  criteria, 2.28
  generally, 2.26–2.27
  impact, 2.29–2.31
  incorporation of buy-to-let business, and, 13.15
  limitations of scope, 2.32–2.33
  'slice of the action' arrangements, 2.34–2.35

Index

Trusts
 choice of entity, 1.5
 finance costs
  discretionary trusts, 3.27–3.29
  IIP trusts, 3.24–3.26
  introduction, 3.22
 stamp duty land tax, 14.34

Uncertain consideration
 stamp duty land tax, 14.18–14.21

Valuation
 inheritance tax
  discounts, 12.20–12.22
  generally, 12.17–12.19
  liabilities, 12.23–12.24
  related property, 12.25–12.30

Value added tax (VAT)
 furnished holiday lettings, 6.15
 generally, 15.1–15.5
 incorporation of buy-to-let business, 13.65
 non-resident landlords, 9.21

Wear and tear allowance
 concession, 5.15–5.16
 introduction, 5.13–5.14
 legislative basis, 5.17–5.18
 overview, P.11
 withdrawal, 5.19–5.21

Woodlands
 generally, 15.14